DISCARDED
COLLEGE
LIBRARY

289.4
Sw3p
v. 2

POSTHUMOUS
THEOLOGICAL WORKS

POSTHUMOUS
THEOLOGICAL
WORKS

OF

EMANUEL SWEDENBORG

PROPHETS AND PSALMS
SCRIPTURE CONFIRMATIONS
PRECEPTS OF THE DECALOGUE
MARRIAGE
INDEXES ON MARRIAGE
BRIEF BIBLIOGRAPHY OF SWEDENBORG'S WORKS
INDEX OF PUBLICATIONS

VOLUME II.

JOHN WHITEHEAD
EDITOR AND TRANSLATOR

Standard Edition

SWEDENBORG FOUNDATION
INCORPORATED
NEW YORK

Established in 1850

First published in U.S.A., 1914

12th Printing 1978

ISBN: 0—87785—074—7 (Student), 2 Vol. set 0—87785—075—5
0—87785—077—1 (Trade), 2 Vol. set 0—87785—078—X

Library of Congress Catalog Card Number 38-24293

Manufactured in the United States of America

EDITOR'S CRITICAL NOTES.

Page	Line		Page	Line	
473	16	The *MS.* has n. 769–763; Worcester has n. 569–763; Index under *Amor Conjugialis* has n. 569–763.	480	11	The *MS.* here reads *non exscriptum est videatur prius..et concedetur;* Worcester has, *num exscriptum est videatur ..et concidetur.*
473	17	The *MS.* has n. 564–852; Worcester has n. 765–882. Index under *Similitudo* has n. 765–882.	481	10	The *MS.* has n. 439; Worcester has n. 447.
				15	The *MS.* has n. 818–822 underlined, also the following n. 847–851.
474	11	The *MS.* has n. 1419; Worcester has n. 1819; Index under *Violatio* has n. 1819.	482	14	The *MS.* has *amor scortatorius;* Worcester has *amor scortationis.*
475	30	The *MS.* has *cavernam,* a cavern; *C. L.* n. 521 has *cavernam;* Worcester has *cavernis,* in caverns.	484	15	The *MS.* has *quae vocantur;* Worcester has *quae sunt.*
			486	2	In the *MS.* after spiritual Swedenborg wrote *suo modo,* "in their manner;" but he crossed out these words.
477	5	The *MS.* has *Scripserit varia;* Worcester omits *varia.*
477	15	The *MS.* has *tres coetus,* three assemblies; *C. L.* n. 421 also has *tres coetus;* Worcester has *tres caelos,* three heavens.		35	The *MS.* has *conjugialis;* Worcester gives *pulchritudinis,* referring to index under INTELLECTUS, where the same passage gives *pulchritudinis,* "beauty."
	31	*MS.* has n. 1641; Index under *Anima* has n. 1641; Worcester has n. 1691.	494	22	The *MS.* has *supremo;* Worcester has *superiore.*
	last	*Spectans de blatta,* Worcester thus reads the *MS.,* with which we agree. In *C. L.* 329 we read, *et tunc videbant blattam.*	495	27	The *MS.* has *illae;* Worcester has *illorum.*
			504	7	The *MS.* has *sit vitium;* Worcester has *sint vitia.*
479	17	In the *MS., pag. 20, seq.* is written in the margin.		8	The *MS.* has 962; Worcester has 992.
480	5	The *MS.* has p. 90; Worcester reads n. 90.	506	8	The *MS.* has *magnis civitatibus,* which Worcester omits.
	7	The *MS.* has p. 91; Worreads n. 91.	507	29	The *MS.* has *inde;* Worcester has *in.*
	9	The *MS.* has p. 92; Worreads n. 92; the letter p. in the *MS.* in these places is imperfect.	508	35	The *MS.* has *et communicatur;* Worcester has *et coram* [*Domino*] *uniantur.*

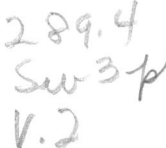

POSTHUMOUS THEOLOGICAL WORKS

Page	Line	
510	4	The *MS.* has 371; Worcester has 373.
514	4	The *MS.* has 575; Worcester has 573.
	36	The *MS.* has 1217 but reference to same number under BESTIA is 1251.
518	7	The *MS.* has *conjugialis*; Worcester omits it.
526	5	The *MS.* has *fructificationis*; Worcester has *prolificationis*.
527	2	The editor of the *MS.* inserts *Deliciae*; Worcester prefers *felicia*.
528	5	The *MS.* has *interior*; Worcester has *internae*.
531	9	The *MS.* has *et*; Worcester has *ex*.
532	29	A word is crossed out in the *MS.* which Worcester retains, deciphering it as *proprias*.
537	last	See under STORGE, where we read *modo*.
543	8	The *MS.* has *sed*; Worcester has *seu*.
	22	The *MS.* has *voluntatis*, but *intellectus* is evidently intended, which Worcester adopts.
544	21	The *MS.* has 1873; under CONJUGIALE it is 1813.
549	18	The *MS.* has *mens fit*; Worcester has *moralis seu*.

Page	Line	
550	3	See First Index under CONJUGIAL LOVE, also *C. L.* 293, 294.
	23	"*Qui*," which is a doubtful reading.
551	7	"*Non*," "not," is not in the original *MS.* See First Index under CONJUGIAL LOVE.
551	10	"*Non*," "not," is not in the original *MS.* See First Index under CONJUGIAL LOVE.
554	29	In the *MS.* there is a word blotted, possibly *haec*, "these," which Worcester omits.
555	7	The *MS. sint.* Worcester has *si*, probably a printer's error.
	21	The *MS.* has 43; Worcester has 45.
558	29	The *MS.* has 522; possibly it should be 52. The figure is crossed by the d in line below.
	32	The *MS.* has *animabus*; Worcester has *animalibus*.
560	19	The *MS.* has *Verum*.; Worcester has *bonum*, which is evidently meant.
560	29	The *MS.* has *sibi*, which Worcester omits.

GENERAL INDEX

	PAGE
SUMMARIES OF THE INTERNAL SENSE OF THE PROPHETS AND PSALMS	1
SCRIPTURE CONFIRMATION OF NEW CHURCH DOCTRINE	313
THE PRECEPTS OF THE DECALOGUE	427
MARRIAGE	431
INDEXES TO ANGELIC WISDOM CONCERNING MARRIAGE	467
FIRST INDEX	481
SECOND INDEX	549
A BRIEF BIBLIOGRAPHY OF SWEDENBORG'S WORKS	563
INDEX OF SWEDENBORG'S WORKS PUBLISHED BY THE SWEDENBORG FOUNDATION, INCORPORATED	583

Summaries of the Internal Sense

OF

THE PROPHETICAL BOOKS
THE PSALMS OF DAVID
HISTORICAL PARTS OF THE WORD

A POSTHUMOUS WORK OF

EMANUEL SWEDENBORG

TRANSLATED BY

E. J. E. SCHRECK

CONTENTS.

	page
EDITOR'S PREFACE,	v
INTRODUCTION,	viii
INTIMATIONS OF THIS LITTLE WORK FOUND ELSEWHERE,	xv
LIST OF BOOKS TO BE PUBLISHED,	2
TABLE OF SUBJECTS,	3
THE LORD'S STATE OF HUMILIATION,	4
THE PROPHETICAL BOOKS:	
CONTENTS OF THE PROPHETICAL BOOKS,	6
ISAIAH,	7
JEREMIAH,	34
LAMENTATIONS,	60
EZEKIEL,	62
DANIEL,	83
HOSEA,	90
JOEL,	95
AMOS	97
OBADIAH,	101
JONAH,	102
MICAH,	104
NAHUM,	107
HABAKKUK,	108
ZEPHANIAH,	110
HAGGAI,	112
ZECHARIAH,	113
MALACHI,	118
THE PSALMS OF DAVID,	123
HISTORICAL PARTS OF THE WORD:	
INTRODUCTION,	163
GENESIS,	165
INDEX OF WORDS AND SUBJECTS,	171
INDEX OF SCRIPTURE PASSAGES,	312

EDITOR'S PREFACE.

This work, which was left in manuscript by Swedenborg, appears to have been written before the year 1763, as the list of books "To be Published" would indicate.

It is impossible to reproduce accurately the peculiar features of the manuscript, in type, and the student is therefore referred to the phototyped edition, published by the Academy of the New Church in the year 1896. Still a description of the manuscript seems necessary for those who may not have access to the phototyped edition.

The work lacks a title. In previous editions it was entitled "*A Summary Exposition of the Internal Sense of the Prophetical Books of the Word of the Old Testament, and also of the Psalms of David*," which has been changed to the one used in this edition, suggested by *The Doctrine concerning the Sacred Scripture* (n. 97).

The first page of the manuscript is divided into lateral halves or columns, by a perpendicular line drawn from the top to the bottom of the page. About the middle of the first half is the list of works "To be Published," which will be found on page 3 of the present edition, and which is similar to the one embodied in Swedenborg's preface to *The Doctrine of the New Jerusalem concerning the Lord*, where it is introduced with the words, "Now, pursuant to the command of the Lord, who has been revealed to me, the following works will be published."

In the lower corner of the same column is the "Table of Subjects," printed on our folder attached to page 4.

In the second column are the references to "The Lord's State of Humiliation," and separated from it by a considerable space are the references to the Psalms; both of which groups of memoranda will be found on page 4 of this edition.

The summaries begin on the second page of the manuscript, having at their head the list of six topics to be found on our page 7.

The "Table of Subjects" is printed on a folder in this edition, in order to facilitate reference, since these seventeen subjects are referred to in the margin of every line of the manuscript, and give the contents of the lines. The chapters are not broken into paragraphs, but summary follows summary continuously throughout the chapter, and in this manner one or two of the marginal references frequently indicate the contents of two or more propositions, or summaries, which are given, in whole or in part, on the line. It was found impossible to reproduce this arrangement in type, and a plan was adopted for this edition, which appeared to be the nearest and best approach to the manuscript. Each summary is printed in a paragraph by itself, with the marginal references belonging to it. This plan presents the additional advantage of making reference to chapter and verse, as well as to subject, very easy. But this plan made it necessary for the editor to exercise his judgment in assigning the marginal references to each separate summary. In many cases this has resulted in a more frequent repetition of the references than actually occurs in the manuscript. Wherever, in this respect, a question may arise in the mind of the reader, recourse must be had to the original manuscript or its facsimile.

Owing, presumably, to the difficulties just adverted to, the references were removed from the margin in the first Latin edition (London, 1784) and in all the English editions, and (except in the edition published in London, 1887) they were made the basis of two indexes, one of which gives the chapters and verses in their order, with the corresponding references to the subjects in the Table, while the other presents the subjects in their order, and classifies all the chapters and verses under them. These indexes are rendered unnecessary by our return to Swedenborg's own plan.

An index to the text of the summaries, however, was considered highly important and useful, and great pains have been taken in the elaboration of such a one. Owing to the succinct wording of the summaries, this index partakes largely of the nature of a Concordance. The compiler has endeavored to make it also a topical index, and has arranged the entries under the respective subjects as analytically as was possible, so that it may prove of real value in the study and understanding of the sacred contents of the prophets and psalms.

The preliminary " INTIMATIONS OF THIS LITTLE WORK FOUND IN OTHER WORKS BY EMANUEL SWEDENBORG," have been gathered together for this edition, for the better appreciation of the summaries in the light of the Heavenly Doctrines of the New Jerusalem themselves.

The Bibles principally used by Swedenborg were the Latin translation by Sebastian Schmidius originally published in Strassburg in 1696, and a later edition of the same translation, printed in parallel columns with the Hebrew text and published at Leipsic in the year 1740. The division into chapters and verses in the Hebrew-Latin edition varies in at least one instance from that of the sole-Latin edition (see, for instance, *Isaiah* xv.). Both differ frequently from the division adopted in the English Bibles. In order to prevent the confusion experienced heretofore in the use of this little work in Bible study, the English division has been adopted in this translation, all the references to chapters and verses being changed in adaptation to the English Bibles. The divisions of the Hebrew and Latin Bibles, as given in the manuscript, are noted in smaller type, "H.B." standing for Hebrew Bible (meaning also the edition of Schmidius of 1740), and "L.B." standing for the sole-Latin Bible (edition of 1696).

The grouping of verses in the Hebrew Bible is more logical than

EDITOR'S PREFACE.

that in the English Bible. See the summaries of *Isa.* viii., lxiii., lxiv.; *Jer.* viii., ix.; *Ezek.* xx., xxi.; *Daniel* iii., iv.; *Hosea* xiii., xiv.; *Jonah* i., ii.; *Micah* iv., v.; *Nahum* i., ii.; *Malachi* iii., iv. As to the difference in the verse divisions of the Psalms in the Hebrew and English Bibles, see the note on back of the title page to the Psalms.

After completing the summaries of the Prophets and the Psalms, Swedenborg began giving the summaries of the internal sense of the historical portions of the Word, and introduced them with a preface— a feature lacking in the earlier Parts. Perhaps the memoranda on the first pages were intended as material for one. It has seemed so to us, and we have therefore used them as the basis for an introduction to the work, designed more especially for such readers as have not yet the knowledge of the Doctrines of the New Church which is required for an intelligent use of this book.

In presenting this important little volume to the public in its new dress, we feel constrained to join in the following devout sentiment with which the first Latin edition was introduced by the editor:

"TO THE KIND READER.

"Among some of Swedenborg's letters we found the following remarkable and noteworthy reference about the present work :

"'Once when I was reading this book, celestial angels were present with me, who rejoiced greatly at heart over my intention of publishing it for the common good of the New Church of the Lord Jesus Christ.'

"In order that the joy of the celestial angels may not be vain, we adjudged it highly necessary to make this very useful little book public. Deign to receive the new treasure with a thankful mind, use it with a pious and sincere heart, and live forever."

E. J. E. S.

INTRODUCTION.

The Summaries contained in this work presuppose some knowledge respecting the general subject of the internal sense of the Word of God.

The Sacred Scripture contains an internal or spiritual sense, which differs from the literal sense in the same way that the things of heaven differ from the things of the world. The literal sense, by which is to be understood the meaning which ordinarily comes to the reader as he peruses the narratives and prophecies of the Scriptures, treats, for the most part, of occurrences in the natural world, such as the history of the Israelitish people, and the history and deeds of our Lord and Saviour. But the internal sense treats of things heavenly and Divine, that is to say, of such things as relate to the soul-life of man, to the church as a spiritual entity, to the angelic life in heaven, and to the inner life of our Lord Jesus Christ.

The natural sense as a whole is said to "correspond" to the spiritual sense, every single particular of the literal sense corresponding to some detail of the internal sense.

The existence of an internal sense may be perceived from many passages in the Scriptures.

On the occasion of the memorable journey which the Lord Jesus Christ took after His resurrection, when He met and accompanied the two Apostles on their way to Emmaus,

"Beginning at Moses and all the Prophets, He expounded unto them in all the Scriptures the things concerning Himself" (*Luke* xxiv. 27).

The Lord Jesus Christ here indicates that all the Scriptures treat of Him; and if all, then even those passages from the surface meaning or literal sense of which this may not appear, in some hidden way still treat of Him. The memoranda on page 4 refer to evidences of this great and most important truth respecting the Lord, which is fundamental to the Christian Church, and essential to its life and prosperity. In keeping with this vital truth, the term "the Lord" is uniformly used in this and all the other works of the New Jerusalem to designate the Lord God Jesus Christ. He is the God of the Sacred Scripture. He is the One and Eternal God incarnate, who assumed the flesh for the purpose of revealing Himself in His own Personality to mankind, and of meeting, through the assumed human, the hells, whose influence, like that of a successful rebel host, at that time dominated mankind, to the exclusion of all heavenly and even Divine influences. The incarnation was for the further purpose of overcoming the hells, and reducing them to subjection and obedience to the Lord. The conflict with the hells, their overthrow, the consequent establishment of order in the spiritual world, the formation of a New Heaven, and the derivation therefrom of a new spiritual church on earth to take the place of the Jewish Church, that had come to a miserable end,—all taken together constituted the Divine work of Redemption. These things are treated of throughout the Scriptures. They are brought to view in a general way by the summaries that make up this book.

The Lord's Divinity was proclaimed by the angelic messenger who was sent to announce His conception to the virgin Mary,

> "The angel Gabriel said unto Mary, The Holy Spirit shall come upon thee, and the virtue of the Most High shall overshadow thee; wherefore also the Holy Thing that shall be born of thee shall be called the Son of God" (*Luke* i. 5).

The babe born of Mary was conceived,—not, as we have been led to conclude from the theology hitherto prevailing in the Christian Church, by an eternal God the Son, the second in a supposed trinity of Divine Persons,—but by the Most High, the only God Himself; the "Son of God" being the appellation given to the human nature born of Mary: the clothing in which the Most High deigned to appear to men, a clothing woven of Mary's blood and substance.

Every human being derives his soul from the father, and his body from the mother. The soul is a graft of the father's soul, and, like the parent soul, it is not inherently possessed of life, but is a spiritual organism receptive of the life that inflows into all of God's creatures from Him who is the one and only source of life. In the case of Jesus Christ, His soul was not from the Father; it was the Father Himself, for the Infinite cannot be divided, there can be no off-shoot from It: "The Holy Spirit" came upon Mary, "the virtue of the Most High overshadowed" her, therefore the Holy Thing born of her was called "the Son of God." The soul of Jesus Christ was God Himself. For this reason,

> The Child born to us, the Son given to us, is called "God,.. the Father of eternity" (*Isa.* ix. 6).

The Lord Jesus Christ testified that the soul that dwelt within Him was the everlasting Father, when He said,

> "The Father that dwelleth in Me, He doeth the works" (*John* xiv. 10).

No man would say of his parent that he dwells within him, for the soul of a mortal is not the father, but from the father. And since the Father was in the Lord Jesus Christ, as the soul is in the body, therefore when Philip, who had heard Him say so much about the Father, finally asked Him, "Show us the Father," the Lord answered,

> "Have I been so long time with you, and hast thou not known Me, Philip? he that hath seen Me hath seen the Father; how sayest thou then, Shew us the Father?" (*John* xiv. 8, 9.)

The Father and the Son are frequently spoken of as though they were two distinct beings, and Jesus Christ Himself frequently prayed

INTRODUCTION.

to the Father and referred to Him as to a Person different from Himself. This form of speech is often employed in the following Summaries, in adaptation to the language of the New Testament, and we read of many Psalms that they are "prayers of the Lord to the Father." Occasionally the explanation is suggested that this means that the Human prayed to the Divine.

The human assumed by the Infinite God was at first merely human and finite, and hence such a distinction existed between this human and the inner Divine Soul, that, in states when the distinction was very evident, the intercourse between the two is represented as the speech between two distinct persons. The human, being assumed from a finite human being who shared the hereditary taint of the house and family of David, was itself full of inherited inclinations to evil. But these inherited forms were successively put off, and to the extent in which they were put off, interior and finally Divine forms took their place from the Divine that dwelt within: This process involved alternating states. In the one state the Human prayed to the Divine (or the "Son" to the "Father"). In the other state the Human spake with the authority and power of the Divine Itself. The first state, in which "He poured out His soul unto death" (*Isa.* liii. 12), is called the state of "exinanition," or of "humiliation;" the other state is called the state of "glorification." The death of merely finite tendencies, resulting finally in the death or dissipation of the very material of which the body had been organized, while the body itself remained as an organization of Divine substance, involved the resurrection of this body of organized "flesh and blood," which flesh and blood was now no longer material, but Divine—the Divine Human.

Without the state of humiliation the Lord could not have been crucified, but this state of final exinanition was followed by the state of complete glorification, which, being the state in which the human was lifted up from its finite state into the infinite glory of the Divine Itself, and thus united to It, is also called the state of "union." The Lord was in this state when He was transfigured before the three disciples on the Mount, and also when He performed miracles, and whenever He said that the Father and He were one, and that the Father was in Him and He in the Father, that all things of the Father are His; and, when the union was completed, that He had power over all flesh (*John* xvii. 2), and all power in heaven and earth (*Matth.* xxviii. 18).

The glorification of the Son, or the union of the Human with the Divine, is the very climax of the inner history of the Lord; it is the most excellent of all teachings of the church; it calls for the profoundest veneration. In the following work, summaries that tell of it are especially marked by an "N.B." placed opposite them in the margin by Swedenborg. (See Psalms ii. 10–12; xxiv. 7–10; xlv. 7, 8; lxxii. 17; lxxxix. 26–29, 35–37; cx. 4–7; cxxxii. 9, 10.)

This sublime teaching of the New Jerusalem has been treated of at some length in this Introduction, because it is necessary to a proper understanding of the Summaries, and also because these two states are especially referred to in the memoranda on page 4, where some of the places in the Gospels, as also in the Psalms, referring to these two states, are noted by Swedenborg. These citations are doubtless inserted here in order to show the internal and essential unity of the Word of both Testaments: one in that they both witness to the love and wisdom and life of the one Lord God Jesus Christ, who is the true God and eternal life, the God of both Testaments.

The passages in the Gospels refer to the records of the Lord's prayers to the Father, indicating the state of His humiliation and the intimate connection of such prayers with the succeeding state of union with the Divine, or glorification of the Human. While the literal sense of the Gospels thus witnesses to the two states of the Lord in His Human, the internal sense of the Old Testament, summarized in this work, notably of the Psalms, treats of the same states with great fulness.

The passages in the Psalms referred to on page 4, clear away any doubt that the internal sense of the Psalms so treats of the Lord. Let us consider them.

In Psalm lxix. 21 we read, "They gave me gall for my meat; and in my thirst they gave me vinegar to drink." The enlightenment vouchsafed to even the most simple reader enables him to recognize in this verse a prophecy of the Lord Jesus when He was brought to Golgotha to be crucified, and

"They gave Him vinegar to drink mingled with gall" (*Matt.* xxvii. 34).

David, writing the Psalm from inspiration, represented the Lord who was to come into the world, and by referring to his own personality, foretold what would happen to Him who was to be

"The root and offspring of David" (*Rev.* xxii. 16), but who was, nevertheless, David's Lord (*Mark* xii. 36, 37).

The verse in the Psalm is not true literally, but it is true prophetically. We are reminded here of the statement in the present work prefatory to the summaries of the Psalms,

"It should be known, that as by David the Lord is meant, so where David speaks in the Psalms, the Lord is signified in the spiritual sense."

The same remarks apply to the next reference on page 4, Psalm xxii. 16–18, "Dogs have compassed me about, the assembly of the malignant have surrounded me: they pierced my hands and my feet. I may tell all my bones; they look, they stare upon me. They parted my garments among them, and cast lots upon my vesture." There is no historical evidence, and not the slightest probability, that David, even when most harrassed by his enemies, had his hands and feet pierced, and that his garments were divided among his enemies, and lots cast upon his vesture. But when the Lord Jesus Christ was crucified, the nails pierced His hands and feet; and

They "parted His garments, casting lots: that it might be fulfilled which was spoken by the prophet, They parted My garments among them, and upon My vesture did they cast lots" (*Matt.* xxvii, 35).

Here David is called outright a prophet. What he had said about himself was not literally true, but it was prophetic of what was done to the Lord. Thus David, as a prophet, represented the Lord.

In Psalm xxxv. 19, David says, "Let not them that are mine enemies of a lie rejoice over me: neither let them wink with the eye that hate me without a cause." On the memorable occasion of the Last Supper, when the Lord foretold His death, and the hatred borne Him, saying,

> "If I had not done among them the works which none other man did, they had not had sin, but now have they both seen and hated both Me and My Father;" He added, "But that the Word might be fulfilled that is written in their Law, They hated Me without a cause" (*John* xv. 24, 25),

So the Lord Jesus Christ fulfilled in His own Person what David had said of himself in a representative capacity, and the Lord's fulfilment carried with it all the import of Divine love and mercy that had aroused the malignant hatred of His wicked and causeless enemies.

And finally, the words in Psalm cxviii. 22, 23, "The stone rejected of the builders is become the head of the corner; this is the Lord's doing, it is wonderful in our eyes," are quoted by the Lord (*Matt.* xxi. 42), as applying to Himself.

Since, then, from the recorded fulfilment of these Old Testament prophecies it is clear that David wrote prophetically of the Lord, representing Him in his own person, we may justly conclude that all of the Psalms treat of the Lord, and that this is what is meant by the Lord's expounding "in all the Scriptures the things concerning Himself." And if David so represented the Lord when he spoke in the Psalms, why not when he is spoken of in the two books of *Samuel* and in *Kings?* David's enemies represented the Lord's enemies, not only the Jews, that, like dogs, compassed Him about and clamored for His life, but principally the powers of evil in hell from whom come evil influences to men on earth. David's prayers and lamentations represented the Lord's prayers and temptations; David's victories over his enemies represented the Lord's victories over the hells, over Satan and the Devil; David's exultant Psalms voiced prophetically the joy of the Lord over the accomplishment of the glorious work of redemption. And since David as king and as prophet represented the Lord, is it unreasonable to conclude that all the other prophets and kings likewise represented Him? The hard things that the prophets often bore but represented the cruel things which the Word, and thus the Lord as the Word, bore from His rebellious and sinful people. The prophets represented the Lord; the people, and even the land itself, represented the church.

Everything written in the Word has reference to the Lord:

> "From *Isaiah* to *Malachi* there is not anything which is not about the Lord, or in the opposite sense, opposed to the Lord" (*Doctrine concerning the Lord*, n. 2).

The state of the church is gauged by its knowledge and acknowledgment of the Lord, and therefore the Word treats also of the states of

INTRODUCTION.   xiii

the church. In the following Summaries, while those of the Psalms treat more especially of the Lord, those of the Prophets treat more especially of the states of the church. All the spiritual contents of the prophetical books may be summed up in the six propositions given on page 6, stated more fully in the extract from the *Doctrine concerning the Lord* (n. 3), quoted on page xv.

The internal sense of the Word, being free from the many paradoxes and appearances of truth of the literal sense, and presenting the Divine truth in the light in which it appears to the angels in heaven, constitutes the doctrine of genuine truth for the church. For this reason the general summing up of the internal sense on page 6 agrees perfectly with "The Faith of the New Heaven and the New Church in its Universal Form," which is prefaced as "face, gate, and summary" to *The True Christian Religion, containing the Universal Theology of the New Church*, where it is given in the following comprehensive form:

"The Lord from eternity, who is Jehovah, came into the world that He might subjugate the hells and glorify His Human. Without this no mortal could have been saved; and they are saved who believe in Him."

The topics on page 6, which stand at the head of the Summaries in the manuscript, are given in a more amplified form on the preceding page of the manuscript, where we find a list of sixteen subjects (see folder, page 4), giving thus more fully the universals of the faith of the New Heaven and the New Church. The relation of this "TABLE OF SUBJECTS" to the Summaries is described in the EDITOR'S PREFACE.

In conclusion, a word respecting the rank of this work in the order pervading the theology of the New Church, and respecting its use to the expositor of the Word, and to every reader of our Heavenly Father's Book.

The place of this work in the general system of the Doctrines of the New Jerusalem is made clear by an analysis of those works which present the internal sense in serial form, namely, the *Arcana Coelestia*, the *Apocalypse Revealed*, and the *Apocalypse Explained*. The *Apocalypse Revealed* offers a good example. Here, at the head of every chapter, we find the "Spiritual Sense of the contents of the whole chapter;" then follow the "Contents of the single verses," and finally the elaborate explanation adapted to the reason and understanding of man, and confirmations and illustrations from the literal sense of the Word and from the phenomena of nature and experiences of human life. The Summaries contained in the work before us answer to the "Contents of the whole chapter." These Summaries give, therefore, the key to the internal sense of all the Prophets and Psalms.

These contents are the guide for applying the science of correspondences which gives the spiritual signification of the particular words of Sacred Scripture. By following this guide, the danger of violating the spiritual sense by exploring it from one's own intelligence may be guarded against, of which danger we have the following wholesome warning:

"By means of some correspondences known to man he can pervert that sense, and even force it to confirm falsity; and this would be to offer violence to Divine Truth, and thus also to heaven in which it dwells" (*True Christian Religion*, n. 208, 230).

The use of the Summaries in connection with the reading of the Sacred Scriptures, seems to be indicated in teachings like the following :

"The Word conjoins man to heaven, and through heaven with the Lord, since all things in the sense of the letter correspond to things celestial and spiritual in which are the angels, with whom there is no communication if the Word is applied only according to the letter, and not at the same time according to some doctrine of the church, which is the internal of the Word" (*Arcana Coelestia*, n. 9410).

"From the first chapter of *Isaiah* to the last of *Malachi*, and in the *Psalms of David*, every verse communicates with some society of heaven, and thus the whole Word with the universal heaven" (*True Christian Religion*, n. 272).

"If man knew that there is an internal sense, and would think from some knowledge of it when he is reading the Word, he would come into interior wisdom ; and would be still more conjoined with heaven because he would thereby enter into ideas like the angelic ones" (*Heaven and Hell*, n. 310; cf. *Arcana Coelestia*, n. 3316).

E. J. E. S.

INTIMATIONS OF THIS LITTLE WORK FOUND IN OTHER WORKS OF EMANUEL SWEDENBORG.

[CONCERNING THE LORD, n. 37.]

It is allowable to mention that it has been granted me to go through all the Prophets and the Psalms of David, and to examine each single verse, and to see what is there treated of, and it was seen that nothing else is treated of but the church established and to be established by the Lord, the Lord's advent, combats, glorification, redemption and salvation, and heaven from Him, together with their opposites. Because all of these are the Lord's works it appeared that the whole Sacred Scripture is concerning the Lord, and hence that the Lord is the Word.

[CONCERNING THE LORD, n. 2.]

Because the Word is the Lord Himself, therefore each and every thing of the Word has been written about Him alone; from *Isaiah* to *Malachi* there is not any thing that is not concerning the Lord, or in the opposite sense, against the Lord.

[CONCERNING THE LORD, n. 3.]

It shall here be told briefly what respecting the Lord is treated of in all the Prophets of the Old Testament, from *Isaiah* to *Malachi*, in general and specifically.

(I.) That the Lord came into the world in the fulness of times, which was when He was no longer recognized by the Jews, and because of this, when nothing of the church yet remained, and unless the Lord had then come into the world and revealed Himself, man would have perished in eternal death; for He says in *John*:

"Unless ye believe that I am, ye shall die in your sins" (viii. 24).

(II.) That the Lord came into the world to effect a last judgment, and thereby subjugate the hells then dominant, which was done by combats, that is, by temptations admitted into His human from the mother, and by continual victories at that time; and unless the hells had been subjugated no man could have been saved.

(III.) That the Lord came into the world to glorify His Human, that is unite it to the Divine which was in Him from conception.

(IV.) That the Lord came into the world to establish a new church, which should acknowledge Him as the Redeemer and Saviour, and be redeemed and saved by love and faith in Him.

(V.) That at the same time He set heaven in order, so that it might make one with the church.

(VI.) That the passion of the cross was the last combat or temptation, by which He fully conquered the hells, and fully glorified His Human.

[THE TRUE CHRISTIAN RELIGION, n. 272; CONCERNING THE SACRED SCRIPTURE, n. 113.]

By much experience it has been granted me to know that by means of the Word man has communication with heaven. While I read the Word through from the first chapter of *Isaiah* to the last of *Malachi*, and the *Psalms of David*, and kept my thought on their spiritual sense, it was given me to perceive clearly that every verse communicated with some society of heaven, and thus the whole Word with the universal heaven; from which it was evident, that as the Lord is the Word, heaven is also the Word, since heaven is heaven from the Lord, and the Lord, through the Word, is all in all of heaven.

[CONCERNING THE WORD, n. 10.]*

That all things of the Word correspond to all things of heaven has been granted me to perceive from this, that every chapter in the prophetic Word corresponds to a particular society of heaven; for when I went through the propheticals of the Word from *Isaiah* to *Malachi*, it was granted me to see that the societies of heaven were stirred up in their order and that they perceived the spiritual sense corresponding to them; from these and from other evidences it was made clear to me that there is a correspondence of the entire heaven with the Word in a series.

[*See also* n. 18; *and* CONCERNING THE SACRED SCRIPTURE, n. 64.]

[CONCERNING THE SACRED SCRIPTURE, n. 97.]

The Divine truth in the Word and its character are depicted by the "cherubs" in the first and in the ninth and tenth chapters of *Ezekiel;* but because the significance of each single part of the description of them can be known only to him to whom the spiritual sense has been opened, it has been disclosed to me what all those things that are said of the "cherubs" in the first chapter of *Ezekiel* signify in brief, which are these:

The external Divine sphere of the Word is described (verse 4);
It is represented as a man (verse 5);
Conjoined to things spiritual and celestial (verse 6);
The natural of the Word, what it is (verse 7);
The spiritual and celestial of the Word conjoined to its natural, what it is (verses 8, 9);
The Divine love of celestial, spiritual and natural good and truth therein, separately and together (verses 10, 11);
They look to a one (verse 12);
The sphere of the Word from the Lord's Divine good and Divine truth, from which the Word has its life (verses 13, 14);

---

* A work not yet published in the English language. Published in Latin in 1854.

INTIMATIONS.

> *The doctrine of good and truth in the Word and from the Word* (verses 15-21);
> *The Divine of the Lord above it and in it* (verses 22, 23);
> *And from it* (verses 24, 25);
> *The Lord is above the heavens* (verse 26);
> *And the Divine love and Divine wisdom is His* (verses 27, 28).

These summaries have even been compared with the Word in heaven, and are in conformity with it.

[*See also* THE APOCALYPSE REVEALED, n. 239.]

[THE APOCALYPSE REVEALED, n. 859.]

.... As the spiritual sense has been disclosed to me, it shall be opened ...what those things signify that are contained in chapters xxxviii. and xxxix. of *Ezekiel*. In chapter xxxviii. in *Ezekiel* are these things:

> *Those are treated of who are in the sense of the letter of the Word only, and in a worship therefrom that is external without any internal; this is "Gog"* (verses 1, 2);
> *All things and each thing of that church will perish* (verses 3-7);
> *That worship will invade the church, will vastate it, and thus it will be in externals without internals* (verses 8-16);
> *The state of the church is consequently changed* (verses 17-19);
> *The truths and goods of religion will therefore perish, and falsities will take their place* (verses 20-23).

In chapter xxxix. of the same are these things:

> *Those who are in the sense of the letter of the Word only and in external worship will come into the church: these are "Gog;" but they will perish* (verses 1-6);
> *This will take place when the Lord comes and establishes a church* (verses 7, 8);
> *This church will then disperse all their evils and falsities* (verses 9, 10);
> *It will utterly destroy them* (verses 11-16);
> *The new church that will be established by the Lord will be instructed in truths and goods of every kind, and will be imbued with goods of every kind* (verses 17-21);
> *And the former church will be destroyed on account of evils and falsities* (verses 23, 24);
> *Then a church will be gathered together by the Lord from all nations* (verses 25-29).

But something shall be said about those who are in an external worship without internal spiritual worship,....

[THE APOCALYPSE REVEALED, n. 43.]

In *Zechariah* (chap. iv.), the "candlestick" signifies a new church to be established by the Lord, since it signifies the new house of God, or the new temple, as appears from what there follows, and by the "house of God" or the "temple" is signified the church, and in the highest sense the Divine

Human of the Lord, as He Himself teaches (*John* ii. 19-21, and elsewhere). But it shall be told what is signified in order in chapter iv. of *Zechariah*, when the "candlestick" was seen by him:

> *The things contained in verses* 1 *to* 7 *signify the enlightenment of the new church by the Lord from the good of love by means of truth,* "*olive trees*" *signifying here the church in respect to good of love;*
>
> *The things in verses* 8 *to* 10 *signify that these things are from the Lord,* "*Zerubabel,*" *who was to build the house, thus the church, representing the Lord;*
>
> *The things in verses* 11 *to* 14 *signify that in that church will also be truths from a celestial origin.*

This explanation of that chapter has been given to me through heaven by the Lord.

[THE APOCALYPSE REVEALED, n. 707.]

In *Zechariah* (chap. xii.)...the coming of the Lord and the end of the Jewish Church and the beginning of a new church to be established by the Lord, also the collision between those churches are treated of. .... As the series of things in that chapter and in the two that follow in that prophet has been disclosed to me through the spiritual sense, it shall be stated, but in a brief summary. In chapter xii., in *Zechariah*, in the spiritual sense it is set forth:

> *That the Lord is to form a new church* (verse 1);
>
> *That there will then be nothing of doctrine in the old church, and therefore they will shun it* (verses 2, 3);
>
> *That there will be no longer any understanding of truth except with those who are in the Word, and who are of the new church* (verse 4);
>
> *That these will learn good of doctrine from the Lord* (verse 5);
>
> *That the Lord, by means of the truths of the Word, will then destroy all falsities, so that the doctrine of the new church may teach nothing but truth* (verses 6, 7);
>
> *That the church will then be in doctrine concerning the Lord* (verse 8);
>
> *That then He will destroy all men and all things opposed to that doctrine* (verse 9);
>
> *And that there will then be a new church from the Lord* (verse 10);
>
> *And that all things and each thing of the church will then be in mourning* (verses 10-14).

These are the contents of chapter xii. in the spiritual sense. The contents of the following chapter (xiii.) are as follows:

> *That the Word will be for the new church, and it will be open to them* (verse 1);
>
> *That falsities of doctrine and of worship will be utterly destroyed* (verses 2, 3);
>
> *That the old prophetic or doctrinal will cease; and that falsities of doctrine will be no more* (verses 4, 5);
>
> *That the Lord will be slain by those who are in the old church with the intention that those who believe in Him may be scattered* (verses 6, 7);

INTIMATIONS.

That those who are of the devastated church will perish, and that those who are of the new church are to be purified and taught by the Lord (verses 8, 9).

These are the contents of chapter xiii. in the spiritual sense. The contents of chapter xiv. are as follows:

Concerning the combats of the Lord against the evil, and their dispersion (verses 1-5);
That there will then be no truth, but from the Lord [there will be] Divine truth (verses 6, 7);
That Divine truth will go forth from the Lord (verses 8, 9);
That truth will be multiplied in the new church, and there will be no falsity of evil there (verses 10, 11);
That he who fights against these truths will place himself in falsities of every kind (verse 12);
That there will then be a destruction of all things of the church (verses 13-15);
That there will then be a drawing near to the worship of the Lord, even by nations that are external natural (verses 16-19);
That there will then be intelligence from good of charity, from which is worship (verses 20, 21).

These are the contents of the three chapters xii., xiii., xiv. of *Zechariah* in the spiritual sense, that have been disclosed, because in them the last state of the old church and the first state of the new church is treated of.

SUMMARIES OF THE INTERNAL SENSE

OF

The Prophetical Books
The Psalms of David
Historical Parts of the Word

[From the Author's Manuscript.]

TO BE PUBLISHED:

1 Concerning the Lord.
2 Concerning the Sacred Scripture or concerning the Word of the Lord.
3 All things of religion and of the worship of God in one complex in the Decalogue.
4 Concerning Faith.

---

5 Angelic wisdom concerning the Divine Providence.
6 Angelic wisdom concerning the Divine omnipotence and omniscience, and concerning infinity and eternity.
7 Angelic wisdom concerning life.
8 Angelic wisdom concerning the Divine love and Divine wisdom.

[Table of Subjects.]

[The gothic figures (**1, 17, 5·7·8**, etc.,) in the margin of the following pages refer to the Subjects on this folder.]

The things that follow [in this little work treat of]:

1. The Lord's advent.
2. The successive vastation of the church.
3. The church totally devastated, and its rejection.
4. The rejection of the Lord by the church.
5. Temptations of the Lord in general.
6. Temptations even to despair.
7. The combats of the Lord with the hells.
8. Victory over them, or their subjugation.
9. The passion of the cross.
10. The glorification of the Human of the Lord, or its union with the Divine.
11. A new church in place of the former.
12. A new church together with a new heaven.
13. The state of humiliation before the Father.
*15. A last judgment by the Lord.
16. Celebration and worship of the Lord.
17. Redemption and salvation by the Lord.

---

* EDITOR'S NOTE.—No. 14 is crossed out by Swedenborg in his MS., and is never referred to in the text. It reads, " The state of union with His Divine," which is the same as No. 10.

THE LORD'S STATE OF HUMILIATION.

HIS PRAYING TO THE FATHER.

He prayed to the Father
 (*Matthew* xiv. 23; *John* xvii. 9, 15, 20; *Luke* v. 16; xxii. 37–47; *Mark* i. 35; vi. 46; xiv. 32–39);
and upon the cross, that He be not forsaken; and elsewhere.

He was then conjoined to His Divine: as when He was baptized heaven was opened
     (*Luke* iii. 21);
when He was transfigured He also prayed
     (*Luke* ix. 28, 29);
and when He prayed concerning glorification it was said that He was glorified and should be glorified further
     (*John* xii. 28).

If they asked [anything] in the name of the Lord, that He would do [it]
     (*John* xiv. 13, 14).

From David:
 They gave Him gall [*Ps.* lxix. 21 (H.B. 22)].
 They divided His garments [*Ps.* xxii. 18 (H.B. 19)].
 They hated Him without a cause [*Ps.* xxxv. 19].
 The stone that the builders rejected (*Ps.* cxviii. 21, 22).

The Prophetical Books

[*CONTENTS OF THE PROPHETICAL BOOKS.*]

[See Doctrine concerning the Lord, n. 3.]

I. THE CHURCH DEVASTATED.

II. COMBATS WITH THE HELLS, OR TEMPTATIONS.

III. THE LAST, WHICH WAS THE PASSION OF THE CROSS.

IV. THE GLORIFICATION OF THE HUMAN.

V. A NEW CHURCH.

VI. A NEW HEAVEN.

Isaiah.

Chapter I.

Verses   Subjects*
1–8   **3** The church has been vastated by evil of life,
9   **3** so that there is little of a residue.
10–15   **3** Therefore their external worship is of no avail.
16–19   **3** Exhortation that they should repent of the evil of life, and thus they will receive good.
20–23   **3** They falsify the Word.
24–27   **1·11** The Lord when He comes will destroy them, and will establish the church with others :
28–31   **3** This when nothing of the church remains with them.

Chapter II.

1–5   **1·12** The coming of the Lord, and a new heaven and a new church at that time, are openly treated of,
6–9   **1·3** because in the former church there is nothing but falsity and evil of falsity.
10–18   **1·3·15** The coming of the Lord is openly treated of: He will destroy all who are in the love of self and in the pride of their own intelligence.
10, 19–21   **15** The last judgment is openly treated of, and the casting down of the evil into hell.
22   **15** Something concerning the separation of the good from them.

Chapter III.

1–7   **2** There will be a lack of knowledges (*cognitiones*) of good and truth,
8–12   **2** because they are in evils and in things falsified.

---

* Editor's Note.—The figures in this column index the general subject or subjects of each line in the manuscript, and refer to the Table of Subjects on the folder attached to page 4.

Verses   *Subjects*
13, 14   15 The Lord will come to judgment,
15–26   15 and He will cast into hell those who have perverted the truths of the Word.

Chapter IV.

1–3   12 There will then be from the Lord a new thing of the church,
4–6   12 and providence that the Word be not perverted still further.

Chapter V.

1, 2   2 A church full of truths and goods from the Word was instituted by the Lord.
3, 4, 7   2 It became perverted.
[5, 6,] 7–15   2 It is destroyed still further by falsifications of the truth and good of the Word.
16, 17   1·11 The Lord will come and give the church to others.
[18,19,] 20–30   15 Those who perverted the truths and goods of the church will perish from falsities and evils of every kind.

Chapter VI.

1–4   [1] The Lord appeared in the midst of His Divine truth, which is the Word.
5–8   2 The doctrine of the church, derived from the Word not understood, was impure.
9–13   2 It is foretold that all understanding of the Word would perish, so that at last it would no longer be known what truth and good are in the church.

Chapter VII.

1–6   2 Ignorance of truth and non-understanding of the Word will enter and begin to destroy the church.
7–9   3·2 It is foretold that this will not take place as yet,
10–16   3·1 but it will at the time when the Lord comes into the world.
17–20   2·3 Then all understanding of the Word will be perverted by knowledges (*scientifica*) and by reasonings from them, until nothing remains.

Verses	Subjects	
21, 22	11·3	Then truth will be taught in all abundance.
23, 24	11·3	The church will then be wholly devastated.
25	11·3	It will be otherwise with those who receive.

Chapter VIII.

1–4	2·3	It is foretold that before that time knowledge (*cognitio*) and perception of truth will perish,
5, 6	2·3	because they are not willing to understand the Word in simplicity.
7–12	2·3	By reasonings from falsities the whole church will perish, until conjunction with God will no longer take place;
13–16	4	and they will not know the Lord, who is the Word and the church.
17–21	11	Nevertheless, others will know the Lord, who reject falsities, and put away things falsified,
CH. IX. 1 H.B. viii. 23	11	and who, by combats against evils and falsities, receive reformation;
CH. VIII. 22 H.B. viii. 22	3	although the church there is nothing but falsity.

Chapter IX.

1	11	[See above, before chap. viii., verse 22.]
2–4 H.B. ix. 1–3	1·11	The coming of the Lord, and the new church which will receive Him,
5 H.B. 4	1·11	but not the old church, which has been destroyed.
6, 7 H.B. 5, 6	11	The Lord, who is described, will do all things, and He will protect from falsities and evils.
8–21 H.B. 7–20	3	The old church, from its own intelligence, will falsify and pervert every truth and good of the Word and thus of the church, even until nothing remains.

Chapter X.

1, 2	2	The further vastation of the church, by their taking away stealthily from others the truths and goods of the church.
3, 4	5·2	They will perish at the time of the last judgment.

Verses	Subjects	
5–11	2	They pervert truths by reasonings from their own intelligence.
12–19	15·3	At the time of the last judgment such are to be utterly destroyed by the Lord, so that scarcely anything of natural truth will remain with them.
20–22, 24	17·3 12	Those who believe in the Lord are to be saved, and to be protected lest they be taken captive by confirmations of falsity through reasonings;
23, 25–34	12	because the whole church has been devastated by knowledges (*scientifica*) that pervert the truths of the church and confirm falsities.

CHAPTER XI.

1   THE COMING OF THE LORD.

1–5	15	He will judge from Divine wisdom; and will save the faithful and destroy the unfaithful.
6–9	12	The state of innocence that those in the heavens have who trust in Him.
10–12	11·12	Those who are in falsities from ignorance, and have not suffered themselves to be led astray by falsities and evils, will draw near to the Lord.
13–15	11·12	The church will then understand the Word, and will shake off falsities of every kind.
16	11·12	These falsities will no longer hurt them

CHAPTER XII.

1–6	16	Confession and celebration of the Lord on account of salvation.

CHAPTER XIII.

IN THIS CHAPTER, CONCERNING THE ADULTERATION OF GOOD AND TRUTH, WHICH IS "BABEL" [OR "BABYLON"].

1–3	1	The Lord will come in Divine power,
4–9	15	for grievous judgment upon those that have utterly departed, to destroy them,
10–12	15	because there is no longer any good and truth remaining with them.
13–18	15	Therefore all will perish with their evils and falsities,
19–22	15	and abide in hell, where there are direful and horrid evils and falsities.

Chapter XIV.

Verses *Subjects*
1–3   **12** The new church that is to be established.
4–6   **15·3** The judgment upon those who have adulterated the goods of the church and profaned its truths, which are "Babel" [or "Babylon"].
7–12, }   **15·3** The casting of them down into hell, where they are
15–21 }   the worst of all.
13, 14   **15·3** Their pride, that they wish to have dominion with God over heaven.
22, 23   **15·3** Their horrible end.
24–27   **15·3** Those who by reasonings from their own intelligence destroy the truths of the Word and profane them, are to be destroyed.

28–32   **15** THE JUDGMENT UPON THOSE WHO MAKE RELIGION TO CONSIST IN
L.B. XV. 1–5   NOTHING BUT KNOWLEDGES (*cognitiones*). THESE KNOWLEDGES ARE "PHILISTEA."

30, 32   **12** When they are removed the church will be safe.
L.B. XV. 3, 5

Chapter XV.

15·3 THE LAST JUDGMENT UPON THOSE WHO HAVE REJECTED THE GOODS OF CHARITY, AND HAVE PERVERTED THE GOODS OF THE WORD, WHO ARE MEANT BY "MOAB."

1–9   **15·3** Their destruction.
L.B. xvi. 1–9

Chapter XVI.

1, 2   **4** The Lord is not acknowledged by them.
L.B. 10, 11
3–5   **15** They will remain until the coming of the Lord, and
L.B. 12–14   are then to be judged.
6–14   **15** Of what quality they are, and of what quality they
L.B. 15–23   will be after their end.

Chapter XVII.

2 THOSE WHO PLACE RELIGION IN NOTHING BUT KNOWING KNOWLEDGES (*scientia cognitionum*), WHICH IS "DAMASCUS."

1, 2   **2** They are to be destroyed.
3   **11·2** This [knowledge] will be serviceable to the new church.
4–6   **11·2** The knowledge of knowledges will then be rare,

Verses	Subjects	
7, 8	11·2	but they are to be instructed by the Lord.
9–14	11·2	Those who do not suffer themselves to be instructed by the Lord will lack all things, and will seize upon falsities for truths.

Chapter XVIII.

<blank> 2 THOSE WHO ARE WILLING TO BE IN BLIND IGNORANCE RESPECTING THE THINGS OF SALVATION. SUCH ARE "CUSH" [OR "ETHIOPIA"].

1, 2	2	Their quality.
3–6	3	When the church will be established, they will be rejected as worthless.
7	11	On the other hand, those who are in ignorance from not having the church, will draw near to the Lord.

Chapter XIX.

<blank> 2 THOSE WHO, OUT OF A MERE SCIENCE OF SUCH THINGS AS BELONG TO THE WORD AND THE CHURCH, MAKE A RELIGION FOR THEMSELVES, AND ENTER INTO IT; THIS RELIGION IS "EGYPT."

1–4	2	From this come controversies and heresies; and such men enter into falsities of every kind.
5–10	2	All truths will perish with them.
[11,]12–15	2·3	Insanity will take the place of intelligence.
15–17	15	They will perish.
18–22	11	Such knowledges (*scientifica*) will be of use in the future, when they have been instructed in truths by the Lord.
23–25	11·12	Then the spiritual, rational, and knowing faculties will act in unity.

Chapter XX.

<blank> 2·3 THE SAME.

1–6	2·3	In consequence of their having been deprived of truths, they will be led astray by reasonings and will be devastated by them of every good of religion.

Chapter XXI.

1–4	3	Natural good will no longer remain.
5–7	1·11	Expectation of the Lord, when the natural [of man] will first be imbued with truths from good;

Verses	Subjects	
8–10	II	then the rational,
9	3	so far as adulteration of good and truth ceases.
11, 12	II	The coming of the Lord is expected.
13, 14	2·II	Then those who are in ignorance will have knowledges (*cognitiones*) of good and truth.
15–17	II·2·3	He will come when all knowledges (*cognitiones*) of truth and good perish, until very little is left.

Chapter XXII.

2   SELF INTELLIGENCE.

1–7	2	The truths of the church are destroyed thereby.
8–12	2	The externals of the church are wholly destroyed thereby, until they come into ignorance concerning the Lord.
13–15	2	From the delights of falsity, they will then destroy the senses of the Word.
16–19	2	They will perish.
20–24	2	The power of the Word will remain, guarded by the Lord.
25	2	This also will perish in the church.

Chapter XXIII.

2 THE CHURCH WHICH IS TO BE DEVASTATED AND WHICH HAS BEEN DEVASTATED IN RESPECT TO ALL KNOWLEDGES (*cognitiones*) OF GOOD AND TRUTH. THIS IS "TYRE."

1–9	2	There is no longer any truth of the church through knowledges (*cognitiones*), as before.
10–14	2	It will be vastated still further by reasonings from falsities.
15–17	1·2·3	The devastation of knowledges (*cognitiones*) of truth will extend, and it will last until the coming of the Lord.
18	II	The knowledges (*cognitiones*) will then be of service to others.

Chapter XXIV.

1–13	3	The church in general is utterly devasted, insomuch that there is no longer anything of the church remaining, but in its place falsity and evil.
14–16	II	Those who are outside of the church will receive enlightenment from the Lord.
16–20	3	The church will utterly perish, and is to be destroyed.

14   SUMMARIES OF THE INTERNAL SENSE.

Verses   Subjects
21, 22   15 They are to be cast into hell.
22, 23   11-12 There will be a new church from the Lord in place of the old.

Chapter XXV.

1   16 Confession of the Lord,
2   3 after all things of the church had utterly perished.
3–5   11 They shall not then perish; and those who are outside of the church shall draw near, and shall be protected that they be not infested by them.
6–8   11 The Lord will disclose truths to them, and will take away the blindness that has arisen.
9, 10   16 Confession of the Lord by them.
10–12   3 Adulteration of the good of the church and of the Word will be utterly destroyed.

Chapter XXVI.

1–4   16 Glorification of the Lord because of the doctrine of truth from Him, which they will receive and confess.
5, 6   3 The old church, being utterly destroyed, is rejected.
7–9   1 Consequently the coming of the Lord will then be expected.
10, 11   4 The wicked will not receive.
12, 13   11 The Lord alone will teach all things.
14, 15   15 Those who by persuasion establish falsity of doctrine, are to be utterly rejected by the judgment.
16–18   11 They could not grow better prior to this, owing to the ignorance in which they are.
19   11 Nevertheless, they are to be instructed, and will receive life.
19–21   15 They are to be preserved, while, in the meantime, those who are in the persuasion of falsity are to be destroyed by the last judgment.

Chapter XXVII.

1   2 There is no longer any truth or good in the natural man.
2, 3   11 Nevertheless the truth of the church must be guarded.

ISAIAH XXIX. 15

Verses	Subjects	
4, 5	15	Every evil and falsity will be destroyed on the day of judgment.
6	11	Afterwards there will be a new church
7, 8	11	with those in whom truths have not been completely lost.
8–12	15	In time all true worship will perish, with all truth and good : they will perish on the day of judgment.
12, 13	11	Afterwards there will be a new church that will confess the Lord.

CHAPTER XXVIII.

2 THOSE WHO FROM THEIR OWN INTELLIGENCE HAVE FALSIFIED TRUTHS. THESE ARE "THE DRUNKARDS OF EPHRAIM."

1, 2	2	Falsities will break in.
3, 4	2	Truths will perish.
5[, 6]	11	The Lord will teach truths when He comes.
7, 8	3	Then all doctrine will be full of falsities and evils,
9, 10	3	so that they cannot be instructed and taught.
11–13	3	They will reject.
14–16	4	They will laugh to scorn those things that are of heaven and the church, and will reject those things that are of the Lord.
17–21	4·2	Although they will reprobate and not understand, nevertheless they must be taught.
22–29	2·3	They will be taught constantly, and yet will not receive.

CHAPTER XXIX.

3 THE LOST DOCTRINE OF TRUTH OF THE CHURCH. THIS IS "ARIEL."

1–4	3	It will perish even until it is not anything.
5, 6	2·3	Falsities will gain strength and pervert still further, even until the church perishes.
7, 8	2·3	Falsity will appear as truth.
9–12	2·3	Because of falsities they are unable to see truths.
13	2·3	There is external worship without internal.
14	2·3	There is no longer any understanding of truth.
15, 16	3	They will entertain sinister thoughts about God.
17–19	3·11	When the old church perishes, a new one is to be established by the Lord.
20, 21	3	All who are against truth and good will perish.
22–24	11	It will be otherwise with those who will receive the

Chapter XXX.

Verses	Subjects	
1–5	2	Those who trust in the knowledge (*scientia*) of the natural man, thus in their own intelligence, lead themselves astray.
6	2	The learned or the self-taught:
7–10	2	they are led astray by knowledges (*scientiae*), and they recede from the Word,
11	2	and from the Lord.
12–14	2	Thus they have no truth and thus again no good.
15	2	They should have trust in the Lord.
16, 17	2	Those who trust in themselves and in their own learning have no intelligence whatever.
18, 19	11	The Lord turns Himself to those who trust in Him.
20, 21	11	They will be instructed.
22	11	They will then reject those things pertaining to self-intelligence.
23–26	11	They will then have truth in all abundance, and wisdom.
27, 28	15·3	When those who are in the falsities of evil will perish,
29, 30	11	they will then come into the delights of truth and good, from the Lord.
30, 31	15	There will be a judgment on those who trust in themselves.
32, 33	15	Those who have thereby adulterated the Word, will be cast into hell.

Chapter XXXI.

1	4	Those who trust in their own learning from self-intelligence, and not in the Lord,
2	2·4	are against Him; wherefore they have evil.
3	2	They have no understanding of truth, but will fall into falsities.
4	15	They are to be destroyed at the time of judgment.
5, 6	11	The Lord will then protect those in whom is the church from Him.
7	11	Then they will reject falsities and evils.
8, 9	15	Those who trust in themselves will perish.
9	11	There will be good from the Lord in the new church.

Chapter XXXII.

Verses   *Subjects*

1	1	When the Lord will reign by means of the Divine truth,
2–4	II	truth will be acceptable, and there will be understanding of truth,
5	II	and pretense will cease.
6, 7	3	Then the falsespeaker will speak falsities, and the malevolent will do evils,
8	II	and vice versa.
9–12	II[?3]	Then all things of the church will cease,
13, 14	[3]	and falsity will be everywhere,
15–18	II	even until there is Divine truth from the Lord; then there will be truth and good, and protection from falsities.
19	3	Falsity will continue even unto the end.
20	II	Not so with those who love truth and good.

Chapter XXXIII.

1	3	Those who by falsities vastate the truths of the church.
2	II	The Lord when He comes, will protect His own.
3, 4	3	The vastators will be dispersed by Him.
5, 6	II	They will have protection from the Lord by means of Divine truth.
7–9	3	Devastation of the truth of the church will then continue.
10	4	They will not care for the Lord.
11, 12	15·3	Falsities and evils will consume all things of the church.
13, 14	15	They will fear the last judgment.
15–17	II·17	Those who do good are to be saved by the Lord.
18, 19	II	They will not listen to falsities nor believe them.
20–22	II	They will be of the Lord's church, and there they will have from the Lord an abundance of all things of truth,
23, 24	II	and of all things of good; and thus no more evil.

Chapter XXXIV.

1–8	15	A last judgment upon all who are in evil and in falsities therefrom, is described.

Verses	Subjects	
9–15	15	Having been cast down into hell they will abide in horrid falsities and evils to eternity.
16	15	This has been foretold.
17	11	It will be otherwise with those who are not such.

Chapter XXXV.

1–3	11	Those who are outside of the church, and do not have the Word, are to be accepted, that they may become a church, and all things of heaven are to be given to them.
[4,] 5	11	The Lord will protect and liberate the latter from the infernals,
6–9	11	and while in the midst of them they are to be protected and saved.
10	11	The church will consist of them, and they will have the good of the church.

Chapter XXXVI.

1	2	Reasonings from falsities have perverted the doctrinals of the church,
2–6	2	by means of knowledges (*scientifica*) falsely applied,
7	2·3	and by abrogation of the representative worship,
8–10	2·3	and in consequence, the church has gone away into what is perverse;
11, 12	2·3	the result of this was mere evils and falsities,
13–20	2·3	even so that they blasphemed the Lord, [maintaining] that He had no power.
21, 22	2·3	This has been made manifest.

Chapter XXXVII.

1–5	3	Of those who repented, and consulted truths of doctrine,
6, 7	3·2·4	and perceived that those who blasphemed the Lord will perish.
8–13	3·4	They blasphemed still more violently, as [in the assertion] that He could be of no avail whatever against them.
14–20	3·11	Those who consulted doctrine from the Word repented, and prayed unto the Lord for help against the blasphemers,

Verses	Subjects	
21–27	3·15·4	and received answer in their heart, that those who blasphemed the Lord will perish; and this blasphemy is likewise treated of.
28, 29	3·15·4	Therefore it will go no farther,
30–32	11	because a new church will come into existence in its time;
33–35	2	and therefore the old church will not be destroyed as yet;
36–38	2[?3]	nevertheless, they are to be utterly destroyed.

Chapter XXXVIII.

1–6	2	They repented: therefore they were protected from destruction;
7, 8	1	therefore the time of the coming of the Lord has been protracted.
9–15	2	The church will nevertheless depart.
16–20	2	They are exhorted to repent.
21, 22	2	There is still natural good with some.

Chapter XXXIX.

1–7	3	It is foretold that they will adulterate all the goods of the Word and profane its truths, until nothing of good and truth is left, which is "Babel" [or "Babylon"];
8	2	but not as yet,

Chapter XL.

1–5	1·2·11	The coming of the Lord is foretold, when the good are to be saved, and the evil will perish.
6–8	2	Every truth will be banished.
9–11	1·11	Prediction concerning the coming of the Lord, and the salvation of those who receive Him,
12–14	16	because He is almighty and all-knowing.
15–18	16	All men and all things against Him are nothing worth.
19, 20	16	One's own intelligence is nothing worth.
21–25	16	Dominion over all things is the Lord's, and without Him, all things fall.
26	16	He rules the heavens.

Verses	Subjects	
27	16	Why the church is ignorant of this.
28, 29, 31	16·11	The Lord upholds the church with those who look to Him.
30	2	Those who do not [look to Him], have no power, but fall.

Chapter XLI.

1–3	15	Concerning a last judgment executed by the Lord from His Human, in which He was while in the world.
4	[15·10]	[He executed the judgment] by means of His Divine.
5–7	4	Those who were in self-intelligence opposed themselves to Him.
8–10, 13, 14	10	His Human was strengthened by His Divine.
11, 12	7	They will be of no avail whatever against Him.
15, 16	8	They will be totally dispersed.
16, 17	11	Those who confide in the Lord will not fail.
18–20	11	They will have truths and goods in all abundance.
[21,] 22–24	11	The rest will not know, and will have no power.
25, 26	11	Those who are in ignorance of truth, will come to the Lord:
27	11	the church will consist of these.
28, 29	11	Of themselves they are [nothing] but falsity and evil.

Chapter XLII.

1–4	1·11	Concerning the Lord, in whom is the Divine, that He will gently lead and teach.
5–8	1·11	He will save by virtue of His Divine.
9–12	1·11	The coming of the Lord is foretold, and the joy of those who will draw nigh to Him, who had previously lived in ignorance.
13–15	7	He will fight for them against the hells, which He will conquer, and He will destroy their power.
16	11	Those who are in ignorance are then to be enlightened.
17	3	Those who trust in their own intelligence, and thus in falsities, are to be driven away.
18–20	1·6·4	The Lord's patience and tolerance is described,
21	1·6·4	and also His justice.

Verses	Subjects
22–24	**11** Then those who were of the church despoiled them of all truths, and they became averse to them.
25	**9·4** He suffered direful things from them, and endured these things.

Chapter XLIII.

1	**17** Redemption and salvation of those who will be of the new church from the Lord.
2	**11** Falsities and evils will not hurt them.
3–8	**11** Those from every quarter and of every kind will come to Him.
9	**11** This has been foretold.
10–13	**1** He Himself, who is to come, has foretold it.
14	**3** He will destroy all who adulterate and profane the goods and truths of the church.
15	**1** It will be He Himself,
16, 17	**8** who saves His own, and destroys all the power of hell.
18–21	**11** From Him will be a new thing, and a new church of those who had previously been in no truths whatever.
22–27	**4** The church itself did not worship Him, but they wearied Him with sins, which He bore with, from the beginning and also afterwards.
28	**3** Therefore He will utterly reject the church.

Chapter XLIV.

1–4	**1·11** Those who will acknowledge the Lord will receive the Holy Spirit.
5–7	**1** He is Jehovah who has foretold that He will do this.
8	**1** There is no other God.
9–11	**4** Those who do not worship Him alone are falsifiers.
12–20	**2** Those who frame for themselves something else of religion from their own intelligence make falsity to appear as truth, and evil as good, whence they have a *quasi* divine worship.
21, 22	**2** To the Jewish church: it should refrain from such things.
23, 24	**11·10** To the new church: the Lord alone is the God of heaven and earth.
25	**3** He rejects such, because they are insane from self-intelligence,

Verses	Subjects	
26	11	when He establishes His church,
27	3	and destroys the old church.
28	11	This is from the Lord through the Divine Human, who is meant by "Cyrus" in this place.

Chapter XLV.

Of the Lord in respect to the Divine Human, who is "Cyrus."

1, 2	8	From His Divine He has omnipotence against all things of hell.
3	8·10	He has Divine Wisdom,
4	8·10	through His Divine, even to ultimates.
5, 6	10	He is none other than Jehovah; let all men know this.
7	10	From Him are all things.
8	17	Let them receive Him, that they may be saved.
9–11	10	Doubt whether it be so and why it is so, ought not to be entertained,
12	10	for He Himself is the God of heaven,
13	17	and thus He will save men, for they have been bound by the hells.
14	11	Those who are in ignorance and natural will draw near.
15	17	Whence salvation thus comes has been hidden.
16	4	Those who are in falsities will recede.
17	17	Those who are of His church are saved.
18	17	The reason why they are thus saved is that man has been born for heaven.
19	17	This has been foretold in the Word.
20	11·4	Those who are in good draw near, and those who are in evil recede.
21, 22	11·17	The Lord should be received, because He alone is God, and from Him alone is salvation.
23–25	17	In Him alone is all the life of heaven,
24	4	and that life is not in those who are against Him.

Chapter XLVI.

	2·3	Of the profanation of truth, which is "Bel."
1	2·3	They have affections of falsity and evil.
2	2·3	They are no longer able to understand truth.
3–5	17	Those who are not of such a character have been led by the Lord and are led by Him.

Verses	Subjects	
6, 7	2·3	The rest take goods and truths from the Word, and profane them, and make for themselves a religion in which there is no life.
8–12	2·3	They ought to consider, that there is no other religion than that which is commanded in the Word, where all truths are.
13	1·17	The coming of the Lord from whom is salvation, is near at hand.

Chapter XLVII.

	8·15	Of those who adulterate good and profane truth, who are meant by "Babel" [or "Babylon"].
1	8·15	These no longer have dominion.
2, 3	8·15	They may frame falsities of faith and evils of love; but these will be destroyed until they are not,
4	8·15	by the Lord,
5	8·15	Those who profane will be thrust down.
6	3	These falsities and evils have invaded the church, and perverted it.
7	8·15	They believe that they have dominion over all men,
8, 9	8·15	and that their dominion will not cease, by reason of the heinous inventions of worship in which they trust.
10, 11	8·15	They will be utterly destroyed, because they have exalted themselves above all in the world.
12–15	8·15	All the fictions and inventions of worship will avail nothing, because they will be cast down into hell.

Chapter XLVIII.

	2	Exhortation to the church that is adulterating the goods and profaning the truths of the Word, that they should desist.
1, 2	2	It has been granted them that they may be the church, and that they may acknowledge the Lord, but in vain.
3, 4	2	They have turned away, and this has been declared to them,
5	2	lest, haply, they should believe that they themselves are superior to others,
6, 7	2	and have not known this,
8	2	and yet they have been such from the beginning.
9–11	2	They are not yet to be destroyed, for His own reasons, and the time will yet be prolonged.

24 SUMMARIES OF THE INTERNAL SENSE.

Verses Subjects
12, 13 **10·16** Be it known to them that He is the God of heaven and earth.
14–17 **1** He is the Lord who will come among those who are adulterating and profaning the Word, and will declare this to them :
18, 19 **2** if they had obeyed Him they would have had the goods and truths of the church in all abundance :
20, 21 **2** if they would leave the adulterations and falsifications of the Word, and the pride of having dominion, they would be in everything of the church.
22 **2** But the church is not with them, because they have turned away.

CHAPTER XLIX.

17 OF REDEMPTION AND SALVATION BY THE LORD. "ISRAEL" HERE MEANS THE LORD.

1–3 **17·11** He will give the doctrine concerning God.
4 **4** It is to no purpose in the church.
5, 6 **11** A church with every thing belonging to it is to be established by Him.
7 **11·17** They should submit themselves to Him.
7–11 **17·11** He will teach them all the truths of salvation.
12 **11** Those who are far removed from truths will draw near,
13 **11** and they will have joy on this account.
14–16 **11** Let them not believe that the Lord does not remember them ; He remembers them constantly.
17, 19 **11** Falsities and evils will be removed.
18 **11** Approach from all parts to the church.
19, 20 **12** Heaven will be enlarged for them.
21–23 **11** A multitude of those who have not had the Word and hence neither the truths of the church, will draw near, and will worship the Lord, and will be instructed in Divine truths.
24, 25 **11·17** Evils from hell will not break in upon them.
26 **17** Those will be removed from them, who endeavor to introduce evil and falsity ; these will be in the hells.

CHAPTER L.

1 **3** The former church is rejected.
2, 3 **3** There is not one there who is obedient, not one who

Verses	Subjects	
		believes that the Divine has power to save, wherefore all things of the church are hidden from them.
4, 5	[1]	The Lord has taught constantly.
6, 7	9	They have treated the Lord wickedly, but He has endured it.
8, 9	10	Through the Divine in Himself He has become justice.
9	15	Those who are against Him will perish by falsities from evil.
10	11	Those who are far removed from truths will trust in Him and will acknowledge Him,
11	15	and the rest, with their evils and the falsities therefrom, will be cast down into hell.

CHAPTER LI.

1, 2	17	The worshipers of God look unto the Lord from whom, and to the church through which [come reformation and regeneration]:
3	17	because the Lord will fill them with intelligence, and will make them happy:
4, 5	17·11	because from Him is all good and truth, and in Him does every nation trust;
6	17	nothing abides to eternity except that which is from Him.
7, 8	17	Let those who love good look to Him, and make nothing of the oppositions of men, because they will perish, owing to falsities and evils.
9–11	17	To the Lord, because he has Divine power, that He may act, because He has strength to remove the hells, that they may joyfully pass over without harm.
12, 13	17	There is nothing to fear from the evils thence arising, nor from infestation by them.
14, 15	17·8	The Lord will lead them forth safe, however much hell may resist.
16	17·8·12	From His Divine He will set heaven and the church in order,
17, 18	11	constituted of those who have been in falsities of ignorance.
19, 20	2	Heretofore there has been a lack of truth and good, a source of falsities beyond measure.

Verses	Subjects	
21, 22	3	These the Lord will take away,
23	3	and they will be given to those who contemptuously reject the good.

Chapter LII.

1	11	To the New Church: let it embrace the doctrine of truth, that falsities may not break in,
2	11	and let it reject falsities,
3	11	by which they have been made captive, and from which they will be freed.
4	11	Because they have been imbued with knowledges (*cognitiones*) of falsity confirmed by reasonings,
5	11	therefore there is evil and ignorance of God;
6, 7	11·1	but they will know their God when He comes into the world,
8, 9	11·1	when He will restore the church,
10	1	and will manifest Himself;
11	11	and then they will forsake the religiosities in which there are such falsities.
12, 13	11·1	The Lord will lead them out by degrees.
14	1	He will appear in humility.
14, 15	11·1	Then those who are in goods and truths will see and draw near.

Chapter LIII.

	13·4	OF THE LORD'S APPEARANCE IN THE STATE OF HUMILIATION.
1	13·4	It is scarcely believed that the omnipotence of God is in the Lord,
2, 3	13·4	because He will appear as vile, and therefore to be despised;
4	13·4	and He appeared as if the Divine were not in Him,
5	17	and yet through it is salvation.
6–8	9	He bore all things even to the passion of the cross,
9	8	and subjugated the hells.
10, 11	9·11	Through the passion of the cross a new church will come into existence;
12	9·8	and because he bore such things He will go forth a Victor.

Chapter LIV.

1-3	11	Those with whom the church had not before existed will have many truths of the church, which will be multiplied.
4, 5	10·17	The former falsities will not be remembered, because the Lord will be the God of the church.
5, 6	11	They have been for some time as though without God.
7, 8	11	This came to pass when there was no church, although it is to be restored by the Lord:
9, 10	11	at a time when there is no truth, whereas afterwards it will not be lacking.
11-13	11·17	The doctrinals will be full of spiritual and celestial truths from the Lord.
14, 15	17·3	Falsities from hell will no longer be feared.
16, 17	17·3·15	Those who are against the church because of these falsities will be cast into hell.

Chapter LV.

1	11·17	They will receive truths from the Lord gratis.
2	11·17	They will reject such things as have no spiritual life in them.
3, 4	11·17	Truth, in which there is life, and by which there is conjunction, will be given by the Lord.
5, 6	11	Those will draw nigh to the Lord who had not known Him before.
7	11	Concerning repentance.
8, 9	17	The way by which is salvation is not known:
10, 11	17	it is effected through the coming of the Lord.
12	17	Through this alone is heavenly happiness,
13	11·17	and instead of evil and falsity there is good and truth to eternity.

Chapter LVI.

1	1·17	The Lord the Saviour will come.
2	10·17	Happy is he who esteems holy the union of the Divine and the Human, and of the Lord with the church;
3	10·17	and let no one believe that he is separated from the Lord.

Verses	Subjects	
4, 5	11·10	Strangers, who esteem that union holy, are to be received into the church in preference to others,
6, 7	11	and those also, who are in falsities from ignorance are to be introduced, and their worship will be accepted.
8, 9	11	The rest are also to be brought near,
10, 11	11·2	because they have been seduced by those who have evil cupidities,
12	2	and who lust for nothing else than to be insane in falsities.

Chapter LVII.

1, 2	2·3	Truth and good and life are no longer in them,
3	3	because they have falsified and adulterated them,
4	3	speaking against the Divine.
5	3	They love all falsities whatsoever, and destroy all truths whatsoever,
6	3	and worship those things that come from their own intelligence,
7	3	and extol doctrine derived therefrom even to worshipping it,
8	3	and have published it before all, and have extended it to falsities of every kind,
9	3	and call them heavenly goods and truths, and adore them with all submission:
10	3·4	They have not retracted, because this was from their own intelligence.
11, 12	3·4	This they have done because they have not consulted the Lord, who might teach them.
13, 14	3·11	Falsities will destroy them: it is otherwise with those who so love the Lord that He may teach them truths and remove falsities.
15	11	The Lord does this with those who are humble at heart,
16, 17	3	He is not able to do this for those who are wise from what is their own (*proprium*),
18[, 19]	11	but only for those who grieve over it:
20, 21	3	not with those who bring forth from their natural nothing but evils and falsities, from which they are never removed.

Chapter LVIII.

Verses | Subjects
| |
1 | 2 The iniquity of the old church, which is to be disclosed.
2 | 2 They are as those who love truth,
3 | ıı and as those who are converted;
4 | ıı but their conversion originates in evil.
5, 6 | ıı Conversion does not consist in speaking in a devout manner, but in shunning evils,
7 | ıı and in exercising charity:
8–11 | ıı then they will have truths in abundance, and the Lord will be with them;
12 | ıı thus the church will be with them, and they will restore all things of the church.
13, 14 | ıı·ıo If they regard the union of the Lord with the church as holy, they will come into heaven.

Chapter LIX.

1, 2 | 2 The Lord hears and is able to do all things, but falsities and evils stand in the way.
3, 4 | 2 By these, truths have been falsified, and this is the source of evils of life and falsities of doctrine.
5 | 2 They hatch out such things as captivate and deceive, and afterwards kill.
6 | 2 Those things with them that are of doctrine and of life are of no avail for anything.
7 | 2 They are diligent at perverting, whence comes vastation.
8 | 2 He that follows, destroys the truths of the church in himself.
9, 10 | 2 For this reason they are in falsities and see nothing in noonday light.
11 | 2 Hence there is no salvation,
12–15 | 2·4 because there is nothing but evils, and a turning away from truths, thus from the Lord.
16, 17 | 2·4·7 Inasmuch as no one was in truth, and no one was on the Lord's side, He alone fought from Divine truth with His own power,
18 | 7 seemingly from revenge;
19, 20 | 17 therefore Divine worship belongs to Him, for from Him is redemption,

Verses *Subjects*
21   17   and from His Divine is every truth of the church to eternity.

Chapter LX.

1, 2	1-3	The Coming of the Lord with Divine truth, when there is nothing but falsity and evil of falsity.
2	10	The Divine is in the Lord only.
3–5	11	They will draw nigh to Him from all parts in great numbers, even those who are external,
6, 7	11	and they will worship the Lord from good and truth.
8	11	Those who are in the shade of truth will draw near.
9, 10	11	The truths of the church and the church will be in them.
11, 12	11	There will be a continual approach for the sake of salvation.
13	11	The spiritual-moral will draw near,
14	11	even those who had not known the Lord before,
15, 16	11	and these will learn spiritual truths from the Lord.
17	11-17	Their natural will become spiritual:
18	11-17	perversion of truth and good will be no more,
19	11-17	nor the love of evil and falsity, but love to the Lord,
20	11-17	and this to eternity,
21, 22	11-17	in heaven with growing intelligence.
22	[1-]11-17	These things will be when the Lord comes.

Chapter LXI.

1–3	1-11-15	The coming of the Lord, to save those who are ignorant of truth and who desire it, and when the judgment is to be executed,
4	11	then the things of the church which have perished are to be restored:
5	11	externals of the church:
6	11	internals of the church:
7	11	more than ever before.
8	11	Conjunction by means of their truths and goods.
9	11	These to be acknowledged.
10, 11	11-1	Such things of the church will exist, when the Lord comes.

Chapter LXII.

<small>Verses   Subjects</small>

            1-11 THE COMING OF THE LORD AND THE CHURCH AT THAT TIME, AND ITS QUALITY.

1–3   **1-11** A church will come into existence which will acknowledge the Lord; the very truths of heaven will be in it, and more than before.

4, 5   **11-17** They will not be separated from the Lord, as before, but conjoined with Him.

6, 7   **11-17** This gospel will be preached even until it takes place.

8, 9   **11-17** Then the truths of the Word will not be for those who falsify them, but for those who receive them.

10   **1** Preparation is being made,

10, 11 **1** and announcement that the Lord will come,

12   **11** and that that church will be from Him.

Chapter LXIII.

            1-7   THE LORD AND HIS COMBATS.

1   **1-7** The Lord as to the Divine truth, or the Word, from which He has Divine power.

2   **3** The Word has been wholly adulterated and destroyed.

3–6   **3.7.17** No one is in truths, and therefore the Lord alone has fought and conquered, that the faithful may obtain salvation.

7, 8   **17** This has been done from mercy, that those who wish to receive truth may be saved by Him,

9   **17** that He, from Divine love, might lead them.

10   **17** Those who were formerly of His church have turned away.

11–14 **17** Yet, before that church existed, He led men, and protected them in the midst of hell.

15, 16 **17.16** Prayer to the Lord that He may have pity, because He alone has redeemed them.

17, 18 **17.7** Otherwise they would have perished, and hell would have had dominion over them.

19   **17.7** When the Lord comes there will be power.
<small>H B. 19 (first part)</small>

Chapter LXIV.

1   **17.7** When the Lord comes there will be power.
<small>H.B. lxiii. 19 (last part)</small>

2, 3   **7.15** The Lord causes the infernals to perish, when He comes with Divine power.
<small>H.B. 1, 2</small>

32   SUMMARIES OF THE INTERNAL SENSE.

Verses	Subjects	
4 H.B. 3	17	This has not been heard or done before.
5 H.B. 4	17	Thus He saves the faithful.
6, 7 H.B. 5, 6	17·1	All are in sins, and there is safety for no one, unless He come,
8 H.B. 7	17	and yet all have been created by Him,
9 H.B. 8	11	Oh! that He might therefore have regard to them,
10, 11 H.B. 9, 10	3	when all things of the church have been laid waste.
12 H.B. 11		The Lord cannot endure this.

CHAPTER LXV.

1–5	4	The Lord had been present with those who are against Him, who are in dire loves of falsity and evil, and who reject Him.
6, 7	3	They will perish in consequence of their contrary worship:
8–10	11	still, not all things of the church will perish, because there must be a church;
11, 12	3	but those who have perverted the Word will perish because of falsities.
13, 14	3·11	They will become wretched; others, happy.
15, 16	11	They will be conjoined with the Lord.
17, 18	11	The Lord will establish a new church,
19–21	11	in which will be all goods and truths, thus all things of heaven;
22, 23	11·17	and that church will not perish.
24	11·17	The Lord will teach.
25	11·17	Falsities and evils will no longer destroy.

CHAPTER LXVI.

1, 2	11·12	Heaven and the church are with those who live in humility and in accordance with the commandments.
3	3	It is otherwise with those who have perverted all worship into evil.
4	3	Those things will be requited them because they have not obeyed.
5	11	Those who are outside of the church will obey and will be received in their stead.
6	3	Destruction of the evil.

ISAIAH LXVI.

Verses	Subjects	
7, 8	11·3	Before they perish, the church is established among others,
9	11·3	and will be established.
10, 11	11	They will drink in Divine truth with joy.
12–14	11	They will have all goods and truths.
14, 15	3	Those who are against them will come to an end;
16	3	and those will perish
17	3	who have perverted the holy things of the church.
18	11	Men will draw near to the Lord from all parts,
19	11	and from every religion.
20	11	They will be in all truth of doctrine of the church,
21	11	and in its good.
22	11·17	Those things which are of heaven and the church will abide with them.
23	11	They will continually worship the Lord.
24	4	Those who have rejected Him will remain forever in their falsities and evils.

Jeremiah.

CHAPTER I.

Verses	Subjects	
1–3	2	The perverted state of the church.
4–8	11	Of the Lord, who is here meant by "Jeremiah :" He will be born, in order that He may teach all men Divine truth.
9, 10	11·2	From His Divine He will teach the truths and goods of the church, and will destroy falsities and evils.
11, 12	2	Truths of every good have been given them through the Word;
13	2	but they have perverted them;
14, 15	2	which is the source of all kinds of falsities that are contrary to the truths of the church,
16	2	and from this arises a contrary worship.
17–19	5·7·8	The Lord will admit them to fight against Him, and they will succumb, because the Divine is the Lord's.

CHAPTER II.

11·2   THE CHURCH ESTABLISHED AMONG THE ANCIENTS :

1–3	11·2	Its primitive state when it was defended from falsities and evils.
4–6	2	For no reason they departed from Him who had led and protected them,
7, 8	2	and had taught them all things of the church, which they nevertheless perverted, both its truths and its goods, by departing from the Lord.
9	2	Still He will teach them with difficulty.
10, 11	4	No nation has changed its religion as they have done.
12, 13	4	It is horrible, their rejecting the Lord, and their hatching falsities of doctrine for themselves.
14, 15	3	Consequently the church and its doctrine have been devastated
16	3	by falsities out of the natural man.

Verses	Subjects	
17	4·3	This has taken place because they have rejected the Lord
18	4·3	by means of knowledges (*scientifica*) and reasonings.
19, 20	4	They draw punishments upon themselves, because they have separated themselves from the Lord, and have worshipped things infernal,
21	3	and even though genuine truths have been given to them, yet they have become such.
22, 23	3	Howsoever they may worship in like ways in externals, yet interiorly they are infernal.
24, 25	3	They desire eagerly to be in falsities and evils, and shun truths and goods.
26, 27	3	Evils and falsities are their worship.
28	3	This is true of all of them.
29, 30	3	They are not willing to return, even when chastised.
31, 32	3	Nevertheless they have not been forsaken by the Lord, but they have forsaken Him.
33, 34 [35?]	3	They fight to confirm falsities and evils by falsifications of the Word.
36	3	And they have confirmed them by reasonings from the natural man.
37	3	And yet confirmations are of no avail.

Chapter III.

The Spiritual Church, or the Truths of the Church.

1, 2	2	They have departed and falsified truths.
3	2	They are unwilling to understand truths.
4, 5	2	They have merely acknowledged the Word outwardly in the letter, and not even with the Word [in mind], but with falsities.
6, 7	2	The church in respect to truths, has falsified truths, and has not been willing to be reformed.
7–9	2	The celestial church, that is, the church in respect to good has done likewise: as the spiritual church has falsified truths, so the celestial church has adulterated goods.
10, 11	2	They worship falsities of evil, and have perverted goods more than truths.
12–14	2[·ıı]	Exhortation to reject falsity and to receive truth, that there may be conjunction and a church,
15	[ıı]	and that there may then be knowledge (*cognitio*).
16, 17	ı·ıı	When the Lord comes there will no longer be the

Verses	Subjects	
		representative of a church, but a church, wherein the Lord Himself will be in place of that representative.
18	11	Then truth and good will make one.
19	11	Those who will draw near shall be adopted as children by the Lord;
20[, 21]	3	but the church has become perverted.
22–25	11	Those who will be of the new church will acknowledge and confess that they have falsities and evils.

Chapter IV.

1, 2	2	Exhortation to refrain from evils and to acknowledge the Lord, from whom those who are in goods and truths will have salvation.
3, 4	2	Unless they refrain and turn back, they will utterly perish.
5, 6	2	Those who will acknowledge must be removed while the destruction lasts,
7	3	because devastation of all things of the church is at hand,
8	3	which does not come to an end through outward mourning,
9, 10	3	nor through complaints that they are perishing, although it is said in the Word that they shall be saved.
11, 12	3	It is answered that they are not willing to acknowledge and receive.
13	3	Falsities are breaking in.
14, 15	3	Corruption of the church
16	3	in respect to doctrine,
17	3	in respect to the Word.
18–21	3	Lamentation thereat.
22	3	There is no longer any understanding of truth.
22–27	3	All things of the church have been destroyed, even until nothing remains,
28, 29	3	and the church has become none.
30	3	The things of the church could not have been restored among them in any way.
31	11	Despair of those of whom the new church will consist.

Chapter V.

Verses	Subjects
1, 2	**2** There is no truth in doctrine or in the church, and if they believe, it is falsity.
3	**2** They were urged by punishments, but still they did not receive.
4, 5	**2** This non-reception is due, not to simplicity, but to application and industry;
6	**2** therefore all falsities and evils of falsity have broken in upon them.
7, 8	**2** They have rejected all mercy, because they have perverted all truths and goods, which they had in all abundance.
9, 10	**2** Therefore they cannot but perish,
11, 12	**2** for they have acknowledged evils and falsities as goods and truths, because they have departed from the Lord,
13	**2** and have annihilated the Word.
14–17	**2** Therefore infernal evil will invade them, and will still further destroy all the goods and truths of the church;
18	**2** but not quite, as yet.
19, 20	**2** This comes upon them because they have forsaken the Lord,
21–24	**2** and yet it is in their power to know that the Lord alone can do all things, but they are unwilling to know that He is God from whom are all truths and goods.
25–27	**2** This has come to pass because it is delightful to them to pervert and deceive.
27, 28	**2** and for this reason they are held in esteem.
29	**3** They cannot but perish,
30, 31	**3** because all goods and truths from firsts to lasts have been perverted in such wise; also because all of them, from the highest to the lowest, do thus.

Chapter VI.

2 THOSE WHO HAVE CONJUNCTION WITH THE LORD IN THE LOWEST HEAVEN; THESE ARE MEANT BY "THE CHILDREN OF BENJAMIN."

1, 2	**2** The church among them is destroyed by falsities of evil.
3–5	**2** They no longer have truth and good, but falsity and evil, and these destroy them.
6, 7	**2** By means of these the church amongst them is destroyed.

Verses	Subjects	
8, 9	2	There are still some truths: let them beware lest they destroy them;
10	3	but they hearken not.
11	3	Therefore all things are being destroyed.
12	11	Thus others are being received in their stead.
13, 14	3	Because everything there has been so perverted that there is no protection against falsity,
15	3	which they do not acknowledge to be falsities,
16, 17	3	and they repudiate truths,
18, 19	3	therefore they will come to an end;
20	3	hence they regard the works of their worship as of no value.
21	3	Destruction comes upon them
22, 23	3	through falsities, from which they reason against the truths of the church.
24–26	3	Those who are separated and grieve over them.
27–30	3	The perverse are tested, and found incapable of restoration.

Chapter VII.

3 Those who are in the lowest heaven with whom is the church in respect to good.

1, 2	3	To such:
3	3	let them look to truths and goods;
4	3	let them not believe that the church is with them:
5, 6	3	unless they live according to the commandments, and do no violence to the Word,
7	3	goods and truths do not cause them to be a church.
8–10	3	If the life is contrary to the commandments, there is no church worship.
11	3	The church of the Lord is not with those who profane holy things.
12–15	3	By such profanation the destruction of the church is brought about, as elsewhere, so also here.
16	3	Intercession is of no avail,
17–19	3	because it is certain that they profane the truths and goods of heaven.
20	3	Hence is the destruction of all.
21–24	3	They rely on externals of worship, which are of no account, because they have no internals of worship.
25, 26	2	They have obstinately rejected internals, even from the beginning.

Verses	Subjects	
27–31	15	Since their reformation is vain, everything of their worship is rejected, because they profane all things of the church.
32, 33	15	They will be cast into hell, where there is nothing but falsity and evil.
34	15	Thus that church will perish.

Chapter VIII.

1, 2	15	The profaners of truth will be cast into hell, and abide in their profanities.
3	15	And all their remains will likewise perish.
4–6	3	They are such that they cannot be converted and led back.
7–9	3	They are not willing to know any truth from the Word, but reject it.
10	3	Therefore the things they have will be given to others.
11, 12	3	They defend their falsities, and call them truths of the church; they do not want it to be otherwise.
13	3	Therefore, because they no longer have truth or good, they will perish.
14, 15	3	They have recourse to the Word, but in vain.
16, 17	3	Then fallacies of the sensual man, and reasonings therefrom will destroy them, and infect them with poison.
18–22, CH. IX. 1 H.B. 18-23	11	Reciprocal grief and lamentation, that the time is so long drawn out before a new church consisting of others can be established.

Chapter IX.

1 H.B. viii. 23	11	[See above, end of chapter viii.]
2, 3 H.B. ix. 1, 2	3	In the church is nothing but what is falsified and evil therefrom, because they depart from the Lord.
4–6 H.B. 3-5	3	One falsity comes from another even until there is nothing but falsity in which [they are].
7, 8 H.B. 6, 7	3	When they are being taught they feign that they wish it, but they do not.
9 H.B. 8	3	Must they not perish?
10–12 H.B. 9-11	3	Grief because of the destruction of all things of the church, even until nothing remains.

Verses	Subjects	
13–15 H.B. 12–14	3	Because they have repudiated the Word, and have obeyed their own lusts, they are in falsities of evil;
16 H.B. 15	3	and therefore they will be destroyed by evils, and falsities therefrom.
17–19 H.B. 16–18	3	Lamentation over devastation.
20, 21 H.B. 19, 20	3	Lamentation that from this there is destruction,
22 H.B. 21	3	because they have infernal evil and falsity.
23, 24 H.B. 22, 23	15·11	Let it be known that everything of truth and good, and hence everything of power and wisdom, is from acknowledgment of the Lord.
25, 26 H.B. 24, 25	15	The coming of the Lord to judgment upon all who are in externals without internals.

CHAPTER X.

1, 2	3	Let not those be feared who wish to prevail by their own intelligence and by means of artifices.
3–5	3	It is described how they make evil to appear like good, and make themselves appear powerful,
6, 7	16	whereas the Lord alone has power.
8, 9	3	To do this they abuse the Word;
10	16	but the Lord alone reigns,
11	4	and those who do not acknowledge Him, vanish.
12, 13	16	All truth is from the Lord.
14, 15	2·3	Self-intelligence amounts to nothing at all: it will perish.
16	11	It is otherwise with a church that trusts in the Lord.
17, 18	11·3	The preparation of these during the destruction of the former.
19–21	3·11·4	Grief because of the backsliding of the church from the Lord, and its vastation,
22	3	Their end.
23–25	11	Prayer to the Lord that they may not perish together with the evil.

CHAPTER XI.

1–3	3	Let them do the commandments and acknowledge the Lord; this is meant by the "covenant."
4	3	It was with them when they were reformed.
5, 6	3	Every good and truth of the church is theirs by means of it.

Verses	Subjects	
7, 8	3	This they were often told, but they did not obey,
9, 10	3	but all did the contrary, and acknowledged another god.
11–13	3	Therefore there is no help for them, because they all love falsities and worship other gods.
14	3	Intercession will not avail.
15,16[,17]	3	They have profaned the church and its good and truth.
18, 19	9	This was made manifest by their delivering the Lord up to death.
20	15	Therefore retribution awaits them.
21	4	They do not wish to hear about the Lord.
22, 23	15	They will perish by means of falsities on the day of judgment.

Chapter XII.

1, 2	11·1	The church that expects the Lord asks why the wicked flourish.
3	1·1	Oh! that He would come, and that the evil might be removed.
4	3	Because there are no longer truths and goods with them,
5	3	they have self-intelligence,
6	3	and they wish to know nothing more.
7–12	3	The church where the Word is turns against the Lord, and has embraced falsities, whence she has been utterly desolated and vastated.
13	3	Goods are turned into evils.
14, 15	3	Therefore they are to be expelled, and others, of whom the church is to be formed, are to be accepted in their place.
16, 17	3	As long as they acknowledge the Lord they will remain.

Chapter XIII.

1–7	2	That the truth of the church would gradually perish by means of reasonings from the natural man, was represented by the "girdle of linen."
8–11	2	The like has come to pass with the church where the Word is, where they have backslidden from the Lord, and consequently from truths;
12, 13	2	and afterwards there were falsities for truths,

Verses	Subjects	
14	2	and consequent destruction.
15, 16	2	Let them beware lest mere falsity take the place of truth.
17	2	Grief on this account.
18, 19	2	It may be seen that all truth of the Word perishes.
20	3	Falsities take the place of truth.
21	3	Hence destruction is at hand.
22	15·3	The cause of this is, that they are interiorly evil and hence become also outwardly evil.
23	15·3	It cannot be otherwise;
24, 25	15·3	therefore destruction visits them, because they have forsaken the Lord, and hence they have falsities;
26, 27	3	and in consequence their interiors, which are evil, will be laid open.

Chapter XIV.

1–3	2	Truth is wholly lacking in the church.
4–6	2	He that seeks does not find it.
7–9	2	Prayer to the Lord to have pity.
10	2	Answer is made, that they have backslidden;
11, 12	2	therefore no attention is given either to their prayer or to their worship.
13	2	They are flattered into believing that there is no lack and no desolation of truth.
14–16	3	This is from their doctrine of falsity, which will perish, and together with it, those who live according to it.
17, 18	3	Grief that there is no truth either in the church or in doctrine.
19	9·3	Complaint thereat.
20–22	9·3	Prayer for them.

Chapter XV.

1	3	Answer is made, that no intercession for them can be of any avail.
2, 3	15	They will be cast into hell, where are falsities and evils of every kind.
4, 5	3	They are to be driven out from the church,
6	3	because they have backslidden.
7	3	They have no truth.
8	3	Because there is no truth, there is falsity.

Verses	Subjects	
9, 10	3	The church with them has come to an end.
11	15	At the time of the judgment they will be destroyed.
12–14	3	Having been destroyed by falsities from the natural man, they have no truths from the Word: these will be taken away from them.
15, 16	1·7	The Lord, and His combats from Divine truth.
17, 18	7	His grief over their falsities.
19–21	8	His victory over them.

CHAPTER XVI.

1–3	3	There is no conjunction of the Lord with that church, because no truths and goods are there.
4	15	They cannot but be cast into hell.
5–7	15	No compassion can be shown.
8	3	Because no good and truth can be received by them,
9	3	all conjunction with the Lord has perished with them.
10, 11	3	This comes of their having departed from worshipping the Lord; hence their worship is not worship of God;
12	3	therefore every one wishes to be wise from himself;
13	15	consequently they must be in hell.
14, 15	11	Others are to be brought to the church by the Lord,
16[, 17]	11	both those who are natural and those who are rational.
18	3	Retribution will visit those who have previously profaned the church.
19–21	11	Those of whom the church will consist will acknowledge the Lord.

CHAPTER XVII.

1, 2	3	It is in their internals to worship only externals.
3	3	All true knowledges (*scientifica*) will be taken away;
4	3	but not yet. They will come into hell.
5, 6	3	Because they trust in themselves, they perceive nothing of truth and good.
7, 8	11	On the other hand, those who trust in the Lord always have good and truth.
9, 10	3	The Lord knows what lies hidden interiorly, howsoever the external may appear.

Verses	Subjects	
11	3	The truths which they learn are of no use to them.
12, 13	15	Because the Lord is heaven and the church, those who depart from Him are damned.
14–18	3	Prayer to the Lord, and acknowledgment, that the evil may be removed.
19, 20	3	The Lord, to those who are in externals:
21–24	16	that they ought to acknowledge His Divine, which is meant by the "sabbath," and not violate it;
25	16	then they will possess an understanding of the Word,
26	16	and then their worship will be from truths.
27	2	If they will not acknowledge, the externals will perish from internals.

Chapter XVIII.

1–4	11	It is represented that those who are in falsities and evils can be reformed by the Lord.
5–8	11	Therefore those who are converted after repentance, are accepted by the Lord, although they are in falsities and evils.
9, 10	3	On the other hand, those who are in truths and in good, and do evil, perish.
[11,]12,13	3	Those who are in the church are told to repent and be converted; but they will not,
14–16	3	because they love falsities of every kind, and thereby annihilate the church with themselves.
17	3	Therefore they will be destroyed.
18	3	They exalt themselves against the Lord and consequently against His Word, despising Him, and falsifying it.
19, 20	3	Lamentation over this.
21, 22	3	They have no truth of the church, and they act craftily.
23	3	They cannot be forgiven.

Chapter XIX.

1	3	The Church has been instituted;
2, 3	3	but they have destroyed its truths by dire falsities, and therefore the church has perished.

Verses	Subjects
4, 5	3 They have forsaken the Lord, and have loved evils that gush forth from the love of self.
6	3 Therefore the church is no longer there, but hell.
7, 8	3 There they will be among profaners,
9	3 where there is deadly hatred for one another.
9–11	3 It is represented that the church there has been destroyed, so that it cannot be restored.
12, 13	3 Hell is actually there, because there is nothing but the lust of the love of self.
14, 15	3 This was foretold to them through the Word.

CHAPTER XX.

1–3	3 They blaspheme the Word.
4	3 They will come among those who blaspheme and adulterate the Word.
5	3 They will disperse all the truths and goods of the Word,
6	3 and will thus perish with these.
7–10	3 Lamentation over the blasphemies against the Lord, and against the Word;
11–13	3 and the Lord's confidence during combats, that the Word is being protected.
14–18	3 Despair that the Word is so treated.

CHAPTER XXI.

1, 2	3 The hell of blasphemers of the Lord and of profaners of the Word was present.
3–5	3 The Lord cannot turn this away, because they ally it to themselves.
6	3 Everything that they have is such;
7	3·15 and they will all perish.
8–10	3·15 Those who study the Word are worse off, because they study it from something profane that is within.
11, 12	3·15 There is no good and truth.
13	3·15 Their heart is stubborn.
14	3·15 Hence their destruction.

Chapter XXII.

Verses	Subjects	
1, 2	2	To those in the church who possess a knowledge (*scientia*) of things.
3, 4	2	If they do according to the truths of the Word and the knowledge (*scientia*) they possess, and do not pervert these, they will have intelligence.
5, 6	2	Otherwise all of their intelligence will perish,
7–9	2	and everything pertaining to their knowledge (*scientia*), because they have separated themselves from the Lord.
10	2	There is no restitution.
11, 12	2	The church no longer consists of such,
13, 14	2	because they have made a religion for themselves by reasonings from falsities.
15, 16	2	Those who were before them in the church were not of such a character;
17	3	but they perverted the church by falsities of every kind.
18, 19	3	There can be no pity, but they must be cast out as profane.
20, 21	3	They are unwilling to give heed to the Word,
22	3	because they have been imbued with falsities of religion.
23, 24	3·15	They can have no protection through the Word, howsoever they acknowledge it with their lips.
25–27	3	They will come among those who profane the Word, and by means of it make for themselves a religion that is contrary to the truths of the church, from which religion they cannot recede.
28–30	3	They have not a truth which has not been perverted and profaned.

Chapter XXIII.

1, 2	3	Against those who have perverted the good of the Word, and by means of it have destroyed the church, who are meant by the "shepherds."
3, 4	11	They will perish, and the Lord will establish a church from others, who will teach and learn its good.
5, 6	11	The Lord will do this, and then those who are of His church will be saved.
7[, 8]	16·11	Then they will acknowledge that the Lord is Jehovah, and that the church is His.

JEREMIAH XXIV.

Verses	Subjects	
9	3	Against those who pervert the truths of the Word, who are meant by the "prophets."
10	3	From their perversions the church is full of falsities and is perverted,
11	3	and there is no longer truth or good, excepting such as is external.
12	15·3	Because they do not see truths, they perish on the day of judgment.
13	3	Truths are perverted by false principles, which are of religion.
14	3	But the Word is perverted, this is the worst.
15	3	They will possess nothing but falsity,
16, 17	3	which they also confirm from the Word,
18	3	saying, that it is Divine.
19, 20	15	They will perish on the day of judgment.
21, 22	3	They learn from themselves, and not from the Lord; if they learned from the Lord, they would depart from evils :
23, 24	3	thus the Lord would be with them.
25, 26	3	They pervert by means of false interpretation.
27	3	Hence they have no understanding of truth,
28, 29	3	because they have none from the Lord, who also is the Word, in which truth from Him makes itself manifest.
30, 31	3	Those who call themselves enlightened pervert truth still more,
32	3	whereas they are not enlightened.
33	3	The Divine truth shows that they have gone back.
34	3	He who says otherwise will suffer.
35, 36	3	Moreover they will not know what Divine truths is;
37–40	3	and because they call that which is false, Divine truth, the truth of the church will be removed from them : hence their destruction.

Chapter XXIV.

1–3	2·11	After that the whole church had adulterated and profaned the Word, it was represented that part of them were of such a character that they could be reformed, but part could not; these are meant by the "two baskets of figs, in one of which were good ones, and in the other bad ones."
4–7	2·11	Those who could be reformed, were those who had been completely vastated, so that they did not

Verses	Subjects	
	11	know what is true and what is good; these can at last be taught, can acknowledge the Lord, can be received, and can become a church.
8, 9	3	But those who could not be reformed, were those who desired still to be in worship from the Word, which worship they would then continually profane.
9, 10	3	With these, everything holy would be profaned, and they would perish.

CHAPTER XXV.

1–3	11·2	The Lord to those with whom the church has been instituted.
4–7	2	He taught them continually by the Word, that they should refrain from evils, and not go away to any other worship than that of the Lord; but they did not obey.
8–11	2	Therefore everything of the church among them will perish; and they will be in temptations from those who profane things holy.
12	2·11	Retribution will afterwards visit the tempters.
13, 14	2·11	It will so come to pass.
15–27	3	Knowledges (*cognitiones*) of truth and good, and also truths of every kind and sort will perish.
28–30	3	This cannot otherwise than come to pass, even with those who are in knowledges (*cognitiones*) from the Word.
31–33	3	There is no longer any truth that has not been profaned.
34–38	11	Lamentation by those who are in good, and in truths therefrom.

CHAPTER XXVI.

1–5	2	Exhortation by the Lord to repent, and live according to His commandments in the Word.
6	2	Otherwise the church with them will be destroyed.
7–9	9	Evil and falsity of religion condemned Him to death,
10–16	9	but because He spoke from the Divine, the truths of the church acquitted Him.
17–19	9	An instance of their not condemning to death one who spoke from inspiration,

Verses	Subjects
20–23	**9** excepting one who spoke falsely.
24	**9·3** The Lord was not condemned on account of the people.

CHAPTER XXVII.

1–8	**3** Since there is an end to the church, and to all things of it, they ought no longer to be there, lest they should profane it; therefore they were carried off to "Babylon," where they could not profane its holy things, and those who would not go, were profaners, and will perish.
9–11	**3** Those who teach anything else, teach falsities.
12, 13	**3** All with whom the church has been instituted will depart, or otherwise they would profane it, and will perish.
14, 15	**3** Let them not believe anything else.
16–21	**3** Nothing of things holy, not even of its externals, will remain, because it has been profaned.
22	**11** The church will be constituted of others, after it has been delivered from the profane.
	3 This was because the land of Canaan and all things therein represented the church, and as these are mentioned by name in the Word, those who profaned holy things could not be tolerated there.

CHAPTER XXVIII.

1–17	**2** They understood the Word in a contrary sense, and from this they persuaded themselves that the profanities of their religion were the holy things of the church, and consequently they were not to be carried away from the land; but they were told that they had persuaded themselves of falsities.

CHAPTER XXIX.

1–7	**11** Those in spiritual captivity are told that they should study truths and do goods, and continue in them,
8, 9	**11** and not become imbued with falsities,
10–15	**11** since when their spiritual captivity ceases, a new

Verses	Subjects	
		church will be instituted of those who are of such a character, and who acknowledge the Lord.
16–19	3	Those who were formerly of the church will profane the holy things of the church, and will therefore perish.
20–23	3	Those who have falsely interpreted the Word are condemned.
24–32	3	Those who persuasively established falsities, will abide in falsities, and will not perceive truth.

Chapter XXX.

1–3	11	Establishment of the church with those who have been in spiritual captivity, or in ignorance of truth.
4–7	15	Then the last judgment will be executed with those who are of the church.
8, 9	11	Then they are to be brought to the church, and will worship the Lord.
10, 11	11	Then their spiritual captivity will cease.
12–15	11·3	They have been infested by evils and falsities, and there is no remedy,
16	3	but those who have destroyed, will be destroyed.
17, 18	11	There will be a remedy from the Lord, who will restore the church.
19, 20	11	They will be perfected in truths, and it will last.
21, 22	11·1	This will be done by the Lord, when He will come, and He will be their God.
23, 24	15	He will execute judgment upon the wicked.

Chapter XXXI.

	1·11	OF THE NEW CHURCH THAT WILL BE ESTABLISHED BY THE LORD. THIS IS MEANT BY "ISRAEL" AND "ZION."
1	1·11	The Lord will be their God.
2–5	11	The loved one will receive the goods of the church.
6–8	11	They are to be brought near.
9	11	They will come, and will understand truths.
10, 11	11·17	The redeemed will be guarded against falsities,
12–14	11·17	and will receive things spiritual and celestial.
15	11	They are as dead,
16, 17	11	but they will finally return.

JEREMIAH XXXIII. 51

Verses	Subjects
18–21	" They will come out of ignorance of truth into the truths of heaven.
22	" They will understand them.
23–28	" They will be imbued with wisdom.
29, 30	" They will have no falsity of evil.
31–34	" They will be conjoined with the Lord, and from that conjunction truths will be inscribed on their life.
35–37	" This will be established to eternity.
38–40	" They will have abundant and extended doctrine of life.

CHAPTER XXXII.

1–5	3	Indignation that the Jewish church will be destroyed,
6–15	"	Yet the Lord's church will be preserved.
16–22, 25	"	Prayer that it may be preserved,
23–25	3	but the former church will be destroyed,
26–33	3	and it will be reproved because of its evils, which have also been with them from the beginning, although they had the Word, and doctrine from it.
34, 35	3	They have profaned holy things.
36–40	"	When this has been done, a new church is to be instituted, which will be conjoined with the Lord. and will not be separated from Him.
41, 42	"	They will have every good.
43, 44	"	They will then have everything of the church.

CHAPTER XXXIII.

1–5	" A new church. It will be established when the former church has been destroyed.
6–9	" After its destruction those are to be brought near who are to be led out of falsities,
10, 11	" who will worship the Lord from an affection for truth and good,
12, 13	" and who will be in truths of every kind after the former church has ceased to be.
14–16	I·" This will take place when the Lord comes, who will institute it.
17, 18	" Then truth and good will not be wanting.
19–21	" The spiritual and the natural will be in agreement.

Verses Subjects

22	**11**	Then there will be truths in all abundance.
23–26	**11**	Unless spiritual and natural truth and good become concordant, there can be no church.

Chapter XXXIV.

1–7	**3·11**	The Jewish church will be destroyed, although its truth will be preserved.
8–11	[**11**]	Those who are of the church will be free,
12–16	**3**	but they have of themselves become slaves.
17–19	**3**	They will be slaves to falsities, because they have departed from conjunction with the Lord;
20	**3**	and because of profanation of truth.
21, 22	**3**	Therefore they will die the death of profaners.

Chapter XXXV.

1–10	**11**	Those who are of the Lord's celestial church are represented by the "children of Jonadab," who were to "drink no wine, nor build a house, nor sow seed, nor plant vineyards," which signifies to learn truths and retain them in the memory, which belongs to the spiritual church; but that they should "dwell in tents," which signifies to receive in the life and obey.
11	**11**	From this they will have the celestial church.
12–16	**3**	The Jewish church does not receive nor obey, although they are taught continually.
17	**3**	Therefore they will perish.
18, 19	**11**	But those who obey will be in the celestial church.

Chapter XXXVI.

1–10	**3**	The destruction of the Jewish church and nation is foretold, and it is impressed upon them that they should repent.
11–16	**3**	They might know it to be true.
17, 18	**3**	It was foretold by the Lord.
19–24	**3**	They rejected it by profaning it;

Verses	Subjects	
25, 26	3	likewise the Word.
27, 28, 32	11	The Divine truth will not perish.
29–31	3	Because they have made themselves obstinate, the destruction of the church and of the kingdom is imminent.

Chapter XXXVII.

2 THOSE WHO REMAINED OF THE DEVASTATED CHURCH PROFANED THE HOLY TRUTHS OF THE CHURCH BY REASONINGS FROM KNOWLEDGES (*scientifica*).

1, 2	2	Those who remained did not live according to the truths of doctrine from the Word.
3, 4	2	They had regard to doctrinals.
5	2	They consulted knowledges (*scientifica*).
6–10	2	It is foretold that they will be destroyed by reasonings from knowledges.
11–16	2	Thus doctrine was repudiated and falsified.
17–21	2	Truths were perverted, but not goods with the truths, until there was a lack of goods.

Chapter XXXVIII.

1–3	2	Those who have not yet been vastated, will be vastated.
4–6	2	They made themselves still more obstinate, by perverting doctrine from the Word, and defiling it.
7–13	2	The remnants that were not utterly falsified, were nevertheless tainted with falsities.
14–18	2	If they pervert them still farther, they will perish.
19–21	2	Otherwise, if those remnants are not so perverted, they will not perish.
22, 23	2	It is foreseen that all things of the church will be perverted.
24–28	2	This was hidden from them.

Chapter XXXIX.

1–3	2	By reasonings from falsities the remnants of doctrine will perish.

Verses	Subjects	
4–8	2	They have been wholly falsified, even until there is no truth in them.
9, 10	2	The simple understanding of the Word had not yet been devastated,
11–14	2·II	because they were not in reasonings from falsities, but only in externals of doctrine.
15–18	2	The remnant of doctrine will be falsified, but not yet.

CHAPTER XL.

1–6	2	The simple understanding of the Word according to doctrine will still remain.
7–12	2	Beside the simple understanding, reasonings from falsities have been tolerated, which were commingled.
13–16	2	They began to be imbued with falsities of faith.

CHAPTER XLI.

1–3	2	Further falsification of truth,
4–7	2	and abolition of worship from this,
8	2	with some exception,
9	2	by means of falsities of faith,
10	2	and by means of falsification of truth.
11–15	2	But there were still remains,
16–18	2	some of which were perverted by knowledges (*scientifica*) of the natural man.

CHAPTER XLII.

1–6	2	The remains or those left consulted doctrine,
7–22	2	but they were told, that if they would continue simply in their external worship, and would not consult knowledges (*scientifica*) of the natural man, they would be saved; if they should consult them, all truth and good of worship would perish.

Chapter XLIII.

Verses — *Subjects*

1–4 — **2** But this was not done.

5–7 — **2** They consulted the knowledges (*scientifica*) of the natural man.

8–13 — **2** Thus they will perish by reasonings from these, and the knowledges themselves would be perverted by adapting them to falsities.

Chapter XLIV.

1–6 — **3** Much of the church perished by departure from the Lord and by falsities of every kind.

7–10 — **3** Now nearly all things left perish by means of knowledges (*scientifica*) of the natural man, nor do they refrain for fear of destruction,

11–14 — **3** because they consult knowledges, and thus there is scarcely any residue.

15–19 — **3** They make themselves obstinate, and love things that have been falsified by knowledges.

20–23 — **3** Their destruction in consequence of this foretold,

24–27 — **3** even until nothing of the church was left,

28 — **3** except a few things.

29, 30 — **3** True knowledges (*scientifica vera*) are perverted by reasonings therefrom.

Chapter XLV.

1–5 — **3** Prediction that the whole church will be destroyed.

Chapter XLVI.

3 THE NATURAL OF MAN WILL PERISH BY REASONINGS FROM KNOWLEDGES (*scientifica*).

1–6 — **3** All such knowledges are no longer of any avail, because they have been destroyed by means of reasonings.

7–10 — **3** Pride in these will be lowered, and they will become falsities.

11, 12 — **3** They cannot be healed, because the church has been destroyed by means of these falsities.

13–19 — **3** The whole natural perishes, nor is there anything there but falsity and evil.

Verses | Subjects
20–24　**3·11** All its learning which confirms falsities will perish.
25, 26　**3·11** The like will happen to others who trust in knowledges (*scientifica*).
27, 28　**11** It is otherwise with those who are in spiritual captivity, who will constitute the church.

Chapter XLVII.

1–7　**3** All who are in faith alone, so-called, will lapse into mere falsities, until they have no knowledges (*cognitiones*) of truth and good; and they will perish on
　　15 the day of judgment.

Chapter XLVIII.

3 OF THOSE WHO ADULTERATE THE GOODS OF THE WORD AND OF THE CHURCH, WHO ARE MEANT BY "MOAB."

1–5　**3** The destruction of all things with those who adulterate the goods of the church and of the Word.
6–9　**3** All truths have been destroyed thereby.
10, 11　**3** It has not been devastated for a long time, and therefore the evil is worse.
12–16　**3** Nevertheless they will perish with their falsities.
17–26　**3** There will be devastation of all things of truth with them.
27, 28　**3** They are against the church, because against truths.
29　**3** Its pride.
30–34　**3** Grief on account of all this,
35–38　**3** because there is nothing but evil,
39–42　**3** because there is no longer any good or truth of the Word.
43–46　**3** Every remnant of truth and good, which is untouched, is adulterated at the same time.
47　**11** Those who have not adulterated will be amended.

Chapter XLIX.

3 OF THOSE WHO FALSIFY THE TRUTHS OF THE WORD AND OF THE CHURCH, WHO ARE MEANT BY "THE CHILDREN OF AMMON."

1　**3** They falsify truths.
2　**3** Truths and goods with them will be destroyed.
3　**3** Mourning over this.

Verses	Subjects	
4, 5	3	They will be dispersed.
6	11	Those who have not falsified truths will be accepted.

    3 OF THOSE WHO HAVE FALSIFIED THE EXTERNAL OF THE WORD, WHO ARE MEANT BY "EDOM."

7, 8	3	They will be destroyed by things falsified.
9–13	3	Nothing of truth remains.
14–18	3	Their total destruction.
19–22	15	The last judgment is executed upon them, and they are cast down into hell.

    3 OF THOSE WHO PERVERT THE KNOWLEDGES (*cognitiones*) OF TRUTH, WHO ARE MEANT BY "DAMASCUS."

23–26	3	The doctrine of truth has been destroyed thereby.
27	3	They will perish.

    3 OF THOSE WHO PERVERT THE KNOWLEDGES (*cognitiones*) OF GOOD, WHO ARE MEANT BY "ARABIA."

28–30	3	They have destroyed the knowledges (*cognitiones*) of good and truth by reasonings.
31–33	3	Their destruction.

    3 OF THE FALSIFICATION OF DOCTRINE, WHICH IS MEANT BY "ELAM."

34–36	3	The falsities of their doctrine will be dispersed.
37, 38	3	They will perish,
39	11	except those who have not falsified.

CHAPTER L.

    3 OF THOSE WHO HAVE ADULTERATED AND FALSIFIED THE GOODS AND TRUTHS OF THE CHURCH, WHO ARE MEANT BY "BABYLON" AND "CHALDEA."

1–3	3	They will no longer have any good or truth.
4–7	11	Then those who are in ignorance of good and truth, because of a lack of them, will be brought to the Lord.
8	11	They will depart from "Babylon."
9, 10	3	"Babylon" will perish,
11	3	because they have vastated the church.
12, 13	3	It is without any truth.
14–16	15	Their destruction at the time of judgment,
17	15·3	because she has destroyed the church.
18–20	3·11	After "Babylon" has been destroyed, a new church will be established, which will be acceptable to the Lord.

Verses	Subjects	
21-24	3	"Babylon" will be destroyed because she is against the Lord.
25-30	3	They are to be wholly destroyed,
31, 32	3	on account of the love of ruling,
33, 34	3	because they do not refrain from destroying the church which the Lord establishes and redeems.
35-38	3	All things appertaining to them from firsts to lasts have been destroyed by means of falsities.
39, 40	3	They have horrible falsities and evils.
41-46	15	The last judgment upon them.

CHAPTER LI.

3 OF THOSE WHO BY TRADITIONS OR REASONINGS FROM THE NATURAL MAN HAVE PERVERTED THE TRUTHS AND GOODS OF THE CHURCH, WHO ARE HERE MEANT BY "BABYLON."

1-4	3	All truths of doctrine with them will be destroyed.
5	3	The Jewish church is such, and is against the Lord.
6	3	Let them beware of such.
7-10	3	Those who are there are vastated by such things, and they do not refrain.
11-13	2·3	They pervert truths and goods, which they have in abundance.
14-18	2	They have the Word so that they can be wise, but they falsify it.
19-23	15	When the judgment overtakes them from the Lord, all things appertaining to them, from firsts to lasts, are to be scattered.
24-26	15	Their destruction will come, because they have destroyed everything of the church.
27-29	3	They will seize upon falsities of every kind.
30-32	2	Hence they will no longer have any power.
33	15	Her last time is coming.
34-40	15	They will perish because they have destroyed the church.
41-44	15	They will be destroyed by mere falsities.
45-50	15	Let them not come near those who are of the church, lest they perish together with them.
51-53	15	They cannot resist, however much they trust in themselves.
54-58	15	Those who trust in their own falsities, will come to nothing, and will be destroyed.

Verses	Subjects	
59–61	15	This is told to those, who in the church have been taken captive by such, and who have become "Babylon."
62–64	15	They are to be cast into hell.

Chapter LII.

1–7	3	After the Jewish church has been wholly devastated in respect to all truths and goods by traditions or by reasonings from falsities,
8–11	3	the church is destroyed, until nothing of it is left remaining.
12–23	3	The destruction of all things of the church in general and in particular is described.
24–27	3	They can no longer be taught from the Word.
28–30	11	Their quality.
31–34	11	Beginning of the establishment of the church.

Lamentations.

CHAPTER I.

Verses *Subjects*
1–3   **3** The church and its doctrine from the Word, which had been dominant, but now enslaved and laid waste.
4, 5   **3** All of its truths and goods are perverted.
6   **3** There is no power against the hells.
7–11   **3** All things of the church have been devastated, and hence it is in evils and falsities.
12–16   **3** Its grief on account of the devastation.
17–22   **3** There is no help from heaven.

CHAPTER II.

1–9   **3** Because all truths and goods have been destroyed, that church has been rejected by the Lord, and there is damnation.
10–12   **3** Grievous mourning of the church on account of the devastation.
13–15   **3** The church has no conjunction with the Lord, because it is wholly perverted, and hence rejected.
16, 17   **3** Evils prevail.
18–22   **3** Lamentation of the church over her devastation.

CHAPTER III.

1–64 } **7·6** Description of the combats of the Lord with hells,
[–66] }   which were especially from the Israelitish and Jewish church, with despair, because all had been in evils and in falsities therefrom, and against the
    13 Lord: He invokes the Father that He may not be forsaken, and that He may conquer and subjugate these hells. These things in a summary.

Chapter IV.

Verses	Subjects
1–3	**3** Holy truths and goods turned into falsities,
4	**3** so that there is a lack of all of them.
5–8	**3** Their spiritual things have become infernal.
9, 10	**3** Affections of truth have become cupidities of falsity.
11	**3** They were against the Lord.
12–14	**3** They falsified the truths of the Word.
15	**3** It was impure.
16, 17	**3** The Word was rejected owing to their own intelligence.
18, 19	**3** Nothing of the church was left, and therefore came their destruction.
20	**9** The Lord was rejected.
21, 22	**3** The external of the church was also vastated.

Chapter V.

1–5	**3** Lamentation to God, that there is a lack of everything of the church,
6–9	**3** because of falsities and evils.
10–18	**3** They have become infernal.
19–22	**11** Prayer to the Lord, that the former church may be restored.

Ezekiel.

Chapter I.

Verses	Subjects	
1–3	10	Prophecy concerning the Lord in respect to the Word.
4	10	The Divine external sphere of the Word.
5	10	A representative of it as a man.
6	10	Conjunction of celestial and spiritual things there.
7	10	The quality of the natural of the Word.
8, 9	10	Its spiritual and celestial which are conjoined.
10, 11	10	The love of spiritual good and truth, and the love of natural good and truth; their distinction and oneness.
12	10	The turning or looking of all toward one.
13, 14	10	The sphere of the Word from Divine good and Divine truth, from which is the life of the Word.
15–21	10	The doctrine of good and truth acting in unity with the Word.
22, 23	10	The Divine above and in the Word.
24, 25	10	It is Divine truth (*verum*), and its influx.
26	10	The Lord above the heavens.
27, 28	10	The Divine love and the Divine truth (*veritas*) pertaining to Him.

Chapter II.

1, 2	1·2	The Word from the Lord to the prophet,
3–5	1·2	respecting the Jewish church, that it did not receive the Word.
6, 7	2	It was against the Word and the Lord.
8–10	2	There is everywhere in the Word a lamentation over that church.

Chapter III.

Verses *Subjects*

1–3   **2** He should be instructed in the Word, which in itself is delightful.

4–7   **2·11** He should teach those that have the Word, and consequently are able to live according to the Divine commandments, but they do not so live; while with others it would be otherwise.

8, 9   **2** He should not fear their obduracy,

10, 11   **2** but should teach them.

12, 13   **2** It is perceived that the state of the church has been changed entirely in respect to the Word and doctrine from the Word.

14, 15   **2** He was indignant that it should be so.

16, 17   **2** But that he might represent the Word,

18–21   **2** he would be guilty if he did not reveal their falsities and evils, and not guilty if he did reveal them.

22, 23   **2·16** It is according to the sense of the letter, which he must explain.

24–27   **16** He must not speak from himself, but from the Lord.

Chapter IV.

2   REPRESENTATION OF THE PERVERTED CHURCH IN THE CHURCH.

1, 2   **2** He should represent the falsities of the church, and the church besieged by them.

3   **2** He should represent the hardness of their heart, from which it is that they have no fear;

4–8   **2** he should also represent the church besieged by falsities of evil and evils of falsity.

[9–]14–16   **2** He should represent the falsification and adulteration of the sense of the letter of the Word,

17   **2** by which everything of the church has perished.

Chapter V.

2   IT IS REPRESENTED HOW THEY HAVE DESTROYED THE SENSE OF THE LETTER.

1, 2   **2** In part they have adulterated the sense of the letter, in part have falsified it, and in part forsaken it; nevertheless, they will continue to falsify it.

3, 4   **2** They will profane all the truths of the church.

5–7   **3** Because they have perverted the truths of the church more than others,

Verses	Subjects	
8–10	**3**	falsities have destroyed goods, and evils truths until nothing of good and truth is left;
11, 12	**3**	and because they have destroyed the church by profaning it, they will perish, as above.
13	**11**	Afterward the church will be instituted among others,
14–17	**3**	since all things of the Word, of doctrine and of the church have previously been consummated by profanities, and by evils and falsities.

CHAPTER VI.

3 TO ALL WHO ARE IN EVIL LOVE AND IN FALSITIES FROM SUCH LOVE IN THE CHURCH.

1–3	**3**	They will perish by reason of falsities.
4–6	**3**	All of the worship derived from truth and good has been destroyed, because there is nothing but evil and falsity.
7–10	**3·11**	Those who depart from evils and falsities will not perish.
11	**3**	Lamentation over this
12–14	**3**	that all who are in evils and falsities will be destroyed.

CHAPTER VII.

15 THE LAST JUDGMENT.

1–4	**15**	They are to be destroyed on the day of the last judgment.
5–13	**1·15**	This will take place when the Lord comes.
14, 15	**1·15**	Then they will perish by their evils, falsities, and profanities.
16	**3**	Some will be left,
17–19	**3**	but even these will have no truth or good.
20–22	**3**	They will draw near to those who have perverted all things of the church.
23, 24	**3**	Falsification of the Word.
25–27	**3**	They cannot repent, because they cannot be led away from evils and falsities.

Chapter VIII.

Verses Subjects
   3   PROFANATION OF WHAT IS HOLY.

1, 2	**1**	The Lord is represented in respect to Divine love,
3, 4	**3**	and it is shown how the holy of the Word has been profaned:
5, 6	**3**	namely, that they have separated themselves from the holy of the worship of the church.
7–10	**3**	Diabolical loves have perverted the lowest sense of the Word.
11, 12	**3**	They have instituted a worship in accordance with those loves,
13, 14	**3**	by adulterating all things of good,
15, 16	**3**	and adoring the devil in place of the Lord.
17, 18	**3**	They have closed against themselves the way to all mercy.

Chapter IX.

   15   VISITATION AND JUDGMENT UPON THOSE WHO ARE OF THE CHURCH.

1–3	**15**	Exploration of their quality as respects the Word.
4	**15**	Separation of the evil and the good.
5, 6	**15**	Destruction of those in whom there is no good or truth.
7	**15**	Judgment upon the evil.
8–11	**15**	There is no compassion, because there is nothing but what has been profaned.

Chapter X.

   11   THE INSTITUTION OF THE CHURCH BY MEANS OF THE WORD AND BY MEANS OF DOCTRINE THEREFROM.

1, 2	**11**	The Divine spiritual of the Word there forming the church, is described,
3–5	**11**	from which the internal and the external of the church is full of the Divine;
6–8	**11**	from this the doctrine is Divine.
9, 10	**11**	Doctrine from the Word, which is spiritual within.
11	**11**	It should act in unity with the Word.
12, 13	**11**	It is full of Divine truths.
14, 15	**11**	[It is known] from the Word, that it is such inwardly and outwardly.

Verses	Subjects	
16, 17	II	Doctrine is from the Word.
18–20	II	Influx of the Lord therefrom into the church.
21, 22	II	Conjunction of all things of the Word, and consequent life.

CHAPTER XI.

2   DOCTRINE FALSIFIED.

1–3	2	Beginning of the perversion of the church by means of falsities (the "caldron" here meaning doctrine, and the "flesh" the people),
4–7	2	by falsifications of the truth of doctrine.
8–11	3	It will be even worse, and they will perish by reason of things falsified,
12	3	because they will pervert all things.
13–16	3·II	All who are in falsities must be scattered: the church will consist of few.
17–20	II	A new church will be instituted by the Lord, which will be in truths from Him,
21	3	at the time when the former church is being destroyed.
22, 23	II	The Word will enlighten the new church.
24, 25	II	This is made manifest to those who are in spiritual captivity.

CHAPTER XII.

3   VASTATION OF THE CHURCH, AND FULFILLMENT OF THE PROPHECY.

1, 2	3	They are opposed to the Lord and the Word.
3–12	3	It is represented that the church has departed from them, through the falsification of the Word in respect to the sense of the letter, until there is no longer any church.
13	3	They have destroyed the chief truths by reasonings from the natural man,
14–16	3	and consequently the remaining truths, so that there is little left.
17–20	3	It is not known what good and truth are.
21–25	1	The coming of the Lord will not be delayed.
26–28	2·1	It is vain for them to say that the prophecies of the Word concerning the Lord will be fulfilled after a long time.

Chapter XIII.

Verses *Subjects*
2   THE DOCTRINE OF THE CHURCH FALSIFIED.

Verses		
1–3	2	Respecting those who from their own intelligence hatch out doctrine, or falsify doctrine.
4, 5	15	They do not stand in the day of judgment.
6, 7	2	They say that it is the Word of the Lord, and yet it is not.
8, 9	2	They will be shut out from the church.
10–12	2	They falsely interpret the truths of the Word.
13–15	3	They will be destroyed.
16	3	They will have no protection against the hells.
17	3	The affection for falsifying.
18, 19	3	From such affections arise persuasions of falsity, by which they lead astray.
20–23	3·II	They will perish, and those who do not suffer themselves to be led astray will be protected.

Chapter XIV.

1–4	2	Those who depart from the worship of the Lord have no enlightenment from the Word.
5	2	The church is of this description.
6, 7	2	If they do not become converted, they cannot be enlightened in truths from the Word,
8	2	and the church will be devastated,
9, 10	[2?]	until there be nothing of the doctrine of truth in it.
11	I·II	They must not go back, but must acknowledge the Lord.
12–14	3	When there is no longer any truth or good in the church, intercession will not avail in the least.
15, 16	3	Neither will intercession be of any avail when evil desires take possession of the church.
17, 18	3	So likewise when falsities take possession of the church;
19, 20	3	likewise when adulteration of good takes possession of it.
21–23	3·II	When these have taken possession of the church, another church will be established, on which the Lord will have mercy.

Chapter XV.

Verses *Subjects*
1–3   **3** There is no longer any spiritual good;
4, 5   **3** none whatever, since that good has been utterly destroyed by evil love.
6   **3** Such are those who are in the church.
7, 8   **3** From evil love they will perish, and thus they will have no church.

Chapter XVI.

    2 THE SUCCESSIVE STATES OF THE JEWISH CHURCH.

1, 2   **2** There was nothing in it but falsity and evil.
3–6   **2** It was forsaken by the Lord from the beginning, because it was without anything of the church.
7–12   **2** After a time truths and goods of every kind and species were given to it through the Word, and thus evils and falsities were removed.
13, 14   **2** Thus it could have been in intelligence.
15–20   **2** It falsified all things of the Word.
21, 22   **2** It extinguished truths and goods, and became as in the beginning.
23–25   **2** It turned truths into falsities,
26–28   **2** by knowledges (*scientifica*) of the natural man, by traditions, and by reasonings from them,
29, 30   **2** finally profaning [truths].
31   **2** It exalted itself above all men.
32–34   **2** It obtruded its falsities on others.
35–42   **3** They will utterly perish by the falsities by which the truths of the Word have been destroyed.
43–45   **3** Thus they will be as in the beginning.
46–52   **3** The like has come to pass with the Israelitish church, but in a less degree.
53–55   **11** Nevertheless the church in general shall be restored.
56–58   **11** It is everywhere better than in the Jewish church.
59–63   **11** A new church is to be instituted among others.

Chapter XVII.

HOW THE ANCIENT CHURCH WAS INSTITUTED BY THE LORD, AND WHAT IT BECAME AMONG THE JEWISH NATION (THE "EAGLE" MEANING THE UNDERSTANDING, AND "LEBANON" THE RATIONAL OF THE CHURCH).

Verses	*Subjects*	
1–3	II·2	Those who were in the capacity to understand were brought to the church.
4, 5	II·2	They were brought into the Lord's spiritual church, and instructed.
6	II·2	They became the church.
7, 8	II·2	Others succeeded, who had not the rational of the understanding, of whom the church was to consist, and to whom all Divine truths were given, because the Word was given them,
9, 10	2	but they utterly rejected all things of the church, so that they could not but be devastated of them.
11–13	2	They destroyed them by reasonings from the natural man,
14	2	excepting as yet a few,
15, 16	2	who, however, were natural external without an internal.
17, 18	2	Therefore they have destroyed those things which were of the church.
[19?] 20, 21	2	They will perish by means of reasonings from the natural man, and will therefore be dispersed.
22–24	II	The Lord will establish a new church of others, in their place.

Chapter XVIII.

1, 2	2·II	It is said, If the fathers are evil their offspring also are evil:
3, 4	2·II	but the offspring are not condemned on the father's account, but everyone on his own account.
5–9	2·II	There are some of the offspring who do not commit evils, or act contrary to the goods and truths of the church, and these are saved.
10–13	2·II	It is otherwise with the offspring who commit evils, or act contrary to the goods and truths of the church; these are condemned.
14–17	II	But he who does not do this is saved,
18	2	although the fathers are condemned.
19, 20	2	Every one is dealt with according to his deeds.

Verses	Subjects	
21–23	2	The impious man who is converted is saved,
24	2	while the pious man, if he becomes impious, is condemned.
25–29	2	Both are of Divine justice.
30–32	2	Exhortation to be converted, because the Lord wishes the salvation of all.

CHAPTER XIX.

1, 2	2	The first thing of the church among the fathers of the Israelitish nation was destructive of all things of the church.
3	2	That nation was likewise destroying all things of the church.
4–7	2	They were natural external, and opposed to all things of the church, and therefore they became perverted and were destroyed,
[?8,] 9	2	and afterwards they were wholly destroyed by means of reasonings from the natural man.
10, 11	2	The ancient church was in Divine truths,
12–14	2	but in the Israelitish and Jewish church all Divine truth was perverted and rejected.

CHAPTER XX.

2   SUCCESSIVE STATES OF THE JEWISH CHURCH.

1–3	2	Those who are of the Jewish church worship the Lord with the mouth and not with the heart.
4	2	The first of them, that is, their fathers.
4–9	2	They worshipped other gods, and did not depart from them, however much admonished, because they were natural external: this concerning them when in Egypt.
10–12	2	They were let into temptations, and then instructed. Also, respecting conjunction of the Lord with the church.
13	2	And they cannot even thus be brought to the worship of the Lord.
14–17	2	Although they were of such a character, yet they were not cast off.
18–20	2	Their offspring were instructed in like manner.
21–24	2	They in like manner reprobated all things of the church.

Verses	Subjects	
25, 26	2	In consequence they had representatives different from the former good ones, because they had profaned them; this concerning them in the wilderness.
27–29	2	When they had been introduced into the land of Canaan, they worshipped other gods in every way.
30, 31	2	They profaned things holy.
32–36	2.3	They are to be cast out of the church, because they have been such from the beginning.
37–39	3	They will not return to the church, but will be among the profaners of the holy things of the church.
40–42	11	A new church will be instituted, which will worship the Lord,
43, 44	11	and they will acknowledge their evils, and at the same time the Lord's mercy.

3   THE CHURCH HAS PERISHED BY REASON OF FALSITIES.

45, 46 H.B. xxi. 1, 2	3	An external or natural church, which is able to be in the light of truth.
47, 48 H.B. xxi. 3, 4	3	It is destroyed by evil love.
49, CH. XXI. 1–3 H.B. xxi. 5–8	3	It is the Jewish nation, which is here further treated of.

Chapter XXI.

1–3 H.B. 6–8	3	[See above, end of chapter xx.]
4, 5 H.B. 9, 10	3	They will all perish by means of falsities of evil.
6, 7 H.B. 11, 12	3	Grief of doctrine.
8–11 H.B. 13–16	3	Destruction by means of interior falsities of evil.
12, 13 H.B. 17, 18	3	Grief of the church because they cannot be converted.
14–17 H.B. 19–22	3	All things that remain will also perish, owing to falsities still more interior.
18–22 H.B. 23–27	3	Destruction will come by reasonings from falsities, and yet they will have worship, but from these falsities.
23, 24 H.B. 28, 29	3	Their worship will be vain.
25–27 H.B. 30–32	1·3	That church will come to its end when the Lord comes.
28, 29 H.B. 33, 34	3	It will be the same with those who have falsified the sense of the letter of the Word.
30–32 H.B. 35–37	15	They will be cast into hell.

Chapter XXII.

Verses	Subjects	
1, 2	2	The church adulterating truths and goods of doctrine.
3–6	2	It is coming nearer to its end.
7–9	2	They destroy truths and goods by means of it.
10–12	2	They have been guilty of various adulterations of truth and good.
13–16	3	They are destroyed.
17–22	3	Falsities and evils of every kind are mixed with truths and goods.
23–25	3	The truth of the Word has been adulterated,
26	3	also its good;
27–29	3	likewise the remaining things which, though false and evil, have been made to appear as though they were true and good.
30	3	Nothing is left over.
31	15	They will perish in hell.

Chapter XXIII.

2 THE CHURCH WHICH IS IN TRUTH, AND THE CHURCH WHICH IS IN GOOD.

1, 2	2	There are two churches, one which is in truth, which is "Samaria," and the other which is in good, which is "Jerusalem."
3, 4	2	Both are external natural, perverted in the beginning.
5–8	2·3	"Samaria" falsified the truths of the Word by reasonings from knowledges (*scientifica*);
9, 10	2·3	thus she became corrupted.
11–13	2·3	"Jerusalem" likewise falsified truths,
14–17	2·3	and adulterated goods also by various means.
18	2	Thereby she separated herself from the Lord,
[19,]20,21	2	and defiled truths and goods still further by knowledges (*scientifica*) of the natural man.
22–25	15	They will wholly perish on the day of judgment.
26, 27	15	Thus the truths and goods of the church will no longer be perverted.
28–31	15	They will be in hell where there is nothing but evils and falsities.
32–34	15	They will also be in the falsification of all truth;
35	4	and this, because they have denied the Lord.
36–39	3	They have destroyed all the holy things of the church.

Verses	Subjects	
40–42	**3**	They boasted before others because of their having the Word and the holy things of the church,
43–45	**3**	although these were entirely falsified and adulterated.
46–49	**3·11**	Falsities and evils will destroy all things of the church among them, and such must be separated that they may no longer mislead.

Chapter XXIV.

1, 2	**3**	The end of the church among the Jewish nation.
3–5	**2**	Through the Word truths together with goods have been given them, also the Divine presence.
6–8	**2**	They are filthy by reason of the adulteration and profanation of truth and good.
9–12	**2**	The Lord has labored with all His might, that they might grow better,
13	**2**	but it could not be done;
14	**3**	therefore they will die in their profanities.
15–17	**3**	Everything of the church will be taken away from them, and yet there will be no grief on that account.
18, 19	**1·3**	This will take place when the Lord comes into the world.
[20,] 21–23	**1·3**	Then He will destroy all the worship of that church, and there will be no grief on that account.
24–27	**1·11**	When the Lord comes, those who will be led to the new church will be instructed.

Chapter XXV.

1, 2	**2**	Against those who are in the sense of the letter of the Word, and who pervert the truths of religion by things which do not belong to religion, who are meant by the "children of Ammon:"
3–5	**2**	because they wonder at the destruction of the church they will not know truths:
6, 7	**2**	because they have rejoiced over this, they will pervert truths.
8–11	**2**	Still more when they pervert goods of the church.
12–14	**3·15**	Of those who destroy the external of the Word and of doctrine: they will be rejected for a like reason.
15–17	**3·15**	Those who by falsities of faith devastate the church will be devastated and perish on the day of judgment.

Chapter XXVI.

Verses — Subjects

— **2** Of the church as to knowledges (*cognitiones*) of truth, which is meant by "Tyre."

1, 2 — **2** They imagine that all things of the church consist in knowledges (*cognitiones*).

3, 4 — **2** Thereby come falsities, which destroy the ultimates of doctrine.

5, 6 — **2** These and also affections for truth are destroyed by knowledges (*scientifica*).

7–12 — **2** Much reasoning from the natural man will destroy all truths, from which comes self-intelligence.

13, 14 — **3** Thus all affection for spiritual truth will perish, so that nothing of the church will any longer remain.

15–18 — **3·15** Their end will be in hell, which will cause the rest of them to be in terror.

19–21 — **15·11** When they have been cast into the hells, the knowledges (*cognitiones*) of truth will be evident to those who will be in heaven and in the church.

Chapter XXVII.

1, 2 — **2** Further concerning the church in respect to knowledges (*cognitiones*) of truth, which is "Tyre."

3–9 — **2** The ancient church had knowledges of truth and good of every kind and species, and by means of them it had intelligence.

10, 11 — **2** Truths that protected that church.

12, 13 — **2** Acquisitions and communications of all the knowledges.

14–20 — **2** Knowledge (*scientia*), intelligence and wisdom by means of them.

21–23 — **2** Divine worship from them.

24, 25 — **2** Truths and goods of every kind and thus everything of the church acquired by means of them.

26–29 — **2** Through natural knowledges (*scientiae*) they have perished.

30–34 — **2** Lamentation over their destruction,

35, 36 — **2** and that it is the countenance of hell.

Chapter XXVIII.

Verses   *Subjects*

1–5   **2** Since they believe that they are learned from mere knowledges (*cognitiones*), and say in their heart that they are most intelligent from themselves,

6–10   **2·3** therefore they will falsify all knowledges (*cognitiones*) of truth, and will perish thereby.

11   **2** Respecting learning from the Word.

12   **2** From the Word they have all truths and goods of heaven and of the church;

12–18   **2** in consequence of which they were in intelligence at first, but afterwards this was dissipated by means of their pride.

19, 20   **3** Natural love consumed all things of the church, resulting in their destruction.

21–23   **2** Of the understanding of truth, which is meant by "Zidon:" it will perish by means of falsities.

24   **3** Their destruction, lest the church should be still further destroyed.

25, 26   **11** A new church will come into existence, when the former has been condemned.

Chapter XXIX.

1–3   **2** Of the natural man who, in things Divine, trusts nothing but his knowledges (*scientifica*).

4, 5   **2** Such will pervert the truths of the church by applying their knowledges to falsities.

6, 7   **3** Because truths have been perverted in this manner, all power, which is of truth, has been destroyed in their case,

8–12   **3** and all truth will be utterly devastated, until they will no longer have truth.

13–16   **11** Nevertheless something of a church will be established out of those who are natural and in knowledges (*scientifica*).

17, 18   **11** Reasonings from knowledges (*scientifica*) of the natural man will not destroy knowledges (*cognitiones*) of truth with them;

19, 20   **2** but these will be destroyed by reasonings from the natural man with those who trust knowledges (*scientifica*) alone, and have perverted the truths of the church.

Verses	Subjects
21	**11** Those who are of the church that the Lord will establish will have truths of doctrine.

CHAPTER XXX.

1–5	**1·3** The coming of the Lord when all things of the church have been destroyed by knowledges (*scientifica*) of the natural man.
6–9	**3** Then all who trust in these knowledges will perish through evil loves.
10–12	**3** By such the truths of the church will be destroyed through reasonings from the natural man, derived from falsities, even until there is nothing left but falsities.
13–19	**3·15** All things which are of the knowledge (*scientia*) of the natural man, of every sort, will become hell.
20–23	**3** They will have no truth, thus no power.
24–26	**3** This will take place through reasonings from the natural man.

CHAPTER XXXI.

1, 2	**11** Of the natural man who is in knowledges (*scientifica*).
3–9	**11** In the ancient church a rational flourished that was derived from knowledges (*scientifica*) of every kind, through their confirming, by means of these, the Divine things of the church; and from this source they had spiritual intelligence.
10–13	**3** The pride of self-intelligence, from which comes a trust in learning, has wholly cast them down from intelligence, and has deprived them of all the truths of the church.
14	**3·15** They are cast into hell, that they may no longer destroy.
15–18	**3·15** There they are shut up, lest, while continuing in their falsifications, they should spread their falsities abroad.

Chapter XXXII.

Verses *Subjects*

3 LAMENT OVER THOSE WHO BY KNOWLEDGES (*scientiae*) HAVE PERVERTED THE HOLY THINGS OF THE CHURCH.

1, 2   3 They pervert all truths of the church.

3–8   3 They fall into all falsities of evil, until they no longer see what is good and true.

9, 10   3 Those who are outside the church are horrified at their falsities.

11, 12   3 They destroy all things of the church by reasonings from the natural man.

13–16   15 They shall be cast into hell, that they may no longer pervert truths in those who are in an affection for truth.

17–23   15 In hell they will be associated with those who have profaned the holy things of the Word;

24, 25   15 also with those who have falsified truths of doctrine;

26–30   15 with those who have falsified the sense of the letter of the Word.

31, 32   15 All of these will be with those who by knowledges (*scientiae*) have perverted the holy things of the church, and thus they will be separated from those who are of the church, lest they persecute them.

Chapter XXXIII.

2   OF THOSE WHO INSTRUCT AND ARE INSTRUCTED.

1–5   2 Those who are instructed by the preacher concerning falsities and do not take heed, perish;

6, 7   2 when the preacher sees falsities and does not give instruction concerning them, he perishes.

8, 9   2 The same is true of every one who teaches doctrine, when he teaches and is not heard, or when he does not teach.

10, 11   2 So now in the church, they must be taught in order that they may be converted, because the Lord wishes the salvation of all.

12–16   2 If the evil man becomes good, his evil is forgiven; if the good man becomes evil, his good is not regarded.

17–20   2 These things are Divine justice.

21–26   2 A perverted church declares that they are the

Verses	Subjects	
		church, because they have the Word; nevertheless they falsify the Word, worship another god and do evil,
27–29	3	and will perish by reason of falsities of evil,
30–33	3	notwithstanding their hearing the Word, and being in external worship.

Chapter XXXIV.

1–4	2	Respecting teachers who regard their own good only, and not the good of the church.
5, 6	2	In consequence those who are of the church come into an evil life.
7–10	3	Being such, everything of the church is taken from them.
11–16	II	When the Lord comes into the world He will gather the church together, and will teach it Divine truths.
16, 17	3·II	The evil among them He will separate.
18–20	3	Evil shepherds destroy everything of the church,
21	[3]	and destroy the simple.
22–25	I·II	When the Lord comes He will teach and save these.
26–31	II	He will both teach them and protect them from falsities, and they will acknowledge Him.

Chapter XXXV.

3   RESPECTING FALSITIES OF FAITH.

1–5	3	All truth of faith among them perishes through falsities.
6–9	3	Falsification of the Word from this, until there is nothing but falsity.
10	3	They claim that the church is with them.
11–13	3	They speak against the church and against the Lord.
14, 15	3	When the church comes into existence, they will be devastated in respect to everything of the Word.

Chapter XXXVI.

3   THE PERVERTED CHURCH IN GENERAL.

1, 2	3	It has been destroyed by evils and falsities.
3–7	3	Because it has been destroyed even to its ultimates, those that have been destroyed will perish.

Verses	Subjects	
8–12	ii	A new church will be established by the Lord, which will be in truths and goods.
13–15	ii	The evils and falsities of the perverted church will no longer do any harm.
16–19	2	That perverted church will perish utterly.
20–23	2	Yet it will still be tolerated because of the Word, and because the Lord is known by means of the Word.
24–30	ii	A new church will then be established, which, being freed from falsities and evils, will be in truths and goods, and will acknowledge the Lord.
31, 32	ii	It will reject evils.
33–36	ii	Its intelligence will gradually grow by means of Divine truths.
37, 38	ii	The Lord will be acknowledged in it, and there will be the worship of Him.

Chapter XXXVII.

1, 2	3	It is represented that the church was destitute of all life from good and truth.
3–6	ii	It is foretold that a new church will come into existence, in which will be life.
7, 8	ii	This also came to pass when that church was first instructed in truths, and was thus made fit for receiving,
9, 10	ii	and it then received life.
11–14	i·ii	Thus the Lord did when He came into the world, and a new church was established by Him.
15–20	ii	There were two churches, the celestial and the spiritual, and the two together were one.
21–25	ii	This will be under the Lord, and the two will become one church from the Lord, and will be protected from infernal evils and falsities.
26–28	ii	The church will be different because the conjunction will be different.

Chapter XXXVIII.

1, 2	2	Those who are in the mere sense of the letter of the Word, and in a worship therefrom which is external without an internal, are meant by "Gog."

Verses	Subjects	
3–7	2	Everything and all things of that worship will perish.
8–16	2	That worship will possess the church, and will vastate it, and it will thus be in externals without internals.
17–19	2	The state of the church will therefore be changed.
20–23	2	And the truths and goods of religion will perish in consequence, and falsities will succeed in their place.

CHAPTER XXXIX.

1–6	2	Those who are in the mere sense of the letter and in external worship, will come into the church,
	3	but will perish. These are meant by "Gog."
7, 8	3·1·11	This will take place when the Lord comes and establishes the church.
9, 10	3	This church will then disperse all the evils and falsities of such,
11–16	3	and will wholly destroy them.
17–21[,22]	11	The new church that will be established by the Lord will be imbued with goods of all kinds,
23, 24	3	and the former church will be destroyed because of evils and falsities.
25–29	11	The Lord will then gather together a church from all nations.

CHAPTER XL.

1	12	Respecting a new church from the Lord, after the Jewish church has been destroyed.
2–5	12	What its quality will be.
6–23	12	All things of doctrine in respect to celestial good and truth:
24–34	12	all things of it in respect to spiritual good and truth:
35–49	12	all things of it in respect to external good and truth.

CHAPTER XLI.

1–26	12	All things of worship of the internal church in respect to good and truth.

Chapter XLII.

Verses   *Subjects*
1–20   12 All things of worship of that external church in respect to good and truth.

Chapter XLIII.

1–11   12 The Word in that church, in respect to the sense of its letter.
12–27   12 Worship of the Lord from good of love in that church.

Chapter XLIV.

1–3   12 Every good of the church and of worship is from the Lord.
4–8   12 The Jewish nation destroyed the church.
9–14   12 That nation will [not] be in that church,
15–31   12 but others, of whom the new church will consist, which will acknowledge the Lord; concerning which, and its life, doctrine, worship and ministry.

Chapter XLV.

1–5   12 Concerning that church: its outmosts will be holy.
6–8   12 The holy of doctrine.
9–25   12 Its statutes.

Chapter XLVI.

1–3   12 Influx of the Lord from Divine love.
4–24   12 Worship of the Lord there.

Chapter XLVII.

1–12   12 Influx of Divine good and Divine truth from the Lord; from this influx the angels of the three heavens, and men, have spiritual life, and from the Divine good and Divine truth they have intelligence and charity.

Verses   *Subjects*

13–23   **12** Inheritances or partitions of the church and heaven according to goods and truths in the whole complex, which is "according to the tribes of Israel."

Chapter XLVIII.

1–8   **12** That partition continued,

9–20   **12** for those who are in the third heaven, who are the "priests and Levites."

21, 22   **12** The Lord is in the midst of them.

23–29   **12** The further partition or inheritance continued.

30–34   **12** The knowledges (*cognitiones*) of that church, which are introductory truths.

35   **12** This church is the Lord's church.

Daniel.

Chapter I.

Verses	Subjects	
1, 2	2	When the church among the Jewish nation had been destroyed, "Babylon" appropriated to herself all things pertaining to it.
3–21	2	She wished to know all things of the church, and to acquire an understanding of them, and this was the beginning of "Babylon."

Chapter II.

1, 2	2	The future character of "Babylon" foretold.
3–11	2	This was not known to those who made common cause with "Babylon."
12, 13	2	They were blinded,
14–30	2	but it was disclosed by revelation from the Lord to those who were of the church.
31–35	2	The progress of the Babylonish religion follows: first the rulers would learn and teach the goods and truths of heaven and the church; and afterwards they would backslide, until nothing remained except what was adulterated, thus what
	1	was merely false and evil, and then the Lord would come.
36–38	2	First the Word will be taught there according to truths of doctrine drawn from it.
39	2	Afterwards the church will prevail, not from spiritual good, but from natural good.
40–43	3	Finally all good and truth will be changed by adulterations into evil and falsity, prevailing only through civil diabolic power.
44, 45	1·3·11	Then the Lord will come, and destroy that religion, and will institute a church that will be in Divine truth from Him.

Verses	Subjects	
46–49	2	This was the beginning of "Babylon," when it worshipped the God of heaven, and magnified doctrine from the Word.

CHAPTER III.

1, 2	2	"Babylon" was minded to depart from the worship of the Lord to the worship of another god, which is the "statue of gold set up by Nebuchadnezzar."
3–7	2, 15	All such agreed together, threatening all that they would otherwise be cast into hell.
8–12	11	Those rulers who worshipped the Lord did not obey;
13–21	3·11	they were therefore excommunicated and condemned to hell by "Babylon," together with all things of the Lord's church;
22–25	11	but still no harm came to them, and it was clearly seen that they were protected by the Lord.
26–30 CH. IV. 1–3 H.B. 26–33	11	"Babylon" was compelled by this to acknowledge and worship the Lord.

CHAPTER IV.

1–3 H.B. iii. 31–33	11	[See above, end of chapter iii.]
	2	IT IS FORETOLD WHAT "BABYLON" WILL BE, AND WHITHER THEIR MIND WAS MOVED.
4–7 H.B. 1–4	2	This was not known to those who were "Babylon."
8, 9 H.B. 5, 6	2	It was known to those who were of the Lord's church.
10–12 H.B. 7–9	2	They purposed to have dominion over heaven and the church when that religion should extend over much territory.
13, 14 H.B. 10, 11	2	Then they would no longer have any goods and truths of heaven and the church.
15–17 H.B. 12–14	2	Nevertheless the Word would remain with them, although perverted.
18, 19 H.B. 15, 16	11	Then those who were of the Lord's church perceived what those of the Babylonish religion were interiorly, and how far they wished to extend their dominion.

DANIEL VI.

Verses	Subjects	
20–33 H.B. 17-30	2	They were so stupid in respect to the truths and goods of the church, as to be no longer men, and this fact was confirmed from heaven, where they were seen to be such.
34–37 H.B. 31-34	2	They feared as yet to extend their dominion over heaven and the church, but acknowledged the Lord before those who were under obedience to them.

Chapter V.

1–4	3	"Babylon" profaned all things of heaven and of the church.
5, 6	3	It was perceived from the Word, that it was profane,
7–9	3	but it was not perceived by the primates who were in that religion.
10–24	3	It was confirmed by those who were in the truths of the church, that it was contrary to the Word for them to have exalted themselves above the Lord, and that thus they profaned things holy.
25–28	3	That religion was at an end because there was no longer good and truth of the church.
29, 30	3	Thus everything of the church there, came to an end.
31 CH. VI. 1–3 H.B. vi. 1-4	2	Worship of the Lord was thought about, as in the church.

Chapter VI.

1–3 H.B. 2-4	2	[See above, end of chapter v.]
4–9 H.B. 5-10	2	They deliberated about this, and concluded that they should be worshipped in place of the Lord;
10–17 H.B. 11-18	2	which decree being gainsaid by those who were of the Lord's church, it was ordained that they should undergo the punishment of the inquisition, which is "the lion's den into which Daniel was cast;"
18–23 H.B. 19-24	11	but still they were guarded by the Lord, that they might not undergo that punishment;
24 H.B. 25	15	but on the contrary, those who invented that crime were cast into hell,
25–28 H.B. 26-29	11	and those who were in worship of the Lord were saved.

Chapter VII.

Verses	Subjects	
1–3	2	Revelation concerning the successive changes of state of the church :
4	2	*The first*, while they were in the understanding of truth :
5	2	*The second*, when they studied only the sense of the letter of the Word :
6	2	*The third*, when the sense of the letter of the Word was falsified, and falsity was made to appear as truth :
7	3	*The fourth*, when there was faith alone, which destroyed all things of the church,
8	3	and which was confirmed by the sense of the letter of the Word;
9, 10	3	they were judged from the Word,
11	3	and that faith was wholly destroyed,
12	3	and [those who were in] the former [states] were judged according to their life,
13, 14	11	and the church became the Lord's.
15, 16	2	Further explanation of those things :
17, 18	2	four successive states of the church are meant ;
19–21	2	the last state is faith alone confirmed by reasonings and by the Word falsified, by virtue of which they would prevail ;
22	11	and this until the Lord shall institute the church
23, 24	[3]	which has been destroyed by faith alone,
25	3	and which despises the Lord Himself.
26, 27	15	Finally those who are in faith alone will be judged,
	11	and a new church will be established by the Lord.
28		Thus comes the end.

Chapter VIII.

11 Prediction concerning the church in respect to charity and in respect to faith.

1–3	11	The church which is in faith and in charity, and its power.
4	11	It will increase in truths and goods.
5	2	Faith alone will wholly destroy charity.

Verses	Subjects	
6–10	2	It will prevail through reasonings, by which it will dissipate the truths of doctrine that are derived from the Word.
11, 12	2	It will destroy the worship of the Lord, together with Divine truths.
13, 14	1	This will go on until the coming of the Lord.
15–19	2·1	It is further explained, that this will be when the Lord comes.
20–25	3·4	Faith alone will destroy the church, and despise the Lord.
26	3	This is the end of the church.
27	3	It is a sad time.

CHAPTER IX.

1·3   THE COMING OF THE LORD, AND THE END OF EACH CHURCH, THE OLD AND THE NEW.

1–3	1·3	Revelation respecting the end of the church.
4–19	3	Confession respecting the Jewish church destroyed.
20–23	[1]	Revelation.
24	15	After the church has been consummated, the judgment will come, and the Word will cease, and
	10	the Lord will glorify His Human.
25	11	Afterwards a new church will be established, but not easily.
26	3	Afterwards falsity will invade that church and will destroy it.
27	11·3	Still there will be a reformation, but this church will also perish from mere falsities and evils (*Matt.* xxiv. 15).

CHAPTER X.

1–6	1	Manifestation of the Lord,
7–21	11	to reveal those things that will be in the new church respecting such as are in faith alone, and respecting such as are in truths from good, who are meant here by "Michael."

Chapter XI.

Verses *Subjects*

11-2 THE "KING OF THE SOUTH" HERE MEANS THE CHURCH WHICH IS IN TRUTHS OF FAITH FROM GOOD OF CHARITY, AND THE "KING OF THE NORTH" MEANS THE RELIGION THAT IS IN FAITH SEPARATE FROM CHARITY: HOW THE CHANGES FOLLOWED EACH OTHER DID NOT APPEAR IN THE WORLD, BUT IN HEAVEN.

Verses		
1–4	3	The church among the Jewish nation will be destroyed.
5	11	Then a new church will be established, which will be in faith from charity.
6	11-3	Charity will be conjoined to faith, but faith will prevail;
7–9	11	and yet with some charity will prevail, and will therefore be the first thing of the church.
10–12	3	Their posterity will fight for faith and will conquer.
13–16	3	Faith will gain strength against charity and consequent faith, and will overcome the latter.
17	3	The dogma followed that charity is from faith.
18–20	2	Contention about various sayings respecting this subject from the Word.
21–23	2-11	They simulated the dogma of charity, from which they had a *quasi* consociation.
24–26	2	Confirmations from the Word in favor of charity were explained perversely, and they destroyed faith originating in charity.
27, 28	2	Painful conjunction.
29–31	2	Faith broke up the painful conjunction, adulterated the Word itself, and thus destroyed the church.
32–35	2	It was objected to by many, nevertheless they were overcome.
36, 37	2	Finally faith alone obtained,—a religion which destroys all fear of God and the whole church.
38, 39	2	It worships another god than the Lord.
40, 41	2	Thus faith originating in charity was subjugated.
41	11	Nevertheless those who believe the Word in simplicity will remain.
42, 43	2	Faith alone will also destroy by reasonings from the natural man.
44, 45	2	When the end comes, those who are natural sensual will be persistent.

Chapter XII.

Verses	Subjects	
1	11·1	Near the end, a new church will begin, in which the Lord will be worshipped, and the faith of charity will be received.
2, 3	11	Then those who are in that faith will come into heaven, but not the rest.
4	11	They will become intelligent.
5–7	3	All this will come to pass at the consummation.
8, 9	11	This revelation is from the Lord.
10	11	The evil will not understand, but the good.
11–13	11	The beginning of that church.

Hosea.

Chapter I.

Verses   Subjects
1–3	3	The prophet represented the falsification of the Word with the Jewish nation.
3–5	3·1	That profane church will be destroyed when the Lord comes.
6	3·1	No pity is possible;
7	1·11	but the Lord will pity those who will be of His new church.
7–9	3	When nothing of the church will any longer remain,
10, 11	11	then the new church will grow, and will acknowledge the Lord.

Chapter II.

1–4	11·2	Exhortation to abstain from the falsifications of the Word, otherwise there will be no church, but it will be without goods and truths, as before.
5–7	11·2	They will become as before when they loved evil and falsity, but they will be withheld.
8	11·2	They will return to God whom they worshipped at that time, and from whom they received good, not knowing that this was from the Lord;
9–13	11·2	but because they still did not worship Him, but another god, goods and truths will be vastated.
14–17	11	Those who will be of the new church, are to be purified by temptations, and prepared,
18–20	11	and a new church constituted of such will come into existence, which will acknowledge the Lord.
21–23	11	Then they will receive all things of heaven and the church.

Chapter III.

Verses   *Subjects*
          ‖   A NEW CHURCH TO BE ESTABLISHED BY THE LORD.

1–5   ‖ They will live for a long time without the truths and goods of the church, but they will become a church from the Lord, when He comes, and will acknowledge Him.

Chapter IV.

1–3   3 There is in the church nothing but evil and falsity from the falsified Word;

4–9   3 and because nothing of the law and doctrine remains, the church has been destroyed.

10–12   3 Because they have falsified the Word they are no longer able to understand truth, but will behold falsity.

13   3 For this reason their worship will be from falsities.

14   3 Will they not perish on this account?

15–19   3 Likewise those in the spiritual church: these will go away into falsities.

Chapter V.

1–3   3 Those who represented the celestial things of the church and those who represented its spiritual and intellectual things, falsified and adulterated the truths of the Word.

4   3 They cannot turn back,

5–9   3 but all will perish.

10–14   3 They no longer have any understanding of truth, but in place of truth they understand falsity.

15   ‖ Nevertheless there will be a new thing of the church.

Chapter VI.

1–3   ‖ A new church will be established, which will acknowledge the Lord:

4–6   ‖ it will understand truth,

7–10   3 as there are perversities in the former church,

11   ‖ when the new church will be established.

Chapter VII.

Verses   *Subjects*

1–5   **3** They have perverted all the truths of the Word and of doctrine.
6–10   **3** They have perverted them by evil loves,
11   **3** and by the knowledges (*scientifica*) of the natural man.
12–16   **3** Therefore they cannot be led back, because they are in falsities.

Chapter VIII.

1–7   **3** They have perverted the church: they have turned its goods and truths into evils and falsities.
8–11   **3** By reasonings from the natural man they have put off everything of the church,
12–14   **3** and also everything of the worship of the church; therefore they cannot but perish.

Chapter IX.

1–3   **3** They have falsified the truths of the church, therefore the church has been destroyed, and they will be natural, abiding only in reasonings from the natural man.
4, 5   **3** Consequently there is no Divine worship.
6   **3** All truth and good is turned into falsity and evil.
7–9   **3** They will perish on the day of judgment.
10–13   **3** The first of them were also such, they had no understanding of truth; so also their posterity, although instructed.
14–17   **3** The posterity of these cannot but become such.

Chapter X.

1–3   **3** The church that was devastated in respect to truths, has a worship similar to this one, and they say that they have truth.
4, 5   **3** At heart they worship another god.
6   **3** They will reason against truths.
7, 8   **3·15** They will be cast into hell, where there is such [evil].

HOSEA XIII. 93

Verses	Subjects
9, 10	2 The evils of punishment come upon them, but in vain.
11, 12	2 They have been taught truths and goods, and admonished,
13–15	2 and yet they persisted in falsities of evil. Their destruction, in consequence, on the day of judgment.

CHAPTER XI.

1	1 That "Israel" the Lord was "brought down into Egypt," means that they were instructed in the first principles of the church.
2	11 They were there in natural desire and knowledge (*scientia*).
3, 4	11 They were instructed in cognitions and knowledges (*scientiae*).
5–8	11 When they have become spiritual, they will no longer be natural, since they will thus destroy truths and the understanding of them ;
9–11	11 but from their having been in knowledges (*scientiae*) they will have intelligence from the Lord.
12 H.B. xii. 1	2 The understanding of the Word was falsified, although the Word is the Lord's.

CHAPTER XII.

1 H.B. 2	2 Falsities grow by reasonings originating in the delights of the natural man.
2–5 H.B. 3–6	2 The Lord strove with the posterity of Jacob, from their infancy.
6, 7 H.B. 7, ?	2 Exhortation to be converted, and not falsify truths.
8–14 H.B. 9–15	2 The church gloried in its possession of the Word, and on account of their representative worship, and they were continually guarded by the Lord ; and yet they falsified and adulterated the Word and the worship.

CHAPTER XIII.

1–3	2 From their self-intelligence they have perverted all Divine worship, and hence will perish,

Verses	Subjects	
4	16	yet the Lord alone is God.
5, 6	2	When they became rich in knowledges (*cognitiones*) from the Word, they forsook the Lord by reason of their self-glorification.
7–9	3	Hence their destruction,
10, 11	3	because there is no longer any truth of the church.
12, 13	3	The truth of the church has been interiorly destroyed.
14, 15	2	They are to be kept from destruction, until all truth of the church has been destroyed.
16 H.B. xiv. 1	4	Those who have worshipped another god, will perish.

Chapter XIV.

1–3 H.B. 2–4	11	Exhortation to be converted.
3 H.B. 4	17	because salvation comes from no other source.
4–7 H.B. 5–8	11	Thus they will be received into the church, and instructed in its truths and goods.
8 H.B. 9	11	Falsities will be rejected,
9 H.B. 10	11	and in consequence there will be understanding from rational light.

Joel.

Chapter I.

Verses	Subjects
1–3	**2** To all who are of the church.
4	**2** Falsity from the sensual man and afterwards evil therefrom has consumed all things of the church.
5–7	**2** Let them repent, for evil from the sensual man has destroyed the different things of the church.
8–13	**2** Mourning over the destruction of the goods and truths of the church.
14	**2** Exhortation to be converted,
15	**1** and to reflect that thus will be the last time, when the Lord will come,
16, 17	**3** and that everything of the church has been devastated;
18–20	**3** for which reason there is lamentation.

Chapter II.

1, 2	**1-15** The Lord will come and will execute judgment,
2, 3	**3** when falsity and evil from the sensual had destroyed the whole church.
4–9	**3** Falsity of evil will destroy all things of it by various insanities.
10	**3** All good and truth has been dispersed, together with the knowledges (*cognitiones*) of them.
11	**7** The Lord will fight with them.
12–17	**2** Exhortation to be converted to Him, to repent, and to be wise.
18, 19	**11** The Lord will establish the church, to which He will give its goods and truths,
20	**11** and will remove falsities of evil, and thus hell.
21–25	**11** They will have trust in the Lord, from which they will have goods and felicities,
26, 27	**11** and acknowledgment from the heart.

SUMMARIES OF THE INTERNAL SENSE.

Verses Subjects

28, 29 **11** By His Divine the Lord will fill those who are of
H.B. iii. 1, 2 that church with all things, and will vivify them.

30, 31 **3·15** Falsities of evil and evils of falsity will dissipate in-
H.B. iii. 3, 4 flux on the day of judgment,

32 **17** but those who acknowledge and worship the Lord
H.B. iii. 5 will be saved.

CHAPTER III.
H.B. iv.

1 **11** Then the church will be gathered together,

2, 3 **15** and then judgment will be executed upon those who have scattered the goods and truths of the church:

4–8 **15** upon those who are in knowledges (*cognitiones*) alone and in faith alone, and have thereby destroyed the truths of the Word and of doctrine.

9–12 **15** Combat of good and truth against evils and falsities at that time.

13–15 **3** Then evil is consummated.

16, 17 **11** This is from the Lord, whom they will then also acknowledge, and from whom is the church.

18, 19 **11** The Lord will then teach them the Word, and falsifications of the Word will be removed.

20, 21 **11** Then the church will be the Lord's, and from the Word.

Amos.

Chapter I.

Verses	Subjects	
1, 2	1	[The teaching of] the Lord about the Word and doctrine from the Word:
3-5	3	About those who pervert knowledges (*cognitiones*) from the Word which are of service to doctrine, and who thus turn away also the good of those knowledges: these will perish.
6-8	3	About those who apply the Word to a heretical falsity: these will perish.
9, 10	3	About those who pervert knowledges (*cognitiones*) of good and truth, and thereby do injury to the external sense of the Word.
11, 12	3	About those who pervert the sense of the letter of the Word by falsity, by which doctrine perishes.
13-15	3·15	About those who falsify the truths of the sense of the letter of the Word: they do not resist in the day of combat, but destroy the truth of doctrine.

Chapter II.

1-3	2	About those who adulterate the good of the sense of the letter of the Word: these destroy the good and truth of the church.
4, 5	2	About those who destroy the celestial things of the Word: they destroy both its celestial and its spiritual things.
6-8	2	About those who destroy the spiritual things of the church: these go away in consequence into falsities of every kind.
9-11	2	The Lord entirely removed falsities of evil when the church was instituted among them, and they were instructed.
[?12]13-16	2·15	Nevertheless that church perverted all things, and hence it has become like one who has truth, and yet is without truth, and thus perishes in the time of judgment.

Chapter III.

Verses	Subjects	
1, 2	3	The church was instituted solely with the Israelitish nation, therefore falsities and evils must be examined there.
3–6	3	There cannot be at the same time a church and not a church, nor truths and at the same time falsities, without truths being snatched away.
7, 8	3	The Lord will surely reveal this;
9, 10	3	for from this it is clear how the church is devastated.
11	3	Therefore the truths of the church perish from falsities,
12	3	and the goods and truths of the Word will be carried off by them;
13–15	3	so also all things of the church.

Chapter IV.

1–3	2	Those who pervert the doctrine of the church: they will also fall into falsities in outermost things.
4–6	2	They worship in externals according to the statutes, which will be similar [to genuine worship], but only in outermost things.
7, 8	2	Some things true will remain, when the rest are false, in consequence of which truths will have no power.
9,	3	Afterward all things of the church are falsified,
10, 11	3	and finally they are profaned by sensual knowledges (*scientifica*), the profanation extending to all things of the church, so that there is hardly anything left.
12, 13	3	Exhortation to turn themselves to the Lord.

Chapter V.

1–3	2	Lamentation over the church because it has been successively devastated.
4–9	2	Exhortation to seek the Lord, that all things of the church may not perish through evils and falsities.
10–13	2	They reject truths because they are in self-intelligence.
14, 15	2	Exhortation to be converted.

Verses	Subjects	
16–20	3	Lamentation over the destruction of the church, and over their own destruction, when the Lord comes.
21, 22	2	Their worship cannot be accepted.
23–25	2	It will be accepted if they have good and truth.
26, 27	2	Otherwise they are deprived of all knowledge (*cognitio*) of truth and good.

Chapter VI.

3   Of the spiritual church which was instituted.

1, 2	3	It turned out worse than the religions of other nations.
3–6	3	It possesses all things of the church in abundance; they think nothing of the destruction of the church.
7–9	3	Therefore all things will perish,
10–12	3	until nothing remains:
13, 14	3	for the reason that they acquired those things from what is their own.

Chapter VII.

1	3	The church grew from externals to externals.
[?2–]4–6	3	When externals were lost, there was a restoration.
7–9	3	When inmosts were reached, all things were destroyed, because they were contrary to God,
10–13	3	and contrary to all things of doctrine;
[?14]15,16	3	so that there was no longer any doctrine.
17	3	The church with all things pertaining to it will perish.

Chapter VIII.

1	11	A new thing of the church comes into existence.
2, 3	3	The old church comes to an end,
4–6	3	when there is nothing but adulteration of good and truth.
7–10	15	Therefore they will perish on the day of judgment.
11–14	3·15	Then there will no longer be any good or truth.

Chapter IX.

Verses	Subjects	
1–5	15	The last judgment upon them, and whithersoever they may flee, nowhere will there be an escape
6	II	from the Lord, who causes a church to be.
7	II·2	There were also churches before, which were devastated.
8–10	2·II	Yet the church will not perish, but those who are in it perish.
11, 12	II	A new church will be instituted by the Lord, which will acknowledge the Lord.
13–15	II	The doctrine of truth, and the understanding of it, will be in that church.

Obadiah.

Verses	Subjects	
	2	OF THOSE WHO ARE IN SELF-INTELLIGENCE AND PERVERT THE SENSE OF THE LETTER OF THE WORD; THESE ARE "EDOM."
1–3	**2**	They must be combated, because they believe themselves to be more intelligent than others.
4, 5	**2**	They defend falsities by natural light, but they will perish, and with them, the falsities themselves.
6	**2**	They have pride.
7	**2**	They have no truths.
8, 9	**15**	They will perish on the day of judgment, because they have oppressed the church.
10–14	**3**	They destroy the church still further, and this is their delight.
15, 16	**15**	Destruction will come upon them on the day of judgment.
17	**11**	A new church will come into existence
18	**11**	in place of the former church, which is condemned.
19–21	**11**	The new church will be in the understanding of truth, and those that are in it will be saved.

Jonah.

Chapter I.

Verses   Subjects

ii The conversion of the nations, which are meant by "Nineveh."

1–3   **ii·2** Those who were of the Jewish nation were commanded to teach the Word to the nations round about, but they would not, and thus they kept the Word among themselves alone.

4–6   **2** Knowledges (*cognitiones*) began to perish with them, and yet they lived unconcernedly.

7–9   **ii·2** The nations perceived that the state of the church was perverted among themselves, because of the loss of knowledges (*cognitiones*) among the Jews, and that the latter were unwilling to impart them to others outside of themselves.

10–13   **ii·2** They should reject those things which were from the Jewish nation, because they were falsified, so that they might be saved.

14–16   **17** They prayed unto the Lord for salvation, which was effected for them, when the falsities from the Jewish nation had been removed.

17   **7·6** [See next chapter.]

Chapter II.

CH. I. 17, **7·6** Prophecy concerning the Lord's combats with the hells, and concerning His most grievous temptations at the time, and concerning His state at the time; the "three days and nights during which Jonah was in the bowels of the fish," signify the entire duration of the combat with the hells.
CH. II. 1–10
H.B. 1–11

Chapter III.

Verses   *Subjects*
1–10   **11** The nations, hearing from the Word of God about their sins, and that they would perish, were converted after repenting, and were heard by the Lord, and saved.

Chapter IV.

1–4   **2** The Jewish nation became very angry at the salvation of the nations.
5–11   **2** A representation of their being inflamed thereat.

Micah.

Chapter I.
Verses   *Subjects*
             1   THE CHURCH IN RESPECT TO THE DOCTRINE OF TRUTH AND GOOD.

1, 2	**1**	The descent of the Lord from heaven, and His coming into the world.
3	**12**	The state of heaven then became changed.
4–7	**3**	Then all the representatives of the church, which had been totally falsified, will be destroyed.
8–12	**3**	Consequent mourning, and that it will extend even to those who were in celestial good.
13–15	**3**	Hence even these will begin to be perverted.
16	**3**	Consequently they also will suffer deprivation of all truth.

Chapter II.

1, 2	**3**	Concerning thought with the intention of doing evil, that they also do it from the will.
3–5	**3**	Hence the church has become perverted.
6, 7	**3**	There is no longer any use to teach any except those who obey;
8, 9	**3**	therefore they do evils of every kind.
10, 11	**3**	They will perish, because they cannot be taught.
12, 13	**11**	Such things do not invade those who will be of the Lord's new church.

Chapter III.
             3   THE PERVERTED CHURCH.

1–3	**3**	They have destroyed all truths and goods even to the last things of the church.
4	**3**	Then they are not heard by the Lord.
5–7	**3**	Because they have perverted all things of the Word and of doctrine, they can no longer see and receive anything of truth and good.

Verses	Subjects	
8	1	The Lord in respect to the Word which He will declare unto them.
9–11	3	They falsify all the truths and goods of the Word, and yet they say, that God is with them.
12	3	Therefore the whole church will be destroyed.

CHAPTER IV.

1, 2	II·1	A new church will be established by the Lord when He comes into the world, and it will be formed out of the nations.
3, 4	II	Falsities and evils will no longer be there, but truths and goods,
5, 7, 10	II	under the Lord.
6, 7	II	Those who are in externals, and those who from ignorance are in things not true and good, will draw near.
8–10	II	Truths and goods with them will grow.
10–12	II	Falsities will not enter and destroy.
13	II	Falsities will be destroyed among them,

CHAPTER V.

1	II	however much they may infest.
2 (H.B. iv. 14)	1	The coming of the Lord who is the **God of the church**,
3, 4 (H.B. v. 1)	II	who will gather the church together and teach those who are in it.
5, 6 (H.B. 2, 3)	17	He will utterly destroy reasonings from falsities.
7 (H.B. 4, 5)	17	Then there will be salvation in that church,
8 (H.B. 6)	3	but in the church in the Jewish nation there will be nothing but falsities of evil.
9 (H.B. 7)	II	This church will have no power over the Lord's church,
10–15 (H.B. 8)	3	and it will perish with all its falsities and evils.
(H.B. 9–14)		

CHAPTER VI.

2   AGAINST THE JEWISH NATION.

1–4	2	The Lord offered every good to them.
5	2	He protected them.

Verses	Subjects	
6–8	2	The Lord is not approached by externals of worship, but by internals, which are of truth and good.
9	2	The life of truth and good should be loved,
10, 11	2	and not the life of falsity and evil.
12	2	There is falsification of truth with them.
13	2	They could not be brought back by punishments;
14–16	2	therefore it must needs be that this church, having been overthrown, should perish.

CHAPTER VII.

1–4	3	There is no longer any truth or good in the church: therefore the last time has come upon it.
5, 6	3	Then falsities and evils will combat amongst themselves, and against truths and goods.
7–9	II	Then the church will come, which will be in the light of truth, from the Lord.
10	3	The old church will be destroyed.
11, 12	II	A new church will be established, gathered from every nation,
13	[3]	when the old has been destroyed.
14, 15	II	It will be taught and led.
16, 17	II	Infernal things will be removed from it.
18–20	II	The Divine compassion will be there.

Nahum.

Chapter I.

Verses *Subjects*
1, 2   **15** The last judgment upon those who are in evils.
3–6   **15.3** By virtue of His presence all things are revealed, and those who are of the perverted church will not endure.
7   **ii** The Lord will protect those who trust in Him,
8–11   **3** but those who are in falsities and evils will perish;
12–14   **ii** those, however, who are not of that church, and are in falsities from ignorance, will be received, and their falsities will be removed.
15   **i·ii** [See next chapter.]

Chapter II.

CH.I.15,   **i·ii** The Lord's coming and the new church from Him,
CH.II.1–3   and the protection of that church by Him.
H.B. ii. 1–4
3–6   **15.3** On the day of judgment those will perish who have
H.B. 4–7   destroyed the church, and they will be cast into hell with tumult.
7–10   **3** All things of the church will be taken away from them.
H.B. 8–11
11–13   **3** Then they will no longer destroy the church and
H.B. 12–14   its sanctities.

Chapter III.

15.3 RESPECTING THOSE WHO HAVE FALSIFIED AND ADULTERATED THE WORD.

1–4   **15.3** They will perish in hell.
5–7   **15.3** All their adulterations will be revealed, and they will perish.
8–10   **15.3** Knowledges (*cognitiones et scientifica*) will not save, because they will be dissipated,
11, 12   **15.3** because they will not protect them from perishing by falsities of evil,
13–17   **15.3** howsoever they have confirmed themselves by them, but in vain;
18   **15.3** neither will reasonings save.
19   **15.3** There is nothing of soundness, therefore their destruction.

Habakkuk.

Chapter I.

Verses	Subjects	
	3	OF VIOLENCE AND INJUSTICE.
1–5	3	Justice and truth perish. Grief on the part of the Lord, and directed to the Lord.
6–11	3	The Jewish church profaned all the truths and goods of the Word and of the church.
12–17	3	The Lord's grief continued, that the evil prevail over the good, and destroy them.

Chapter II.

1–3	1	The coming of the Lord: what will then take place.
4, 5	3	The love of self: it grows, and man grows vile therefrom.
6, 7	3	He is held in contempt by others,
8	3	and they pervert the goods and truths of the church.
9, 10	3	They are in their own intelligence, owing to which they are puffed up.
11	3	They judge from externals alone.
12, 13	3	A curse rests upon those who hatch doctrine out of falsities.
14	1	When the Lord comes,
15–17	3	he who leads others astray, will then be ashamed,
18, 19	3	and falsities will then profit him nothing.
20	1·3	This, when the Lord is in His Human.

Chapter III.

1–4	1	Prediction that the Lord will come into the world, to whom belongs Divine truth and good.
5–7	3	He will examine the church: it is not a church.

Verses	Subjects	
8–9	3	He will by His Divine truth dissipate the falsities of evil.
10–15	15	Judgment upon them, combat with them, their destruction, and their being cast into hell.
16, 17	3	Grief on account of their state, that there is no longer anything of the church.
18, 19	17	Then those who at heart acknowledge the Lord will be saved.

Zephaniah.

Chapter I.

Verses   *Subjects*
1–3   **2** All knowledge (*cognitio*) and understanding of truth will perish.
4–6   **2** The church will perish because it is in mere falsities and evils in respect to doctrine and in respect to worship.
7, 8   **1** The Lord will come and gather together to the church.
9–11   **15** Then those who have adulterated the truths of the Word will perish, and are to be cast into hell.
12–13   **3** No truth will then be left in the church.
14–17   **15** They will perish on the day of the judgment by the Lord.
18   **15** They cannot be preserved.

Chapter II.

1–3   **15** They ought to be converted before the Lord comes to judgment,
4–6   **15** for the evil will then perish on account of evils and falsities of many kinds.
7   **16**[?**17**] Then some are to be saved.
8–10   **15.3** Those who have adulterated the Word will utterly perish.
11   **15.3** They will perish that whoever is able may acknowledge the Lord.
12–15   **15.3** Those who have falsified the knowledges (*cognitiones*) of truth, by means of reasonings and knowledges (*scientifica*), and have thus destroyed the church, will utterly perish.

Chapter III.

Verses	Subjects	
1–4	3	Everything of the doctrine of truth and good has been perverted.
5	1	When the Lord comes He will investigate.
6–8	15	The evil will perish and are to be cast into hell.
9, 10	11	Then a new church made up of those who acknowledge the Lord will arise.
11, 12	11·16[?17]	Those who are in falsities of evil must be separated, and thus the few must be saved.
13–20	11	Then there will be a new church of those who will acknowledge the Lord, and He will remove evils and falsities from them; concerning this church.

Haggai.

Chapter I.

Verses   *Subjects*
1–4   **1-3** They believe that the Messiah will come to exalt them to glory, and yet the church among them has been devastated.
5, 6   **3** They could no longer be taught by the Word.
7–9   **3** The church cannot be instituted among them, because every one looks to himself and not to the Lord;
10, 11   **3** therefore no truth or good can be received by them.
12–15   **II** The church will be instituted among those who are wise from the Word.

Chapter II.

1–3   **2** The church when first instituted was full of truths; at the present day it is devastated.
4, 5   **II** Nevertheless a church will be instituted.
6–9   **I** When the Lord comes into the world, this church will be an interior church.
10–14   **3** An external without an internal is of no use, and still less when the external has been falsified; so is it in the former church,
15–17   **3** where truth has been turned into falsity, in which there is hardly anything of the church,
18, 19   **3** although there are truths in abundance in the Word.
20–22   **3** All things of the former church will be destroyed.
23   **II** The church will be among others.

Zechariah.

Chapter I.

Verses	Subjects	
1–4	2	Those who were descended from Jacob were instructed in the things of the church, from the very beginning, but in vain.
5, 6	2	Therefore what happened to them was according to the Word.
7–10	2	The successive states of the church even to the end are represented, what was their understanding of the Word.
11	2	It is found that there is no church.
12, 13	II	A new church which will be from the Lord.
14–16	II·3	The Lord will institute a new church when the former church has been completely perverted.
17	II·3	He will institute it in place of the former.
	II	A NEW CHURCH FROM THE LORD.
18–21 H.B. ii. 1–4	3	Falsities of evil which have destroyed everything of the church.

Chapter II.

1, 2 H.B. 5, 6	II	Quality of the church about to be instituted, in respect to truth and good.
3–5 H.B. 7–9	II	It will be vastly multiplied, and the Lord will be in it.
6–9 H.B. 10–13	II·3	Those who have profaned holy things are to be separated and dispersed.
10–13 H.B. 14–17	1·II	The Lord will come, and those who are of the new church will acknowledge Him, and He will be with them.

Chapter III.

	II	OF THE NEW CHURCH.
1, 2	II·2	Infernal falsity from the former church will infest the new church which the Lord will establish.

Verses	Subjects
3–5	II In this church there will be falsities of ignorance, which will be removed, and truths will be given in their place.
6–10	II They will have understanding of truth from the Lord, to the extent in which they depart from falsities.

Chapter IV.

1–7	II Enlightenment of the new church by the Lord from the good of love by means of truth.
8–10	II This is from the Lord.
11–14	II There will also be in it truths from a celestial origin.

Chapter V.

1–4	3 Rejection of the Jewish church, because they have utterly perverted the church.
5–8	3 They have destroyed every good.
9–11	3 They will profane its truth still further.

Chapter VI.

1–7	II The doctrine of the new church from truths which are from the good of love and charity.
8	II It will be with those who are in ignorance of truth.
9–14	II A representative that the new church is from the Lord, with all the good and truth in it.
15	II The church will be constituted of those who are without the church.

Chapter VII.

1–7	2 The Jews desiring that after the Babylonish captivity the church might be with them, but this will not take place, because they have not turned away from falsities and evils.
8–12	2 They were told, that they should keep the statutes, but they did not.
13, 14	2 Therefore the church will not be with them, but they will be dispersed.

Chapter VIII.

Verses   *Subjects*
- 1–3   **11** The Lord will institute a church in which will be the doctrine of truth and good,
- 4–6   **11** where there will be wisdom and innocence.
- 7–9   **11** Men are to be brought to it from all parts, and it will acknowledge the Lord.
- 10   **3** There has been heretofore no protection from falsities of evil, which are from hell.
- 11, 12   **11** It will be different in this church, where truths and goods will continue.
- 13–17   **3·11** As the former church has perished through falsities of evil, so this one will continue in truths and goods.
- 18, 19   **11** It will be in humiliation and in the affection for truth.
- 20–23   **11** It will grow and will increase in numbers from all who worship the Lord and love the Word.

Chapter IX.

- 1, 2   **11** The new church will be in knowledges (*cognitiones*) from the Word.
- 3, 4   **3** Those who are in knowledges from the Word will destroy them.
- 5, 6   **3** Likewise those who are in faith alone.
- 7, 8   **3** They shall perish lest they ruin the church still further.
- 9   **1** The Lord will come with Divine truth.
- 10, 11   **3·11** After the old church has perished, a new one will be instituted subject to the Lord, who will reign over it.
- 12–16   **11** The Lord will fill them with truths, and will protect them.
- 17   **11** They will possess intelligence.

Chapter X.

- 1   **17** The Lord will spiritually bless those who seek Him.
- 2, 3   **3** Those who have the Word are in falsities of evil and will perish.
- 4–6   **11** Those who are in celestial good, of whom the church will consist where the Lord is, will fight
-      **11·7** against falsities of evil; so also will those who are in spiritual good.

Verses	Subjects
7-10	**11** They are to be gathered together out of every religion, and taught.
11	**11** The Lord will protect them from falsities that are from hell,
12	**[11]** because they worship the Lord.

Chapter XI.

1-3	**3**	Every external of the church has been devastated.
4, 5	**3**	Care is to be taken lest those who are in good be destroyed by them.
6	**2**	Falsities destroy the church.
7, 8	**2**	There are none to lead the people any longer,
9	**2**	but only such as destroy.
10, 11	**3**	The Lord's conjunction with them has been sundered.
12, 13	**4·9**	The Lord was betrayed by the Jews, because He taught them.
14	**4·9**	The conjunction of truth and good has been sundered.
15-17	**3**	The teacher and the leader destroy all things of the church by falsities of evil.

Chapter XII.

1	**11**	The Lord forms the church.
2, 3	**3**	Nothing of the doctrine of truth will be in the church, therefore they will shun it.
4	**3·11**	There is no understanding of truth any longer, except with those who are in the Word and of the new church.
5	**11**	Then they will learn the good of doctrine from the Lord.
6, 7	**11**	Then the Lord will destroy all falsities by the truths of the Word, lest doctrine should teach something else.
8	**11**	Then the church will be in doctrine respecting the Lord.
9	**3**	Then all men or all things that are contrary to that doctrine will be destroyed.
10	**11**	Then there will be a new church from the Lord.
10-14	**3**	All things and every single thing of the church will mourn.

Chapter XIII.

Verses	Subjects	
1	11	Then the Word will be for the Lord's new church.
2, 3	3	Falsities of doctrine and worship will both be utterly destroyed.
4, 5	3	Prophecy will cease, and there will be no more falsity of doctrine.
6, 7	9	Those with whom the church will be at the time will slay the Lord, with the intention of scattering those who believe in Him.
8, 9	3·11	Those who are of the devastated church will perish, and those who are of the new church are to be purified, and taught by the Lord.

Chapter XIV.

1–5	7	The Lord's combats against the wicked, and their dispersion.
6, 7	3·12	Then there will be no truth, but in the Lord there will be Divine truth.
8, 9	12	Then Divine truth will proceed from the Lord.
10, 11	12	Truth will be multiplied in the new church, and no falsity of evil will be there.
12	3	He who fights against those truths, will plunge into falsities of every kind.
13–15	3	Then follows the destruction of the church.
16–19	11	Then they will draw near to the worship of the Lord, even those from the nations who are external natural.
20, 21	11	Then from the good of charity, from which proceeds worship, there will be intelligence.

Malachi.

Chapter I.

Verses	Subjects
1, 2	**II** The Lord has instituted a church with those who could be in external truth, but who were not in external good.
3, 4	**3** All external good has been destroyed, and hence also external truth.
5, 6	**3·4** Although the church is there, yet they do not acknowledge the Lord.
7, 8	**4** They worship the Lord from evil and not from good,
9, 10	**3** Therefore their worship is not accepted.
11	**II** Those who are outside of the church worship the Lord,
12–14	**4** but those who are within the church profane worship, and do not worship the Lord.

Chapter II.

1–4	**4** Unless they worship the Lord, all worship will be perverted and profane.
5–7	**4** Through the Word it is granted them to have conjunction with the Lord, who is here meant by "Levi."
8–10	**4** They have departed from the Word, and have thereby dissolved the conjunction.
11	**3·4** They have worshipped another god, whence came profanation;
12	**3** wherefore they will perish.
13	**3** Therefore their external worship is not accepted.
14–16	**3** They have severed themselves from the church,
17	**3** even by their calling evil good.

Chapter III.

[1,] 2, 3	**II** The Lord will come into the world, and will teach the Word in its purity.

Verses	Subjects	
4	**11**	The church, doctrine and worship will then be as they had been among the ancients.
5, 6	**15 2**	The Lord will then execute judgment upon all who have adulterated and destroyed the truths of the church.
7	**2·3**	They have done this from the beginning, and do not desist from it,
8, 9	**3·2**	nor do they desist from adultery, therefore this will bring about their ruin.
10–12	**2**	If they had lived according to the statutes, they would have been in the good of the church.
13–15	**2**	They have confirmed themselves in this, that good is of no profit and that evil does no harm, because the good and the wicked are alike prosperous.
16	**11·1**	It is otherwise with those who trust in the Lord:
17	**11·1**	they will be blessed of the Lord when He comes.
18	**3·11**	Then the difference will be seen,

CHAPTER IV.

2 H.B. iii. 20	**17**	and the good will be saved,
[?1,] 3 H.B. iii. [?19,] 21	**15**	and then the evil will be cast into hell,
4 H.B. iii. 22	**15·3**	because they have annulled the Word.
5[,6] H.B. iii. 23[, 24]	**1**	John the Baptist will be sent before the Lord, lest that nation should then perish.

The Psalms of David

The titles which appear in the common English Bibles at the head of many Psalms, in Roman type, are part of the sacred text, and contain an internal sense like every other portion of the Word of God, as is evident from their being referred to in these Summaries of the Internal Sense,—most noticeably in Psalm xcii., where the first summary refers exclusively to the title,—and as is likewise evident from the fact that the title of Psalm xviii. constitutes the first verse of the twenty-second chapter of 2 *Samuel*. These titles (if such they may be called) do not appear as titles in the Hebrew text, but often they are part of the first verse; often they constitute the first verse entirely; and sometimes, as in Psalms li., lii., liv., lx., they constitute the first two verses. These titles are uniformly referred to under the letter "*t.*" in the following pages.

The Psalms of David.

It should be known that as by "David" the Lord is meant, so where David speaks in the Psalms, the Lord is signified in the spiritual sense, as in many other places, which are to be adduced. [For these passages, see *The Doctrine of the New Jerusalem respecting the Lord*, n. 43, 44; *The Apocalyse Explained*, n. 205.—EDITOR.]

Psalm I.

Verses	Subjects	
1–3	11	The man who does not live ill is regenerated by the Word of the Lord,
4, 5	3·15	but he who lives ill, perishes on the day of judgment,
6	15	for the Lord knows everyone.

Psalm II.

1, 2	2	Those who should be in the truths and goods of the church are against the Lord;
3, 4	3	but men should separate themselves from these, because they are nothing before the Lord,
5	3	and they will be destroyed.
6–8	1·11	The Lord will put on the Human and will establish the church,
9	3	and will disperse falsities that are from evil.
10–12 N.B.	10·1	Let them therefore acknowledge and worship the Divine Human of the Lord, lest they perish.

Psalm III.

title, 1–8 H.B. 1–9	5·13	Respecting the Lord, when He was in temptations and subjugated the hells, and was then in a state of humiliation, in which He prayed to the Father.

Psalm IV.

Verses   *Subjects*
t., 1, 2   **6** Respecting the Lord, when in great temptations.
H.B. 1-3
3   **1** They should fear Him, for He has protection
H.B. 4   from the Father.
4–8   Exhortation to repent.
H.B. 5-9

Psalm V.

t., 1–3, 7,
8, 11, 12 } **13** Prayer of the Lord to the Father for help
H.B. 1-4, 8, 9, 12, 13
4–6, 9, 10   **7** against the evil, falsifiers and hypocrites.
H.B. 5-7, 10, 11

Psalm VI.

t., 1–7   **13·6** Prayer of the Lord to the Father, when He was
H.B. 1-8   in the last state of temptations, which state is despair,
8–10   **8** and being helped, He repressed the hells.
H.B. 9-11

Psalm VII.

t., 1–2,
6–11, 17 } **13·7** Prayer of the Lord to the Father for help against the hells—
H.B. 1-3, 7-12, 18
3, 4, 8–10   **13·7** for He is just, and there is no evil in Him—
H.B. 4, 5, 9-11
5   **8** that the hells may not prevail,
H.B. 6
12–16   **8** but may be conquered.
H.B. 13-17

Psalm VIII.

t., 1–3, 9   **13·7** A song in praise of the Father by the Lord to
H.B. 1-4, 10   regard His innocence, and give help against the hells.
4, 5   **13** The state of humiliation of the Lord is described.
H.B. 5, 6
6–8   **10** The state of His glorification is described.
H.B. 7-9

Psalm IX.

<small>Verses   Subjects</small>
t., 1–8, } **16·13·8** Thanksgiving and joy of the Lord that the evil
19, 20 } have been judged and destroyed,
<small>H.B. 1–9, 20, 21</small>
9,10[–14,18] **8** and the good have been delivered;
<small>H.B. 10, 11[–15, 19]</small>
15–17 **8** and thanksgiving of the latter that the evil have
<small>H.B. 16–18</small> been conquered and cast into hell.

Psalm X.

1–4   } **3·15** The evil do evil to the good and deny God, and
[–11] }   are hypocrites and deceitful.
12–18 **15** Prayer to the Father, for their requital, and for judgment upon them.

Psalm XI.

t., 1–5 **7** The Lord arouses Himself to fight for the good
<small>H.B. 1–5</small> against the evil.
6, 7 **8** The evil will perish as a consequence of justice.

Psalm XII.

t., 1–4 **3** There are no longer any good, but only hypocrites.
<small>H.B. 1–5</small>
5–8 **11** The Lord will to eternity deliver the good as against
<small>H.B. 6–9</small> the evil.

Psalm XIII.

t., 1–4 **6** The state of the Lord's temptations, and the grievous
<small>H.B. 1–5</small> insurrection of the infernals against Him.
5, 6 **8** He has confidence respecting the victory.
<small>H.B. 6</small>

Psalm XIV.

t., 1–3 **3** There is no longer any understanding of truth or
<small>H.B. 1–3</small> will of good whatever.
4, 5 **4** They do not acknowledge God.

Verses   *Subjects*
6   **3** They are against good and truth.
7   **17** The Lord will save those who are of the church, whence they will have joy from Him.

Psalm XV.

t., 1–5   **11** Those who love the neighbor and God, will be of
H.B. 1–5   the Lord's church.

Psalm XVI.

t., 1, 2   **8·11** The Lord's trust in Himself,
H.B. 1, 2
3–5   **8·11** for delivering the good, whom the evil infest.
6–8   **8·11** His is the Divine and Divine power.
8–10
[?9–11] } **10** His Human glorified will rise again.

Psalm XVII.

t., 1–5   **10** The Lord concerning the integrity of His life,
H.B. 1–5
6   **10** from the Divine in Himself;
6–10   **8** from which He is sustained against the evil who rise up against Him,
11, 12   **9** and wish to slay Him;
13   **9** by whom, nevertheless, He cannot be hurt:
14   [?**9**] and yet they possess the Word.
15   **10** He will be glorified.

Psalm XVIII.

t., 1–3, 6   **8** Confidence of the Lord from His Divine, against
H.B. 1–4, 7   the hells.
4–6   **7** Combats of the Lord with the hells.
H.B. 5–7
7–14   **8** In zeal He has subjugated them and laid them low.
H.B. 8–15
15   **8** Thus the Divine truth appears.
H.B. 16
16–19   **8** From His Divine He has prevailed over them.
H.B. 17–20
20–26[27],
30, 32 } **8** Justice and integrity belonged to the Lord,
H.B. 21–27[28], 31, 33
28, 29   **8** also Divine truth.
H.B. 29, 30

PSALM XXI. 127

Verses	Subjects	
31 H.B. 32	**8**	He is the only God.
32–36 H.B. 33-37	**8**	He fights from His Divine,
37–40 H.B. 38-41	**8**	and subjugates the hells.
41 H.B. 42	**8**	They have no saviour,
42, 45 H.B. 43, 46	**8**	therefore they will be destroyed.
43, 44 H.B. 44, 45	**11**	Then there will be a new church which will acknowledge and worship the Lord.
46–50 H.B. 47-51	**16·17**	A song of that church in praise of the Lord on account of redemption.

Psalm XIX.

t., 1–4 H.B. 1-5	**11**	The Divine truth will go forth in every direction.
5, 6 H.B. 6, 7	**12**	This truth will go forth from the Lord from the first things to the last things of heaven and the church.
7–11 H.B. 8-12	**12**	This Divine truth perfects man, because it is wisdom.
12, 13 H.B. 13, 14	**12**	There will be no pride.
14 H.B. 15	**12**	Thus there will be what is pure and acceptable.

Psalm XX.

t., 1–4 H.B. 1-5	**16·17**	A song in praise of the Lord, that He sustains the church,
5, 6, 9 H.B. 6, 7, 10	**17**	that salvation is from Him,
7, 8 H.B. 8, 9	**17·3**	that those are saved who trust in Him, and those perish who trust in themselves.

Psalm XXI.

	10	RESPECTING THE LORD:
t., 1–6 H.B. 1-7	**10**	From His Divine He has all good and truth, thus honor and glory.
7–12 H.B. 8-13	**8·15**	He will overthrow all who are against Him on the day of judgment.
13 B.B. 14	**15**	Those who are with Him will be glad, because of His power.

Psalm XXII.

Verses Subjects
                9   The state of the Lord's passion.

[*t.*,1–]3–5, **9** Prayer to the Father that He be not forsaken,
8[, 11]
H.B. [1–]4–6, 9[, 12]

6, 7   **4** seeing that he was more despised than all others,
H.B. 7, 8

9, 10 **9** that He was the Father's from conception,
H.B. 10, 11

12–15 **9** that those who are of the church, where the Word
H.B. 13–16   is, have condemned Him to death,

16, 17 **9** that they have crucified Him,
H.B. 17, 18

18   **9** that they have divided His garments, or dissipated
H.B. 19   the truths of His Word.

19–21 **6·9** Supplication that He may not be forsaken.
H.B. 20–22

22, 23, 25 **11** A church [will come into existence] from this [that
H.B. 23, 24, 26   the Lord was assisted by the Father],

24   **9** and He endured [the temptation] by power from His
H.B. 25   Divine.

26–31 **11** Through this there will be a church that will be
H.B. 27–32   gathered together from all parts, and it will worship Him.

Psalm XXIII.

       12   Concerning the Lord:

t., 1–3 **12** He teaches and leads to the truths and goods of
H.B. 1–3   heaven and the church;

[4], 5   **12** hence there will be no fear of the hells, for He guards, and imparts good and truth in abundance,

6   **12** in heaven with the Lord to eternity.

Psalm XXIV.

t., 1–3 **11** Respecting the church which is from the Lord
H.B. 1–3   through the Word:

4–6   **11** those who are not in falsities and evils will be in it;

7–10 **11·17** they will receive the Lord, who has conquered the
  N.B.   hells and glorified His Human.

Psalm XXV.

Verses   Subjects
t., 1–3   **16·11** Prayers of the church to the Lord, that they may
H.B. 1-3   be protected from the hells,
4–6   **16·11** that they may be taught truths,
7–11   **17** that their sins may be forgiven from mercy.
12–14   **17** Thus they will have good, and conjunction.
15–20   **7** Prayer of the church to the Lord, and in the highest sense, of the Lord to the Father, that, because He alone fights, He may assist against the hells,
21   **17** for perfection is His,
22   **17** and thus there is redemption.

Psalm XXVI.

t.,1–6,11 **16·7** To the Lord belong perfection, purity and innocence.
H.B. 1-6, 11
7, 8   **16·7** He has the Divine love of saving.
9, 10   **17·7** He is in combats with the malicious.
11, 12   **17** There is redemption when He conquers.

Psalm XXVII.

t., 1–3   **7** What the Lord says to the Father: He does not
H.B. 1-3   fear the hells which fight against Him:
4–10, 13, 14 }   **10** His union with the Father,
11, 12   **8** whereby He will subjugate the hells.

Psalm XXVIII.

t., 1–5   **13·8** Prayer of the Lord to the Father that the hypo-
H.B. 1-5   crites may be subjugated.
6–8   **8** He will assist and will prevail.
9   **17** May those be saved who are in the truths and good of the church.

Psalm XXIX.

t., 1–4   **10·11** Those who are in truths from the Word will adore
H.B. 1-4   the Lord who is the Word.
5–11   **10·11** The power of Divine truth from the Lord.

Psalm XXX.

<small>Verses Subjects</small>
t., 1–12 **10·9** The glorification of the Human of the Lord after
<small>H.B. 1–13</small>   He has suffered temptations, even the last of them which was that of the cross.

Psalm XXXI.

t., 1–4   **13·7** Prayer of the Lord to the Father, that He may be
<small>H.B. 1–5</small>   protected from those who devise evil,
5   **9·4** and who want to slay Him ;
<small>H.B. 6</small>
6–10   **9·4** whence He has grief of heart ;
<small>H.B. 7–11</small>
11–13   **9·4** they treat Him with contumely, as upon the cross ;
<small>H.B. 12–14</small>
14–21   **9** through trust in the Father He is delivered ;
<small>H.B. 15–22</small>
22   **6** from despair He imagines Himself to be forsaken,
<small>H.B. 23</small>   but He is not.
23, 24   **6** Let there be trust in the Lord.
<small>H.B. 24, 25</small>

Psalm XXXII.

t., 1, 2   **6** The just man is happy.
<small>H.B. 1, 2</small>
3, 4   **6** The grievousness of temptations is described.
5–7   **6** Confession of infirmities, and deliverance.
8, 9   **6** He is wise.
10, 11   **6** Let there be trust.

Psalm XXXIII.

1–9   **16** A song in praise of the Lord because the church is from Him through the Word.
10, 11   **3·11** Howsoever much the evil may fight against it, still it will continue.
12–15   **11** Happy are they who are of that church.
16, 17   **11** Self-intelligence effects nothing.
18–22   **17** Those are saved who trust in the Lord.

Psalm XXXIV.

t., 1–11 **16·11** Song in praise of the Lord because He delivers
<small>H.B. 1–12</small>   those who trust in Him, from all evil.
12–22   **11·3** He saves the good, and the evil perish.
<small>H.B. 13–23</small>

Psalm XXXV.

Verses   *Subjects*
t., 1–9   **7·8** The combats of the Lord against the hells, and
H.B. 1–9   their subjugation and overthrow.
10–16   **9·4** They purpose putting Him to death for desiring their good, which causes Him grief.
17,18[,24] **4·8** Prayer that He may be preserved from them, whence He will have joy.
19–21, 25   **4** They blaspheme Him.
22,23[,26] **8** From His Divine He will overcome them.
27, 28   **16** Hence the justice of the Lord will be praised in song.

Psalm XXXVI.

t., 1–4   **4** Respecting hypocrites, that they think evil.
L.B. 1–5
5–9   **16** It ought to be acknowledged that all good and truth is from the Lord.
L.B. 6–10
10   **16** Those who acknowledge the Lord possess all good and truth.
L.B. 11
11, 12   **17** The Lord protects from evil, and the evil perish.
L.B. *12

Psalm XXXVII.

         3·8·11 Comparison of the lot of the evil with the lot of the good.

t., 1, 2, 8–10, ⎫
12–15,17,20, ⎬ **3·8·15** Although the evil flourish for a short time,
21, 28,32,35, ⎪   yet they perish, and are cast down into
36, 38 ⎭   hell.
H.B. 1, 2, 8–10, *etc.*
3–7, 11, 16, ⎫
18,19,22–31, ⎬ **11·17** The good are saved by the Lord, and taken
[33,] 34, 37, ⎪   up into heaven.
39, 40 ⎭

Psalm XXXVIII.

t., 1–10   **6·9** The grievousness of the Lord's temptations is described.
H.B. 1–11
11, 12   **6·9** Those who are of the church purpose to have Him put to death.
H.B. 12, 13

---

* This is the division in the sole-Latin Schmidius Bible. In the Hebrew-Latin Bible verse 12 is divided into two verses numbered 12 and 13.—Editor.

Verses   *Subjects*
13, 14   **6·9** He bears all things with tolerance.
H.B. 14, 15
9, 15–22   **6·9** Trust in the Father that the hells will not pre-
H.B. 10, 16–23   vail.

Psalm XXXIX.

t., 1–3, 8–11 **6** The Lord's tolerance in the state of temptations.
H.B. 1–4, 9–12
4–7   **6** He desires the end of the temptations.
H.B. 5–8
12, 13   **9** Prayer to the Father that He be not forsaken.
H.B. 13, 14

Psalm XL.

t., 1–5   **13** Thanksgiving and celebration of the Father, that
H.B. 1–6   He has helped Him.
6–8   **13** He came into the world, as is written in the
H.B. 7–9   Word, that He might do the will of the Father.
9, 10   **11** He also preached the gospel of the kingdom of
H.B. 10, 11   God, and taught.
12–15, 17   **9** Trust from His Divine against those who pur-
H.B. 13–16, 18   pose to put Him to death,
16   **11·16** and let those who worship the Lord rejoice in
H.B. 17   Him.

Psalm XLI.

t., 1–3   **5** He who is in temptations, and consequent afflic-
H.B. 1–4   tion, is always upheld and thereby vivified.
4–7   **5** The hells among themselves devise evils against
H.B. 5–8   the Lord,
8   **5** and think that He is to be utterly destroyed:
H.B. 9
9   **5·4** so also do those who are of the church where the
H.B. 10   Word is.
10, 11   **4** They will not succeed, and will themselves be
H.B. 11, 12   destroyed.
12, 13   **8** Perfection belongs to the Lord.
H.B. 13, 14

Psalm XLII.

t., 1–6   **6** The state of grief and perturbation of the Lord
H.B. 1–7   from temptations, with trust from the Divine.

Verses	Subjects	
7–10 H.B. 8-11	**6**	The growing grievousness of the temptations even to despair.
11 H.B. 12	**8**	Confidence from the Divine that He will be raised up.

Psalm XLIII.

1, 2	**6·13**	Grievousness of the Lord's temptations even to despair.
3, 4	**6·13**	Prayer to the Father that Divine truth may comfort Him.
5	**6·13**	Consolation.

Psalm XLIV.

t., 1–4 H.B. 1-5	**11**	The church was established by the Lord among the ancients, evils having been cast out.
5–8 H B. 6-9	**11**	This was done by God, and not by man.
9–12, 19 H.B. 10-13, 20	**3·6**	Nevertheless the hells now prevail against Him as if there were no Divine presence, whence it is that there is no church.
13–16 H.B. 14-17	**6·3**	He is blasphemed by the evil in the church,
17–21 H.B. 18-22	**10**	notwithstanding that perfection is His.
22 H.B. 23	**10**	He is so treated on account of the Divine;
23, 26 H.B. 24, 27	**6**	therefore may the Divine bring Him help.
24, 25 H.B. 25, 26	**6**	He is in the last state of temptations, as if He were forsaken.

Psalm XLV.

	16	THE GLORIFICATION OF THE HUMAN OF THE LORD, AND HEAVEN AND THE CHURCH FROM HIM.
t., 1 H. B. 1, 2	**16**	A magnificent word respecting the Lord, and respecting conjunction with Him.
2 H.B. 3	**16**	The Divine truth is His alone.
3–5 H.B. 4-6	**8**	He has powerfully conquered the hells by means of Divine truth.
6 H.B. 7	**10**	The kingdom is His to eternity.
7, 8 **N.B.** H.B. 8, 9	**10**	He has thereby made the Human Divine:

Verses	Subjects	
8 H.B. 9	10·12	thus heaven and the church are His, and they are in Divine truths from Him :
9 H.B. 10	12	thus also there are affections for truth, and in these are the societies of heaven.
10 H.B. 11	11	Of the church where the Word is : it should depart from the affections of the natural man ;
11 H.B. 12	11	thus will it be the church of the Lord,
12–14 H.B. 13-15	11	and thus it will have cognitions of truth and good, with subservient knowledges (*scientiae*) .
15 H.B. 16	11·16	so there will be conjunction with the Lord in heaven.
16 H.B. 17	11·16	It will possess primary truths.
17 H.B. 18	11·16	The whole church will serve the Lord.

Psalm XLVI.

t., 1–3, 6, 7 H.B. 1-4, 7, 8	15	There will be protection from the Lord when the last judgment comes and continues.
5, 6 H.B. 6, 7	17	Those who are of the church and in the doctrine of truth will be saved by the Lord when He comes.
8, 9 H.B. 9, 10	17	They will have no fear of the hells nor of infestations therefrom.
10, 11 H.B. 11, 12	17	This is from the Lord.

Psalm XLVII.

11   THE LORD'S KINGDOM.

t., 1, 2 H.B. 1-3	16·11	A song in praise of the Lord, that He reigns over the church,
3 H.B. 4	16·11	that He will remove falsities and evils ;
4, 5 H.B. 5, 6	16·11	that He will establish a church.
6 H.B. 7	16	He is therefore to be praised in song,
7, 8 H.B. 8, 9	16·11·12	because His kingdom is over the whole church,
9 H.B. 10	16·11·12	and over the heavens.

Psalm XLVIII.

Verses	Subjects	
t., 1–3, 8 h.b. 1–4, 9	12	The spiritual kingdom of the Lord, how admirable!
4–7 h.b. 5–8	12	It will dissipate all falsities.
9, 10 h.b. 10, 11	1·10	This is the Divine Human.
11–13 h.b. 12–14	10·12	From this are all things of heaven and of the church,
14 h.b. 15	16	because the Lord reigns there.

Psalm XLIX.

t., 1–4 h.b. 1–5	2	Let there be attention to the following:
5, 6 h.b. 6, 7	2	Respecting those who are merely natural, and boast of knowledges (*scientifica*) and their own intelligence.
7–9 h.b. 8–10	2	No salvation comes from that source.
10–13 h.b. 11–14	2·15	However much they may boast of such things, they perish,
14 h.b. 15	2·15	and come into hell.
15 h.b. 16	17	Salvation is solely in the Lord.
16–20 h.b. 17–21	2	Knowledge (*scientia*) and one's own intelligence does not save after death.

Psalm L.

t., 1–6 h.b. 1–6	1·15	The Lord will come for judgment to those with whom is the church.
7–13	2	The Lord does not desire sacrifices and external worship.
14, 15	2	He desires confession of the heart.
16–20	2	External worship is of no avail, so long as evils are committed.
[21,] 22	2	They do evils, and therefore evil befalls them.

Psalm LI.

Verses	Subjects	
t., 1–5 H.B. 1–7	13	Prayer that He may be purified of the infirmities derived from the mother.
6–10 H.B. 8–12	13	If He be purified of them He will be pure,
11, 12 H.B. 13, 14	10	and He is holy.
13–15 H.B. 15–17	10	So will He teach Divine truths.
16, 17 H.B. 18, 19	11	Not external, but internal worship.
18, 19 H.B. 20, 21	11	He will institute a church, in which will be worship from good.

Psalm LII.

t., 1–6 H.B. 1–8	15·3	Respecting hypocrites: they will be in hell and will perish.
7 H.P. 9	15	So likewise those who trust in their own intelligence.
8, 9 H.B. 10, 11	11·17	Those who trust in the Lord will flourish.

Psalm LIII.

t., 1–3 H.B. 1–4	3	Every one has departed from God, there is no one left.
4, 5 H.B. 5, 6	3	They have destroyed the church without any cause.
6 H.B. 7	11	Therefore there will be a new church from the Lord.

Psalm LIV.

t., 1–3 H.B. 1–5	13·9	Prayer to the Father that He may assist against those that wish to destroy them.
4, 5 H.B. 6, 7	3·8	He assists against them, and they will perish.
6, 7 H.B. 8, 9	8	A song in praise of assistance.

Psalm LV.

t., 1–5, 9 H.B. 1–6, 10	6·13	The grievousness of temptations is described, in which He prays to the Father.

PSALM LIX.

Verses	Subjects	
6–8 H.B. 7–9	6·13	He would fain give up the combats because of their grievousness.
9–14 H.B. 10–15	7	The malice of the hells is described.
15 H.B. 16	7	They will be cast down into hell.
16–18, 22 H.B. 17–19, 23	7	Prayer to the Father, and He will bring help
19–21, 23 H.B. 20–22, 24	7	against the evil and hypocrites.

PSALM LVI.

t., 1–4, 10, 11 H.B. 1–5, 11, 12	5	Temptations of the Lord, in which He has confidence in the Father.
5, 6 H.B. 6, 7	7	Malice of the infernals.
7, 8 H.B. 8, 9	13	O that the Father would help in affliction!
9 H.B. 10	13	He will help.
12, 13 H.B. 13, 14	8	Song of praise for protection.

PSALM LVII.

t., 1–5 H.B. 1–6	13·7	Prayer to the Father when in the combats of temptations with the hells which attack Him.
4, 6 H.B. 5, 7	7	Their malice against Him.
7, 8 H.B. 8, 9	8	Confidence from His Divine.
9–11 H.B. 10–12	8	A song in praise of the Father for this reason.

PSALM LVIII.

t., 1–9 H.B. 1–10	4	Against those who were of the church, who cherished evil thoughts against the Lord: they are in mere falsities of evil, of which they perish,
10, 11 H.B. 11, 12	11	so that those who are in good may come into the church.

PSALM LIX.

t., 1–6 H.B. 1–7	13·9	Prayer to the Father concerning those who are then of the church: they wish to destroy and slay Him, although He is innocent.
7 H.B. 8	7·9	They fight from falsities against truths.

138   SUMMARIES OF THE INTERNAL SENSE.

Verses	Subjects	
8–10 H.B. 9–11	7·9	Confidence in the Father.
11 H.B. 12	7·9	He prays for them.
12, 13 H.B. 13, 14	8	They destroy themselves
14, 15 H.B. 15, 16	8	by malice.
16, 17 H.B. 17, 18	8	Confidence respecting help.

PSALM LX.

t., 1–3 H.B. 1–5	6	Lamentation of the Lord, that He has been forsaken, together with the church.
4, 5 H.B. 6, 7	6	Confidence respecting deliverance.
6–9 H.B. 8–11	11·10	A church internal and external is being instituted. In the highest sense respecting the Human of the Lord, that it will be made Divine,
10 H.B. 12	11·10	from His own power,
11, 12 H.B. 13, 14	11·10	and from His Divine.

PSALM LXI.

| *t.*, 1–5
H.B. 1–6 | 16·10 | The Lord's song in praise of the Father because of help, |
| 6–8
H.B. 7–9 | 16·10 | and because of union. |

PSALM LXII.

| *t.*,1, 2, 5–8,
11, 12
H.B. 1–3, 6–9, 12, 13 | 8 | Confession that the Divine alone has power, and from it there is help. |
| 3, 4, 9
H.B. 4, 5, 10 | 8 | They are of no avail against the Divine. |

PSALM LXIII.

t., 1–8 H.B. 1–9	10	The desire and love of the Lord to be united to His Divine.
9, 10 H.B. 10, 11	3	Those who lie in wait for Him will perish by falsities of evil.
11 H.B. 12	17·15	Then there will be salvation from the Lord, and rejection of the evil.

Psalm LXIV.

Verses	Subjects	
t., 1-6 H.B. 1-7	4	The lying in wait of the evil against the Lord.
7, 8 H.B. 8, 9	4	They will perish.
9, 10 H.B. 10, 11	17	Thus the good will be saved.

Psalm LXV.

t., 1-13 H.B. 1-14	10·11	From the uniting of the Divine and the Human in the Lord will be a church that will be in all truth from the Lord, and safe from infestation from falsities.

Psalm LXVI.

t., 1-5 H.B. 1-5	11·16	Joy that there is a new church that trusts in the Lord,
6, 7	11·16	who will save it from evils.
8-12	19	The Lord was united to His Divine by means of grievous temptations.
13-17	19	Thus Divine truth from the Lord is with men.
[?18], 19, 20	13	This has been done through His perfection.

Psalm LXVII.

t., 1-5, 7 H.B. 1-6, 8	11·12	The whole church will acknowledge and worship the Lord from joy of heart.
6 H.B. 7	11·12	Everything of the church will be theirs.

Psalm LXVIII.

t., 1, 2 H.B. 1-3	8	The hells will be subjugated.
3-5, 31 H.B. 4-6, 32	11	Those who are in good, will acknowledge the Lord, who is Divine truth itself;
5, 6 H.B. 6, 7	11	He will be their protection;
7-11 H.B. 8-12	11	He will regenerate them.
12-14 H.B. 13-15	3	It will not be so with the rest, although they have the Word.

SUMMARIES OF THE INTERNAL SENSE.

Verses	*Subjects*	
15–17 H.B. 16-18	11	Respecting the church from the Lord, from whom is everything of doctrine.
18–23 H.B. 19-24	17	He snatched them out of the hand of the infernals.
24–29 H.B. 25-30	16	Song in praise of the Lord on this account.
30 H.B. 31	16	The natural man will be subdued.
32–35 H.B. 33-36	10·16	Song in praise of the Divine power of the Lord [acquired by Him] through union [with the Father].

Psalm LXIX.

t., 1–4 H.B. 1-5	6	The temptation-combats of the Lord even to despair,
5 H.B. 6	6	even to the thought of withdrawal ;
6, 7 H.B. 7, 8	6	but He endured for the sake of those who awaited salvation.
8–12 H.B. 9-13	4	He is shamefully treated by those with whom was the church.
13–20 H.B. 14-21	4	Prayer to the Father for help, lest these prevail
21 H.B. 22	4 9	When He desired the good and truth of the church, they gave Him falsity and evil, as upon the cross, gall and vinegar.
22–28 H.B. 23-29	3	For this reason they are being destroyed.
29–31 H.B. 30-32	11	When He is delivered, the gospel will be preached,
32–36 H.B. 33-37	11·17	because then those who are of the church will be saved, and will worship Him.

Psalm LXX.

t., 1–3, 5 H.B. 1-4, 6	8·13·5	Prayer to the Father for help against the hells,
4 H.B. 5	17	that those who worship Him may have salvation.

Psalm LXXI.

1–4,[5,] 7, 12, 14 }	13·7	Confidence that the Father will assist Him.
6, 7	10	He was the Father's from birth.
9–11	9	Let not the hells say that He has been forsaken by God.

Verses	Subjects	
13	8	Thus they withdraw,
8, 15–19 } 22–24 }	8	and the name of God will be preached,
20, [21,] 24	8	when He has gained the victory.

Psalm LXXII.

t., 1, 2, 4 H.B. 1, 2, 4	12	The kingdom of the Lord.
3,6,7,15,16	12	The happy state of those who are of His kingdom.
5	12·16	Worship of Him from love and faith from eternity, and thereafter.
8–12	12·16	The greatness and extension of His dominion.
12–14	17	Protection and redemption.
17 N.B.	17·10	They have acknowledged the Divine Human from eternity, in which is all of salvation.
18, 19	16·17	A song of praise to Him.

Psalm LXXIII.

t., 1–9 H.B. 1–9	2	A matter of wonder to some, that the evil vaunt themselves and prosper.
10–14	2	Whereby the good are led astray, imagining that good is of no use, neither affliction.
15–20, 27	2	But afterward it is granted them to know that the evil are nevertheless devastated and consumed.
21, 22	2	They do not know this;
23–26	17	but the good are always upheld and live with God.

Psalm LXXIV.

t., 1–9 H.B. 1·9	3	The church with all things appertaining to it has been utterly destroyed, and its holy things profaned, they saying in their heart that religion is not anything.
2, 10, 11	11	Prayer to the Lord to bring help.
12–15	8	Before this He has overthrown the hells,
16, 17	11	and before this, being protected, He has established a church :
18–21	11	let there therefore be compassion, that the church perish not
22, 23	3	through the uprising of the evil.

Psalm LXXV.

Verses	Subjects	
t., 1–3 H.B. 1–4	1·11	When the Lord comes He will raise up the fallen church.
4–6 H.B. 5–7	3	Let not the evil exalt themselves above the good,
7 H.B. 8	15·17	for the judgment comes, in which the evil perish and the good are saved.
8, 10 H.B. 9, 11	15	The evil will then perish through direful falsities,
9 H.B. 10	11	but the good will worship the Lord.

Psalm LXXVI.

t., 1–4 H.B. 1–5	11	The Lord is in His church; protection there against falsities and evils.
5, 6 H.B. 6, 7	3	There is no longer any truth in the Jewish church.
7–10, 12 H.B. 8–11, 13	15·17	The Lord will effect a judgment, in which the evil will perish and the good will be saved.
11 H.B. 12	[16]	Let the Lord be worshipped.

Psalm LXXVII.

t., 1–9 H.B. 1–10	6	State of temptation of the Lord even to despair, whether the Father would give help;
10–15 H.B. 11–16	6·11	strengthening Himself from His Divine from things past, that those that had prayed for it had been saved,
16–19 H.B. 17–20	8	and that power was His through Divine truth,
20 H.B. 21	17	and that the church was preserved.

Psalm LXXVIII.

t., 1–7 H.B. 1–7	2	The Word was given to the children of Jacob, and they were confirmed in it by means of miracles;
8–10	2	but their fathers and the children had gone back, and had not lived according to it,
11–31	2	the miracles in the desert even having no effect: all of which involved how the Lord teaches and leads those whom He calls to His church. All these things recited.

Verses	Subjects	
32–37	**2**	On account of the miracles they returned, indeed, but only with the mouth, not with the heart.
38–40	**2**	The Lord forgave them.
41–51	**2**	Again they were seemingly converted when they recalled the miracles in Egypt, all of which involve the removal and dispersion from them of the hells. A recital of these things.
52–55	**2**	The Lord thus led them unto the land which was the seat of the church.
56–58	**2**	Yet they backslid and worshipped another god.
59–64	**2·3**	Therefore they were forsaken by the Lord, and delivered over to their falsities and evils; this of themselves.
65–67	**3**	Thus they were rejected.
68–72	**11**	Therefore a new church was instituted, which would worship the Lord, and which the Lord could lead.

Psalm LXXIX.

t., 1–4 H.B. 1–4	**3**	Falsifications of the Word and direful evils have destroyed the church.
5–12	**11·3** **15·8**	The cry of the church for help, that she be not destroyed at the same time, and her prayer that those who have ruined the church be removed.
13	**11·16**	Thus there will be worship of the Lord.

Psalm LXXX.

t., 1–3, 7 H.B. 1–4, 8	**11·16**	Prayer of the new church to the Lord, to come and lead,
4–6 H.B. 5–7	**2**	because they are in affliction:
8–11 H.B. 9–12	**2**	He has instituted a church and reformed it by truths from the Word,
12, 13 H.B. 13, 14	**2**	and yet falsities begin to destroy it.
14–19 H.B. 15–20	**11**	May the Lord come and restore it, and may it thus be vivified.

Psalm LXXXI.

Verses	Subjects	
t., 1–4 H.B. 1–5	16·11	Song in praise of the Lord by His church.
5–7 H.B. 6–8	11	When called upon and when He has proved man, He delivers him from the hells.
8–11 H.B. 9–12	3	The church among the children of Israel has gone back, and worships another god;
12 H.B. 13	2	therefore they have been left to themselves.
13–16 H.B. 14–17	2	If they had obeyed, the hells would have been removed from them, and they would have enjoyed every good.

Psalm LXXXII.

t., 1 H.B. 1	11	The Lord to the church, in which is the Word, from which it is possible to be in Divine truths:
2–4	11	let them not do evils, but goods;
5	11	because they do not do goods, the church is tottering;
6, 7	11	thus, although they possess the Word, they will perish.
8	15	Prayer that the Lord may come and effect the judgment.

Psalm LXXXIII.

	7	COMBATS OF THE LORD WITH THE HELLS.
t., 1–5 H.B. 1–6	7	The hells wish to destroy all things of the church.
6–8 H.B. 7–9	7	The hells that rise up against the Lord are enumerated.
9–11 H.B. 10–12	7·8	They will be cast down and subjugated
12 H.B. 13	7·8	from the places where they have made seeming heavens for themselves.
13–17 H.B. 14–18	7·8	Prayer to the Lord to overthrow them,
18 H.B. 19	8·16	that it may be known that power belongs to the Lord alone.

Psalm LXXXIV.

Verses	Subjects	
t., 1–4 H.B. 1–5	**11**	Love and desire for the church and heaven.
5–7 H.B. 6–8	**11·17**	Because of trust in the Lord, the church will increase in truths and goods.
8–12 H.B. 9–13	**11·17**	Her happiness arises from trust in the Lord.

Psalm LXXXV.

t., 1–7 H.B. 1–8	**13·15**	Prayer of the Lord to the Father, to institute a new church after judgment has been executed upon the evil.
8–13 H.B. 9–14	**11**	Perception from His Divine, that a church will arise and flourish, which will acknowledge the Lord, walking in truths.

Psalm LXXXVI.

t., 1–8 H.B. 1–8	**13·5**	Prayer of the Lord to the Father for help in temptations,
[9, 10,] 11, 12	**11·16**	because thus there will be worship of the Lord, and confession of Him;
13, 14	**7**	the hells are in insurrection;
15–17	**8**	by His help they will be overthrown.

Psalm LXXXVII.

t., 1–7 H.B. 1–7	**16·11**	Song in praise of the Lord by a new church that will be gathered together from all parts.

Psalm LXXXVIII.

t.,1–9,13–18 H.B. 1–10, 14–19	**13·7**	In temptations that continue even to despair, the Lord addresses the Father, that He is seemingly overcome by the infernals.
10–12 H.B. 11–13	**7**	God has no glory from the hells.

Psalm LXXXIX.

Verses	Subjects	
t., 1, 2	**13·10·16**	All Divine truth is from the Lord.
H.B. 1–3		
3–5	**10·16**	The Divine truth is from Him because there is oneness with the Divine Human.
H.B. 4–6		
6–9, 13	**10·16**	Thus the Lord has all power.
H.B. 7–10, 14		
10–14	**10·16·12**	All of heaven and the church is from Him.
H.B. 11–15		
15–18	**12·16**	Happy is he who trusts in the Lord.
H.B. 16–19		
19–25	**10·16**	The Father to the Lord, or His Divine to His Human: that by oneness with Him He has omnipotence over the hells.
H.B. 20–26		
26–29, 35–37	**N.B. 10·16**	There will be eternal oneness with Him.
H.B. 27–30, 36–38		
30–37	**10**	Even if those of the church should fail there will be eternal oneness with Him.
H.B. 31–38		
38–42	**4**	Of the Jewish nation: It has destroyed conjunction with Him, because it has destroyed the church.
H.B. 39–43		
43–45	**4**	It has utterly repudiated Him.
H.B. 44–46		
46–48	**13**	Prayer to the Father, that, unless He assist, no one will have eternal life.
H.B. 47–49		
49	**10**	Unless oneness be effected,
H.B. 50		
49–51	**10·8**	the hells will otherwise prevail.
H.B. 50–52		
52	**10·8**	He assists.
H.B. 53		

Psalm XC.

t., 1–6	**16**	Man is nothing of himself, but the Lord alone [is of Himself].
H.B. 1–6		
7–11	**11**	The church perishes,
12–13	**17**	unless restored by the Lord
14	**10**	by means of His coming.
14–17	**17**	Thence is salvation.

Psalm XCI.

1	**10**	Song in praise of the Father by the Lord, who is to be made one with Him.
2–6	**10**	Thus there will be protection from every attack.

PSALM XCIV.

Verses	Subjects	
7–9	**8**	Thus there will be no uprising of the hells,
10	**11**	not even against the church.
11, 12	**12**	Thus heaven will serve Him.
13–16	**8·10**	There will be no fear from the hells, when the Divine has been made one with the Human.

Psalm XCII.

t., H.B. 1	**10**	The oneness of the Divine of the Lord with His Divine Human, which is the "sabbath."
1–5 H.B. 2–6	**10**	Song in praise of the co-operation of the Father with Him.
6 H.B. 7	**3**	The evil do not understand this.
7–9 H.B. 8–10	**3**	Although the evil flourish, yet they perish.
10, 11 H.B. 11, 12	**10·8**	Thus He has Divine omnipotence against those that rise up against Him,
12–14 H.B. 13–15	**11**	from which the church will flourish,
15 H.B. 16	**11·16**	and will sing praises to the Lord.

Psalm XCIII.

1, 2	**10·12**	Through the oneness of the Divine and the Human in the Lord, heaven and the church will endure to eternity.
3, 4	**12**	The joy of those who are in Divine truths from this source.
5	**12**	The Word established in the church.

Psalm XCIV.

OF THE JEWISH NATION: IT DESTROYED THE CHURCH.

1, 2	**15**	O that judgment may be executed upon them!
3–11	**3**	Because that nation has destroyed the church, neither does it fear God, although He sees all things.
12–15	**11·15**	For the sake of the church the Lord will come to judge.
16–19	**6·9**	The Divine of the Lord gives help against the evil and in temptation.
20, 21	**6·9**	The evil rise up and wish to kill,
22, 23	**4·8**	but through help from His Divine they will perish.

Psalm XCV.

Verses	Subjects	
1	16	Song in praise of the Lord :
2–5	16	Omnipotence belongs to Him ;
6, 7	16	He is to be worshipped in humility.
8–10	3·4	Let them not be like the nation sprung from Jacob, who estranged themselves from the Lord,
11	3·4	and with whom, for this reason, there is no conjunction whatever.

Psalm XCVI.

1–9	16	Song in praise of the Lord by His church, that to Him alone belong power and glory.
10–12	15·12	He will come to judgment, that heaven and the church may worship Him from joy of heart.
13	15	He will come to judgment.

Psalm XCVII.

1–6	11·16	Joy of the church over the coming of the Lord, with whom is Divine truth.
7	3	All who are in falsities will be removed.
8, 9	10·16	Joy that the Lord is the God of heaven and the church.
10–12	11·12	He will protect those who are in truths from Him

Psalm XCVIII.

	1·10	THE COMING OF THE LORD AND THE GLORIFICATION OF HIS HUMAN:
t., 1	1·10	He will then have power.
H.B. 1		
2	1·10·17	Hence is salvation.
3	17	The predictions are to be fulfilled.
4–8	16	Song of praise to Him and joy on that account.
9	15	He comes to judgment.

Psalm XCIX.

1, 2	16	Song in praise of the Lord who is the Word and the God of the church.
3, 5, 9	16	He should be worshipped,

Verses	Subjects	
4	16	because power and justice belong to Him.
6, 7	16	The Word is from Him.
8	17	He is the Redeemer.

Psalm C.

t., 1–3 H.B. 1–3	16·17	Song in praise of the Lord, that He is to be worshipped with the heart, because He is the Former of the church.
4, 5	16·11	Let them draw near to Him through the truths of the Word, and confess Him.

Psalm CI.

	15	SOMETHING CONCERNING JUDGMENT BY THE LORD.
t., 1 H.B. 1	16	He is to be celebrated.
2, 3, 6, 7	16	His perfection, and He loves those that are perfect.
4, 5	3	He rejects the evil and the haughty.
8	3	The evil will perish when the Lord comes.

Psalm CII.

t., 1–11 H.B. 1–12	13·6	Prayer of the Lord when He was in temptations even to despair, which state is described.
12–18 H.B. 13–19	11	Nevertheless, those that are out of the church expect compassion, that they may become a church.
19–22 H.B. 20–23	11	He hears and has compassion, and a church is formed of such.
23, 24 H.B. 24, 25	6	Let Him not fail in temptations before that comes to pass,
25–28 H.B. 26–29	11·12	that heaven and the church perish not, but may be established.

Psalm CIII.

t., 1–7 H.B. 1–7	16·17	Song in praise of the Lord on account of redemption and reformation.
8–18	16·17	These are from mercy, because He knows the infirmities of man.
19–22	16·17	The heavens and the earths are His, therefore He should be celebrated.

Psalm CIV.

Verses	Subjects
	16 Song in praise of the Lord.
1–4	**16** From Him are Divine truths, or the Word.
5–9	**16·11** Of the sense of the letter of the Word, on which the church is founded :
10–23	**16·11** from this all are taught, every one according to the state of his intelligence :
24–30	**16·11** from this are the knowledges (*cognitiones*) of truth and good, from which is spiritual nourishment.
31–35	**17** May the good be saved, and the evil perish !

Psalm CV.

	11 The establishment of the church by the Lord, and the reformation of the natural man.
1–7	**11·16** Song in praise of the Lord and of His works for the establishment of the church.
8–15	**11** The establishment of the church in the beginning, and her protection from falsities of evils.
16	**3** When there was no longer any truth,
17, 18	**4** the Lord came, and they afflicted Him ;
19–22	**10** but He afterwards became the God of heaven and earth.
23, 24	**11** Hence those who were of the church were natural, and in knowledges (*scientifica*) ;
25–36	**11** therefore their natural has been purged of falsities and evils of every kind, which infested : these here treated of ;
37–41	**11** afterwards truth and good, and protection from falsities, are granted them,
42–45	**11** and He causes them to be a church.

Psalm CVI.

	3 Of the church instituted among the Jewish nation : it became perverted and revolted.
1–5	**13·11** Prayer of the Lord to the Father to give help, that He might see the church established.
6–8	**3** Although those who were of the church beheld Divine miracles, they backslid, and yet they were preserved,

PSALM CVIII.   151

Verses	Subjects	
9–34	**3**	as at the sea Suph and afterwards in the desert, (many [instances here recounted],) nevertheless they rebelled.
35–39	**3**	They totally destroyed and profaned the truths and goods of the church.
40–43	**3**	Therefore the church with them was forsaken by the Lord, and destroyed.
44–46	**11**	Then those who were out of the church were heard,
47, 48	**11**	and a church constituted of them will arise and will worship the Lord.

PSALM CVII.

1–3	**11·17**	A new church, which the Lord has redeemed.
4–8	**11**	They are in falsities of ignorance, but in a desire for truth and good.
9–15	**11**	They are in ignorance and in lack of truth.
16–21	**11**	They have no spiritual nourishment, although they will have it through the Word.
22–31	**11**	When they were in knowledges (*cognitiones*), they were admitted into temptations, and preserved.
[32,] 33, 34,39,40	**16·3**	Song in praise of the Lord, that those who were of the devastated church have been rejected,
35–38, 41–43	**11**	and that those who are of the new church have been accepted, with whom truths and goods will be multiplied.

PSALM CVIII.

t., 1–5 H.B. 1–6	**13·3·8**	Prayer of the Lord to the Father to give help, and show His power,
6 H.B. 7	**8**	that those who are to be of the church may be delivered.
7 H.B. 8	**3**	Answer, that the former church will be destroyed,
8, 9 H.B. 9, 10	**11**	and an internal and an external church will be instituted.
10–13 H.B. 11–14	**10**	The Human will become Divine when the hells have been subjugated.

Psalm CIX.

Verses   *Subjects*
               4   OF THE PERVERTED JEWISH CHURCH.

t., 1–6   **4** It repudiated the Lord, and considered Him vile,
H.B. 1–6   and hated Him.

7–12   **15·11** They will perish in the judgment, and there will be others in their place, who will be received, and a church established with them.

13–20   **4·3·4** Their posterity will likewise perish, because they are in falsities of evil, and because they reject the Lord.

21–25   **13·4** To the Father for help, because He is considered vile, and as nothing.

26–29   **3** Let them be put to shame.

30, 31   Song in praise of the Father, because He gives help.

Psalm CX.

t., 1–3   **8** Victory of the Lord over the hells, owing to
H.B. 1–3   which He has dominion over heaven and earth.

4–7 **N.B.** **8·10** From this He has authority over the hells.

Psalm CXI.

1–4   **16** Celebration and confession of the Lord;
5–9   **17** He redeemed men, and saves to eternity;
10   **17** to worship Him is wisdom.

Psalm CXII.

1–7, 9   **17** He that trusts in the Lord and lives well will be saved.

8, 10   **17** He will have no fear of the hells, however much they may rise up against him.

Psalm CXIII.

1–5   **16** Song in praise of the Lord, because He is omnipotent;
6   **1** because He came into the world;
7–9   **17** because He will save those who will be of His church.

Psalm CXIV.

Verses	Subjects
1, 2	**11** The church established by the Lord from the nations.
3–6	**11** Its falsities have been removed, and the goods of love and charity take their place,
7, 8	**11** because the church is from the Lord, who will instruct those that are in ignorance.

Psalm CXV.

1–3	**16** Omnipotence belongs to the Lord.
4–8	**16** From what is his own, man is nothing but falsity of evil.
9–11	**16** The trust of all who are in truths and goods should be in the Lord.
12–15, 18	**17** The Lord will save them.
16	**17** Heaven and the church are His.
17	**16·17** Those who do not trust in the Lord will not be saved.

Psalm CXVI.

1–11	**6** Song in praise of the Father by the Lord, that He gave help in grievous temptations;
12–19	**6·16** thus the Divine will be worshipped in the Lord.

Psalm CXVII.

1, 2	**5** Song of praise to the Father by the Lord, that He gave help in temptations.

Psalm CXVIII.

1–4	**11** Song of praise to the Father by the Lord, for the church;
5–9	**5** He helped Him in His distresses;
10–14	**5** the evil fought against Him, but He was helped by the Divine.
15, 16	**10·16** Joy because there is Divine power through His Human.
17	**10·16** The Divine truth is from Him.
18–22	**17** He it is through whom is all salvation.

SUMMARIES OF THE INTERNAL SENSE.

Verses	Subjects	
22–25	**10**	It is the Divine Human from His Divine in Himself, which is the source.
26–29	**16**	Happy is he who confesses and worships the Lord.

PSALM CXIX.

1–176	**16**	The Lord fulfilled the Law, or the Word, from its firsts to its lasts, and therefore He was hated,
	5	and suffered temptations, and thus made the
	10	Human one with His Divine.*

PSALM CXX.

| t., 1–7 | **13.4** | To the Father, against those in the perverted church, who secretly try to destroy Him. |
| H.B. 1–7 | | |

PSALM CXXI.

| t., 1–8 | **13.5** | [Prayer] to the Father to keep [Him]. |
| H.B. 1–8 | | |

PSALM CXXII.

| t., 1–9 | **11.16** | Joy of the Lord over the new church where He reigns. |
| H.B. 1–9 | | |

PSALM CXXIII.

| t., 1–4 | **13.4** | [Prayer] to the Father to be present, because He has been utterly rejected by the Jewish nation. |
| H.B. 1–4 | | |

PSALM CXXIV.

t., 1–5	**13.5**	To the Father that He may be preserved in temptations
H.B. 1–5		
6–8	**5**	from the deceitful and hypocrites.

---

* The following words are here crossed out in the manuscript: "The initial letters here signify such things as are meant by them in the spiritual world." This note refers to the Hebrew initial letters of the verses, which follow the order of the Hebrew alphabet, the first eight verses beginning each with Aleph, the second eight with Beth, etc. This is indicated in the English Bible by the names of the Hebrew letters to be found as inscriptions over the successive groups of eight verses. See more on this subject in *The Apocalypse Revealed*, n. 38.—EDITOR.

Psalm CXXV.

Verses   *Subjects*
t., 1–5   **11** From the Lord the new church is kept from fals-
H.B. 1–5   ities of evil.

Psalm CXXVI.

t., 1–4   **16·11** Joy of the nations with whom a new church will
H.B. 1–4   arise.
5   **11** It will be instructed.

Psalm CXXVII.

t., 1, 2   **16·11** All things of the church are from the Lord, and
H.B. 1, 2   nothing from man.
3, 4   **16·11** He who is in truths from the Lord, remains safe.

Psalm CXXVIII.

t., 1–6   **11** Happy is he who is of the Lord's church, for
H.B. 1–6   good in abundance is there.

Psalm CXXIX.

t., 1–3   **2** From the beginning they have done exceeding
H.B. 1–3   great evil to the church,
4–8   **11** but, after a vain effort, they were compelled to
            retreat.

Psalm CXXX.

t., 1–4   **16** Prayer to the Lord that they may be preserved.
H.B. 1–4
5–8   **1·17** The coming of the Lord and redemption is ex-
            pected.

Psalm CXXXI.

Of the Lord:

t., 1, 2   **10·17** He operated from His Human: He indeed op-
H.B. 1, 2   erated through influx from the Divine, but not
            from the Divine alone.
3   **11** Let the trust of the church be in Him.

Psalm CXXXII.

OF THE LORD:

Verses	Subjects	
t., 1–5 H.B. 1–5	11	He will not rest until He sees His church established.
6, 7	16	He was born in Bethehem, let us adore Him,
8	10	for He united His Divine to His Human.
9, 10 N.B.	16	Let them worship Him from good and from truth.
11, 12	16·17	It is an eternal truth, that those who worship Him will be saved.
13, 14	11	The Lord dwells in His church because He loves her;
15, 16	11	because there He dwells in truths and goods.
17, 18	11	For this reason she will be in power and in light against falsities of evil.

Psalm CXXXIII.

t., 1 H.B. 1	11·12	Good itself is the conjunction of good and truth,
2	11·12	for the good of love flows into the truths of the external or natural man.
3	12·17	The truth of good is from heaven upon those who are in the church, in which is salvation.

Psalm CXXXIV.

t., 1 H.B. 1	16·3	Song in praise of the Lord by those who worship Him, when the church has been devastated.
2, 3	16	Let them worship the Lord, who is the God of heaven and the church.

Psalm CXXXV.

1–3	11·16	Song in praise of the Lord in His Divine Human,
4	11	who institutes the church,
5	16	and who alone is God,
6, 7	11	who alone teaches the church external and internal truths,
8–11	17	who delivers the natural man from falsities of evil,
12	17·11	and there implants the church.
13	17·11	This is done by the Lord,
14	17·11	who leads her.

Verses	Subjects	
15–18	**16**	One's own intelligence effects nothing.
19–21	**16**	The spiritual and celestial church worships the Lord who is the God of the church.

Psalm CXXXVI.

1–3	**16**	Let them confess the Lord, who alone is God and Lord,
4–6	**12**	who, by means of the Divine truth, has formed heaven and the church,
7–9	**12**	from whom is all truth of doctrine, and good of love, and knowledge (*cognitio*) of these:
10–22	**11·12**	who delivers the natural man from falsities of evil, and there establishes the church, and dissipates evils of every kind.
23–26	**16·12**	Celebration and confession of Him who delivers from falsities and evils, and grants truths and goods,
1–26	**12**	and this from pure mercy.

Psalm CXXXVII.

1–6	**11**	Lamentation by the nations who are in falsities from ignorance, because they do not have the Word.
5, 6	**11**	Of these a church will be formed by the Lord, which He will love.
7–9	**3**	Those who have devastated the church will perish.

Psalm CXXXVIII.

16   SONG IN PRAISE OF THE LORD BY THE CHURCH.

t., 1–5 H.B. 1–5	**10·16**	The Lord ought to be worshipped from the Word, where is His Divine truth.
6–8	**17**	Those who are humble will have salvation from the Lord, and life and protection.

Psalm CXXXIX.

10   SONG IN PRAISE OF THE FATHER BY THE LORD.

t., 1–5 H.B. 1–5	**10**	He knows everything of His thought and will because He is made one with Him;
6–10	**10·16**	omniscience and omnipresence belong to Him;

Verses	Subjects	
11, 12	**10·16**	enlightenment in the natural is from Him;
13–15	**11·12·10**	by Him He was formed and from Him He is pure;
16–18	**10**	hence all things of the Father are united with Him;
19–22	**10**	the Lord rejects all evil and falsity from Himself;
23, 24	**10**	perfection belongs to Him.

PSALM CXL.

t., 1–8 H.B. 1–9	**13·4**	Prayer of the Lord to the Father to be delivered from falsifiers and hypocrites, who purpose evil against Him in the perverted church.
9–11 H.B. 10–12	**3**	They perish through their falsities and evils,
12, 13 H.B. 13, 14	**17**	and those who confess the Lord are saved.

PSALM CXLI.

t., 1, 2 H.B. 1, 2	**13**	Prayer of the Lord to the Father, to have regard to His perfection;
[3,] 4, 5	**16·10**	He has nothing in common with those who are in evils, because He has been made one with His Divine;
6, 7	**10·4**	His words, which are Divine, they have made of no account.
8–10	**8**	Confidence that their evil thoughts and intentions, by which they themselves perish, do no harm.

PSALM CXLII.

t., 1–3 H.B. 1–4	**13·5**	Prayer of the Lord to the Father, to give help in temptations,
4, 5 H.B. 5, 6	**4**	because He is known by no one except the Father only, in whom is His trust.
6, 7 H.B. 7, 8	**5·11**	May He be delivered from temptations, and come among those who acknowledge Him.

PSALM CXLIII.

t., 1, 2 H.B. 1, 2	**13**	Prayer of the Lord to the Father, that He who is true and just, may hear,
3, 4, 7	**5**	that He may not fail in temptations.

Verses	Subjects	
5, 6	**11**	He longs for the ancient state in respect to the church.
8–12	**8**	He has confidence of being delivered from the hells, by which He is assaulted mightily.

Psalm CXLIV.

t., 1, 2 H.B. 1, 2	**13·7**	To the Father, that He may be a help to Him in His combats,
3, 4	**13·7**	for without Him He has no power.
5–8, 11	**7**	O that He may be delivered from the hells which assault Him with falsities!
9, 10	**17**	Thus He would have salvation,
12–14	**12**	and thus would Divine truth and Divine good be His and from Him.
15	**12**	Happy is he who acknowledges Him.

Psalm CXLV.

t., 1–7 H.B. 1–7	**16**	Song in praise of the Lord because of His works and His justice;
8, 9	**16**	because of His mercy.
10–12	**12**	All who are in the heavens will confess Him,
13	**12**	because His kingdom is eternal.
14–16	**12·11**	He raises up sinners, and leads them into truths that they may live.
17		He is Divine.
18, 20	**17·3**	He saves those who believe in Him, and those who do not believe perish.
21	**16**	He is to be worshipped.

Psalm CXLVI.

1, 2	**16**	Song in praise of the Lord:
3, 4	**16**	Man from his own is nothing.
5, 6	**16·11**	Happy is he who trusts in the Lord, who is the God of heaven and earth,
7–9	**16·11**	who teaches and leads all who are in falsities from ignorance, and who desire truths.
10	**11·12**	He reigns to eternity.

Psalm CXLVII.

Verses	Subjects	
1, 2, 7 [, 12]	16	Song in praise of the Lord by His church,
3, 4	17	who reforms by knowledges (*cognitiones*) of truth,
5	17	who alone is able to do this,
6, 8, 9	11	who teaches truths to those who are in ignorance.
10, 11	11	One's own intelligence is nothing, but that which is from the Lord is something.
13–15	16	The church will worship the Lord who protects her, and teaches the Word.
16–18	11	The Lord disperses ignorance by means of the Word.
19, 20	11	All this He does for His church.

Psalm CXLVIII.

1–6	16·12	All who are in the heavens and on the earths should worship the Lord from goods and truths that are from Him:
7–10	16·12	all who are in the lowest parts of heaven and the church should worship Him from truths and goods of every kind:
11, 12	16·12	in general from the understanding and will of truth and good:
13, 14	17	because salvation is by means of those things that He gives.

Psalm CXLIX.

1–4	16·12	The Lord is to be worshipped from an affection for truth and good, because He loves them,
5, 6	8	because Divine truth belongs to them,
7–9	8	and by that the hells are restrained.

Psalm CL.

1, 2	12·16	The Lord ought to be worshipped because He is omnipotent:
3–6	12·16	He ought to be worshipped from every affection for good and truth.

Historical Parts of the Word

THE HISTORICAL PARTS OF THE WORD.

The historical parts of the Word, like the prophetical parts, contain a spiritual sense within themselves, in which there is nothing historical of the world, as in the sense of the letter, but there are heavenly things which relate to the church, and in the highest sense to the Lord, just like the prophetical parts. The historical parts there are representative, and all the senses with their expressions are correspondences.

It ought to be known, that all the churches, down to the coming of the Lord, were representative church s:—they represented the church, and in the highest sense, the Lord; it is from this that the Word is spiritual and Divine. But the representative churches ceased when the Lord came into the world, because all things of the Word, those that are prophetical, as also those that are historical, signified and represented Him: and this is why the Lord is called "the Word."

There were three notable changes of the representative churches: the first, which was before the "flood," shall be called the Most Ancient Church; the second, which was after the "flood," the Ancient Church; and the third, which followed the Ancient, the Israelitish and Jewish Church.

The Most Ancient Church is described briefly by "Adam" and his posterity; the Ancient Church, by "Noah" and his posterity; and the Israelitish and Jewish Church by the historical portions of the Word.

The former churches are described in like manner, but by more interior correspondences, in the Word that is mentioned by Moses; but this Word has been effaced, and in its place the Word was given that exists at the present day.

The church that followed these three is the Christian Church, which church is internal, differing from the Jewish Church as a moonlight night differs from a dark night. But as this church has come to its end, by the accomplishment of the last judgment, a new church is now being instituted by the Lord, which is called, in the Apocalypse, the "New Jerusalem," to which the things that are being published by me at the present day will be of service: it is also being instituted elsewhere.

The historical parts of the Word involve in a summary the things that follow.

Genesis.

Chapter I.

Verses
[1–31] In the spiritual sense the new creation or the regeneration of the men of the Most Ancient Church is here described: the process of their regeneration from firsts to lasts is here contained in its order.

Chapter II.

[1–25] The intelligence and wisdom of those men, while they were being regenerated, is described; for that church was a celestial church, the first of all on this earth.

Chapter III.

[1–24] Fall and end of that church, as they departed from the celestial to the natural man, from this they had intelligence from what was their own (*proprium*) in place of intelligence from the Lord.

Chapter IV.

[1–26] Division of that church, which took place between those who made everything of the church and thus of salvation to consist in the mere doctrine and knowledge (*scientia*) of cognitions (who were "Cain"); and those who made it to consist also in a life of love and charity (who were "Abel"); and, abstractly, that a mere knowledge (*scientia*) of doctrinals, like faith alone, when all of religion is made to consist in it alone, slays charity. But those who made a church out of mere doctrine, and did not at the same time make it consist in life, were rejected.

CHAPTER V.

Verses
[1–32]   Divisions and changes in that church are described, being meant by the "posterity of Adam from Sheth."

CHAPTER VI.

1–6[?7] ⎫
10–12   ⎬   End of that church, when there was no longer any truth or good, because they were in their own intelligence ;
[?11–13] ⎭

[8–10, ⎫   and the beginning of a new church, which is meant
14–22] ⎭   by "Noah" and his "three sons."

CHAPTER VII.

[1–24]   The destruction of the Most Ancient Church is described by the "flood," and the beginning of a new one, by the "ark" and its preservation.

CHAPTER VIII.

[1–22]   The end of the Most Ancient Church, and the beginning of the Ancient Church.

CHAPTER IX.

1–17   Precepts and statutes for that church.
18–28[29] That church is "Noah," its celestial is "Shem," its spiritual is "Japheth," and its natural is "Ham."

CHAPTER X.

[1–32]   As that church spread over a great part of the Asiatic world, and consequently there were divisions, these are described by the "posterity of Noah," or of his "three sons."

CHAPTER XI.

1–9   The beginning of Babylon, and its destruction.

GENESIS XV. 167

Verses
[10–32] Continuation respecting the various states of that church and the nature of them even to the end, when it became idolatrous and magical.

CHAPTER XII.

1–8 The institution of the Israelitish and Jewish church, which was from Eber, and therefore was called the Hebrew church, and its first institution from Abram, who was commanded to go into the land of Canaan, for the reason that all places in that land, and those round about it, had been allotted spiritual significations by the men of the Most Ancient Church, and these were to be mentioned by name in the new Word that was to be written among them, in which the names of those places were to be employed.

[9–20] The first instruction of that church, which is the instruction of the natural man, by means of knowledges *(scientiae)* which are meant by "Egypt," in which country Abram was at that time.

CHAPTER XIII.

[1–18] Growth in the knowledges *(cognitiones)* of the church, and separation of spiritual knowledges which are "Abram," from natural knowledges which are "Lot."

CHAPTER XIV.

1–17 Combat in the natural man, between the truths and goods and the evils and falsities there, and when victory hung on the side of the evil or of hell, the spiritual man attacked them and overthrew them.

18–24 Thus the natural man became spiritual-natural, and removed evils and falsities from himself.

CHAPTER XV.

1–6 Since there was as yet only multiplication of truth, and not the fructification of good, and thus not

Verses

        the church, he was urgent that the church might exist with him;

7–21   but it is foretold what the church and its conjunction with the Lord would be, namely, that it would be perverted.

CHAPTER XVI.

[1–16]   Conjunction of the truth and good of the natural man, from which there would be only an external church, which is rational.

But concerning all this see the Arcana Cælestia, where [it is explained that] these things pertaining to the church, signify things pertaining to the Lord; for all things of the Word in the spiritual sense treat of the church and heaven, but in the celestial sense of the Lord.

Indexes

INDEX OF WORDS AND SUBJECTS.

Only the text of the Summaries has been indexed, the marginal references being left out of consideration, as they constitute an index by themselves.

The references are to the divisions by chapters and verses as found in the common English Bible.

ABBREVIATIONS.—"*ib.*"= *the same book and chapter as in the previous reference.*
"*and prec.*" = *together with the preceding verse or verses.*
"*and fol.*" = *together with the following verse or verses.*

Abel.—"Abel" signifies those who made the church and thus salvation to consist also in a life of love and charity (*Gen.* iv.).

Abolition.—Abolition of worship from falsification of truth (*Jer.* xli. 4–7).

Abram.—First institution of the Israelitish and Jewish Church from Abram, who was commanded to go into the land of Canaan, etc. (*Gen.* xii. 1–8).
"Abram" means spiritual knowledge (*Gen.* xiii.).

Abrogation.—Abrogation of representative worship (*Isa.* xxxvi. 7).

Absolve (*see* **Acquit**).

Abstain.—Exhortation to abstain from the falsification of the Word, otherwise there will be no church, but it will be without good and truths, as before (*Hos.* ii. 1–4).

Abuse.—Abuse of the Word (*Jer.* x. 8, 9).

Accept (*see also* **Convert, Receive**).
Because they worship the Lord from evil and not from good, their worship is not accepted (*Mal.* i. 9, 10).
Those who have not falsified truths will be accepted (*Jer.* xlix. 6).
Those who are of the new church have been accepted (*Ps.* cvii. 35–38, 41–43).

Acceptable (*Ps.* xix. 14).
Unacceptable worship (*Amos* v. 21, 22); it will be accepted if they have good and truth (*ib.* 23–25).

Acknowledgment (*see also* **Lord,** ACKNOWLEDGMENT OF).
Acknowledgment to the Lord (*Jer.* xvii. 14–18).
Acknowledgment of goods and truths (*Isa.* lxi. 9).
It ought to be acknowledged that all good and truth is from the Lord (*Ps.* xxxvi. 5–9).
The new church will have acknowledgment from the heart from their trust in the Lord (*Joel* ii. 26, 27, *and prec.*).
Those who will be of the new church will acknowledge and confess that they have falsities and evils (*Jer.* iii. 22–25).
Acknowledgment of one's evils and at the same time of the Lord's mercy (*Ezek.* xx. 43, 44).
Acknowledgment with the lips of no avail (*Jer.* xxii. 23, 24).
Falsities not acknowledged as such (*Jer.* vi. 15).
Unwillingness to acknowledge and receive (*Jer.* iv. 11, 12).
They have acknowledged evils and falsities as goods and truths, because they have departed from the Lord (*Jer.* v. 11, 12).

SUMMARIES OF THE INTERNAL SENSE.

Adam.—The Most Ancient Church is briefly described by "Adam" and his posterity (p. 163).

Acquit.—Because He spoke from the Divine, the truths of the church acquitted Him (*Jer.* xxvi. 10-16).

Admire.—How admirable is the spiritual kingdom of the Lord (*Ps.* xlviii. *t.*, 1-3, 8).

Admonition (*Hos.* x. 11, 12).

Adopt.—Those who draw near will be adopted as children by the Lord (*Jer.* iii. 19).

Adure (*see also* **Worship**).

Those who are in truths from the Word will adore the Lord who is the Word (*Ps.* xxix. *t.*, 1-4).

The Lord was born in Bethlehem, Let us adore Him, for He united His Divine to His Human (*Ps.* cxxxii. 6-8).

Adulteration (*see also* **Falsification**).

Adulteration of good and truth meant by "Babylon" (*Isa.* xiii.; xiv.; xxxix. 1-7; xlvii.; *Jer.* l.; *Dan.* ii. 31-43).

Adulteration of the goods of the Word and of the church meant by "Moab" (*Jer.* xlviii).

Those who are of the church will come among those who blaspheme and adulterate the Word (*Jer.* xx. 4).

Adulteration of the goods of the Word foretold (*Isa.* xxxix).

Those who adulterate the good of the Word are exhorted to desist (*Isa.* xlviii.).

Those who adulterate the good of the sense of the letter of the Word destroy the good and truth of the church (*Amos* ii. 1-3).

Adulteration of the good of the church and of the Word will be utterly destroyed (*Isa.* xxv. 10-12; xliii. 14).

Respecting those who have falsified and adulterated the Word. Full description (*Nahum* iii. 1-19).

The Lord will execute judgment upon all who have adulterated and destroyed the truths of the church (*Mal.* iii. 5, 6).

They have done this from the beginning, and do not desist from it, nor do they desist from adulteration, therefore this will bring about their ruin (*ib.* 7-9).

Those who have adulterated the truths of the Word will perish, and are to be cast into hell (*Zeph.* i. 9-11).

Those who have adulterated the Word will utterly perish (*Zeph.* ii. 8-10).

Those who, by trusting in themselves, have adulterated the Word, will be cast into hell (*Isa.* xxx. 32, 33).

Adulteration in the Christian church (*Dan.* xi. 29-31).

Adulteration of the sense of the letter of the Word, represented (*Ezek.* iv. 9-16; v. 1, 2).

Adulteration of goods by the celestial church (*Jer.* iii. 7-9).

When adulteration of good possesses the church intercession will be of no avail (*Ezek.* xiv. 19, 20, *and prec.*).

When there is nothing but adulteration of good and truth, the old church comes to an end (*Amos* viii. 4-6 *and prec.*).

The church adulterating truths and goods of doctrine (*Ezek.* xxii. 1, 2, *ana fol.*).

In the Babylonish religion at last nothing remained but what was adulterated, thus what was merely false and evil (*Dan.* ii. 31-35, 40-43).

Adulteration of good and truth ceases (*Isa.* xxi. 9).

Advent (*see* **Lord,** COMING OF).

Affection.—The Lord ought to be worshipped from every affection for good and truth (*Ps.* cl. 3-6).

Worship from the affection of truth and good (*Jer.* xxxiii. 10, 11).

Affections for truth come from the Lord's having made the Human Divine, and in these affections are the societies of heaven (*Ps.* xlv. 9).

INDEX OF WORDS AND SUBJECTS. 173

The new church will be in affection of truth (*Zech.* viii. 18, 19).
How those who are in an affection for truth are protected from perverters (*Ezek.* xxxii. 13–16).
Affections for truth destroyed by knowledges (*scientifica*) (*Ezek.* xxvi. 5, 6).
All affection for spiritual truth will perish (*Ezek.* xxvi. 13, 14).
Affections of truth have become cupidities of falsity (*Lam.* iv. 9, 10).
Affections of the natural man should be left (*Ps.* xlv. 10).
Affection for falsifying (*Ezek.* xiii. 17–19).
Affection of falsity and evil with those who profane truths (*Isa.* xlvi. 1).

Affliction.—The Lord came, and they afflicted Him (*Ps.* cv. 17, 18).
O that the Father would help in affliction! (*Ps.* lvi. 7, 8.)
The new church in affliction (*Ps.* lxxx. 4–6).
The good are led astray, imagining that affliction is of no use (*Ps.* lxxiii. 10–14).
He who is in temptations, and consequent affliction, is always upheld and thereby vivified (*Ps.* xli. *t.*, 1–3).

Against (*contra*) (*see also* **Help, Opposition, Rejection**).
They are against good and truth (*Ps.* xiv. 6).
Against the church because against truths (*Jer.* xlviii. 27, 28).
The natural external opposed to all things of the church (*Ezek.* xix. 4–7).
They are opposed to the Lord and the Word (*Ezek.* xii. 1, 2).
Against God (*Amos* vii. 7–9).
The church where the Word is turns against the Lord, etc. (*Jer.* xii. 7–12).
Against the Lord (*Lam.* iii; iv. 11; *Ps.* lxiv. *t.*, 1–6).
The Jewish Church was against the Word and the Lord (*Ezek.* ii. 6, 7).
They speak against the church and against the Lord (*Ezek.* xxxv. 11–13).
The life of heaven is not in those who are against the Lord (*Isa.* xlv. 24).
The hells among themselves devise evils against the Lord (*Ps.* xli. 4–7).
The hells that rise up against the Lord are enumerated (*Ps.* lxxxiii. 6–8).
Against those who were of the church, who cherished evil thoughts against the Lord, etc. (*Ps.* lviii. *t.*, 1–9 *and fol.*).
Those who should be in the truths and goods of the church are against the Lord, but they are nothing before Him and will be destroyed (*Ps.* ii. 1–5).
All men or all things that are contrary to the doctrine respecting the Lord, will be destroyed (*Zech.* xii. 9).
Contrary to all things of doctrine (*Amos* vii. 10–13).
All did the contrary, and acknowledged another God (*Jer.* xi. 9–10).

All.—All things of the church are from the Lord, and nothing from man (*Ps.* cxxvii. *t.*, 1, 2).
All men and all things are nothing worth against the Lord (*Isa.* xl. 15–18).
All things fall without the Lord (*Isa.* xl. 21–25).
All things are from the Lord (*Isa.* xlv. 7).
All things of heaven and the church will be received by the new church (*Hos.* ii. 21–23).
All who are of the church are addressed (*Joel* i. 1–3).
All who are in the heavens and on the earths should worship the Lord from goods and truths that are from Him (*Ps.* cxlviii. 1–6).
All who are in the lowest parts of heaven and the church should worship Him from truths and goods of every kind (*Ps.* cxlviii. 7–10).
All things of the church carried off by falsities (*Amos* iii. 13–15).
All things of the-church falsified (*Amos* iv. 9); and finally profaned (*ib.* 10, 11).
All things and every single thing of the church will mourn *Zech.*) xii. 10–14).

Alphabet (*Ps.* cxix. *note*).

Amend (*emendare*).—Those who have not adulterated will be amended (*Jer.* xlviii. 47).
Ammon.—"Children of Ammon" mean those who falsify the truths of the Word and of the church (*Jer.* xlix. 1-6).
"Children of Ammon" mean those who are in the sense of the letter of the Word and pervert the truths of religion by things which do not belong to religion (*Ezek.* xxv. 1, 2).

Ancient. ANCIENT CHURCH.
The church established among the Ancients (*Jer.* ii.).
Ancient Church a representative church (p. 163).
The church was established by the Lord among the ancients, evils having been cast out (*Ps.* xliv. *t.*, 1-4).
How the Ancient Church was instituted by the Lord and what it became among the Jewish nation (*Ezek.* xvii.).
It was in Divine truths (*Ezek.* xix. 10, 11).
It had knowledges (*cognitiones*) of truth and good of every kind and species, and by means of them it had intelligence (*Ezek.* xxvii. 3-9).
Truths that protected the Ancient Church (*Ezek.* xxvii. 10, 11).
In the Ancient Church a rational flourished that was derived from, etc. (*Ezek.* xxxi. 3-9).
The Ancient Church had spiritual intelligence (*Ezek.* xxxi. 3-9).
Beginning of the Ancient Church (*Gen.* vi. 8-10, 14-22; viii.).
Precepts and statutes for that church (*Gen.* ix. 1-17).
Its celestial ("Shem"), spiritual ("Japheth"), and natural ("Ham") (*Gen.* ix. 18-29).
Divisions of that church in Asia (*Gen.* x.).
Beginning of Babylon, and its destruction (*Gen.* xi. 1-9).
The end in idolatry and magic (*Gen.* xi. 10-32).
The Lord longs for the ancient state in respect to the church (*Ps.* cxliii. 5, 6).
When the Lord comes, the church, doctrine and worship will be as they had been among the ancients (*Mal.* iii. 4).

ANCIENT WORD.
The former churches are described in the Word that is mentioned by Moses; but this Word has been effaced (p. 164).
Angel.—Angels of the three heavens and men have spiritual life from the influx of Divine good and truth from the Lord, and from the Divine good and Divine truth they have intelligence and charity (*Ezek.* xlvii. 1-12).
Anger (*excandescentia*).—The Jewish nation became very angry at the salvation of the nations (*Jonah* iv. 1-4).
Anguish (*see* ***Distress***).
Annihilation. ⎫ —Annihilating the church (*Jer.* xviii. 14-16).
Annul (*annihilo*). ⎭ Annulling the Word (*Jer.* v. 13; *Mal.* iv. 4).
Announcement.—Announcement that the Lord will come, and that that church will be from Him (*Isa.* lxii. 10-12).
Answers TO PRAYERS (*see also* ***Prayer***).
(*Ps.* liv. 4, 5; lv. 16-18, 22; lvi. 7-9; lxxvii. 10-15; lxxxv.; lxxxix. 46-48, 52; cii. 12-22; cviii. *t.*, 1-9; cix. 21-31).
Answer to the complaints of those who perish (*Jer.* iv. 9-12).
Apathy.—They think nothing of the destruction of the church (*Amos* vi. 3-6).
Apparent heavens (*see* ***Seeming heavens***).
Appear.—Falsity made to appear like truth, and evil made to appear like good (*Isa.* xliv. 12-20; *Jer.* x. 3-5).
Application (*studium*).—Non-reception due to application (*Jer.* v. 4, 5).
Approach (*see* ***Draw near, Ignorance***).
Arabia.—Those who pervert the knowledges of good are meant by "Arabia" (*Jer.* xlix. 28-33).

INDEX OF WORDS AND SUBJECTS.

Arcana Coelestia.—For the spiritual and celestial senses of *Genesis*, see the *Arcana Caelestia* (p. 168).
Ariel.—"Ariel" signifies the lost doctrine of truth of the church (*Isa.* xxix).
Ark (Noah's).—"Ark" means the beginning of a new church (the Ancient) (*Gen.* vii.).
Artifice (*ars*).—Those who wish to prevail by artifices. General subject (*Jer.* x.). (*See further under* **Prevail**.)
Asia.—The Ancient Church spread over a great part of the Asiatic world (*Gen.* x.).
Ask (*quaero*).—The church that expects the Lord, asks why the wicked flourish (*Jer.* xii. 1, 2).
    He that seeks the truth does not find it (*Jer.* xiv. 4–6).
Assault (*impugno*).—The hells mightily assault the Lord (*Ps.* cxliii. 8–12).
    O that He may be delivered from the hells which assault Him with falsities! (*Ps.* cxliv. 5–8, 11.)
Assist (*see* **Help**).
Association (*see* **Consociation**).
Atheist.—The evil deny God (*Ps.* x. 1–11).
Attack (*insultus*) (*see also* **Assault, Overthrow**).
    Protection from every attack (*Ps.* xci. 2–6).
Attention.—Let there be attention to the contents of *Psalm* xlix.
Authority (*potestas*).—The Lord has authority over the hells in consequence of His victory over them (*Ps.* cx. 4–7 *and prec.*).
Aversion to truths (*Isa.* xlii. 22–24).

Babel } (*see also* **Captivity, Worship**).
Babylon } "Babylon" signifies adulteration of good and truth (*Isa.* xiii., xiv.; *Jer.* l.).
    Beginning of "Babylon," and its destruction (*Gen.* xi. 1–9).
    "Babylon" fully treated of seriatim in *Dan.* i.–vi., *which see*.
    Babylon will perish (*Jer.* l. 9, 10); because they have vastated the church (*ib.* 11); it is without truth (*ib.* 12, 13); their destruction at the time of judgment (*ib.* 14–16, 18–24).
    Warning not to come near "Babylon" (*Jer.* li. 45–50).
    Babylonish captivity (*Zech.* vii. 1–7).
    Carried off to "Babylon" so as not to be able to profane the holy things of the church (*Jer.* xxvii. 1–8).
Backslide (*see* **Depart** (*recedo*)).
Baptism (*see* **John the Baptist**).
Basket.—Who are meant by the "two baskets of figs" (*Jer.* xxiv. 1–3).
Bear (*see* **Endure**).
Beatitude (*see* **Happiness**).
Beginning (*inchoatio*).—Beginning of Babylon (*Gen.* xi. 1–9).
—— (*initium*).—Beginning of a new church (the Ancient) described by the "ark" and its preservation (*Gen.* vii.).
    Beginning of the establishment of the church (*Jer.* lii. 31–34).
    Beginning of the New Church (the New Jerusalem) (*Dan.* xii. 11–13).
—— (*principium*).—Beginning of a new church, which church is meant by "Noah" and his "three sons" (*Gen.* vi. 8–10, 14–22).
    End of the Most Ancient Church, and the beginning of the Ancient Church (*Gen.* viii.).
    The establishment of the church in the beginning, and her protection from falsities of evils (*Ps.* cv. 8–15).
    They have obstinately rejected internals, from the very beginning (*Jer.* vii. 25, 26).

From the beginning they have done exceeding great evil to the church (*Ps.* cxxix. *t.*, 1–3).

Evils have been with them from the beginning, although they had the Word and doctrine from it (*Jer.* xxxii. 26–33).

Bel.—" Bel " signifies the profanation of truth (*Isa.* xlvi).

Believe (*see also* **Faith, Trust**).

In the former church there is no one who believes that the Divine has power to save, therefore, etc. (*Isa.* l. 2, 3).

Those with whom the church will be at the time will slay the Lord, with the intention of scattering those who believe on Him (*Zech.* xiii. 6, 7).

The Lord saves those who believe in Him, and those who do not believe perish (*Ps.* cxlv. 18–20).

Those who believe in the Lord are saved, etc. (*Isa.* x. 20–22, 24).

Benjamin.—" Children of Benjamin " mean those who have conjunction with the Lord in the lowest heaven (*Jer.* vi.).

Bethlehem.—The Lord was born in Bethlehem, let us adore Him (*Ps.* cxxxii. 6, 7).

Betray.—The Lord was betrayed by the Jews, because He taught them (*Zech.* xi. 12, 13).

Birth of the Lord.—He was the Father's from birth (*Ps.* lxxi. 6, 7).

Blaspheme.—They blaspheme the Lord (*Ps.* xxxv. 19–21, 25; *see also the following chapters throughout: Isa.* xxxvi., xxxvii.; *Jer.* xx., xxi.).

The Lord is blasphemed by the evil in the church, notwithstanding that perfection is His (*Ps.* xliv. 13–21). He is so treated on account of the Divine (*ib.* 22).

They blaspheme the Lord, that He has no power (*Isa.* xxxvi. 13–20).

They blaspheme Him still more violently, as that He can be of no avail whatever against them (*Isa.* xxxvii. 8–13).

Those who blaspheme will perish (*ib.* 6, 7).

Blasphemy of the Lord stopped (*ib.* 28, 29).

Blasphemy of the Word (*Jer.* xx.).

Blasphemers described (*Jer.* xxi.).

Blessedness (*see* **Happiness**).

Bless (*benedico*).—The Lord will spiritually bless those who seek Him (*Zech.* x. 1.).

Blindness (*see also* **See**).

The Lord will take blindness away (*Isa.* xxv. 6–8).

Those who pervert all truths of the church fall into all falsities of evil, until they no longer see what is good and true (*Ezek.* xxxii. 3–8).

Those who are meant by " Babylon " were blinded (*Dan.* ii. 12, 13).

Boast (*gloriari*).—Respecting those who boast of knowledges (*scientifica*) and their own intelligence, etc. (*Ps.* xlix. 5, 6 *and fol.*); they perish and come into hell (*ib.* 10–14).

The evil vaunt themselves (*Ps.* lxxiii. *t.*, 1–9); but they are devastated and consumed (*ib.* 15–20, 27).

—— (*se jactare*).—They boast before others because of the possession of the Word, and of the holy things of the church (*Ezek.* xxiii. 40–42).

Bound.—Men who have been bound by the hells will be saved by the Lord (*Isa.* xlv. 13).

Bring (*see* **Lead**).

Build (*see* **Drink**).

Cain.—" Cain " signifies those who made everthing of the church and thus of salvation to consist in mere doctrine and knowledge of cognitions (*Gen.* iv.).

Caldron (*olla*).—" Caldron " or " pot " signifies doctrine (*Ezek.* xi. 1–3).

Call upon.—When called upon and when He has proved man, the Lord delivers him from the hells (*Ps.* lxxxi. 5–7).

Canaan.—Abram was commanded to go into the land of Canaan for the reason that all places in that land, and those round about it, had been allotted spiritual significations by the men of the Most Ancient Church, and these were to be mentioned by name in the new Word that was to be written among them, in which the names of those places were to be employed (*Gen.* xii. 1–8).

The land of Canaan and all things therein represented the church, and as these are mentioned by name in the Word, those who profaned holy things could not be tolerated there (*Jer.* xxvii. *end*).

Canaan as the seat of the church (*Ps.* lxxviii. 52–55).

Capacity (*facultas*).—Those who were in the capacity to understand were brought to the church (*Ezek.* xvii. 1–3); and instructed (*ib.* 4, 5).

Captivity (*see* ***Free***).

Captivity effected by confirmations of falsity through reasonings (*Isa.* x. 20–22, 24).

Captivity effected by falsities (*Isa.* lii. 3).

Concerning such as are in spiritual captivity (*Jer.* xxix.).

Establishment of the church with such (*Jer.* xxix. 10–15; xxx; xlvi. 27, 28).

Respecting those who in the church have been taken captive and become "Babylon" (*Jer.* li. 59–61).

Manifestation to those who are in spiritual captivity (*Ezek.* xi. 24, 25).

Care is to be taken lest those who are in good be destroyed, etc. (*Zech.* xi. 4, 5).

Cast down (*dejicio*) (*see also* ***Overthrow***).

They will be cast down from the place where they have made seeming heavens for themselves (*Ps.* lxxxiii. 9–11, 12).

Celebration (*see* ***Song of praise***, *also* ***Confession***, ***Glorification***).

Celestial
Celestial Church } (*see* ***Fall***; ***Word***, CELESTIALS OF).

The Most Ancient Church was a celestial church, the first of all on this earth (*Gen.* ii.).

Celestial of the Ancient Church is meant by "Shem" (*Gen.* ix. 18–29).

Those who represented the celestial things of the church, etc. (*Hosea* v. 1–3).

Mourning over the destruction of the representatives of the church reaches even to those who were in celestial good (*Micah* i. 8–12). Hence even these will begin to be perverted, and will suffer deprivation of all truth (*ib.* 13–16).

The celestial church has adulterated goods (*Jer.* iii. 7–9).

The celestial church and spiritual church were one (*Ezek.* xxxvii. 15–20); and will become one church under the Lord, and will be protected from infernal evils and falsities (*ib.* 21–25).

Those who are in celestial good, of whom the church will consist where the Lord is, will fight against falsities of evil (*Zech.* x. 4–6).

The celestial church represented by the "children of Jonadab" (*Jer.* xxxv.).

The celestial church do not learn truths and retain them in the memory, but receive in the life and obey, which is meant by "dwelling in tents" (*Jer.* xxxv. 1–10, 11).

Those who will obey will be in the celestial church (*Jer.* xxxv. 18, 19).

The spiritual and celestial church worships the Lord who is the God of the church (*Ps.* cxxxv. 19–21).

They will receive things spiritual and celestial (*Jer.* xxxi. 12–14).

Conjunction of celestial and spiritual things in the Word (*Ezek.* i. 6; 8, 9).

All things of doctrine as to celestial good and truth (*Ezek.* xl. 6–23).

Truths from a celestial origin will be in the new church (*Zech.* iv. 11–14).

Celestial Sense (*see* **Word**).
Chaldea.—Those who have adultered and falsified the goods and truths of the church, are meant by "Babylon" and "Chaldea" (*Jer.* l.).
Change (*see also* **Division**).
Change of state of the church (*Ezek.* iii. 12, 13; xxxvii. 26-28; xxxviii. 17-19).
No nation has changed its religion as they have done (*Jer.* ii. 10, 11).
Charity (*see also* **Good, Love**).
Angels and men have intelligence and charity from the Divine good and Divine truth (*Ezek.* xlvii. 1-12).
From the good of charity, from which is worship, there will be intelligence (*Zech.* xiv. 20, 21).
The church which is in faith and in charity, and its power (*Dan.* viii. 1-3). It will increase in goods and truths (*ib.* 4).
Faith alone will wholly destroy charity (*Dan.* viii. 5).
History of charity and faith in the Christian church (*see Dan.* xi. and xii.).
Charity slain when religion is made to consist in merely knowing doctrinals (*Gen.* iv.).
Rejection of goods of charity (*Isa.* xv.).
Chastise.—They are not willing to return, even when chastised (*Jer.* ii. 29, 30).
Chief truths (*see* **Truths**).
Children (*see* **Adopt**).
Christian Church (*see also* **New Church**).
The Christian church followed the three ancient churches. It is internal, etc. (p. 164).
Though no pity is possible when the Jewish Church is destroyed, the Lord will pity those who will be of His new church (*Hos.* i. 7 *and prec.*).
When nothing of the church will any longer remain [among the Jews] then the new church will grow, and will acknowledge the Lord (*Hos.* i. 10, 11, *and prec.*).
When the church among the Jewish nation has been destroyed, a new church will be established which will be in faith and charity (*Dan.* xi. 5). Its successive states fully described (*ib.* 6-45; xii. 11-13).
Salvation in that church (*Micah* v. 7).
History of the Christian Church (*Dan.* ix.-xii.).
The Christian Church not easily established (*Dan.* ix. 25).
After its establishment, falsity will invade and destroy it (*Dan.* ix. 26).
The Reformation will take place, but this church will also perish from mere falsities and evils (*Dan.* ix. 27).
The Christian Church has come to its end by the accomplishment of the last judgment (p. 164).
Church (*see **Christian Church, Deliverance, Desolation, Destruction, Devastation, Celestial Church, Establishment, Evil and Falsity, Externals, Ignorance, Institution, Internals, Jewish Church, Lord,** Coming of, **Order, Perish, Perversion, Perverted Church, Prayers of Church, Preservation, Representative Churches, Restoration, Spiritual Church, Successive, Good, Ultimate heaven***).

THE LORD AND THE CHURCH.

The Lord is the church (*Isa.* viii. 13-16; *Jer.* xvii. 12, 13).
All of heaven and the church is from Him (*Ps.* lxxxix. 10-14).
Heaven and the church from the Lord (*Ps.* xlv.).
The church is from the Lord (*Joel* iii. 16, 17).
The church will be the Lord's and from the Word (*Joel* iii. 20, 21).
The church is the Lord's (*Jer.* xxiii. 7, 8).
The Lord causes a church to be (*Amos* ix. 6).
The church became the Lord's (*Dan.* vii. 13, 14).

THE WORD AND THE CHURCH.

The church is from the Lord through the Word (*Ps.* xxxiii. 1–9; xxiv. *t.*, 1–3).
The Lord forms the church (*Zech.* xii. 1).
The church formed by the Lord through Divine truth (*Ps.* cxxxvi. 4–6).
The church will be in doctrine respecting the Lord (*Zech.* xii. 8).
The church is founded on the sense of the letter of the Word (*Ps.* civ. 5–9).
Divine truth from the Lord from the first things to the last things of heaven and the church (*Ps.* xix. 5, 6).
The church partitioned according to goods and truths in the whole complex (*Ezek.* xlvii. 13–23).

THE LORD'S GLORIFICATION AND THE CHURCH.

Through the oneness of the Divine and the Human in the Lord, heaven and the church will endure to eternity (*Ps.* xciii, 1, 2).
From the Lord's making the Human Divine, heaven and the church are His, and they are in Divine truths from Him (*Ps.* xlv. 8).
From the uniting of the Divine and the Human in the Lord will be a church that will be in all truth from the Lord, and safe from infestation from falsities (*Ps.* lxv).
A church from this, that the Lord was assisted by the Father (*Ps.* xxii. 22–31).
The church from the Lord (*Ps.* lxviii. 15–17); He snatched them out of the hand of the infernals (*ib.* 18–23).
The church was preserved (*Ps.* lxxvii. 20).
The church will flourish from the Lord's omnipotence (*Ps.* xcii. 12–14).
The church will be in power and in light against falsities of evil (*Ps.* cxxxii. 17, 18).

WORSHIP OF THE LORD BY THE CHURCH.

The Lord will come to judgment, that heaven and the church may worship Him from joy of heart (*Ps.* xcvi. 10–12).
The whole church will acknowledge and worship the Lord from joy of heart (*Ps.* lxvii. *t.*, 1–5, 7); everything of the church will be theirs (*ib.* 6).
The whole church will serve the Lord (*Ps.* xlv. 17).
Song of praise to the Father by the Lord, for the church (*Ps.* cxviii. 1–4).
All things of the church are from the Lord, and nothing from man (*Ps.* cxxvii. *t.*, 1, 2).
The Lord dwells in His church because He loves her; because there He dwells in truths and goods (*Ps.* cxxxii. 13–16).
What the Lord does for His church (*Ps.* cxlvii. 19, 20, *and prec.*).

END OF THE CHURCH.

The church at the time of the Lord's coming (*Isa.* lxii).
End of each church, the old (*i. e.* the Jewish) and the new (*i. e.* the Christian) (*Dan.* ix.).
There were also churches before, which were devastated (*Amos* ix. 7).
The church has departed through falsification of the Word as to the sense of the letter (*Ezek.* xii. 3–12).
The church and its doctrine from the Word, which had been dominant, but now, etc. (*Lam.* i. 1–3).
Corruption of the church (*Jer.* iv. 14, 15); in respect to doctrine (*ib.* 16); in respect to the Word (*ib.* 17).
The church does not profit by the doctrine concerning God (*Isa.* xlix. 4).
Since there was as yet only multiplication of truth, and not the fructification of good, and thus not the church, he was urgent that the church might exist with him (*Gen.* xv. 1–6).

But it is foretold what the church and its conjunction with the Lord would be, namely, that it would be perverted (*ib.* 7-24).

Those who are in the church are told to repent and be converted, but they will not (*Jer.* xviii. 11-16).

Of the church as to knowledges (*cognitiones*) of truth (*Ezek.* xxvi., xxvii., xxviii.).

Imagining that all things of the church consist in knowledges (*cognitiones*), they come into falsities which destroy the ultimates of doctrine, which, together with affections for truth are destroyed by knowledges (*scientifica*). Finally all affection for spiritual truth perishes so that nothing of the church remains (*Ezek.* xxvi. 1-14).

Everything of the church acquired by means of knowledges (*cognitiones*) (*Ezek.* xxvii. 24, 25).

It no longer consists of such as possess knowledge and do not according to it (*Jer.* xxii. 11, 12, *and prec.*).

Much of it perished by departure from the Lord and by falsities of every kind (*Jer.* xliv. 1-6).

Nothing but falsity in the church (*Isa.* viii. 22; xxxii. 13, 14).

Those who were of the church despoiled them of all truths (*Isa.* xlii. 22-24).

The church became perverted (*Isa.* v. 1, 2).

Its destruction by falsifications (*Isa.* v. 5-15).

The church destroyed by ignorance of truth and non-understanding of the Word (*Isa.* vii. 1-16).

The church in respect to the knowledges (*cognitiones*) of truth is the countenance of hell (*Ezek.* xxvii. 35, 36).

Church and religiosity contrasted (*Dan.* xi.).

The church and "Babylon" contrasted (*Dan.* ii., iii.; iv. 4-9).

Although the church is there, yet they do not acknowledge the Lord (*Mal.* i. 5, 6).

Those who are within the church profane worship, and do not worship the Lord (*Mal.* i. 12-14).

Those who are of the church come into an evil life in consequence of teachers regarding their own good and not the good of the church (*Ezek.* xxxiv. 5, 6, *and prec.*).

A perverted church declares that they are the church, because they have lthe Word, etc. (*Ezek.* xxxiii. 21-26).

Cim that the church is with them, yet they speak against the church and aagainst the Lord (*Ezek.* xxxv. 10-13).

The church is not with them unless they live according to the commandments and do no violence to the Word (*Jer.* vii. 4-6).

Nochurch unless spiritual and natural truth and good become concordant (*Jer.* xxxiii. 23-26).

The Lord will not regenerate those who are not good, although they have the Word (*Ps.* lxviii. 12-14).

The Lord to the church in which is the Word (*Ps.* lxxxii. *t.*, 1); because they do not do goods, the church is tottering (*ib.* 5); thus, although they possess the Word they will perish (*ib.* 6, 7).

It perishes by reasonings from falsities (*Isa.* viii. 7-12). (*See further under* **Perish**).

Against those who were of the church, who cherished evil thoughts against the Lord (*Ps.* lviii. *t.*, 1-9).

The Lord is blasphemed by the evil in the church (*Ps.* xliv. 13-16).

The Lord is shamefully treated by those with whom was the church (*Ps.* lxix. 8-12).

Those who are of the church purpose to have the Lord put to death (*Ps* xxxviii. 11, 12).

Those who are of the church where the Word is think that the Lord is to be utterly destroyed, and will themselves be destroyed (*Ps.* xli. 10, 11, *and prec.*).

Those who are of the church wish to destroy and slay the Lord (*Ps.* lix. *t.*, 1–6).

The Lord will come for judgment to those with whom is the church (*Ps.* l. *t.*, 1–6).

The church will not perish, but those who are in it perish (*Amos* ix. 8–10).

It has become none (*Isa.* i. 28–31; xxiv. 1–13; xxxii. 9–12; *Jer.* iv. 28, 29; xviii. 14–16; *Lam.* iv. 18, 19; *Zech.* i. 11; *Hab.* iii. 5–7).

No church unless they abstain from falsifications of the Word (*Hosea* ii. 1–4).

It is not with those who profane holy things (*Jer.* vii. 11).

Whence it is that there is no church (*Ps.* xliv. 9–12, 19).

Those who are in the church have utterly destroyed spiritual good by evil love (*Ezek.* xv. 6 *and prec.*); hence there is no church (*ib.* 7, 8).

The church has been forsaken (*Ps.* lx. *t.*, 1–3).

Destruction of the church (*Ps.* lxxiv. *t.*, 1–9).

The church is no longer there, but hell (*Jer.* xix. 9–13).

There cannot be at the same time a church and not a church, without truths being snatched away (*Amos* iii. 3–6).

RESTORATION OF THE CHURCH.

There must be a church (*Isa.* lxv. 8–10).

The church perishes, unless restored by the Lord by means of His coming (*Ps.* xc. 7–14).

Let not heaven and the church perish, but be established (*Ps.* cii. 25–28).

The church where the Word is should depart from the affections of the natural man; thus it will be the church of the Lord, etc. (*Ps.* xlv. 10, 11 *and fol.*).

The church will consist of few (*Ezek.* xi. 13–16).

Those who love the neighbor and God, will be of the Lord's church (*Ps.* xv. *t.*, 1–5).

The church is with those who live in humility and in accordance with the commandments (*Isa.* lxvi. 1, 2).

Those who had the capacity to understand became a church (*Ezek.* xvii. 6).

Those who are of the church are saved (*Isa.* xlv. 17).

CHURCH FORMED OF THE REMNANT.

Falsity must be rejected and truth received, that there may be a church (*Jer.* iii. 12–14).

The church safe on removal of "Philistia" (*Isa.* xiv. 30, 32).

Reception into the church after conversion (*Hosea* xiv. 4–7).

Those who have been completely vastated, so as not to know what is true and what is good, can at last be taught, can acknowledge the Lord, can be received, and can become a church (*Jer.* xxiv. 4–7).

The Lord causes them to be a church, after the natural has been purged of falsities and evils (*Ps.* cv. 42–45 *and prec.*).

The Lord upholds the church with those who look to Him (*Isa.* xl. 28, 29, 31).

Those who are of the church and in the doctrine of truth will be saved by the Lord when He comes (*Ps.* xlvi. 5, 6).

Then those who are of the church will be saved, and will worship the Lord (*Ps.* lxix. 32–36).

Then the church will be gathered together (*Joel* iii. 1).

A church will arise and flourish, which will acknowledge the Lord, walking in truths (*Ps.* lxxxv. 8–13).

Church of the Gentiles.

The church is given to others (*Isa.* v. 16, 17; *Jer.* viii. 10; xxx.). (*See further under* **Others**.)

A church will be constituted of those who are without the church (*Zech.* vi. 15).

A church formed of those that are out of the church (*Ps.* cii. 12–22).

A church to be formed by the Lord of nations who are in falsities from ignorance, because they and do not have the Word, and this church He will love (*Ps.* cxxxvii. 5, 6, *and prec.*).

Church of the Gentiles, described (*Ps.* cxiv.).

The Lord to those with whom the church has been instituted (*Jer.* xxv. 1–3).

Character of the New Church.

(*See also under* **New Church**.)

The church is the means (*Isa.* li. 1, 2).

A church internal and external is being instituted (*Ps.* lx. 6–9).

It will understand the Word, etc. (*Isa.* xi. 13–15).

The Divine spiritual of the Word forming the church (*Ezek.* x. 1, 2); from which the internal and the external of the church is full of the Divine (*ib.* 3–5).

The church in respect to the doctrine of truth and good (*Micah* i.).

The church which is in truths of faith from good of charity, is meant by the "King of the south" (*Dan.* xi.).

The Lord is in His church; protection there against falsities and evils (*Ps.* lxxvi. *t.*, 1–4).

The church will be different because the conjunction will be different (*Ezek.* xxxvii. 26–28).

The church will be as among the ancients (*Mal.* iii. 4).

Love and desire for the church and heaven (*Ps.* lxxxiv. *t.*, 1–4); from trust in the Lord, the church will increase in truths and goods (*ib.* 5–7); her blessedness arises from trust in the Lord (*ib.* 8–12).

Growth of the church in goods and truths (*Dan.* viii. 4).

The truth of good is from heaven upon those who are in the church, in which is salvation (*Ps.* cxxxiii. 3).

Good in abundance is in the Lord's church (*Ps.* cxxviii.).

Wherein the church consists (*Gen.* iv.).

Church Universal and Church Specific.

The nations round about the Jewish nation perceived that the state of the church was perverted among themselves, because of the loss of knowledges (*cognitiones*) among the Jews (*Jonah* i. 7–9).

Two Churches.

There are two churches, one which is in truth, which is "Samaria," and the other which is in good, which is "Jerusalem" (*Ezek.* xxiii.).

Their history (*ib.* 1–49).

There were two churches, the celestial and the spiritual, and the two together were one (*Ezek.* xxxvii. 15–20).

Prediction concerning the church in respect to charity and in respect to faith (*Dan.* viii.). Its successive states described (*ib.* 1–27).

The land which was the seat of the church (*Ps.* lxxviii. 52–55).

(The term "church" used for the evil and the good, in the same Psalm, *Ps.* lxxix.).

Things pertaining to the church signify things pertaining to the Lord (p. 168).

Civil.—Civil diabolical power, in the Babylonish religion (*Dan.* ii. 40–43).

INDEX OF WORDS AND SUBJECTS.

Cleanse (*see* **Purge**).
Cognition (*see* **Knowledge** (*cognitio*)).
Co-operation.—Co-operation of the Father with the Lord (*Ps.* xcii. 1–5).
Combats (*see* **Fight against**; **Lord**, COMBATS OF; **Overthrow, Subjugate**).

COMBAT AGAINST EVILS AND FALSITIES.

Combats against evils and falsities prepare for reformation (*Isa.* ix. 1).
Combat of good and truth against evils and falsities (*Joel* iii. 9–12).
The Lord alone fights and therefore assists against the hells (*Ps.* xxv. 15–20).
Those who are in celestial good will fight against falsities of evil; so also will those who are in spiritual good (*Zech.* x. 4–6).
Combat with those who are in falsities of evil (*Hab.* iii. 10–15).
Those who are meant by "Edom" must be combatted because they believe themselves to be more intelligent than others (*Obad.* 1–3).
Combat in the natural man (*Gen.* xiv. 1–17).

COMBAT AGAINST TRUTHS AND GOODS.

They fight from falsities against truths (*Ps.* lix. 7).
He who fights against the truths of the new church will plunge into falsities of every kind (*Zech.* xiv. 12).
Those who falsify the truths of the sense of the letter of the Word do not resist in the day of combat, but destroy the truth of doctrine (*Amos* i. 13–15).
They fight to confirm falsities and evils by falsifications of the Word (*Jer.* ii. 33–35).
In the last time of the church falsities and evils will combat amongst themselves and against truths and goods (*Micah* vii. 5, 6).

Comfort (*conforto*) (*see also* **Strengthen, Consolation**).
Prayer to the Father that Divine truth may comfort Him (*Ps.* xliii. 3, 4).
Coming (*see* **Lord**, COMING OF).
Commandments (*see* **Statutes**).
Heaven and the church are with those who live in accordance with the commandments (*Isa.* lxvi. 1, 2; *Jer.* vii. 5, 6).
Exhortation by the Lord to live according to His commandments in the Word (*Jer.* xxvi. 1–5).
To do the commandments and acknowledge the Lord is meant by the "covenant" (*Jer.* xi. 1–3).
Commingle.—Reasonings from falsities commingled with the simple understanding of the Word (*Jer.* xl. 7–12).
Falsities and evils of every kind commingled with truths and goods (*Ezek.* xxii. 17–22).
Common cause (*see* **Unity**).
Comparison of the lot of the evil with the lot of the good (*Ps.* xxxvii.).
Compassion (*miseratio*) (*see* **Pity**).
Complaint (*querela*).—Complaint at there being no truth in the church or in doctrine (*Jer.* xiv. 19).
Complaints of the wicked that they perish although it is said in the Word that they shall be saved (*Jer.* iv. 9, 10).
Conception (*see* **Lord**, CONCEPTION OF).
Concordance.—Concordance of spiritual and natural truth and good (*Jer.* xxxiii. 23–26).
Condemn (*damno*) (*see also* **Lord** SLAIN).
Because the Lord is heaven and the church, those who depart from Him are damned (*Jer.* xvii. 12, 13).
The offspring are not condemned on the father's account (*Ezek.* xviii. 1–4).
Those who commit evils, or act contrary to the goods and truths of the church are condemned (*Ezek.* xviii. 10–13).

If the pious man becomes impious he is condemned (*Ezek.* xviii. 24).

Those who have falsely interpreted the Word are condemned (*Jer.* xxix. 20–23).

There is damnation because all truths and goods have been destroyed (*Lam.* ii. 1–9).

The former church condemned (*Ezek.* xxviii. 25, 26; *Obad.* 18).

Confession (*see also* **Lord**, CONFESSION OF).

The Lord desires confession of heart (*Ps.* l. 14, 15).

Let them draw near to the Lord through the truths of the Word, and confess Him (*Ps.* c. 4, 5).

Let them confess the Lord, who alone is God and Lord (*Ps.* cxxxvi. 1–3).

Happy is he who confesses and worships the Lord (*Ps.* cxviii. 26–29).

All who are in the heavens will confess the Lord because His kingdom is eternal, etc. (*Ps.* cxlv. 10–13 *and fol.*).

Confessing the Lord (*Isa.* xxv; xxvii. 12, 13; *Ps.* cxi. 1–4).

Confession and celebration of the Lord on account of salvation (*Isa.* xii.).

They confess the doctrine of truth (*Isa.* xxvi. 1–4).

Confession that the Divine alone has power, and from it there is help (*Ps.* lxii. *t.*, 1, 2, 5–8, 11, 12).

Confession of the Lord who delivers from falsities and evils, and grants truths and goods (*Ps.* cxxxvi. 23–26).

Those who confess the Lord are saved (*Ps.* cxl. 12, 13).

Those who will be of the new church will acknowledge and confess that they have falsities and evils (*Jer.* iii. 22–25).

Confession of infirmities and deliverance (*Ps.* xxxii. 5–7).

Confession respecting the Jewish church destroyed (*Dan.* ix. 4–19).

Confidence (*see* **Trust**; **Lord**, TRUST OF).

Confirmation.—Confirmation of Divine things of the church by knowledges (*scientifica*) produced a rational and also spiritual intelligence (*Ezek.* xxxi. 3–9).

Confirmation from heaven (*Dan.* iv. 20–33).

It was confirmed by those who were in the truths of the church that self-exaltation was contrary to the Word (*Dan.* v. 10–24).

The children of Jacob were confirmed in the Word by means of miracles (*Ps.* lxxviii. *t.*, 1–7).

Confirmations from the Word in favor of charity explained perversely (*Dan.* xi. 24–26).

Confirmations of falsity captivate (*Isa.* x. 20–22, 24).

Falsity confirmed by learning (*Jer.* xlvi. 20–24).

Faith alone confirmed by the sense of the letter of the Word (*Dan.* vii. 8).

Faith alone confirmed by reasonings and by the Word falsified (*Dan.* vii. 19–21).

Falsity confirmed from the Word (*Jer.* xxiii. 15; 16, 17; 18).

Falsities and evils confirmed by falsifications of the Word (*Jer.* ii. 33–35).

Falsities and evils confirmed by reasonings from the natural man (*Jer.* ii. 36).

Confirmations are of no avail (*Jer.* ii. 37).

Confirmations by knowledges do not protect those who have falsified and adulterated the Word (*Nahum* iii. 11–17).

The church devastated by knowledges (*scientifica*) that confirm falsities (*Isa.* x. 23, 25–34).

They have confirmed themselves in this, that good is of no profit and that evil does no harm, because the good and the evil are alike prosperous (*Mal.* iii. 13–15).

Conjunction (*see also* **Lord**, GLORIFICATION OF; **Separation, Sever**).

Conjunction of celestial and spiritual things in the Word (*Ezek.* i. 6; 8, 9).

Conjunction of all things of the Word, and consequent life (*Ezek.* x. 21, 22).
Truth by which there is conjunction (*Isa.* lv. 3, 4).
Falsity must be rejected and truth received that there may be conjunction and a church (*Jer.* iii. 12-14).
How they will have conjunction (*Ps.* xxv. 12-14 *and prec.*).
Conjunction of the truth and good of the natural man, from which there would be only an external church, which is rational (*Gen.* xvi).
Conjunction of good and truth constitutes good itself (*Ps.* cxxxiii. *t.*, 1).
Conjunction by truths and goods (*Isa.* lxi. 8).

CONJUNCTION WITH THE LORD.

Conjunction with the Lord in heaven; how it comes about (*Ps.* xlv. 15 *and prec.*)
From conjunction with the Lord truths will be inscribed on their life (*Jer.* xxxi. 31-34).
The church will be different because the conjunction will be different (*Ezek.* xxxvii. 26-28).
Conjunction of the Lord with the church (*Ezek.* xx. 10-12).
Conjunction with the Lord (*Isa.* lxii. 4, 5; *Jer.* xxxi. 31-34; xxxii. 36-40).
Conjunction with the Lord in the lowest heaven ("Children of Benjamin,") (*Jer.* vi.).
A magnificent word respecting conjunction with the Lord (*Ps.* xlv. *t.*, 1).
Conjunction with the Lord through the Word (*Mal.* ii. 5-7).
This conjunction is dissolved by departure from the Word (*ib.* 8-10).

CONJUNCTION WITH THE LORD DESTROYED.

Consequence of departing from conjunction with the Lord (*Jer.* xxxiv. 17-19).
Conjunction with the Lord would be perverted (*Gen.* xv. 7-24).
Conjunction of the Lord with them has been sundered (*Zech.* xi. 10, 11).
The conjunction of truth and good has been sundered (*Zech.* xi. 14).
Conjunction with the Lord destroyed (*Ps.* lxxxix. 38-42).
Conjunction with the Lord has perished, why (*Jer.* xvi. 9, 8, *and fol.*).
No conjunction with the Lord, because no truths and good are there (*Jer.* xvi. 1-3).
The church has no conjunction with the Lord, because it is wholly perverted and hence rejected (*Lam.* ii. 13-15).
No conjunction whatever with those who, like the nation sprung from Jacob, have estranged themselves from the Lord (*Ps.* xcv. 8-11).
Painful conjunction in the Christian Church (*Dan.* xi. 27-31).

Conquer (*see* **Lord**, HIS VICTORY OVER THE HELLS; **Overcome**).
Consociation.—A *quasi* consociation from simulating the dogma of charity (*Dan.* xi. 21-23).
Consociation in hell (*Ezek.* xxxii. 17-30).
Consolation (*consolatio*) (*see also* **Comfort**) (*Ps.* xliii. 5; *see also Isa.* xlix. 14-16).
Consult.—The remains consult doctrine (*Jer.* xlii. 1-6).
Told not to consult the knowledges of the natural man (*ib.* 7-22).
Evil consequences of consulting knowledges (*Jer.* xliii., xliv. 11-14 *and prec.*).
Consume (*consumo*).—The evil, though they prosper, are nevertheless devastated and consumed (*Ps.* lxxiii. 15-20, 27, *and prec.*).
Falsities and evils will consume all things of the church (*Isa.* xxxiii. 11, 12).
Falsity from the sensual man and afterwards evil therefrom has consumed all things of the church (*Joel* i. 4).
Consummation.—All things of the Word, of doctrine and of the church have been consummated by profanities and by evils and falsities (*Ezek.* v. 14-17).

Evil consummated (*Joel* iii. 13-15).
After the church has been consummated, the judgment will come, and the Word will cease, and the Lord will glorify His Human (*Dan.* ix. 24).
Contempt (*contemtus*). ⎫ —Contempt for the Lord (*Jer.* xviii. 18).
Despise (*contemno*). ⎭ The Lord was despised more than all others (*Ps.* xxii. 6, 7).
The good rejected with contempt (*Isa.* li. 23).
The man who is in the love of self is held in contempt by others (*Hab.* ii. 6, 7).
Controversy.—Controversies and heresies. Their origin (*Isa.* xix. 1-4).
Contrary (*see* **Against**).
Contumely.—They treat the Lord with contumely (*Ps.* xxxi. 11-13).
Conversion   ⎫ (*see also* **Exhortation, Miracles, Repent**).
Turning back ⎬ Exhortation to be converted to the Lord (*Amos* iv. 12, 13).
Turning away ⎭ Exhortation to be converted (*Amos* v. 14-15; *Hosea* xiv. 1-3; *Joel* i. 14).
Exhortation to be converted to the Lord, to repent, and to be wise (*Joel* ii. 12-17).
Exhortation to be converted to the Lord and not falsify truths (*Hosea* xii. 6, 7).
They ought to be converted before the Lord comes to judgment (*Zeph.* ii. 1-3).
Exhortation to be converted, because the Lord wishes the salvation of all (*Ezek.* xviii. 30-32).
In the church they must be taught, in order that they may be converted, because the Lord wishes the salvation of all (*Ezek.* xxxiii. 10, 11).
Conversion does not consist in speaking in a devout manner, but in shunning evils and exercising charity (*Isa.* lviii. 5-7).
Unless they refrain from evils and turn back, they will utterly perish (*Jer.* iv. 3, 4).
Without conversion, no enlightenment (*Ezek.* xiv. 6, 7).
The impious man who is converted, is saved (*Ezek.* xviii. 21-23).
Those who are converted after repentance, are accepted by the Lord, although they are in falsities and evils (*Jer.* xviii. 5-8).
Those who are in the church are told to repent and be converted; but they will not (*Jer.* xviii. 11-13).
Profaners are such that they cannot be converted and led back (*Jer.* viii. 4-6).
Grief of the church because they cannot be converted (*Ezek.* xxi. 12, 13).
The church could not be with the Jews after the Babylonish captivity, because they did not turn away from falsities and evils (*Zech.* vii. 1-7).
Conversion in the old church originates in evil (*Isa.* lviii. 4).
Conversion of the nations, who are meant by "Nineveh" (*Jonah* i.-iv.).
The nations, hearing from the Word of God about their sins, and that they would perish, were converted after repenting, and were heard by the Lord, and saved (*Jonah* iii. 1-10).
Correspondence.—The expressions of the historical and prophetical parts of the Word are correspondences (p. 163).
The former churches are described in like manner, but by more interior correspondences, in the Word that is mentioned by Moses (p. 164).
Corruption.—The church which is in truth became corrupted by falsifying the truths of the Word by reasonings from knowledges (*Ezek.* xxiii. 5-8).
Covenant.—The "covenant" means doing the commandments and acknowledging the Lord, etc. (*Jer.* xi. 1-3, *and fol.*).
Craft (*astus*) (*see also* **Artifice**).
They act craftily (*Jer.* xviii. 21, 22).
Creation (*see also* **Regeneration**).
All have been created by the Lord (*Isa.* lxiv. 8).

Cross, Crucifixion (*see* **Lord,** PASSION OF THE CROSS; *also* **Lord** SLAIN).
Cry.—Cry of the church for help, that she be not destroyed (*Ps.* lxxix. 5–12).
Cunning (*see* **Artifice, Craft**).
Cupidity ⎫ (*cupiditas*).—Natural desire and knowledge (*Hosea* xi. 2).
Desire ⎬ Because they have repudiated the Word, and have obeyed their own
Lust ⎭ lusts, they are in falsities of evil, etc. (*Jer.* ix. 13–15 *and fol.*).
   Affections of truth have become cupidities of falsity (*Lam.* iv. 9, 10).
   Intercession is of no avail when evil cupidities have possession of the church (*Ezek.* xiv. 15, 16).
   Eager desire to be in falsities and evils (*Jer.* ii. 24, 25).
   Those led astray who have evil cupidities and desire nothing else but to be insane in falsities (*Isa.* lvi. 10–12).
Curse.—A curse rests upon those who hatch doctrine out of falsities (*Hab.* ii 12, 13).
Cyrus.—"Cyrus" represents the Lord in respect to the Divine Human (*Isa.* xliv. 28; xlv.).

Damascus.—"Damascus" means those who place religion in nothing but knowledge of cognitions (*Isa.* xvii.).
   "Damascus" means those who pervert the knowledges of truth (*Jer.* xlix. 23–27).
Damn (*see* **Condemn**).
Daniel.—The "lion's den into which Daniel was cast" means the punishment of the inquisition which those suffered who were of the Lord's church, and opposed the Babylonish decree to worship the men of that religion (*Dan.* vi. 10–17).
David.—It should be known that as by "David" the Lord is meant, therefore where David speaks in the Psalms, the Lord is signified in the spiritual sense (p. 123).
Dead.—Those of the new church are as dead (*Jer.* xxxi. 15).
   The death of profaners (*Jer.* xxxiv. 21, 22).
   Those of the Jewish church die in their profanities (*Ezek.* xxiv. 14).
Deceive (*fallo*).—Things that deceive are hatched out (*Isa.* lix. 5).
   It is delightful to them to pervert and deceive (*Jer.* v. 25–27).
Deceitful (*dolosus*).—The evil do evil to the good and deny God, and are hypocrites and deceitful (*Ps.* x. 1–11).
   To the Father, that He may be preserved from the deceitful (*Ps.* cxxiv. 6–8).
Decree.—Decree of the Babylonish religion that they should be worshipped in place of the Lord (*Dan.* vi. 4–9); enforced by the inquisition (*ib.* 10–17).
Defence.—The church defended from falsities and evils (*Jer.* ii. 1–3).
   Profaners defend their falsities and call them truths of the church (*Jer.* viii. 11, 12).
Defile (*conspurco*).—Defilement of doctrine from the Word (*Jer.* xxxviii. 4–6).
   Truths and goods defiled by knowledges (*scientifica*) of the natural man. (*Ezek.* xxiii. 19–21).
   They are filthy by reason of the adulteration and profanation of truth and good (*Ezek.* xxiv. 6–8).
Delay (*see* **Protraction**)
Delight (*jucundum*) (*see* **Reasonings**; **Falsity,** DELIGHT OF).
   To be imbued with the Word is in itself delightful (*Ezek.* iii. 1–3).
   Those who trust in the Lord will come into delights of truth and good (*Isa.* xxx. 29, 30).
   Delight of perverting and deceiving (*Jer.* v. 25–27); its consequence (*ib.* 14–17).

SUMMARIES OF THE INTERNAL SENSE.

To destroy the church is delightful to the self-intelligent (*Obad.* 10–14).
Deliver (*libero*) (*see also* **Free ; Lord,** PRAYER OF, TO THE FATHER ; **Snatch**).
The Lord's confidence respecting deliverance (*Ps.* lx. 4, 5).
Confession of infirmities, and deliverance (*Ps.* xxxii. 5, 7).
When the Lord is delivered the gospel will be preached, etc. (*Ps.* lxix. 29–31 *and fol.*).
Deliverance of the good (*Ps.* ix. 9, 10–14, 18).
Deliverance of the good, whom the evil infest (*Ps.* xvi. 3–5).
The Lord will to eternity deliver the good as against the evil (*Ps.* xii. 5–8).
Deliverance of those who are to be of the church (*Ps.* cviii. 6).
The Lord delivers from all evil those who trust in Him (*Ps.* xxxiv. *t.* 1–11).
The Lord delivers from the hells, when He has been called upon and has proved man (*Ps.* lxxxi. 5–7).
The Lord delivers the natural man from falsities of evil (*Ps.* cxxxv. 8–11; cxxxvi. 10–22).
Deliverance from falsities and evils by the Lord (*Ps.* cxxxvi. 23–26).
The church to consist of others after she has been delivered from the profane (*Jer.* xxvii. 22).
Those outside the church to be delivered from the infernals (*Isa.* xxxv. 4, 5).
The new church being freed from falsities and evils will be in truths and goods (*Ezek.* xxxvi. 24–30).
The new church delivered from falsities (*Isa.* lii. 3).
—— (*eximo*).—Through trust in the Father He is delivered (*Ps.* xxxi. 14–21).
Denial (*see also* **God,** WORSHIP OF OTHER GODS ; **Lord,** DENIAL OF).
Denial of God (*Ps.* x. 1–11).
Depart (*abeo*).—The Lord taught them continually by the Word that they should not go away to any other worship than that of the Lord (*Jer.* xxv. 4–7).
Those who depart from the worship of the Lord have no enlightenment from the Word (*Ezek.* xiv. 1–4 *and fol.*).
They have departed and falsified truths (*Jer.* iii. 1, 2).
Result of departing from worshipping the Lord (*Jer.* xvi. 10, 11, *ana prec.*).
All with whom the church has been instituted will depart, or otherwise they would profane it and will perish (*Jer.* xxvii. 12, 13).

——) (*recedo*) (*see also under* **Fall**).
Backslide (They must not go back, but must acknowledge the Lord (*Ezek.*
Retreat (xiv. 11).
Withdraw) The Divine truth shows that the so-called enlightened have gone back (*Jer.* xxiii. 33).
Result of backsliding (*Jer.* xiv. 10–12).
Departure from the Lord, for no reason (*Jer.* ii. 4–6).
Departure from the Lord causes much of the church to perish (*Jer.* xliv. 1–6).
Departure from the Lord causes the acknowledgment of evils and falsities as goods and truths (*Jer.* v. 11, 12).
Departure from the Lord causes perversion of all the goods and truths of the church (*Jer.* ii. 7, 8).
Departure from the Lord causes that nothing but what is falsified and evil therefrom is in the church (*Jer.* ix. 2, 3).
Because the Lord is heaven and the church, those who depart from Him are damned (*Jer.* xvii. 12, 13).
Departure from the Lord and from truths (*Jer.* xiii. 8–11).
They have departed from the Word, and have thereby dissolved the conjunction with the Lord (*Mal.* ii. 8–10).

The church has departed from them, through the falsification of the Word, etc (*Ezek.* xii. 3–12).

Every one has departed from God, there is not one left (*Ps.* liii. *t.*, 1–3).

Grief at the church's departure from the Lord (*Jer.* x. 19–21).

Backsliders to be driven out of the church (*Jer.* xv. 4–6). They have no truth (*ib.* 7).

Afterwards the rulers of the Babylonish religion backslide until nothing remains but what is adulterated (*Dan.* iii. 31–35).

"Babylon" was minded to depart from the worship of the Lord to the worship of another god (*Dan.* vii. 1, 2).

Although those who were of the church beheld Divine miracles, they backslid (*Ps.* cvi. 6–8 *and fol.*).

The fathers and the children among the Israelites had gone back and had not lived according to the Word (*Ps.* lxxviii. 8–10); though led unto the land which was the seat of the church they backslid and worshipped another god (*ib.* 56–58).

The church among the children of Israel has gone back and worships another god, etc. (*Ps.* lxxxi. 8–11 *and fol.*).

The Lord's temptations even to despair even to the thought of withdrawal (*Ps.* lxix. 5 *and prec.*).

After a vain effort the evildoers were compelled to retreat (*Ps.* cxxix. 4–8).

The hells withdraw (*Ps.* lxxi. 13).

The church where the Word is should depart from the affections of the natural man (*Ps.* xlv. 10).

To the extent in which they depart from falsities they will have understanding of truth (*Zech.* iii. 6–10).

Those who depart from evils and falsities will not perish (*Ezek.* vi. 7–10).

Deprive (*orbo*).—Pride of self-intelligence deprive them of all truths of the church (*Ezek.* xxxi. 10–13).

Desire (*desiderium*).—Desire and love of the Lord to be united to His Divine (*Ps.* lxiii. *t.*, 1–8).

When the Lord desired the good and truth of the church they gave Him falsity and evil (*Ps.* lxix. 21).

The Lord longs for the ancient state in respect to the church (*Ps.* cxliii. 5, 6).

Love and desire for the church and heaven (*Ps.* lxxxiv. *t.*, 1–4).

The new church is in falsities of ignorance, but in the desire for truth and good (*Ps.* cvii. 4–8).

The Lord teaches and leads all who are in falsities from ignorance, and who desire truths (*Ps.* cxlvi. 7–9).

Desist (*see* **Refrain**).

Desolation.—Utter desolation of the church consequent on embracing falsities (*Jer.* xii. 7–12).

They are flattered by their doctrine of falsity that there is no desolation of truth (*Jer.* xiv. 13).

Despair (*see* **Lord**, TEMPTATIONS EVEN TO DESPAIR).

Despair that the Word is blasphemed (*Jer.* xx. 14–18).

Despair of those of whom the new church will consist (*Jer.* iv. 31).

Despise (*see* **Contempt**).

Destroy (*deleo*).—Destruction of the old church (*Isa.* xliv. 27).

—— (*deperdo*).—Confession respecting the Jewish Church destroyed (*Dan.* ix. 4–19).

All external good has been destroyed, and hence also external truth (*Mal.* i. 3, 4).

SUMMARIES OF THE INTERNAL SENSE.

Destruction of church as to externals and finally as to inmosts (*Amos* vii. 2-9).
They have falsified the truths of the church, therefore the church has been destroyed, etc. (*Hosea* ix. 1-3).
They are to be kept from destruction (*interitus*) until all the truth of the church has been destroyed (*Hosea* xiii. 14, 15).
They cannot be healed because the church has been destroyed by falsities (*Jer.* xlvi. 11, 12).
Destroyed by falsities from the natural man, they have no truths from the Word (*Jer.* xv. 12-14).
Knowledges have been destroyed by means of reasonings (*Jer.* xlvi. 1-6).
Spiritual good has been utterly destroyed by evil love (*Ezek.* xv. 4, 5).
Such as destroy all manner of truths (*Isa.* lvii. 5).

—— (*destruo*).—Destruction of the Most Ancient Church is described by the "flood" (*Gen.* vii.).
Destruction of "Babylon" (*Gen.* xi. 1-9).
All things of the church destroyed by the Israelitish nation and the fathers thereof (*Ezek.* xix. 1-14).
Destruction of the Jewish Church and nation foretold, although its truth will be preserved (*Jer.* xxxiv. 1-7; xxxvi.).
Destruction of the church among the Jewish nation (*Dan.* xi. 1-4).
Indignation that the Jewish Church should be destroyed (*Jer.* xxxii. 1-5).
The Jewish nation destroyed the church (*Ezek.* xliv. 4-8; *Ps.* xciv.); because it did so, neither does it fear God, although He sees all things (*Ps.* xciv. 3-11).
The Jewish Church, destroyed, must perish (*Micah* vi. 14-16).
Destruction of every good by the Jews (*Zech.* v. 5-8).
The profane (Jewish) church will be destroyed when the Lord comes (*Hosea* i. 3-5).
When the church among the Jewish nation had been destroyed, "Babylon" appropriated to herself all things pertaining to it (*Dan.* i. 1, 2).
Destruction of the Babylonish religion at the coming of the Lord (*Dan.* ii. 44, 45).
Destruction of all the representations of the church, which had been totally falsified (*Micah* i. 4-7); affects even those who are in celestial good (*ib.* 8-12).
A new church after the Jewish Church has been destroyed (*Ezek.* xl. 1).
The old church will be destroyed (*Micah* vii. 10).
The former church will be destroyed (*Isa.* i. 24-27; xxiv. 16-20; xxvi. 5, 6; xxxvii. 36-38; *Jer.* xxxii. 23-25; xlv.; *Ezek.* xi. 21; *Ps.* cviii. 7).
All things of the former church will be destroyed (*Hag.* ii. 20-22).
Destruction of the church delayed (*Isa.* xxxvii. 33-38).
Infernal evil invades and still further destroys all the goods and truths of the church (*Jer.* v. 14-17).
Utter destruction of the church with all things appertaining to it (*Ps.* lxxiv. *t.*, 1-9).
All things of the church have been destroyed (*Jer.* iv. 22-27; lii. 8-11).
Those who are of the perverted church have destroyed all truths and goods even to the last things of the church (*Micah* iii. 1-3).
The hells wish to destroy all things of the church (*Ps.* lxxxiii. *t.*, 1-5).
Evil shepherds destroy everything of the church, and destroy (*perdo*) the simple (*Ezek.* xxxiv. 18-21).
Destruction of the church follows when men fight against truths (*Zech.* xiv. 13-15).
Further destruction of the church by falsifications (*Isa.* v. 5-15).
Destruction by means of interior falsities of evil (*Ezek.* xxi. 8-11).
Falsities of evil have destroyed everything of the church (*Zech.* i. 18-21).

INDEX OF WORDS AND SUBJECTS. 191

Falsity of evil will destroy all things of the church by various insanities (*Joel* ii. 4-9).

All things of the church destroyed by reasonings from the natural man (*Ezek.* xvii. 11-13; 17, 18).

Utter destruction by means of reasonings from the natural man (*Ezek.* xix. 8, 9; xxix. 19, 20).

Destruction of all things of the church by knowledges (*scientifica*) of the natural man (*Ezek.* xxx. 1-5).

Destroying the church by falsifying the knowledges (*cognitiones*) of truth, etc. (*Zeph.* ii. 12-15).

Destruction of the church by faith (*Dan.* xi. 29-31).

Falsifications of the Word and direful evils have destroyed the church (*Ps.* lxxix. *t.*, 1-4); the cry of the church for help that she be not destroyed at the same time (*ib.* 5-12).

Truths of doctrine destroyed (*Jer.* li. 1-4).

Destruction of the truths of the Word and of doctrine, by knowledges (*cognitiones*) alone and faith alone (*Joel* iii. 4-8).

Faith alone will wholly destroy charity (*Dan.* viii. 5); it will destroy the worship of the Lord together with Divine truths (*ib.* 11, 12).

Faith alone destroyed all things of the church (*Dan.* vii. 7); and the church (*ib.* 23, 24).

The religion of faith alone destroys all fear of God, and the whole church (*Dan.* xi. 36, 37).

Faith from charity has been destroyed by perverse explanations of the Word (*Dan.* xi. 24-26).

Because they falsify all the truths and goods of the Word and yet say that God is with them, the whole church will be destroyed (*Micah* iii. 12, *and prec.*).

Destruction of power of truth by perversion of truths (*Ezek.* xxix. 6, 7).

Those who destroy the spiritual things of the Word go away, in consequence, into falsities of every kind (*Amos* ii. 6-8).

Those who destroy the celestial things of the Word destroy also its spiritual things (*Amos* ii. 4; 5).

The church destroyed by perverting the good of the Word (*Jer.* xxiii. 1, 2).

The senses of the Word will be destroyed through delights of falsity (*Isa.* xxii. 13-15).

How they have destroyed the sense of the letter (*Ezek.* v.).

Truth of the Word destroyed by falsities (*Ezek.* xvi. 35-42).

Truths of the Word destroyed by reasonings from self-intelligence (*Isa.* xiv. 24-27).

Because nothing of the law and doctrine remains the church has been destroyed (*Hosea* iv. 4-9).

Destruction of worship (*Ezek.* vi. 4-6).

They have destroyed the church without any cause (*Ps.* liii. 4, 5).

The church will be destroyed unless they repent and live according to the commandments (*Jer.* xxvi. 6).

All things are being destroyed because they hearken not (*Jer.* vi. 11).

Those who are of the church will be destroyed, because, loving falsities of every kind, they will not repent nor be converted (*Jer.* xviii. 17 *and prec.*).

Because opposed to all things of the church they became perverted and were destroyed (*Ezek.* xix. 4-7).

The former church will be destroyed because of evils and falsities (*Ezek.* xxxix. 23, 24).

They have destroyed all the holy things of the church (*Ezek.* xxiii. 36-39).

Evil from the sensual man has destroyed the different things of the church (*Joel* i. 5-7; ii. 2, 3).

Destruction of church by evil love (*Ezek.* xx. 47, 48).
They totally destroyed and profaned the truths and goods of the church (*Ps.* cvi. 35-39).
Distruction of the church by profanation (*Jer.* vii. 12-15; *Ezek.* v. 11, 12).
Destruction of all things of the church in general and in particular (*Jer.* lii. 12-23).
Because all truths and goods have been destroyed the church has been rejected, etc. (*Lam.* ii. 1-9).
Mourning over the destruction of the goods and truths of the church (*Joel* i. 8, 13).
Lamentation over the destruction of the church and their own destruction (*interitus*) when the Lord comes (*Amos* v. 16-20).
Conjunction with the Lord destroyed because the church is destroyed (*Ps.* lxxxix. 38-42).
On the day of judgment those will perish who have destroyed the church; (*Nahum* ii. 3-6); then they will no longer destroy the church and its sanctities (*ib.* 11-13).
The Lord will execute judgment upon all who have adulterated and destroyed the truths of the church (*Mal.* iii. 5, 6).
All men or all things that are contrary to the doctrine respecting the Lord will be destroyed (*Zech.* xii. 9).
Destruction of those who are of the devastated church (*Hab.* iii. 10-15).
Those who falsify doctrine will be destroyed (*Ezek.* xiii. 13-15).
Falsities of doctrine and of worship will both be utterly destroyed (*Zech.* xiii. 2, 3).
The Lord will utterly destroy reasonings from falsities (*Micah* v. 5, 6).
Destruction of those who are in false persuasion (*Isa.* xxvi. 19-21).
Destruction of the evil (*Ps.* ix. *t.*, 1-8, 19, 20).
The Lord will destroy all who adulterate and profane the goods and truths of the church (*Isa.* xliii. 14).
The Lord will destroy all who are in the love of self and in pride (*Isa.* ii. 10-18).
Those who pervert truths by reasonings from their own intelligence will be utterly destroyed by the Lord, so that scarcely anything of natural truth will remain with them (*Isa.* x. 12-19).
Destruction of those who trust in their own learning (*Isa.* xxxi. 4).
Destruction of those who have utterly departed (*Isa.* xiii. 4-9).
The Lord will destroy falsities and evils (*Jer.* i. 9, 10).
Destruction of "Damascus" (*Isa.* xvii. 1, 2).
Destruction of "Babylon" (*Jer.* l. 18-20 *and fol.*).
Destruction of the hells because they have no saviour (*Ps.* xviii. 41, 42, 45).
The Lord will destroy the power of the hells (*Isa.* xlii. 13-15; xliii. 16, 17).
The Lord will destroy all falsities by the truths of the Word, lest doctrine should teach something else (*Zech.* xii. 6, 7).
Falsities will be destroyed with those who are of the new church (*Micah* iv. 13).

Destruction ⎫ (*exitium*) (*see also under* **End**).
End ⎬ End of those who are in the ultimate heaven, why (*Jer.* vi. 18,
Ruin ⎭ 19 *and prec.*).

Destruction of those who pervert the knowledges of good ("Arabia") (*Jer.* xlix. 31-33).
Destruction of the church where there is no truth (*Jer.* xv. 11).
Destruction of those who pervert the truths of the Word (*Jer.* xxiii. 37-40).
Total destruction of those who have falsified the external of the Word ("Edom") (*Jer.* xlix. 14-18).

End of the church which is in self-intelligence (*Jer.* x. 22).

Destruction in consequence of falsities (*Jer.* xiii. 21).

Destruction because they have forsaken the Lord and hence have falsities (*Jer.* xiii. 24, 25).

Destruction in consequence of obstinacy and love of things falsified by knowledges (*Jer.* xliv. 20-23).

Destruction resultant on natural love consuming all things of the church (*Ezek.* xxviii. 19, 20).

Destruction because of interior and exterior evil (*Jer.* xiii. 22).

Destruction of all things, with those who adulterate the goods of the church and of the Word (*Jer.* xlviii. 1-5).

Destruction of "Babylon" at the time of the judgment (*Jer.* l. 14-16; because they have destroyed (*destruo*) all things of the church (*Jer.* li. 24-26).

Grief because of the destruction of all things of the church (*Jer.* ix. 10-12).

Horrible end of "Babylon" (*Isa.* xiv. 22, 23).

(*interitus*).—Destruction of those with whom there is no good or truth (*Ezek.* ix. 5, 6).

They are to be kept from destruction until all truth of the church has been destroyed (*deperdo*) (*Hosea* xiii. 14, 15).

Destruction lest the church be still further destroyed (*perdo*) (*Ezek.* xxviii. 24).

Destruction consequent on falsities (*Jer.* xiii. 14).

Destruction by mere falsities (*Jer.* li. 41-44).

Destruction because there is nothing of soundness (*Nahum* iii. 19).

Destruction of those who by falsities of faith devastate the church (*Ezek.* xxv. 15-17).

Destruction by reasonings from falsities (*Ezek.* xxi. 18-22).

The destruction on the day of judgment of such as persisted in falsities of evil (*Hosea* x. 13-15).

Because they forsook the Lord by reason of their glorifying themselves for their wealth of knowledges, and hence there was no longer any truth in the church, they were destroyed (*Hosea* xiii. 5-11).

Destruction will come upon the self-intelligent on the day of judgment (*Obad.* 15, 16).

Destruction of self-intelligence (*Jer.* x. 14, 15).

Destruction of the church and of the kingdom is imminent, because they have made themselves obstinate (*Jer.* xxxvi. 29-31).

Destruction is brought about by not desisting from adulteration (*Mal.* iii. 8, 9).

Destruction because nothing of the church was left (*Lam.* iv. 18, 19).

Destruction because they have infernal evil and falsity (*Jer.* ix. 20-22).

Destruction of the evil (*Isa.* lxvi. 6).

Destruction of all, consequent on profanation (*Jer.* vii. 20).

Destruction of blasphemers and profaners (*Jer.* xxi. 14).

Remains of profaners of truth perish (*Jer.* viii. 1, 2).

Destruction on the day of judgment by the Lord (*Zeph.* i. 14-17).

Destruction of those in the ultimate heaven (*Jer.* vi. 21).

Those who acknowledge the Lord must be removed while the destruction lasts (*Jer.* iv. 5, 6).

Preparation of the new church during the destruction of the former (*Jer.* x. 17, 18).

Destroy
Ruin. } (*perdo*).—Ignorance of truth and non-understanding of the Word will enter and begin to destroy the church (*Isa.* vii. 1-6); it is foretold that this will not take place as yet (*ib.* 7-9); but it will be when the Lord will come into the world (*ib.* 10-16).

Care is to be taken lest those who are in good be destroyed by those who have devastated the external of the church (*Zech.* xi. 4, 5).

SUMMARIES OF THE INTERNAL SENSE.

The evil prevail over the good and destroy them (*Hab.* i. 12-17).
Evil shepherds destroy (*destruo*) everything of the church, and destroy the simple (*Ezek.* xxxiv. 18-21).
There are none to lead the people any longer, but only such as destroy (*Zech.* xi. 9).
The teacher and the leader destroy all things of the church by falsities of evil (*Zech.* xi. 15-17).
They shall perish lest they destroy the church still further (*Zech.* ix. 7, 8).
Destruction (*interitus*) lest the church should be still further destroyed (*Ezek.* xxviii. 24).
Knowledges (*cognitiones*) from the Word destroyed by those who are in them (*Zech.* ix. 3, 4).
Destruction of truth of doctrine (*Amos* i. 13-15).
The truth of the church interiorly destroyed (*Hosea* xiii. 12, 13).
They are diligent at perverting, hence vastation (*Isa.* lix. 7); he who follows destroys the truths of the church with himself (*ib.* 8).
Those who are in faith alone will destroy knowledges (*cognitiones*) from the Word (*Zech.* ix. 5, 6).
Falsities destroy the church (*Zech.* xi. 6).
Fallacies and reasonings destroy (*Jer.* viii. 16, 17).
Faith alone will destroy the church (*Dan.* viii. 20-25).
All things of the church destroyed by reasonings from the natural man (*Ezek.* xxxii. 11, 12).
The self-intelligent destroy the church still further, and this is their delight (*Obad.* 10-14).
Destruction of good and truth of the church (*Amos* ii. 1-3).
Prayer that those who have ruined the church be removed (*Ps.* lxxix. 5-12).
The perverted church has been destroyed by evils and falsities (*Ezek.* xxxvi. 1, 2).
Because it has been destroyed even to its ultimates, those who have been destroyed will perish (*Ezek.* xxxvi. 3-7).
Falsity and evil destroy those who are in the lowest heaven (*Jer.* vi. 3-5).
They who by reasonings from their own intelligence destroy (*destruo*) the truths of the Word, and profane them, are to be destroyed (*Isa.* xiv. 24-27).
Ignorance of truth and non-understanding of the Word will destroy the church when the Lord comes into the world (*Isa.* vii. 1-6; 10-16).
At the coming of the Lord He will destroy the unfaithful (*Isa.* xi. 1-5).
Those who are then of the church wish to destroy and slay the Lord (*Ps.* lix. *t.*, 1-6).
Those in the perverted church secretly try to destroy the Lord (*Ps.* cxx.).
Prayer to the Father that He may assist against those who wish to destroy Him (*Ps.* liv. *t.*, 1-3).
Those who wish to kill the Lord destroy themselves by malice (*Ps.* lix. 12-15).
Those who are against the Lord will be destroyed (*Ps.* ii. 5).
They are being destroyed for giving the Lord falsity and evil when He desired the good and truth of the church (*Ps.* lxix. 22-28 *and prec.*).
The hells think that the Lord is to be utterly destroyed (*Ps.* xli. 8); they will not succeed, but will themselves be destroyed (*ib.* 10, 11).
Falsities begin to destroy the new church (*Ps.* lxxx. 12, 13).
Falsity will destroy the Christian Church (*Dan.* ix. 26).
Falsities will not enter and destroy the new church (*Micah* iv. 10-12).
No more destruction by falsities and evils (*Isa.* lxv. 25).

Devastation (*see also* **Destroy, Lamentation, Mourning, Perversion, Truth and Good**).
The evil, though they prosper, are nevertheless devastated and consumed (*Ps.* lxxiii. 15-20, 27).

INDEX OF WORDS AND SUBJECTS.

How the church is devastated (*Amos* iii. 9, 10).
Lamentation over successive devastation of the church (*Amos* v. 1-3).
The church will be devastated if they be not converted (*Ezek.* xiv. 8).
They could not but be devastated of all things of the church, because they rejected them (*Ezek.* xvii. 9, 10).
Every external of the church has been devastated (*Zech.* xi. 1-3).
Exhortation to reflect that everything of the church has been devastated (*Joel* i. 16, 17).
No devastation for a long time, hence the evil is worse (*Jer.* xlviii. 10, 11).
Devastation of all truth among those who pervert it by applying knowledges (*scientifica*) to falsities (*Ezek.* xxix. 8-12 *and prec.*).
The whole church has been devastated by knowledges (*scientifica*) that pervert, etc. (*Isa.* x. 23, 25-34).
Devastation of the church in respect to knowledges (*cognitiones*) of truth and good "Tyre" (*Isa.* xxiii.).
Devastation of knowledges (*cognitiones*) of truth will extend and last until the coming of the Lord (*Isa.* xxiii. 15-17).
Those who possess knowledge (*scientia*) but do not according to it, have not a truth which has not been perverted and profaned (*Jer.* xxii. 28-30 *and prec.*).
Nothing of the doctrine of truth will be in the church, therefore they will shun it (*Zech.* xii. 2, 3).
Devastation by traditions or by reasonings from falsities (*Jer.* lii. 1-7).
Devastation of all things of truth with those who adulterate, etc. (*Jer.* xlviii. 17-26).
There is no longer any truth in the church (*Hosea* xiii. 10, 11).
Devastation of the truth of the church will continue (*Isa.* xxxiii. 7-9).
The church that was devastated as to truths say they have truths, etc. (*Hosea* x. 1-3 *and fol.*).
Devastation of the church and its doctrine in consequence of rejecting the Lord and hatching falsities (*Jer.* ii. 14, 15; 17).
Devastation by falsities out of the natural man (*Jer.* ii. 16).
When there was no longer any truth the Lord came and they afflicted Him, etc. (*Ps.* cv. 16-18 *and fol.*).
Devastation of every good of religion by reasonings (*Isa.* xx.).
All things of the church will be taken away from those who have dedestroyed the church (*Nahum* ii. 7-10).
Devastation of all things of the church is at hand (*Jer.* iv. 7).
The church in general is utterly devastated (*Isa.* xxiv. 1-13).
Utter devastation of the church (*Isa.* vii. 23, 24).
Devastation when the Lord comes into the world (*Ezek.* xxiv. 18, 19).
When the church comes into existence, they will be devastated in respect to everything of the Word (*Ezek.* xxxv. 14, 15).
Those who were of the devastated church have been rejected (*Ps.* cvii. 32-34, 39, 40).
Those who by falsities of faith devastate the church will be devastated and perish on the day of judgment (*Ezek.* xxv. 15-17).
Those who have devastated the church will perish (*Ps.* cxxxvii. 7-9).
Those who are of the devastated church will perish (*Zech.* xiii. 8, 9).
Devastation of the church among the Jews (*Haggai* i. 1-4).
The church at the present day is devastated (*Haggai* ii. 1-3).
All things of the church have been devastated, and hence it is in evils and falsities (*Lam.* i. 7-11); grief on this account (*ib.* 12-16).
Lamentation over devastation (*Jer.* ix. 17-19).
Devastation does not come to an end through outward mourning (*Jer.* iv. 8); nor through complaints that they are perishing, etc. (*ib.* 9, 10).
Song in praise of the Lord by those who worship Him, when the church has been devastated (*Ps.* cxxxiv. *t.*, 1).

Devil (*see also* **Infernals**).

A devil adored in place of the Lord (*Ezek.* viii. 15, 16).

Devise (*machino*).—The hells among themselves devise evils against the Lord (*Ps.* xli. 4–7).

His prayer for protection from those who devise evil (*Ps.* xxxi. *t.*, 1–4).

Diabolic (*see also under* **Evil Love**).

Civil diabolic power in the Babylonish religion (*Dan.* ii. 40–43).

Direful.—Direful things suffered by the Lord (*Isa.* xliii. 25).

Direful evils have destroyed the church (*Ps.* lxxix. *t.*, 1–4).

Discouragement (*see* **Despair**).

(*See also Ps.* lv. 6–8).

Disjunction (*see* **Separation**).

Disobedience (*see also* **Obedience, Hearken**).

The Jews were told to keep the statutes, but they did not (*Zech.* v. 8–12).

Disperse (*discuto*).—The Lord disperses ignorance by means of the Word (*Ps.* cxlvii. 16–18).

Disperse \
Scatter } (*dispergo*) (*see also under* **Dissipate**).

All good and truth has been dispersed, together with the knowledges of them (*Joel* ii. 10)

Those with whom the church will be at the time will slay the Lord with the intention of scattering those who believe in Him (*Zech.* xiii. 6, 7).

Those who are in falsities must be scattered (*Ezek.* xi. 13–16).

The Lord's combats with the evil, and their dispersion (*Zech.* xiv. 1–5).

Total dispersion of those who opposed the Lord (*Isa.* xli. 15, 16).

Dispersion of those who falsify the truths of the Word (*Jer.* xlix. 4, 5).

Dispersion of vastators by the Lord (*Isa.* xxxiii. 3, 4).

Dispersion of those who have profaned holy things (*Zech.* ii. 6–9).

Dispersion of the Jews because they did not keep the statutes (*Zech.* vii. 13–14).

Dissipate (*dissipo*) (*see also* **Influx**).

Dispersion of the hells from the children of Israel involved in the conversion of the Israelites when they recalled the miracles in Egypt (*Ps.* lxxviii. 41–51).

Dissipation of knowledges (*scientifica et cognitiones*) (*Nahum* iii. 8–10).

Dissipation of the truths of the Word meant by "dividing the Lord's garments" (*Ps.* xxii. 18).

The Lord dissipates evils of every kind (*Ps.* cxxxvi. 10–22).

The Lord will, by His Divine truth, dissipate the falsities of evil (*Hab.* iii. 8, 9).

The spiritual kingdom of the Lord will dissipate all falsities (*Ps.* xlviii. 4–7).

Distinction.—Distinction between loves of natural and of spiritual good and truth (*Ezek.* i. 10, 11).

Distress (*angustia*).—The Father helped the Lord in His distresses (*Ps.* cxviii. 5–9).

Disturbance (*see* **Perturbation**).

Divine.—The Lord is Divine (*Ps.* cxlv. 17).

Divine Good.—From the Lord is Divine truth and Divine good; how (*Ps.* cxliv. 12–14 *and prec.*).

The influx of Divine good and Divine truth from the Lord; from them angels and men have intelligence and charity (*Ezek.* xlvii. 1–12).

Divine Human (*see also* **Lord**, DIVINE HUMAN OF).

The spiritual kingdom is the Divine Human (*Ps.* xlviii. 9, 10).

Divine Love (*see further under* **Love**).

Divine love of saving belongs to the Lord (*Ps.* xxvi. 7, 8).

Divine Operation.—The Lord operated from His Human; He indeed operated through influx from the Divine, but not from the Divine alone (*Ps.* cxxxi. *t.*, 1, 2).

Divine Power (see also *Power*).
  Power belongs to the Lord (*Ps.* xcvi. 1-9; xcix. 4); and to Him alone (*Ps.* lxxxiii. 18).
  Divine power belongs to the Lord (*Isa.* li. 9-11; *Ps.* xvi. 6-8).
  The Lord's own power (*Ps.* lx. 10).
  Omnipotence belongs to the Lord (*Ps.* xcv. 2-5; cxv. 1-3).
  Omnipotence of the Lord (*Jer.* v. 21-24; *Ps.* cxiii. 1-5; *Isa.* xl. 12-14); all men and all things are nothing against Him (*Isa.* xl. 15-18).
  The Lord will come in Divine power (*Isa.* xiii. 1-3).
  When the Lord comes and glorifies His Human He will have power, etc. (*Ps.* xcviii. *t.*, 1 *and fol.*).
  When the Lord comes with Divine power He causes the infernals to perish (*Isa.* lxiv. 2, 3).
  Without the Father the Lord has no power (*Ps.* cxliv. 3, 4).
  The Divine alone has power (*Ps.* lxii. *t.*, 1, 2, 5-8, 11, 12).
  The Lord as to the Divine truth, or the Word, from which He has Divine power (*Isa.* lxiii. 1).
  The omnipotence of God is scarcely believed to be in the Lord (*Isa.* liii. 1).
  Denial of the Lord's power (*Isa.* xxxvi. 19-20; xxxvii. 8-13).
  It is in their power to know that the Lord alone can do all things, but they are unwilling to know that He is God, etc. (*Jer.* v. 21-24).
  Prayer of the Lord to the Father to show His power (*Ps.* cviii. *t.*, 1-5).
  The Lord has omnipotence against all things of hell from His Divine (*Isa.* xlv. 1, 2).
  By oneness with the Divine the Human has omnipotence over the hells (*Ps.* lxxxix. 19-25).
  The Lord has all power from the oneness with the Divine Human (*Ps.* lxxxix. 6, 9, 13).
  The Lord has Divine power from the Word (*Isa.* lxiii. 1).
  The Lord has power through Divine truth (*Ps.* lxxvii. 16-19).
  The Lord alone fought from Divine truth with His own power (*Isa.* lix. 16, 17).
  The Lord alone has power (or prevails) (*Jer.* x. 6, 7).
  The Lord alone is able to reform by knowledges (*cognitiones*) of truth (*Ps.* cxlvii. 3, 4; 5).
  How the Lord has Divine omnipotence against those that rise up against Him (*Ps.* xcii. 10, 11 *and prec.*); from which the church will flourish (*ib.* 12-14); and will sing praises to the Lord (*ib.* 15).
  The Lord ought to be worshipped because He is omnipotent (*Ps.* cl. 1, 2).
  From the Lord's power those who are with Him will be glad (*Ps.* xxi. 13).
  Joy because there is Divine power through His Human (*Ps.* cxviii. 15, 16).
  Song in praise of the Divine power of the Lord acquired by Him through union with the Father (*Ps.* lxviii. 32-35).
  Without the Lord all things fall (*Isa.* xl. 21-25).
  The Lord labored with all His might that they might grow better, but it could not be done (*Ezek.* xxiv. 9-13).
  The Lord's omnipotence impeded by falsities and evils (*Isa.* lix. 1, 2).
  Those who pervert and profane can have no protection through the Word (*Jer.* xxii. 23, 24).
  The Lord cannot turn the hell of blasphemers and profaners away because they ally it to themselves (*Jer.* xxi. 3-5).
Divine Presence (see *Presence*).
Divine Spiritual (see *Word*).
Divine Truth (see also *Word*, *Truth*).
  The Lord is Divine truth itself (*Ps.* lxviii. 3-5, 31).
  Divine truth (*veritas*) pertaining to the Lord (*Ezek.* i. 27, 28).
  Divine truth (*verum*) belonged to the Lord (*Ps.* xviii. 28, 29); and to Him alone (*Ps.* xlv. 2).

Divine truth and good belongs to the Lord (*Hab.* iii. 1-4).
The Lord appeared in the midst of His Divine truth (*Isa.* vi. 1-4).
Divine truth and its influx (*Ezek.* i. 24, 25).
All Divine truth is from the Lord (*Ps.* lxxxix. *t.*, 1, 2; cxviii. 17).
Divine truths, or the Word, are from the Lord (*Ps.* civ. 1-4).
Divine truth given because the Word was given (*Ezek.* xvii. 7, 8).
From the Word it is possible to be in Divine truths (*Ps.* lxxxii. *t.*, 1).
The Lord has formed heaven and the church by means of Divine truth (*Ps.* cxxxvi. 4-6).
Intelligence grows through Divine truths (*Ezek.* xxxvi. 33-36).
Divine truth was in the Ancient Church, but it was perverted and rejected in the Israelitish and Jewish Church (*Ezek.* xix. 10-14).
Divine truth destroyed by faith alone (*Dan.* viii. 11, 12).
Divine truth will not perish (*Jer.* xxxvi. 27, 28, 32; *cf.* xxxiv. 1-7).
The Lord ought to be worshipped from the Word, where is His Divine truth (*Ps.* cxxxviii. *t.*, 1-5).
Joy of the church over the coming of the Lord, with whom is Divine truth (*Ps.* xcvii. 1-6).
The Lord will come with Divine truth (*Zech.* ix. 9).
Divine truth taught when the Lord comes into the world (*Ezek.* xxxiv. 11-16).
Where there is Divine truth there will be truth and good (*Isa.* xxxii. 15-18).
The Lord will teach Divine truths (*Ps.* li. 13-15).
Divine truth belongs to them, by which the hells are restrained (*Ps.* cxlix. 5-9).
The Lord will reign through Divine truth (*Isa.* xxxii. 1).
There will be no truth, but in the Lord there will be Divine truth; and Divine truth will proceed from Him (*Zech.* xiv. 6-9).
Protection through Divine truth (*Isa.* xxxiii. 5, 6).
The Lord will, by His Divine truth, dissipate the falsities of evil (*Hab.* iii. 8-9).
Divine truth and Divine good are the Lord's and from Him, when He has been delivered from the hells which assault Him with falsities (*Ps.* cxliv. 12-14 *and prec.*).
He has powerfully conquered the hells by means of Divine truth (*Ps.* xlv. 3-5).
The Lord had power through Divine truth (*Ps.* lxxvii. 16-19).
The power of Divine truth from the Lord (*Ps.* xxix. 5-11).
The Divine truth appears in consequence of the subjugation of the hells (*Ps.* xviii. 15 *and prec.*).
Joy of those who are in divine truths from the oneness of the Divine and the Human in the Lord (*Ps.* xciii. 3, 4).
There is oneness with the Divine Human, therefore the Divine truth is from Him (lxxxix. 3-5).
From the Lord's making the Human Divine, heaven and the church are in Divine truths from Him (*Ps.* xlv. 8 *and prec.*).
Divine truth from the Lord is with men owing to the Lord being united to His Divine by means of grievous temptations (*Ps.* lxvi. 13-17 *and prec.*).
Divine truth will go forth from the Lord in every direction, from the first things to the last things of heaven and the church, and it perfects man, because it is wisdom (*Ps.* xix. *t.*, 1-11).

Divine Will.—The Lord wills the salvation of all (*Ezek.* xviii. 30-32; xxxiii. 10, 11).

(*See further under* **Lord. Divine Love, Will, Desire**).

Divine Wisdom.—The Lord will judge from Divine wisdom (*Isa.* xi. 1-5).
The Lord has Divine wisdom (*Isa.* xlv. 3); through His Divine, even to ultimates (*ib.* 4).

Divine Zeal.—The Lord will not rest until He sees His church established (*Ps.* cxxxii. *t.*, 1–5).

Division.—Division of the Most Ancient Church, as between the mere doctrine and knowledge of cognitions, and the life of love and charity (*Gen.* iv.).

Divisions and changes in the Most Ancient Church meant by the "posterity of Adam from Sheth" (*Gen.* v.).

Divisions and changes in the Most Ancient Church meant by the "posterity of Noah," or of his "three sons" (*Gen.* x.).

Do (*facio*).—If they do according to the truths of the Word and the knowledge they possess, and do not pervert these, they will have intelligence (*Jer.* xxii. 3, 4).

Those in spiritual captivity are told to study truths and do goods, and continue in them (*Jer.* xxix. 1–7).

Doctrine (*see* **Perversion, Teach, Truth**).

Doctrine concerning God given by the Lord (*Isa.* xlix. 1–3).

The church will be in doctrine respecting the Lord (*Zech.* xii. 8).

Doctrine of good and truth acting in unity with the Word (*Ezek.* i. 15–21).

Doctrine should act in unity with the Word (*Ezek.* x. 11).

Doctrine is Divine from the Divine spiritual of the Word (*Ezek.* x. 6–8).

Doctrine from the Word is spiritual within (*Ezek.* x. 9, 10).

Doctrine full of Divine truths (*Ezek.* x. 12, 13).

From the Word, that doctrine is inwardly and outwardly full of Divine truths (*Ezek.* x. 14, 15).

From the Lord is all truth of doctrine (*Ps.* cxxxvi. 7–9).

The Lord, respecting doctrine from the Word (*Amos* i. 1, 2).

Doctrine is from the Word (*Ezek.* x. 16, 17).

Everything of doctrine is from the Lord (*Ps.* lxviii. 15–17).

Influx from the Lord therefrom into the church (*Ezek.* x. 18–20).

Doctrinals will be full of spiritual and celestial truths from the Lord (*Isa.* liv. 11–13).

All things of doctrine in respect to celestial, spiritual, and external good and truth (*Ezek.* xl. 6–49).

Doctrine of life abundant and extensive (*Jer.* xxxi. 38–40).

The holy of doctrine (*Ezek.* xlv. 6–8).

Those who are in the doctrine of truth will be saved by the Lord when He comes (*Ps.* xlvi. 5, 6).

Doctrine of truth will be received and confessed (*Isa.* xxvi. 1–4).

Doctrine of truth to be embraced by the new church (*Isa.* lii. 1).

The simple were not in reasonings from falsities, but only in externals of doctrine (*Jer.* xxxix. 11–14).

The doctrine of the new church from truths which are from the good of love and charity will be with those who are in ignorance of truth (*Zech.* vi. 1–8).

Doctrine of the new church (*Ezek.* xliv. 15–31).

Doctrine of truth and good in the new church (*Zech.* viii. 1–3).

Doctrine of truth will be in the new church (*Amos* ix. 13–15).

Those who are of the church that the Lord will establish will have truths of doctrine (*Ezek.* xxix. 21).

The church in respect to the doctrine of truth and good (*Micah* i.).

The new church will be in all truth and good of doctrine of the church (*Isa.* lxvi. 20, 21).

They will learn the good of doctrine from the Lord (*Zech.* xii. 5).

The Word will be taught according to the truths of doctrine drawn from it (*Dan.* ii. 36–38).

The simple understanding of the Word according to doctrine (*Jer.* xl. 1–6).

Doctrine will be as among the ancients (*Mal.* iii. 4).

There will be no more falsity of doctrine (*Zech.* xiii. 4, 5).
Falsities of doctrine will be utterly destroyed (*Zech.* xiii. 2, 3).
The Lord will destroy all falsities by the truths of the Word, lest doctrine should teach something else (*Zech.* xii. 6, 7); then the church will be in doctrine respecting the Lord (*ib.* 8); and all men or all things that are contrary to that doctrine will be destroyed (*ib.* 9).
Doctrine from the Word was magnified in the beginning of the Babylonish religion (*Dan.* ii. 46-49).
Doctrine from the Word even in the former, evil, church (*Jer.* xxxii. 26-33).
Mere doctrine, or mere knowledge of doctrinals, like faith alone, slays charity. Such are rejected (*Gen.* iv.).
No life according to the truths of doctrine from the Word (*Jer.* xxxvii. 1, 2).
The things which are of doctrine with them are of no avail (*Isa.* lix. 6).
Contrary to all things of doctrine, so that there was no longer any doctrine (*Amos* vii. 10-16).
Doctrine of truth lost (*Isa.* xxix.).
Doctrine of truth destroyed by perversion of knowledges of truth (*Jer.* xlix. 23-26).
Truths of doctrine that are derived from the Word are dissipated by reasonings (*Dan.* viii. 6-10).
Truths of doctrine among perverters, destroyed (*Jer.* li. 1-4).
Truths of doctrine destroyed by knowledges alone and faith alone (*Joel* iii. 4-8).
Doctrine from self-intelligence extolled, worshipped, published and extended (*Isa.* lvii. 7, 8).
Truths of doctrine falsified (*Ezek.* xxxii. 24, 25).
Doctrine of the church falsified (*Ezek.* xiii.).
Doctrine falsified (*Ezek.* xi.).
Doctrine repudiated and falsified; how (*Jer.* xxxvii. 11-16 *and prec.*).
Doctrine of the church impure (*Isa.* vi. 5-8).
Doctrinals of the church perverted by reasonings from falsities (*Isa.* xxxvi. 1-7).
Everything of the doctrine of truth and good has been perverted (*Zeph.* iii. 1-4).
All things of doctrine perverted leads to blindness (*Micah* iii. 5-7).
Doctrine from the Word perverted and defiled (*Jer.* xxxviii. 4-6).
Doctrine corrupted (*Jer.* iv. 16).
Truths and goods of doctrine adulterated (*Ezek.* xxii. 1, 2).
Mere falsities and evils in respect to doctrine (*Zeph.* i. 4-6).
All doctrine will be full of falsities and evils when the Lord comes (*Isa.* xxviii. 7, 8).
Those who destroy the external of doctrine will be rejected (*Ezek.* xxv. 12-14).
Falsities which destroy the ultimates of doctrine (*Ezek.* xxvi. 3, 4).
Ultimates of doctrine destroyed by knowledges (*scientifica*) (*Ezek.* xxvi. 5, 6).
Truth of doctrine destroyed (*Amos* i. 13-15).
Doctrine perishes by perversion of the sense of the letter of the Word (*Amos* i. 11, 12).
The remnants of doctrine will be destroyed by reasonings from falsities (*Jer.* xxxix. 1-3); but not yet (*ib.* 15-18).
Nothing of the doctrine of truth will be in the church, therefore they will shun it (*Zech.* xii. 2, 3).
Because nothing of the law and doctrine remains, the church has been destroyed (*Hosea* iv. 4-9).
Falsity of doctrine established by persuasion (*Isa.* xxvi. 14, 15).

INDEX OF WORDS AND SUBJECTS. 201

Doctrine of falsity flatters them that there is no lack and desolation of truth (*Jer.* xiv. 13–16).

A curse rests on those who hatch doctrine out of falsities (*Hab.* ii. 12–13).

Doctrine of falsity will perish and, together with it, those who live according to it (*Jer.* xiv. 14–16).

Doctrinals regarded by those that remained of the devastated church (*Jer.* xxxvii. 3, 4).

Truths of doctrine consulted by those who repented (*Isa.* xxxvii. 1–5, 14–20).

Doctrine meant by " caldron " (*Ezek.* xi. 1–3).

Dominion (*dominium, dominor*) (*see also* **Kingdom, Prevail**).

" Babylon " wish to have dominion with God over heaven (*Isa.* xiv. 13, 14).

"Babylon" purposed to have dominion over heaven and the church when that religion should extend over much territory (*Dan.* iv. 10–12); the effect (*ib.* 13–37); they feared to do so as yet (*ib.* 34–37).

Dominion taken from " Babylon " (*Isa.* xlvii. 1); their vain belief about their dominion (*ib.* 7–11).

The church and its doctrine from the Word which had been dominant, but now, etc. (*Lam.* i. 1–3).

Dominion of the Lord over heaven and earth in consequence of His victory over the hells (*Ps.* cx. *t.*, 1–3).

The Lord has dominion over all things, and without Him all things fall (*Isa.* xl. 21–25).

Greatness and extension of the Lord's dominion (*Ps.* lxxii. 8–12).

Dominion over all things belongs to the Lord (*Isa.* xl. 21–25).

Doubt.—Doubt ought not to be entertained (*Isa.* xlv. 9–11).

Draw near (*accedo*) (*see also* **Ignorance**).

Approach to the Lord from every quarter and from every religion (*Isa.* xliii. 3–8; xlix. 12–23; lx. 3–5; lxvi. 18, 19).

Those will draw nigh to the Lord who had not known Him before (*Isa.* lv. 5, 6).

Men will draw near to the worship of the Lord, even those from the nations who are external-natural (*Zech.* xiv. 16–19).

Those who are in the shade of truth will draw near (*Isa.* lx. 8).

Those who are in goods and truths will draw near (*Isa.* lii. 14, 15).

Those who will draw near shall be adopted as children by the Lord (*Jer.* iii. 19).

Let them draw near to the Lord through the truths of the Word (*Ps.* c. 4, 5).

Continual approach for the sake of salvation (*Isa.* lx. 11, 12).

Drink.—To " drink wine, build a house, sow seed, and plant vineyards," signifies to learn truths and retain them in the memory, which belongs to the spiritual church (*Jer.* xxxv. 1–10).

Drive out (*expello*).—Backsliders to be driven out of the church (*Jer.* xv. 4–6).

Those who were of the church are to be expelled (*Jer.* xii. 14, 15).

Drunkards.—" Drunkards of Ephraim " means those who from their own intelligence have falsified truths (*Isa.* xxviii.).

Dwell.—To " dwell in tents " signifies to receive in the life and obey (*Jer.* xxxv. 1–10).

The Lord dwells in His church because He loves her; because there He dwells in truths and goods (*Ps.* cxxxii. 13–16).

Earth (*terra*) (*see also* **All**).

The heavens and the earths are the Lord's, therefore He should be praised in song (*Ps.* ciii. 19–22).

Eagle.—"Eagle" means the understanding (*Ezek.* xvii.).
Eber.—Institution of the Israelitish and Jewish Church which was from Eber (*Gen.* xii. 1–8).
Edom.—Those who have falsified the external of the Word are meant by "Edom," *general subject* (*Jer.* xlix. 7–22).
Of those who are in self-intelligence and pervert the sense of the letter of the Word, who are "Edom" (*Obad.* 1–21).
Egypt.—First instruction of the church, which is that of the natural man by knowledges (*scientiae*), which are "Egypt," in which Abram was (*Gen.* xii. 9–20).
That "Israel" (the Lord) was "brought down into Egypt," means that they were instructed in the first principles of the church (*Hosea* xi. 1).
Of those who make to themselves a religion out of the mere knowledge (*scientia*) of such things as appertain to the Word and the church, and who enter into it, which (religion) is "Egypt," *general subject* (*Isa.* xix).
Elam.—"Elam" means the falsification of doctrine (*Jer.* xlix. 34–49).
Elevate (*see* **Raise up.**)
Embrace.—Embracing falsities (*Jer.* xii. 7–12).
End (*desino*).—The church with the backsliders has come to an end (*Jer.* xv. 9, 10).
—— (*exitium*) (*see* **Destruction** (*exitium*)).
—— (*finis*) (*see also* **Destruction, Fall, Last time**).
End of the Most Ancient Church, when there was no longer any truth or good, because they were in their own intelligence (*Gen.* vi. 1–7, 10–13).
End of the Most Ancient Church (*Gen.* viii.).
End of the Ancient Church when it became idolatrous and magical (*Gen.* xi. 10–22).
Falsity will continue unto the end (*Isa.* xxxii. 19).
End of the church (*Dan.* vii. 28; viii. 26).
End of the church, old and new (*Dan.* ix.).
End of the old church (*Amos* viii. 2, 3); when there is nothing but adulteration of good and truth (*ib.* 4–6).
End of the Babylonish religion because there is no longer any good and truth of the church (*Dan.* v. 25–30).
Endure (*suffero*) (*see also* **Tolerance**).
The Lord cannot endure the vastation of the church (*Isa.* lxiv. 12).
—— (*sustineo*) (*see also* **Uphold**).
The Lord enduring evil treatment (*Isa.* l. 6, 7).
The church wearied Him with sins, which He endured from the beginning and also afterward (*Isa.* xliii. 22–27).
He suffered direful things of them, and endured them (*Isa.* xlii. 25).
The Lord bears all things with tolerance (*Ps.* xxxviii. 13, 14).
The Lord endured for the sake of those who awaited salvation (*Ps.* lxix. 6, 7).
The Lord endured all things even to the passion of the cross (*Isa.* liii. 6–8); and because He endured such things He goes forth as the Conqueror (*ib.* 12).
Enemies.—The Lord prays for His enemies (*Ps.* lix. 11).
Enjoy (*fruor*).—If they had obeyed they would have enjoyed every good (*Ps.* lxxxi. 13–16).
Enlighten (*illustro*).—Those who call themselves enlightened pervert truth still more, whereas they are not enlightened (*Jer.* xxiii. 30–32).
Those who depart from the worship of the Lord have no enlightenment from the Word (*Ezek.* xiv. 1–4); unless they become converted (*ib.* 6, 7).
Those outside the church will receive enlightenment from the Lord (*Isa.* xxiv. 14–16).

Enlightenment of those who are in ignorance (*Isa.* xlii. 16).
Enlightenment of the new church by the Lord from the good of love by means of truth (*Zech.* iv. 1-10).
The Word will enlighten the new church (*Ezek.* xi. 22, 23).
Enlightenment in the natural is from the Lord (*Ps.* cxxxix. 11, 12).

Ephraim (*see* **Drunkard**).

Establish (*instauro*) (*meaning, To raise up, Institute*) (*see also* **Church, Institute, New Church, New Heaven, New Thing, Restore**).
The church was established by the Lord among the ancients, evils having been cast out (*Ps.* xliv. *t.*, 1-4); this was done by God, and not by man (*ib.* 5-8).
A church is established when evil desires, falsities and adulteration of good have possession of the former church (*Ezek.* xiv. 21-23).
The church established among others, before the destruction of the evil (*Isa.* lxvi. 7-9).
When the perverted church perishes, a new church will be established by the Lord, which will be in truths and goods (*Ezek.* xxxvi. 8-12, 24-30).
A new church to be established by the Lord when those who are in faith alone have been judged (*Dan.* vii. 26, 27).
A new church will be established after the church among the Jewish nation has been destroyed (*Dan.* xi. 5).
The Lord will establish a church to whom He will give the goods and truths thereof, and will remove falsities of evil, and thus hell, etc. (*Joel* ii. 18-20 *and fol.*).
The Lord will establish a new church of others in place of the former (*Ezek.* xvii. 22-24).
The Lord will establish the church with others (*Isa.* i. 24-27).
The Lord will establish the church from others, who will teach and learn its good (*Jer.* xxiii. 3, 4).
A church with everything belonging to it is to be established by the Lord (*Isa.* xlix. 5, 6; *cf. Jer.* xxxii. 43, 44).
A new church will be established, gathered from every nation, when the old has been destroyed (*Micah* vii. 11-13).
A new church will be established out of the nations by the Lord when He comes into the world (*Micah* iv. 1, 2); *fully described* (*ib.* 3-13; v).
Establishment of the church from the nations (*Ps.* cxiv. 1, 2).
A new church will be established, but not easily, after consummation, judgment, and the glorification of the Lord's Human (*Dan.* ix. 25).
When the Lord comes there will be a church in which the Lord Himself will be in place of the representative of a church (*Jer.* iii. 16, 17); then truth and good will make one (*ib.* 18).
A new church will be established which will acknowledge the Lord (*Hosea* vi. 1-3, 11).
A new church to be established by the Lord; they will live for a long time without the truths and goods of the church, but they will become a church from the Lord, when He comes, and will acknowledge Him (*Hosea* iii. 1-5).
The new church, which the Lord will establish, will be infested, etc. (*Zech.* iii. 1, 2).
Those who will be of the church which the Lord will establish, will have truths of doctrine (*Ezek.* xxxix. 21).
The new church to be established by the Lord, which is "Israel" and "Zion," *fully described* (*Jer.* xxxi.).
The Lord will put on the Human and will establish the church (*Ps.* ii. 6-8).
The Lord will establish the church (*Ps.* xlvii. 4, 5).
Prayer of the Lord to the Father to give help that He might see the church established (*Ps.* cvi. 1-5).

The Lord being protected has established the church (*Ps.* lxxiv. 16, 17).

The church established with those who have been in spiritual captivity or in ignorance of truth (*Jer.* xxx. 1-3).

Establishment of the church by the Lord (*Ps.* cv.); song in praise of the Lord for His works for the establishment of the church (*ib.* 1-7); its establishment in the beginning (*ib.* 8-15).

Beginning of the establishment of a church (*Jer.* lii. 31-34).

Something of a church will be established out of those who are natural and in knowledges (*scientifica*) (*Ezek.* xxix. 13-16).

The Lord establishes the church in the natural man (*Ps.* cxxxvi. 10-22).

When the Lord came into the world and established a new church He instructed it in truths and made it fit for receiving life (*Ezek.* xxxvii. 11-14 *and prec.*).

Establish (*stabilio*) (*meaning*, *To make firm*, *Steadfast*, etc.).

May heaven and the church be established (*Ps.* cii. 25-28).

The Lord will not rest until He sees His church established (*Ps.* cxxxii. *t.*, 1-5).

The Word established in the church (*Ps.* xciii. 5).

(The state of conjunction, etc., of the new church) will be established (*stabile*) to eternity (*Jer.* xxxi. 35-37).

Esteem (*aestimo*).—They are esteemed for perverting and deceiving (*Jer.* v. 27, 28).

Eternity.—The Divine Human from eternity (*Ps.* lxxii. 17).

Unless the Father assist, no one will have eternal life (*Ps.* lxxxix. 46-48).

Eternal oneness with the Father (*Ps.* lxxxix. 26-29, 35-37).

The Lord reigns to eternity (*Ps.* cxlvi. 10).

The Lord's kingdom is eternal (*Ps.* cxlv. 13).

The kingdom is the Lord's to eternity (*Ps.* xlv. 6).

Worship of the Lord from love and faith from eternity and thereafter (*Ps.* lxxii. 5).

The state of conjunction, etc., of the new church will be stable to eternity (*Jer.* xxxi. 35-37).

Ethiopia.—"Ethiopia" means those who are willing to be in blind ignorance, etc. (*Isa.* xviii.).

Evangelization ⎫ (*see also* **Instruct**, **Teach**).
Gospel ⎭ Those who were of the Jewish nation were commanded to teach the Word to the nations round about, but they would not, and thus kept the Word among themselves alone (*Jonah* i. 1-3).

This gospel will be preached until it takes place (*Isa.* lxii. 6, 7).

The gospel will be preached when He is delivered (*Ps.* lxix. 29-31).

The Lord preached the gospel of the kingdom of God, and taught (*Ps.* xl. 9, 10).

Evil (*malum*) (*see also subsequent headings, also* **Infernal**).

Let them not do evils, but goods (*Ps.* lxxxii. 2-4).

If the evil man becomes good his evil is forgiven (*Ezek.* xxxiii. 12-16; *cf.* xviii. 21-23); this is of Divine justice (*Ezek.* xxxiii. 17-20).

The man who does not live ill is regenerated by the Word of the Lord; but he who lives ill perishes on the day of judgment (*Ps.* i. 1-5).

Those who commit evils, or act contrary to the goods and truths of the church, are condemned (*Ezek.* xviii. 10-13).

Those who are in truths and in good, and do evil, perish (*Jer.* xviii. 9, 10).

The last judgment upon those who are in evils (*Nahum* i. 1, 2).

Evils destroy those who have repudiated the Word, and have obeyed their own lusts (*Jer.* ix. 16).

Concerning thought with the intention of doing evil, that they also do it from the will (*Micah* ii. 1, 2).

They worship the Lord from evil and not from good (*Mal.* i. 7, 8).
External worship is of no avail, so long as evils are committed (*Ps.* l. 16–20).
Evils have destroyed truths (*Ezek.* v. 8–10).
Evils cause lack of knowledges of good and truth (*Isa.* iii. 1–12).
Evil due to knowledges of falsity confirmed by reasonings (*Isa.* lii. 4).
Evil does no harm—so maintain those who have adulterated the truths of the church (*Mal.* iii. 13–15).
Evil made to appear as good (*Isa.* xliv. 12–20; *Jer.* x. 3–5).
By calling evil good they have severed themselves from the church (*Mal.* ii. 17).
Evil from the sensual man has consumed all things of the church (*Joel* i. 1–4; *cf.* ii. 2, 3); it has destroyed the different things of the church (*Joel* i. 5–7).
Because they are interiorly evil and hence also become outwardly evil, destruction is at hand (*Jer.* xiii. 22).
From the beginning they have done exceeding great evil to the church (*Ps.* cxxix. *t.*, 1–3).
Evils have been with them from the beginning, although they had the Word, and doctrine from it (*Jer.* xxxii. 26–33).
They do evils of every kind (*Micah* ii. 8, 9).
They do evils, and therefore evil befalls them (*Ps.* l. [21,] 22).
Evils prevail (*Lam.* ii. 16, 17).
Nothing but evil (*Jer.* xlviii. 35–38).
Evil consummated (*Joel* iii. 13–15).
The hells among themselves devise evils against the Lord (*Ps.* xli. 4–7).
Protection from those who devise evil (*Ps.* xxxi. *t.*, 1–4).
Those who did evil to the church, after a vain effort, were compelled to retreat (*Ps.* cxxix. 4–8).
The Lord protects from evil (*Ps.* xxxvi. 11, 12).
The Lord rejects all evil and falsity from Himself (*Ps.* cxxxix. 19–22).
Evils of every kind dissipated by the Lord (*Ps.* cxxxvi. 10–22).
The Lord has nothing in common with those who are in evils, because He has been made one with His Divine (*Ps.* cxli. 3–5).
No evil in the Lord (*Ps.* vii. 3, 4, 8–10).
The Lord will save the new church from evils (*Ps.* lxvi. 6, 7).

Evil and Falsity (*see also* **Falsity and Evil, Removal**).
Evils and falsities infest (*Jer.* xxx. 12–15).
Evils and falsities acknowledged as goods and truths (*Jer.* v. 11, 12).
Evils and falsities the result of false reasonings and perverseness (*Isa.* xxxvi. 11, 12).
There is in the church nothing but evil and falsity from the falsified Word (*Hosea* iv. 1–3).
Evils and falsities are their worship (*Jer.* ii. 26, 27; 28).
The church will disperse all the evils and falsities of those who are in the mere sense of the letter and in external worship (*Ezek.* xxxix. 9, 10).
Every evil and falsity will be destroyed on the day of judgment (*Isa.* xxvii. 4, 5).
Evils and falsities will perish (*Isa.* xiii. 13–18).
Direful and horrid evils and falsities are in hell (*Isa.* xiii. 19–22).

Evil of Falsity (*see also* **Falsity of Evil**).
Evils of falsity have broken in upon them (*Jer.* v. 6).

Evil of Life.—Evil of life vastated the church (*Isa.* i. 1–8). .
Exhortation to repent of evil of life, and thus they will have good (*Isa.* i. 16–19).
Evil life in the church results from teachers regarding their own good only, and not the good of the church (*Ezek.* xxxiv. 5, 6); hence everything of the church is taken from them (*ib.* 7–10).

Evil Love (*see under* **Love**, *for* LOVE OF EVIL).
> To all who are in evil love and in falsities from such love in the church (*Ezek.* vi.).
> Diabolical loves have perverted the lowest sense of the Word (*Ezek.* viii. 7-10).
> How a worship in accordance with diabolical love was instituted (*Ezek.* viii. 11-18).
> Evil love has destroyed spiritual good (*Ezek.* xv. 4, 5).
> They will perish from evil love (*Ezek.* xv. 7, 8).
> Evil love has destroyed the external or natural church (*Ezek.* xx. 47, 48).
> All who trust in knowledges will perish through evil loves (*Ezek.* xxx. 6-9).
> All the truths of the Word and of doctrine perverted by evil loves (*Hosea* vii. 6-10).

Evil (the) (*malus*) (*see also* **Help, Wicked**).
> He who lives ill perishes on the day of judgment (*Ps.* i. 4, 5).
> The evil will not understand, but the good (*Dan.* xii. 10).
> The evil do not understand the co-operation of the Father with the Lord (*Ps.* xcii. 6).
> The evil infest the good (*Ps.* xvi. 3-5).
> However much the evil fight against the church, still it will be (*Ps.* xxxiii. 10, 11).
> The Lord's words, which are Divine, have become of no account with the evil (*Ps.* cxli. 6, 7); their evil thoughts and intentions, by which they themselves perish, do no harm (*ib.* 8).
> The evil do evil to the good and deny God, and are hypocrites and deceitful (*Ps.* x. 1-11).
> The Lord is blasphemed by the evil in the church (*Ps.* xliv. 13-16).
> The evil prevail over the good and destroy them (*Hab.* i. 12-17).
> Prayer to the Lord that the evil may be removed (*Jer.* xvii. 14-18).
> May the evil perish! (*Ps.* civ. 31-35).
> Comparison of the lot of the evil with the lot of the good; although the evil flourish for a short time, yet they perish and are cast down into hell; the good are saved, etc. (*Ps.* xxxvii.).
> Although the evil flourish, yet they perish (*Ps.* xcii. 7-9).
> The evil vaunt themselves and prosper (*Ps.* lxxiii. *t.*, 1-9); but they are nevertheless devastated and consumed (*ib.* 15-20, 27); they do not know this (*ib.* 21, 22).
> Let not the evil exalt themselves above the good (*Ps.* lxxv. 4-6); for the judgment comes, in which the evil perish and the good are saved (*ib.* 7; lxxvi. 7-10, 12); the evil will then perish through direful falsities (lxxv. 8, 10).
> The good separated from the evil (*Isa.* ii. 22).
> The evil in the church will be separated by the Lord (*Ezek.* xxxiv. 16, 17).
> The evil recede (*Isa.* xlv. 20).
> The evil have closed against themselves the way to all mercy (*Ezek.* viii. 17, 18).
> The Lord rejects the evil (*Ps.* ci. 4, 5); they will perish when He comes (*ib.* 8).
> At the coming of the Lord the evil will perish (*Isa.* xl. 1-5).
> The evil will perish as a consequence of justice (*Ps.* xi. 6, 7).
> The evil will perish at the judgment on account of evils and falsities of many kinds (*Zeph.* ii. 4-6).
> The evil will perish and are to be cast into hell (*Zeph.* iii. 6-8).
> The evil will be cast into hell, because they have annihilated the Word (*Mal.* iv. 1, 3, 4).

The evil cast into hell (*Isa.* ii. 10, 19–21).
The evil lie in wait against the Lord and will perish (*Ps.* lxiv. *t.*, 1–8).
Uprising of the evil (*Ps.* lxxiv. 22, 23).
The evil rise up against the Lord and wish to slay Him, but cannot hurt Him (*Ps.* xvii. 6–13).
The evil rise up and wish to kill (*Ps.* xciv. 20, 21); but through help from His Divine they will perish (*ib.* 22, 23).
Prayer to the Lord to the Father for help against the evil (*Ps.* v. *t.*, 1–10).
Prayer to the Father for help against the evil (*Ps.* lv. 19–21, 23).
The Lord fights for the good against the evil (*Ps.* xi. *t.*, 1–5).
The Lord's combats against the evil, and their dispersion (*Zech.* xiv. 1–5).
The evil have been conquered and cast into hell (*Ps.* ix. 15–17).
The evil perish (*Ps.* xxxiv. 12–22; xxxvi. 11, 12).
Destruction (*interitus*) of the evil (*Isa.* lxvi. 6).

Exalt (*see* **Self-exaltation**).

Examine (*lustro*).—The Lord will examine the church (*Hab.* iii. 5–7).
The church was instituted solely with the Israelitish nation, therefore falsities and evils must be examined there (*Amos* iii. 1, 2).

Excommunication (*Dan.* iii. 13–21).

Exemption (*see* **Deliver**).

Exhortation (*exhortatio, hortatio*) (*see also* **Warning**).
The Lord to those with whom the church has been instituted; *general subject* (*Jer.* xxv.).
Exhortation to repent (*Ps.* iv. 4–8).
Let them be converted (*Amos* v. 14, 15).
Exhortation to be converted to the Lord (*Hosea* xiv. 1–3; *Amos* iv. 12, 13).
Exhortation to be converted to the Lord, to repent, and to be wise (*Joel* ii. 12–17).
Exhortation to be converted, because the Lord wishes the salvation of all (*Ezek.* xviii. 30–32).
Exhortation to be converted and to reflect on the last time and the Coming of the Lord, etc. (*Joel* i. 14 *and fol.*).
Let them not destroy the few truths still left (*Jer.* vi. 8, 9).
Exhortation to be converted and not falsify truths (*Hosea* xii. 6, 7).
Exhortation to abstain from the falsifications of the Word, etc. (*Hosea* ii. 1–4 *and fol.*).
Exhortation (*hortatio*) to reject falsity and to receive truth, that there may conjunction and a church (*Jer.* iii. 12–14).
Exhortation (*hortatio*) by the Lord to repent, and live according to His commandments in the Word (*Jer.* xxvi. 1–5).
Exhortation (*hortatio*) to repent of the evil of life (*Isa.* i. 16–19; xxxviii. 16–20).
Exhortation to desist from evils and to acknowledge the Lord, etc. (*Jer.* iv. 1, 2).
Exhortation to the church that adulterates the truths and profanes the goods of the church, to desist (*Isa.* xlviii.).
Exhortation (*hortatio*) to seek the Lord, lest all things of the church perish by evils and falsities (*Amos* v. 4–9).

Expect (*see also* **Lord**, COMING OF).
The coming of the Lord and redemption is expected (*Ps.* cxxx. 5–8).
The church that expects the Lord asks, etc. (*Jer.* xii. 1–3).
Those who are out of the church expect compassion that they may become a church (*Ps.* cii. 12–18).

Explain (*explico*).—He must explain the sense of the letter (*Ezek.* iii. 22, 23).

Explore (*see also* **Examine**).
Exploration of their quality as respects the Word (*Ezek.* ix. 1–3).

Expel (see **Drive out**).
Extension.—Extension of the Lord's dominon (*Ps.* lxxii. 8–12).
External (see also **Interior**; **Natural external**; **Word**, EXTERNAL OF; **Worship**, EXTERNAL OF; **Outermosts**).
  The Lord to those who are in externals (*Jer.* xvii. 19, 20).
  Those who are in externals will draw near to the new church (*Micah* iv. 6, 7).
  The simple are in externals of doctrine (*Jer.* xxxix. 11–14).
  An internal and an external church will be instituted (*Ps.* cviii. 8, 9).
  The Lord, to those who are in externals (*Jer.* xvii. 19, 20).
  Externals will perish from internals if they do not acknowledge the Divine of the Lord (*Jer.* xvii. 27).
  Externals without an internal (*Ezek.* xxxviii. 1, 2; 8–16).
  Externals of the church restored (*Isa.* lxi. 5, 8).
  The church grew from externals to externals (*Amos* vii. 1); when externals were lost, there was a restoration (*ib.* 2–6); when inmosts were reached, all things were destroyed, etc. (*ib.* 7–9).
  External of the church also vastated (*Lam.* iv. 21, 22).
  Every external of the church has been devastated (*Zech.* xi. 1–3).
  An external without an internal is of no use, and still less when the external has been falsified (*Haggai* ii. 10–14).
  Externals of the church destroyed by self-intelligence (*Isa.* xxii. 8–12).
  Judgment upon those who are in externals without internals (*Jer.* ix. 25, 26).
  From the conjunction of truth and good of the natural man there would be only an external church, which is rational (*Gen.* xvi.).
  An external or natural church which can be in the light of truth (*Ezek.* xx. 45, 46) is destroyed by evil love (*ib.* 47, 48).
  A church internal and external (*Ps.* lx. 6–9).
External good (see also **External truth**).
  External good and truth (*Ezek.* xl. 35–49).
External man (see **Natural man**).
External natural (see also **Nations**).
  External natural (*Ezek.* xxiii. 3, 4).
External truth.—The Lord has instituted a church with those who could be in external truth, but who were not in external good; all external good has been destroyed, and hence also external truth (*Mal.* i. 1–4).
  The Lord in His Divine Human alone teaches the church external and internal truths (*Ps.* cxxxv. 6, 7).
  Devastation does not come to an end through outward mourning (*Jer.* iv. 8).

Faculty (see **Capacity**).
Fail (see **Want** (*deficio*)).
Faith (see also **Believe, Falsities of Faith, Truths of Faith, Trust**).
  Worship of the Lord from love and faith (*Ps.* lxxii. 5).
Faith from charity (see also **Truths from good**).
  A new church (the Christian) will be established which will be in faith from charity (*Dan.* xi. 5).
  Faith of charity will be received in the new church (*Dan.* xii. 1).
  Those who are in that faith will come into heaven, but not the rest (*Dan.* xii. 2, 3); and they will become intelligent (*ib.* 4).
Faith Alone.—The fourth state of the church was when there was faith alone, which destroyed all things of the church (*Dan.* vii. 7), and which was confirmed by the sense of the letter of the Word (*Dan.* vii. 8).
  The fourth or last state of the church is faith alone confirmed by **reasonings** and by the Word falsified, etc. (*Dan.* vii. 19–21).

Revelation respecting such as are in faith alone (*Dan.* x. 7–21).
The ascendency of faith alone in the Christian Church fully described (*see Dan.* xi. and xii.).
Faith separate from charity meant by the "King of the North" (*Dan.* xi.).
Faith alone will prevail through reasonings by which it will dissipate the truths of doctrine, etc. (*Dan.* viii. 6–10).
Faith alone will also destroy by reasonings from the natural man (*Dan.* xi. 42, 43).
Those who are in faith alone will destroy knowledges (*cognitiones*) from the Word (*Zech.* ix. 5, 6).
All those who are in faith alone, so-called, will lapse into mere falsities, until they have no knowledges of truth and good; and they will perish on the day of judgment (*Jer.* xlvii.).
Faith alone will wholly destroy charity (*Dan.* viii. 5).
Faith alone will destroy the worship of the Lord together with Divine truths (*Dan.* viii. 11, 12).
Faith alone will destroy the church and despise the Lord (*Dan.* viii. 20–25).
Faith alone destroys all fear of God, and the whole church (*Dan.* xi. 36, 37).
Faith alone has destroyed the church (*Dan.* vii. 23, 24).
Judgment upon those who are in faith alone and have thereby destroyed the truths of the Word and of doctrine (*Joel* iii. 4–8).
Those who are in faith alone will be judged, etc. (*Dan.* vii. 26, 27).
Faith alone was wholly destroyed (*Dan.* vii. 11).

Faithful (*see* **Salvation**).

Fall.—Fall and end of Most Ancient Church as they departed from the celestial to the natural man, from this they had intelligence from what was their own in place of intelligence from the Lord (*Gen.* iii.).
When the Lord comes He will raise up the fallen church (*Ps.* lxxv. *t.*, 1–3).

Fallacy.—Fallacies of the sensual man and reasonings therefrom destroy and poison (*Jer.* viii. 16, 17).

False heavens (*see* **Seeming heavens**).

Falsespeaker (*Isa.* xxxii. 6–8).

Falsifiers.—Those who do not worship the Lord alone are falsifiers (*Isa.* xliv. 9–11).
Prayer of the Lord for deliverance from falsifiers and hypocrites who purpose evil against Him in the perverted church (*Ps.* cxl. *t.*, 1–8); they perish through their falsities and evils (*ib.* 9–11).
Prayer for help against falsifiers (*Ps.* v. *t.*, 1–12).

Falsify (*see also* **Adulteration, Drunkard, Word**).
Affection for falsifying (*Ezek.* xiii. 17).
From affections for falsifying arise persuasions of falsity (*Ezek.* xiii. 18, 19).
The spiritual church falsified truths (*Jer.* iii. 6, 7; 7–9).
Truth turned into falsity (*Haggai* ii. 15–17).
They have falsified truths (*Jer.* iii. 1, 2).
The further falsification of truth (*Jer.* xli. 1–3).
Because they have falsified and adulterated truth and good there is no longer truth and good and life in them (*Isa.* lvii. 3 *and prec.*).
Falsification of all truth consequent on denial of the Lord (*Ezek.* xxiii. 35).
Abolition of worship by falsification of truth (*Jer.* xli. 10).
They have falsified the truths of the Word (*Lam.* iv. 12–14).
Falsification of truths of the Word by reasonings from knowledges (*scientifica*) (*Ezek.* xxiii. 5–8).
They loved things falsified by knowledges (*scientifica*) (*Jer.* xliv. 15–19).
Those who have falsified the knowledges (*cognitiones*) of truth by means

of reasonings and knowledges (*scientifica*), and have thus destroyed the church, will utterly perish (*Zeph.* ii. 12–15).

Of those who falsify the truths of the Word and of the church, who are meant by the "Children of Ammon." *General subject* (*Jer.* xlix. 1–6).

Respecting those who have falsified and adulterated the Word; *full description* (*Nahum* iii. 1–19).

Falsifications of the Word and direful evils have destroyed the church (*Ps.* lxxix. *t.*, 1–4).

They falsify all the truths and goods of the Word, and yet they say that God is with them (*Micah* iii. 9–11).

They fight to confirm evils and falsities by falsifications of the Word (*Jer.* ii. 33–35).

Falsification of truth is the source of evils of life and falsities of doctrine (*Isa.* lix. 3, 4).

There is in the church nothing but evil and falsity from the falsified Word (*Hosea* iv. 1–3).

Because they have falsified the Word they are no longer able to understand truth, but will behold falsity (*Hosea* iv. 10–12). For this reason their worship will be from falsities (*ib.* 13).

Falsification of all things of the church (*Amos* iv. 9).

In the church is nothing but what is falsified and evil therefrom; why (*Jer.* ix. 2, 3).

Because they are in evils and in things falsified there will be a lack of knowledges (*cognitiones*) of good and truth (*Isa.* iii. 1–7, 8–12).

Of those who falsify the external of the Word, meant by "Edom" (*Jer.* xlix. 7–22).

Falsification of the sense of the letter (*Ezek.* v. 1, 2).

Falsification and adulteration of the sense of the letter of the Word, represented (*Ezek.* iv. 9–16).

Those who have falsified the sense of the letter of the Word will be cast into hell (*Ezek.* xxi. 28–32).

In hell with those who have falsified the sense of the letter of the Word (*Ezek.* xxxii. 26–30).

Falsification and adulteration of the Word by the Jews (*Hosea* xii. 8–14).

Falsification of truth with the Jewish nation (*Micah* vi. 12).

Falsification of the Word with the Jewish nation represented by the prophet Hosea (*Hosea* i. 1–3).

Those who represented the things of the church falsified and adulterated the truths of the Word (*Hosea* v. 1–3).

Falsification of the representatives of the church (*Micah* i. 4–7).

Falsifications of the Word will be removed (*Joel* iii. 18, 19).

Doctrine of the church falsified (*Ezek.* xiii.).

Those who hatch out doctrine from their own intelligence, or falsify doctrine (*Ezek.* xiii. 1–3).

Doctrine has been repudiated and falsified by reasonings from scientifics (*Jer.* xxxvii. 11–16).

Falsification of doctrine meant by "Elam" (*Jer.* xlix. 34–39). The falsities will be dispersed (*ib.* 34–36). They will perish (*ib.* 37, 38), except those who have not falsified (*ib.* 39).

Remnant of doctrine will be falsified, but not as yet (*Jer.* xxxix. 15–18).

Remnants of doctrine have been utterly falsified so that there is no more truth in them (*Jer.* xxxix. 4–8).

In hell with those who have falsified truths of doctrine (*Ezek.* xxxii. 24, 25).

Falsity (*falsum*) (*see subsequent headings. See also* **Captivity, Doctrine, Fear, Heresy, Ignorance, Insane, Love, Perish, Perversion, Reasoning, Rejection**).

Falsities of the church represented (*Ezek.* iv. 1, 2).
Those who are instructed by the preacher concerning falsities and do not take heed perish (*Ezek.* xxxiii. 1–5).
When the preacher sees falsities and does not give instruction concerning them, he perishes (*Ezek.* xxxiii. 6, 7).
Falsities arise from thinking that the church consists in knowledges (*cognitiones*), which falsities destroy the ultimates of doctrine (*Ezek.* xxvi. 3, 4).
Those who are in mere knowledge enter into falsities of every kind (*Isa.* xix. 1–4).
Falsity will break in (*Isa.* xxviii. 1, 2).
Falsities are breaking in (*Jer.* iv. 13).
One falsity comes from another even until there is nothing but falsity (*Jer.* ix. 4–6).
Falsities grow by reasonings originating in the delights of the natural man (*Hosea* xii. 1).
Falsities will gain strength and pervert still farther, until the church perishes (*Isa.* xxix. 5, 6).
Falsities seized upon in place of truths (*Isa.* xvii. 9–14).
They fight from falsities against truths (*Ps.* lix. 7).
Falsities contrary to truths of the church, from perversion of goods and truths (*Jer.* i. 14, 15).
Falsities for truths (*Jer.* xiii. 12, 13; 20).
Falsities succeed in place of truths and goods, where there has been merely external worship (*Ezek.* xxxviii. 20–23).
Falsities not acknowledged to be such (*Jer.* vi. 15).
Falsity made to appear as truth in the third state of the church (*Dan.* vii. 6).
Falsity made to appear as truth (*Isa.* xliv. 12–20).
Falsity will appear as truth (*Isa.* xxix. 7, 8).
Falsities called truths of the church (*Jer.* viii. 11, 12).
Because of falsities they are unable to see truths (*Isa.* xxix. 9–12).
Falsities of every kind cause much of the church to perish (*Jer.* xliv. 1–6).
Falsities beyond measure owing to lack of truth and good (*Isa.* li. 19, 20).
When falsities take possession of the church intercession will not be of any avail (*Ezek.* xiv. 17, 18).
They possess nothing but falsity (*Jer.* xxiii. 15).
Falsity confirmed from the Word (*Jer.* xxiii. 16, 17).
Delights of falsity will destroy the senses of the Word (*Isa.* xxii. 13–15).
Degrees of interiority of falsities (*Ezek.* xxi. 8–11; 14–17).
Falsity from the sensual man has consumed all things of the church (*Joel* i. 4; *cf.* ii. 2, 3).
Falsities have destroyed goods (*Ezek.* v. 8–10).
Falsities destroy the church (*Zech.* xi. 6).
Falsities cause the church to perish (*Ezek.* xx. 45 to xxi. 32).
Their rejecting the Lord and hatching falsities is horrible (*Jer.* ii. 12, 13).
Falsity will continue until the end (*Isa.* xxxii. 19).
The Lord will destroy all falsities by the truths of the Word (*Zech.* xii. 6, 7).
Falsities of doctrine and worship will both be utterly destroyed (*Zech.* xiii. 2, 3).
At the judgment the evil will perish through direful falsities (*Ps.* lxxv. 8, 10).
Those who are in falsities will recede (*Isa.* xlv. 16).
The Israelites forsaken by the Lord and delivered over to their falsities and evils (*Ps.* lxxviii. 59–64).
All falsities dissipated by the spiritual kingdom of the Lord (*Ps.* xlviii. 4–7).

SUMMARIES OF THE INTERNAL SENSE.

Falsities taken away and given to those who contemptuously reject the good (*Isa.* li. 21–23).
All who are in falsities will be removed (*Ps.* xcvii. 7).
Falsity must be rejected and truth received (*Jer.* iii. 12–14).
Falsities will be shaken off (*Isa.* xi. 13–15).
Others who know the Lord, who reject falsities and put away things falsified (*Isa.* viii. 17–21).
After the destruction of the former church those who are to be led out of falsities are to be brought near (*Jer.* xxxiii. 6–9).
Infernal falsity from the former church will infest the new church (*Zech.* iii. 1, 2).
Falsities will not enter and destroy the new church but will be destroyed, however much they may infest (*Micah* iv. 10–13; v. 1).
Falsities will no longer hurt (*Isa.* xi. 16).
Falsities will profit nothing when the Lord comes (*Hab.* ii. 18, 19).
Falsities will not be remembered. Why? (*Isa.* liv. 4, 5).
There will be no falsity with those who love truth and good (*Isa.* xxxii. 20).
He who fights against the truths of the new church, will plunge into falsities of every kind (*Zech.* xiv. 12).
The Lord will protect them from falsities that are from hell (*Zech.* x. 11).
Falsities begin to destroy the new church (*Ps.* lxxx. 12, 13).
Falsity will invade the Christian Church and destroy it (*Dan.* ix. 26).

Falsity and Evil (*see also* **Confirmation, Desire, Doctrine, Evil and Falsity, Infestation, Own, Perversion, Protection**).
Men of the church of themselves are nothing but falsity and evil (*Isa.* xli. 28, 29).
It is represented that those who are in falsities and evils can be reformed by the Lord (*Jer.* xviii. 1–4).
Falsities and evils of the church must be revealed (*Ezek.* iii. 18–21).
Falsities and evils (see *Jer.* xviii. 5–8, *under* **Conversion**).
Falsities and evils lead astray (*Isa.* xi. 10–12).
Falsities and evils cause lack of everything of the church (*Lam.* v. 1–9).
In the last time of the church falsities and evils will combat amongst themselves and against truths and goods (*Micah* vii. 5, 6).
Falsity and evil in place of truth and good, and they destroy (*Jer.* vi. 3–5).
Falsities and evils of every kind mixed with truths and goods (*Ezek.* xxii. 17–22).
Affections for falsity and evil with those who profane truths (*Isa.* xlvi. 1).
Falsities and evils will consume all things of the church (*Isa.* xxxiii. 11, 12).
Nothing but falsity and evil in the natural (*Jer.* xlvi. 13–19).
Nothing but falsity and evil in the church (*Ezek.* xvi. 1, 2).
Falsity and evil in place of the church (*Isa.* xxiv. 1–13).
Falsities and evils cause destruction (*Isa.* v. 18–30).
Horrid falsities and evils to eternity (*Isa.* xxxiv. 9–15).
Falsity und evil given to the Lord when He desired the good and truth of the church (*Ps.* lxix. 21).
Those who are in falsities and evils will perish (*Nahum* i. 8–11).
Falsities and evils will be destroyed by the Lord from His Divine (*Jer.* i. 9, 10).
Falsities and evils to be removed by the Lord (*Ps.* xlvii. 3).
Those who are not in falsities and evils will be in the church (*Ps.* **xxiv.** 4–6).
Protection from falsities and evils (*Isa.* ix. 6, 7).
Falsities and evils rejected by the new church (*Isa.* xxxi. 7).
Falsities and evils will not hurt the new church (*Isa.* xliii. 2).

Falsities and evils will be no longer in the new church (*Micah* iv. 3, 4).
Falsities and evils will no longer destroy (*Isa.* lxv. 25).
Falsity of Doctrine —Falsities of doctrine will be dispersed (*Jer.* xlix. 34-36).
There will be no more falsity of doctrine (*Zech.* xiii. 4, 5).
Falsity of Evil.—Heretofore no protection from falsities of evil which are from hell (*Zech.* viii. 10).
Those who have the Word are in falsities of evil and will perish (*Zech.* x. 2, 3).
Those who are in celestial good will fight against falsities of evils. So also will those who are in spiritual good (*Zech.* x. 4-6).
The Lord entirely removed falsities of evil when the church was instituted among them (*Amos* ii. 9-11).
Those who pervert truths fall into all falsities of evil (*Ezek.* xxxii. 3-8).
Because they have repudiated the Word and obeyed their own lusts, they are in falsities of evil (*Jer.* ix. 13-15).
Falsities of evil destroy those who have repudiated the Word, and have obeyed their own lusts (*Jer.* ix. 13-16).
The posterity of the Jewish Church will perish, because they are in falsities of evil (*Ps.* cix. 13-20).
Falsity of evil will destroy all things of the church by various insanities (*Joel* ii. 4-9).
The teacher and the leader destroy all things of the church by falsities of evil (*Zech.* xi. 15-17).
Falsities of evil have destroyed everything of the church (*Zech.* i. 18-21).
Falsities of evil worshipped (*Jer.* iii. 10, 11).
Falsities of evil cause those who were of the church to perish (*Ps.* lviii. t., 1-9).
Destruction of the church in the lowest heaven by falsities and evil (*Jer.* vi. 1, 2).
Falsities of evil and evils of falsity will dissipate influx on the day of judgment (*Joel* ii. 30, 31).
Those who lie in wait for the Lord will perish by falsities of evil (*Ps.* lxiii. 9, 10).
Those who are in falsities of evil will perish (*Isa.* xxx. 27, 28).
Those who are in evil love and in falsities from such love in the church will perish by reason of falsities (*Ezek.* vi. 1-3).
All will perish by means of falsities of evil (*Ezek.* xxi. 4, 5; xxxiii. 27-29).
The Lord in His Divine Human delivers the natural man from the falsities of evil (*Ps.* cxxxv. 8-13).
The Lord delivers the natural man from falsities of evil (*Ps.* cxxxvi. 10-22).
The Lord will, by his Divine truth, dissipate the falsities of evil (*Hab.* iii. 8-9).
Falsities of evil will be dispersed by the Lord (*Ps.* ii. 9).
From the Lord the new church is kept from falsities of evil (*Ps.* cxxv.).
Protection of the church from falsities of evils (*Ps.* cv. 8-15).
The church will be in power and light against falsities of evil; why (*Ps.* cxxxii. 17, 18 *and prec.*).
Those who are of the new church will have no falsity of evil (*Jer.* xxxi. 29, 30).
No falsity of evil will be in the new church (*Zech.* xiv. 10, 11).
Falsity of Faith.—Beginning to be imbued with falsities of faith (*Jer.* xl. 13-16).
Falsities of faith (*Ezek.* xxxv.).
Abolition of worship by falsities of faith (*Jer.* xli. 4-7).
Devastation of the church by falsities of faith (*Ezek.* xxv. 15-17).

Falsity from Ignorance (*see also* **Ignorance**).
  Lamentation by the nations who are in falsities from ignorance, because they do not have the Word (*Ps.* cxxxvii. 1-6).
  Those in falsities from ignorance will draw near to the Lord (*Isa.* xi. 10-12).
  Those who are in falsities from ignorance will be received by the Lord, and their falsities will be removed (*Nahum* i. 12-14).
  The Lord teaches and leads all who are in falsities from ignorance, and who desire truths (*Ps.* cxlvi. 7-9).
  Falsities of ignorance will be in the new church, but they will be removed, and truths will be given in their place (*Zech.* iii. 3-5).
  The new church is in falsities of ignorance, but in desire for truth and good (*Ps.* cvii. 4-8).
  From His Divine the Lord will set in order heaven and the church for those who have been in falsities of ignorance (*Isa.* li. 16-18).
  Those who are in falsities from ignorance are to be introduced, and their worship will be accepted (*Isa.* lvi. 6, 7).

Father (*see also* **Adopt**).
  If fathers are evil, the offspring are not condemned on that account (*Ezek.* xviii. 1-4).
  Fathers of the Israelitish nation (*Ezek.* xix. 1, 2).
  Fathers of the Jewish Church (*Ezek.* xx. 4).

Father (*see* **Lord**, THE DIVINE OF).

Fear.—The prophet not to fear their obduracy (*Ezek.* iii. 8, 9).
  It is from their hardness of heart that they have no fear (*Ezek.* iv. 3).
  Because the Jewish nation has destroyed the church, neither does it fear God (*Ps.* xciv. 3-11).
  Fear of God destroyed by faith alone (*Dan.* xi. 36, 37).
  Fear of the last judgment (*Isa.* xxxiii. 13, 14).
  Fear of destruction does not cause them to refrain (*Jer.* xliv. 7-10).
  They should fear the Lord, for He has protection from the Father (*Ps.* iv. 3).
  Let not those be feared who wish to prevail by their own intelligence and by artifices (*Jer.* x. 1, 2).
  Falsities from hell will no longer be feared (*Isa.* liv. 14, 15).
  He that trusts in the Lord and lives well will have no fear of the hells, however much they may rise up against him (*Ps.* cxii.).
  There will be no fear of the hells, for the Lord guards, etc. (*Ps.* xxiii. 4, 5).
  No fear of the hells nor of infestations therefrom (*Isa.* li. 12, 13; *Ps.* xlvi. 8, 9).
  There will be no fear from the hells, when the Divine has been made one with the Human (*Ps.* xci. 13-16).
  No fear of the hells with the Lord (*Ps.* xxvii. *t.*, 1-3).

Feign (*see* **Pretend**).

Felicity } (*felicitas*) (*see also* **Happy** (*beatus*)).
Happiness } The new church will have felicities from their trust in the Lord (*Joel* ii. 21-25).
  Heavenly happiness is only through the coming of the Lord (*Isa.* lv. 12).
  Happy is he who esteems holy the union of the Divine and the Human, and of the Lord with the church (*Isa.* lvi. 2).

Figs.—Who are meant by the "two baskets of figs" (*Jer.* xxiv. 1-3).

Fight (*see* **Combat**; **Lord**, COMBATS OF).

Fight against (*repugno*).—Howsoever much the evil may fight against the church, still it will be (*Ps.* xxxiii. 10, 11).

Firm (to make) (*see* **Establish** (*stabilo*)).

First (*see also* **Law, Ultimates**).
  First things of heaven and the church (*Ps.* xix. 5, 6).

First thing of the church among the fathers of the Israelitish nation was destructive of all things of the church (*Ezek.* xix. 1, 2).

Goods and truths from firsts to lasts have been perverted (*Jer.* v. 30, 31).

Fish (*see Jonah* i. 17, ii. 1-10).

Flattery.—Flattery (from the doctrine of falsity) of those who are devastated as to truth (*Jer.* xiv. 13).

Flesh.—" Flesh ", signifies the people (*Ezek.* xi. 1-3).

Flood.—" Flood " means the destruction of the Most Ancient Church (*Gen.* vii.).

Flourish (*see also* **Prosper**).

The church which awaits the Lord asks why the wicked flourish (*Jer.* xii. 1, 2).

Although the evil flourish, yet they perish (*Ps.* xcii. 7-9).

Although the evil flourish for a short time, yet they perish, and are cast down into hell (*Ps.* xxxvii.).

A church will arise and flourish (*Ps.* lxxxv. 8-13).

The church will flourish from the Lord's omnipotence (*Ps.* xcii. 12-14).

Those who trust in the Lord will flourish (*Ps.* lii. 8, 9).

Foresee (*see also* **Predict**).

It is foreseen that all things of the church will be perverted (*Jer.* xxxviii. 22, 23).

Foretell (*see also* **Predict**).

Forgive (*condono*).—They cannot be forgiven (*Jer.* xviii. 23).

The Lord forgave the backsliding (*Ps.* lxxviii. 38-40).

If the evil man becomes good, his evil is forgiven (*Ezek.* xxxiii. 12-16).

—— (*remitto*).—Prayers of the church that their sins may be forgiven from mercy (*Ps.* xxv. 7-11).

Form.—The Lord was formed by the Father, and from Him He is pure (*Ps.* cxxxix. 13-15).

The Lord forms the church (*Zech.* xii. 1).

The Lord is the former of the church (*Ps.* c. *t.*, 1-3).

Former Church (*see also* **Destroy, Old Church, Jews,** *etc.*).

The former church will be reproved because of its evils, etc. (*Jer.* xxxii. 26-33).

In the former church there is nothing but falsity and evil of falsity (*Isa.* ii. 6-9).

Prayer to the Lord that the former church may be restored (*Lam.* v. 19-22).

In the former church was the external without an internal, truth being turned into falsity, etc. (*Haggai* ii. 10-19).

All things of the former church will be destroyed (*Haggai* ii. 20-22).

The former church rejected (*Isa.* l. 1).

The former church will be destroyed (*Ps.* cviii. 7).

Forsake (*desero*) (*see also* **Despair**).

They forsook the Lord by reason of their self-glorification (*Hosea* xiii. 5, 6).

The Lord is in the last state of temptations, as if He were forsaken (*Ps.* xliv. 24, 25).

Prayer to the Father that He be not forsaken (*Ps.* xxxix. 12, 13).

Prayer of the Lord to the Father that he be not forsaken (*Ps.* xxii. *t.*, 1-5, 8, 11).

Supplication (*precatio*) that He be not forsaken (*Ps.* xxii. 19-21).

Forsake (*relinquo*).—The Israelites were forsaken by the Lord and delivered over to their falsities and evils; this of themselves (*Ps.* lxxviii. 59-64).

The Jewish Church was forsaken by the Lord from the beginning, because it was without any thing of the church (*Ezek.* xvi. 3-6).

The church among the Jews was forsaken by the Lord and destroyed (*Ps.* cvi. 40-43).

They have not been forsaken by the Lord, but they have forsaken Him (*Jer.* ii. 31, 32).
They have forsaken the Lord (*Jer.* xiii. 24, 25; xix. 4, 5); the consequence (*Jer.* v. 19, 20; xiii. 24-26).
Lamentation of the Lord that He has been forsaken, together with the church (*Ps.* lx. *t.*, 1-3).
Let not the hells say that He has been forsaken by God (*Ps.* lxxi. 9-11).

Found (*fundo*).—The church is founded on the sense of the letter of the Word (*Ps.* civ. 5-9).

Four.—Four successive states of the church revealed (*Dan.* vii. 1-14; 17, 18).

Free (*see also* **Deliver, Slave**).
Those who are of the church will be free (*Jer.* xxxiv. 8-11).

Free Will.—The offspring are not condemned on their father's account (*Ezek.* xviii.).

Fructification (*see* **Multiplication**).

Fulfil (*see* **Prophecy**).
Predictions are to be fulfilled (*Ps.* xcviii. 3).
The Lord fulfilled the Law, or the Word, from its firsts to its lasts, etc. (*Ps.* cxix.).

Garment.—They have divided the garments of the Lord, or dissipated the truths of His Word (*Ps.* xxii. 18).

Gather (*congrego*).—Through the Lord's enduring by power from His Divine, a church will be gathered together from all parts (*Ps.* xxii. 26-31).
They are to be gathered together out of every religion, and taught (*Zech.* x. 7-10).

Gentile (*see* **Church, Draw near, Establish, Ignorance, Nations, Others, Outside**).
Those who are far from truths will draw near (*Isa.* xlix. 12).
Those who are remote from truths will trust in Him and acknowledge Him (*Isa.* l. 10).
Strangers who esteem the union of the Divine and the Human holy, to be received in preference to others (*Isa.* lvi. 4, 5).
Those with whom the church was not previously will have many truths of the church (*Isa.* liv. 1-3).

Genuine Truth.—Though genuine truths have been given them, yet they have become devastated (*Jer.* ii. 21).

Gift.—Gifts from the Lord (*Ps.* cxlviii. 13, 14).

Girdle.—The "girdle of linen" represented the truth of the church, etc. (*Jer.* xiii. 1-7).

Gladness (*laetitia*) ⎫ (*see also* **Joy**).
Rejoice (*laetor*) ⎭ Those who are with the Lord will be glad from His power (*Ps.* xxi. 13).
Because they rejoice at the destruction of the church, they will pervert truths (*Ezek.* xxv. 6, 7).

Glory (*see also* **Boast**).
Glory belongs to the Lord alone (*Ps.* xcvi. 1-9).
The Lord has glory from His Divine (*Ps.* xxi. *t.*, 1-6).
God has no glory from the hells (*Ps.* lxxxviii. 10-12).

Glorification (*see* **Lord,** GLORIFICATION OF).

Glorification (*see also* **Confession, Song of Praise**).
Glorifying the Lord because of the doctrine of truth from Him (*Isa.* xxvi. 1-4).

Go away (*see* **Depart** (*abeo*)).

Go back (*see* **Depart** (*recedo*)).

Go forth (*exeo*).—The Divine truth will go forth in every direction (*Ps.* xix. *t.*, 1-4).

God (*see* **Fear, Lord, Name of God, Omniscience**, *etc.*).
> They will know their God when He comes into the world (*Isa.* lii. 6, 7).
> Doctrine concerning God given by the Lord (*Isa.* xlix. 1-3).
> The Lord is the only God (*Ps.* xviii. 31).
> The Lord alone is God (*Isa.* xlv. 21, 22; *Hosea* xiii. 4).
> The Lord alone is God and Lord (*Ps.* cxxxvi. 1-3).
> There is no other God but the Lord (*Isa.* xliv. 8).
> The Lord Himself is the God of heaven (*Isa.* xlv. 12).
> The Lord will be the God of the church (*Isa.* liv. 4, 5).
> The Lord will be the God of the new church (*Jer.* xxx. 21, 22; *Jer.* xxxi. 1).
> The Lord, after being afflicted, became the God of heaven and earth (*Ps.* cv. 19-22).
> The Lord alone is the God of heaven and earth (*Isa.* xliv. 23, 24; xlviii. 12, 13).
> The Lord is the God of heaven and the church (*Ps.* xcvii. 8, 9; cxlvi. 5; cxxxiv. 2, 3).
> The Lord is the God of the church (*Micah* v. 2; *Ps.* xcix. 1, 2; cxxxv. 19-21).
> The Lord is God from whom are all truths and goods (*Jer.* v. 21-24).
> God sees all things (*Ps.* xciv. 3-11).
> God and not man establishes the church (*Ps.* xliv. 5-8).
> In the beginning of the Babylonish religion, the God of heaven was worshipped (*Dan.* ii. 46-49).
> They falsify all the truths and goods of the Word, and yet they say, that God is with them (*Micah* iii. 9-11).
>
> WORSHIP OF OTHER GODS.
>
> Denial of God (*Ps.* x. 1-11).
> They do not acknowledge God (*Ps.* xiv. 4, 5).
> Other worship than that of the Lord forbidden (*Jer.* xxv. 4-7).
> The perverted church worships another god (*Ezek.* xxxiii. 21-26).
> The church among the children of Israel worship another god (*Ps.* lxxxi. 8-11).
> Worship of another god (*Ezek.* xxxiii. 21-26; *Hosea* x. 4, 5).
> Worship of other gods (*Jer.* xi. 11-13).
> Faith alone worships another god than the Lord (*Dan.* xi. 38, 39).
> Because they did not worship the Lord, but another god, goods and truths will be vastated (*Hosea* ii. 9-13).
> Those who have worshipped another god will perish (*Hosea* xiii. 16).
> Worship of another god, whence came profanation, and therefore they will perish (*Mal.* ii. 11, 12).
> Worship of men (*Dan.* vi. 4-9).

Gog.—Those who are in the mere sense of the letter of the Word, and in a worship therefrom, which is external without an internal, are meant by "Gog" (*Ezek.* xxxviii. 1, 2 *and fol.*; xxxix. 1-6). They will come into the church, but will perish (*Ezek.* xxxix. 1-6 *and fol.*).

Good (*bonum*) (*see subsequent headings. See also* **Celestial, Good (the), Multiplication, Natural Good, Spiritual Good, Salvation**).
> Good itself is the conjunction of good and truth, for the good of love flows into the truths of the external or natural man (*Ps.* cxxxi i. *t.*, 1, 2).
> If the good man becomes evil, his good is not regarded (*Ezek.* xxxiii. 12-16; *cf.* xviii. 24).
> Let them not do evils, but goods (*Ps.* lxxxii. 2-4); because they do not do goods, the church is tottering (*ib.* 5).
> If they had obeyed, the hells would have been removed from them, and they would have enjoyed every good (*Ps.* lxxxi. 13-16).

If they had lived according to the statutes, they would have been in the good of the church (*Mal.* iii. 10-12).

Good is of no profit,—so say those who have adulterated the truths of the church (*Mal.* iii. 13-15).

Goods were not perverted with the truths, until there was a lack of goods (*Jer.* xxxvii. 17-21).

Care is to be taken lest those who are in good be destroyed by those who have devastated the external of the church (*Zech.* xi. 4, 5).

Goods turned into evil (*Jer.* xii. 13).

Every good offered by the Lord to the Jewish nation (*Micah* vi. 1-4).

Every good is destroyed by the Jews (*Zech.* v. 5-8).

No good or truth among blasphemers and profaners (*Jer.* xxi. 11, 12).

Those who are in good draw near (*Isa.* xlv. 20).

Those who do good will be saved by the Lord (*Isa.* xxxiii. 15-17). They will not listen to falsities nor believe them (*ib.* 18, 19). They will be of the Lord's church (*ib.* 20-22). They will have abundance of all things of truth (*ib.* 20-22); and of all things of good (*ib.* 23, 24).

The new church will have every good (*Jer.* xxxii. 41, 42).

Those who are in good can come into the church, when those of the church who thought evils against the Lord perished (*Ps.* lviii. 10, 11 *and prec.*).

Those who are in good will acknowledge the Lord who is Divine truth itself (*Ps.* lxviii. 3-5, 31).

Good consequent on repentance (*Isa.* i. 16-19).

How they will have good (*Ps.* xxv. 12-14).

The new church will have goods from their trust in the Lord (*Joel* ii. 21-25).

Good in abundance is in the Lord's church (*Ps.* cxxviii.).

Good and Truth (*see* **Adulteration, Natural, Perversion, Spiritual, Truth and Good**).

All good and truth is from the Lord (*Isa.* li. 4, 5).

It ought to be acknowledged that all good and truth is from the Lord (*Ps.* xxxvi. 5-9); those who acknowledge Him possess all good and truth (*ib.* 10).

Good itself is the conjunction of good and truth (*Ps.* cxxxiii. *t.*, 1).

Goods and truths of heaven and the church first taught in the Babylonish religion (*Dan.* ii. 31-35). But they had them no longer when they strove for dominion over heaven and the church (*Dan.* iv. 13, 14).

Every good and truth of the church is theirs by means of the covenant (*Jer.* xi. 5, 6).

It is not known what good and truth are (*Ezek.* xii. 17-20).

They are against good and truth (*Ps.* xiv. 6).

Goods and truths of the church turned into evils and falsities (*Hosea* viii.) 1-7).

Good and truth of the church destroyed; how (*Amos* ii. 1-3).

Goods and truths have all been destroyed by infernal evil (*Jer.* v. 14-17).

Goods and truths from firsts to lasts have been perverted (*Jer.* v. 30, 31).

All good and truth has been dispersed (*Joel* ii. 10).

No good and truth remaining any longer (*Isa.* xiii. 10-12).

No good and truth of the Word any longer (*Jer.* xlviii. 39-42).

No good and truth of the church any longer (*Dan.* v. 25-28).

Good and truth no longer (*Amos* viii. 11-14).

Good and truth of the church desired by the Lord (*Ps.* lxix. 21.

The Lord has all good and truth from His Divine (*Ps.* xxi. *t.*, 1-6).

The Lord will give goods and truths to the church which He establishes (*Joel* ii. 18, 19).

Good and truth in abundance imparted by the Lord (*Ps.* xxiii. 4, 5).

All the good and truth in the new church is from the Lord (*Zech.* vi. 9-14).

All goods and truths in the new church (*Isa.* lxvi. 12-14).
Good and truth to eternity instead of evil and falsity (*Isa.* lv. 13).
Good and truth of doctrine, celestial, spiritual, and external (*Ezek.* xl. 6-49).
Worship from good and from truth (*Ps.* cxxxii. 9, 10).
Goods and truths (*see Ps.* cxlviii. *under* **Worship**).
All things of worship of the internal church in respect to good and truth *Ezek.* xli. 1-26); the same of the external church (*Ezek.* xlii. 1-20).

Good of Charity (*see under* **Charity**. *See also* **Good of Love**).

Good of the Church (*see also* **Church**).
Good of the church contrasted with one's own good (*Ezek.* xxxiv. 1-4).
Good of the church and of worship is from the Lord (*Ezek.* xliv. 1-3).
The loved one will receive goods of the church (*Jer.* xxxi. 2-5).
Good of the church taught and learned (*Jer.* xxiii. 3, 4).

Good of Doctrine (*see* **Doctrine**, GOOD OF).

Good of Knowledges (*cognitiones*) (*Amos* i. 3-5).

Good of Love.—From the Lord is all good of love (*Ps.* cxxxvi. 7-9).
From the good of love by means of truth comes enlightenment from the Lord (*Zech.* iv. 1-10).
Goods of love and charity take the place of falsities that have been removed (*Ps.* cxiv. 3-6).
Good of love flows into the truths of the external or natural man (*Ps.* cxxxiii. 2).
The doctrine of the new church from truths which are from the good of love and charity (*Zech.* vi. 1-7).
Worship from the good of love in the new church (*Ezek.* xliii. 12-27).

Good of the Word (*see* **Word**).

Good (the) (*bonus*).—The good are led astray by the prosperity of the evil, imagining that good is of no use, neither affliction (*Ps.* lxxiii. 10-14); but afterwards it is granted them to know that the evil are nevertheless devastated and consumed (*ib.* 15-20, 27); but the good are always upheld and live with God (*ib.* 23-26).
The good and the evil are alike prosperous—so say those who have adulterated the truths of the church (*Mal.* iii. 13-15).
Let not the evil exalt themselves above the good (*Ps.* lxxv. 4-6); for the judgment comes, in which the evil perish and the good are saved (*ib.* 7); the good will worship the Lord (*ib.* 9; *cf.* lxxvi. 7-12).
Comparison of the lot of the evil with the lot of the good. . . . . The good are saved by the Lord and taken up into heaven (*Ps.* xxxvii.).
The evil do evil to the good (*Ps.* x. 1-11).
The good, whom the evil infest, are delivered by the Lord (*Ps.* xvi. 3-5).
The Lord fights for the good against the evil (*Ps.* xi. *t.*, 1-5).
The Lord will to eternity deliver the good as against the evil (*Ps.* xii. 5-8).
The good separated from the evil (*Isa.* ii. 22).
The good will be saved and the evil will be cast into hell (*Mal.* iv. 1-3).
May the good be saved (*Ps.* civ. 31-35).
The good to be saved at the coming of the Lord (*Isa.* xl. 1-5).
The good will be saved (*Ps.* lxiv. 9, 10).
The good are saved by the Lord (*Ps.* xxxiv. 12-22).
The good will understand (*Dan.* xii. 10).
Deliverance of the good; and their thanksgiving that the evil have been conquered and cast into hell (*Ps.* ix. 9-18).

Gospel (*see* **Evangelization, Preach**).

Great.—Greatness and extension of the Lord's dominion (*Ps.* lxxii. 8-12).

Grief (*dolor*) (*see also* **Lamentation**; **Lord**, GRIEF OF; **Mourning**).
Grief on the part of the Lord, and directed to the Lord (*Hab.* i. 1-5).
Grief on account of falsity (*Jer.* xiii. 17).

Grief that there is no truth either in the church or in doctrine (*Jer.* xiv. 17, 18).

Grief of doctrine (*Ezek.* xxi. 6, 7).

Grief because of the backsliding of the church from the Lord, and its vastation (*Jer.* x. 19–21).

Grief on account of devastation (*Jer.* xlviii. 30–34; *Lam.* i. 12–16).

Grief on account of there being no longer anything of the church (*Hab.* iii. 16, 17).

Grief because of the destruction of all things of the church (*Jer.* ix. 10–12).

Reciprocal grief and lamentation that the time is so long drawn out, etc. (*Jer.* viii. 18–22; ix. 1).

Those who are separated grieve over the wicked (*Jer.* vi. 24–26).

Grief of the church because they cannot be converted (*Ezek.* xxi. 12, 13).

No grief on account of the utter desolation of the church (*Ezek.* xxiv. 15–17).

Grow (*see also* **Multiplication**).

The new church will grow when nothing of the church remains in the old (*Hosea* i. 10, 11).

The new church will grow and will be multiplied from all who worship the Lord and love the Word (*Zech.* viii. 20–23).

From trust in the Lord the church will grow in truths and goods (*Ps.* lxxxiv. 5–7).

Growth in the knowledges (*cognitiones*) of the church (*Gen.* xiii.).

Truths and goods with those who are of the new church will grow (*Micah* iv. 8–10).

Guard (*custodio*) (*see* **Protect; Word,** POWER OF).
Keep

Prayer to the Father to keep Him (*Ps.* cxxi.).

The truth of the church must be guarded (*Isa.* xxvii. 2, 3).

Those who were of the Lord's church guarded by Him that they might not undergo the punishment of the inquisition (*Dan.* vi. 18–23).

The redeemed will be guarded against falsities (*Jer.* xxxi. 10, 11).

From the Lord the new church is kept from falsities of evil (*Ps.* cxxv.).

There will be no fear of the hells, for the Lord guards (*Ps.* xxiii. 4, 5; cf. *Isa.* li. 12, 13).

Ham.—"Ham" is the natural of the Ancient Church (*Gen.* ix. 18–29).

Happy (*beatus*) (*see also* **Felicity, Intelligence**).
Blessed

The just man is happy (*Ps.* xxxii. *t.*, 1, 2).

Those who have not perverted the Word will be happy (*Isa.* lxv. 13, 14).

Those who trust in the Lord will be blessed of Him when He comes (*Mal.* iii. 17).

Happy is he who acknowledges the Lord (*Ps.* cxliv. 15).

Happy is he who confesses and worships the Lord (*Ps.* cxviii. 26–29).

Happy is he who trusts in the Lord (*Ps.* lxxxix. 15–18).

Happy is he who trusts in the Lord, who is the God of heaven and earth (*Ps.* cxlvi. 5, 6).

Happiness arises from trust in the Lord (*Ps.* lxxxiv. 8–12).

Happy is he who is of the Lord's church, for good in abundance is there (*Ps.* cxxxviii. *t.*, 1–6).

Happy are they who are of the church which is from the Lord through the Word (*Ps.* xxxiii. 12–15).

The happy state of those who are of the Lord's kingdom (*Ps.* lxxii. 3, 6, 7, 15, 16).

Hardness (*durities*) (*see also* **Obduracy**).

Hardness of heart represented, from which it is that they have no fear (*Ezek.* iv. 3).

INDEX OF WORDS AND SUBJECTS.

Harm (*laedo*).—Confidence of the Lord that the evil thoughts and intentions, by which the evil themselves perish, do no harm (*Ps.* cxli. 8–10).
—— (*noceo*).—The evils and falsities of the perverted church will no longer do any harm (*Ezek.* xxxvi. 13–15).

Harmony (*see* **Concordance**).

Hate.—The Lord fulfilled the Law, and therefore was hated, etc. (*Ps.* cxix.).
The Jewish Church hated the Lord (*Ps.* cix. *t.*, 1–6).
Deadly hatred for one another among profaners (*Jer.* xix. 9).

Haughty (*elatus*) (*see also* **Pride, Self-exaltation**).
The Lord rejects the haughty (*Ps.* ci. 4, 5).

Heal.—They cannot be healed, because the church has been destroyed by means of falsities (*Jer.* xlvi. 11, 12).

Hear (*audio*).—That the Lord causes the infernals to perish when He comes with Divine power has not been heard before (*Isa.* lxiv. 4 *and prec.*).
Hearing the Word and being in external worship is of no avail to the perverted church (*Ezek.* xxxiii. 30–33).
Unwillingness to hear about the Lord (*Jer.* xi. 21).
Consequence of not hearkening to the teacher of doctrine (*Ezek.* xxxiii. 8, 9).
Those who are of the perverted church are not heard by the Lord (*Micah* iii. 4).

Hearken (*ausculto*).—They hearken not (*Jer.* vi. 10). The consequence (*ib.* 11 *and fol.*).

Heart.—Conversion with the mouth, not with the heart (*Ps.* lxxviii. 32–37).
Worship with the mouth, not with the heart (*Ezek.* xx. 1–3).

Heaven (*see* **All, Dominion, Ignorance, Innocence, Order**).
The Lord above the heavens (*Ezek.* i. 26).
The descent of the Lord from heaven, and His coming into the world (*Micah* i. 1, 2). The state of heaven then became changed (*ib.* 3).
The Lord is heaven and the church (*Jer.* xvii. 12, 13).
The Lord alone is the God of heaven (*Isa.* xliv. 23, 24; xlv. 12).
Heaven ruled by the Lord (*Isa.* xl. 26).
Heaven and the church are the Lord's (*Ps.* cxv. 16).
All of heaven and the church is from the Lord (*Ps.* lxxxix. 10–14).
Heaven and the church from the Lord (*Ps.* xlv.).
From the Lord's making the Human Divine, heaven and the church are His and they are in Divine truths from Him (*Ps.* xlv. 8); from the same cause there are affections of truth therefrom, and in these are the societies of heaven (*ib.* 9).
All things of heaven and the church from the Divine Human (*Ps.* xlviii. 11–13).
Through the oneness of the Divine and the Human in the Lord, heaven and the church will endure to eternity (*Ps.* xciii. 1, 2).
Heaven formed by the Lord through Divine truth (*Ps.* cxxxvi. 4–6).
Divine truth from the Lord from the first things to the last things of heaven and the church (*Ps.* xix. 5, 6).
The three heavens (*Ezek.* xlvii. 1–12).
Heaven partitioned according to goods and truths in the whole complex (*Ezek.* xlvii.13–23); further partition (*Ezek.* xlviii. 1–20, 23–29).
Heaven will serve the Lord (*Ps.* xci. 11, 12).
Man has been born for heaven (*Isa.* xlv. 18, 19).
The Lord teaches and leads to the truths and goods of heaven and the church (*Ps.* xxiii. *t.*, 1–3).
Heaven and the church with those who live in humility and in accordance with the commandments (*Isa.* lxvi. 1, 2, 22).
The life of heaven in the Lord alone (*Isa.* xlv. 23–25).
Love and desire for the church and heaven (*Ps.* lxxxiv. *t.*, 1–4).
The life of heaven is not in those who are against the Lord (*Isa.* xlv. 24).

Those who are in the faith of charity will come into heaven (*Dan.* xii. 2, 3).
The good are taken up into heaven (*Ps.* xxxvii.).
The heavens and the earths are the Lord's, therefore He should be praised in song (*Ps.* ciii. 19-22).
All who are in the heavens will confess the Lord (*Ps.* cxlv. 10-12).
In heaven with the Lord to eternity (*Ps.* xxiii. 6).
The Lord will come to judgment, that heaven and the church may worship Him from joy of heart (*Ps.* xcvi. 10-12).
Let not heaven and the church perish, but be established (*Ps.* cii. 25-28).
Effect of last judgment on those who will be in heaven (*Ezek.* xxvi. 19-21).
Heaven will be enlarged for them (*Isa.* xlix. 19, 20).
Heavenly Marriage (*see* **Conjunction, Good Will**).
Hebrew Alphabet (*Ps.* cxix. *note*).
Hebrew Church, so called from "Eber" (*Gen.* xii. 1-8).
Hell (*see also* **Bound, Combat, Destroy, Fear, Infernal, Lord,** TEMPTATION OF; **Lord,** VICTORY OF; **Overthrow, Perish, Remove, Restrain, Subjugate, Uprising**).
Nothing but evils and falsities in hell (*Ezek.* xxiii. 28-31).
Nothing but falsity and evil in hell (*Jer.* vii. 32, 33).
Hell eternal (*Isa.* xxxiv. 9-15).
Hell is actually there, because there is nothing but the lust of the love of self (*Jer.* xix. 12, 13).
Those who endeavor to introduce evil and falsity will be in the hells (*Isa.* xlix. 26).
Those who adulterate good and truth will abide in hell (*Isa.* xiii. 19-22).
Those who adulterate good and truth will perish in hell (*Ezek.* xxii. 31).
Those who wish to be wise of themselves must be in hell (*Jer.* xvi. 13).
Those who worship only externals will come into hell (*Jer.* xvii. 4).
The self-intelligent shut up in hell lest, while continuing in their falsifications, they should spread their falsities abroad (*Ezek.* xxxi. 15-18).
All things which are of knowledge (*scientia*) of the natural man will become hell (*Ezek.* xxx. 13-19).
The end of those who are in mere knowledges (*cognitiones*) will be in hell (*Ezek.* xxvi. 15-18).
The church in respect to knowledges (*cognitiones*) is the countenance of hell (*Ezek.* xxvii. 35, 36).
The church which was in good, now in hell (*Ezek.* xxiii. 28-31).
Hell in place of the church, why (*Jer.* xix. 6).
Although the church was established by the Lord among the ancients, yet the hells now prevail against Him, etc. (*Ps.* xliv. 9-12, 19).
Hells from the Jewish and Israelitish Church (*Lam.* iii. 1-66).
Dominion of hell (*Isa.* lxiii. 17, 18).
God has no glory from the hells (*Ps.* lxxxviii. 10-12).
Let not the hells say that He has been forsaken by God (*Ps.* lxxi. 9, 11).
The malice of the hells described (*Ps.* lv. 9-14).
The hells among themselves desire evils against the Lord, and think that He is to be utterly destroyed (*Ps.* xli. 4-8).
The hells wish to destroy all things of the church (*Ps.* lxxxiii. *t.*, 1-5).
The hells mightily assault the Lord (*Ps.* cxliii. 8-12).
The hells that rise up against the Lord are enumerated (*Ps.* lxxxiii. 6-8).
The hells are of no avail against the Divine (*Ps.* lxii. 3, 4, 9).
Prayer for help against the hells, that they may not prevail, but be conquered (*Ps.* vii. *t.*, 1-17).
The hells will not prevail (*Ps.* xxxviii. 9, 15-22)
The hells removed by the Lord (*Isa.* li. 9-11).
Power of the hells destroyed by the Lord (*Isa.* xlii. 13-15; xliii. 16, 17)

The hells have no saviour, wherefore they will be destroyed (*Ps.* xviii 41, 42, 45).
Those who have falsified and adulterated the Word will perish in hell (*Nahum* iii. 1 4).
Hell of blasphemers and profaners cannot be turned away by the Lord, because they ally it to themselves (*Jer.* xxi. 1–5).
The worst in hell (*Isa.* xiv. 7–12, 15–21).
The Lord has authority over the hells (*Ps.* cx. 4–7).
The Lord's omnipotence against all things of hell (*Isa.* xlv. 1, 2).

—— (*cast into*).—Cast into hell (*Isa.* xxiv. 21, 22; liv. 16, 17; *Hab.* iii. 10–15).
They will be cast down into hell (*Ps.* lv. 15).
The evil have been conquered and cast into hell (*Ps.* ix. 15–17).
The evil cast into hell (*Isa.* ii. 10, 19–21).
Although the evil flourish for a short time, yet they perish, and are cast down into hell (*Ps.* xxxvii.).
The evil will perish and are to be cast into hell (*Zeph.* iii. 6–8).
They cannot but be cast into hell (*Jer.* xvi. 4).
Cast into hell, where there is nothing but falsity and evil (*Jer.* vii. 32, 33).
When they have been cast into the hells the knowledges (*cognitiones*) of truth will be evident to those who will be in heaven and in the church (*Ezek.* xxvi. 19–21).
The self-intelligent cast into hell that they may no longer destroy (*Ezek.* xxxi. 14).
Those who are against the church because of falsities will be cast into hell (*Isa.* liv. 16, 17)
Those in evil and falsity therefrom cast into hell (*Isa.* xxxiv. 9–15).
Those who have falsified the external of the Word are cast into hell (*Jer.* xlix. 19–22).
Those who have falsified the sense of the letter of the Word are cast into hell (*Ezek.* xxi. 30–32).
Those who pervert shall be cast into hell, that they may no longer pervert truths in those who are in an affection for truth (*Ezek.* xxxii. 13–16).
The evil will be cast into hell, because they have annihilated the Word (*Mal.* iv. 1, 3, 4).
Those who adulterate the Word cast into hell (*Isa.* xiv. 7–12, 15–21; xxx. 32, 33).
Those who have adulterated the truths of the Word to be cast into hell (*Zeph.* i. 9–11).
Those who have become "Babylon" are cast into hell (*Jer.* li. 62–64).
Those who invented the inquisition were cast into hell (*Dan.* vi. 24).
Those who worship another god and reason against truth will be cast into hell where there is such evil (*Hosea* x. 7, 8).
Profaners cast into hell (*Jer.* viii. 1, 2).
Backsliders cast into hell (*Jer.* xv. 2, 3).
Those who have destroyed the church cast into hell with tumult, on the day of judgment (*Nahum* ii. 3–6).

Help (*adjuvo*).—The Father helped the Lord in His distresses (*Ps.* cxviii. 5–9).
The evil fought against Him, but He was helped by the Divine (*Ps.* cxviii. 10–14).
Being helped, the Lord repressed the hells (*Ps.* vi. *t.*, 8–10).
Song in praise of the Lord thas He gave help in grievous temptations (*Ps.* cxvi. 1–11).

—— } (*assisto*) (*see also* **Song of Paise**).
Assist } A song in praise of the Father by the Lord to give help against the hells (*Ps.* viii. *t.*, 1–3, 9).
Prayer of the church to the Lord, and in the highest sense, of the Lord to the Father, that because He alone fights, He may assist against the hells (*Ps.* xxv. 15–20).

Prayer of the Lord to the Father, to give help in temptations, because He is known by no one except the Father only, in whom is His trust (*Ps.* cxlii. *t.*, 1–3).

Prayer of the Lord to the Father for help in temptations, etc. (*Ps.* lxxxvi. *t.*, 1–8 *and fol.*).

Prayer to the Father for help, lest the evil prevail (*Ps.* lxix. 13–20).

Prayer of the Lord to the Father for help against the hells, that they may not prevail, but be conquered (*Ps.* vii. *t.*, 1–17).

Prayer of the Lord to the Father for help against the evil, falsifiers, and hypocrites (*Ps.* v. *t.*, 1–10).

Prayer to the Father, that He may assist against those who wish to destroy Him (*Ps.* liv. *t.*, 1–3).

Prayer to the Father for help, because He is considered vile, and as nothing (*Ps.* cix. 21–25); let them be put to shame (*ib.* 26–29).

Prayer of the Lord to the Father, to give help and show His power, that those who are to be of the new church may be delivered (*Ps.* cviii. *t.*, 1–6).

Prayer to the Father for help against the hells, that those who worship Him may have salvation (*Ps.* lxx.).

Prayer of the Lord to the Father to give help, that He might see the church established (*Ps.* cvi. 1–5).

Prayer to the Father, that, unless He assist, no one will have eternal life (*Ps.* lxxxix. 46–48); He assists (*ib.* 52).

Confidence that the Father will assist Him (*Ps.* lxxi. 1–5, 7, 12, 14).

Despair whether the Father would give help (*Ps.* lxxvii. *t.*, 1–9).

The Father will assist (*Ps.* xxviii. 6–8).

The Father assists against those that wish to destroy Him, and they will perish (*Ps.* liv. 4, 5); a song in praise of assistance (*ib.* 6, 7).

The Divine of the Lord gives help against the evil and in temptation (*Ps.* xciv. 16–19).

Song in praise of the Father because He gives help (*Ps.* cix. 30, 31).

Song in praise of the Father by the Lord that He gave help in temptations (*Ps.* cxvii.).

The Lord alone fights, and therefore alone can assist (*Ps.* xxv. 15–20).

—— (*auxilium, auxilior*).—They have no help, because all love falsities and worship other gods (*Jer.* xi. 11–13).

No help from heaven (*Lam.* i. 17–22).

The Divine alone has power, and from it there is help (*Ps.* lxii. *t.*, 1, 2, 5–8, 11, 12).

Prayer to the Father that He may be a help to Him in His combats, for without Him He has no power, etc. (*Ps.* cxliv. *t.*, 1–4 *and fol.*).

Prayer to the Father, and He will bring help against the evil and hypocrites (*Ps.* lv. 23).

O that the Father would help in affliction! (*Ps.* lvi. 7, 8;) He will help (*ib.* 9).

Through help from the Divine of the Lord the evil will perish (*Ps.* xciv. 22, 23).

Song in praise of the Father, that He has helped Him (*Ps.* xl. *t.*, 1–5).

The Lord's song in praise of the Father because of help and because of union (*Ps.* lxi. *t.*, 1–8).

—— (*opitulor*).—May the Divine bring Him help! (*Ps.* xliv. 23, 26.)

—— (*ops*).—Prayer (*precatio*) to the Lord to bring help (*Ps.* lxxiv. 2, 10, 11).

Prayer (*precatio*) unto the Lord for help against blasphemers (*Isa.* xxxvii. 14–20); the answer (*ib.* 21–27).

Hereditary (*see* **Mother**).

Hereditary evil (*Ezek.* xviii.).

Heresy (*see also* **Controversy**).

Those who apply the Word to a heretical falsity will perish (*Amos* i. 6–8).

INDEX OF WORDS AND SUBJECTS.

Hidden.—Whence salvation comes has been hidden (*Isa.* xlv. 15).
   Perversion of all things of the church was hidden from them (*Jer.* xxxviii. 24-28).
High.—From the highest to the lowest, all pervert (*Jer.* v. 30, 31).
Historical.—Historical parts of the Word, like the prophetical parts, contain a spiritual sense; its character described (p. 163).
   Historical things in the Word are representative (p. 163).
   The Israelitish and Jewish Church is described by the historical portions of the Word (p. 163).
Holy.—The Lord is holy (*Ps.* li. 11, 12).
   Holy things of the church profaned (*Ps.* lxxiv. *t.*, 1-9).
   Destruction of holy things of the church (*Ezek.* xxiii. 36-39).
   Utter falsification and adulteration of the holy things of the church (*Ezek.* xxiii. 43-45).
   (After the judgment) they shall no longer destroy the holy things of the church (*Nahum* ii. 11-13).
   The ultimates of the new church will be holy (*Ezek.* xlv. 1-5).
   The holy of doctrine (*Ezek.* xlv. 6-8).
Holy Spirit.—Those who acknowledge the Lord will receive the Holy Spirit (*Isa.* xliv. 1-4).
Honor.—The Lord has honor from His Divine (*Ps.* xxi. *t.*, 1-6).
Hope (*see* ***Trust***).
Horror.—Those who are outside of the church are horrified at the falsities of those who pervert all truths of the church (*Ezek.* xxxii. 9, 10).
   Horrid falsities and evils (*Isa.* xxxiv. 9-15).
Hosea.—The prophet Hosea represented the falsification of the Word with the Jewish nation (*Hosea* i. 1-3).
House (*see* ***Drink***).
Human (*see* ***Lord***, HUMAN OF).
Humiliation (*see* ***Lord***, HUMILIATION OF).
   The new church will be in humiliation (*Zech.* viii. 18, 19).
Humility.—The Lord is to be humbly worshipped (*Ps.* xcv. 6, 7).
   Those who are humble will have salvation from the Lord, and life and protection (*Ps.* cxxxviii. 6-8).
   The Lord teaches those who are humble in heart (*Isa.* lvii. 15).
   Heaven and the church are with those who live in humility (*Isa.* lxvi. 1, 2).
Hypocrisy (*see* ***Interiors***).
Hypocrites (*see also* ***Falsifiers***).
   Hypocrites (*Ps.* x. 1-11; lv. 19-21, 23).
   There are no longer any good, but only hypocrites (*Ps.* xii. *t.*, 1-4).
   Hypocrites think evil (*Ps.* xxxvi. *t.*, 1-4).
   Hypocrites will be in hell and will perish (*Ps.* lii. *t.*, 1-6).
   Prayer for help against hypocrites (*Ps.* v. *t.*, 1-10).
   To the Father, that He may be preserved from the deceitful and hypocrites (*Ps.* cxxiv. 6-8).
   Prayer of the Lord to the Father that the hypocrites may be subjugated (*Ps.* xxviii. *t.*, 1-5).

Idolatry (*see also* ***God***, *last two references*).
   End of the Ancient Church, when it became idolatrous (*Gen.* xi. 10-32).
Ignominy (*see* ***Shame***).
Ignorance (*see also* ***Falsity from Ignorance, Instruct, Teach, Truth***).
   Why the church is ignorant of the Lord's omnipotence and omniscience (*Isa.* xl. 27).
   They could not grow better prior to this, owing to ignorance (*Isa.* xxvi. 16-18).

Those who are in ignorance and natural, will draw near (*Isa.* xlv. 14).
Those who are in ignorance from not having the church will draw near to the Lord (*Isa.* xviii. 7).
Those who are in ignorance of the truth will come to the Lord (*Isa.* xli. 25, 26; xlii. 9–12).
Their joy (*Isa.* xlii. 9–12).
Those who had not known the Lord before will draw near (*Isa.* lx. 14).
Those who from ignorance are in things not true and good, will draw near (*Micah* iv. 6, 7)
Those who are in ignorance of good and truth, because of a lack of them, will be brought to the Lord (*Jer.* l. 4–7); they will depart from "Babylon" (*ib.* 8).
Those who are in ignorance will have knowledges (*cognitiones*) of good and truth (*Isa.* xxi. 13, 14).
Those who are in ignorance are to be enlightened (*Isa.* xlii. 16).
Those who are in ignorance of truth to be saved by the Coming of the Lord (*Isa.* lxi. 1–3).
The new church in ignorance and in lack of truth (*Ps.* cvii. 9–15).
Establishment of the church with those who have been in spiritual captivity, or in ignorance of truth (*Jer.* xxx. 1–3).
The doctrine of the new church from truths which are from the good of love and charity will be with those who are in ignorance of truth (*Zech.* vi. 1–8).
The Lord disperses ignorance by means of the Word (*Ps.* cxlvii. 16–18).
Out of ignorance of truth into the truths of heaven (*Jer.* xxxi. 18–21).
Self-intelligence leads to ignorance concerning the Lord (*Isa.* xxii. 8–12).
Ignorance of God due to knowledges of falsity confirmed by reasonings (*Isa.* lii. 5).
Those who pervert truths will not know what Divine truth is (*Jer.* xxiii. 35, 36).
Those who are willing to be in blind ignorance (*Isa.* xviii.).

Illustration (*see* **Enlighten**).
Imbue (*see also* **Instruct**).
They began to be imbued with falsities of faith (*Jer.* xl. 13–16).
Because imbued with falsities of religion, they are unwilling to give heed to the Word (*Jer.* xxii. 22).
Because they have been imbued with knowledges of falsity confirmed by reasonings, there is evil and ignorance of God (*Jer.* lii. 4, 5).
Not become imbued with falsities (*Jer.* xxix. 8, 9).
The prophet should be imbued with the Word, which in itself is delightful (*Ezek.* iii. 1–3).
Those of the new church will be imbued with wisdom (*Jer.* xxxi. 23–28).

Impious (*see* **Wicked**).
Implant.—The Lord in His Divine Human implants the church in the natural man (*Ps.* cxxxv. 12, 13).
Implore (*see* **Pray** (*imploro*)).
Impure (*Lam.* iv. 15).
Incarnation (*see* **Descent**; **Lord,** COMING OF).
Increase (*see* **Grow**).
Indignation.—Indignation at change of state of the church (*Ezek.* iii. 14, 15).
Indignation that the Jewish Church will be destroyed (*Jer.* xxxii. 1–5).
Industry.—Non-reception due to industry (*Jer.* v. 4, 5).
Infernal (*see also* **Hell**).
Infernal evil and falsity (*Jer.* ix. 22).
Infernal evil invades and still further destroys all the goods and truths of the church (*Jer.* v. 14–17).
Infernal things will be removed from the new church (*Micah* vii. 16, 17).

—— **(the)**.—They have become infernal (*Lam.* v. 10-18).
  Malice of the infernals (*Ps.* lvi. 5, 6).
  Protection, deliverance and salvation from the infernals (*Isa.* xxxv. 4-9).
  The Lord snatched them out of the hand of the infernals (*Ps.* lxviii. 18-23).
Infestation.—Infestation by evils and falsity, and no remedy (*Jer.* xxx. 12-15).
  From the uniting of the Divine and the Human in the Lord will be a church that will be safe from infestation from falsities (*Ps.* lxv.).
  The evil infest the good (*Ps.* xvi. 3-5).
  Infestation by falsities (*Micah* v. 1).
  Infernal falsity from the former church will infest the new church which the Lord will establish (*Zech.* iii. 1, 2).
  Protection against infestation (*Isa.* xxv. 3-5).
  No fear of infestation (*Isa.* li. 12, 13).
  No fear of infestations from the hells (*Ps.* xlvi. 8, 9).
  The natural purged of falsities and evils of every kind, which infested (*Ps.* cv. 25-36).
Infidel.—The church with all things appertaining to it has been utterly destroyed, and its holy things profaned, they saying in their heart that religion is not anything (*Ps.* lxxiv. *t.*, 1-9).
Infirmity.—The Lord knows the infirmities of man (*Ps.* ciii. 8-18).
  Confession of infirmities, and deliverance (*Ps.* xxxii. 5-7).
Influx (*see also* **Operation**).
  Influx of the Lord from Divine love (*Ezek.* xlvi. 1-3).
  Influx of Divine truth (*Ezek.* i. 24, 25).
  Influx of Divine good and Divine truth from the Lord. From this influx angels and men have spiritual life (*Ezek.* xlvii. 1-12).
  Influx of the Lord into the church from doctrine from the Word (*Ezek.* x. 18-20).
  The good of love flows into the truths of the external or natural man (*Ps.* cxxxiii. 2).
  Falsities of evil and evils of falsity will dissipate influx on the day of judgment (*Joel* ii. 30, 31).
Inform (*see* **Instruct**).
Inhabit (*see* **Dwell**).
Inheritance.—Inheritances or partitions of the church and heaven according to goods and truths in the whole complex (*Ezek.* xlvii. 13-23; xlviii. 1-20, 23-29).
Iniquity.—Iniquity of the old church is to be disclosed (*Isa.* lviii. 1).
Injustice (*Hab.* i.).
Inmost.—When the church was destroyed (*deperdo*) even to inmosts, all things were destroyed (*destruo*) (*Amos* vii. 2-9).
Innocence.—Innocence belongs to the Lord (*Ps.* xxvi. *t.*, 1-6, 11).
  Innocence of the Lord (*Ps.* lix. *t.*, 1-7).
  Those who are then of the church wish to destroy and slay the Lord, although He is innocent (*Ps.* lix. *t.*, 1-6).
  Song in praise of the Father by the Lord to regard His innocence (*Ps.* viii. *t.*, 1-3, 9).
  The state of innocence in the heavens (*Isa.* xi. 6-9).
  Wisdom and innocence will be in the new church (*Zech.* viii. 4-6).
Inquisition.—Undergoing the punishment of the inquisition is meant by "the lion's den into which Daniel was cast" (*Dan.* vi. 10-17); still they were guarded by the Lord that they might not undergo that punishment (*ib.* 18-23); but those who invented that crime were cast into hell (*ib.* 24).
Insanity.—Insanities from falsity of evil (*Joel* ii. 4-9).
  Insanity will take the place of intelligence (*Isa.* xix. 11-15).
  Insanity from self-intelligence (*Isa.* xliv. 25).

Those who lust after being insane in falsities (*Isa.* lvi. 12).

Insist (*insisto*) (*see also* **Urgent**).
When the end comes, those who are natural-sensual will be persistent (*Dan.* xi. 44, 45).

Inspiration.—Speaking from inspiration (*Jer.* xxvi. 17-19).

Institute } (*instituo*) (*see also* **Establish, Church,** etc.).
Institution —Institution of the Israelitish and Jewish Church which was from Eber, and its first institution from Abram, etc. (*Gen.* xii. 1-8).

The church was instituted solely with the Israelitish nation (*Amos* iii. 1, 2).

Of the church instituted among the Jewish nation (*Ps.* cvi.).

Institution of the church (*Jer.* xix. 1; xxxiii. 14-16).

A church full of truths and goods from the Word was instituted by the Lord (*Isa.* v. 1, 2).

The church cannot be instituted among them because every one looks to himself and not to the Lord (*Haggai* i. 7-9); it will be instituted among those who are wise from the Word (*ib.* 12-15).

Faith alone prevails until the Lord institutes the church (*Dan.* vii. 22).

A new church to be instituted among others (*Ezek.* xvi. 59-63).

New church to be instituted when the former church has profaned holy things (*Jer.* xxxii. 36-40; *see also Ezek.* v. 13-17).

The Lord will institute a new church when the former church has been completely perverted (*Zech.* i. 14-17 *and fol.*).

Quality of the church about to be instituted in respect to truth and good (*Zech.* ii. 1, 2).

After the old church has perished, a new one will be instituted under the Lord, who will reign over it (*Zech.* ix. 10, 11).

The Lord will come and destroy the Babylonish religion, and will institute a church that will be in Divine truths from Him (*Dan.* ii. 44, 45).

A new church will be instituted by the Lord, which will be in truths from Him (*Ezek.* xi. 17-20), while the former church is being destroyed (*ib.* 21).

The Lord entirely removed falsities of evil when the church was instituted among them, and they were instructed (*Amos* ii. 9-11).

A new church will be instituted by the Lord, which will acknowledge the Lord (*Amos* ix. 11, 12).

The Lord will institute a church in which will be the doctrine of truth and good (*Zech.* viii. 1-3).

A new church instituted by means of the Word and by means of doctrine therefrom (*Ezek.* x.).

A new church instituted which would worship the Lord, and which the Lord could lead (*Ps.* lxxviii. 68-72).

The Lord will institute a church, in which will be worship from good (*Ps.* li. 18, 19).

A new church to be instituted which will worship the Lord, and will acknowledge its evils and at the same time the Lord's mercy (*Ezek.* xx. 40-44).

Prayer of the Lord to the Father, to institute a new church after judgment has been executed upon the evil (*Ps.* lxxxv. *t.*, 1-7).

The Lord in His Divine Human institutes the church (*Ps.* cxxxv. 4).

A church internal and external is being instituted (*Ps.* lx. 6-9; cviii. 8, 9).

The Lord has instituted a church with those who could be in external truth, but who were not in external good, etc. (*Mal.* i. 1, 2, *and fol.*).

The Lord has instituted a church and reformed it by truths from the Word, and yet falsities begin to destroy it (*Ps.* lxxx. 8-13).

The church, when first instituted, was full of truths; at the present day it is devastated (*Haggai* ii. 1-3); nevertheless a church will be instituted (*ib.* 4, 5).

The new church, meant by the "New Jerusalem," is also being instituted elsewhere (p. 164).

Instruct (*erudio*) (*see also* **Evangelization, Imbue, Teach**).
Those who trust in the Lord to be instructed (*Isa.* xxx. 20, 21).

—— (*informo*).—The descendants of Jacob were instructed in the things of the church from the very beginning, but in vain (*Zech.* i. 1–4).

When the church was first instructed in truths it was made fit for receiving life (*Ezek.* xxxvii. 7–14).

Instruction of the new church when the Lord comes (*Ezek.* xxiv. 24–27).

Instruction by the Lord (*Isa.* xvii. 7–14).

After conversion they will be received into the church and instructed in its truths and goods (*Hosea* xiv. 4–7).

Instruction in truths by the Lord (*Isa.* xix. 18–22).

Concerning the duties of those who instruct and are instructed (*Ezek.* xxxiii.).

(*instruo*).—The first instruction of the Israelitish and Jewish Church, which is the instruction of the natural man by means of knowledges (*scientiae*) which are meant by "Egypt" (*Gen.* xii. 9–20).

They had no understanding of truth, although instructed (*Hosea* ix. 10–13).

The new church from the nations will be instructed (*Ps.* cxxvi. 5).

The Lord will instruct those that are in ignorance (*Ps.* cxiv. 7, 8).

Those in ignorance are to be instructed (*Isa.* xxvi. 16–19); in Divine truths (*Isa.* xlix. 21–23).

Those who had the capacity to understand were instructed (*Ezek.* xvii. 4, 5).

Instruction in the first principles of the church ("Israel in Egypt") (*Hosea* xi. 1).

Instruction in cognitions and knowledges (*scientiae*) (*Hosea* xi. 3, 4).

Instruction (*instructio*) consequent on temptation (*Ezek.* xx. 10–12).

The Lord entirely removed falsities of evil when the church was instituted among them, and they were instructed (*Amos* ii. 9–11).

Insurrection (*see* **Uprising**).

Integrity (*see* **Perfection**).

Intellectual.—Those who represented the intellectual things of the church, etc. (*Hosea* v. 1–3).

Intelligence (*see also* **Insane, Self-intelligence**).
Intelligence of the men of the Most Ancient Church (*Gen.* ii.).

Those who trust in themselves and in their own learning have no intelligence (*Isa.* xxx. 16, 17).

Intelligence dissipated by pride (*Ezek.* xxviii. 12–18; *cf.* xxxi. 10–13).

If they do according to the truths of the Word and the knowledge they possess, and do not pervert these, they will have intelligence (*Jer.* xxii. 3, 4); otherwise all of their intelligence will perish (*ib.* 5, 6).

Spiritual intelligence from knowledges (*scientifica*) of every kind through confirming, by means of these, the Divine things of the church (*Ezek.* xxxi. 3–9).

From their having been in knowledges (*scientiae*) they will have intelligence from the Lord (*Hosea* xi. 9–11).

Intelligence by means of knowledges (*cognitiones*) (*Ezek.* xxvii. 3–9; 14–20; xxviii. 12–18).

Every one taught according to the state of his intelligence (*Ps.* civ. 10–23).

Intelligence through truths and goods from the Word (*Ezek.* xvi. 13, 14).

Intelligence grows through Divine truths (*Ezek.* xxxvi. 33–36).

Intelligence which is from the Lord is of value, but not self-intelligence (*Ps.* cxlvii. 10, 11).

Those who are in the faith of charity will become intelligent (*Dan.* xii. 4).

From the good of charity, from which is worship, there will be intelligence (*Zech* xiv. 20, 21).

The Lord fills those who looks to Him with intelligence and makes them happy (*Isa.* li. 3).

Those who will be of the new church will possess intelligence (*Zech.* ix. 17).

Angels and men have intelligence and charity from the Divine good and Divine truth (*Ezek.* xlvii. 1–12).

In heaven with increasing intelligence (*Isa.* lx. 21, 22).

Intend ⎫ (*intendo*).—The evil intentions by which the evil themselves perish,
Purpose ⎬ do no harm (*Ps.* cxli. 8–10).
Intention ⎭ Falsifiers and hypocrites who purpose evil against the Lord (*Ps.* cxl. *t.*, 1–8).

Those who are of the church purpose to have the Lord put to death (*Ps.* xxxviii. 11, 12).

The hells purpose putting the Lord to death for desiring their good (*Ps.* xxxv. 10–16).

Trust from His Divine against those who purpose to put Him to death (*Ps.* xl. 12–15, 17).

Intercession.—Intercession of no avail (*Jer.* xi. 14; xv. 1).

Intercession is of no avail when there is no longer any truth or good in the church (*Ezek.* xiv. 12–14).

Intercession is of no avail when evil desires take possession of the church (*Ezek.* xiv. 15, 16), or falsities (*ib.* 17, 18), or adulteration of good (*ib.* 19, 20).

Intercession is of no avail, because it is certain that they profane the truths and goods of heaven (*Jer.* vii. 16–19).

Interior.—The Lord knows what lies hidden interiorly howsoever the external may appear (*Jer.* xvii. 9, 10).

Interiors, which are evil, will be laid open (*Jer.* xiii. 26, 27).

—— **church.**—When the Lord comes into the world the church will be an interior church (*Haggai* ii. 6–9).

Internal (*see also* **External**).

Internals rejected, even from the beginning (*Jer.* vii. 25, 26).

It is in their internals to worship only externals (*Jer.* xvii. 1, 2).

Internals of the church more than ever before (*Isa.* lxi. 6, 7).

Internals of worship are of truth and good (*Micah* vi. 6–8).

—— **church.**—A church internal and external instituted (*Ps.* lx. 6–9; cviii. 8, 9).

All things of worship of the internal church in respect to good and truth (*Ezek.* xli. 1–26).

—— **truth.**—The Lord in His Divine Human alone teaches the church external and internal truths (*Ps.* cxxxv. 6, 7).

Interpret.—Perversion by false interpretation (*Jer.* xxiii. 25, 26).

Those who have falsely interpreted the Word are condemned (*Jer.* xxix. 20–23).

False interpretation of the truths of the Word (*Ezek.* xiii. 10–12).

Introductory truth.—The knowledges (*cognitiones*) of the new church are introductory truths (*Ezek.* xlviii. 30–34).

Invasion.—Invasion by infernal evil (*Jer.* v. 14–17).

Invoke (*see* **Call upon**).

Irreligion (*Ps.* lxxiv. *t.*, 1–9).

Irruption.—Irruption of falsities (*Jer.* iv. 13).

Irruption of falsities and evils of falsity (*Jer.* v. 6).

Israel.—"Israel" means the Lord (*Isa.* xlix.).

"Israel," the Lord (*see Hosea* xi. 1, *under* **Egypt**).

"Israel" means the new church that will be established by the Lord (*Jer.* xxxi.).

INDEX OF WORDS AND SUBJECTS. 231

Israelites, Israelitish Nation, Israelitish Church, Israelitish and Jewish Church (*see also* **Samaria, Jews**).
Israelitish and Jewish Church a representative church (p. 163).
Israelitish and Jewish Church is described by the historical portions of the Word (p. 163).
Israelitish and Jewish Church was from Eber, and was therefore called the Hebrew Church. Its first institution from Abram, etc. (*Gen.* xii. 1–8).
The first thing of the church among the fathers of the Israelitish nation was destructive of all things of the church (*Ezek.* xix. 1, 2); that nation also destroyed all things of the church (*ib.* 3).
They were natural-external and opposed to all things of the church, therefore they became perverted and were destroyed (*Ezek.* xix. 4–7).
The church was instituted solely with the Israelitish nation, therefore falsities and evils must be examined there (*Amos* iii. 1, 2).
The Word was given to the children of Jacob, and they were confirmed in it by means of miracles; but their fathers and the children had gone back, and had not lived according to it; the miracles in the desert even having no effect, etc. (*Ps.* lxxviii.).
First instruction of the Israelitish and Jewish Church (*Gen.* xii. 9–20).
Those who were descended from Jacob, were instructed in the things of the church from the very beginning, but in vain; therefore what happened to them was according to the Word; their successive states even to the end, etc. (*Zech.* i. 1–11).
The church among the children of Israel has gone back, and worship another god, etc. (*Ps.* lxxxi. 8–11 *and fol.*).
All Divine truth perverted and rejected in the Israelitish and Jewish Church (*Ezek.* xix. 12–14).
The Israelitish Church had a similar fate as the Jewish Church, but in less degree (*Ezek.* xvi. 46–52).
Hells from the Israelitish and Jewish Church (*Lam.* iii.).

Jacob, Children of (*see Israelites*).
Japheth.—"Japheth" means the spiritual of the Ancient Church (*Gen.* ix. 18–29).
Jehovah (*see also* **Lord**, AS JEHOVAH AND GOD).
The Lord is Jehovah who has foretold that He would grant the Holy Spirit (*Isa.* xliv. 5–7); there is no other God (*ib.* 8).
The Lord is none other than Jehovah; let all men know this (*Isa.* xlv. 5, 6).
They will acknowledge that the Lord is Jehovah (*Jer.* xxiii. 7, 8).
Jeremiah.—"Jeremiah" represents the Lord (*Jer.* i. 4–8).
Jerusalem.—"Jerusalem" means the church which is in good (*Ezek.* xxiii. 1, 2); its history (*ib.* 3, 4, 11–13, *and fol.*).
Jews.
Jewish Nation. —(*For further references see under* **Perish**; *see also* **Israelites**).
Jewish Church. The Lord strove with the posterity of Jacob from their infancy (*Hosea* xii. 2–5).
There is no longer any truth in the Jewish Church (*Ps.* lxxvi. 5, 6).
The Jewish Church should refrain from, etc. (*Isa.* xliv. 21, 22).
The Jewish Church does not receive nor obey, although they are taught continually (*Jer.* xxxv. 12–16). Therefore they will perish (*ib.* 17).
Destruction of the Jewish Church and nation foretold (*Jer.* xxxvi. 1–10).
The church among the Jewish nation will be destroyed (*Dan.* xi. 1–4).
The Jewish Church will be destroyed, although its truth will be preserved (*Jer.* xxxiv. 1–7).
In the church in the Jewish nation there will be nothing but falsities of

evil (*Micah* v. 8-15); it will have no power over the Lord's church, (*ib.* 9); and will perish with all its falsities and evils (*ib.* 10-15).

Indignation that the Jewish Church should be destroyed (*Jer.* xxxii. 1-5).

The church gloried in its possession of the Word, and on account of this representative worship, and they were continually guarded by the Lord; and yet they falsified and adulterated the Word and the worship (*Hosea* xii. 8-14).

Those who were of the Jewish nation were commanded to teach the Word to the nations round about, but they would not (*Jonah* i. 1-3); (*see the effect and subsequent events fully described in Jonah* i.-iv.).

Against the Jewish nation (*Micah* vi.); its character fully described (*see ib.* 1-16).

Of the church instituted among the Jewish nation; it became perverted and revolted (*Ps.* cvi.); although they beheld Divine miracles, they backslid, and yet they were preserved (*ib.* 6-8); as at the sea Suph and afterwards in the desert, nevertheless they rebelled (*ib.* 9-34); they totally destroyed and profaned the truths and goods of the church (*ib.* 35-39); therefore the church with them was forsaken by the Lord, and destroyed (*ib.* 40-43).

The Jews desiring that after the Babylonish captivity the church might be with them, but this will not take place, because they have not turned away from falsities and evils (*Zech.* vii. 1-7). They were told to keep the statutes, but they did not (*ib.* 8-12); therefore the church will not be with them, but they will be dispersed (*ib.* 13, 14).

The prophet Hosea represented the falsification of the Word with the Jewish nation (*Hosea* i. 1-3). That profane church will be destroyed when the Lord comes, no pity being possible (*ib.* 3-6).

Successive states of the Jewish Church (*Ezek.* xvi. 1-45; xx.).

It is everywhere better than in the Jewish Church (*Ezek.* xvi. 56-58).

The Jewish Church did not receive the Word (*Ezek.* ii. 3-5).

The Jewish Church was against the Word and the Lord (*Ezek.* ii. 6, 7).

The Jewish Church wholly devastated by traditions or by reasonings from falsities (*Jer.* lii. 1-7); the consequences (*ib.* 8-27).

All truths of doctrine with the Jewish Church are destroyed, and it is against the Lord (*Jer.* li. 5).

The perverted Jewish Church (*Ps.* cix.); it repudiated the Lord and considered Him vile, and hated Him (*ib. t.*, 1-6); they will perish in the judgment, etc. (*ib.* 7-12 *and fol.*).

The Jewish nation has utterly rejected the Lord (*Ps.* cxxiii.).

The Lord was betrayed by the Jews, because He taught them (*Zech.* xi. 12, 13).

The Jewish nation has destroyed conjunction with the Lord, because it has destroyed the church (*Ps.* lxxxix. 38-42).

The Jewish nation destroyed the church (*Ezek.* xliv. 4-8; *Ps.* xciv.); O that judgment may be executed upon them! (*Ps.* xciv. 1, 2;) because that nation has destroyed the church, neither does it fear God, although He sees all things (*ib.* 3-11).

Confession respecting the Jewish Church destroyed (*Dan.* ix. 4-19).

Rejection of the Jewish Church because they have utterly perverted the church (*Zech.* v. 1-4); they have destroyed every good (*ib.* 5-8); and will profane its truth still further (*ib.* 9-11).

The Jewish church profaned all the truths and goods of the Word and of the church (*Hab.* i. 6-11).

When the church among the Jewish nation had been destroyed, "Babylon" appropriated to herself all things belonging to it (*Dan.* i. 1, 2).

End of the church among the Jewish nation (*Ezek.* xxiv. 1, 2).

The Jews believe that the Messiah will come to exalt them to glory, and

INDEX OF WORDS AND SUBJECTS.

yet the church among them has been devastated (*Haggai* i. 1–4; *see further ib.* 5–15).

John the Baptist will be sent before the Lord lest that nation should then perish (*Mal.* iv. 5, 6).

A new church after the Jewish church has been destroyed (*Ezek.* xl. 1).

The Jewish nation will not be in the new church (*Ezek.* xliv. 9–14).

Let them not be like the nation sprung from Jacob, who estranged themselves from the Lord (*Ps.* xcv. 8–10); and with whom, for this reason, there is no conjunction whatever (*ib.* 11).

John the Baptist.—John the Baptist will be sent before the Lord, lest the Jewish nation should then perish (*Mal.* iv. 5, 6).

Jonadab.—"The children of Jonadab" represented those who are of the celestial church, *general subject* (*Jer.* xxxv.).

Joy (*gaudium*) ⎫ (*see also* **Gladness, Song of Praise,** *etc.*).
Rejoice (*gaudeo*) ⎭—The Lord will come to judgment, that heaven and the church may worship Him from joy of heart (*Ps.* xcvi. 10–12).

Joy of the church over the coming of the Lord, with whom is Divine truth (*Ps.* xcvii. 1–6).

Joy of those who will draw nigh to the Lord (*Isa.* xlii. 9–12; xlix. 13).

Joy of the nations with whom a new church will arise (*Ps.* cxxvi. *t.*, 1–4).

Joy that there is a new church that trusts in the Lord (*Ps.* lxvi. *t.*, 1–5).

Joy of the Lord over the new church where He reigns (*Ps.* cxxii.).

Joy on account of the fulfilment of predictions (*Ps.* xcviii. 4–8).

Joy of the Lord because He is preserved from the hells (*Ps.* xxxv. 17, 18, 24).

Joy because there is Divine power through the Lord's Human (*Ps.* cxviii. 15, 16).

Joy that the Lord is the God of heaven and the church (*Ps.* xcvii. 8, 9).

Joy from the Lord (*Ps.* xiv. 7).

Let those who worship the Lord rejoice in Him (*Ps.* xl. 16).

The whole church will acknowledge and worship the Lord from joy of heart (*Ps.* lxvii. *t.*, 1–5, 7).

Joy of those who are in Divine truths (*Ps.* xciii. 3, 4, *and prec.*).

Judge.—Those who are in the love of self and in self-intelligence judge from externals alone (*Hab.* ii. 11).

Judgment (*see* **Last Judgment**).

Just.—May the Father, who is true and just, hear (*Ps.* cxliii. *t.*, 1, 2).

The Lord is just (*Ps.* vii. 3, 4, 8–10).

The just man is happy (*Ps.* xxxii. *t.*, 1, 2); and wise (8, 9).

Justice (*see also* **Injustice**).

Justice perishes (*Hab.* i. 1–5).

It is of Divine justice that the impious man who is converted is saved, and the pious man who becomes impious, is condemned (*Ezek.* xviii. 25–29; *cf.* xxxiii. 12–20).

Through the Divine in Himself, the Lord has become justice (*Isa.* l. 8, 9).

The justice of the Lord is described (*Isa.* xlii. 21).

Justice belongs to the Lord (*Ps.* xcix. 4).

Justice belonged to the Lord (*Ps.* xviii. 20–27, 30, 32).

The justice of the Lord will be praised in song (*Ps.* xxxv. 27, 28).

Song in praise of the Lord because of His justice (*Ps.* cxlv. *t.*, 1–7).

Keep (*see* **Guard**).
Kill (*occido*) ⎫ (*see* **The Lord,** SLAIN; *see also* **Destroy**
Put to Death (*mortem condemno*) ⎬ (*perdo*)).
King.—"King of the South" means the church which is in truths of faith from good of charity (*Dan.* xi.).

"King of the North" means the religion that is in faith separate from charity (*Dan.* xi.).

Kingdom (*regnum*) \
Reign (*regno*) } (*see also* **Dominion, Evangelization, New Church, Spiritual Kingdom, The Lord** AS GOD). \
Rule (*rego*) / The Lord rules the heavens (*Isa.* xl. 26).

The kingdom of the Lord (*Ps.* xlvii.); song in praise of the Lord that He reigns over the church (*ib.* 1–3); and over the heavens (*ib.* 9).
The Lord will reign over the new church (*Zech.* ix. 10, 11).
The Lord reigns in His spiritual kingdom (*Ps.* xlviii. 14).
The Lord alone reigns (*Jer.* x. 10).
The Lord will reign by means of Divine truths (*Isa.* xxxii.).
The Lord reigns to eternity (*Ps.* cxlvi. 10).
The kingdom is the Lord's to eternity (*Ps.* xlv. 6).
The Lord's kingdom is eternal (*Ps.* cxiv. 13).
The kingdom of the Lord, and the happy state of those who are of His kingdom (*Ps.* lxxii. *t.*, 1–4, *etc.*).

Know (*cognosco*).—No one knows the Lord but the Father only, in whom is His trust (*Ps.* cxlii. 4, 5).
They do not know the Lord, who is the Word and the church (*Isa.* viii. 13–16);
Yet others who reject falsities and remove things falsified know the Lord (*Isa.* viii. 17–21).
They will know their God when He comes into the world (*Isa.* lii. 6, 7).

Knowledge (*cognitio*) (*see also* **Knowledge** (*scientia*), **Church, Rich, Natural knowledge**).

Of the church as to the knowledges of truth, which is meant by "Tyre" (*Ezek.* xxvi., xxvii., xxviii.).
Knowledges of every kind and species, in the ancient church, and intelligence by means of them (*Ezek.* xxvii. 3–9).
They imagine that all things of the church consist in knowledges (*Ezek.* xxvi. 1, 2).
When they have been cast into the hells, the knowledges of truth will be evident to those who will be in heaven and in the church (*ib.* 19–21).
Acquisitions and communications of all knowledges (*Ezek.* xxvii. 12, 13). Knowledge (*scientia*) intelligence and wisdom by means of them (*ib.* 14–20; *cf.* 3–9).
Divine worship from knowledges (*Ezek.* xxvii. 21–23).
A religion that consists in nothing but knowledges of good and truth (*Isa.* xiv. 28–32).
Truths and goods of every kind, and thus everything of the church acquired by means of knowledges (*Ezek.* xxvii. 3–9).
Those who believe themselves learned from mere knowledges will falsify all knowledges of truth and will perish thereby (*Ezek.* xxviii. 6–10).
Knowledges from the Word of service to doctrine, are perverted, and their good is turned away (*Amos* i. 3, 5).
Those who pervert knowledges of good are meant by "Arabia" (*Jer.* xlix. 28–33); they have destroyed the knowledge of good and truth by reasonings (*ib.* 28–30); their destruction (*ib.* 31–33).
Those who pervert knowledges of truth are meant by "Damascus" (*Jer.* xlix. 23–27); the doctrine of truth has been destroyed thereby (*ib.* 23–26); they will perish (*ib.* 27).
The church will be devastated, and devastated as to all knowledges of truth and good is "Tyre" (*Isa.* xxiii.).
There is no longer any truth of the church by means of knowledges, as before (*Isa.* xxiii. 1–9).
Those who have falsified the knowledges of truth by means of reasonings and knowledges (*scientifica*) and have thus destroyed the church, will utterly perish (*Zeph.* ii. 12–15).

INDEX OF WORDS AND SUBJECTS. 235

Imbued with knowledges of falsity confirmed by reasonings (*Isa.* lii. 4).
Lack of knowledges of good and truth, because they are in evils and in things falsified (*Isa.* iii. 1-12).
Deprived of all knowledge of truth and good (*Amos* v. 26, 27).
All knowledge of truth will perish (*Zeph.* i. 1-3).
Knowledges of truth and good of every kind and sort will perish (*Jer.* xxv. 15-30).
Knowledges will not save those who have falsified and adulterated the Word, because they will be dissipated (*Nahum* iii. 8-12).
All knowledges of good and truth have been dispersed (*Joel* ii. 10).
Knowledges began to perish with the Jews, yet they lived unconcernedly (*Jonah* i. 4-6).
Loss of knowledges among the Jews caused perversion of the state of the church among the nations round about (*Jonah* i. 7-9).
Judgment upon those who are in knowledges alone (*Joel* iii. 4-8).
At the coming of the Lord those who are in ignorance will have knowledges of good and truth (*Isa.* xxi. 13, 14).
He will come when all knowledges of truth and good perish, until very little is left (*Isa.* xxi. 15-17).
From the Lord is all knowledge of the truth of doctrine and the good of love (*Ps.* cxxxvi. 7-9).
Falsity must be rejected and truth received, that there may be knowledge (*Jer.* iii. 15).
By departing from the affections of the natural man the church will have cognitions of truth and good with subservient knowledge (*scientiae*) (*Ps.* xlv. 12-14).
Knowledges of the new church, which are introductory truths (*Ezek.* xlviii. 30-34).
From the sense of the letter of the Word are the knowledges of truth and good, from which is spiritual nourishment (*Ps.* civ. 24-30).
The new church will be in knowledges from the Word (*Zech.* ix. 1, 2).
Those who are in knowledges from the Word will destroy these knowledges (*Zech.* ix. 3, 4).
When those of the new church were in knowledges, they were admitted into temptations, and preserved (*Ps.* cvii. 22-31).
Growth in the knowledges of the church, and separation of spiritual knowledges ("Abram") from natural knowledges ("Lot") (*Gen.* xiii.).

Knowledge of cognitions (*scientia cognitionum*) (*Gen.* iv.).
Those who place religion in nothing but knowledge of cognitions (*Isa.* xvii.); they are to be destroyed (*ib.* 1, 2).
The knowledge of cognitions will be serviceable to the new church (*Isa.* xvii. 3).
The knowledge of cognitions will be rare (*Isa.* xvii. 4-6).
Those in knowledge of cognitions to be instructed by the Lord (*Isa.* xvii. 7, 8).
The fate of those in knowledge of cognitions who do not suffer themselves to be instructed (*Isa.* xvii. 9-14).

Know (*scio*).—Let all men know that the Lord is none other than Jehovah (*Isa.* xlv. 5, 6).
Let it be known that every thing of truth and good, and hence every thing of power and wisdom is from the acknowledgment of the Lord (*Jer.* ix. 23, 24).
Those who will not confide in the Lord will not know (*Isa.* xli. 21-24).
They do dot know the way by which is salvation (*Isa.* lv. 8, 9).
They might know it to be true that the Jewish Church and nation will be destroyed (*Jer.* xxxvi. 11-16).
Because they wonder at the destruction of the church they will not know truths (*Ezek.* xxv. 3-5).

Knowledge (*scientia*) (*see also* **Knowledge** (*cognitio*), **Seduction**).
  Those who out of a mere knowledge of such things as belong to the Word and the church make a religion for themselves and enter into it (*Isa.* xix., xx.).
  Cognitions have perished through natural knowledges (*Ezek.* xxvii. 26–29).
  All knowledge (*scientia*) perishes because they have separated themselves from the Lord (*Jer.* xxii. 7–9).
  Those who by knowledges pervert the holy things of the church (*Ezek.* xxxii.).
  To those in the church who are in the knowledge of things (*Jer.* xxii. 1, 2); if they do according to the truths of the Word and their knowledge, and do not pervert them, they will have intelligence (*ib.* 3, 4); otherwise all of their intelligence and knowledge will perish, because they have separated themselves from the Lord, etc. (*ib.* 5–9 *and fol.*).
  Instruction of the natural man by means of knowledges, which are meant by "Egypt" (*Gen.* xii. 9–20).
  They were in natural desire and knowledge (*Hosea* xi. 2); they were instructed in cognitions and knowledges (*ib.* 3, 4); from this that they were in knowledges, they will have intelligence from the Lord (*ib.* 9–11).
  Cognitions of good and truth with subservient knowledges (*Ps.* xlv. 12–14).
  Knowledge, intelligence and wisdom by means of cognitions (*Ezek.* xxvii. 14–20).

—— (*scientificum*) (*see also* **Natural Man, Reason**).
  Knowledge does not save after death (*Ps.* xlix. 16–20).
  All true knowledges will be taken away (*Jer.* xvii. 3, 4).
  The natural man, in things Divine, trusts nothing but his knowledges (*Ezek.* xxix. 1–3).
  Those who trust in knowledges will perish (*Jer.* xlvi. 25, 26).
  Knowledges of the natural man have destroyed all things of the church (*Ezek.* xxx. 1–5). All who trust them will perish through evil loves (*ib.* 6–9). Those who trust in knowledges will destroy the truths of the church through reasonings from the natural man derived from falsities (*ib.* 10–12). They will have no truth, thus no power (*ib.* 20–23).
  True knowledges are perverted by reasonings therefrom (*Jer.* xliv. 29, 30).
  Knowledges are no longer of any avail, because they have been destroyed by means of reasonings (*Jer.* xlvi. 1–6).
  Respecting those who boast of knowledges, etc. (*Ps.* xlix. 5, 6, *and fol.*); they perish and come into hell (*ib.* 10–14).
  Knowledges destroying affections for truth (*Ezek.* xxvi. 5, 6).
  Knowledges of the natural man have defiled truths and goods (*Ezek.* xxiii. 19–21).
  All the truths of the Word and of doctrine perverted by knowledges of the natural man (*Hosea* vii. 11 *and prec.*).
  Knowledges pervert all understanding of the Word (*Isa.* vii. 17–20).
  Knowledges that pervert truths, etc., devastate the whole church (*Isa.* x. 23, 25–34).
  Knowledges falsely applied have perverted the doctrinals of the church (*Isa.* xxxvi. 2–6 *and prec.*).
  Knowledges will become falsities (*Jer.* xlvi. 7–10).
  Truths turned into falsities by knowledges (*Ezek.* xvi. 23–28).
  Loving things that have been falsified by knowledges (*Jer.* xliv. 15–19).
  Those who have falsified the knowledges (*cognitiones*) of truth by means of reasonings and knowledges and have thus destroyed the church, will utterly perish (*Zeph.* ii. 12–15).
  Knowledges will not save those who have falsified and adulterated the Word, because they will be dissipated (*Nahum* iii. 8–12).
  Rejection of the Lord by means of knowledges (*Jer.* ii. 18).

INDEX OF WORDS AND SUBJECTS.

Knowledges consulted by those who remained of the devastated church (*Jer.* xxxvii. 5; xlii. 1-6). The evil consequences (*Jer.* xlii. 7-22; xliii., xliv. 11-14).

Knowledges of the natural man perverted remains (*Jer.* xli. 16-18).

Knowledges of the natural man perverted by adapting them to falsities (*Jer.* xliii. 8-13).

Knowledges will be of use in future (*Isa.* xix. 18-22).

The spiritual, rational, and knowing faculties will act in unity (*Isa.* xix. 23-25).

Those who were of the church were natural and in knowledges (*Ps.* cv. 23, 24).

Reasonings from knowledges of the natural man will not destroy knowledges (*cognitiones*) of truth with the new church (*Ezek.* xxix. 17, 18); but they will, in the case of those who trust knowledges alone and have perverted the truths of the church (*ib.* 19-20).

Labor (*laboro*).—The Lord has labored with all His might, that they might grow better (*Ezek.* xxiv. 9-12).

Lack (*see* **Want**).

Lament (*lamentum*).—Lament over those who by knowledges (*scientiae*) have perverted the holy things of the church (*Ezek.* xxxii.).

Lamentation (*lamentatio*) (*see also* **Grief**).

Lamentation that they exalt themselves against the Lord and His Word (*Jer.* xviii. 19, 20).

Lamentation over the Jewish Church, everywhere in the Word (*Ezek.* ii. 8-10).

Lamentation to God, that there is a lack of everything of the church (*Lam.* v. 1-5).

Lamentation over the destruction of the knowledges (*cognitiones*) of truth (*Ezek.* xxvii. 30-34).

Lamentation at the corruption of the church, doctrine and Word (*Jer.* iv. 18-21).

Lamentation over the church because it has been successively devastated (*Amos* v. 1-3).

Lamentation over the destruction of the church and over their own destruction (*Amos* v. 16-20).

Lamentation over the devastation of the church (*Joel* i. 18-20).

Lamentation over devastation (*Jer.* ix. 17-19); and over destruction (*ib.* 20, 21; *Ezek.* vi. 11-14).

Lamentation of the church over her devastation (*Lam.* ii. 18-22).

Lamentation of the Lord, that He has been forsaken, together with the church (*Ps.* lx. *t.*, 1-3).

Lamentation by the nations who are in falsities from ignorance, because they do not have the Word (*Ps.* cxxxvii. 1-6).

Lamentation by those who are in good, and in truths thereform (*Jer.* xxv. 34-38).

Last Judgment (*see* **Destroy, Disperse; Hell,** CAST INTO; **Institute, Perish, Reject**).

The last judgment (*Zeph.* i. 14-17; *Isa.* ii. 10, 19-21; xxiv. 21, 22; *Ezek.* vii.).

They ought to be converted before the Lord comes to judgment (*Zeph.* ii. 1-3).

After the church has been consummated, the judgment will come, etc. (*Dan.* ix. 24).

Something concerning judgment by the Lord (*Ps.* ci.).

Prayer that the Lord may come and effect the judgment (*Ps.* lxxxii. 8).

O that judgment may be executed upon the Jewish nation which destroyed the church! (*Ps.* xciv. 1, 2.)

For the sake of the church the Lord will come to judge (*Ps.* xciv. 12–15).

The Lord will come to judgment, that heaven and the church may worship Him from joy of heart (*Ps.* xcvi. 10–12); He will come to judgment (*ib.* 13).

The Lord will come and will execute judgment (*Joel* ii. 1, 2; *Isa.* iii. 13, 14; xiii.; lxi. 1–3; *Ps.* xcviii. 9).

The Lord will come for judgment to those with whom is the church (*Ps.* l. *t.*, 1–6).

A last judgment when the Lord comes (*Ezek.* vii. 5–13).

Those of the old church will fear the last judgment (*Isa.* xxxiii. 13, 14).

Every evil and falsity will be destroyed on the day of judgment (*Isa.* xxvii. 4, 5).

The Lord will judge from Divine wisdom (*Isa.* xi. 1–5).

Those who were in faith alone were judged from the Word (*Dan.* vii. 9, 10).

Last judgment upon those who have falsified the external of the Word (*Jer.* xlix. 19–22).

Those who establish falsity of doctrine to be rejected by the judgment (*Isa.* xxvi. 14, 15).

Those who pervert the truths of the Word will perish on the day of judgment (*Jer.* xxiii. 19, 20).

Falsities of evil and evils of falsity will dissipate influx on the day of judgment (*Joel* iii. 30, 31).

Because they do not see truths they perish on the day of judgment (*Jer.* xxiii. 12).

When the Lord comes He will execute judgment upon all who have adulterated and destroyed the truths of the church (*Mal.* iii. 5, 6).

The last judgment upon those who have scattered the goods and truths of the church (*Joel* iii. 2, 3); upon those who are in knowledges (*cognitiones*) alone and in faith alone, etc. (*ib.* 4–8).

Destruction on the day of judgment of such as persisted in falsities of evil (*Hosea* x. 13–15)

Judgment upon those who are in falsities of evil, combat with them, their destruction, and their being cast into hell (*Hab.* iii. 10–15).

Judgment upon those who trust in themselves (*Isa.* xxx. 30–33; xxxi. 4).

The self-intelligent will perish on the day of judgment, because they have oppressed the church (*Obad.* 8, 9; 15, 16).

Last judgment by the Lord from His Human through His Divine, upon those who were in self-intelligence (*Isa.* xli. 1–16).

Last judgment upon those who from their own intelligence hatch out doctrine and falsify doctrine (*Ezek.* xiii. 4, 5).

Those who are in faith alone will perish on the day of judgment (*Jer.* xlvii.).

Last judgment upon those who are of the church (*Jer.* xxx. 4–7; *Ezek.* ix.).

Last judgment upon those who are in externals without internals (*Jer.* ix. 25, 26).

On the day of judgment those will perish who have destroyed the church, and they will be cast into hell. Their lot described (*Nahum* ii. 3–13).

Those of the old church perish at the time of the last judgment (*Isa.* x. 3, 4, 12–19; *Ezek.* vii. 1–4).

Last judgment upon those who have utterly departed (*Isa.* xiii. 4–9).

They will perish on the day of judgment (*Amos* viii. 7–10).

Last judgment upon all who are in evil and in falsity therefrom (*Isa.* xxxiv.).

All true worship, with all truth and good, will perish on the day of judgment (*Isa.* xxvii. 8–12).

He who lives ill perishes on the day of judgment (*Ps.* i. 1–3).
Last judgment upon those who are in evils (*Nahum* i. 1, 2).
Last judgment on the evil (*Ps.* x. 12–18).
The Lord will execute judgment upon the wicked (*Jer.* xxx. 23, 24).
The Lord will separate the evil among the church (*Ezek.* xxxiv. 16, 17).
At the judgment the evil perish and the good are saved (*Ps.* lxxv. 7; lxxvi. 7–10, 12).
The Lord will overthrow all who are against Him on the day of judgment (*Ps.* xxi. 7–12).
Judgment upon "Philistia" (*Isa.* xiv. 28–32).
Last judgment upon "Moab" (*Isa.* xv., xvi.).
Judgment upon "Babylon" (*Jer.* l. 14–16, 41–46).
When the judgment overtakes "Babylon" all things appertaining to them, from firsts to lasts, are to be scattered (*Jer.* li. 19–23).
Whithersoever they may flee, nowhere will there be an escape (*Amos* ix. 1–5).
Those who will acknowledge must be removed while the destruction lasts (*Jer.* iv. 5, 6).
Those who are being instructed are to be preserved, while in the meanwhile those who are in the persuasion of falsity are destroyed, by the last judgment (*Isa.* xxvi. 19–21).
There will be protection from the Lord when the last judgment comes and continues (*Ps.* xlvi. *t.*, 1–3, 6, 7).
Thanksgiving and joy of the Lord that the evil have been judged and destroyed, and the good have been delivered; and thanksgiving of the latter that the evil have been conquered and cast into hell (*Ps.* ix. *t.*, 1–20).
When they have been cast into the hells, the knowledges (*cognitiones*) of truth will be evident to those who will be in heaven and in the church (*Ezek.* xxvi. 19–21).
The Christian Church has come to an end by the accomplishment of the last judgment (p. 164).

Last things (*see* **Ultimates**).

Last time (*ultimum tempus*).—Exhortation to reflect that thus the last time comes when the Lord comes (*Joel* i. 15).
Last time has come upon the church because there is no longer any truth or good in it (*Micah* vii. 1–4).

Laugh to scorn (*irrideo*).—They will laugh to scorn those things that are of heaven and the church (*Isa.* xxviii. 14–16).

Law.—Because nothing of the law and doctrine remains, the church has been destroyed (*Hosea* iv. 4–9).
The Lord fulfilled the Law, or the Word, from its firsts to its lasts (*Ps.* cxix.).

Lead (*duco*) (*see* **Teach**).
The Lord leads from Divine love (*Isa.* lxiii. 9).
The Lord leads the church (*Ps.* cxxxv. 14).
The Lord will gently lead (*Isa.* xlii. 1–4).
The Lord leads by degrees (*Isa.* lii. 12, 13).
The Lord leads to the truths and goods of heaven and the church (*Ps.* xxiii. *t.*, 1–3).
The Lord led men (*Isa.* lxiii. 11–14).
The Lord led and protected, yet they departed from Him (*Jer.* ii. 4–6).
There are none to lead the people any longer, but only such as destroy (*Zech.* xi. 7–9).
The teacher and the leader destroy all things of the church by falsities of evil (*Zech.* xi. 15–17).
The new church prays to the Lord to come and lead, because they are in affliction (*Ps.* lxxx. *t.*, 1–7)

Those who do not profane truth have been led by the Lord and are led by Him (*Isa.* xlvi. 3-5).

The Lord raises up sinners and leads them into truths, that they may live (*Ps.* cxlv. 14-16).

Those are to be brought near who are to be led out of falsities (*Jer.* xxxiii. 6-9).

Men are to be led together from all parts to the new church (*Zech.* viii. 7-9).

A new church instituted which He could lead (*Ps.* lxxviii. 68-72).

The new church will be taught and led (*Micah* vii. 14, 15).

Lead astray (*auferro*).—Deprived of truths, reasonings lead them astray (*Isa.* xx.).

—— (*seduco*).—The evil vaunt themselves and prosper, whereby the good are led astray, imagining that good is of no use, neither affliction (*Ps.* lxxiii. 10-14).

Those who trust in the knowledge of the natural man, thus in their own intelligence, lead themselves astray (*Isa.* xxx. 1-5).

The learned are led astray by knowledges and recede from the Word and the Lord (*Isa.* xxx. 7-10, 11).

Led astray through persuasions of falsity (*Ezek.* xiii. 18, 19).

Led astray by those who have evil cupidities (*Isa.* lvi. 10, 11).

When the Lord comes, he who leads others astray will be ashamed (*Hab.* ii. 15-17).

Separation to prevent seduction (*Ezek.* xxiii. 46-49).

Those who do not suffer themselves to be led astray will be protected (*Ezek.* xiii. 20-23).

Those who are in falsities from ignorance and have not suffered themselves to be led astray by falsities and evils will draw near to the Lord (*Isa.* xi. 10-12).

Lead back (*reduco*).—They cannot be led back, because they are in falsities (*Hosea* vii. 12-16).

Profaners cannot be led back (*Jer.* viii. 4-6).

Learn (*addisco*).—To learn truths and retain them in the memory belongs to the spiritual church (*Jer.* xxxv. 1-10).

—— (*disco*).—They learn from themselves and not from the Lord; if they learned from the Lord they would depart from evils (*Jer.* xxiii. 21, 22).

Others will learn the good of the church (*Jer.* iii. 3, 4).

They will learn the good of doctrine from the Lord (*Zech.* xii. 5).

Learned (*eruditus*). } —Concerning those who believe that they are learned
Learning (*eruditio*). } from mere knowledges (*cognitiones*) (*Ezek.* xxviii. 1-5, *and fol.*).

The learned, or self-taught; they are led astray by knowledges and recede from the Word and from the Lord. They have no truth and thus no good. They should have trust in the Lord. They have no intelligence whatever (*Isa.* xxx. 6-17).

Those who trust in their own learning from self-intelligence (*Isa.* xxxi.; *Ezek.* xxviii.; xxxi. 10-13).

All the learning of the natural of man which confirms falsities will perish (*Jer.* xlvi. 20-24).

Learning from the Word (*Ezek.* xxviii. 11).

Leave (*relinquo*).—Because they have gone back and worship another god they have been left to themselves (*Ps.* lxxxi. 12).

Lebanon.—" Lebanon " means the rational of the church (*Ezek.* xvii.).

Left (*residuum*).—Things that are left (*see* **Residue**, *see also* **Remains**).

Letter.—The letters of the Hebrew alphabet signify such things as are meant by them in the spiritual world (*Ps.* cxix. *note*).

Levi.—" Levi " means the Lord in *Mal.* ii. 5, 7.

Levites.—" Priests and Levites " mean the third heaven (*Ezek.* xlviii. 9-20).

Liberate (*see* **Deliver**).
Lie in wait (*insidior*).—The lying in wait of the evil against the Lord (*Ps.* lxiv. 1., 1–6).
  Those who lie in wait for Him will perish by falsities of evil (*Ps.* lxiii. 9, 10).
Life ⎫ (*see also* **Obedience, Vivify, Walk**).
Live ⎭ Life of heaven is in the Lord alone (*Isa.* xlv. 23–25).
  Life consequent on conjunction of all things of the Word (*Ezek.* x. 21, 22).
  Life of love and charity (*Gen.* iv.).
  Angels and men have spiritual life from the influx of Divine good and Divine truth from the Lord (*Ezek.* xlvii. 1–12).
  Truth in which is life (*Isa.* lv. 3, 4).
  He that trusts in the Lord and lives well will be saved (*Ps.* cxii. 1–7, 9).
  The good are always upheld and live with God (*Ps.* lxxiii. 23–26).
  Those who are humble will have life from the Lord (*Ps.* cxxxviii. 6–8).
  The man who does not live ill is regenerated by the Word of the Lord, but he who lives ill perishes on the day of judgment (*Ps.* i. 1–5).
  The life of truth and good should be loved, and not the life of falsity and evil (*Micah* vi. 9–11).
  The Lord raises up sinners, and leads them into truths that they may live (*Ps.* cxlv. 14–16).
  Exhortation to live according to the commandments (*Jer.* xxvi. 1–5).
  No church unless they live according to the commandments (*Jer.* vii. 4–7).
  If the life is contrary to the commandments there is no church worship (*Jer.* vii. 8–10).
  Those who have the Word are able to live according to the Divine commandments, but they do not so live (*Ezek.* iii. 4–7).
  They did not live according to the Word (*Ps.* lxxviii. 8–10).
  If they had lived according to the statutes, they would have been in the good of the church (*Mal.* iii. 10–12).
  The remains did not live according to the truths of doctrine from the Word (*Jer.* xxxvii. 1, 2).
  The church was destitute of all life from good and truth (*Ezek.* xxxvii. 1, 2).
  Truth and good and life no longer in them (*Isa.* lvii. 1, 2); why (*ib.* 3, 4).
  Things that have no spiritual life to be rejected (*Isa.* lv. 2).
  Life of heaven is not in those who are against the Lord (*Isa.* xlv. 24).
  Life of the new church (*Ezek.* xliv. 15–31).
  Life will be in the new church when first instructed in truths and made fit for receiving (*Ezek.* xxxvii. 3–10).
Light (*lumen*) (*see* **Natural light**).
—— (*lux*).—Light of truth (*Ezek.* xx. 45, 46).
  The new church in the light of truth, from the Lord (*Micah* vii. 7–9).
  From the Lord's dwelling in truths and goods the church will be in light against falsities of evil (*Ps.* cxxxii. 17, 18, *and prec.*).
  Rational light (*Hosea* xiv. 9).
Linen (*see* **Girdle**).
Lion's den (*see* **Daniel**).
Literal sense (*see* **Word**).
Long for (*see* **Desire**).
Look (*specto*).—Looking of all toward one (*Ezek.* i. 12).
  Every one looks to himself and not to the Lord, therefore the church cannot be instituted among them, and no truth and good can be received by them (*Haggai* i. 7–11).
  The worshippers of God look to the Lord (*Isa.* li. 1, 2).

The Lord upholds the church with those who look to Him (*Isa.* xl. 28, 29, 31).
Those who do not look to the Lord have no power, but fall (*Isa.* xl. 30).
Let them look to truths and goods (*Jer.* vii. 3).
May the Lord have regard to them (*Isa.* lxiv. 9-11).
Lord* (*see also* **Adore, Conjunction, Deliver, Divine Power, Divine Truth, Divine Wisdom, Divine Zeal, Endure, Guard, Innocence, Justice, Love, Omnipotence, Perfection, Presence, Redemption, Salvation, Song of Praise, Subjugate, Teach, Tolerance, Uphold, Worship,** beside subjects referred to under the following sub-divisions).

COMING OF THE LORD.

The coming of the Lord predicted (*Hab.* iii. 1-4).
The descent of the Lord from heaven, and His coming into the world (*Micah* i. 1, 2); effect upon heaven and the church fully described (*ib.* 3-16).
The coming of the Lord who is the God of the church (*Micah* v. 2).
The Lord will be born that He may teach all men Divine truth (*Jer.* i. 4-8).
The Lord the Saviour will come (*Isa.* lvi. 1).
No safety without the coming of the Lord (*Isa.* lxiv. 6, 7).
Through the coming of the Lord is salvation (*Isa.* lv. 10, 11); through this alone is heavenly happiness (*ib.* 12).
The coming of the Lord, from whom is salvation, is near at hand (*Isa.* xlvi. 13).
The coming of the Lord protracted (*Isa.* xxxviii. 7, 8).
The coming of the Lord will not be delayed (*Ezek.* xii. 21-25, 26-28).
What the Lord will do when He comes (*Jer.* xxx. 21, 22; *Hab.* iii. 1-19).
What will then take place when the Lord comes (*Hab.* ii. 1-3).
The coming of the Lord foretold, when the good will be saved and the evil will perish (*Isa.* xl. 1-5, 9-11).
The coming of the Lord foretold (*Isa.* xlii. 9-12).
The evil will perish when the Lord comes (*Ps.* ci. 8).
Exhortation to reflect on the coming of the Lord (*Joel* i. 15).
Ignorance of truth and non-understanding of the Word will destroy the church when the Lord comes into the world (*Isa.* vii. 10-16).
The coming of the Lord when all things of the church have been destroyed by knowledges of the natural man (*Ezek.* xxx. 1-5).
The Lord will come when all knowledges of good and truth perish, until very little is left (*Isa.* xxi. 15-17).
The Lord will come among those who adulterate and profane the Word (*Isa.* xlviii. 14-17).
Devastation of the church by faith alone continues until the Lord comes (*Dan.* viii. 13-19).
Manifestly of the coming of the Lord; that He will destroy all who are in the love of self and in the pride of self-intelligence (*Isa.* ii. 10-18).
Destruction of the church when the Lord comes (*Amos* v. 16-20).
The Jewish Church will come to its end at the coming of the Lord (*Ezek.* xxi. 25-27).
Destruction of worship of Jewish Church at the coming of the Lord (*Ezek.* xxiv. 20-23).
The profane (Jewish) church will be destroyed when the Lord comes (*Hosea* i. 3-5; *see further under* **Destroy**).
At the coming of the Lord there will be no longer the representative of a church but a church, wherein the Lord Himself will be in place of that representative (*Jer.* iii. 16, 17).

---

* It should be borne in mind that wherever the term "Lord" is used in this work it means our Lord God and Saviour Jesus Christ.—COMPILER.

Prayer that the Lord may come and effect the judgment (*Ps.* lxxxii. 8).
Prayer that the Lord may come and remove the evil (*Jer.* xii. 3).
The Lord will come and will execute judgment (*Joel* ii. 1, 2).
The coming of the Lord to judgment (*Isa* iii. 13, 14; xiii. 1–22; xvi. 3–14).
Coming of the Lord with Divine truth, when there is nothing but falsity and evil of falsity (*Isa.* lx. 1, 2).
The Lord will come with Divine truth (*Zech.* ix. 9).
Coming of the Lord in Divine power (*Isa.* xiii. 1–3; lxiii. 19).
The coming of the Lord; He will judge from Divine wisdom; and will save the faithful, and destroy the faithless (*Isa.* xi. 1–5).
Coming of the Lord to judgment upon all who are in externals without internals (*Jer.* ix. 25, 26).
When the Lord comes He will protect His own (*Isa.* xxxiii. 2).
When the Lord comes He will investigate (*Zeph.* iii. 5).
When the Lord comes, he who leads others astray will be ashamed, and falsities will then profit him nothing (*Hab.* ii. 14–19).
May the Lord come and restore the church, and may it thus be vivified (*Ps.* lxxx. 14–19).
When the Lord comes He will raise up the fallen church (*Ps.* lxxv. *t.*, 1–3).
Coming of the Lord to restore the church (*Ps.* xc. 14 *and prec.*).
When the Lord comes He will destroy them and establish the church with others (*Isa.* i. 24–27; *see further under* **Establish**).
The Lord will come and will give the church to others (*Isa.* v. 16, 17).
The coming of the Lord and redemption is expected (*Ps.* cxxx. 5–8).
The coming of the Lord expected (*Isa.* xxi. 5–7, 8–10; 11, 12; xxvi. 7–9).
They will know their God when He comes into the world (*Isa.* lii. 6, 7).
When nothing remains but what is adulterated, the Lord will come (*Dan.* ii. 31–35); He then will institute a church that will be in Divine truth from Him (*ib.* 44, 45).
Coming of the Lord and end of each church, the old and the new (*Dan.* ix.).
When the Lord comes and establishes the church those who are in the mere sense of the letter and in external worship will perish (*Ezek.* xxxix. 7, 8, *and prec.*).
The coming of the Lord to save those who are in ignorance of truth and desire for it, and when the judgment is to be performed (*Isa.* lxi. 1–3).
A new church will be established out of the nations by the Lord when He comes into the world (*Micah* iv. 1, 2).
He will gather the church together and teach those who are in it (*Micah* v. 3, 4).
The Lord will come and gather together the church (*Zeph.* i. 7, 8).
The Lord will come, and those who are of the new church will acknowledge Him, and He will be with them (*Zech.* ii. 10–13).
The Lord's coming and the new church from Him (*Nahum* i. 15; ii. 1–3).
When the Lord comes into the world He will institute a church which will be an interior church (*Haggai* ii. 6–9).
How the Lord institutes the church when He comes (*Jer.* xxxiii. 14–16 *and prec.*).
When the Lord comes He will then gather the church together on earth and will teach it Divine truths (*Ezek.* xxxiv. 11–16).
He will then teach, save and protect the simple (*Ezek.* xxxiv. 22–31).
When the Lord comes those who will be led into the new church will be instructed (*Ezek.* xxiv. 24–27).

The Lord will come into the world, and will teach the Word in its purity, etc. (*Mal.* iii. 1–3 *and fol.*).

Those who are of the church and in the doctrine of truth will be saved by the Lord when He comes (*Ps.* xlvi. 5, 6).

Manifestly of the coming of the Lord and the new heaven and the new church at that time (*Isa.* ii. 1–5; ix. 2–4).

Blessings when the Lord comes (*Isa.* lx. 22 *and prec.*).

When the Lord comes the natural will first be imbued with truths from good (*Isa.* xxi. 5–7).

Joy of the church over the coming of the Lord, with whom is Divine truth (*Ps.* xcvii. 1–6).

When the Lord came He instructed the church in truths and made it fit for receiving life (*Ezek.* xxxvii. 11–14 *and prec.*).

He came into the world, as is written in the Word, that He might do the will of the Father (*Ps.* xl. 6–8).

When there was no longer any truth, the Lord came and they afflicted Him (*Ps.* cv. 17, 18, *and prec.*); but He afterwards became the God of heaven and earth (*ib.* 19–22).

The coming of the Lord and the glorification of His Human (*Ps.* xcviii.).

The Lord came into the world, and is therefore praised in song (*Ps.* cxiii. 6 *and prec.*).

THE HUMAN OF THE LORD.

(See also subsequent sub-headings).

What will take place when the Lord is in His Human (*Hab.* ii. 20 *and prec.*).

The Lord will put on the Human and will establish the church (*Ps.* ii. 6–8); and disperse falsities that are from evil (*ib.* 9); they should therefore acknowledge and worship the Divine Human of the Lord, lest they perish (*ib.* ii. 10–12).

Relationship of the Divine and the Human (*Ps.* cxxxix.).

The Lord's Human strengthened by His Divine (*Isa.* xli. 8–10, 13, 14; *cf. Ps.* lxxvii. 10–15; *and see further under* **The Divine**).

The Lord operated from His Human; He indeed operated through influx from the Divine, but not from the Divine alone (*Ps.* cxxxi. *t.*, 1, 2).

The Lord executed a last judgment from His Human, in which He was while in the world, by means of His Divine (*Isa.* xli. 1–4).

Joy because there is Divine power through His Human (*Ps.* cxviii. 15, 16).

THE DIVINE HUMAN.

They have acknowledged the Divine Human from eternity, in which is all of salvation (*Ps.* lxxii. 17).

Institution of the church and destruction of the old by the Lord through the Divine Human (*Isa.* xliv. 28).

Song in praise of the Lord in His Divine Human, who institutes the church, and who alone is God, who alone teaches the church external and internal truths, who delivers the natural man from falsities of evil, and there implants the church (*Ps.* cxxxv. 1–12).

It is the Divine Human from His Divine in Himself which is the source (*Ps.* cxviii. 22–25).

The spiritual kingdom is the Divine Human (*Ps.* xlviii. 9, 10).

The Lord in respect to the Divine Human is meant by "Cyrus" (*Isa.* xlv.).

THE DIVINE OF THE LORD; OR, THE FATHER.

The Divine above and in the Word (*Ezek.* i. 22, 23).

The Lord came into the world that He might do the will of the Father (*Ps.* xl. 6–8).

INDEX OF WORDS AND SUBJECTS. 245

The Lord was the Father's from conception (*Ps.* xxii. 9, 10).
He was the Father's from birth (*Ps.* lxxi. 6, 7).
It appeared as if the Divine were not in the Lord (*Isa.* liii. 4).
Confession that the Divine alone has power, and from it there is help (*Ps.* lxii. *t.*, 1, 2, 5–8, 11, 12).
The Divine of the Lord gives help against the evil and in temptation (*Ps.* xciv. 16–19).
The Lord has protection from the Father (*Ps.* iv. 3).
Without the Father the Lord has no power (*Ps* cxliv. 3, 4).
The Lord endured by power from His Divine (*Ps.* xxii. 24).
The Lord in temptations strengthening Himself from His Divine, etc. (*Ps.* lxxvii. 10–15; *cf. Isa.* xli. 8–10, 13, 14).
From the Lord's Divine His Human will be made Divine (*Ps.* lx. 11, 12).
Co-operation of the Father with the Lord (*Ps.* xcii. 1–5).
The Father knows everything of the Lord's thought and will, because He is made one with Him, etc. (*Ps.* cxxxix. *t.*, 1–5 *and fol.*).
The Father to the Lord, or His Divine to His Human; that by oneness with Him He has omnipotence over the hells, etc. (*Ps.* lxxxix. 19–25, *and fol.*).
The Lord has omnipotence against all things of hell from His Divine (*Isa.* xlv. 1, 2).
The hells are of no avail against the Divine (*Ps.* lxii. 3, 4, 9).
The Divine and Divine power are the Lord's (*Ps.* xvi. 6–8).
The Lord executed a last judgment from His Human through His Divine (*Isa.* xli. 4).
The Lord will save from His Divine (*Isa.* xli. 5–8).
From His Divine the Lord has all good and truth, thus honor and glory (*Ps.* xxi. *t.*, 1–6).
The Lord has Divine wisdom through His Divine even to outmosts (*Isa.* xlv. 3, 4).
From His Divine the Lord sets heaven and the church in order (*Isa.* li. 16).
By His Divine the Lord will fill those who are of the new church with all things, and will vivify them (*Joel* iii. 28, 29).
The Divine of the Lord in His Human (*Ps.* xvii. 6).
The Divine is in the Lord (*Isa.* xlii. 1–4).
The Divine is in the Lord only (*Isa.* lx. 2).
The Divine will be worshipped in the Lord (*Ps.* cxvi. 12–19).
The Divine of the Lord ought to be acknowledged, which is the "sabbath," and not violated (*Jer.* xvii. 21–24).

THE DIVINE LOVE, WILL, DESIRE AND ZEAL.

The Lord represented as to Divine love (*Ezek.* viii. 1, 2).
Divine love appertaining to the Lord (*Ezek.* i. 27, 28).
Influx of the Lord from Divine love (*Ezek.* xlvi. 1–3).
Divine love of saving belongs to the Lord (*Ps.* xxvi. 7, 8).
The Lord desires the ancient state in respect to the church (*Ps.* cxliii. 5, 6).
The Lord wills the salvation of all (*Ezek.* xviii. 30–32; xxxiii. 10, 11).
From mercy, that He might lead them from Divine love (*Isa.* lxiii. 9).
Efforts of the Divine love to save illustrated in the case of the Jewish Church (*see Ezek.* xx.; xxiv. 9–12).
They purpose putting Him to death for desiring their good (*Ps.* xxxv. 10–16).
The Father knows everything of the Lord's thought and will, because He is made one with Him (*Ps.* cxxxix. *t.*, 1–5).
The Lord desires the end of the temptations (*Ps.* xxxix. 4–7).
Zeal of the Lord (*Ps.* xviii. 7–14).

THE LORD REJECTED.

(*See also under* **Against**).

When the Lord came they afflicted Him (*Ps.* cv. 17, 18).

The Lord is despised by those who exalt themselves (*Jer.* xviii. 18).

The Lord despised by faith alone (*Dan.* vii. 25; viii. 20-25).

The Lord considered vile, hated, repudiated and rejected (*Ps.* cix. *t.*, 1-6, 13-25).

They will be in the falsification of all truth because they have denied the Lord (*Ezek.* xxiii. 35).

The church did not worship the Lord, but wearied Him with sins, which He endured, from the beginning and also afterward (*Isa.* xliii. 22-27).

The Lord suffered direful things and endured them (*Isa.* xlii. 25).

THE LORD SLAIN.

Those who want to slay the Lord (*Ps.* xxxi. 5).

The evil wish to slay the Lord (*Ps.* xvii. 11, 12).

The evil rise up and wish to slay (*Ps.* xciv. 20, 21).

Those who are then of the church wish to destroy and slay the Lord (*Ps.* lix. *t.*, 1-6).

Those who are of the church where the Word is think that the Lord is to be utterly destroyed (*Ps.* xli. 9 *and prec.*).

Those who are of the church purpose to have the Lord put to death (*Ps.* xxxviii. 11, 12).

Those with whom the church will be at the time will slay the Lord, with the intention of scattering those who believe in Him (*Zech.* xiii. 6, 7).

The hells purpose putting the Lord to death for desiring their good (*Ps.* xxxv. 10-16).

Trust from His Divine against those who purpose to put Him to death (*Ps.* xl. 12-15, 17).

Evil and falsity of religion condemned the Lord to death (*Jer.* xxvi. 7-9); but because He spoke from the Divine, the truths of the church acquitted Him (*ib.* 10-16); an instance of their not condemning to death one who spoke from inspiration (*ib.* 17-19).

The Lord was not condemned on account of the people (*Jer.* xxvi. 24).

Those who are of the church where the Word is, have condemned Him to death (*Ps.* xxii. 12-15).

The Lord delivered up to death. In this way profanation manifested itself (*Jer.* xi. 18, 19, *and prec.*).

They treated the Lord wickedly, but He endured it (*Isa.* l. 6, 7).

THE PASSION OF THE CROSS.

(*See also sub-heading* TEMPTATIONS EVEN TO DESPAIR).

The passion of the cross (p. 4; *Ps.* xxxi. 11-13).

He endured all things even to the passion of the cross (*Isa.* liii. 6-8).

The Lord suffered temptations, even to the last of them, which was that of the cross (*Ps.* xxx. *t.*, 1-12).

They crucified Him (*Ps.* xxii. 16, 17); they divided His garments, or dissipated the truths of the Word (*ib.* 18). He endured by power from the Divine (*ib.* 24).

They gave Him falsity and evil, as, upon the cross, gall and vinegar (*Ps.* lxix. 21).

Through the passion of the cross, a new church will come into existence (*Isa.* liii. 10, 11).

COMBATS OF THE LORD.

(*See also* **Insurrection** *and sub-headings* TEMPTATIONS OF THE LORD, TEMPTATIONS EVEN TO DESPAIR).

The Lord and His combats (*Isa.* lxiii.).
Combats of the Lord with the hells (*Ps.* xviii. 4-6; lxxxiii.).
The Lord will admit them to fight against Him (*Jer.* i. 17-19).
Prophecy concerning the Lord's combats with the hells. Jonah's "three days and nights in the bowels of the fish" signify the entire duration of the combat with the hells (*Jonah* i. 17; ii. 1-10).
The Lord will fight with those who are in falsity of evil (*Joel* ii. 11).
The Lord arouses Himself to fight for the good against the evil (*Ps.* xi. *t.*, 1-5).
The Lord is in combats with the malicious (*Ps.* xxvi. 9, 10).
Description of the combats of the Lord with hells which were especially from the Israelitish and Jewish Church, etc. (*Lam.* iii. 1-66).
The evil fought against Him, but He was helped by the Divine (*Ps* cxviii. 10-14).
The Lord fights from the Divine (*Ps.* xviii. 32-36).
As no one was in truth, and no one was on the Lord's side, He alone fought from Divine truth with His own power (*Isa.* lix. 16, 17); seemingly from revenge (*ib.* lix. 18).
Combats of the Lord from Divine truth (*Jer.* xv. 15, 16).
The Lord alone fought and conquered, that the faithful may obtain salvation (*Isa.* lxiii. 3-6).
The Lord will fight for the new church against the hells, which He will conquer (*Isa.* xlii. 13-15).
The Lord does not fear the hells which fight against Him (*Ps.* xxvii. *t.*, 1-3).
The Lord's confidence during combats, that the Word is being protected (*Jer.* xx. 11-13).
The Lord's combats against the evil, and their dispersion (*Zech.* xiv. 1-5).
Combats of the Lord against the hells, and their subjugation and overthrow (*Ps.* xxxv. *t.*, 1-9).
The temptation combats of the Lord even to despair, even to the thought of withdrawal, etc. (*Ps.* lxix. *t.*, 1-5, *and fol.*).
The Lord would fain give up the combats because of their grievousness (*Ps.* lv. 6-8).

TEMPTATIONS OF THE LORD.

(*See also sub-headings* PRAYER OF THE LORD TO THE FATHER, *also* **Help, Prove**).
The Lord fulfilled the Law, or the Word, from its firsts to its lasts, and therefore He was hated, and suffered temptations, and thus made the Human one with the Divine (*Ps.* cxix.).
Prayer to the Father when in the combats of temptations with the hells, which attack Him (*Ps.* lvii. *t.*, 1-5).
The Lord's temptations, when He subjugated the hells and was then in a state of humiliation, in which He prayed to the Father (*Ps.* iii. *t.*, 1-8).
Temptations of the Lord, in which He has confidence in the Father (*Ps.* lvi. *t.*, 1-4, 10, 11).
Song of praise to the Father by the Lord, that He gave help in temptations (*Ps.* cxvii.).

THE LORD'S TEMPTATIONS EVEN TO DESPAIR.

Prophecy of the Lord's most grievous temptations (*Jonah* i. 17; ii. 1-10).
The state of the Lord's temptations, and the grievous insurrection of the infernals against Him (*Ps.* xiii. *t.*, 1-4).
The grievousness of the Lord's temptations is described (*Ps.* xxxviii. *t.*, 1-10; xxxii. 3, 4).

Respecting the Lord, when in great temptations (*Ps.* iv. *t.*, 1, 2).
The grievousness of temptations is described, in which He prays to the Father (*Ps.* lv. *t.*, 1–5, 9).
The Lord would fain give up the combats because of their grievousness (*Ps.* lv. 6–8; *compare Ps.* lxix. 5).
The growing grievousness of the Lord's temptations even to despair (*Ps.* xlii. 7–10).
Grievousness of the Lord's temptations even to despair (*Ps.* xliii. 1, 2).
The Lord's temptations even to despair (*Ps.* cii. *t.*, 1–11).
The last state of temptations is despair (*Ps.* vi. *t.*, 1–7).
Despair of the Lord because all of the Israelitish and Jewish Church had been in evils and in falsities therefrom and against the Lord, etc. (*Lam.* iii.).
Despair of the Lord, that the Word is blasphemed (*Jer.* xx. 14–18).
Let not the Lord fail in temptations before a new church is formed (*Ps.* cii. 23, 24).
In temptations that continue even to despair, the Lord addresses the Father, that He is seemingly overcome by the infernals (*Ps.* lxxxviii. *t.*, 1–9, 13–18).
State of temptation of the Lord even to despair whether the Father would give help, etc. (*Ps.* lxxvii. *t.*, 1–9, *and fol.*).
He is in the last state of temptations, as if He were forsaken (*Ps.* xliv. 24, 25).
From despair He imagines Himself to be forsaken, but He is not (*Ps.* xxxi. 22).
The Lord's tolerance in a state of temptations (*Ps.* xxxix. *t.*, 1–3, 8–11); the Lord desires the end of the temptations (*ib.* 4–7).
The state of grief and perturbation of the Lord from temptations, with trust from the Divine (*Ps.* xlii. *t.*, 1–6).
Glorification of the Human of the Lord, after He has suffered temptations, even to the last of them which was that of the cross (*Ps.* xxx. *t.*, 1–12).
The Lord was united to His Divine by means of grievous temptations (*Ps.* lxvi. 8–12); thus Divine truth from the Lord is with men (*ib.* 13–17).

THE LORD'S HUMILIATION.

State of the Lord's humiliation (p. 4).
Appearance of the Lord in the state of humiliation (*Isa.* liii.).
The Lord will appear in humility (*Isa.* lii. 14).
The state of humiliation of the Lord is described (*Ps.* viii. 4, 5).
The Lord's humiliation before the Father (*Ps.* iii. *t.*, 1–8).

GRIEF OF THE LORD.

Grief on the part of the Lord and directed to the Lord (*Hab.* i. 1–5).
Grief of the Lord over their falsities (*Jer.* xv. 17, 18).
His grief that justice and truth perish, and that the evil prevail over the good and destroy them (*Hab.* 1–5, 12–17).
Grief of the Lord from temptations, with trust from the Divine (*Ps.* xlii. *t.*, 1–6).
Grief of heart of the Lord (*Ps.* xxxi. 6–10).
Grief of the Lord, because they purpose putting Him to death for desiring their good (*Ps.* xxxv. 10–16).

PRAYER (*oratio*) OF THE LORD TO THE FATHER.

(*For full additional references under this head, see* **Help**).
Prayer of the Lord to the Father (p. 4; *Ps.* iii. *t.*, 1–8).
Prayer that He may be purified of the infirmities derived from the mother (*Ps.* li. *t.*, 1–5).

INDEX OF WORDS AND SUBJECTS.

Prayer of the Lord to the Father, that He who is true and just may hear (*Ps.* cxliii. *t.*, 1, 2); that He may not fail in temptations (*ib.* 4, 7); He longs for the ancient state in respect to the church (*ib.* 5, 6).

Prayer to the Father to keep Him (*Ps.* cxxi.).

Prayer of the Lord to the Father, to have regard to His perfection (*Ps.* cxli. *t.*, 1, 2).

Prayer that He may be preserved from the hells, whence He will have joy (*Ps.* xxxv. 17, 18[, 24]).

Prayer to the Father that Divine truth may comfort Him (*Ps.* xliii. 3, 4).

Prayer to the Father that the evil may be requited and judged (*Ps.* x. 12–18).

Prayer to the Father when in the combats of temptations with the hells which attack Him (*Ps.* lvii. *t.*, 1–5).

What the Lord says (*sermo*) to the Father; He does not fear the hells which fight against Him (*Ps.* xxvii. *t.*, 1–3).

Prayer to the Father against those in the perverted church, who secretly try to destroy Him (*Ps.* cxx.).

Prayer to the Father concerning those who are then of the church, who wish to destroy Him, etc. (*Ps.* lix. *t.*, 1–6, *and fol.*).

May He be delivered from temptations, and come among those who acknowledge Him (*Ps.* cxlii. 6, 7).

O that He may be delivered from the hells which assault Him with falsities (*Ps.* cxliv. 5–8, 11).

Prayer of the Lord to the Father to be delivered from falsifiers and hypocrites, who purpose evil against Him in the perverted church (*Ps.* cxl. *t.*, 1–8).

Prayer to the Father that He may be preserved in temptations from the deceitful and hypocrites (*Ps.* cxxiv.).

Prayer of the Lord to the Father, that the hypocrites may be subjugated (*Ps.* xxviii. *t.*, 1–5).

Prayer to the Father in temptations which continued even to despair, that He was seemingly overcome by the infernals (*Ps.* lxxxviii.).

Prayer to the Father that He be not forsaken (*Ps.* xxii. *t.*, 1–5, *and fol.*; xxxix. 12, 13).

The Lord invokes the Father that He may not be forsaken, but that He may conquer and subjugate the hells, which were especially from the Israelitish and Jewish Church (*Lam.* iii.).

Prayer to the Father to be present, because He has been utterly rejected by the Jewish nation (*Ps.* cxxiii.).

Prayer of the Lord to the Father, that He may be protected from those who devise evil, and who want to slay Him, etc. (*Ps.* xxxi. *t.*, 1–4, *and fol.*).

Prayer of the Lord to the Father for those who wish to kill Him (*Ps.* lix. 11).

The Lord prays to the Father during grievous temptations (*Ps.* lv. *t.*, 1–5, 9).

Prayer of the Lord to the Father, when He was in the last state of temptations, etc. (*Ps.* vi. *t.*, 1–7).

Prayer of the Lord when He was in temptations, even to despair, which state is described (*Ps.* cii. *t.*, 1–11).

Prayer of the Lord to the Father, to institute a new church after judgment has been executed upon the evil (*Ps.* lxxxv. *t.*, 1–7).

TRUST (OR CONFIDENCE) (*fiducia*) OF THE LORD.

No one knows the Lord but the Father only, in whom is His trust (*Ps.* cxlii. 4, 5).

Confidence in the Father (*Ps.* lix. 8–10).

Confidence of the Lord from His Divine (*Ps.* lvii. 7, 8; xlii. *t.*, 1–6).

Trust of the Lord from His Divine against the hells (*Ps.* xviii. *t.*, 1-3, 6).
The Lord has confidence in the Father during temptations (*Ps.* lvi. *t.*, 1-4, 10, 11).
Confidence that the Father will assist Him (*Ps.* lxxi. 1-5, 7, 12, 14).
Confidence respecting help (*Ps.* lix. 16, 17).
Trust from His Divine against those who purpose to put Him to death (*Ps.* xl. 12-15, 17).
The Lord cannot be hurt by the evil who rise up against Him and wish to slay Him (*Ps.* xvii. 13 *and prec.*).
Trust in the Father that the hells will not prevail (*Ps.* xxxviii. 9, 15-22).
Confidence that their evil thoughts and intentions, by which they themselves perish, do no harm (*Ps.* cxli. 8-10).
Confidence respecting deliverance (*Ps.* lx. 4, 5).
The Lord has confidence of being delivered from the hells, by which He is assaulted mightily (*Ps.* cxliii. 8-12).
The Lord is delivered (*exemptus*) through trust in the Father (*Ps.* xxxi. 14-21).
The Lord has confidence respecting the victory (*Ps.* xiii. 5, 6).
Confidence from the Divine that He will be raised up (*Ps.* xlii. 11).
The Lord's trust in Himself for delivering the good whom the evil infest (*Ps.* xvi. *t.*, 1, 2; 3-5).
The Lord's confidence during combats, that the Word is being protected (*Jer.* xx. 11-13).

THE LORD'S VICTORY OVER THE HELLS.

(*See also* **Help** (*adjuvo*), **Lord,** CONFIDENCE OF; **Overcome, Overthrow, Subjugate**).
The Lord's victory over the hells (*Ps.* vii. 12-16; ix. 15-17).
The Lord will conquer the hells and destroy their power (*Isa.* xlii. 13-15).
They will succumb, because the Divine is the Lord's (*Jer.* i. 17-19).
The Lord's victory over those who are in falsities (*Jer.* xv. 19-21).
Redemption when the Lord conquers (*Ps.* xxvi. 11, 12).
Because the Lord endured such things (as the passion of the cross) He goes forth the victor (*Isa.* liii. 12).
Being helped, the Lord repressed the hells (*Ps.* vi. 8-10).
The Lord has conquered the hells (*Ps.* xxiv. 7-10).
The Lord has powerfully conquered the hells by means of Divine truth (*Ps.* xlv. 3-5).
The Lord alone fought and conquered (*Isa.* lxiii. 3-6).
Victory of the Lord over the hells, owing to which He has dominion over heaven and earth (*Ps.* cx. *t.*, 1-3); and authority over the hells (*ib.* 4-17).
The name of God will be preached when He has gained the victory *Ps.* lxxi. 8, 15-24).

CONFESSION AND THANKSGIVING BY THE LORD.

(*For additional references see* **Song of Praise** (*celebratio*), **Help.**)
Confession of the Lord resultant upon the Father helping Him in temptations (*Ps.* lxxxvi 9-12).
Thanksgiving of the Father that He has helped Him (*Ps.* xl. *t.*, 1-5).
Thanksgiving and joy of the Lord that the evil have been judged and destroyed, and the good have been delivered (*Ps.* ix. *t.*, 1-14, 18-20).

GLORIFICATION OF THE HUMAN OF THE LORD; OR, UNITION
(OR ONENESS (*unitio*)) WITH THE DIVINE.

Glorification of the Human of the Lord, or unition with the Divine (p. 4).
Glorification of the Human of the Lord (*Ps.* xcviii.).
The Lord will be glorified (*Ps.* xvii. 15).
After the church has been consummated, the judgment will come, and the

INDEX OF WORDS AND SUBJECTS.

Word will cease, and the Lord will glorify His Human (*Dan.* ix. 24).
Respecting the Human of the Lord, that it will be made Divine (*Ps.* lx. 6-9); from His own power (*ib.* 10); and from His Divine (*ib.* 12).
Glorification of the Human of the Lord after He has suffered temptations, even to the last of them (*Ps.* xxx. *t.*, 1–12).
The human will become Divine when the hells have been subjugated (*Ps.* cviii. 10–13).
The Lord has glorified His Human (*Ps.* xxiv. 7–10).
The state of the glorification of the Lord is described (*Ps.* viii. 6–8).
The Lord has made the Human Divine (*Ps.* xlv. 7, 8); from this heaven and the church are His, and they are in Divine truths from Him (*ib.* 8); from the same cause there are affections for truth, and in these are the societies of heaven (*ib.* 9).
The Lord's Human, glorified, will rise again (*Ps.* xvi. 8–11).
Desire and love of the Lord to be united (*uniri*) to His Divine (*Ps.* lxiii. *t.*, 1–8).
The Lord to be made one (*uniri*) with the Father (*Ps.* xci. 1).
Union (*unio*) of the Lord with the Father (*Ps.* xxvii. 4–10, 13, 14).
Unless oneness (*unitio*) be effected with the Father, the hells will prevail (*Ps.* lxxxix. 49–51).
There will be no fear from the hells when the Divine has been made one (*uniri*) with the Human (*Ps.* xci. 13–16).
The oneness (*unitio*) of the Divine of the Lord with His Divine Human, which is the "sabbath" (*Ps.* xcii. *t.*).
How all things of the Father are united (*uniri*) with the Lord (*Ps.* cxxxix. 16–18 *and prec.*).
Oneness (*unitio*) with the Divine Human, therefore Divine truth is from Him (*Ps.* lxxxix. 3–5); and thus the Lord has all power (*ib.* 6–9, 13).
From the uniting (*unitio*) of the Divine and the Human in the Lord will be a church that will be in all truth from the Lord, and safe from infestation from falsities (*Ps.* lxv.).
The Lord was united (*uniri*) to His Divine by means of grievous temptations (*Ps.* lxvi. 8–12); thus Divine truth from the Lord is with men (*ib.* 13–17).
By oneness (*unitio*) with the Father, or the Divine, the Lord, or the Human, has omnipotence over the hells (*Ps.* lxxxix. 19–25); there will be eternal oneness with Him (*ib.* 26–29, 35–37); even if those of the church should fail there will be eternal oneness with Him (*ib.* 30–37).
Through the union (*unitio*) of the Divine and the Human in the Lord, heaven and the church will endure to eternity (*Ps.* xciii. 1, 2); the joy of those who are in Divine truths from this source (*ib.* 3, 4).
The Lord united (*uniri*) His Divine to His Human (*Ps.* cxxxii. 8).
The Lord has nothing in common with those who are in evils, because He has been made one (*uniri*) with His Divine (*Ps.* cxli. 3–5).
The Father knows everything of the Lord's thought and will, because He is made one (*uniri*) with Him (*Ps.* cxxxix. *t.*, 1–5).
The Lord's song in praise of the Father because of union (*unio*) (*Ps.* lxi. 6–8).
Song in praise of the Divine power of the Lord through union (*unio*) (*Ps.* lxviii. 32–36).
Happy is he who regards holy the union (*unio*) of the Divine and the Human, and of the Lord with the church (*Isa.* lvi. 2); let not any one believe that He is separated from the Divine (*ib.* 3); strangers who regard that union holy will be received into the church rather than others, etc. (*ib.* 4, 5).
If they regard the union (*unio*) of the Lord with the church as holy, they will come into heaven (*Isa.* lviii. 13, 14).

THE LORD AS THE WORD.

*(See also **Teach, Lead.**)*
Prophecy concerning the Lord in respect to the Word (*Ezek.* i. 1–3).
The Lord is called the Word because all things of the Word signified and represented Him (p. 163).
The Lord in respect to the Word; or, the glorification of His Human (*Ezek.* i. 1–3; *note marginal reference*).
The Lord in respect to the Word, which He will declare unto them (*Micah* iii. 8).
The Lord is the Word (*Jer.* xxiii. 28, 29; *Ps.* xcix. 1, 2).
The Lord is the Word and the church (*Isa.* viii. 13–16).
The Lord as to the Divine truth, or the Word, from which He has Divine power (*Isa.* lxiii. 1).
The Lord is Divine truth itself (*Ps.* lxviii. 3–5, 31).
The Lord appeared in the midst of His Divine truth, which is the Word (*Isa.* vi. 1–4).
From the Lord are Divine truths, or the Word (*Ps.* civ. 1–4).
All truth is from the Lord (*Jer.* x. 12, 13).

THE LORD AS JEHOVAH AND GOD.

*(For full additional references on the subject of the Lord as the God of heaven and the church see under **God**, see also **Omniscience, Divine, Power, Kingdom, Worship.**)*
The Lord after being afflicted became the God of heaven and earth (*Ps.* cv. 19–22).
The Divine will be worshipped in the Lord (*Ps.* cxvi. 12–19).
The Lord is Jehovah (*Isa.* xliv. 5–7; xlv. 6); let all men men know this (*Isa.* xlv. 5, 6; *cf. Jer.* xxiii. 7, 8).
The Lord alone is (*Ps.* xc. *t.*, 1–6).
The Lord above the heavens (*Ezek.* i. 26).
The Lord is heaven and the church, therefore those depart from Him are damned (*Jer.* xvii. 12, 13).
Heaven and the church are the Lord's (*Ps.* cxv. 16).
The Lord He should be received, because He alone is God, and from Him alone is salvation (*Isa.* xlv. 21, 22).
In the Lord alone is the life of heaven (*Isa.* xlv. 23–25).
Under the Lord (*Micah* iv. 5, 7, 10).
The Lord is God from whom are all truths and goods (*Jer.* v. 21–24).
From the Lord are all things (*Isa.* xlv. 7).
The Lord is the origin of good (*Zech.* iv. 8–10).
Worshippers of God should look to the Lord, who is the source (*Isa.* li. 1, 2).
The Lord seen (*Dan.* x. 1–6).

ACKNOWLEDGMENT OF THE LORD.

No acknowledgment of the Lord among "Moab" (*Isa.* xvi. 1, 2).
Although the church is there, yet they do not acknowledge the Lord (*Mal.* i. 5, 6).
How "Babylon" was compelled to acknowledge and worship the Lord (*Dan.* iii. 26–30; iv. 1–3).
Acknowledgment of the Lord on the part of "Babylonians" before those who were under obedience to them (*Dan.* iv. 34–37).
Exhortation to acknowledge the Lord (*Jer.* iv. 1, 2).
Let them not go back, but acknowledge the Lord (*Ezek.* xiv. 11).
Let them acknowledge and worship the Divine Human of the Lord, lest they perish (*Ps.* ii. 10–12).
So long as they acknowledge the Lord, those of the vastated church will remain (*Jer.* xii. 16, 17).

Those who are completely vastated can at last acknowledge the Lord (*Jer.* xxiv. 4–7).
Those who do not acknowledge Him, vanish (*Jer.* x. 11).
They will perish that whoever is able may acknowledge the Lord (*Zeph.* ii. 11).
When the old church is at an end those who at heart acknowledge the Lord will be saved (*Hab.* iii. 18, 19).
The Lord's Divine ought to be acknowledged and not violated (*Jer.* xvii. 21–24); then they will possess understanding of the Word (*ib.* 25); and then their worship will be from truths (*ib.* 26). If they will not acknowledge the Divine of the Lord the externals will perish from the (evil) internals (*ib.* 27).
May the Lord be delivered from temptations, and come among those who acknowledge Him (*Ps.* cxlii. 6, 7).
The Lord perceives that a church will come into existence which will acknowledge Him (*Ps.* lxxxv. 8–13).
A church will exist which will acknowledge the Lord (*Isa.* lxii. 1–3).
A new church will be instituted which will acknowledge the Lord (*Amos* ix. 11, 12).
Acknowledgment of the Lord by the new church when delivered from falsities and evils (*Ezek.* xxxvi. 24–30, 37, 38).
Those who are in good will acknowledge the Lord, who is Divine truth itself (*Ps.* lxviii. 3–5, 31).
The simple will acknowledge the Lord at His coming (*Ezek.* xxxiv. 26–31).
Those who are far removed from truths will acknowledge the Lord (*Isa* l. 10).
Those of whom the church will consist will acknowledge the Lord (*Jer.* xvi. 19–21).
A new church of those who will acknowledge the Lord (*Zeph.* iii. 9–20).
The new church will acknowledge the Lord (*Ezek.* xliv. 15–31; *Hosea* i. 10, 11; ii. 18–20; iii. 1–5; vi. 1–3; *Zech.* viii. 7–9).
The new church will acknowledge and worship the Lord (*Ps.* xviii. 43, 44).
They will acknowledge the Lord from whom is the church (*Joel* iii. 16, 17).
They will acknowledge that the Lord is Jehovah and that the church is His (*Jer.* xxiii. 7, 8).
They have acknowledged the Divine Human from eternity, in which is all of salvation (*Ps.* lxxii. 17).
The whole church will acknowledge and worship the Lord from joy of heart (*Ps.* lxvii. *t.*, 1–5, 7).
Those who acknowledge and worship the Lord will be saved (*Joel* ii. 32).
Happy is he who acknowledges the Lord (*Ps.* cxliv. 15).
Those who acknowledge the Lord possess all good and truth (*Ps.* xxxvi. 10).
Those who will acknowledge the Lord will receive the Holy Spirit (*Isa.* xliv. 1–4).
Acknowledging the Lord and doing the commandments meant by the "covenant" (*Jer.* xi. 1–3; *see the whole chapter*).
From acknowledgment of the Lord is everything of truth and good, and hence everything of power and wisdom (*Jer.* ix. 23, 24).

REPRESENTATIVES OF THE LORD.

The Lord meant by "Cyrus" (*Isa.* xliv. 28; xlv).
The Lord meant by "Levi" (*Mal.* ii. 5–7).
The Lord meant by "David" (p. 123).
Things pertaining to the church signify things pertaining to the Lord (p. 168).

The Lord in respect to Divine love represented (*Ezek.* viii. 1, 2).
Lot (*sors*).—The lot of the evil compared with the lot of the good (*Ps.* xxxvii.).
Lot (*Lothus*).—"Lot" means natural knowledges (*Gen.* xiii.).
Love (*see also* **Evil love, Desire, Cupidity, Divine Love,** *etc.*).
Natural love has consumed all things of the church, resulting in their destruction (*Ezek.* xxviii. 19, 20).
Those in love of falsity and evil (*Isa.* lxv. 1–5).
Love of evil and falsity to be no more (*Isa.* lx. 19).
Love of things that have been falsified by knowledges (*Jer.* xliv. 15–19).
Love of falsities of every kind causes unwillingness to repent and be converted (*Jer.* xviii. 11–16).
By loving falsities of every kind they annihilate the church in themselves (*Jer.* xviii. 14–16).
Because they all love falsities and worship other gods, they have no help (*auxilium*) (*Jer.* xi. 11–13).
The love of self grows, and man grows vile therefrom (*Hab.* ii. 4, 5). Such a man further and fully described (*see ib.* 6–20).
They have loved evils that gush forth from the love of self (*Jer.* xix. 4, 5).
All who are in the love of self will be destroyed by the Lord (*Isa.* ii. 10–18).
Hell is actually there, because there is nothing but the lust of the love of self (*Jer.* xix. 12, 13).
Love of ruling causes the destruction of "Babylon" (*Jer.* l. 31, 32 *and prec.*).

Love of spiritual good and truth, and the love of natural good and truth; their distinction and oneness (*Ezek.* i. 10, 11).
There will be no falsity with those who love truth and good (*Isa.* xxxii. 20).
Love of the Lord in place of love of evil and falsity (*Isa.* lx. 19, 20).
The life of truth and good should be loved, and not the life of falsity and evil (*Micah* vi. 9, 11).
Those who love the neighbor and God will be of the Lord's church (*Ps.* xv. *t.*, 1–5).
Those who made the church to consist in doctrine and a life of love and charity signified by "Abel" (*Gen.* iv.).
Word of the Lord from love and faith (*Ps.* lxxii. 5).
Love of the Word in the new church (*Zech.* viii. 20–23).

The Lord in respect to Divine love (*Ezek.* viii. 1–2).
The Lord loves to be united to His Divine (*Ps.* lxiii. *t.*, 1–8).
Love and desire for the church and heaven (*Ps.* lxxxiv. *t.*, 1–4).
The Lord loves those that are perfect, and rejects the evil and the haughty (*Ps.* ci. 2–8).
* The Lord will love the church formed by Him of the nations who are in falsities of ignorance (*Ps.* cxxxvii. 5, 6, *and prec.*).
The Lord loves them, therefore He should be worshipped from affection for truth and good (*Ps.* cxlix. 1–4).
The loved one (*Jer.* xxxi. 2–5).

Lowest heaven (*see* **Ultimate heaven**).
Lowest parts (*see* **Ultimates**).
Lumen (*see* **Natural light**).
Lust (*see* **Cupidity**).

Magic.—End of the Ancient Church, when it became magical (*Gen.* xi. 10–32).
Magnificent.—A magnificent word respecting the Lord, and respecting conjunction with Him (*Ps.* xlv. *t.*, 1).
Malevolent (*Isa.* xxxii. 6–8).
Malice.—Malice of the hells described (*Ps.* lv. 9–14).
  Malice of the infernals (*Ps.* lvi. 5, 6).
  Malice of the hells against the Lord (*Ps.* lvii. 4, 6).
  The Lord in combats with the malicious (*Ps.* xxvi. 9, 10).
  Those who wish to kill the Lord destroy themselves by malice (*Ps.* lix. 12–15).
Man (*see also under* ***Angel, Own***).
  Man has been born for heaven (*Isa.* xlv. 18).
  Man is nothing of himself (*Ps.* xc. *t.*, 1–6).
  All things of the church are from the Lord, and nothing from man (*Ps.* cxxvii. *t.*, 1, 2).
  Man does not establish the church, but God (*Ps.* xliv. 5–8).
  The Word represented as a man (*Ezek.* i. 5).
Manifest (*manifesto*).—Manifestation of the total devastation of the church (*Isa.* xxxvi. 21, 22).
  Profanation of good and truth by the church made manifest by their delivering up the Lord to death (*Jer.* xi. 15–19).
  The Lord will manifest Himself (*Isa.* lii. 10).
  Manifestation of the Lord (*Dominus visus*) to reveal, etc. (*Dan.* x. 1–21).
Marriage.—When the Lord comes and establishes a church truth and good will make one (*Jer.* iii. 18; *see further under* ***Union***).
Memory.—To learn truths and retain them in the memory belongs to the spiritual church (*Jer.* xxxv. 1–10).
Mercy (*misericordia*) (*see also* ***Pity*** (*miseratio*)).
  They have closed against themselves the way to all mercy (*Ezek.* viii. 17, 18).
  They rejected all mercy because they perverted all truths and goods which they had in all abundance (*Jer.* v. 7,8).
  The new church will acknowledge their evils, and at the same time the Lord's mercy (*Ezek.* xx. 43, 44).
  Prayers of the church to the Lord that their sins may be forgiven from mercy (*Ps.* xxv. 7–11).
  What the Lord does from pure mercy (*Ps.* cxxxvi. 1–26; *Isa.* lxiii. 7, 8).
  Redemption and reformation are from mercy, because the Lord knows the infirmities of man (*Ps.* ciii. 8–18).
  Mercy of the Lord on the new church (*Ezek.* xiv. 21–23).
  Song in praise of the Lord because of His mercy (*Ps.* cxlv. 8, 9).
Messiah.—They believe that the Messiah will come to exalt them to glory (*Hag.* i. 1–4).
Michael.—"Michael" means such as are in truths from good (*Dan.* x. 7–21).
Ministry (*ministerium*) (*see also* ***Preacher, Shepherd, Teacher***).
  The ministry of the new church (*Ezek.* xliv. 15–31).
Miracle.—The children of Jacob confirmed in the Word by means of miracles (*Ps.* lxxviii. *t.*, 1–7).
  Although those who were of the church beheld Divine miracles, they backslid, and yet they were preserved (*Ps.* cvi. 6–8); as at the sea Suph and afterwards in the desert frequently, nevertheless they rebelled (*ib.* 9–34).
  Miracles in the desert had no effect on the backsliding Israelites (*Ps.* lxxviii. 11–31); on account of the miracles they returned indeed, but only with the mouth, not with the heart (*ib.* 32–37); again they were seemingly converted when they recalled the miracles in Egypt (*ib.* 41–51).

Mislead (see **Lead astray**).
Missions (see **Evangelization**).
Mix (*commingo*) (see **Commingle**).
Moab.—" Moab" means those who have rejected the goods of charity, and have perverted the goods of the Word (*Isa.* xv., xvi.).
"Moab" means those who adulterated the goods of the Word and of the church (*Jer.* xlviii.).
Moderator (see **Ruler**).
Moral (see **Spiritual Moral**).
Most Ancient Church (see also **Canaan**).
The Most Ancient Church was a representative church (p. 163).
The Most Ancient Church is briefly described by "Adam" and his posterity (p. 163).
The Most Ancient Church was a celestial church (*Gen.* ii.).
Regeneration of the men of the Most Ancient Church (*Gen.* i.).
Their intelligence and wisdom (*Gen.* ii.).
Its fall and end (*Gen.* iii.).
Divisions of that church (*Gen.* iv., v.).
Its destruction (*Gen.* vii.).
Its end (*Gen.* vi. 1–7, 11–13; viii.).
Mother.—Prayer that He may be purified of the infirmities derived from the mother (*Ps.* li. *t.*, 1–5).
Mourn (*lugeo*), **Mourning** (*luctus*).
Mourning over the destruction of the representatives of the church will extend even to those who were in celestial good (*Micah* i. 8–12).
Mourning over destruction of truths and goods with the "children of Ammon" (*Jer.* xlix. 3).
Mourning over the destruction of the goods and truths of the church (*Joel* i. 8–13).
All things and every single thing of the church will mourn (*Zech.* xii. 10–14).
Grievous mourning of the church on account of the devastation (*Lam.* ii. 10–12).
The devastation does not come to an end through outward mourning (*Jer.* iv. 8).
Multiplication.—There was as yet only multiplication of truth and not the fructification of good, and thus not the church (*Gen.* xv. 1–6).
The church will be vastly multiplied (*Zech.* ii. 3–5).
Multiplication of truths (*Isa.* liv. 1–3).
Multiplying of truths and goods (*Ps.* cvii. 35–38, 41–43).

Name (see also **Canaan**).
The name of God will be preached when He has gained the victory (*Ps.* lxxi. 8, 15–24).
Nation (*gens*) (see also **Gentiles**, *etc.*).
Conversion of the nations (*Jonah* i.–iv.).
The Jews were commanded to teach the Word to the nations round about, but they would not (*Jonah* i. 1–3).
The nations perceived that the the state of the church was perverted among themselves, because of the loss of knowledges among the Jews, etc. (*Jonah* i. 7–9); their further history fully described (see i.–iv.).
Lamentation by the nations who are in falsities from ignorance; of these a church will be formed by the Lord, which He will love (*Ps.* cxxxvii. 1–6).

INDEX OF WORDS AND SUBJECTS. 257

Even those from the nations who are external-natural will draw near (*Zech.* xiv. 16-19).

A new church will be established out of the nations by the Lord when He comes into the world (*Micah* iv. 1, 2).

Joy of the nations with whom a new church will arise (*Ps.* cxxvi. *t.*, 1-4); it will be instructed (*ib.* 5).

The church established by the Lord from the nations (*Ps.* cxiv. 1, 2).

Natural (*naturalis*).—Those who are merely natural, etc. (*Ps.* xlix. 5, 6, *and fol.*).

They will be merely natural, abiding only in reasonings from the natural man (*Hosea* ix. 1-3).

Those who are in ignorance, and natural, will draw near (*Isa.* xlv. 14).

The natural to be brought to the church by the Lord (*Jer.* xvi. 16, 17).

Those who were of the church were natural, and in knowledges (*scientifica*) (*Ps.* cv. 23, 24); therefore their natural has been purged of falsities and evils of every kind which infested (*ib.* 25-36); afterward truths and good, and protection from falsities are granted them (*ib.* 37-41); and He causes them to be a church (*ib.* 42-45).

—— **(the)** (*naturale*).—The natural of the Ancient Church is meant by "Ham" (*Gen.* ix. 18-29).

The natural of man will perish by reasonings from knowledges; *general subject* (*Jer.* xlvi.).

The whole natural perishes, nor is there anything there but falsity and evil (*Jer.* xlvi. 13-19).

The natural to be first imbued with truths from good (*Isa.* xxi. 5-7).

Enlightenment in the natural is from the Lord (*Ps.* cxxxix. 11, 12).

The natural to become spiritual (*Isa.* lx. 17).

—— *external.*—The natural external without an internal (*Ezek.* xvii. 15, 16).

The natural external is opposed to all things of the church (*Ezek.* xix. 4-7).

The Jews did not depart from worship of other gods, however much admonished, because they were natural external (*Ezek.* xx. 4-9).

—— *good.*—In the progress of the Babylonish religion, the church prevails, not from spiritual good, but from natural good (*Dan.* ii. 39).

—— *knowledges* meant by "Lot" (*Gen.* xiii.).

—— *light* (*lumen*).—The self-intelligent ("Edom") defend falsities by natural light (*Obad.* 4, 5).

—— *love* (*see also under* **Love**).

Love of natural good and truth and its distinction from the love of spiritual good and truth, and its oneness therewith (*Ezek.* i. 10, 11).

Natural good will no longer remain (*Isa.* xxi. 1-4).

Natural good still with some (*Isa.* xxxviii. 21, 22).

—— *man* (*see also preceding topics, and* **Fall, Knowledges, Reasoning, Lead astray**).

There is no longer any truth or good in the natural man (*Isa.* xxvii. 1).

Falsities out of the natural man devastate (*Jer.* ii. 16).

Falsities from the natural man destroy (*Jer.* xv. 12-14).

Knowledges of the natural man perverted remains (*Jer.* xli. 16-18).

Knowledges of the natural man should not have been consulted. The consequence (*Jer.* xlii., xliii.).

Of the natural man who, in things Divine, trusts nothing but his knowledges (*scientifica*) (*Ezek.* xxix. 1-3 *and fol.*).

Something of a church will be established out of those who are natural and in knowledges (*scientifica*) (*ib.* 13-16).

Of the natural man who is in knowledges (*scientifica*) (*Ezek.* xxxi. 1, 2).

The church where the Word is should depart from the affections of the natural man (*Ps.* xlv. 10).

The natural man will be subdued (*Ps.* lxviii. 30).

Instruction of the natural man (*Gen.* xii. 9-20).
Combat in the natural man (*Gen.* xiv. 1-17).
How the natural man became spiritual-natural, and removed evils and falsities from himself (*Gen.* xiv. 18-24 *and prec.*).
Conjunction of truth and good of the natural man, from which there would be only an external church, which is natural (*Gen.* xvi.).
Reformation of the natural man (*Ps.* cv.).
The good of love flows into the truths of the external or natural man (*Ps.* cxxxiii. 2).
The Lord alone delivers the natural man from falsities of evil, and there implants the church (*Ps.* cxxxv. 8-13).
The Lord delivers the natural man from falsities of evil, and there establishes the church, and dissipates evils of every kind (*Ps.* cxxxvi. 10-22).
—— -*sensual.*—When the end comes, those who are natural-sensual will be persistent (*Dan.* xi. 44, 45).
—— *truth.*—There is scarcely any natural truth remaining (*Isa.* x. 12-19).
Unless spiritual and natural truth and good become concordant, there can be no church (*Jer.* xxxiii. 23-26).

Neighbor.—Those who love the neighbor and God will be of the Lord's church (*Ps.* xv. *t.*, 1-5).

New church (see also **Acknowledge, Christian Church, Church, Confess, Despair, Establish, Good, Ignorance, Institute, Lord,** GLORIFICATION OF; **Nations, New Jerusalem, Receive, Redemption**).
General subject (*Jer.* xxxiii.).
A new church will be instituted by the Lord (*Amos* ix. 11, 12).
A new church to be instituted (*Jer.* xxix. 10-15).
A new church from the Lord (*Zech.* i. 12-21; ii., iii., iv., vi., viii., etc., *which see for particulars.*
A new church to be established by the Lord (*Hosea* iii.).
A new church to be established (*Isa.* xiv. 1-3; xviii. 3-6; xliv. 26; lxv. 17, 18; lxvi. 7-9).
A new church to be established is meant by "Israel" and "Zion" (*Jer.* xxxi.).
The time is long drawn out before a new church consisting of others can be established (*Jer.* viii. 18-22; ix. 1).
A new church in place of the old (*Isa.* xxiv. 22, 23).
A new church will come into existence in place of the former church, which is condemned (*Obad.* 17, 18).
A new church will come into existence when the former has been condemned (*Ezek.* xxviii. 25, 26).
There will be a new church from the Lord because they have destroyed the former (*Ps.* liii. 6 *and prec.*).
A new church from the Lord on the destruction of the old (*Zech.* xii. 10).
When the evil perish and are cast into hell, a new church made up of those who acknowledge the Lord will arise (*Zeph.* iii. 6-20).
A new church established when the old perishes (*Isa.* xxix. 17-19; xxxvii. 30-35).
A new church established when the former has been destroyed (*Jer.* xxxiii. 1-5).
On the destruction of the hells there will be a new church which will acknowledge and worship the Lord (*Ps.* xviii. 43, 44).
A new church at the last judgment (*Isa.* xxxiv. 17).
A new church after the judgment (*Isa.* xxvii. 6-12, 13).
A new church established after destruction of "Babylon" (*Jer.* l. 18-20).
Through the passion of the cross a new church will come into existence (*Isa.* liii. 10, 11).
A new church with those with whom truths have not been completely lost (*Isa.* xxvii. 7, 8).

A new church of those who obey (*Isa.* lxvi. 5).
A new church of those who had previously been in no truths whatever (*Isa.* xliii. 18-21).
A new church will be gathered together from all parts (*Ps.* lxxxvii.).
A new church gathered together by the Lord from all nations (*Ezek.* xxxix. 25-29).
Those outside of the church shall draw near, etc. (*Isa.* xxv. 3-5; xxxv.; xlii. 9-12).
Those outside of the church will receive enlightenment from the Lord (*Isa.* xxiv. 14-16).
A new church which the Lord has redeemed (*Ps.* cvii. 1-3); they are in falsities of ignorance, but in a desire for truth and good, etc. (*ib.* 4-8 *and fol.*).
A new church to be formed of those in ignorance (*Isa.* xviii. 7; xli. 25, 26; 27; *see also Isa.* xlix. 12).
To the new church: The Lord alone is the God of heaven and earth (*Isa.* xliv. 23, 24).
The new church will receive the Lord (*Isa.* ix. 2-4).
The new church trusts in the Lord (*Isa.* xxx. 18, 19).
Joy that there is a new church that trusts in the Lord, who will save it from evils (*Ps.* lxvi. *t.,* 1-5).
The new church prays to the Lord to come and lead (*Ps.* lxxx. *t.,* 1-3, 7).
The new church is the Lord's church (*Ezek.* xlviii. 35).
The new church will acknowledge and confess that they have evils and falsities (*Jer.* iii. 22-25).
Those who will be of the new church are to be purified by temptations, and prepared, and a new church constituted of such will come into existence, which will acknowledge the Lord, etc. (*Hosea* ii. 14-20 *and fol.*).
The new church will shake off falsities of every kind (*Isa.* xi. 13-15).
The new church will reject falsities and evils (*Isa.* xxxi. 7).
Falsities and evils will not hurt the new church (*Isa.* xliii. 2).
The new church will disperse all the evils and falsities of those who are in the mere sense of the letter and in external worship (*Ezek.* xxxix. 9, 10); and will wholly destroy them (*ib.* 11-16); and will be imbued with goods of all kinds (*ib.* 17-22).
A new church will come when the former church is devastated; it will be in the light of truth, from the Lord, it will be taught and led; infernal things will be removed from it, and the Divine compassion will be there (*Micah* vii. 7-20).
A new church from the Lord, after the Jewish Church has been destroyed. Its quality; and its doctrine in respect to celestial, spiritual and external good and truth (*Ezek.* xl. 1-49).
Worship of the internal church (*Ezek.* xli.); and of the external church xlii.).
Worship from the good of love (*Ezek.* xliii. 12-27).
The Word in the sense of the letter there (*Ezek.* xliii. 1-11).
The knowledges (*cognitiones*) of that church, which are introductory truths (*Ezek.* xlviii. 30-34).
When the Lord comes, those who will be led to the new church will be instructed (*Ezek.* xxiv. 24-27).
A new church will come into existence in which will be life (*Ezek.* xxxvii. 3-6).
The new church will be instructed and receive life (*Isa.* xxvi. 19).
The new church will be instructed (*Isa.* xxx. 20, 21).
Knowledge of cognitions will be serviceable to the new church (*Isa.* xvii. 3).
Knowledges (*cognitiones*) will be serviceable to the new church (*Isa.* xxiii. 18).

The Lord will disclose truths to the new church (*Isa.* xxv. 6-8).
The new church will understand truths (*Isa.* xxix. 22-24).
The new church will be in truths from the Lord (*Ezek.* xi. 17-20).
It will be enlightened by the Word (*Ezek.* xi. 22, 23).
The new church will understand the Word (*Isa.* xi. 13-15).
The doctrine of truth, and the understanding of it, will be in the new church (*Amos* ix. 13-15).
The Word will be for the Lord's new church (*Zech.* xiii. 1).
The new church will be in all truth and good of doctrine of the church (*Isa.* lxvi. 20, 21).
The new church will drink in Divine truth with joy (*Isa.* lxvi. 10, 11).
The new church will have all goods and truths (*Isa.* lxvi. 12-14).
Those who are of the new church have been accepted, with whom truths and goods will be multiplied (*Ps.* cvii. 35-38, 41-43).
The very truths of heaven will be in the new church, and more than before (*Isa.* lxii. 1-3).
In the new church will be all goods and truths, thus all things of heaven (*Isa.* lxv. 19-21).
The new church will have truth and good, and be protected from falsities (*Isa.* xxxii. 15-18).
The new church will be protected by the Lord (*Isa.* xxxi. 5, 6; xxxv. 4-9).
The Jewish Church will have no power over the Lord's church (*Micah* v. 9).
Evils described that do not invade those who will be of the Lord's new church (*Micah* ii. 12, 13).
The new church will come into delights of truth and good from the Lord (*Isa.* xxx. 29, 30).
Those things which are of heaven and the church will abide with them (*Isa.* lxvi. 22).
The new church is beloved, and will receive the goods of the church (*Jer.* xxxi. 2-5).
The new church will have good from the Lord (*Isa.* xxxi. 9).
Concerning the new church, and its life, doctrine, worship and ministry (*Ezek.* xliv. 15-31); its ultimates will be holy (xlv. 1-5); its statutes (*ib.* 9-25).
The new church will be conjoined with the Lord, and will not be separated from Him (*Jer.* xxxii. 36-40).
By His Divine the Lord will fill those who are of that church with all things, and will vivify them (*Joel* ii. 28, 29).
Joy of the Lord over the new church where He reigns (*Ps.* cxxii.).
The new church will continually worship the Lord (*Isa.* lxvi. 23).
The new church will not perish (*Isa.* lxv. 22, 23).
Reasonings from knowledges (*scientifica*) of the natural man will not destroy knowledges (*cognitiones*) of truth in the new church (*Ezek.* xxix. 17, 18).
The new church will be in the understanding of truth, and those that are in it will be saved (*Obad.* 19-21).
The new church (meaning the Christian Church), its end (*Dan.* ix.).

New Heaven.—Innocence in the new heaven (*Isa.* xi. 6-9).
A new heaven and a new church (*Isa.* ii. 1-5).

New Jerusalem.—A new church is now being instituted by the Lord, which is called, in the *Apocalypse*, the New Jerusalem, to which the things published by Swedenborg will be of service. It is also being instituted elsewhere (p. 164).
Near the end (of the Christian Church) a new church will begin, in which the Lord will be worshipped, and the faith of charity will be received (*Dan.* xii. 1; *see further ib.* 2-13).

New thing (*novum*).—There will be a new thing of the church (*Isa.* iv. 1-3; xliii. 18-21; *Hosea* v. 15; *Amos* viii. 1).
Nineveh.—"Nineveh" means the nations who are converted (*Jonah* i.).
No one.—No one is in truths (*Isa.* lxiii. 3-6).
  No one is obedient, no one believes that the Divine has power to save (*Isa.* l. 2, 3).
Noah.—The Ancient Church is briefly described by "Noah" and his posterity (p. 163).
  "Noah" and his "three sons" mean a new church (*Gen.* vi. 8-10, 14-22).
  "Noah" means the Ancient Church (*Gen.* ix. 18-29).
North (*see* **King**).
Nothing (*see also* **Annul**).
  Those who are against the Lord are nothing before Him (*Ps.* ii. 3, 4).
  Man from his own is nothing (*Ps.* cxlvi. 3, 4).
  Man is nothing of himself, but the Lord alone (*Ps.* xc. *t.*, 1-6).
Nourishment.—Spiritual nourishment is from the knowledges (*cognitiones*) of truth and good from the sense of the letter of the Word (*Ps.* civ. 24-30).
  A new church who have no spiritual nourishment, although they will have it through the Word (*Ps.* cvii. 16-21).

Obduracy (*obfirmatio*) (*Ezek.* iii. 8, 9).
Obey (*see also* **Disobedience, Hearken, Life**).
  The Lord taught them continually from the Word, etc., but they did not obey (*Jer.* xxv. 4-7; *cf. Jer.* xi. 7, 8).
  Not one who is obedient (*Isa.* l. 2, 3).
  Consequence of disobedience (*Isa.* lxvi. 4; *Jer.* xxv. 8-11).
  Because they obeyed their lusts they are in falsities of evil (*Jer.* ix. 13-15).
  If they had obeyed, the hells would have been removed from them, and they would have enjoyed every good (*Ps.* lxxxi. 13-16).
  There is no longer any use to teach any except those who obey (*Micah* ii. 6, 7).
  Those outside of the church will obey (*Isa.* lxvi. 5).
  To receive in the life and obey belongs to the celestial church (*Jer.* xxxv. 1-10; 18, 19).
  Obedience to the Lord results in an abundance of goods and truths (*Isa.* xlviii. 18, 19).
Obstinate (*see also* **Rejection**).
  They made themselves obstinate (*Jer.* xliv. 15-19).
  They made themselves still more obstinate, by perverting doctrine from the Word and defiling it (*Jer.* xxxviii. 4-6).
  Because they made themselves obstinate the destruction of the church and of the kingdom is imminent (*Jer.* xxxvi. 29-31).
Obtrude.—Obtrusion of falsities on others (*Ezek.* xvi. 32-34).
Old Church (*see also* **Church, Destroy, Devastate, Former Church, New Church, Perish, Perversion, Vastation**).
  The old church will falsify and pervert (*Isa.* ix. 8-21).
  The iniquity of the old church which is to be disclosed (*Isa.* lviii. 1).
  The old church will be destroyed (*Micah* vii. 10); when it has been destroyed a new church will be established, gathered from every nation (*ib.* 11-13).
  The old church being utterly destroyed is rejected (*Isa.* xxvi. 5, 6).
  End of the old church (meaning the Jewish Church) (*Dan.* ix.).
  When the old church perishes, a new one is to be established by the Lord (*Isa.* xxix. 17-19).

The old church will not receive the Lord (*Isa.* ix. 5).
Old Testament (*see* **Canaan**).
Omnipotence (*see* **Divine Power**).
Omnipresence (*see also* **Presence**).
   Omnipresence belongs to the Father (*Ps.* cxxxix. 6-10).
Omniscience.—The Lord knows every one (*Ps.* i. 6).
   The Lord knows what lies hidden interiorly, howsoever the external may appear (*Jer.* xvii. 9, 10).
   God sees all things (*Ps.* xciv. 3-11).
   The Lord hears all things (*Isa.* lix. 1, 2).
   The Lord is omniscient (*Isa.* xl. 12-14).
   Omniscience belongs to the Father (*Ps.* cxxxix. 6-10).
One (*unum*) (*see also* **Lord**, GLORIFICATION OF).
Unity—The turning or looking of all (loves) toward one (*Ezek.* i. 12).
   The spiritual, rational and knowing faculties will act in unity (*Isa.* xix. 23-25).
   The doctrine of good and truth acting in unity (*unum ago*) with the Word (*Ezek.* i. 15-21; x. 11).
   When the Lord comes truth and good will make one (*Jer.* iii. 18).
   There were two churches, the celestial and the spiritual, and the two together were one (*Ezek.* xxxvii. 15-20); and will become one from the Lord (*ib.* 21-25).
   Of those who made common cause (*unum facio*) with "Babylon" (*Dan.* ii. 3-11).
Oneness (*unitio*) (*see also* **Lord**, GLORIFICATION OF).
   Oneness of love of spiritual and love of natural good and truth (*Ezek.* i. 10, 11).
Opposition (*see also* **Against**).
   Opposition of men amounts to nothing, because they perish owing to evils and falsities (*Isa.* li. 7, 8).
Operation (*see* **Divine Operation**).
Oppression.—Oppression of the church by the self-intelligent (*Obad.* 8, 9).
Order.—From His Divine the Lord will set heaven and the church in order (*Isa.* li. 16).
Origin.—The Lord the origin of the good of love (*Zech.* iv. 8-10).
Other god (*see* **God**, *at end;* **Idolatry**).
Others (*see also* **Outside the church**).
   The Lord will establish a new church of others (*Ezek.* xvii. 22-24).
   The church will be among others (*Haggai* ii. 23).
   The church to be formed of others (*Jer.* xii. 14, 15).
   Others are to be brought to the church by the Lord (*Jer.* xvi. 14, 15, *and fol.*).
   Others, not the Jews, will be in the new church (*Ezek.* xliv. 15-31).
   Others will be received in place of the Jews, and a church will be established with them (*Ps.* cix. 7-12).
   The things which profaners have will be given to others (*Jer.* viii. 10).
   The church will be constituted of others, after it has been delivered from the profane (*Jer.* xxvii. 22; *see also Ezek.* v. 13-17).
   Others received instead of those of the devastated church (*Jer.* vi. 12); why (*ib.* 13 *and fol.*).
   Others do not live like those who have the Word (*Ezek.* iii. 4-7).
   Others will teach and learn the good of the church (*Jer.* xxiii. 3, 4).
Outcasts (*Ezek.* xx. 32-36).
Outermost things (*extrema*).—Those who pervert the doctrine of the church will also fall into falsities in outermost things (*Amos* iv. 1-3).
   Worship only in outermost things (*Amos* iv. 4-6).
Outmosts (*see* **Ultimates**).

Outside the church (*see also* **Gentiles, Nations, Others**).
    Those who are outside the church are horrified at the falsities of those who pervert all truths of the church (*Ezek.* xxxii. 9, 10).
    Those who are outside the church worship the Lord (*Mal.* i. 11).
    Those that are out of the church expect compassion, that they may become a church (*Ps.* cii. 12-18).
    When the Jewish Church was destroyed, those who were out of the church were heard (*Ps.* cvi. 44-46 *and prec.*); and a church constituted of these will arise and will worship the Lord (*ib.* 47, 48).

Overcome (*supero*) (*see* **Lord**, VICTORY OF).
    From His Divine, the Lord will overcome the hells (*Ps.* xxxv. 22, 23[, 26]).

Overthrow (*prosterno*) (*see also* **Cast down**).
    When victory hung on the side of the evil or of hell, the spiritual man attacked them and overthrew them (*Gen.* xiv.).
    Prayer to the Lord to overthrow the hells (*Ps.* lxxxiii. 13-17).
    Owing to the Lord's help the hells will be overthrown (*Ps.* lxxxvi. 15-17).
    The Lord will overthrow all who are against Him on the day of judgment (*Ps.* xxi. 7-12).
    Overthrow of the hells (*Ps.* xxxv. *t.*, 1-9).
    The Lord has overthrown the hells (*Ps.* lxxiv. 12-15).

Own (*proprium*) (*see also* **Self-intelligence**).
    Man from his own is nothing (*Ps.* cxlvi. 3, 4).
    From what is his own man is nothing but falsity of evil (*Ps.* cxv. 4-8).
    The Lord cannot teach those who are wise from what is their own (*Isa.* lvii. 16, 17).
    They acquired those things from what is their own, therefore all things have perished (*Amos* vi. 13, 14).

Partition (*see* **Inheritance**).
Passion of the Cross (*see* **Lord**, THE PASSION OF THE CROSS).
Past.—In temptations the Lord strengthens Himself from His Divine, from things past, that those that had prayed for it had been saved, etc. (*Ps.* lxxvii. 10-15 *and fol.*).
Patience (*see* **Tolerance**).
    Patience of the Lord (*Isa.* xlii. 18-20).
Perceive.—Those who persuade to falsities will not perceive truths (*Jer.* xxix. 24-32).
    No perception with those who trust in themselves (*Jer.* xvii. 5, 6).
    Perception of truth will perish (*Isa.* viii. 1-4).
    Those who were of the Lord's church perceived interior character of "Babylonians" (*Dan.* iv. 18, 19).
    It was perceived from the Word that it was profane (*Dan.* v. 5, 6); but not by the primates who were in the Babylonish religion (*ib.* 7-9).
    Perception that those who blaspheme the Lord will perish (*Isa.* xxxvii. 6, 7).
    Perception of the Lord from His Divine, that a church will arise and flourish, etc. (*Ps.* lxxxv. 8-13).
Perdition (*see* **Destroy** (*perdo*)).
Perfection } (*integritas*).—Perfection belongs to the Lord (*Ps.* xviii. 20-27, 30,
Integrity } 32; xxv. 21; xxvi. *t.*, 1-6, 11; xli. 12, 13; xliv. 17-21; cxxxix. 23, 24).
    The Lord's perfection, and what it accomplished (*Ps.* lxvi. 18-20 *and prec.*).
    The Lord's perfection, and He loves those that are perfect (*Ps.* ci. 2, 3, 6, 7).

Prayer of the Lord to the Father to have regard to His perfection (*Ps.* cxli. *t.*, 1, 2).

The Lord, concerning the integrity of His life, from the Divine in Himself (*Ps.* xvii. *t.*, 1–6).

Perfect (*perficio*).—The Divine truth perfects man, because it is wisdom (*Ps.* xix. 7–11).

They will be perfected in truths (*Jer.* xxx. 19, 20).

Perish } (*pereo*) (*see also* **Evil, Falsifiers, Hypocrites, Knowledge** (*sci-*
Be Destroyed } *entia*), **Last Judgment, Old Church**).

All knowledge (*cognitio*) and understanding of truth will perish (*Zeph.* i. 1–3).

Knowledges (*cognitiones*) of truth and good, and also truths of every kind and sort will perish (*Jer.* xxv. 15–27).

Doctrine perishes by the perversion of the sense of the letter of the Word (*Amos* i. 11, 12).

The doctrine of truth will perish until it is nothing (*Isa.* xxix. 1–4).

The remnants of doctrine will be destroyed by reasonings from falsities (*Jer.* xxxix. 1–3).

Understanding of truth will perish by means of (*per*) falsities (*Ezek.* xxviii. 21–23).

All intelligence will perish, when (*Jer.* xxii. 5, 6 *and prec.*).

The infernals perish (*Isa.* lxiv. 2, 3).

Justice and truth perish (*Hab.* i. 1–5).

Truths will perish (*Isa.* xxviii. 3, 4).

The truths of the church perish from (*a*) falsities (*Amos* iii. 11).

The power of the Word will perish (*Isa.* xxii. 25).

Falsities gain strength and pervert still further, until the church perishes (*Isa.* xxix. 5, 6).

Truths and goods of religion perish where there has been merely external worship (*Ezek.* xxxviii. 20–23).

Truth and good of worship perish if the knowledges of the natural man are consulted (*Jer.* xlii. 7–22).

All the learning of the natural man which confirms falsities will perish (*Jer.* xlvi. 20–24).

Truth of the church perishes gradually by means of (*per*) reasonings from the natural man (*Jer.* xiii. 1–7).

They will perish by means of (*per*) reasonings from the natural man (*Ezek.* xvii. 19–21).

The natural of man will perish by (*per*) reasonings from knowledges (*Jer.* xlvi.).

The whole natural perishes, etc. (*Jer.* xlvi. 13–19).

Those who have falsified the knowledges (*cognitiones*) of truth by means of reasonings and knowledges (*scientifica*), and have thus destroyed the church, will utterly perish (*Zeph.* ii. 12–15).

Destruction by (*per*) reasonings from (*ex*) knowledges (*scientificis*) (*Jer.* xxxvii. 6–10).

Those who pervert knowledges (*cognitiones*) from (*e*) the Word, etc., will perish (*Amos* i. 3–5).

Those who pervert the knowledges of truth ("Damascus") will perish (*Jer.* xlix. 27).

Those who make a religion out of mere knowledge (*scientia*) will perish (*Isa.* xix. 15–17).

Those who are in mere knowledges (*cognitiones*) and in faith alone shall perish lest they ruin the church still further (*Zech.* ix. 7, 8).

Those who are in faith alone will perish (*Jer.* xlvii.).

Those who falsify doctrine will perish (*Ezek.* xiii. 20–23).

Those who trust in themselves perish (*Ps.* xx. 7, 8).

Those in self-intelligence will perish (*Isa.* xxii. 16–19).

The self-intelligent ("Edom") will perish, and with them the falsities which they defend (*Obad.* 4, 5).
They will perish on the day of judgment, because they have oppressed the church (*Obad.* 8, 9).
Truths of the church perish through self-intelligence (*Isa.* xxii. 1–12).
Everything of the church has perished through the falsification and adulteration of the sense of the letter of the Word (*Ezek.* iv. 17).
Those who have falsified the external of the Word ("Edom") will be destroyed by (*a*) things falsified (*Jer.* xlix. 7, 8).
Those who apply the Word to a heretical falsity will perish (*Amos* i. 6–8).
As they have falsified the Word, etc., will they not perish on this account? (*Hosea* iv. 14.)
Those who have perverted the Word will perish from (*ex*) falsities (*Isa.* lxv. 11, 12).
They will perish on the day of judgment (*Hosea* ix. 7–9).
Those who have the Word are in falsities of evil and will perish (*Zech.* x. 2, 3).
Those who are in falsities of evil will perish (*Isa.* xxx. 27, 28).
Those who are in falsities and evils will perish (*Nahum* i. 8–11).
Men who perish from falsities and evils (*Isa.* li. 7, 8).
They will utterly perish by (*per*) falsities, by which the truths of the Word have been destroyed (*destruo*) (*Ezek.* xvi. 35–42).
They will perish by means of (*per*) falsities (*Jer.* xi. 22, 23).
They will perish by reason of (*ex*) things falsified (*Ezek.* xi. 8–11).
Those who have falsified and adulterated the Word will perish in hell (*Nahum* iii. 1–7).
Those who have adulterated the truths of the Word will perish, and are to be cast into hell (*Zeph.* i. 9–11).
Those who have adulterated truths and goods will perish in hell (*Ezek.* xxii. 31).
Those who adulterated the goods of the Word and of the church ("Moab") perish with their falsities (*Jer.* xlviii. 12–16).
Those who have adulterated and defiled truths and goods will perish on the day of judgment (*Ezek.* xxiii. 22–25).
All that adulterate will perish with their evils and falsities (*Isa.* xiii. 13–18).
Falsities of evil cause those who were of the church to perish (*Ps.* lviii. *t.*, 1–9); so that those who are in good may come into the church (*ib.* 10, 11).
Those who have adulterated the Word will utterly perish (*Zeph.* ii. 8–10); so that whoever is able may acknowledge the Lord (*ib.* 11).
Although they possess the Word they will perish (*Ps.* lxxxii. 6, 7).
Those who have destroyed the good of the church will perish (*Jer.* xxiii. 3, 4).
All who are against truth and good will perish (*Isa.* xxix. 20, 21).
Because they no longer have truth or good they will perish (*Jer.* viii. 13).
They will perish from perverting all Divine worship (*Hosea* xiii. 1–3).
Must they not perish? (*Jer.* ix. 9;) they will be destroyed by evils and falsities therefrom, why (*ib.* 16).
Exhortation to seek the Lord, that all things of the church may not perish through evils and falsities (*Amos* v. 4–9).
Let them acknowledge and worship the Divine Human of the Lord, lest they perish (*Ps.* ii. 10–12).
Those who do not believe in the Lord perish (*Ps.* cxlv. 18, 20).
Those who have worshipped another god will perish (*Hosea* xiii. 16).
They will perish owing to their worshipping another god, whence came profanation (*Mal.* ii. 12).
Those who are against the Lord will perish (*Isa.* lxv. 6, 7).

Those who are against the Lord will perish by (*a*) falsities from evil (*Isa.* l. 9).
Those who wish to destroy the Lord perish (*Ps.* liv. 4, 5).
The evil who lie in wait against the Lord will perish (*Ps.* lxiv. 7, 8).
Those who lie in wait for the Lord will perish from (*ex*) falsities of evil (*Ps.* lxiii. 9, 10).
Much of the church perished by departure from the Lord and by falsities of every kind (*Jer.* xliv. 1–6).
The church in the lowest heaven destroyed by (*per*) falsities of evil (*Jer.* vi. 1, 2).
The church in the lowest heaven, as to good, perishes by profanation (*Jer.* vii. 34).
The church has perished because they have destroyed (*destruo*) its truths by dire falsities (*Jer.* xix. 2, 3).
The church will perish because it is in mere falsities and evils in respect to doctrine and in respect to worship (*Zeph.* i. 4–6).
Doctrine of falsity will perish, and with it those who live according to it (*Jer.* xiv. 14–16).
The church has perished by reason of (*ex*) falsities (*Ezek.* xx. 45—xxi. 32).
The church will perish by reason of (*ex*) falsities of evil (*Ezek.* xxxiii. 27–29).
The perverted church perishes in the time of judgment (*Amos* ii. 12–16).
The church with all things pertaining to it will perish (*Amos* vii. 17).
Why all things will perish (*Amos* vi. 7–14).
All things of the church have utterly perished (*Isa.* xxv. 2).
Those who are of the devastated church will perish (*Zech.* xiii. 8, 9).
Those who have devastated the church will perish (*Ps.* cxxxvii. 7–9).
Those who have destroyed (*destruo*) the church will perish on the day of judgment (*Nahum* ii. 3–6).
Those who have been destroyed (*perdo*) will perish (*Ezek.* xxxvi. 3–7, 16–19).
All will perish (*Hosea* v. 5–9).
All will perish by (*per*) falsities of evil (*Ezek.* xxi. 4, 5).
Those who are instructed by the preacher concerning falsities and do not take heed, perish (*Ezek.* xxxiii. 1–5).
When the preacher sees falsities and does not give instruction concerning them, he perishes (*Ezek.* xxxiii. 6, 7).
They will perish because they cannot be taught (*Micah* ii. 10, 11).
Because they do not see truths they perish on the day of judgment (*Jer.* xxiii. 12).
In consequence of disobedience everything of the church will perish (*Jer.* xxv. 8–11).
They cannot but perish because they have rejected all mercy and perverted all truths and goods (*Jer.* v. 9, 10; 29–31).
They will perish by (*a*) evil love (*Ezek.* xv. 7, 8).
All who trust in knowledges (*scientifica*) of the natural man will perish through (*per*) evil loves (*Ezek.* xxx. 6–9).
Those who have perverted the holy things of the church will perish (*Isa.* lxvi. 16, 17).
Those who blasphemed the Lord will perish (*Isa.* xxxvii. 6, 7; 21–27).
The blasphemers of the Word will perish with the truths and goods of the church which they have dispersed (*Jer.* xx. 6).
Blasphemers of the Lord and profaners of the Word will all perish (*Jer.* xxi. 7).
Those with whom everything holy is profaned perish (*Jer.* xxiv. 9, 10).
Those who are in truths and in good, and do evil, perish (*Jer.* xviii. 9, 10).
Profaners will perish (*Jer.* xxix. 16–19; see also *Ezek.* v. 11, 12).
They will perish by (*per*) evils, falsities, and profanities (*Ezek.* vii. 14, 15).

All conjunction with the Lord has perished (*Jer.* xvi. 9).
Because they have put off everything of the church and of its worship, they cannot but perish (*Hosea* viii. 12-14).
Knowledges (*cognitiones*) began to perish with the Jews (*Jonah* i. 4-6).
The Jewish Church will perish because, though taught continually, they did not receive nor obey (*Jer.* xxxv. 17 *and prec.*).
The Jewish Church will perish in the judgment (*Ps.* cix. 7-12).
The Jewish Church will perish with all its falsities and evils (*Micah* v. 10-15).
It must needs be that the Jewish Church, having been destroyed, should perish (*Micah* vi. 14-16).
The posterity of the Jewish Church will perish, because they are in falsities of evil, and because they reject the Lord (*Ps.* cix. 13-20).
The nations hearing from the Word of God about their sins, and that they would perish, were converted, etc. (*Jonah* iii. 1-10).
Compassion that the church perish not through (*per*) the uprising of the evil (*Ps.* lxxiv. 18-21 *and fol.*).
The church perishes, unless restored by the Lord by means of (*per*) His coming (*Ps.* xc. 7-14).
Let not the Lord fail in temptations lest heaven and the church perish (*Ps.* cii. 25-28 *and prec.*).
Prayer that they may not perish with the evil (*Jer.* x. 23-25).
Those who depart from evils and falsities will not perish (*Ezek.* vi. 7-10).
They will perish on the day of judgment (*Amos* viii. 7-10).
The church will not perish, but those who are in it will perish (*Amos* vii. 8-10).
Not all things of the church will perish, because there must be a church (*Isa.* lxv. 8-10).
The Divine truth will not perish, though the church is destroyed (*destruo*) (*Jer.* xxxvi. 27, 28, 32; 1-10; xxxiv. 1-7).
When an old church perishes a new one is to be established by the Lord (*Isa.* xxix. 17-19).
The new church will not perish (*Isa.* lxv. 22, 23).
The church of the reformation will perish from (*a*) mere falsities and evils (*Dan.* ix. 27).

Permanence.—Nothing abides to eternity except that which is from the Lord (*Isa.* li. 6).

Persecution.—How those who are of the church are protected from persecution by those who have perverted the holy things of the church (*Ezek.* xxxii. 31, 32).

Persist (*see* **Insist**).

Persuade.—Persuasion of falsity arises from affection for falsifying (*Ezek.* xiii. 18, 19).
Those who persuade to falsities will abide in falsities and not perceive truth (*Jer.* xxix. 24-32).
Those who by persuasion establish falsity of doctrine, are to be utterly rejected by the judgment (*Isa.* xxvi. 14, 15, 19-21).
The profaners persuaded themselves of falsities (*Jer.* xxviii.).

Perturbation.—Perturbation of the Lord from temptations, with trust from the Divine (*Ps.* xlii. *t.*, 1-6).

Perverse (*perversum*).—The church gone away into what is perverse (*Isa.* xxxvi. 8-10).
Perversities in the former church (*Hosea* vi. 7-10).
—— (**the**) (*perversus*).—The perverse are tested, and found incapable of restoration (*Jer.* vi. 27-30).

Pervert (*perverto*) (*see also* **Falsify**).
Knowledges (*scientifica*) perverted by adapting them to falsities (*Jer.* xliii. 8-13).

Those who pervert the knowledges (*cognitiones*) of truth are meant by "Damascus" (*Jer.* xlix. 23–27).

About those who pervert the knowledges (*cognitiones*) of good and truth and thereby do injury to the external sense of the Word (*Amos* i. 9, 10).

Perversion of knowledges (*cognitiones*) from the Word which are of service to doctrine (*Amos* i. 3–5).

Truths perverted by applying knowledges (*scientifica*) to falsities (*Ezek.* xxix. 4, 5, *and fol.*).

Perversion of some remains by knowledges (*scientifica*) of the natural man (*Jer.* xli. 16–18).

Concerning those who by knowledges (*scientiae*) pervert the holy things of the church. Their activity and final lot (*Ezek.* xxxii.).

Perversion of doctrine from the Word (*Jer.* xxxviii. 4–6).

Everything of the doctrine of truth and good has been perverted (*Zeph.* iii. 1–4).

Those who pervert the doctrine of the church fall into falsities in outermost things (*Amos* iv. 1–3).

Those who are in the sense of the letter of the Word and pervert the truths of religion, etc. (*Ezek.* xxv. 1, 2).

Those who are in self-intelligence and pervert the sense of the letter of the Word ("Moab") (*Obad.*).

Diabolical loves have perverted the ultimate sense of the Word (*Ezek.* viii. 7–10).

Beginning of the perversion of the church by falsities (*Ezek.* xi. 1–3); by falsifications of truth of doctrine (*ib.* 4–7); it will be still worse, and they will perish by reason of things falsified (*ib.* 8–11); because they pervert all things (*ib.* 12).

Though falsities of evil were entirely removed at the institution of the church yet it perverted all things, etc. (*Amos* ii. 12–16).

Those who call themselves enlightened pervert truths still more (*Jer.* xxiii. 30, 31).

Truths perverted by reasonings from self-intelligence (*Isa.* x. 5–11).

Perversion of the truths of the church (*Ezek.* v. 5–7); its consequence (*ib.* 8–12).

Truths are perverted by false principles which are of religion (*Jer.* xxiii. 13).

Falsities increase and pervert still more until the church perishes (*Isa.* xxix. 5, 6).

Successive perversion until they perish (*Jer.* xxxviii. 4–23).

They perverted the church by falsities of every kind (*Jer.* xxii. 17).

Against those who have perverted the truths of the Word, who are meant by the "prophets;" *general subject* (*Jer.* xxiii. 9–40).

From the perversions by the "prophets" the church is full of falsities and is perverted (*Jer.* xxiii. 10).

They have perverted all the truths of the Word and of doctrine by evil loves, and by the knowledges (*scientifica*) of the natural man (*Hosea* vii. 1–11).

They pervert by false interpretation (*Jer.* xxiii. 25, 26).

Perverting the Word is the worst (*Jer.* xxiii. 14).

Those who have perverted the Word will perish because of falsities (*Isa.* lxv. 11, 12).

They have perverted truths of every good given them through the Word (*Jer.* i. 13); the consequence (*ib.* 14–16).

Holy truths and goods turned into falsities (*Lam.* iv. 1–3).

Because they have rejoiced over the destruction of the church they will pervert truths (*Ezek.* xxv. 6, 7).

It is delightful to them to pervert and deceive (*Jer.* v. 25–27).

INDEX OF WORDS AND SUBJECTS.

They have not any truth that has not been perverted and profaned (*Jer.* xxii. 28–30).
Those who have perverted the holy things of the church will perish (*Isa.* lxvi. 16, 17).
They are diligent at perverting, whence comes vastation (*Isa.* lix. 7).
Perversion of everything takes away protection against falsity (*Jer.* vi. 13, 14).
Perversion of Divine worship from self-intelligence (*Hosea* xiii. 1–3).
Perverting worship into evil (*Isa.* lxvi. 3).
Perversion of truths, but not of goods with the truths, until there was a lack of truths (*Jer.* xxxvii. 17–21).
Those who are in the love of self pervert the goods and truths of the church (*Hab.* ii. 8).
They perverted all the truths and goods of the church by departing from the Lord (*Jer.* ii. 7, 8; *cf. Jer.* v. 7, 8).
They pervert truths and goods, which they have in abundance (*Jer.* li. 11–13).
All the truths and goods of the church perverted (*Lam.* i. 4, 5).
Perversion of goods and truths from firsts to lasts (*Jer.* v. 30, 31).
Perverting truths and goods of church leads to destruction (*Isa.* v. 18–30).
Those who pervert the knowledges of good are meant by "Arabia" (*Jer.* xlix. 28–33).
Against those who have perverted the good of the Word, who are meant by the "shepherds;" *general subject* (*Jer.* xxiii. 1–8).
Those who have perverted the goods of the Word and rejected charity ("Moab"). Their destruction (*interitus*) (*Isa.* xvi. 1–9).
Those who by traditions or reasonings from the natural man have perverted truths and goods of the church ("Babylon") (*Jer.* li.).
Perversion of good worse than perversion of truth (*Ezek.* xxv. 8–11).
Those who pervert goods more than truths (*Jer.* iii. 10, 11).
Even those in celestial good begin to be perverted (*Micah* i. 13–15).
Those who have perverted all things of the church (*Ezek.* vii. 20–22).
They will pervert all things (*Ezek.* xi. 12).
Because opposed to all things of the church they became perverted and were destroyed (*Ezek.* xix. 4–7).
Perversion of the church by the Jews (*Zech.* v. 1–4).
The church instituted among the Jewish nation became perverted and revolted (*Ps.* cvi.).
Perversion of state of church among the nations due to loss of knowledges (*cognitiones*) among the Jews (*Jonah* i. 7–9).
A new church when the former church has been completely perverted (*Zech.* i. 14–16).
No conjunction of the church with the Lord, because it has been utterly perverted, and hence rejected (*Lam.* ii. 13–15).
The conjunction of the church with the Lord would be perverted (*Gen.* xv. 7–24).
Unless they worship the Lord all worship will be perverted and profane (*Mal.* ii. 1–4).
They have perverted the church, etc. (*Hosea* viii. 1–7 *and fol.*).
The church has become perverted (*Jer.* iii. 20, 21; *Isa.* v. 3, 4, 7).
The perverted state of the church (*Jer.* i. 1–3).
Providence lest the Word be perverted further (*Isa.* iv. 4–6).
Perversion of good and truth to be no more (*Isa.* lx. 18).
The truths and goods of the church will no longer be perverted (*Ezek.* xxiii. 26, 27).

Perverted church.—Perverted church in the church, represented (*Ezek.* iv.).
The perverted church *fully described* (*Micah* iii. 1–12).
State and history of the perverted church (*Ezek.* xxxvi. 1–38).

SUMMARIES OF THE INTERNAL SENSE.

The church has become perverted from the intention of doing evil (*Micah* ii. 3–5).
The perverted Jewish church (*Ps.* cix.).
Those in the perverted church secretly try to destroy the Lord (*Ps.* cxx.).
By reason of the Lord's presence all things are revealed, and those who are of the perverted church will not endure (*Nahum* i. 3–6).

Philistea.—"Philistea" means those who make religion to consist in nothing but knowledges (*cognitiones*) (*Isa.* xiv. 28–32).

Pious.—The pious man, if he becomes impious, is condemned (*Ezek.* xviii. 24; *cf.* xxxiii. 12–20).

Pity } (*miseratio*).—No pity possible at the destruction of the Jewish
Compassion } church (*Hosea* i. 6).
There can be no pity, but they must be cast out as profane (*Jer.* xxii. 18, 19).
There can be no pity (*Jer.* xvi. 5–7).
Prayer for pity (*Jer.* xiv. 7–9).
Compassion that the church perish not through the uprising of the evil (*Ps.* lxxiv. 18–21).
There is no compassion, because there is nothing but what has been profaned (*Ezek.* ix. 8–11).
Those that are out of the church expect compassion, that they may become a church (*Ps.* cii. 12–18); He hears and has compassion, and a church is formed of such (*ib.* 19–22).
The Divine compassion will be in the new church (*Micah* vii. 18–20).
The Lord will pity those who will be of His new church (*Hosea* i. 7).

Places (see **Canaan**).
Plant (see **Drink**).
Poison.—Fallacies of the sensual man and reasonings therefrom infect with poison (*Jer.* viii. 16, 17).
Posterity.—"Posterity of Adam from Sheth," means divisions and changes in the Most Ancient Church (*Gen.* v.).
"Posterity of Noah," or of his "three sons," means divisions and changes in the Ancient Church (*Gen.* x.).
Pot (see **Caldron**).
Power (see also **Divine Power, Prevail, Word,** POWER OF).
All power of truth destroyed by perversion of truths (*Ezek.* xxix. 6, 7).
No power against the hells (*Lam.* i. 6).
Power when the Lord comes (*Isa.* lxiii. 19; lxiv. 1).
Power of the hells destroyed by the Lord (*Isa.* xlii. 13–15; xliii. 16, 17).
Power of Divine truth from the Lord (*Ps.* xxix. 5–11).
From the Lord's dwelling in the church she will be in power against falsities of evil (*Ps.* cxxxii. 17, 18).
Power of the church which is in faith and in charity (*Dan.* viii. 1–3).
Everything of power and wisdom is from acknowledgment of the Lord (*Jer.* ix. 23, 24).
It is in their power to know that the Lord alone can do all things, but they are unwilling to know that He is God, etc. (*Jer.* v. 21–24).
Those who do not look to the Lord have no power, but fall (*Isa.* xl. 30).
Those who do not confide in the Lord have no power (*Isa.* xli. 21–24).
Those who trust in knowledges (*scientifica*) of the natural man, will have no power (*Ezek.* xxx. 20–23).
Prayer to the Lord for pity, because He alone has redeemed (*Isa.* lxiii. 15, 16).

Pray for (*imploro*).—Those that prayed for it were saved (*Ps.* lxxvii. 10–15).
Prayer (*oratio*) (see also **Lord,** PRAYER OF; **Help**).
Prayer to the Lord, that they may not perish together with the evil (*Jer.* x. 23–25).
Prayer of the nations to the Lord for salvation (*Jonah* i. 14–16).

Prayer of the church to the Lord, that because He alone fights He may assist against the hells (*Ps.* xxv. 15-20).
—— (*precatio*) (*see also* **Cry**).
Prayer (of the devastated church) to the Lord to have pity (*Jer.* xiv. 7-9); the answer (*ib.* 10-12); prayer for the devastated church (*ib.* 20-22); the answer (*ib.* xv. 1).
No attention paid to the prayer of backsliders (*Jer.* xiv. 10-12).
Prayer of the church that those who have ruined the church be removed (*Ps.* lxxix. 5-12).
Prayer to the Lord that the evil may be removed (*Jer.* xvii. 14-18).
Prayer to the Lord to overthrow the hells (*Ps.* lxxxiii. 13-17).
Prayer that the Lord may come and effect the judgment (*Ps.* lxxxii. 8).
Prayer to the Lord that they may be preserved (*Ps.* cxxx. *t.*, 1-4).
Prayer that the Lord's church may be preserved (*Jer.* xxxii. 16-22, 25).
Prayer to the Lord that the former church may be restored (*Lam.* v. 19-22).
Prayer of the new church to the Lord, to come and lead, etc. (*Ps.* lxxx. *t.*, 1-3, 7, *and fol.*).
—— (*preces*).—Prayers of the church to the Lord, that they may be protected from the hells (*Ps.* xxv. *t.*, 1-3); that they may be taught truths (*ib.* 4-6); that their sins may be forgiven from mercy (*ib.* 7-11).
Preacher (*antistes*) (*see also* **Leader, Ministry, Priest, Primate, Prophet, Ruler, Shepherd, Teacher**).
Those who are instructed by the preacher concerning falsities, and do not take heed, perish (*Ezek.* xxxiii. 1-5).
When the preacher sees falsities and does not give instruction concerning them he perishes (*Ezek.* xxxiii. 6, 7; *cf. Ezek.* iii. 18-21).
Preach (*praedico*) (*see also* **Gospel**).
The name of God will be preached when He has gained the victory (*Ps.* lxxi. 8, 15-24).
Precepts.—Precepts for the Ancient Church (*Gen.* ix. 1-17).
Predict (*see also* **Foresee, Revelation**).
Predictions by the Lord Himself (*Isa.* xliii. 10-13; *Jer.* xxxvi. 17, 18).
Prediction by Jehovah (*Isa.* xliv. 5-7).
Prediction through the Word (*Jer.* xix. 14, 15).
Prediction in the Word (*Isa.* xlv. 19).
Predictions respecting "Babylon" (*Dan.* ii. 1, 2; iv.); unknown to those who were "Babylon," but known to those who were of the Lord's church (*ib.* iv. 4-9).
Prediction that the Lord will come into the world, to whom belongs Divine truth and good, etc. (*Hab.* iii. 1-4 *and fol.*).
The Lord Himself, who is to come, has foretold the new church (*Isa.* xliii. 10-13).
Predictions are to be fulfilled (*Ps.* xcviii. 3).
Predictions (*Isa.* vii. 7-9; viii. 1-4; xxxiv. 16; xxxix.; xl. 1-5; 9-11; xlii. 9-12; xliii. 9; *Jer.* xxxvi. 1-10; xxxvii. 6-10; xliv. 20-23; xlv.; *Ezek.* xxxvii. 3-6; *Dan.* viii.; *Gen.* xv. 7-21).
Preparation (*see also* **Temptation**).
Preparation for the Coming of the Lord (*Isa.* lxii. 10).
Preparation of the new church during the destruction of the former (*Jer.* x. 17, 18).
Presence (*see also* **Omnipresence**).
Presence of the Lord with those who are against Him (*Isa.* lxv. 1-5).
If they learned from the Lord they would depart from evils, and thus the Lord would be with them (*Jer.* xxiii. 21-24).
The hells prevail as if there were no Divine presence (*Ps.* xliv. 9-12, 19).
By virtue of (*ex*) the presence of the Lord all things are revealed, and those who are of the perverted church will not endure (*Nahum* i. 3-6).

Prayer to the Father to be present, because He has been utterly rejected by the Jewish nation (*Ps.* cxxiii.).

The Lord will be in the new church (*Zech.* ii. 3–5, 10–13).

The Lord is in His church (*Ps.* lxxvi. *t.*, 1–4).

The Divine presence through the Word (*Ezek.* xxiv. 3–5).

Present day.—The church when first instituted was full of truth; at the present day it is devastated (*Haggai* ii. 1–3).

Preserve (*conservo*) (see also **Last Judgment**).

Those whose have adulterated the truths of the Word cannot be preserved (*Zeph.* i. 18).

The Jewish Church will be destroyed, although its truth will be preserved (*Jer.* xxxiv. 1–7).

The Lord's church will be preserved (*Jer.* xxxii. 6–15, 25).

As long as those of the vastated church acknowledge the Lord they will remain (*Jer.* xii. 16, 17).

Those who acknowledge the Lord must be removed while the destruction lasts (*Jer.* iv. 5, 6).

—— (*servo*). ⎫ —Although those who were of the church beheld Divine
Save (*servo*). ⎬ miracles they backslid, and yet they were preserved (*Ps.*
Saviour (*servator*). ⎭ cvi. 6–8).

Prayer of the Lord that He may be preserved from the hells, whence He will have joy (*Ps.* xxxv. 17, 18[, 24]).

To the Father that He may be preserved in temptations from the deceitful and hypocrites (*Ps.* cxxiv.).

Prayer to the Lord that they may be preserved (*Ps.* cxxx. *t.*, 1–4).

When they were in knowledges (*cognitiones*) they were admitted into temptations and preserved (*Ps.* cvii. 22–31).

The church was preserved (*Ps.* lxxvii. 20).

The Lord saves the good, and the evil perish (*Ps.* xxxiv. 12–22).

They have no saviour (*Ps.* xviii. 41).

Pretense (*simulatio*).—When they are being taught they pretend that they are willing, but they are not (*Jer.* ix. 7, 8).

Pretense will cease when the Lord reigns (*Isa.* xxxii. 5 *and prec.*).

Prevail (*praevaleo*).—Prayer to the Father for help lest the evil in the church prevail (*Ps.* lxix. 13–20).

Unless oneness be effected the hells will prevail (*Ps.* lxxxix. 49–51).

The Father will prevail (*Ps.* xxviii. 6–8).

—— (*valeo*).—Those who wish to prevail by their own intelligence and by artifices; *general subject* (*Jer.* x.); they are not to be feared (*ib.* 1, 2); how they make evil to appear like good, and make themselves appear powerful (*ib.* 3–5); to do this they abuse the Word (*ib.* 8, 9); but they vanish (*ib.* 11).

The Lord alone has power (or prevails) (*Jer.* x. 6, 7).

Pride.—Pride of those who are meant by "Moab" (*Jer.* xlviii. 29).

Pride of those who are meant by "Babylon" (*Isa.* xiv. 13, 14; xlviii. 20, 21).

Pride of the self-intelligent (*Obad.* 6).

Pride of self-intelligence dissipates intelligence (*Ezek.* xxviii. 12–18; *cf.* xxx. 10–12).

Pride in knowledges will be brought down (*Jer.* xlvi. 7–10).

All who are in pride of self-intelligence to be destroyed by the Lord (*Isa.* ii. 10–18).

There will be no pride (*Ps.* xix. 12–13).

Priest (see also **Leader, Ministry, Preacher, Primate, Prophet, Ruler, Shepherd, Teacher**).

"Priests and Levites" mean the third heaven (*Ezek.* xlviii. 9–20).

Primary (see **Truths**).

Primate (*see also* ***Priest, Ruler,*** *etc.*).
    Profanation not perceived by the primates of the Babylonish religion (*Dan.* v. 7–9).
Primitive.—Primitive state of the church among the ancients (*Jer*. ii. 1–3).
Principal (*see* ***Chief***).
Principle.—Truths are perverted by false principles which are of religion (*Jer.* xxiii. 13).
Proceed (*see* ***Go forth***).
Profanation.—Finally profaning (*Ezek.* xvi. 29, 30).
    Profanation of all things of the church by sensual knowledges (*scientifica*) (*Amos* iv. 10, 11).
    Those who possess knowledge, and do not according to it, but pervert the truths of the Word and the knowledges must be cast out as profane (*Jer.* xxii. 18, 19; 25–27).
    The Jewish Church profaned all the truths and goods of the Word and of the church (*Hab.* i. 6–11).
    Profanation of representatives (*Ezek.* xx. 25, 26).
    The Jewish Church will die in their profanities (*Ezek.* xxiv. 14).
    Since there is an end to the church, and to all things of it, they ought no longer to be there, lest they should profane it; therefore they were carried off to Babylon, where they could not profane the holy things, and those who would not go were profaners and will perish (*Jer.* xxvii. 1–8; *see also the rest of the chapter*).
    Remains take goods and truths from the Word and profane them, etc. (*Isa.* xlvi. 6, 7).
    Profanation of truths meant by "Babylon" (*Isa.* xxxix. 1–7; xlvii.).
    "Babylon" profaned all things of heaven and the church (*Dan.* v. 1–4); this was perceived from the Word (*ib.* 5, 6); but not by the primates of that religion (*ib.* 7–9).
    Judgment upon those who have profaned the truths of the church ("Babylon") (*Isa.* xiv. 4–6).
    Profanation of truth meant by "Bel" (*Isa.* xlvi.); they have affections of falsity and evil (*ib.* 1); they are no longer able to understand truth (*ib.* 2).
    The truth of the church will be profaned still further (*Zech.* v. 9–11).
    Profanation of all the truths of the church (*Ezek.* v. 3, 4).
    They rejected by profaning (*Jer.* xxxvi. 19–24); likewise the Word (*ib.* 25, 26).
    Slaves to falsities because of profanation of truth (*Jer.* xxxiv. 20).
    There is no longer any truth that has not been profaned (*Jer.* xxv. 31–33).
    They totally destroyed and profaned the truths and goods of the church (*Ps.* cvi. 35–39); therefore the church with them was forsaken by the Lord and destroyed (*ib.* 40–43).
    Intercession of no avail (*Jer.* vii. 16); because it is certain that they profane the truths and goods of heaven (*ib.* 17–19); hence the destruction of all (*ib.* 20).
    The Lord will destroy all who adulterate and profane the goods and truths of the church (*Isa.* xliii. 14).
    Profanation of the church and of its good and truth (*Jer.* xi. 15–17); how manifested (*ib.* 18, 19); consequences (*ib.* 20–23).
    The disobedient will be in temptations from those who profane things holy (*Jer.* xxv. 8–11).
    Those who were formerly of the church will profane the holy things of the church and will therefore perish (*Jer.* xxix. 16–19).
    Profanation of what is holy (*Jer.* xxxii. 34, 35); *general subject* (*Ezek.* viii.).
    Profanation of the holy things of the church, they saying in their heart that religion is not anything (*Ps.* lxxiv. *t.*, 1–9).

Profaners of the holy things of the church (*Ezek.* xx. 30–39).
Profanation of things holy (*Ezek.* xx. 30, 31); caused by self-exaltation above the Lord (*Dan.* v. 10–24).
Profanation of everything holy (*Jer.* xxiv. 9, 10).
Profaners persuaded themselves that the profanities of their religion were the holy things of the church, etc. (*Jer.* xxviii.).
The church of the Lord is not with those who profane holy things (*Jer.* vii. 11); by such profanation the destruction of the church is brought about (*ib.* 12–15).
Those who have profaned holy things are to be separated and dispersed (*Zech.* ii. 6–9).
Profanation came from the worship of another god (*Mal.* ii. 11).
Retribution will visit the profaners (*Jer.* xi. 20; xvi. 18).
Profaning holy truths by reasonings from knowledges (*scientifica*) (*Jer.* xxxvii.).
Profanation causes rejection of worship (*Jer.* vii. 27–31).
Those are to be destroyed who by reasonings from their own intelligence destroy the truths of the Word and profane them (*Isa.* xiv. 24–27).
It is worse with those who study the Word, because they do this from what is profane within (*Jer.* xxi. 8–10).
Profanation of the holy of the Word, by their separating themselves from the holy of the worship of the church (*Ezek.* viii. 3–6).
Those who are within the church profane worship (*Mal.* i. 12–14).
Continual profanation of worship (*Jer.* xxiv. 8, 9).
Unless they worship the Lord all worship will be perverted and profane (*Mal.* ii. 1–4).
Profanation of the church leads to its destruction (*Ezek.* v. 11, 12).
Those who by knowledges (*scientiae*) have perverted all truths of the church will be associated in hell with those who have profaned the holy things of the Word (*Ezek.* xxxii. 17–23).
Retribution will visit those who have previously profaned the church (*Jer.* xvi. 18).
Profaners of truth will be cast into hell and abide in their profanities (*Jer.* viii. 1, 2; 13); and all their remains will likewise perish (*ib.* 3); they cannot be converted and led back (*ib.* 4–6); they are unwilling to know any truth from the Word, but reject it (*ib.* 7–9); they defend their falsities and call them truths of the church (*ib.* 11, 12); they have recourse to the Word in vain (*ib.* 14, 15); fallacies of the sensual man, and reasonings therefrom destroy them, and infect them with poison (*ib.* 16, 17).
In hell among profaners (*Jer.* xix. 7, 8).
Utter profanation, and therefore no compassion (*Ezek.* ix. 8–11).
Hell of blasphemers of the Lord and profaners of the Word was present (*Jer.* xxi. 1, 2; *see also the rest of the chapter*).
The death of profaners (*Jer.* xxxiv. 21, 22).

Promise.—Promise of salvation cannot be fulfilled in the case of those who are not willing to acknowledge and receive (*Jer.* iv. 9–12).

Prophecy (*propheticum*).—Prophecy concerning the Lord in respect to the Word (*Ezek.* i. 1–3).
Prophecy concerning the Lord's combats with the hells (*Jonah* i. 17; ii. 1–10).
It is vain for them to say that the prophecies of the Word respecting the Lord will be filled after a long time (*Ezek.* xii. 26–28).
Prophecy will cease (*Zech.* xiii. 4, 5).
—— (*prophetia*).—Fulfilment of prophecy (*Ezek.* xii.).

Prophet (*see also* **Jeremiah**).
The Word from the Lord to the prophet (*Ezek.* ii. 1, 2).
The prophet should be instructed in the Word, which in itself is delight-

ful (*Ezek*. iii. 1–3); he should teach those that have the Word, and not fear their obduracy (*ib*. 4–11).

The prophet to represent the Word (*Ezek*. iii. 16, 17).

The prophet would be guilty if he did not reveal their falsities and evils, and not guilty if he did reveal them (*Ezek*. iii. 18–21); he must explain the sense of letter (*ib*. 22, 23); he must not speak from himself, but from the Lord (*ib*. 24–27; *cf. Ezek*. xxxiii.).

The prophet Hosea represented the falsification of the Word with the Jewish nation (*Hosea* i. 1–3).

"Prophets" means those who pervert the truths of the Word (*Jer*. xxiii. 9).

Prophetical parts.—The prophetical parts of the Word contain a spiritual sense; its character described (p. 163).

Proprium (see **Own**).

Prosper (*se bene habere*) (see also **Flourish**).

The evil vaunt themselves and prosper (*Ps*. lxxiii. *t*., 1–9); but they are nevertheless devastated and consumed (*ib*. 15–20, 27).

Protect (*protego*).—Protection of the Word (*Jer*. xx. 11–13).

—— (*tutor*) ⎫ (see also **Faith, Fear, Guard, Save**).
Protection (*tutela, tutamen*) ⎬ Protection (*Ps*. lxxii. 12–14).
Safe (*tutus*) ⎭ Truths that protected the Ancient Church (*Ezek*. xxvii. 10, 11).

The celestial and spiritual churches protected from infernal evils and falsities (*Ezek*. xxxvii. 21–25).

The Lord protected the Jewish nation (*Micah* vi. 5).

Knowledges will not protect, even when used as confirmations (*Nahum* iii. 11–17); neither will reasonings (*ib*. 18).

Those who from their own intelligence hatch out doctrine or falsify doctrine will have no protection against the hells (*Ezek*. xiii. 16).

Those who pervert and profane can have no protection through the Word, howsoever they acknowledge it with the lips (*Jer*. xxii. 23, 24).

No protection against falsity owing to perversion of all things (*Jer*. vi. 13, 14).

The Lord led and protected, yet they departed from Him (*Jer*. ii. 4–6).

Prayers of the church to the Lord, that they may be protected (*custodio*) from the hells (*Ps*. xxv. *t*., 1–3).

Prayer for protection (*Ps*. xxxi. *t*., 1–4 *and fol*.).

There will be protection from the Lord when the last judgment comes and continues (*Ps*. xlvi. *t*., 1–3, 6, 7).

The Lord is described, He will do all things and protect (*Isa*. ix. 6, 7).

The Lord has protection from the Father (*Ps*. iv. 3).

The Lord, being protected, has established a church (*Ps*. lxxiv. 16, 17).

Protection from every attack, owing to the union of the Lord to the Father (*Ps*. xci. 2–6).

Song of praise for protection (*Ps*. lvi. 12, 13).

The Lord, who is Divine truth itself, will be the protection of the good (*Ps*. lxviii. 5, 6); but not of the rest, although they have the Word (*ib*. 12–14).

The Lord will protect those who trust in Him, but those who are in falsities and evils will perish (*Nahum* i. 7–11).

Protection of the new church by the Lord (*Nahum* i. 15; ii. 1–3).

There has been no protection from falsities of evil which are from hell, but in the new church it will be different, where truths and goods will continue (*Zech*. viii. 10–12).

The Lord protects from evil, and the evil perish (*Ps*. xxxvi. 11, 12).

Protection of the church from falsities of evils (*Ps*. cv. 8–15).

Protection from falsities (*Isa*. xxxii. 15–18).

Protection from falsities and evils (*Isa*. ix. 6, 7).

The Lord will protect them from falsities that are from hell, because they worship the Lord (*Zech.* x. 11, 12).

When those who make religion to consist merely in knowledges (*cognitiones*) ("Philistea") have been removed by the last judgment, the church will be safe (*tuta*) (*Isa.* xiv. 30, 31).

It was clearly seen that those rulers, in the Babylonish religion, who worshipped the Lord, were protected by Him (*Dan.* iii. 22-25).

Protection of men in the midst of hell (*Isa.* lxiii. 11-14).

How those who are in an affection for truth are protected from perverters (*Ezek.* xxxii. 13-16).

How those who are of the church are protected from being persecuted by those who pervert the holy things of the church (*Ezek.* xxxii. 31, 32).

Those who do not suffer themselves to be led astray will be protected (*Ezek.* xiii. 20-23).

Those who are humble will have protection from the Lord (*Ps.* cxxxviii. 6-8).

Protection owing to repentance (*Isa.* xxxviii. 1-6).

The simple protected by the Lord when He comes (*Ezek.* xxxiv. 26-31).

Protection from falsities granted after the natural has been purged of falsities and evils (*Ps.* cv. 37-41 *and prec.*).

Protection of those in whom is the church from the Lord (*Isa.* xxxi. 5, 6).

The Lord will protect those who will be of the new church (*Zech.* ix. 12-16).

The new church protected from infestation by the old (*Isa.* xxv. 3-5).

Protection from the infernals (*Isa.* xxxv. 4-9).

Protection in the Lord's church against falsities and evils (*Ps.* lxxvi. *t.*, 1-4).

The Lord will protect by Divine truth (*Isa.* xxxiii. 5, 6).

The Lord will protect those who are in truths from Him (*Ps.* xcvii. 10-12).

He who is in truths from the Lord remains safe (*Ps.* cxxvii. 3, 4).

The Lord will protect His own (*Isa.* xxxiii. 2).

The church will worship the Lord who protects her (*Ps.* cxlvii. 13-15).

Protraction.—Protraction of destruction of the old church (*Isa.* xxxvii. 33-35; see also *Hosea* xiii. 14, 15; *Isa.* vii. 7-9).

Protraction of utter devastation of church (*Isa.* xxxix. 8).

Protraction of coming of the Lord (*Isa.* xxxviii. 7, 8).

Protraction of time before a new church can be established (*Jer.* viii. 18-22; ix. 1).

Prove (*probo*).—When the Lord has proved man He delivers him from the hells (*Ps.* lxxxi. 5-7).

Providence (*see also* **Hell,** CAST INTO; **Protect, Protraction**).

Providence lest the Word be perverted still further (*Isa.* iv. 4-6).

The Lord will destroy all falsities by the truth of the Word, lest doctrine should teach something else (*Zech.* xii. 6, 7).

Providence seen in the history of the Jewish Church (*Ezek.* xx; xxiv. 9-12).

Providence in tolerating a perverted church (*Ezek.* xxxvii. 20-23).

They are to be kept from destruction (*interitus*) until all truth of the church has been destroyed (*deperditum*) (*Hosea* xiii. 14, 15).

Those who acknowledge the Lord must be removed while the destruction lasts (*Jer.* iv. 5, 6).

Destruction to prevent further ruin of the church (*Ezek.* xxviii. 24).

They shall perish lest they ruin the church still further (*Zech.* ix. 7, 8; *see further under* **Protraction**).

Separation to prevent seduction (*Ezek.* xxiii. 46-49).

Punishment (*see also* **Retribution**).

Punishments due to separation from the the Lord and worship of things infernal (*Jer.* ii. 19, 20).

Urged by punishments, yet they did not receive (*Jer.* v. 3).
The evils of punishment come upon them, but in vain (*Hosea* x. 9–10).
The Jewish nation could not be brought back by punishments (*Micah* vi. 13).

Pure ⎫ (*see also* **Remove, Temptation**).
Purify ⎭ (*Ps.* xix. 14).
    Prayer that He may be purified of the infirmities derived from the mother (*Ps.* li. *t.*, 1–5); if He be purified of them He will be pure and holy (*ib.* 6–12).
    The Lord is pure from the Father (*Ps.* cxxxix. 13–15).
    Purity belongs to the Lord (*Ps.* xxvi. *t.*, 1–6, 11).
    The Lord will teach the Word in its purity (*Mal.* iii. 1–3).
    Those who are of the new church are to be purified (*Zech.* xiii. 8, 9).

Purge.—The natural has been purged of falsities and evils of every kind, which infested (*Ps.* cv. 25–36).

Purpose (*see* **Intend**; *see also* **Devise, Think**).

Quality.—Quality of the understanding of the Word in the successive states of the church (*Zech.* i. 7–10).
    Quality of the church about to be instituted, in respect to truth and good (*Zech.* ii. 1, 2).

Raise up (*erigo*).—The Lord raises up sinners (*Ps.* cxlv. 14–16).
    The Lord will raise up the fallen church (*Ps.* lxxv. *t.*, 1–3).

Rational (faculty) (*rationale*) (*see also* **External Church, Knowing faculty**).
    The rational is meant by "Lebanon" (*Ezek.* xvii.).
    The rational is to be imbued with truths from good after the natural (*Isa.* xxi. 8–10).
    A rational derived from knowledges (*scientifica*) of every kind through confirming by means of them the Divine things of the church (*Ezek.* xxxi. 3–9).
    Those who had not a rational of the understanding succeeded in the church, but they utterly rejected all things of the church, etc. (*Ezek.* xvii. 7, 8, *and fol.*).

—— **(the)** (*rationalis*).—The rational are to be brought to the church by the Lord (*Jer.* xvi. 16, 17).

—— **light** (*Hosea* xiv. 9).

Reason (*ratiocino*).—They reason from falsities against the truths of the church (*Jer.* vi. 22, 23).
    The church devasted as to truths reasons against truths (*Hosea* x. 6).

Reasonings (*ratiocinia*).—Faith alone prevails through reasonings (*Dan.* viii. 6–10).
    Truths of doctrine from the Word dissipated by faith alone through reasonings (*Dan.* viii. 6–10).
    Reasonings lead astray in consequence of deprivation of truths (*Isa.* xx.).
    Reasonings confirmatory of faith alone (*Dan.* vii. 19–21).
    Reasonings from fallacies of the sensual man destroy and poison (*Jer.* viii. 16, 17).
    Faith alone will destroy by reasonings from the natural man (*Dan.* xi. 42, 43).
    Those who have falsified the knowledges (*cognitiones*) of truth by means of reasonings, etc. (*Zeph.* ii. 12–15).
    Reasonings destroy the knowledges (*cognitiones*) of good and truth (*Jer.* xlix. 28–30).

Reasonings from knowledges (*scientifica*) destroy the natural of man (*Jer.* xlvi.).
Reasonings from knowledges (*scientifica*) have profaned the holy truths of the church (*Jer.* xxxvii.).
Reasonings from knowledges (*scientifica*) pervert all understanding of the Word (*Isa.* vii. 17–20).
Reasonings from true knowledges (*scientifica*) pervert them (*Jer.* xliv. 29, 30).
Reasonings from knowledges (*scientifica*) falsify the truths of the Word (*Ezek.* xxiii. 5–8).
Reasonings from the knowledges (*scientifica*) of the natural man destroy the remains (*Jer.* xliii. 8–13).
Reasonings from scientifics and traditions have turned truths into falsities (*Ezek.* xvi. 23–28).
Those who profane by reasonings from knowledges will be destroyed by reasonings from knowledges (*Jer.* xxxvii. 6–10).
Reasonings from knowledges (*scientifica*) of the natural man: their effect upon the good and on the evil (*Ezek.* xxix. 17, 18; 19, 20). ——
Reasonings from the natural man (*Hosea* ix. 1–3).
Reasonings from the natural man have destroyed the chief truths (*Ezek.* xii. 13); and consequently the remaining truths (*ib.* 14–16).
Reasoning from the natural man will destroy all truths, from which comes self-intelligence (*Ezek.* xxvi. 7–12; *cf.* xxx. 10–12, 20–26).
Reasonings from the natural man destroy all things of the church (*Ezek.* xvii. 11–13, 19–21; xxxii. 11, 12).
Reasonings from the natural man cause the truth of the church to perish (*Jer.* xiii. 1–7).
Reasonings from the natural man pervert truths and goods of the church (*Jer.* li.).
Falsities grow by reasonings originating in the delights of the natural man (*Hosea* xii. 1).
Reasonings from the natural man confirm falsities and evils (*Jer.* ii. 36).
Reasonings from the natural man have destroyed the Israelitish nation (*Ezek.* xix. 8, 9).
By reasonings from the natural man they have put off everything of the church and its worship (*Hosea* viii. 8–11); therefore they cannot but perish (*ib.* 12–14).
Reasonings from self-intelligence pervert truths (*Isa.* x. 5–11).
Reasonings from self-intelligence destroy and profane truths (*Isa.* xiv. 24–27).
Reasonings from falsities tolerated and commingled with the simple understanding (*Jer.* xl. 7–12).
Reasonings from falsities have perverted the doctrinals of the church (*Isa.* xxxvi. 1–7).
Reasonings from falsities destroy the remnants of doctrine (*Jer.* xxxix. 1–3, *et seq.*).
Reasonings from falsities cause the church to perish (*Isa.* viii. 7–12; *Ezek.* xxi. 18–22).
Reasonings confirmatory of falsities (*Isa.* lii. 4).
Reasonings from falsities vastate (*Isa.* xxiii. 10–14; xx.; *cf. Jer.* ii. 18).
Reasonings from falsities devastate (*Jer.* lii. 1–7).
They have made for themselves a religion by reasonings from falsities (*Jer.* xxii. 13, 14).
Reasonings will not protect those who have falsified and adulterated the Word (*Nahum* iii. 18).

Rebel.—Those who were of the Israelitish Church rebelled against the Lord in spite of miracles (*Ps.* cvi. 9–34).

Recede (*see* **Depart**).

Receive (*see also* **Accept, Others**).
    No truth and good can be received where not the Lord, but self, is regarded (*Haggai* i. 10, 11).
    The wicked will not receive (*Isa.* xxvi. 10, 11).
    Because they have perverted all things of the Word and of doctrine they can no longer receive anything of truth and good (*Micah* iii. 5–7).
    The Jewish Church does not receive in the life and obey although taught continually (*Jer.* xxxv. 12–16).
    Urged by punishments still they did not receive (*Jer.* v. 3).
    Non-reception due not to simplicity, but to application and industry (*Jer.* v. 4, 5); the consequence (*ib.* 6).
    They will be taught constantly, but still they will not receive (*Isa.* xxviii. 22–29).
    The Lord should be received, because He alone is God, and from Him alone is salvation (*Isa.* xlv. 21, 22).
    Let them receive the Lord that they may be saved (*Isa.* xlv. 8).
    Those who have been completely vastated can at last be received and become a church (*Jer.* xxiv. 4–7).
    Falsity must be rejected and truth received that there may be conjunction and a church (*Jer.* iii. 12–14).
    Those who are not in falsities and evils will receive the Lord, who has conquered the hells and glorified His Human (*Ps.* xxiv. 7–10).
    Those who receive the Lord will understand truths (*Isa.* xxix. 22–24).
    The redeemed will receive things spiritual and celestial (*Jer.* xxxi. 12–14).
    Reception of the doctrine of truth from the Lord (*Isa.* xxvi. 1–4).
    They will receive truths from the Lord gratis (*Isa.* lv. 1).
    The loved one will receive goods of the church (*Jer.* xxxi. 2–5).
    To receive in the life and obey belongs to the celestial church (*Jer.* xxxv. 1–10).
    Reception of life by the new church (*Isa.* xxvi. 19).

Reciprocal (*see* **Grief**).

Recourse (*recursus*).—Profaners have recourse to the Word, but in vain (*Jer.* viii. 14, 15).

Red Sea (*see* **Sea Suph**).

Redeem   ⎫ (*see also* **Deliver**).
Redeemer ⎬   Redemption is expected (*Ps.* cxxx. 5–8).
Redemption ⎭   There is redemption when the Lord conquers (*Ps.* xxvi. 11, 12).
    The Lord is the redeemer (*Ps.* xcix. 8).
    How there is redemption (*Ps.* xxv. 22).
    The Lord alone redeemed (*Isa.* lxiii. 15, 16).
    Redemption is from the Lord (*Isa.* lix. 19, 20); and from Him alone (lxiii. 15, 16).
    Redemption and protection (*Ps.* lxxii. 12–14).
    The redeemed will be guarded against falsities (*Jer.* xxxi. 10, 11); and will receive things spiritual and celestial (*ib.* 10, 11).
    The Lord has redeemed men and saves to eternity (*Ps.* cxi. 5–9).
    A new church, which the Lord has redeemed (*Ps.* cvii. 1–3).
    A song of the new church in praise of the Lord on account of redemption (*Ps.* xviii. 46–50).
    Song in praise of the Lord on account of redemption and reformation (*Ps.* ciii. *t.*, 1–7); they are from mercy, because He knows the infirmities of man (*ib.* 8–18).

Reflect (*cogito*) (*see* **Think**).

Reform (*see also* **Amend, Depart, Purge**).
    Reformation vain (*Jer.* vii. 27–31).
    Those could be reformed who had been completely vastated, etc. (*Jer.* xxiv. 4–7); those could not be reformed who still desired to be in worship from the Word, which worship they would then profane (*ib.* 8, 9).

280   SUMMARIES OF THE INTERNAL SENSE.

Unwillingness to be reformed (*Jer.* iii. 6, 7).
It is represented that those who are in falsities and evils can be reformed by the Lord (*Jer.* xviii. 1-4).
Reformation received through combats against evils and falsities (*Isa.* ix. 1).
The Lord reforms by knowledges (*cognitiones*) of truth, and is alone able to do this (*Ps.* cxlvii. 5).
Reformation of the natural man (*Ps.* cv.).
The Lord has instituted a church and reformed it by truths from the Word, and yet falsities begin to destroy it (*Ps.* lxxx. 8-13).
The "covenant" (*q. v.*) was with them when they were reformed (*Jer.* xi. 1-3).
Song in praise of the Lord on account of redemption and reformation (*Ps.* ciii. *t.*, 1-7); these are from mercy, because He knows the infirmities of man (*ib.* 8-10).

Reformation (the).—The Reformation foretold, but that this church will also perish from mere falsities and evils (*Matt.* xxiv. 15); (*Dan.* ix. 27).

Refrain (*desisto*).—The Jewish Church should refrain from, etc. (*Isa.* xliv. 21, 22).
Those who were of the church were continually taught by the Lord by the Word to refrain from evils, etc. (*Jer.* xxv. 4-7).
Exhortation to refrain from evils (*Jer.* iv. 1, 2).
Unless they refrain and turn back they will utterly perish (*Jer.* iv. 3, 4).
They do not even refrain for fear of destruction (*Jer.* xliv. 7-10).
They do not refrain (*Jer.* li. 7-10).

Regeneration.—The man who does not live ill is regenerated by the Word of the Lord (*Ps.* i. 1-3).
The Lord, who is Divine truth, will regenerate the good (*Ps.* lxviii. 7-11); but not others, although they have the Word (*ib.* 12-14).
The new creation or regeneration of the men of the Most Ancient Church from first to last (*Gen.* i.).

Reign (see **Kingdom**).

Reject (*rejicio*) (*see also* **Against, Last Judgment**).
Rejection of truth from the Word (*Jer.* viii. 7-9).
Rejection of the Word, owing to their own intelligence (*Lam.* iv. 16, 17).
Rejection of goods of charity (*Isa.* xv.).
They have obstinately rejected internals, even from the beginning (*Jer.* vii. 25, 26).
Rejection of worship because of profanation (*Jer.* vii. 27-31).
Rejection of all things of the church (*Ezek.* xvii. 9, 10).
Rejection by the old church (*Isa.* xxviii. 11-13).
The Lord has been utterly rejected by the Jewish nation (*Ps.* cxxiii.).
The posterity of the Jewish church will reject the Lord (*Ps.* cix. 13-20).
Rejection of the Lord (*Isa.* lxv. 1-5; *Lam.* iv. 20).
The Lord rejected by means of knowledges and reasonings (*Jer.* ii. 17, 18).
Their rejecting the Lord and hatching falsities is horrible (*Jer.* ii. 12, 13).
Those who have rejected the Lord will remain forever in their falsities and evils (*Isa.* lxvi. 24).
Rejecting by profaning (*Jer.* xxxvi. 19-24).
Rejection of the Jewish Church, because they have utterly perverted the church (*Zech.* v. 1-4).
The Israelites rejected (*Ps.* lxxviii. 65-67).
Rejection of the old church (*Isa.* xxvi. 5, 6; xliii. 28; xliv. 25; l. 1; *Lam.* ii. 1-9; 13-15).
Rejection of those who are willing to be in blind ignorance (*Isa.* xviii. 3-6).

Those who made a church out of mere doctrine and did not at the same time make it consist in life, were rejected (*Gen.* iv.).
Those who were of the devastated church have been rejected (*Ps.* cvii. 32–34, 39, 40).
Rejection of the evil (*Ps.* lxiii. 11).
The Lord rejects the evil and the haughty (*Ps..* ci. 4, 5).
Falsity must be rejected and truth received, that there may be conjunction and a church (*Jer.* iii. 12–14).
Falsities will be rejected (*Hosea* xiv. 8).
The will reject such things as have no spiritual life in them (*Isa.* lv. 2).
Rejection of falsities and evils by the new church (*Isa.* xxxi. 7; lii. 2).
The new church will reject evils (*Ezek.* xxxvi. 31, 32).
The Lord rejects all evil and falsity from Himself (*Ps.* cxxxix. 19–22).
——— (*respuo*).—They reject truths because they are in self-intelligence (*Amos* v. 10–13).
Rejoice (*see* **Joy**).
Religion (*religio*) (*see also* **Change**).
A religion that consists in nothing but knowledges (*cognitiones*) (*Isa.* xiv. 28–32).
A religion that consists in nothing but knowledge (*scientia*) (*Isa.* xix.).
Perverting the truths of religion by those things which do not belong to religion (*Ezek.* xxv. 1, 2).
Those who frame something else of religion from their own intelligence (*Isa.* xliv. 12–20).
They have made religion by reasonings from falsities (*Jer.* xxii. 13, 14); contrary to the truths of the church, and they cannot recede from it (*ib.* 25–27).
Devastation of every good of religion (*Isa.* xx.).
Religion said to be not anything (*Ps.* lxxiv. *t.*, 1–9).
There is no other religion but that which is commanded in the Word (*Isa.* xlvi. 8–12).
Wherein does religion consist? (*Gen.* iv.)
They are to be gathered together out of every religion and taught (*Zech.* x. 7–10).
Man will draw near the Lord from every religion (*Isa.* lxvi. 19).
——— (*religiosum*).—Religiosity (*or* "religion") contrasted with "church" (*Dan.* xi.).
The religiosity (*or* religion) which is in faith separate from charity is meant by the "king of the north" (*Dan.* xi.).
Remain (*maneo*).—The simple understanding of the Word according to doctrine will still remain (*Jer.* xl. 1–6).
——— (*remaneo*).—Nothing remains (*Amos* vi. 10–12).
——— (*supersum*).—All things of the church have been destroyed, even until nothing remains (*Jer.* iv. 22–27).
Nothing of the church remains (*Jer.* ix. 10–12).
Remains (*reliquum*) ⎫ (*see also* **Residue**).
Remnant ⎭ —The things that remained that were not utterly falsified were nevertheless tainted with falsities (*Jer.* xxxviii. 7–13).
The remnants of doctrine will perish by reasonings from falsities (*Jer.* xxxix. 1–3).
All things that remain will also perish, owing to falsities still more interior (*Ezek.* xxi. 14–17).
Nothing of truth remains (*Jer.* xlix. 9–13).
Every remnant of truth and good which is untouched is adulterated at the same time (*Jer.* xlviii. 43–46).
All the remains of profaners likewise perish (*Jer.* viii. 3).
Those who remained (*reliqui*) of the devastated church profaned the holy truths of the church by reasonings from knowledges (*Jer.* xxxvii.).

At the last judgment some will be left (*Ezek.* vii. 16); but even these will have no truth or good (*ib.* 17–19); they will draw near to those who have perverted all things of the church, etc. (*ib.* 20–22).

—— (*reliquiae*) (*see also* **Simple**).

There were still remains (*Jer.* xli. 10–15); some of which were perverted by knowledges of the natural man (*ib.* 16–18).

The remains or those things that were left (*residua*) consulted doctrine (*Jer.* xlii. 1–16); they were told to continue simply in their external worship and not consult knowledges, and then they would be saved (*ib.* 7–22); but they consulted them, and will perish (xliii.).

Not all things of the church will perish, because there must be a church (*Isa.* lxv. 8–10).

Something of a church will be established out of those who are natural and in knowledges (*scientifica*) (*Ezek.* xxix. 13–16).

Those who have not falsified will not perish (*Jer.* xlix. 39).

Remedy (*medela*).—No remedy against infestation by evils and falsities (*Jer.* xxx. 12–15); there will be a remedy from the Lord, who will restore the church (*ib.* 17, 18).

Remission of sins (*see* **Forgive**).

Remove (*see also* **Purify**).

If they had obeyed, the hells would have been removed from them (*Ps.* lxxxi. 13–16).

Removal and dispersion of the hells involved in the conversion of the Israelites when they recalled the miracles in Egypt (*Ps.* lxxviii. 41–51).

Prayer for removal of the evil (*Jer.* xii. 3; xvii. 14–18).

All who are in falsities will be removed (*Ps.* xcvii. 7).

The Lord will remove falsities and evils (*Ps.* xlvii. 3).

The Lord will remove falsities of evil and thus hell (*Joel* ii. 20).

Removal of falsities of ignorance (*Zech.* iii. 3–5).

Removal of falsities from the church established by the Lord from the nations (*Ps.* cxiv. 3–6).

Removal of evils and falsities in the new church (*Zeph.* iii. 13–20).

Removal of evils and falsities by truths and goods from the Word (*Ezek.* xvi. 7–12).

Removal of infernal things from the new church (*Micah* vii. 16, 17).

How the natural man removed evils and falsities from himself (*Gen.* xiv. 18–24 *and prec.*).

Repentance (*paenitentia*).—Those who are in the church are told to repent and be converted; but they will not (*Jer.* xviii. 11–13).

Exhortation to repent (*Jer.* xxvi. 1–5; *Joel* ii. 12–17).

Repentance during the devastation of the church (*Isa.* xxxvii. 1–7; 14–20).

Repentance protects from destruction (*Isa.* xxxviii. 1–8).

Of those who are converted after repentance (*Jer.* xviii. 5–8).

The nations, hearing from the Word of God about their sins, and that they would perish, were converted after repenting, and were heard by the Lord and saved (*Jonah* iii. 1–10).

—— (*resipiscentia*). ⎫ —They cannot repent, because they cannot be led away
Repent (*resipisco*). ⎭ from evils and falsities (*Ezek.* vii. 25–27).

Exhortation to repent, for evil from the sensual man has consumed the different things of the church (*Joel* i. 5–7).

Exhortation to repent (*Ps.* iv. 4–8; *Isa.* i. 16–19; xxxviii. 16–20; *Jer.* xxxvi. 1–10).

Repentance (*Isa.* lv. 7).

Represent ⎫ (*see also* **Lord**, *last subheading;* **Prophet**).
Representative ⎭ —The historical things in the Word are representative (p. 163).

A representative of the Word, as a man (*Ezek.* i. 5).

The Lord was represented in respect to Divine love (*Ezek.* viii. 1, 2).

The prophet to represent the Word (*Ezek.* iii. 16, 17).
Representatives among the Israelites different from the former good ones, because they had profaned them (*Ezek.* xx. 25, 26).
A law of representation (*Jer.* xxvii. end).
The prophet Hosea represented the falsification of the Word with the Jewish nation (*Hosea* i. 1-3).
Representation of the perverted church in the church (*Ezek.* iv.).
In is represented how they have destroyed the sense of the letter (*Ezek.* v.).
That the truth of the church would gradually perish by means of reasonings from the natural man was represented by the "girdle of linen" (*Jer.* xiii. 1-7).
Representation of the successive states of the church even to the end (*Zech.* i. 7-10).
It is represented that the church has departed from the Lord and the Word by the falsification of the Word as to the sense of the letter, etc. (*Ezek.* xii. 3-12).
It is represented that the church was destitute of all life from good and truth (*Ezek.* xxxvii. 1, 2).
It is represented that the church has been destroyed so that it cannot be restored (*Jer.* xix. 9-11).
It is represented that those who are in falsities and evils can be reformed by the Lord (*Jer.* xviii. 1-4).
A representation of the Jewish nation's being inflamed at the salvation of the nations (*Jonah* iv. 5-11).
The posterity of Jacob gloried on account of their representative worship (*Hosea* xii. 8-14).
Those who represented the celestial things of the church and those who represented its spiritual and intellectual things, falsified and adulterated the truths of the Word (*Hosea* v. 1-3); they cannot turn back, but all will perish (*ib.* 4-9).
At the coming of the Lord, and the consequent change of state of heaven, all the representatives of the church which had been totally falsified will be destroyed (*Micah* i. 4-7); consequent mourning reaches even to those who were in celestial good (*ib.* 8-12).
A representative that the new church is from the Lord, with all the good and truth in it (*Zech.* vi. 9-14).
—— **church and worship.**—Representative churches described in the Word that is mentioned by Moses (p. 164).
All the churches down to the coming of the Lord were representative churches:—they represented the church, and in the highest sense the Lord; it is from this that the Word is spiritual and Divine (p. 163).
Three notable changes of the representative churches (p. 163).
Representative churches ceased when the Lord came into the world (p. 163).
Representative worship abrogated (*Isa.* xxxvi. 7).
When the Lord comes there will no longer be the representative of a church, but a church wherein the Lord Himself will be in place of that representative (*Jer.* iii. 16, 17).

Reprobate } (*reprobo*).—The former church will be reproved because of its evils,
Reprove } etc. (*Jer.* xxxii. 26-33).
Although they will reprobate and not understand, nevertheless they must be taught (*Isa.* xxviii. 17-21; *cf. Ezek.* xx. 18-24).

Repudiate.—Repudiation of doctrine, how effected (*Jer.* xxxvii. 11-16).
Repudiation of truths (*Jer.* vi. 16, 17).
Because they have repudiated the Word and have obeyed their own lusts they are in falsities of evil (*Jer.* ix. 13-15); and will be destroyed by evils and falsities of evil (*ib.* 16).

The Jewish Church repudiated the Lord (*Ps.* cix. *t.*, 1-6).
The Jewish nation has utterly repudiated the Lord (*Ps.* lxxxix. 43-45).

Repugnance (*see* **Fight against**).

Residue (*residuum*) (*see also* **Remains**).
Little left in vastated church (*Isa.* i. 9; *Ezek.* xii. 14-16).
Nearly all things left perish by means of knowledges of the natural man (*Jer.* xliv. 7-10).
The remains (*reliquiae*) or things that were left (*residua*) consulted doctrine (*Jer.* xlii. 1-16).

Resist.—They cannot resist, however much they trust in themselves (*Jer.* li. 51-53).
The Lord will lead them forth, however much hell may resist (*Isa.* li. 14, 15).

Rest (*quiesco*).—The Lord will not rest until He sees His church established (*Ps.* cxxxii. *t.*, 1-5).

Restore (*reparo*).—When externals were lost, there was a restoration (*Amos* vii. 2-6).
The church has been destroyed so that it cannot be restored (*Jer.* xix. 9-11).

——— (*restauro*).—Prayer that the former church may be restored (*Lam.* v. 19-22).
Restoration of all things of the church (*Isa.* lviii. 12).

——— (*restituo*).   } —The perverse are found incapable of restoration
Restoration (*restitutio*). }   (*Jer.* vi. 27-30).
The things of the church could not have been restored among them in any way (*Jer.* iv. 30).
May the Lord come and restore the new church (*Ps.* lxxx. 14-19).
The Lord will restore the church (*Isa.* lii. 8, 9; liv. 7, 8; *Jer.* xxx. 17, 18; *Ezek.* xvi. 53-55).
The church restored by the Lord by means of His coming (*Ps.* xc. 12-14).
Restoration of the things of the church (*Isa.* lxi. 4).

Restrain (*coerceo*).—The hells are restrained through the Divine truth which is with the men of the church (*Ps.* cxlix. 7-9 *and prec.*).

Resurrection (*see also* **Raise up**).
The Lord's Human, glorified, will rise again (*Ps.* xvi. 8-11).

Retaliation (*see also* **Retribution**).
Those who have destroyed will be destroyed (*Jer.* xxx. 16).
Those who profaned the holy truths of the church by reasonings from knowledges will be destroyed by reasonings from knowledges (*Jer.* xxxvii. 6-10).
Those who have falsified the external of the Word ("Edom") will be destroyed by things falsified (*Jer.* xlix. 7, 8).
Destruction of "Babylon" comes because they have destroyed all things of the church (*Jer.* li. 34-40).

Retreat (*recedo*) (*see* **Depart**).

Retribution (*see also* **Retaliation**).
Retribution will visit the tempters (*Jer.* xxv. 12).
Retribution will visit the profaners who have delivered the Lord up to death (*Jer.* xi. 20).
Retribution will visit those who have previously profaned the church (*Jer.* xvi. 18).
Retribution on the evil (*Ps.* x. 12-18).

Return (*redeo*) (*see* **Conversion**).
They will return to God whom they then worshipped, and from whom they received good, not knowing that this was from the Lord (*Hosea* ii. 8).
Those of the new church will finally return (*Jer.* xxxi. 16, 17).

——— (*reverto*).—They are not willing to return, even when chastized (*Jer.* ii. 29, 30).

Reveal (*see also* ***Predict***).
> The prophet guilty if he did not reveal the falsities and evils of the church (*Ezek.* iii. 11-21; *cf.* xxxiii. 6-9).
> Revelation from the Lord to those who were of the church during the era of "Babylon," (*Dan.* ii. 14-30).
> Revelation concerning the successive changes of state of the church (*Dan.* vii. 1-3, *and fol.*).
> By virtue of the presence of the Lord all things are revealed (*Nahum* i. 3-6).
> Their adulterations will be revealed and they will perish (*Nahum* iii. 5-7).
> The Lord will surely reveal that there cannot be at the same time a church and not a church, etc. (*Amos* iii. 7, 8).
> Revelation respecting the end of the church (*Dan.* ix. 1-3).
> Revelation (*Dan.* ix. 20-23).
> The Lord reveals those things which will be in the new church respecting such as are in faith alone, and respecting such as are in truths from good, who are meant by "Michael" (*Dan.* x. 7-21).
> Revelation about the new church is from the Lord (*Dan.* xii. 8, 9).
> The Lord will disclose truths to the new church (*Isa.* xxv. 6-8).

Revenge.—The Lord fought seemingly from revenge (*Isa.* lix. 18).

Revolt (*deficio*) (*see also* ***Want***).
> The church instituted among the Jewish nation revolted (*Ps.* cvi.).

Rise up (*see* ***Uprising***).

Rich.—The church possesses all things of the church in abundance (*Amos* vi 3-6).
> When they became rich in knowledges (*cognitiones*) from the Word they forsook the Lord by reason of their self-glorification (*Hosea* xiii. 5, 6).

Roman Catholics (*see* ***Babylon, Iniquisition***).

Ruin (*see* ***Destroy*** (*perdo*)).

Rule (*see* ***Love of ruling, Kingdom***).

Ruler (*moderator*).—The rulers of the Babylonish religion at first learn and teach the goods and truths of heaven and the church; but afterwards they backslide, etc. (*Dan.* ii. 31-35).
> Those rulers in the Babylonish religion who worshipped the Lord did not obey the threats of the apostates (*Dan.* iii. 8-12); they were therefore excommunicated and condemned to hell by "Babylon" (*ib.* 13-21); but no harm came to them, for they were protected by the Lord (*ib.* 22-25).

Sabbath.—The Divine of the Lord is the "sabbath" (*Jer.* xvii. 21-24).
> The oneness of the Divine of the Lord with His Divine Human is the "sabbath" (*Ps.* xcii. *t.*).

Sacrifice.—The Lord does not desire sacrifices (*Ps.* l. *t.*, 1-6).

Sad time (*Dan.* viii. 27).

Safe (*salvus*).—The Lord leads men forth safe, however much hell may resist (*Isa.* li. 14, 15).

Safety } (*salus*) (*see also* ***Protect***).
Salvation } Safety for no one unless the Lord comes (*Isa.* lxiv. 6, 7).
> Wherein does salvation consist? (*Gen.* iv.)
> Prayer to the Father that those who worship Him may have salvation (*Ps.* lxx. 4).
> The Lord endured for the sake of those who awaited salvation (*Ps.* lxix. 6, 7).
> All of salvation is in the Divine Human from eternity (*Ps.* lxxii. 17).
> Salvation is from the Lord (*Ps.* xx. 5, 6, 9).
> Salvation is solely in the Lord (*Ps.* xlix. 15).

Salvation is from the Lord alone (*Isa.* xlv. 21, 22).
The Lord wishes the salvation of all (*Ezek.* xviii. 30-32; xxxiii. 10, 11).
All are in sins and there is safety for no one unless the Lord comes (*Isa.* lxiv. 6, 7).
Salvation is by means of those things that the Lord gives (*Ps.* cxlviii. 13, 14).
When there will be salvation in the new church (*Micah* v. 7).
Those who are humble will have salvation from the Lord (*Ps.* cxxxviii. 6-8).
Prayer of the nations to the Lord for salvation, which was effected for them, when the falsities from the Jewish nation had been removed (*Jonah* i. 14-16).

Salvation (*salvatio*) ⎫ (*see also* **Preserve, Safety, Confess, Deliver, Faith, Help,**
Save (*salvo*) ⎭ **Lead, Redeem, Regeneration**).

Whence it is that there is no salvation (*Isa.* lix. 11 *and prec.*).
No salvation from mere natural-mindedness when one boasts of knowledges and his own intelligence (*Ps.* xlix. 7-9 *and prec.*).
Knowledges and self-intelligence does not save after death (*Ps.* xlix. 16-20).
Salvation of the remains dependent upon their abiding simply in their external worship, and not consulting knowledges of the natural man (*Jer.* xlii. 7-22).
Whence comes salvation has been hidden (*Isa.* xlv. 15).
They do not know the way by which is salvation (*Isa.* lv. 8, 9).
Some are to be saved (*Zeph.* ii. 7).
The Lord will save men, for they have been bound by the hells (*Isa.* xlv. 13).
Those who are out of the church are to be protected and saved in the midst of the infernal (*Isa.* xxxv. 6-9).
When the Lord comes He will save the simple (*Ezek.* xxxiv. 22-25).
The way of salvation is through the coming of the Lord (*Isa.* lv. 10, 11; *Ps.* xc. 14-17).
Salvation is from the power which the Lord will have when He comes and glorifies His Human (*Ps.* xcviii. 2 *and prec.*).
Salvation comes when the Lord is delivered from the hells which assault Him with falsities (*Ps.* cxliv. 9, 10, *and prec.*).
The Divine love of saving belongs to the Lord (*Ps.* xxvi. 7, 8).
The Lord is He through whom is all salvation (*Ps.* cxviii. 18-22).
Salvation is from the Lord for those who are in goods and truths (*Jer.* iv. 1, 2).
Salvation is through the Divine in the Lord (*Isa.* liii. 5).
The coming of the Lord, from whom is salvation, is near at hand (*Isa.* xlvi. 13).
Redemption and salvation of the faithful by the Lord (*Isa.* xlix.).
The Lord has redeemed men, and saves to eternity (*Ps.* cxi. 5-9).
Promise of salvation in the Word cannot be fulfilled in the case of those who are not willing to acknowledge and receive (*Jer.* iv. 9-12).
May those be saved who are in the truths and goods of the church! (*Ps.* xxviii. 9.)
May the good be saved and the evil perish! (*Ps.* civ. 31-35.)
When the old church is at an end then those who at heart acknowledge the Lord will be saved (*Hab.* iii. 18, 19).
It is an eternal truth, that those who worship the Lord will be saved (*Ps.* cxxxii. 11, 12).
Those who acknowledge and worship the Lord will be saved (*Joel* ii. 32).
Salvation of those who receive the Lord (*Isa.* xl. 9-11; xlv. 8).
Those who confess the Lord are saved (*Ps.* cxl. 12, 13).

Those who were in the worship of the Lord (in the midst of the Babylonish religion) were saved (*Dan.* vi. 25-28).
Salvation from the Lord, and rejection of the evil (*Ps.* lxiii. 11).
The Lord Himself saves His own, and destroys all power of hell (*Isa.* xliii. 16, 17).
The Lord will save those who are of the church, whence they will have joy from Him (*Ps.* xiv. 7).
Those who are of the Lord's church will be saved (*Jer.* xxiii. 5, 6).
Salvation comes from no other source than turning back to the Lord (*Hosea* xiv. 3).
Salvation is in the church (*Ps.* cxxxiii. 3).
The Lord will save those who are in truths and goods (*Ps.* cxv. 12-15, 18).
Those who are of the church and in the doctrine of truth will be saved by the Lord when He comes (*Ps.* xlvi. 5, 6).
The Lord will save those who will be of His church, and is therefore praised in song (*Ps.* cxiii. 7-9 *and prec.*).
Those who are in the new church will be saved (*Obad.* 19-21).
Redemption and salvation of those who will be of the new church from the Lord (*Isa.* xliii. 1).
The Lord will save the new church from evils (*Ps.* lxvi. 6, 7).
Those who prayed for it were saved (*Ps.* lxxvii. 10-15).
The Lord saves those who believe in Him, and those who do not believe perish (*Ps.* cxlv. 18-20).
Those are saved who trust in the Lord (*Ps.* xx. 7, 8; xxxiii. 18-22).
He that trusts in the Lord and lives well will be saved (*Ps.* cxii. 1-7, 9).
Those who do not trust in the Lord will not be saved (*Ps.* cxv. 17).
How the Lord saves the faithful (*Isa.* lxiv. 5).
The Lord will save the faithful (*Isa.* xi. 1-5).
The Lord alone fought and conquered that the faithful might obtain salvation (*Isa.* lxiii. 3-6).
The Lord will save those who do good (*Isa.* xxxiii. 15-17).
Those who do not commit evils or act contrary to the goods and truths of the church are saved (*Ezek.* xviii. 14-17).
The good will be saved (*Isa.* xl. 1-5; *Ps.* lxiv. 9, 10; *Mal.* iv. 2).
At the judgment the good are saved (*Ps.* lxxv. 7; lxxvi. 7-10, 12).
The good are saved by the Lord, and taken up into heaven (*Ps.* xxxvii.).
Those who are of the Lord's church are saved (*Isa.* xlv. 17); for man is born for heaven (*ib.* 18).
The nations saved after repentance (*Jonah* iii. 1-10; iv. 1-4).

Samaria.—"Samaria" means the church which is in truth (*Ezek.* xxiii. 1, 2); its history (*ib.* 3, 4, *and fol.*).
Sanctities (*see* **Holy**).
Sane (*see* **Sound**).
Save (*servo*) (*see* **Preserve**).
Scatter (*see* **Dispersion**).
Science (*see* **Knowledge** (*scientia*)).
Sea Suph (*Ps.* cvi. 9-34).
Seduce (*see* **Lead astray**).
See (*see also* **Blind, Truth**).
God sees all things (*Ps.* xciv. 3-11).
Because they have perverted all things of the Word and of doctrine they can no longer see and receive anything of truth and good (*Micah* iii. 5-7).
Because they do not see truths they perish on the day of judgment (*Jer.* xxiii. 12).
It may be seen that all truth of the Word perishes (*Jer.* xiii. 18, 19).
Seed (*see* **Drink**).

Seek (*see also* **Ask**).

The Lord will spiritually bless those who seek Him (*Zech.* x. 1).

Seeming heavens (*sicut coeli*).—They will be cast down and subjugated from the places where they have made seeming heavens for themselves (*Ps.* lxxxiii. 9-12).

Self (*see also* **Love of self**).

The men of the new church of themselves are nothing but falsity and evil (*Isa.* xli. 28, 29).

Every one wishes to be wise from himself, why (*Jer.* xvi. 12); consequently they must be in hell (*ib.* 13).

They learn from themselves and not from the Lord (*Jer.* xxiii. 21, 22).

—— **confidence** (*see also under* **Self-intelligence**).

Those who trust in themselves and their own learning have no intelligence whatever (*Isa.* xxx. 16, 17).

Because they trust in themselves they perceive nothing of truth and good (*Jer.* xvii. 5, 6).

They cannot resist, however much they trust in themselves (*Jer.* li. 51-53).

Those who trust in their own falsities will come to nothing, and will be destroyed (*Jer.* li. 54-58).

Judgment on those who trust in themselves (*Isa.* xxx. 30, 31).

Those who trust in themselves perish (*Ps.* xx. 7, 8).

—— **exaltation** (*se exaltare*) (*see also* **Self-glorification**).

The Jewish Church exalted itself above all (*Ezek.* xvi. 31).

It was against the Word if they exalted themselves above the Lord, and thus they profaned things holy (*Dan.* v. 10-24).

—— —— (*se extollere*).—Let not the evil exalt themselves above the good (*Ps.* lxxv. 4-6).

They exalt themselves against the Lord, and consequently against His Word, despising Him and falsifying it (*Jer.* xviii. 18).

—— **glorification** (*gloriatio sui*).—They forsook the Lord by reason of self-glorification in their wealth of knowledges (*Hosea* xiii. 5, 6).

—— **intelligence** (*propria intelligentia*) (*see also* **Lead astray, Learning, Pride, Reasoning, Self-confidence**).

As the men of the Most Ancient Church departed from the celestial to the natural man, they had intelligence from the latter from what was their own (*proprium*) in place of intelligence from the Lord (*Gen.* iii.).

End of the Most Ancient Church, when there was no longer any truth or good, because they were in their own intelligence (*Gen.* vi. 1-7, 10-13).

Self-intelligence comes from reasoning from the natural man, which destroys all truths (*Ezek.* xxvi. 7-12).

Self-intelligence consequent on there being no truths and goods any longer (*Jer.* xii. 5).

Concerning those who believe that they are learned from mere knowledges (*cognitiones*), and say in their heart that they are most intelligent from themselves (*Ezek.* xxviii. 1-5 *and fol.*).

Those who trust the knowledge (*scientia*) of the natural man, thus their own intelligence, lead themselves astray (*Isa.* xxxi. 1-5 *and fol.*). (*See further under* **Trust**.)

Those who are in self-intelligence and pervert the sense of the letter of the Word, who are "Edom" (*Obad.*).

Self-intelligence causes rejection of the Word (*Lam.* iv. 16, 17).

Self-intelligence falsifies and perverts (*Isa.* ix. 8-21).

Of those who from their own intelligence have falsified truths, who are the "drunkards of Ephraim" (*Isa.* xxviii.).

Those who from self-intelligence hatch out doctrine or falsify by doctrine described (*Ezek.* xiii.).

Of self-intelligence (*Isa.* xxii.); truths of the church perish through it (*ib.* 1-7) externals of the church are completely ruined through self-

intelligence, until they come into ignorance respecting God (*ib.* 8–12; *see also following verses*).
They reject truths because they are in self-intelligence (*Amos* v. 10–13).
Worship of things that come from self-intelligence (*Isa.* lvii. 6; 10).
Religion from self-intelligence (*Isa.* xliv. 12–20).
Self-intelligence does not save after death (*Ps.* xlix. 16–20).
Self-intelligence amounts to nothing at all (*Jer.* x. 14, 15; *Isa.* xl. 19, 20).
Self-intelligence effects nothing (*Ps.* xxxiii. 16, 17; cxxxv. 15–18).
Self-intelligence is nothing, but that which is from the Lord is something (*Ps.* cxlvii. 10, 11).
From self-intelligence they are puffed up (*Hab.* ii. 9, 10).
Those who wish to prevail by self-intelligence; *general subject* (*Jer.* x.). (*See further under* **Prevail**.)
Those who were in self-intelligence opposed themselves to the Lord at the last judgment (*Isa.* xli. 5–7); but were of no avail against Him (*ib.* 11, 12); they will be totally dispersed (*ib.* 15, 16).
The Lord rejects those who are insane from self-intelligence (*Isa.* xliv. 25 *and fol.*).
Those who trust in self-intelligence and thus in falsities, are to be driven away (*Isa.* xlii. 17).
Respecting those who boast of their own intelligence (*Ps.* xlix. 5, 6); they perish or come into hell (*ib.* 10–14).
End of the church which is in self-intelligence (*Jer.* x. 14, 15; 22).
From their self-intelligence they have perverted all Divine worship, and hence will perish (*Hosea* xiii. 1–3).
Those who trust in their own intelligence will perish (*Ps.* lii. 7).
The self-intelligent cast into hell, that they may no longer destroy (*Ezek.* xxxi. 14); and there kept shut up lest they spread their falsities abroad (*ib.* 15–18).
Those who trust in the Lord will reject those things that appertain to their own intelligence (*Isa.* xxx. 22).
—— *regard.*—The church cannot be instituted among them, because every one looks to himself and not the Lord (*Hag.* i. 7–9).
Sense of the Letter (*see under* **Word**).
Sensual (*see* **Natural-sensual**).
—— *man* (*see also* **Fallacy**).
Falsity from the sensual man and afterwards evil therefrom has consumed all things of the church (*Joel* i. 4); this evil has destroyed the different things of the church (*ib.* 5–7).
When falsity and evil from the sensual has destroyed the whole church, the Lord comes and executes judgment (*Joel* ii. 2, 3 *and prec.*).
Separate (*separo*).—The church which was in good separated herself from the Lord by falsifying truths and adulterating goods (*Ezek.* xxiii. 18).
They draw punishments to themselves, because they have separated themselves from the Lord and have worshipped things infernal (*Jer.* ii. 19, 20).
Separation of those who have profaned holy thing (*Zech.* ii. 6–9).
Separation of the evil and the good (*Ezek.* ix. 4).
Those who are separated (from those who are in the ultimate heaven) and grieve over them (*Jer.* vi. 24–26).
Separation to prevent seduction (*Ezek.* xxiii. 46–49).
Separation to prevent persecution (*Ezek.* xxxii. 31, 32).
Men should separate themselves from those who are against the Lord because they are nothing before Him and will be destroyed (*Ps.* ii. 1–5).
Let no one believe that he is separated from the Lord (*Isa.* lvi. 3).
The new church will not be separated from the Lord (*Jer.* xxxii. 36–40).
Serve.—The whole church will serve the Lord (*Ps.* xlv. 17).
Heaven will serve the Lord (*Ps.* xci. 11, 12).

SUMMARIES OF THE INTERNAL SENSE.

Sever (*sejungo*).—They have severed themselves from the church (*Mal.* ii. 14–16); even by their calling evil good (*ib.* 17).

Shame.—When the Lord comes, he who leads others astray will be ashamed (*pudeo*) (*Hab.* ii. 15–17).

Let them be put to shame (*pudefio*) who have rejected the Lord (*Ps.* cix. 26–29).

The Lord is shamefully treated (*ig. tominia afficior*) by those with whom was the church (*Ps.* lxix. 8–12).

Shem.—"Shem" means the celestial of the Ancient Church (*Gen.* ix. 18–29).

Shepherd (*see* ***Leader, Minister, Preacher, Teacher***).

"Shepherds" signify those who have perverted the good of the Word, and by means of it have destroyed the church (*Jer.* xxiii. 1, 2).

Evil shepherds destroy (*destruo*) everything of the church (*Ezek.* xxxiv. 18–21); and destroy (*perdo*) the simple (*ib.* 21). (*Cf. Isa.* lvi. 10–12).

Sheth (*see* ***Division***).

Shun (*fugio*) (*see also* ***Abstain, Depart, Refrain, Reject***).

Shunning truths and goods (*Jer.* ii. 24, 25).

They will shun the church because nothing of the doctrine of truth is in it (*Zech.* xii. 2, 3).

The man who does not live ill is regenerated by the Word of the Lord (*Ps.* i. 1–3).

Siege.—Siege of the church by falsities represented (*Ezek.* iv. 1, 2); siege of the church by falsities of evil and evils of falsity represented (*ib.* 7–8).

Signification (*see also* ***Canaan***).

Things pertaining to the church signify things pertaining to the Lord (p. 168).

Simple (*see also* ***Remains***).

The simple understanding of the Word has not yet been devastated (*Jer.* xxxix. 9, 10); why (*ib.* 11–14).

The simple understanding of the Word according to doctrine will still remain (*Jer.* xl. 1–6); beside the simple understanding, reasonings from falsies have been tolerated which were commingled (*ib.* 7–12); they began to be imbued with falsities of faith (*ib.* 13–16).

Those who believe the Word in simplicity (in the devastated Christian Church) will remain (*Dan.* xi. 41).

The simple are destroyed by evil shepherds (*Ezek.* xxxiv. 21); but they will be taught and saved by the Lord, when He comes (*ib.* 22–25); he will teach them and protect them from falsities, and they will acknowledge Him (*ib.* 26–31).

Simplicity.—Non-reception of truth due, not to simplicity, but, etc. (*Jer.* v. 4, 5).

Simulation (*see* ***Pretense***).

Sin ⎱ (*see also* ***Forgive***).
Sinners ⎰ Sins of fathers are not visited on the sons (*Ezek.* xviii.).

All are in sins, and there is safety for none unless the Lord comes (*Isa.* lxiv. 6, 7).

The Lord raises up sinners, and leads them into truths that they may live (*Ps.* cxlv. 14–16).

The nations, hearing from the Word of God about their sins, and that they would perish, repented, etc. (*Jonah* iii. 1–10).

Slave (*servus*). ⎱—Those who are of the church have become slaves (*Jer.*
Enslaved (*serviens*). ⎰ xxxiv. 12–16); they will be slaves to falsities, because they have departed from conjunction with the Lord (*ib.* 17–19); and because of profanation of truth (*ib.* 20).

The church and its doctrine enslaved (*Lam.* i. 1–3).

Slay (*see* ***Lord*** SLAIN).

INDEX OF WORDS AND SUBJECTS. 291

Snatch (*eripio*).—The Lord snatched them out of the hand of the infernals (*Ps.* lxviii. 18–23).
Son (*see* **Adopt**).
Song of praise (*celebratio*). ⎫ The Lord should be praised in song (*Ps.* ci. *t.*, 1).
Sing praises (*celebro*). ⎭ The church will sing praises to the Lord (*Ps.* xcii. 15).

Song in praise of the Lord (*Ps.* lxxii. 18, 19; xcv. 1; cxlvi. 1, 2).
Song in praise of the Lord by a new church, etc. (*Ps.* lxxxvii.).
Song in praise of the Lord by His church (*Ps.* lxxxi. *t.*, 1–4).
Song in praise of the Lord in His Divine Human (*Ps.* cxxxv.).
Song in praise of the Lord who is the Word and the God of the church (*Ps.* xcix.).
Song in praise of the Lord, that Divine truths or the Word are from Him (*Ps.* civ. 1–4).
A song in praise of the Lord because the church is from Him through the Word (*Ps.* xxxiii. 1–9).
Song in praise of the Lord by the church, that He is to be worshipped from the Word, where is His Divine truth (*Ps.* cxxxviii. 1–5); that those who are humble have safety from Him and life and protection (*ib.* 6–8).
Song in praise of the Lord by those who worship Him, when the church has been devastated (*Ps.* cxxxiv. *t.*, 1).
Song of praise to the Lord and joy on account of the fulfilment of predictions (*Ps.* xcviii. 4–8).
Song in praise of the Lord by His church, that to Him alone belong power and glory (*Ps.* xcvi. 1–9).
Song in praise of the Lord: because He is omnipotent (*Ps.* cxiii. 1–5); because He came into the world (*ib.* 6); because He will save those who will be of His church (*ib.* 7–9).
Song in praise of the Divine power of the Lord through union (*Ps.* lxviii. 32–35).
Song in praise of the Lord and of His works for the establishment of the church (*Ps.* cv. 1–7).
Song in praise of the Lord because of His works and His justice, and His mercy (*Ps.* cxlv. *t.*, 1–9).
The justice of the Lord will be praised in song (*Ps.* xxxv. 27, 28).
Song in praise of the Lord, that those who were of the devastated church have been rejected, and that those who are of the new church have been accepted, with whom truths and goods will be multiplied (*Ps.* cvii. 32–43).
A song in praise of the Lord, that He sustains the church, that salvation is from Him for those who trust in Him, while those perish who trust in themselves (*Ps.* xx. *t.*, 1–9).
Song in praise of the Lord, because He delivers those who trust in Him from all evil, etc. (*Ps.* xxxiv. *t.*, 1–11 *and fol.*).
Song in praise of the Lord who delivers from falsities and evils, and grants truths and goods (*Ps.* cxxxvi. 23–26).
Song of the new church in praise of the Lord on account of redemption (*Ps.* xviii. 46–50).
Song in praise of the Lord on account of redemption and reformation, etc. (*Ps.* ciii. *t.*, 1–7 *and fol.*).
Song in praise of the Lord because He snatched them out of the hands of the infernals (*Ps.* lxviii. 24–29 *and prec.*).
Song in praise of the Lord (*Ps.* cxi. 1–4); He redeemed men, and saves to eternity (*ib.* 5–9); toworship Him is widom (*ib.* 8, 10).
Song in praise of the Lord by His church, who alone reforms by knowledges of truth, and teaches truths to those who are in ignorance, etc. (*Ps.* cxlvii. 1–9, 12, *and fol.*).

Song in praise of the Lord, that He is to be worshipped with the heart, because He is the Former of the church (*Ps.* c. *t.*, 1-3).

A song in praise of the Lord, that He reigns over the church, etc. (*Ps.* xlvii. *t.*, 1, 2 *and fol.*); and over the heavens (*ib.* 9).

The heavens and the earths are the Lord's, therefore He should be praised in song (*Ps.* ciii. 19-22).

THE LORD'S SONG IN PRAISE OF THE FATHER.

(*For additional references, see under* **Help**.)

A song in praise of the Father (*Ps.* lvii. 9-11).

Song of praise to the Father by the Lord, for the church (*Ps.* cxviii. 1-4).

Song of praise for protection (*Ps.* lvi. 12, 13).

Song in praise of the co-operation of the Father with the Lord (*Ps.* xcii. 1-5).

Song in praise of the Father by the Lord, who is to be made one with Him (*Ps.* xci. 1).

The Lord's song in praise of the Father because of union (*unio*) (*Ps.* lxi. 6-8).

Song in praise of the Father by the Lord (*Ps.* cxxxix.).

Sound (*sanus*).—There is nothing of soundness (*Nahum* iii. 19).

South (*see* **King**).

Sow (*see* **Drink**).

Sphere (*see also* **Divine truth**).

The Divine external sphere of the Word (*Ezek.* i. 4) ; sphere of the Word from Divine good and Divine truth from which is the life of the Word (*ib.* i. 13, 14).

Spiritual (*spiritualis*) (*see also* **Word**, SPIRITUAL THINGS OF).

Spiritual things have become infernal (*Lam.* iv. 5-8).

Conjunction of celestial and spiritual things in the Word (*Ezek.* i. 6; 8, 9).

They will receive things spiritual and celestial (*Jer.* xxxi. 12-14).

When they have become spiritual, they will no longer be natural, since they will thus destroy truths and the understanding of them (*Hosea* xi. 5-8).

Those who represented the spiritual things of the church, etc. (*Hosea* v. 1-3).

Spiritual knowledges meant by "Abram" (*Gen.* xiii.).

All affection for spiritual truth will perish (*Ezek.* xxvi. 13, 14).

There is no longer any spiritual good (*Ezek.* xv. 1-3); none whatever, since that good has been utterly destroyed by evil love (*ib.* 4, 5).

Unless spiritual and natural truth and good become concordant there can be no church (*Jer.* xxxiii. 23-26).

Spiritual good and truth (*Ezek.* xl. 24-34).

Spiritual and celestial truths from the Lord (*Isa.* liv. 11-13).

Spiritual truths learned from the Lord (*Isa.* lx. 15, 16).

Love of spiritual good and truth (*Ezek.* i. 10, 11).

Those who are in spiritual good will fight against falsities of evil (*Zech.* x. 4-6).

—— (**the**) (*spirituale*) (*see also* **Divine spiritual, Knowing faculty**).

The spiritual and the natural will be in agreement (*Jer.* xxxiii. 19-21).

The spiritual of the Ancient Church is meant by "Japheth" (*Gen.* ix. 18-29).

—— **Church** (*see also* **Samaria**).

The spiritual church which was instituted; *general subject* (*Amos* vi.).

Those who are in the spiritual church will go away into falsities (*Hosea* iv. 15-19).

The spiritual church, or truths of the church, they departed and falsified truths, etc. (*Jer.* iii. 1, 2, *and fol.*).

Those who were in the faculty of understanding were brought into the spiritual church of the Lord (*Ezek.* xvii. 4, *and prec.*).

The spiritual church learn truths and retain them in the memory, which is to "drink wine, build a house, sow seed, and plant vineyards" (*Jer.* xxxv. 1–10).

The celestial church and the spiritual church were one (*Ezek.* xxxvii. 15–20); and will become one church from the Lord and will be protected from infernal evils and falsities (*ib.* 21–25).

The spiritual and celestial church worships the Lord who is the God of the church (*Ps.* cxxxv. 19–21).

—— **kingdom.**—The spiritual kingdom of the Lord, how admirable! (*Ps.* xlviii. *t.*, 1–38); it will dissipate all falsities (*ib.* 4–7); this is the Divine Human (*ib.* 9, 10); from it are all things of heaven and of the church (*ib.* 11–13); because the Lord reigns there (*ib.* 14).

—— **man.**—When victory hung on the side of the evil or of hell, the spiritual man attacked them and overthrew them (*Gen.* xiv. 1–17).

—— **natural.**—How the natural man became spiritual-natural (*Gen.* xiv. 18–24 *and prec.*).

—— **life** (*see* **Life**).

—— **moral.**—The spiritual-moral will draw near (*Isa.* lx. 13).

—— **sense** (*see* **Word**).

States (*see also* **Successive**).

Various states of the Ancient Church and the nature of them, even to the end (*Gen.* xi. 10–32).

From the sense of the letter of the Word all are taught, every one according to the state of his intelligence (*Ps.* civ. 10–23).

Statue.—Statue of gold set up by Nebuchadnezzar signifies the worship of another god (*Dan.* iii. 1, 2).

Statute.—Statutes for the Ancient Church (*Gen.* ix. 1–17).

The Jews were told to keep the statutes, but they did not (*Zech.* vii. 8–12).

If they had lived according to the statutes they would have been in the good of the church (*Mal.* iii. 10–12).

Statutes of the new church (*Ezek.* xlv. 9–25).

Straitness (*see* **Distress**).

Strengthen (*conforto*).—In temptations the Lord strengthens Himself from His Divine from things past, that those that had prayed for it had been saved, etc. (*Ps.* lxxvii. 10–15 *and fol.*).

Stubbornness (*obfirmatio*).—The heart of blasphemers and profaners is stubborn (*Jer.* xxi. 13).

Study.—Those, of blasphemers and profaners, who study the Word are worse off, because they study it from something profane that is within (*Jer.* xxi. 8–10).

Non-reception due to study or, application (*Jer.* v. 4, 5).

Those in spiritual captivity are told to study truths and do goods and continue in them (*Jer.* xxix. 1–7).

Stupid.—Those who were of the Babylonish religion were so stupid in respect to the truths and goods of the church as to be no longer men (*Dan.* iv. 20–33).

Subdue (*domo*) (*see also* **Restrain**).

The natural man will be subdued (*Ps.* lxviii. 30).

Subjugate (*see* **Overcome, Overthrow, Subdue**).

The Human will become Divine when the hells have been subjugated (*Ps.* cviii. 10–13).

The hells will be subjugated (*Ps.* lxviii. *t.*, 1, 2).

They will be cast down and subjugated from their seeming heavens (*Ps.* lxxxiii. 9–12).

Prayer of the Lord to the Father that the hypocrites may be subjugated (*Ps.* xxviii. *t.*, 1–5).

The Lord subjugated the hells (*Isa.* liii. 9; *Ps.* xviii. 37-40).
In zeal the Lord has subjugated the hells and laid them low (*Ps.* xviii. 7-14).
Subjugation of the hells by the Lord (*Ps.* iii. *t.*, 1-8; xxvii. 11, 12; xxxv. *t.*, 1-9).

Submit.—The new church should submit themselves to the Lord (*Isa.* xlix. 7).

Successive.—Successive states of the Jewish Church (*Ezek.* xvi., xx., xxi.).
Successive states of the church which is in truth ("Samaria") and of the church which is in good ("Jerusalem") (*Ezek.* xxiii. 1-49).
Revelation concerning the successive changes of state of the church (*Dan.* vii. 1-3 *and fol.*).
Successive states of the church in respect to charity and in respect to faith (*Dan.* viii. 1-27).
The successive changes in the church did not appear in the world, but in heaven (*Dan.* xi.).
Successive states of the Christian Church (*Dan.* xi. 5-45; xii. 1-13).
Successive states of the church even to the end, what was their understanding of the Word (*Zech.* i. 7-10).
Successive falsification (*Jer.* xl.; ix. 4-6).
Successive deprivation of true knowledges (*Jer.* xvii. 3, 4).
Successive perversion (*Jer.* xxxviii. 14-18).
Successive vastation (*Jer.* xxxviii.).
Successive devastation (*Jer.* iv.; xxxix.).
Successive devastation of the church (*Amos* v. 1-3; vii. 1-7).
Successive devastation of the old church and establishment of the new (*Hosea* ii.).
Successive perishing of truth (*Jer.* xiii. 1-7).
Successive perishing of the church (*Jer.* xiii. 8-11).
Successive destruction (*Jer.* v. 14-18; *Ezek.* xvii. 11-18; xxii.; xxxvi.).
Successive destruction of the church in the lowest heaven (*Jer.* vi.).

Suffer (*see* **Endure**; **Lord**, PASSION OF THE CROSS).

Summary (*summa*) (*Lam.* iii.).
The historical parts of the Word involve in a summary the things that follow (p. 164).

Support (*see* **Uphold**).
Sustain (*see* **Uphold**).
Swedenborg (*see* **New Jerusalem**).

Taint (*conspergo*).—Tainted with falsities (*Jer.* xxxviii. 7-13).

Teach (*see also* **Evangelization** *and* **Instruct**).
In the church they must be taught in order that they may be converted, because the Lord wills the salvation of all (*Ezek.* xxxiii. 10, 11).
The prophet should teach those that have the Word, etc. (*Ezek.* iii. 4-11).
In the Babylonish religion the goods and truths of heaven and the church are first taught (*Dan.* ii. 31-35). First the Word is taught there according to the truths of doctrine drawn from it (*ib.* 36-38).
The Lord taught the church continually by the Word, that they should refrain from evils, and not depart to any other worship than that of the Lord (*Jer.* xxv. 4-7).
The consequence of not consulting the Lord who teaches (*Isa.* lvii. 11, 12, *and prec.*).
Feigned willingness to be taught (*Jer.* ix. 7, 8).
They have been taught truths and goods, but in vain (*Hosea* x. 11-15).
The Lord had taught them all things of the church, which they nevertheless perverted (*Jer.* ii. 7, 8).
Teaching falsities (*Jer.* xxvii. 9-11).

They depart from the Lord; still He will teach them with difficulty (*Jer.* ii. 9).

Although they will reprobate and not understand, nevertheless they must be taught (*Isa.* xxviii. 17–21).

The old church will be taught constantly, and yet they will not receive (*Isa.* xxviii. 22–29; *see also Isa.* l. 4, 5).

When the Lord comes the old church cannot be instructed and taught (*Isa.* xxviii. 9, 10).

They can no longer be taught from the Word (*Jer.* lii. 24–27; *Haggai* i. 5, 6).

They will perish because they cannot be taught (*Micah* ii. 10, 11).

They Lord was betrayed by the Jews because He taught them (*Zech.* xi. 12, 13).

There is no longer any use to teach any except those who obey (*Micah* ii. 6, 7).

Those who have been completely vastated can be taught (*Jer.* xxiv. 4–7).

Others will teach and learn the good of the church (*Jer.* xxiii. 3, 4).

The Lord teaches truths and removes falsities with those who are humble at heart (*Isa.* lvii. 15 *and prec.*); He cannot do it with those who are wise from what is their own (*ib.* 16, 17); but with those who grieve over it (*ib.* 18, 19); not with those who from the natural produce nothing but evils and falsities, from which they are never removed (*ib.* 20, 21).

The Lord will be born in order that He may teach all men Divine truth (*Jer.* i. 4–8).

When the Lord comes He will teach the simple (*Ezek.* xxxiv. 26–31).

The Lord will gather the church together and teach those who are in it (*Micah* v. 3, 4).

When the Lord comes into the world He will gather His church together and will teach it Divine truths (*Ezek.* xxxiv. 11–16).

They are to be gathered together out of every religion, and taught by the Lord (*Zech.* x. 7–10).

The Lord teaches and leads all who are in falsities from ignorance and desire truths (*Ps.* cxlvi. 7–9).

The Lord teaches truths to those who are in ignorance (*Ps.* cxlvii. 6, 8, 9).

How the Lord teaches and leads those whom He calls to His church (*Ps.* lxxviii. 11–31).

Prayers of the church that they may be taught truths (*Ps.* xxv. 4–6).

Those who love the Lord that He may teach truths and remove falsities (*Isa.* lvii. 13, 14).

Those who are of the new church are to be purified and taught by the Lord (*Zech.* xiii. 8, 9).

The Lord alone will teach all things (*Isa.* xxvi. 12, 13).

The Lord will teach (*Isa.* lxv. 24).

The Lord will teach truths when He comes (*Isa.* xxviii. 5, 6).

When the Lord comes truth will be taught in abundance (*Isa.* vii. 21, 22).

The Lord will teach Divine truths (*Ps.* li. 13–15).

The Lord will teach all truths of salvation (*Isa.* xlix. 7–11).

The Lord will teach the Word (*Joel* iii. 18, 19).

The Lord will come into the world, and will teach the Word in its purity (*Mal.* iii. 1–3).

The church will worship the Lord who protects her, and teaches the Word (*Ps.* cxlvii. 13–15).

He will teach from His Divine (*Jer.* i. 9, 10).

The Lord, in whom is the Divine, will gently lead and teach (*Isa.* xlii. 1–4).

The new church will be taught and led (*Micah* vii. 14, 15).

Concerning the Lord's teaching and leading to the truths and goods of heaven and the church, and protecting, etc. (*Ps.* xxiii. *t.*, 1-3 *and fol.*).

The Lord preached the gospel of the kingdom of God, and taught (*Ps.* xl. 9, 10).

The Lord in His Divine Human alone teaches the church external and internal truths (*Ps.* cxxxv. 6, 7).

The Lord teaches about the Word and doctrine from the Word (*Amos* i. 1, 2).

All are taught from the sense of the letter of the Word, every one according to the state of his intelligence (*Ps.* civ. 10-23 *and prec.*).

Teacher (*see also* **Leader, Minister, Preacher, Shepherd**).

Duties and responsibilities of those who teach doctrine and of those who are taught (*Ezek.* xxxiii. 8, 9).

Teachers who regard their own good only, and not the good of the church (*Ezek.* xxxiv. 1-4); in consequence those who are of the church come into an evil life (*ib.* 5, 6).

Temptation (*see also* **Deliver; Lord,** TEMPTATIONS OF, *etc.*; **Prayer, Prove**).

Temptations of the Jewish Church (*Ezek.* xx. 10-12).

The disobedient will be in temptations from those who profane things holy (*Jer.* xxv. 8-11); retribution will afterwards visit the tempters (*ib.* 12).

When they were in knowledges (*cognitiones*) they were admitted into temptations, and preserved (*Ps.* cvii. 22-31).

Those who will be of the new church are to be purified by temptations, and prepared (*Hosea* ii. 14-17).

He who is in temptations, and consequent affliction, is always upheld and thereby vivified (*Ps.* xli. *t.*, 1-3).

Tent.—To "dwell in tents" signifies to receive in the life and obey (*Jer.* xxxv. 1-10).

Terror.—Their end (*exitium*) will be in hell, whence the rest will be in terror (*Ezek.* xxvi. 15-18).

Thanksgiving (*gratiarum actio*) (*see* **Lord,** CONFESSION AND THANKSGIVING BY).

Thanksgiving of the good that the evil have been conquered and cast into hell (*Ps.* ix. 15-17).

Think } (*cogito*) (*see also* **Devise, Intend**).
Reflect } Concerning thought with the intention of doing evil, that they also do it from the will (*Micah* ii. 1, 2).

Hypocrites think evil (*Ps.* xxxvi. *t.*, 1-4).

Against those who were of the church, who thought evils against the Lord (*Ps.* lviii. *t.*, 1-9).

They will entertain sinister thoughts about God (*Isa.* xxix. 15, 16).

The hells think that the Lord is to be utterly destroyed (*Ps.* xli. 8); so also do those who are of the church where the Word is (*ib.* 9); they will not succeed, etc. (*ib.* 10, 11).

Exhortation to reflect that thus will be the last time, when the Lord will come (*Joel* i. 15).

The evil thoughts by which the evil themselves perish do no harm (*Ps.* cxli. 8-10).

The Father knows everything of the Lord's thought and will because He is made one with Him (*Ps.* cxxxix. *t.*, 1-5).

Third heaven.—The third heaven meant by the "Priests and Levites" (*Ezek.* xlviii. 9-20); the Lord is in the midst of them (*ib.* 21, 22).

Three.—The "three days and nights during which Jonah was in the bowels of the fish" signify the entire duration of the Lord's combats with the hells (*Jonah* i. 17; ii. 1-10).

Today (*see* **Present day**).

Tolerate. } —The perverted church still tolerated because of the Word, and
Tolerance. } because the Lord is known by means of the Word (*Ezek.* xxxvi. 20-23).

The Lord's patience and tolerance (*Isa.* xlii. 18–20).
The Lord bears all things with tolerance (*Ps.* xxxviii. 13, 14).
The Lord's tolerance in the state of temptations (*Ps.* xxxix. *t.*, 1–3, 8–11).

Tradition.—Of those who by traditions or reasonings from the natural man have perverted the truths and goods of the church, who are meant here by "Babylon;" *general article* (*Jer.* li.; *cf. Jer.* lii.).

Truths turned into falsities by traditions (*Ezek.* xvi. 23–28).

Tribes of Israel.—The inheritances of the tribes of Israel signify the partitions of the church and heaven (*Ezek.* xlvii. 13–23; xlviii.).

Trust (*fido fiducia*) (*see also* **Lord,** Trust of; *Self-confidence, Self-intelligence*).

Trust in one's learning from self-intelligence (*Isa.* xxxi.; *Ezek.* xxviii., xxxi. 10–13).

Trust in knowledge and self-intelligence leads astray (*Isa.* xxx. 1–5).

Those who trust in knowledges will perish (*Jer.* xlvi. 25, 26).

Let there be trust in the Lord (*Ps.* xxxi. 23, 24; xxxii. 10, 11; *Isa.* xxx. 15).

Let the trust of the church be in the Lord (*Ps.* cxxxi. 3).

Trust in the Lord on the part of those who are far removed from truths (*Isa.* l. 10).

Every nation trusts in the the Lord (*Isa.* li. 4, 5).

The Lord turns Himself to those who trust in Him and instructs them, etc. (*Isa.* xxx. 18–30).

A church which trusts the Lord (*Jer.* x. 16).

Joy that there is a new church that trusts in the Lord (*Ps.* lxvi. *t.*, 1–5).

The Lord will protect those who trust in Him (*Nahum* i. 7).

Those who trust in the Lord will be blessed of Him when He comes, and then the difference between the good and the evil will be seen (*Mal.* iii. 16–18).

The trust of all who are in truths and goods should be in the Lord (*Ps.* cxv. 9–11); He will save them (*ib.* 12–15, 18); those who do not trust in the Lord will not be saved (*ib.* 17).

Those are saved who trust in the Lord, and those perish who trust in themselves (*Ps.* xx. 7, 8).

Those are saved who trust in the Lord (*Ps.* xxxiii. 18–22).

He that trusts in the Lord and lives well will be saved (*Ps.* cxii. 1–7, 9); he will have no fear of the hells, however much they may rise up against him (*ib.* 8, 10).

Those who confide (*confido*) in the Lord will not fail (*Isa.* xli. 16, 17); they will have truths and goods in all abundance (*ib.* 18–20).

Those who trust in the Lord always have good and truth (*Jer.* xvii. 7, 8.

From trust in the Lord, the church will increase in truths and goods (*Ps.* lxxxiv. 5–7).

The new church will have trust in the Lord, from which trust they will have goods and felicities and acknowledgment from the heart (*Joel* ii. 21–27).

Those who trust (*confido*) in the Lord will flourish (*Ps.* lii. 8, 9).

Happy is he who trusts in the Lord, who is the God of heaven and earth (*Ps.* cxlvi. 5, 6).

Happy is he who trusts in the Lord (*Ps.* lxxxix. 15–18).

State of innocence of those in the heavens who trust in the Lord (*Isa.* xi. 6–9).

True (*verus*).—The Father is true and just; may He hear (*Ps.* cxliii. *t.*, 1, 2).

Truth (*veritas*).—It is an eternal truth, that those who worship Him will be saved (*Ps.* cxxxii. 11, 12).

—— (*verum*) (*see also* **Desolation, Divine Truth, Doctrine, External truth, Genuine truth, Internal truth, Light, Multiplication, Natural truth,**

Perish, Pervert, Power, Profane, Receive, Spiritual, Teach, Understand, Union, Want).
Truths that protected the Ancient Church (*Ezek.* xxvii. 10, 11).
The church, when first instituted, was full of truths (*Haggai* ii. 1-3).
Truths of the church (*Jer.* iii.).
Ignorance of truth enters and destroys the church (*Isa.* vii. 1-6).
There is no longer any understanding of truth (*Isa.* xxix. 14).
Truth removed when that which is false is called true (*Jer.* xxiii. 37-40).
There cannot be truths and at the same time falsities, without truths being snatched away (*Amos* iii. 3-6).
Truth is wholly lacking in the church (*Jer.* xiv. 1-3); he that seeks does not find it, etc. (*ib.* 4-6, *etc.*).
Lack of truth (*Ps.* cvii. 9-15).
Truth of the church gradually perishing by means of reasonings from the natural man (*Jer.* xiii. 1-7).
Like one who has truth and yet is without truth (*Amos* ii. 12-16).
No truth with those who trust in knowledges (*scientifica*) (*Ezek.* xxx. 20-23).
No longer any truth through knowledges (*cognitiones*) (*Isa.* xxiii.).
Truths turned into falsities by knowledges, traditions, and reasonings (*Ezek.* xvi. 23-28).
Those who falsify the truths of the sense of the letter of the Word, etc. (*Amos* i. 13-15).
Falsifiers of truths of the Word meant by the "children of Ammon" (*Jer.* xlix. 1-6).
Truths of the Word and of doctrine destroyed by knowledges alone and faith alone (*Joel* iii. 4-8).
Truths from the Word taken away from those who have been destroyed by falsities from the natural man (*Jer.* xv. 12-14).
Truth destroyed by self-intelligence (*Isa.* xxii. 1-7).
No truths with the self-intelligent (*Obad.* 7).
Truths which they learn are of no use to them (*Jer.* xvii. 11).
Truths of the church destroyed through reasonings, etc. (*Ezek.* xxx. 10-12).
Truths of the church destroyed by dire falsities (*Jer.* xix. 2, 3).
Against those who pervert truths of the Word (*Jer.* xxiii. 9-40).
Truths cannot be seen because of falsities (*Isa.* xxix. 9-12).
Despoiled of all truths (*Isa.* xlii. 22-24).
Deprivation of truths causes seduction by reasonings, and devastation (*Isa.* xx.).
Devastation of truth (*Isa.* xxxiii. 7-9).
Every truth will be banished (*Isa.* xl. 6-8).
The truths of the church perish from falsities (*Amos* iii. 11).
Truths perish (*Isa.* xxviii. 3, 4; xix. 5-10).
Truth perishes (*Hab.* i. 1-5).
Truth of the Word has been adulterated (*Ezek.* xxii. 23-45).
All truths destroyed by the adulteration of goods (*Jer.* xlviii. 6-9).
Profanation of truth meant by "Bel" (*Isa.* xlvi.).
Nothing of truth remains (*Jer.* xlix. 9-13).
No truth will be left in the church (*Zeph.* i. 12-13).
No longer any truth in the church: it has been interiorly destroyed (*Hosea* xiii. 10-13).
They have no truth of the church (*Jer.* xviii. 21, 22).
No truths, either in the church or in doctrine (*Jer.* xiv. 17, 18; xv. 7).
No truth in doctrine or in the church, and if they believe it is falsity (*Jer.* v. 1, 2).
Because there is no truth, there is falsity (*Jer.* xv. 8).
Truth no longer in the Jewish Church (*Ps.* lxxvi. 5, 6).

Even those in celestial good will suffer deprivation of all truth (*Micah* i. 16).

The truth of the church must be guarded (*Isa.* xxvii. 2, 3).

Some things true will remain, when the rest are false, in consequence of which truths will have no power (*Amos* iv. 7, 8).

When there was no longer any truth, the Lord came and they afflicted Him, etc. (*Ps.* cv. 16–18 *and fol.*).

He who fights against the truths of the new church will plunge into falsities of every kind (*Zech.* xiv. 12).

There will be no truth, but in the Lord there will be Divine truth (*Zech.* xiv. 6, 7).

Truth will be multiplied in the new church, and no falsity of evil will be there (*Zech.* xiv. 10, 11).

Truths of the Word not for those who falsify, but for those who receive them (*Isa.* lxii. 8, 9).

Truth will be acceptable, and understood when the Lord reigns (*Isa.* xxxii. 2–4).

Those who have been in falsities will be in truths of every kind after the former church has ceased to be (*Jer.* xxxiii. 12, 13).

The Lord leads sinners into truths, that they may live (*Ps.* cxlv. 14–16).

The church reformed by truths from the Word (*Ps.* lxxx. 8–11).

Let them draw near to the Lord through the truths of the Word (*Ps.* c. 4, 5).

Those who are in truths from the Word will adore the Lord who is the Word (*Ps.* xxix. *t.*, 1–4).

The Lord will protect those who are in truths from Him (*Ps.* xcvii. 10–12).

He who is in truths from the Lord remains safe (*Ps.* cxxvii. 34).

A new church walking in truths (*Ps.* lxxxv. 8–13).

Truths will not be lacking (*Isa.* liv. 9, 10).

Truths in abundance for those who are converted (*Isa.* lviii. 8–11).

Truth taught in abundance (*Isa.* vii. 21, 22).

Truth in all abundance for those who trust in the Lord (*Isa.* xxx. 23–26).

Truths in all abundance (*Jer.* xxxiii. 22).

Truths in abundance in the Word (*Haggai* ii. 18, 19).

All truths are in the Word (*Isa.* xlvi. 8–12).

The church will possess primary truths (*Ps.* xlv. 16).

The Lord will fill them with truths (*Zech.* ix. 12–16).

Every truth of the church is from the Lord's Divine to eternity (*Isa.* lix. 21).

They will receive truths from the Lord gratis (*Isa.* lv. 1); truth in which there is life, and by which there is conjunction will be given by the Lord (*ib.* 3, 4).

From the good of love by means of truth comes enlightenment from the Lord (*Zech.* iv. 1–10).

Truths of the external or natural man receive the influx of the good of love (*Ps.* cxxxiii. 2).

—— **and good** (*see also* **Good and truth, Destroy, Knowledge, Multiplication, Pervert, Profane, Spiritual truth, Trust, Worship**).

A church full of truths and goods from the Word was instituted by the Lord (*Isa.* v. 1, 2).

Truths and goods do not cause them to be a church unless they live according to the commandments and do no violence to the Word (*Jer.* vii. 5, 6).

Those who are in truths and goods and do evil perish (*Jer.* xviii. 9, 10).

Truths and goods of the church taken away stealthily (*Isa.* x. 1, 2).

What truth and good are will no longer be known (*Isa.* vi. 9–13).

Truth and good perish, if the knowledges of the natural man are consulted (*Jer.* xlii. 7–22).

The chief truths destroyed by reasonings from the natural man (*Ezek.* xii. 13).
There is no truth and good with the learned (*Isa.* xxx. 12–14).
Truths and goods of religion will perish where there has been merely external worship, and falsities will succeed in their place (*Ezek.* xxxviii. 20–23).
Those who should be in the truths and goods of the church are against the Lord (*Ps.* ii. 1, 2).
They have perverted all truths and goods, which they had in all abundance (*Jer.* v. 7, 8).
All truth and good turned into falsity and evil (*Hosea* ix. 6).
All truths and goods of the Word dispersed by those who blaspheme the Word (*Jer.* xx. 5).
Truths and goods extinguished (*Ezek.* xvi. 21, 22).
Truths and goods will be destroyed with those who falsify the truths of the Word and of the church (*Jer.* xlix. 2).
Truths and gooods destroyed by adulteration (*Ezek.* xxii. 1–31).
No truth and good any longer in the church (*Ezek.* xiv. 12–14).
Truth and good no longer in the church (*Micah* vii. 1–4); then falsities and evils will fight against truths and goods (*ib.* 5, 6).
Truths and goods no longer with them (*Jer.* xii. 4); the consequences (*ib.* 5, 6; xvi. 1–8).
There is no truth and good any longer, excepting such as is external (*Jer.* xxiii. 11).
There is no longer any truth and good in the natural man (*Isa.* xxvii. 1).
Truth and good and life no longer in them (*Isa.* lvii. 1, 2).
No truth or good any longer, because they were in their own intelligence (*Gen.* vi. 1–7, 10–13).
Truths and goods from the Word falsified and perverted (*Isa.* ix. 8–21; *Jer.* i. 13).
Truth and good will perish on the day of judgment (*Isa.* xxvii. 8–12).
All those who are against truth and good will perish (*Isa.* xxix. 20, 21).

Truths and goods of the church will no longer be perverted (*Ezek.* xxiii. 26, 27; *cf. Isa.* lx. 18).
Truth and good of the church is from the Word (*Isa.* ix. 8–21).
All truths and goods of heaven and the church are from the Word (*Ezek.* xxviii. 12).
Truths and goods of every kind and species through the Word (*Ezek.* xvi. 7–12).
Through the Word truths are given together with goods (*Ezek.* xxiv. 3–5).
Truths and goods of every kind acquired by means of knowledges (*cognitiones*) (*Ezek.* xxvii. 24, 25).
Truths and goods should be regarded (*Jer.* vii. 3).
May those be saved who are in the truths and goods of the church (*Ps.* xxviii. 9).
Truth and good granted after the natural has been purged of falsities and evils (*Ps.* cv. 37–41).
Truths and goods granted by the Lord (*Ps.* cxxxvi. 23–26).
Truths and goods in all abundance for those who confide in the Lord (*Isa.* xli. 18–20).
Truth and good will not be wanting (*Jer.* xxxiii. 17, 18).
Everything of truth and good is from acknowledgment of the Lord (*Jer.* ix. 22, 23).
Those who trust in the Lord will come into delights of truth and good (*Isa.* xxx. 29, 30).
Truths and goods of the church will be taught by the Lord from His Divine (*Jer.* i. 9, 10).
Truths and goods in the new church (*Micah* iv. 3, 4); will grow (*ib.* 8–10).

From trust in the Lord the church will increase in truths and goods (*Ps.* lxxxiv. 5–7).
Quality of the church in respect to truth and good (*Zech.* ii. 1, 2).
Truths and good will continue in the new church (*Zech.* viii. 11, 12).
Internals of worship are of truth and good (*Micah* vi. 6–8).
The life of truth and good should be loved (*Micah* vi. 9).
Truth and good will then make one (*Jer.* iii. 18).
Truths and goods of heaven and the church (*Ps.* xxiii. *t.*, 1–3).
Truths and goods the habitation of the Lord (*Ps.* cxxxii. 15, 16).
—— *of faith.*—All truth of faith perishes through falsities (*Ezek.* xxxv. 1–5).
—— *from good* (*see also* **Faith from charity**).
Revelation respecting such as are in truths from good, who are meant by "Michael" (*Dan.* x. 7–21).
Truths of faith from good of charity meant by the "king of the south" (*Dan.* xi.).
The truth of good is from heaven upon those who are in the church, in which is salvation (*Ps.* cxxxiii. 3).
Truths from a celestial origin will be in the new church (*Zech.* iv. 11–14).
The natural will be first imbued with truths from good (*Isa.* xxi. 5–7); then the rational (*ib.* 8–10).
Tumult (*Nahum* ii. 3–6).
Turn (*converto*) (*see also* **Conversion**).
Turning or looking of all toward one (*Ezek.* i. 12).
—— *away* (*converto*).—Those who were formerly of the church have turned away (*Isa.* lxiii. 10).
Turning away (*aversio*) (*see also* **Aversion**).
Turning away from truths, thus from the Lord (*Isa.* lix. 12–15).
Tyre.—"Tyre" means the church devastated in respect to all knowledges (*cognitiones*) of truth and good (*Isa.* xxiii.).
"Tyre" means the church as to knowledges (*cognitiones*) of truth (*Ezek.* xxvi., xxvii., xxviii.).

Ultimates ⎫ (*ultima*) (*see also* **Firsts, Outermosts**).
Last things ⎬ Ultimates of doctrine destroyed by knowledges (*scientifica*)
Lowest parts ⎭ (*Ezek.* xxvi. 5, 6).
They have destroyed all truths and goods even to the last things of the church (*Micah* iii. 1–3).
The ultimates of the new church will be holy (*Ezek.* xlv. 1–5).
Last things of heaven and the church (*Ps.* xix. 5, 6).
All who are in the lowest parts of heaven and the church, etc. (*Ps.* cxlviii. 7–10).
Ultimate heaven.—Those who have conjunction with the Lord in the lowest heaven are meant by the "children of Benjamin" (*Jer.* vi.); their successive destruction treated of (*ib.* 1–30); those who are in the lowest heaven with whom is the church in respect to good (*Jer.* vii.); their successive devastation (*ib.* 1–34).
Unbelief.—Those who do not believe in the Lord perish (*Ps.* cxlv. 18–20).
Understand ⎫ (*see also* **Rational, Truth, Word**).
Understanding ⎭ Understanding is meant by the "eagle" (*Ezek.* xvii.).
Understanding of truth is meant by "Zidon;" it will perish by means of falsities (*Ezek.* xxviii. 21–23).
The first state of the church was while they were in the understanding of truth (*Dan.* vii. 4).
They are not willing to understand the Word in simplicity (*Isa.* viii. 5, 6).
They are not willing to understand truths (*Jer.* iii. 3).
The successive states of the church even to the end are represented; what their understanding of the Word is (*Zech.* i. 7–10).

The understanding of the Word was falsified, although the Word is the Lord's (*Hosea* xi. 12).

In consequence of perverting by false interpretation, there is no understanding of truth, because none from the Lord, etc. (*Jer.* xxiii. 27-29 *and prec.*).

No understanding of truth with those who trust their own learning from self-intelligence (*Isa.* xxxi. 3).

Because they have falsified the Word they are no longer able to understand truth (*Hosea* iv. 10-12).

Those who profane truth are no longer able to understand truth (*Isa.* xlvi. 2).

All understanding of truth will perish (*Zeph.* i. 1-3).

No longer any understanding of truth (*Jer.* iv. 22).

There is no longer any understanding of truth whatever (*Ps.* xiv. *t.*, 1-3).

They no longer have any understanding of truth, but in place of truth they understand falsity (*Hosea* v. 10-14).

The evil do not understand the co-operation of the Father with the Lord (*Ps.* xcii. 6 *and prec.*).

The evil will not understand, but the good (*Dan.* xii. 10).

Understanding of truth from the Lord to the extent in which they depart from falsities (*Zech.* iii. 6-10).

In consequence of rejection of falsities there will be understanding from rational light (*Hosea* xiv. 9).

They would destroy truths and the understanding of truths by being natural (*Hosea* xi. 5-8).

When the Lord reigns there will be understanding of truth (*Isa.* xxxii. 2-4 *and prec.*).

There is no understanding of truth any longer, except with those who are in the Word and of the new church (*Zech.* xii. 4).

Those of the new church will come and will understand truths (*Jer.* xxxi. 9; 22).

Those who receive the Lord will understand truths (*Isa.* xxix. 22-24).

The church will then understand the Word (*Isa.* xi. 13-15).

The new church will understand truth (*Hosea* vi. 4-6).

Understanding of truth in the new church (*Obad.* 19-21).

Understanding of the doctrine of truth will be in the new church (*Amos* ix. 13-15).

The Lord should be worshipped from the understanding and will of truth and good (*Ps.* cxlviii. 11, 12).

Unfaithful (*infideles*).—The Lord will destroy the unfaithful (*Isa.* xi. 1-5).

Union (*see also* **Lord,** GLORIFICATION OF).

The union of the Lord with the church is holy, etc. (*Isa.* lvi. 2).

Unition (*see* **Oneness**).

Unity (*see* **One**).

Unwillingness.—Unwillingness to impart knowledges to others outside of themselves (*Jonah* i. 7-9).

Unwillingness to know any truths from the Word (*Jer.* viii. 7-9).

Unwillingness to be taught (*Jer.* ix. 7, 8).

Unwillingness to understand the Word in simplicity (*Isa.* viii. 5, 6).

Unwillingness to understand truths (*Jer.* iii. 3).

Unwillingness to give heed to the Word (*Jer.* xxii. 20, 21); why (*ib.* 22).

Unwillingness to acknowledge and receive (*Jer.* iv 11, 12).

Unwillingness to know that the Lord is God from whom are all truths and goods (*Jer.* v. 21-24).

Unwillingness to hear about the Lord (*Jer.* xi. 21).

Unwillingness to be reformed (*Jer.* iii. 6, 7).

Unwillingness to repent and be converted (*Jer.* xviii. 11-13); why (*ib.* 14-16).

Unwillingness to know anything more (*Jer.* xii. 6).
Unwillingness to have it otherwise (*Jer.* viii. 11, 12).
Uphold (*sustento*).—The Lord is sustained from His Divine against the evil who
Sustain rise up against Him (*Ps.* xvii. 6-10).
The Lord sustains the church (*Ps.* xx. *t.*, 1-4).
The good are always upheld and live with God (*Ps.* lxxiii. 23-26).
Uphold (*sustineo*).—The Lord upholds the church with those who look to Him (*Isa.* xl. 28, 29, 31).
Uprising (*insurrectio*) (*see also* **Fear**).
Rise up (*insurgo*) Uprising of the evil (*Ps.* lxxiv. 22, 23).
The evil rise up and wish to kill (*Ps.* xciv. 20, 21).
The evil rise up against the Lord and wish to slay Him (*Ps.* xvii. 6-12).
Grievous insurrection of the infernals against the Lord (*Ps.* xiii. *t.*, 1-4).
The hells are in insurrection (*Ps.* lxxxvi. 13, 14).
The hells that rise up against the Lord are enumerated (*Ps.* lxxxiii. 6-8).
How the Lord has Divine omnipotence against those that rise up against Him (*Ps.* xcii. 10, 11, *and prec.*).
No uprising of the hells owing to the union of the Lord to the Father (*Ps.* xci. 7-9 *and prec.*); not even against the church (*ib.* 10).
Urge (*adigo*).—Urged by punishments, still they did not receive (*Jer.* v. 3).
Urgent (*instans*) (*see also* **Insist**).
He was urgent that the church might exist with him (*Gen.* xv. 1-6).

Vastate (*see also* **Devastation, Destroy, Perish,** *etc., etc.*).
Lay waste Of the vastation of the church (*Ezek.* xii.).
Vastation The church and its doctrine enslaved and laid waste (*Lam.* i. 1-3).
Vastation comes from diligent perverting (*Isa.* lix. 7).
Vastation of the church by worship from the mere sense of the letter of the Word (*Ezek.* xxxviii. 8-16).
Vastation by traditions and reasonings (*Jer.* li. 7-10).
The church further vastated by reasonings from falsities (*Isa.* xxiii. 10-14).
Vastation of church consequent on embracing falsities (*Jer.* xii. 7-12).
Because they worshipped another god, goods and truths will be vastated (*Hosea* ii. 9-13).
Further vastation of the church by their taking truths and goods of the church away from others by stealth (*Isa.* x. 1, 2).
The church is laid waste by evils of life (*Isa.* i. 1-8).
All things of the church vastated (*Isa.* lxiv. 10, 11).
Those who have not yet been vastated will be vastated (*Jer.* xxxviii. 1-3).
Grief over withdrawal from the Lord, and vastation of the church (*Jer.* x. 19-21).
Vastators will be dispersed by the Lord (*Isa.* xxxiii. 3, 4).
Those who had been completely vastated, so that they did not know what is true and what is good could be reformed (*Jer.* xxiv. 4-7).
Vaunt (*see* **Boast**).
Victory (*see* **Lord,** VICTORY OF).
Vile.—The Jewish Church considered the Lord vile (*Ps.* cix. *t.*, 1-6); His prayer to the Father for help, because He is considered vile and as nothing (*ib.* 21-25).
The Lord appears as vile (*Isa.* liii. 2, 3).
Man grows vile from the love of self (*Hab.* ii. 4, 5).
Violate.—The Divine of the Lord ought to be acknowledged and not violated (*Jer.* xvii. 21-24).
The Word must not be violated (*Jer.* vii. 5, 6).
Violence (*Hab.* i.).

Visitation.—Visitation upon those who are of the church (*Ezek.* ix.).
Vivify.—May the new church be vivified by the coming of the Lord (*Ps.* lxxx. 14–19).
The Lord will vivify (*Joel* ii. 28, 29).

Walk.—A church walking in truths (*Ps.* lxxxv. 8–13).
Want (*deficio, defectus*) (*see also* **Ignorance, Revolt**).
Lack } Those who do not suffer themselves to be instructed will lack all things
Fail (*Isa.* xvii. 9–14).
    There will be a want of knowledges (*cognitioues*) of good and truth (*Isa.* iii. 1–7); because they are in evils and things falsified (*ib.* 8–12).
    Lack of all holy truths and goods because they have been turned into falsities (*Lam.* iv. 4 *and prec.*).
    They are flattered by the doctrine of falsity that there is no lack of truth (*Jer.* xiv. 13).
    Lack of truth (*Ps.* cvii. 9–15).
    Utter lack of truth in the church (*Jer.* xiv. 1–3).
    Want of truth and goods the source of falsities without measure (*Isa.* li. 19, 20).
    Lack of everything of the church because of falsities and evils (*Lam.* v. 1–9).
    Those who confide in the Lord will not fail (*Isa.* xli. 16, 17).
    Let not the Lord fail in temptations before a new church has been formed (*Ps.* cii. 23, 24, *and prec.*); that heaven and the church perish not (*ib.* 25–28).
    Prayer of the Lord that He may not fail in temptations (*Ps.* cxliii. 3, 4, 7).
Want (*desum*).—Then truth and good will not be wanting (*Jer.* xxxiii. 17, 18).
Lack } Truth will not be lacking in the church restored by the Lord (*Isa.* liv. 9, 10).
Warning (*see also* **Exhortation**).
    Let them not be like the nation sprung from Jacob, who estranged themselves from the Lord, and with whom, for this reason, there is no conjunction whatever (*Ps.* xcv. 8–11).
    Let them beware of those who are against the Lord (*Jer.* li. 6).
    Let them beware not to come near those who are of the church of "Babylon" (*Jer.* li. 45–50).
    Let not mere falsity take the place of truth (*Jer.* xiii. 15, 16).
Wealth (*see* **Rich**).
Weary (*fatigo*).—The church wearied the Lord with sins (*Isa.* xliii. 22–27).
Wicked (*impius*) (*see also* **Evil, The Evil, Perish,** *etc.*).
    The wicked will not receive (*Isa.* xxvi. 10, 11).
    The church which awaits the Lord asks why the wicked flourish (*Jer.* xii 1, 2).
    The Lord will execute judgment upon the wicked (*Jer.* xxx. 23, 24).
    The wicked man who is converted is saved (*Ezek.* xviii. 21–23; *cf.* xxxiii. 12–16).
Will (*see also* **Divine Will, Think, Unwillingness**).
    There is no longer any understanding of truth or will of good whatever (*Ps.* xiv. *t.*, 1–3).
    The Lord should be worshipped from the understanding and will of truth and good (*Ps.* cxlviii. 11, 12).
Wisdom (*see also* **Divine Wisdom, Power, Self**).
    Wisdom of men of Most Ancient Church (*Gen.* ii.).
    Exhortation to be wise (*Joel* ii. 12–17).
    They have the Word so that they can be wise (*Jer.* li. 14–18).
    The Divine truth perfects man because it is wisdom (*Ps.* xix. 7–11).

INDEX OF WORDS AND SUBJECTS.

Wisdom by means of knowledges (*cognitiones*) (*Ezek.* xxvii. 14-20 *and prec.*).
Wisdom for those who trust in the Lord (*Isa.* xxx. 23-26).
The just man is wise (*Ps.* xxxii. 8, 9).
To worship the Lord is wisdom (*Ps.* cxi. 10).
The church will be instituted among those who are wise from the Word (*Haggai* i. 12-15).
Those of the new church will be imbued with wisdom (*Jer.* xxxi. 23-28).
Wisdom and innocence will be in the new church (*Zech.* viii. 4-6).

Withdraw (*see* **Depart**).

Wonder.—Because they wonder at the destruction of the church they will not know truths (*Ezek.* xxv. 3-5).
A matter of wonder to some, that the evil vaunt themselves and prosper, etc. (*Ps.* lxxiii. *t.*, 1-9 *and fol.*).

Word (*see also* **Adulteration, Blaspheme, Canaan, Church, Divine Truth, Falsify, Interpret, Know, The Lord** AS THE WORD, **Love, Pervert, Protect, Simple, Teach, Truth, Truth and good, Understand**).

All the churches down to the coming of the Lord represented the church, and in the highest sense, the Lord; it is from this that the Word is spiritual and Divine (p. 163).
The Word that exists at the present day is given in place of the Ancient Word which has been effaced (p. 164).
The Word called the Law (*Ps.* cxix.).
The Word was given to the children of Jacob, and they were confirmed in it by means of miracles (*Ps.* lxxviii. *t.*, 1-7).
Everywhere in the Word is lamentation over the Jewish Church (*Ezek.* ii. 8-10).
The nations, hearing from the Word of God about their sins, and that they would perish, etc., etc. (*Jonah* iii. 1-10).
The Lord came into the world, as it is written in the Word, to do the will of the Father (*Ps.* xl. 6-8).

THE WORD NOT UNDERSTOOD, FALSIFIED, ETC.

Non-understanding of the Word enters and destroys the church (*Isa.* vii. 1-6).
The Word not understood causes impure doctrine (*Isa.* vi. 5-8).
All understanding of the Word will perish (*Isa.* vi. 9-13).
All understanding of the Word perverted by knowledges and reasonings (*Isa.* vii. 17-20).
By departing from the Word they have dissolved the conjunction with the Lord (*Mal.* ii. 8-10).
They falsify the Word (*Isa.* i. 20-23).
The Word is falsified by those who exalt themselves (*Jer.* xviii. 18).
Falsification of the Word (*Ezek.* vii. 23, 24; xxxv. 6-9).
All things of the Word falsified (*Ezek.* xvi. 15-20).
Senses of the Word destroyed by delights of falsity (*Isa.* xxii. 13-15).
Those who have the Word are in falsities of evil and will perish (*Zech.* x. 2, 3).
The Lord will not regenerate those who are not good, although they have the Word (*Ps.* lxviii. 12-14).
The Word abused for the sake of power (*Jer.* x. 8, 9).
Perverting all things of the Word leads to blindness (*Micah* iii. 5-7).
Providence that the Word be not perverted still further (*Isa.* iv. 4-6).
The Word remained with the Babylonish religion, although perverted (*Dan.* iv. 15-17).
Power of the Word will remain guarded by the Lord (*Isa.* xxii. 20-24).
Power of the Word will perish (*Isa.* xxii. 25).
The Word corrupted (*Jer.* iv. 17).

The Word has been wholly adulterated and destroyed (*Isa.* lxiii. 2).
It is shown how the holy of the Word has been profaned (*Ezek.* viii. 3–6).
The profaners understood the Word in a contrary sense (*Jer.* xxviii.).
The evil wish to slay the Lord and yet they possess the Word (*Ps.* xvii. 14 *and prec.*).
After the church has been consummated the Word will cease (*Dan.* ix. 24).
Annihilation of the Word (*Jer.* v. 13; *Mal.* iv. 4).
"Dividing the Lord's garments" means dissipating the truths of His Word (*Ps.* xxii. 18).

QUALITY OF THE WORD.

The Lord is the Word (*Jer.* xxiii. 28, 29).
The Word is the Lord's (*Hosea* xi. 12).
The Word is from the Lord (*Ps.* xcix. 6, 7; civ. 1–4).
The Word, and doctrine from the Word (*Amos* i. 1, 2).
The Word taught according to the truths of doctrine drawn from it (*Dan.* ii. 36–38).
The Word will be for the Lord's new church (*Zech.* xiii. 1).
The Word established in the church (*Ps.* xciii. 5).
Divine spiritual of the Word forming the church (*Ezek.* x. 1, 2).
Conjunction of all things of the Word, and consequent life (*Ezek.* x. 21. 22).
The church is from the Lord through the Word (*Ps.* xxiv. *t.*, 1–3).
The Lord is known by means of the Word (*Ezek.* xxxvi. 20–23).
Those who are in truths from the Word will adore the Lord who is the Word (*Ps.* xxix. *t.*, 1–4; *see further* **The Lord as the Word**).
Through the Word is conjunction with the Lord (*Mal.* ii. 5–7).
The Lord ought to be worshipped from the Word, where is His Divine truth (*Ps.* cxxxviii. *t.*, 1–5).
There are truths in abundance in the Word (*Haggai* ii. 18, 19). (*See further under* **Truth**, *and* **Truth and good**.)
In the Word truth from the Lord makes itself manifest (*Jer.* xxiii. 28, 29).
From the Word it is possible to be in Divine truths (*Ps.* lxxxii. *t.*, 1).
Through the Word truths together with goods are given; also the Divine presence (*Ezek.* xxiv. 3–5).
Understanding of the Word consequent on acknowledgement of the Lord's Divine (*Jer.* xvii. 25).
The church will understand the Word (*Isa.* xi. 13–15).
Learning from the Word (*Ezek.* xxviii. 11).

GOODS OF THE WORD.

Goods and truths of the Word carried off by falsities (*Amos* iii. 12). (*See further under* **Good and truth**.)
Goods of the Word perverted (*Isa.* xvi.; *Jer.* xxiii.).
Those who adulterate the good of the sense of the letter of the Word (*Amos* ii. 1–3).
Good of the Word has been adulterated (*Ezek.* xxii. 26).
Adulteration of the good of the Word will be utterly destroyed (*Isa.* xxv. 10–12).
The goods of the Word adulterated and its truths profaned (*Isa.* xiv. 4–6; 24–27; xxxix.).
Those who adulterate the goods of the Word and of the church are meant by "Moab" (*Jer.* xlviii.).

THE CELESTIAL SENSE.

The highest sense (*Ps.* lx. 6–9).
All things of the Word in the celestial sense treat of the Lord (p. 168; 163)

Those who destroy the celestial things of the Word destroy also its spiritual things (*Amos* ii. 4, 5).

THE SPIRITUAL SENSE.

In the spiritual sense of the Word there is nothing historical of the world, as in the sense of letter, but heavenly things which relate to the church, (p. 163).

All things of the Word in the spiritual sense treat of the church and heaven (p. 168).

(*See Amos* ii. 4, 5, *above*.)

Those who destroy the spiritual things of the Word go away into falsities of every kind (*Amos* ii. 6–8).

THE EXTERNAL, OR NATURAL, OF THE WORD.

Divine external sphere of the Word (*Ezek.* i. 4); a representation of it as a man (*ib.* 5); conjunction of celestial and spiritual things there (*ib.* 6, *etc., etc.*).

The natural of the Word (*Ezek.* i. 7); its spiritual and celestial which are conjoined (*ib.* 8, 9).

The sphere of the Word from Divine good and Divine truth, from which is the life of the Word (*Ezek.* i. 13, 14).

Those who falsify the external of the Word meant by "Edom;" *general subject* (*Jer.* xlix. 7–22).

Injury done to the external sense of the Word by perversion of knowledges of good and truth (*Amos* i. 9, 10).

Those who destroy the external of the Word and of doctrine will be rejected (*Ezek.* xxv. 12–14).

SENSE OF THE LETTER.

The second state of the church was when they studied only the sense of the letter of the Word (*Dan.* vii. 5).

The third state was when the sense of the letter of the Word was falsified, and falsity was made to appear as truth (*Dan.* vii. 6).

In the fourth state, faith alone was confirmed by the sense of the letter of the Word (*Dan.* vii. 8).

Those who are in the mere sense of the letter of the Word, and in a worship therefrom which is external without an internal, are meant by "Gog" (*Ezek.* xxxviii. 1, 2).

They will come into the church, but will perish when the Lord comes (*Ezek.* xxxix. 1–6 *and fol.*).

The Word outwardly in the letter acknowledged (*Jer.* iii. 4, 5).

Through falsification of the Word in respect to the sense of the letter, the church has departed (*Ezek.* xii. 3–12).

Falsifying the truths of the sense of the letter of the Word (*Amos* i. 13–15).

Perverting the sense of the letter of the Word by falsity (*Amos* i. 11, 12).

Those who are in self-intelligence and pervert the sense of the letter of the Word, who are "Edom" (*Obad.* 1–21).

Against those who are in the sense of the letter of the Word and pervert the truths of religion who are the "children of Ammon" (*Ezek.* xxv. 1, 2).

The sense of the letter falsified and adulterated (*Ezek.* iv. 9–16; v. 1–2; *cf.* xxxii. 26–30).

The lot of those who have falsified the sense of the letter of the Word (*Ezek.* xxi. 28, 29).

Adulterating the good of the sense of the letter of the Word destroys the good and truth of the church (*Amos* ii. 1–3).

It was represented how they destroyed the sense of the letter (*Ezek.* v.).

The sense of the letter to be explained (*Ezek.* iii. 22, 23).
Sense of the letter of the Word in the new church (*Ezek.* xliii. 1-11).
Of the sense of the letter of the Word, on which the church is founded (*Ps.* civ. 5-9); from this all are taught, every one according to the state of his intelligence (*ib.* 10-23); from this are the knowledges of truth and good, from which is spiritual nourishment (*ib.* 24-30).

Words.—The Lord's words, which are Divine, have become of no account with the evil (*Ps.* cxli. 6, 7).
A magnificent word respecting the Lord, and respecting conjunction with Him (*Ps.* xlv. *t.*, 1).

Work (*see* **Labor, Operation**).
Works of worship regarded as of no value (*Jer.* vi. 20).
Works of the Lord for the establishment of the church (*Ps.* cv. 1-7).
Song in praise of the Lord because of His works (*Ps.* cxlv. *t.*, 1-7).

Worse.—There has been no devastation for a long time, and therefore the evil is worse (*Jer.* xlviii. 10, 11).

Worship (*see also* **Adore, God**, *last references*).

WORSHIP BY THE EVIL.

In the beginning of the Babylonish religion, the God of heaven was worshipped (*Dan.* ii. 46-49).
"Babylon" was minded to depart from the worship of the Lord to the worship of another god, which is the "statue of gold set up by Nebuchadnezzar" (*Dan.* iii. 1, 2).
Worship of the Lord thought about in the Babylonish religion (*Dan.* v 31; vi. 1-3); but they concluded that they should be worshipped in place of the Lord (*ib.* 4-9).
How "Babylon" was compelled to acknowledge and worship the Lord (*Dan.* iii. 26-30; iv. 1-3).
Inacceptible worship (*Amos* v. 21, 22); it will be accepted if they have good and truth (*ib.* 23-25).
They worship the Lord from evil and not from good; therefore their worship is not accepted (*Mal.* i. 7-10).
Those who are within the church profane worship, and do not worship the Lord (*Mal.* i. 12-14); unless they worship the Lord, all worship will be perverted and profane (*ib.* ii. 1-4).
Mere falsities and evils in respect to worship (*Zeph.* i. 4-6).
Works of worship regarded as of no value (*Jer.* vi. 20).
No church worship when the life is contrary to the commandments (*Jer.* vii. 8-10).
Worship of the Lord destroyed by faith alone (*Dan.* viii. 11, 12).
They depart from worship of the Lord, hence their worship is not worship of God (*Jer.* xvi. 10, 11). (*See further the last references under* **God**).
Those who depart from worship of the Lord have no enlightenment from the Word (*Ezek.* xiv. 1-4).
The church did not worship the Lord (*Isa.* xliii. 22-27).
Those who do not worship the Lord alone are falsifiers (*Isa.* xliv. 9-11).
A *quasi* Divine worship (*Isa.* xliv. 12-20).
No Divine worship, why (*Hosea* ix. 4, 5 *and prec.*).
Contrary worship (*Jer.* i. 16; *Isa.* lxv. 6, 7).
No attention paid to the worship of backsliders (*Jer.* xiv. 11, 12).
Those who pervert all worship into evil (*Isa.* lxvi. 3).
Evils and falsities are their worship (*Jer.* ii. 26, 27; 28).
Those who desired still to be in worship from the Word, which worship they would then continually profane (*Jer.* xxiv. 8, 9).
Worship of things that come from self-intelligence (*Isa.* lvii. 6).
Worship of falsities of evil (*Jer.* iii. 10, 11).
Worship of things infernal (*Jer.* ii. 19, 20).

Worship in accordance with diabolical loves (*Ezek.* viii. 11–16).
All true worship will perish (*Isa.* xxvii. 8–12).
Worship derived from truth and good had been destroyed (*Ezek.* vi. 4–6).
Worship from falsities (*Hosea* iv. 13; *Ezek.* xxi. 18–22); in vain (*ib.* 23, 24).
Abolition of worship from falsification of truth (*Jer.* xli. 4–7).
Everything of worship rejected because of profanation (*Jer.* vii. 27–31).
They will perish because of contrary worship (*Isa.* lxv. 6, 7).
Divine worship from knowledges (*cognitiones*) (*Ezek.* xxvii. 21–23).
Falsities of worship will be utterly destroyed (*Zech.* xiii. 2, 3).
Worship of Jewish Church destroyed by the Lord at His Coming (*Ezek.* xxiv. 20–23).

WORSHIP BY THE GOOD.

The Lord will come to judgment, that heaven and the church may worship Him from joy of heart (*Ps.* xcvi. 10–12).
Worship of the Lord resultant upon the Father helping the Lord in temptations (*Ps.* lxxxvi. 9–12).
Worship of the Lord on removal of those who have ruined the church (*Ps.* lxxix. 13 *and prec.*).
Prayer that those who worship Him may have salvation (*Ps.* lxx. 4).
It is an eternal truth that those who worship the Lord will be saved (*Ps.* cxxxii. 11, 12).
At the judgment the good will worship the Lord (*Ps.* lxxv. 9).
Song in praise of the Lord by those who worship Him, when the church has been devastated (*Ps.* cxxxiv. *t.*, 1).
The Lord will institute a church in which will be worship from good (*Ps.* li. 18, 19).
A new church instituted which would worship the Lord (*Ps.* lxxviii. 68–72; cvi. 47, 48).
Those who will be gathered from all parts will worship the Lord (*Ps.* xxii. 26–31).
Worshippers of God should look to the Lord from whom, and to the church through which (*Isa.* li. 1, 2).
Those who are outside of the church worship the Lord (*Mal.* i. 11).
They are to be brought to the church, and will worship the Lord (*Jer.* xxx. 8, 9).
The Lord ought to be worshipped because He is omnipotent (*Ps.* cl. 1, 2).
Worship of the Lord results in protection from falsities that are from hell (*Zech.* x. 12 *and prec.*).
Worship will be as among the ancients (*Mal.* iii. 4).
The new church will acknowledge and worship the Lord (*Ps.* xviii. 43, 44).
Let them acknowledge and worship the Divine Human of the Lord lest they perish (*Ps.* ii. 10–12).
The Divine will be worshipped in the Lord (*Ps.* cxvi. 12–19).
Let them worship the Lord, who is the God of heaven and the church (*Ps.* cxxxiv. 2, 3).
Let the Lord be worshipped (*Ps.* lxxvi. 11; cxlv. 21).
Worship belongs to the Lord (*Isa.* lix. 19, 20).
The Lord should be worshipped, because power and justice belong to Him (*Ps.* xcix. 3–5, 9).
The Lord ought to be worshipped from the Word, where is His Divine truth (*Ps.* cxxxviii. *t.*, 1–5).
The church will worship the Lord who protects her, and teaches the Word (*Ps.* cxlvii. 13–15).
The Lord is to be worshipped in humility (*Ps.* xcv. 6, 7).
To worship the Lord is wisdom (*Ps.* cxi. 10).

The Lord is to be worshipped with the heart, because He is the Former of the church (*Ps.* c. *t.*, 1-3).

Let them worship the Lord from good and truth (*Ps.* cxxxii. 9, 10).

Worship of the Lord from good and truth (*Isa.* lx. 6, 7).

Worship from truths consequent on the acknowledgment of the Lord's Divine (*Jer.* xvii. 26 *and prec.*).

The Lord ought to be worshipped from every affection for truth and good (*Ps.* cl. 1, 2).

The Lord is to be worshipped from affection for truth and good (*Ps.* cxlix. 1-4; *Jer.* xxxiii. 10, 11).

Worship from the good of charity (*Zech.* xiv. 20, 21).

Worship of the Lord in the new church (*Isa.* lxvi. 23; *Ezek.* xxxvi. 37, 38; xlvi. 4-24; xliv. 15-31; *Zech.* viii. 20-23; *Dan.* xii. 1).

Worship from the good of love in the new church (*Ezek.* xliii. 12-27).

All who are in the heavens and on the earths should worship the Lord from goods and truths that are from Him (*Ps.* cxlviii. 1-6; all who are in the lowest parts of heaven and the church should worship Him from truths and goods of every kind (*ib.* 7-10); in general from the understanding and will of truth and good (*ib.* 11, 12).

The spiritual and celestial church worships the Lord who is the God of the church (*Ps.* cxxxv. 19-21).

All things of worship of the internal church in respect to good and truth (*Ezek.* xli. 1-26).

Worship of the Lord from love and faith from eternity and thereafter (*Ps.* lxxii. 5).

Happy is he who confesses and worships the Lord (*Ps.* cxviii. 26-29).

Let those who worship the Lord rejoice in Him (*Ps.* xl. 16).

The whole church will acknowledge and worship the Lord from joy of heart (*Ps.* lxvii. *t.*, 1-5, 7).

The Lord is not approached by externals of worship, but by internals, which are of truth and good (*Micah* vi. 6-8).

External Worship.

Worship in externals according to the statutes similar only in outermost things (*Amos* iv. 4-6).

It is in their internals to worship only externals (*Jer* xvii. 1, 2).

External worship without internal (*Isa.* xxix. 13).

External worship of no avail in vastated church (*Isa.* i. 10-15; *Ezek.* xxxiii. 30-33).

Worship with the mouth and not with the heart (*Ezek.* xx. 1-3).

External worship is of no avail, so long as evils are committed (*Ps.* l. 16-20).

Worship in externals interiorly infernal (*Jer.* ii. 22, 23).

Externals of worship are of no account, because there are no internals of worship (*Jer.* vii. 21-24).

Worship from the mere sense of the letter of the Word, which is external without an internal, being meant by "Gog" (*Ezek.* xxxviii. 1, 2); everything and all things of that worship will perish (*ib.* 3-7); it will possess the church and will vastate it (*ib.* 8-16).

Those who are in such worship will come into the church, but will perish at the coming of the Lord (*Ezek.* xxxix. 1-6 *and fol.*).

Their external worship is not accepted because they worshipped another god, whence came profanation (*Mal.* ii. 13 *and prec.*).

The Lord does not desire external worship (*Ps.* l. 7-13).

Not external, but internal worship (*Ps.* li. 16, 17).

All things of worship of the external church as to good and truth (*Ezek.* xlii. 1-20).

Worst.—The Word is perverted, this is the worst (*Jer.* xxiii. 14).
Wretched (*miserus*).—Those who have perverted the Word will become wretched (*Isa.* lxv. 11, 12).

Zeal (*see* **Divine zeal**).
Zidon.—"Zidon" means the understanding of truth; its history (*Ezek.* xxviii. 21–26).
Zion.—"Zion" means the new church that will be established by the Lord (*Jer.* xxxi.).

INDEX OF SCRIPTURE PASSAGES.

Psalms.

	page
xxii. *18,*	4
xxxv. *19,*	4
lxix. *21,*	4
cxviii. *21, 22,*	4

Matthew.

xiv. *23,*	4
xxiv. *15,*	87

Mark.

i. *35,*	4

Luke.

vi. *46,*	4
xiv. *32–39,*	4

Luke.

iii. *21,*	4
v. *16,*	4
ix. *28, 29,*	4
xxii. *37–47,*	4

John.

xii. *28,*	4
xiv. *13, 14,*	4
xvii. *9, 15, 20,*	4

Scripture Confirmations of New Church Doctrine

Scripture Confirmations

OF

New Church Doctrine

(DICTA PROBANTIA)

BEING

PROOF PASSAGES FROM THE
SCRIPTURES

FROM THE LATIN OF

EMANUEL SWEDENBORG

TRANSLATOR'S NOTE.

This little work consists of a collection of passages from the Scriptures under convenient subject headings gathered by Swedenborg for his use in the composition of his works. The original manuscript has no title, and probably was not intended for publication. Dr. Im. Tafel issued an edition of the Latin text at Tübingen, in 1845, and gave it the title *Dicta Probantia* (Proof Passages). In Dr. Tafel's edition, however, the subjects are arranged alphabetically, following the Latin subject headings. In this translation the order of the subjects is that of the original manuscript. The parentheses ( ), at the beginning and the end of certain paragraphs were introduced by Dr. Tafel to indicate that the author had crossed his pen over the parts so marked: it is probable that he did so when he used them in his published writings.

The figures found at the sides of the pages are as in the original manuscript, and refer to the Table of Subjects. We have numbered the chapters with Roman numerals, and have subdivided them with black-letter figures as in Potts' subdivisions, for convenience of reference.

The only English translation heretofore published was issued by the Swedenborg Society of London in 1906, being translated by the Rev. James R. Rendell. In that edition a useful index of the Scripture passages was added. The present translation is a revision of the above. We have retained the title Scripture Confirmations of New Church Doctrine.

JOHN WHITEHEAD.

CONTENTS.

		PAGE
I.	The Apostles—Miracles	323
II.	Christ	324
III.	God the Father, and the Holy Spirit	347
IV.	The Coming of the Lord—The Consummation—The New Church—Christ and the Judgment	350
V.	Faith	382
VI.	Charity and Good Works	385
VII.	Law and Works	388
VIII.	The Gospel	390
IX.	The Last Judgment	390
X.	Baptism	396
XI.	The Lord's Supper	396
XII.	Predestination	397
XIII.	Repentance	398
XIV.	Justification—Regeneration—The Church	398
XV.	Free Will	404
XVI.	Imputation	404
XVII.	Salvation and Heaven	404
XVIII.	Condemnation and Hell	404
XIX.	Redemption	404
XX.	Sin; and Original Sin	411

AUTHOR'S TABLE OF SUBJECTS.

[NOTE.—The Numbers on the margins indicate that a text refers to the subject or subjects in the Table, as well as to that under which it is cited.]

1. The Appearing of the Lord Jehovah.
2. The Morning or Rise.
3. The Day or Progression.
4. The Evening or Vastation.
5. The Night or Consummation.
6. The Coming of the Lord.
7. The Last Judgment.
8. The New Heaven.
9. The New Church.
10. Redemption.

Concerning Miracles.

Jehovah, and God, and the Holy One of Israel are to be found in many places where the Lord and the Father are mentioned, and elsewhere.

Scripture Confirmations of New Church Doctrine.

(DICTA PROBANTIA.)

I. THE APOSTLES. MIRACLES.

1. The apostles are named (*Acts* i. 13, 26).

Judas the traitor burst asunder in the midst, and all his bowels gushed out (*Acts* i. 16–19).

Many miracles and signs were done by the apostles (*Acts* ii. 43). Peter and John healed the lame man sitting at the gate of the temple, therefore all were astonished, but when the priests heard them preaching about Jesus, they laid hands upon them, thrust them into prison, and afterwards having threatened them sent them away because of the people (*Acts* iii. 1–20; iv.). This miracle was done in the name of Jesus Christ (iv. 10, 30).

Many miracles done by the apostles (*Acts* v. 12, 15, 16), but yet they were put in prison by the high priest, and although they were led out thence by an angel miraculously, yet they were beaten, and warned not to preach concerning Jesus (vers. 29–40).

Stephen also did great signs and miracles (*Acts* vi. 8).

Miracles done by Philip (*Acts* viii. 6, 7, 13).

Simon the sorcerer made himself great in Samaria, saying, here is the great power of God; but he was severely reproved by Peter (*Acts* viii. 9, 10, *seq.*, 20–24).

Miracles done by Peter, and also that he raised the dead to life (*Acts* ix. 33, 34, 36–42).

The miracle of Paul, that a certain man was made blind (*Acts* xiii. 11); also others (xix. 11, 12; xx. 9, *seq.;* xxviii. 3, *seq.*, 8).

Miracles done by the disciples, and with Paul (*Acts* xiv. 3, 8–10, 19, 20; xvi. 25, 26, *seq.*).

2. Of those who transform themselves into apostles, as Satan into an angel of light (2 *Cor.* xi. 13–15).

The torments and evils endured by Paul are recounted (2 *Cor.* xi. 24–27, 32, 33).

Paul was in the third heaven and heard ineffable things (2 *Cor.* xii. 2–4).

The messenger of Satan received Paul with blows (2 *Cor.* xii. 7–9).

The coming of the Lord according to the working of Satan in signs and lying miracles (2 *Thess.* ii. 9).

False Christs shall arise, and shall show signs and prodigies (*Matt.* xxiv. 24, 25; *Mark* xiii. 22).

By the prince of the demons, Beelzebub, He casts out demons (*Mark* iii. 22; *Luke* xi. 15, 17, 19).

That they would not hearken to miracles even if one rose from the dead. Abraham to the rich man in hell (*Luke* xvi. 29–31).

The coming of the Lord is in signs and lying miracles (2. *Thess.* ii. 1–11).

II. CHRIST.

1. The Lord is called in many places Jehovah, Jehovah of hosts, and in particular God, the God of Israel, the Holy One, and the Holy One of Israel, and Lord, the Rock, Angel, the Arm of Jehovah, Prophet, the Son of man, while very frequently Jehovah is named, even He, since they are one—the Mighty One of Jacob, the Rock of Jacob. Therefore in general by Jehovah the Father Himself, and Lord are at the same time meant, as is clear from the following passages.

Jesus was taken up into heaven, and a cloud received Him, and then two angels said, This Jesus shall so come as ye have seen him going into heaven (*Acts* i. 9, 11).

Jesus rose from the dead according to the prophecy through David (*Ps.* xvi. 10), and that there Christ is meant and not David (*Acts* ii. 27–29, 31; xiii. 24–37). Then said Jehovah, the Lord said unto my Lord, Sit at My right hand until I make Thine enemies Thy footstool (*Ps.* cx. 1; *Acts* ii. 34, 35).

The Lord our God (*Acts* ii. 39). He is the Lord of all (*Acts* x. 36).

Ye have slain the Prince of life (*Acts* iii. 15).

That when the times of refreshing shall come from the presence of the Lord, he may send Jesus Christ *which* before was preached unto you, whom the heaven must receive until the time of the restitution of all things, which God hath spoken by the mouth of all the prophets from of old (*Acts* iii. 20, 21).

Moses said, The Lord your God will raise up unto you a Prophet from your brethren, unto him ye shall hearken, whatever soul shall not hearken to that Prophet, he shall be destroyed from among the people: all the prophets have foretold him (*Deut.* xviii. 15, 18, 19; *Acts* iii. 22–24).

Prediction from *Isaiah* (liii. 7–9), the Lord would suffer (*Acts* viii. 32, 33).

Christ was the Son of God (*Acts* viii. 37; ix. 20).

Jesus is the Lord of all (*Acts* x. 36). He is the Judge of the living and the dead (ver. 42).

They were called Christians first in Antioch (*Acts* xi. 26).

Paul explains the saying, this day have I begotten thee (*Ps.* ii. 7) as referring to Jesus (*Acts* xiii. 33).

He is called the light of the nations, for salvation to the uttermost part of the earth (*Is.* xlix. 6; *Acts* xiii. 47).

The coming of the Lord for the rebuilding of the ruins (*Amos* ix. 11; quoted *Acts* xv. 16, 17).

Paul said that he was ready to be bound and die for the name of the Lord Jesus (*Acts* xxi. 13).

Paul at Rome preaching the kingdom of God, and teaching the things concerning the Lord Christ (*Acts* xxviii. 31).

In the Acts of the Apostles it is said that they preached the Lord Christ only, and that they should believe in Him, and nowhere that they should believe in God the Father.

2. The Son of God (*Rom.* i. 3, 4).

Called after Jesus Christ, Christians (*Rom.* i. 6) through the faith of Jesus Christ (*Rom.* iii. 22).

Faith in Christ. Through Jesus Christ we have peace toward God, and to God we have access by faith into this grace, and we glory in the hope of the glory of God (*Rom.* v. 1, 2).

By Jesus Christ were we reconciled to God (*Rom.* **v.** 10, 11).

As by one man sin entered into the world, so by the justice of one are we justified (*Rom.* v. 12, 13, 15, 18, 19).

There is no condemnation to them which are in Christ Jesus, who walk not after the flesh, but after the Spirit, in order that the justification of the law might be fulfilled in us, who walk not after the flesh, but after the spirit (*Rom.* viii. 1–4).

Christ is at the right hand of God, who also maketh intercession for us (*Rom.* viii. 34).

Who shall separate us from the love of Christ? Shall tribulation, distress, hunger, death, angels, principalities, height, depth, etc. (*Rom.* viii. 35–39)?

From the fathers Christ is according to the flesh, who is over all; God blessed forever. Amen (*Rom.* ix. 5).

Whosoever shall call upon the name of the Lord, shall be saved (*Rom.* x. 13).

We are one body in Christ; all are members having different gifts according to grace (*Rom.* xii. 5, 6). The gifts which belong to different members are enumerated in a long series (vers. 6, 13).

Put ye on the Lord Jesus Christ (*Rom.* xiii. 14).

Whether we live, we live in the Lord; whether we die, we die in the Lord; therefore, whether we live or die, we are the Lord's. For to this end Christ both died and rose and lived again that He might be Lord both of the dead and of the living (*Rom.* xiv. 8, 9).

It is written, I live, saith the Lord, for every knee shall bow to Me, and every tongue shall confess to God (*Rom.* xiv. 11).

Isaiah saith, there shall be a root of Jesse, and He that shall rise to rule over the nations; in Him shall the nations hope (*Rom.* xv. 12).

The Gospel of Christ (Rom. xv. 19–21).

Chosen and tried in the Lord, in Christ: to work and labor in the Lord (*Rom.* xvi. 8–13).

3. Ye are in Christ Jesus, who of God is made unto us wisdom, and justice, and sanctification, and redemption; according as it is written, He that glorieth, let him glory in the Lord (1 *Cor.* i. 30, 31).

I determined not to know anything among you, save Jesus Christ (1 *Cor.* ii. 2).

For other foundation can no man lay more than that which is laid, which is Jesus Christ. Now if any man build upon this foundation, gold, silver, precious stones, wood, hay, stubble; the day shall declare it because it shall be revealed by fire (1 *Cor.* iii. 11, 12, *seq.*).

All are yours; but ye are Christ's; but Christ is God's (1 *Cor*, iii. 22, 23).

We know that there is no other God but one. For though there be that are called gods, whether in heaven or in earth, as there be gods many and lords many, yet to us there is one God, the Father, of whom are all things, and we in Him; and one Lord Jesus Christ, by whom are all things, and we by Him (1 *Cor.* viii. 4–6).

They drank from the spiritual Rock, the Rock was Christ (1 *Cor.* x. 4).

The head of every man is Christ, the head of Christ is God (1 *Cor.* xi. 3).

As often as ye eat this bread, and drink this cup, proclaim ye the Lord's death *till He come* (1 *Cor.* xi. 26).

No one can say that Jesus is the Lord but in the Holy Spirit (1 *Cor.* xii. 3).

Ye are the body of Christ, and members in part (1 *Cor.* xii. 27).

Christ was seen by many after the resurrection, and in addition to the apostles by five hundred (1 *Cor.* xv. 4–7).

Christ is the image of God (2 *Cor.* iv. 4).

God who gave the light in our hearts, to the enlightening of the knowledge of the glory of God which is in the face of Jesus Christ (2 *Cor.* iv. 6).

God hath reconciled us to Himself by Jesus Christ (2 *Cor.* v. 18–21).

Ye know not your own selves, that Jesus Christ is in you (2 *Cor.* xiii. 5).

4. If any one preacheth any other gospel than that which He preached let him be accursed (*Gal.* i. 8, 9).

I live, no more I, but Christ liveth in me (*Gal.* ii. 20).

The power which God wrought in Christ, wherefore He set Him at His own right hand above the heavens, above all principalities, power and might, etc., and hath put all things under

His feet, and hath given Him to be the head over all things of the church, which is His body, the fullness of Him that filleth all in all (*Eph.* i. 20–23).

Through Christ we have access in one Spirit unto the Father. Christ is the corner stone, by whom the whole building framed together groweth unto an holy temple in the Lord, through whom ye also are builded together into an habitation of God in the spirit (*Eph.* ii. 18, 20–22).

God hath founded all things by Jesus Christ (*Eph.* iii. 9).

One body and one Spirit; one Lord, one faith, one baptism, one God and Father of all; and unto every one of us is given grace according to the measure of the gift of Christ (*Eph.* iv. 4–7).

He that descended is also the same that ascended above all the heavens, that He might fill all things (*Eph.* iv. 10).

For the edifying of the body of Christ, and that the church is the body and Christ the head (*Eph.* iv. 12, 15, 16).

We are members of His body; of His flesh, and of His bones (*Eph.* v. 30).

By faith we have access to Christ in confidence (*Eph.* iii. 12).

Christ is the head of the church, and He is the Saviour of the body (*Eph.* v. 23).

5. I desire you all in the bowels of Jesus Christ (*Phil.* i. 8).

Jesus emptied Himself, taking the form of a servant, wherefore God hath exalted Him and given Him a Name above every name, that at the name of Jesus every knee should bow, in heaven, in earth, and under the earth (*Phil.* ii. 7–11).

The God of faith (*Phil.* iii. 9).

Christ, who is the image of the invisible God, the firstborn of every creature, and that through Him and in Him all things were created (*Col.* i. 15, 16).

Christ is before all things, and all things subsist in Him, and He is the head of the body, the church (*Col.* i. 17, 18, 24).

In Christ doth all fullness dwell, and by Him all things were reconciled to Himself (*Col.* i. 18–20).

In Christ are hid all the treasures of wisdom and of knowledge (*Col.* ii. 3).

In Christ dwelleth all the fullness of the Divinity bodily (*Col.* ii. 9).

Christ sitting on the right hand of God (*Col.* iii. 1; *Heb.* viii. 1; x. 12; xii. 2).

Christ is all in all (*Col.* iii. 11).

That they all may be in one body (*Col.* iii. 15).

Do all things in the name of the Lord Jesus (*Col.* iii. 17).

That from the Lord ye shall receive the reward of the inheritance; ye serve the Lord Christ (*Col.* iii. 24).

Christ is the head of the body (*Col.* ii. 19).

Life is with Christ in God (*Col.* iii. 3).

Concerning the coming of the Lord, see also *Consummation* and *Judgment.*

6. One God, one Mediator, Christ (1 *Tim.* ii. 5, 6).

God was manifest in the flesh, seen, received up (1 *Tim.* iii. 16).

If we are not faithful, He abideth faithful: He cannot deny Himself (2 *Tim.* ii. 13).

They profess that they know God, but in works they deny Him (*Titus* i. 16).

He hath in the last days spoken unto us in the Son whom He hath appointed heir of all things, through whom also He made the worlds (*sæcula*); who being the brightness of His glory and the express image of His person, upholding all things by the word of His power [after] He had by Himself made purification of our sins, sat down on the right hand of the Majesty on high; to whom did He ever say, Thou art my Son, this day have I begotten Thee? (*Ps.* ii. 7) and He saith, Let all the angels of God worship Him (*Ps.* xcvii. 7); and many things in *Hebrews* (i. 2–9, 13).

Thou madest Him a little lower than the angels; Thou crownedst Him with glory and honor, and didst set Him over all the works of Thy hands: Thou hast put all things in subjection under His feet. But we see not yet all things put under Him. It became Him for whom are all things, and through whom are all things, to be the author of their salvation (*Heb.* ii. 7, 8, 10).

He is called the chief priest and the high priest (*Heb.* ii. 17; iii. 1). We have a great chief priest that is passed into the heavens, Jesus the Son of God (*Heb.* iv. 14). Thou art a priest for ever after the order of Melchizedek (*Heb.* v. 10; vi. 20; vii. 1–3, 10, 11, 15, 21). Here concerning the new covenant (*Jer.* xxxi. 10, 11).

7. The Lord who is a living stone, rejected by men, chosen of God, precious, that ye also as living stones may be built up into a spiritual house, to the unbelieving He is a stone of stumbling (1 *Pet.* ii. 4–8).

Acceptable to God through Jesus Christ (1 *Pet.* ii. 5).

He is called the Shepherd and Bishop of souls (1 *Pet.* ii. 25).

Jesus Christ, after He went into heaven was on the right hand of God; angels, authorities and powers being subject unto Him (1 *Pet.* iii. 22).

That God may be glorified by Jesus Christ (1 *Pet.* iv. 11).

God and Jesus our Lord (1 *Pet.* i. 2; 2 *Pet.* i. 1; *James* i. 1).

The eternal kingdom of the Lord and Saviour Jesus Christ (2 *Pet.* i. 11; iii. 2).

The knowledge of Jesus Christ (2 *Pet.* i. 8; ii. 20).

Of the glorification of the Lord seen by the three disciples upon the mount (2 *Pet.* i. 17, 18).

8. He is called Father and Son (1 *John* i. 3; ii. 1; 2 *John* i. 3; 1 *John* ii. 22, 23; *Jude* i. 4).

The Lord is life revealed and made manifest, and God is light (1 *John* i. 2, 5).

He is a propitiation for our sins (1 *John* ii. 2; iv. 10).

For this purpose the Son of God was manifested, that He might destroy the works of the devil (1 *John* iii. 8; iv. 10).

That we shall abide in Christ (1 *John* ii. 5, 6, 24; iii. 6).

He is antichrist, that denieth the Father and the Son: whosoever denieth the Son hath not the Father (1 *John* ii. 22, 23).

He that keepeth His commands dwelleth in Him, and He in him. Hereby we know that we dwell in Him, and He in us. Whosoever shall confess that Jesus is the Son of God, God dwelleth in him, and he in God (1 *John* iii. 24; iv. 13, 15, 16).

He who confesseth Jesus Christ, who lived in the flesh, is of God; he who confesseth not is not of God (1 *John* iv. 2, 3).

Whosoever believeth that Jesus is the Christ (Messiah) is born of God (1 *John* v. 1).

Who hath overcome the world, but he that believeth that Jesus is the Son of God (1 *John* v. 5).

This is the testimony, that God has given to us eternal life, and this life is in His Son. He that hath the Son hath life. He who believeth in the name of the Son of God hath eternal life (1 *John* v. 10-13).

We know that the Son of God is come and hath given us an understanding that we may know [Him that is] true, and we are in [Him that is] true, in His Son Jesus Christ. This is the true God, and eternal life (1 *John* v. 20, 21).

To the only wise God our Saviour, be glory and power (*Jude* 25).

9. His appearance as the Sun shining in his strength (*Rev.* i. 16).

The Lord is described by various names (*Rev.* i. 5).

The representation of Him as the Word (*Rev.* i. 13-18).

If any one will open the door, I will come in to him (*Rev.* iii. 20)..

Honor was given to the Lord from the Word, while He opened the seals of the book, by many animals and elders, and by every creature (*Rev.* v. 9-14).

That no one can interpret the Word, and teach truths from it, except the Lord, is meant by the Lamb opened the seals of the book (*Rev.* v. 1, *seq.*, and vi.).

The Lamb which is in the midst of the throne shall feed them, and shall lead them to living fountains of water (*Rev.* vii. 10, 16, 17).

They are virgins who follow the Lamb whithersoever He goeth (*Rev.* xiv. 4).

An angel flying in the midst of heaven having the everlasting gospel (*Rev.* xiv. 6).

Blessed are the dead who die in the Lord from henceforth (*Rev.* xiv. 13).

Behold a white cloud, and one sitting upon the cloud like unto the Son of man (*Rev.* xiv. 14).

Great are Thy works, Lord God Almighty, just and true are Thy ways, O King of saints. Who shall not glorify Thy name, for Thou only art holy; therefore all nations shall come and adore before Thee, for Thy judgments are made manifest (*Rev.* xv. 3, 4).

The Lamb is Lord of lords and King of kings, and they that are with Him are called, and chosen, and faithful (*Rev.* xvii. 14; xix. 16).

Having the testimony of Jesus. The testimony of Jesus is the spirit of prophecy (*Rev.* xix. 10).

That the Word will be opened by the Lord is meant by the white horse, for He that sitteth upon it is called the Word of God (*Rev.* xix. 10–16).

Behold the tabernacle of God is with men; He will dwell with them (*Rev.* xxi. 3).

The Lord God Almighty and the Lamb are the temple of it. The glory of God will lighten it, and the Lamb is the light thereof (*Rev.* xxi. 22, 23; xxii. 5).

The throne of God and of the Lamb (*Rev.* xxii. 3).

That He it is who is, and was and is to come, Alpha and Omega (*Rev.* i. 4, 8, 11; ii. 8; xi. 17; xxi. 6; xxii. 13).

10. Thou shalt call His name Jesus, He shall save the people from their sins (*Matt.* i. 21).

The wise men came to adore the infant Jesus, and that He would be born in Bethlehem according to *Micah* v. 1 (*Matt.* ii. 1–6).

The wise men adored Him and brought Him gifts (*Matt.* ii. 11).

Jesus said to John, It becometh us so to fulfil all the justice of God (*Matt.* iii. 15).

Jesus said to the devil who was tempting, Thou shalt not tempt the Lord thy God; and again, Thou shalt adore the Lord thy God, and Him only shalt thou serve (*Matt.* iv. 7, 10).

A ruler came and adored Jesus (*Matt.* ix. 18).

He that receiveth Me receiveth Him that sent Me (*Matt.* x. 40).

All things are delivered unto Me by my Father, wherefore come ye all unto Me (*Matt.* xi. 27, 28).

They that were in the ship adored Jesus, saying, Of a truth Thou art the Son of God (*Matt.* xiv. 33). A woman of Canaan (*Matt.* xv. 25), the disciples (*Luke* xxiv. 52), a blind man (*John* ix. 38), adored Him.

Multitudes glorified the God of Israel (*Matt.* xv. 31).

There is one Rabbi and one Master, that is, He teaches what is good and true (*Matt.* xxiii. 8, 10).

Of the sign of the coming of the Lord and of the consummation of the age (*Matt.* xxiv. 1 to end).

Then shall there be wars and rumor, and they will say, I am the Christ; false prophets shall arise and seduce many; signifies the heresies in the first times, which were many (*Matt.* xxiv. 5–14).

The women, running to Jesus, adored Him (*Matt.* xxviii. 9).

He said, All power is given unto Me in heaven and on earth (*Matt.* xxviii. 18; *Ps.* viii. 6, 7).

11. John says, There cometh one after me, the latchets of whose shoes I am not worthy to unloose (*Mark* i. 7; *Matt.* iii. 11).

He is called the Holy One of God (*Mark* i. 24).

He is called the Bridegroom, and they the sons of the bride-chamber (*Mark* ii. 19, 20; *Luke* v. 35).

John shall turn many of the sons of Israel to the Lord their God; but He shall go before Him in the power of Elias to make ready a people for the Lord (*Luke* i. 16, 17). He is called the Lord God.

The angel Gabriel to Mary, Thou shalt conceive. He shall be great, and shall be called the Son of the Highest, of whose kingdom there shall be no end (*Luke* i. 31–33).

The angel said, The Holy Spirit shall come upon thee and the power of the Highest shall overshadow thee: wherefore the Holy One that shall be born of thee shall be called the Son of God (*Luke* i. 35).

Mary said, My spirit hath exulted in God my Saviour (*Luke* i. 47).

He is called the Lord God of Israel and the day-spring from on high (*Luke* i. 68, 78).

The Lord's Christ (*Luke* ii. 26). The Christ of God (*Luke* ix. 20).

He is called the Lord God (*Luke* iv. 12).

He that is not with Me is against Me: and he that gathereth not with Me scattereth abroad (*Matt.* xii. 30; *Luke* xi. 23).

Blessed is the King that cometh in the name of the Lord; when He rode upon an ass into Jerusalem (*Luke* xix. 38; *John* xii. 13, 15).

The Son of man sitting on the right hand of the power of God (*Luke* xxii. 69).

12. The Word was with God, and God was the Word; and all things were made by Him. In Him was life, and the life was the light of men; He was the true Light which lighteth every man: and the Word became flesh (*John* i. 1–14).

This was He who was before me, for He was prior to me. Of His fulness we have all received (*John* i. 15, 16, 27, 30).

No one hath seen God at any time; the only begotten Son of God, who is in the bosom of the Father, hath made Him manifest (*John* i. 18).

Whose shoe's latchet I am not worthy to unloose (*John* i. 27).

The Son of man which is in the heavens (*John* iii. 13, 14).

Light has come into the world. He who does evils hates the light (*John* iii. 19, 20).

He that hath the bride is the bridegroom. Spoken concerning Christ (*John* iii. 29).

He came from heaven and is therefore above all (*John* iii. 31). Spoken concerning Christ.

The Father gave not the Spirit by measure unto Him; the Father gave all things into His hands (*John* iii. 34, 35).

Jesus says that He is equal to the Father; in various places (*John* v. 18–23). That He quickeneth, and that He hath life in Himself, etc. (vers. 21, 26, 27).

The bread of God is He which cometh down from heaven, and giveth life unto the world (*John* vi. 33). He is the bread of life (vers. 35, 50, 51).

Not that any one has seen the Father, save He who is with the Father, He hath seen the Father (*John* vi. 46).

Jesus said I am the light of the world; he that followeth Me shall have the light of life (*John* viii. 12; ix. 5, 39; xii. 35, 36, 46).

Jesus said, Before Abraham was, I am (*John* viii. 56, 58).

He came into the world that the blind might see, and that they which see might become blind (*John* ix. 39).

Jesus said, I and the Father are one (*John* x. 30).

The Father and He are one (*John* x. 30).

He is in the Father and the Father in Him (*John* xiv. 10, 11; x. 38; *Phil.* 1–4; 1 *Cor.* i. 3).

That ye may believe that the Father is in Me and I in the Father (*John* x. 38; xiv. 10, 11).

He that receiveth Me receiveth Him that sent Me (*John* xiii. 20).

Jesus said, Believe in God, believe also in Me (*John* xiv. 1).

Jesus is the way to the Father (*John* xiv. 4–6).

He is the way, the truth and the life (*John* xiv. 6).

Jesus said, He that seeth and knoweth Me, seeth and knoweth the Father (*John* xiv. 7–9).

If ye shall ask of the Father in My name, I will do it (*John* xiv. 13, 14).

Jesus said, Because I live, ye shall live (*John* xiv. 19).

He and the Father will make their abode with them (*John* xiv. 21, 23).

God and Christ [mentioned] together; that I and the Father will come to him (*John* xiv. 23). I and the Father are one (*John* x. 30).

He that hateth Me hateth My Father (*John* xv. 23, 24).

All things that the Father hath are Mine (*John* xvi. 15).

Jesus goes away to the Father (*John* xvi. 5–7, 16, 17, 29), which is to be united to Him.

They should pray in His name, I say not that I will pray the Father for you; the Father Himself loveth you because ye have loved Me (*John* xvi. 26–28). He often says, In His name.

I came forth from the Father, and am come into the world; again I leave the world and go to the Father (*John* xvi. 28–31).

Jesus said, the Father had given Him power over all flesh (*John* xvii. 2).

Jesus will give to them eternal life (*John* xvii. 2) also, the Son from the Father.

God and Jesus Christ [mentioned] together, namely that they both know each other (*John* xvii. 3).

Father glorify Thy Son, that thy Son also may glorify Thee. Now therefore do Thou, O Father, glorify Me with Thine own self with the glory which I had with Thee before the world was (*John* xvii. 1, 5).

N. B. Arcanum. By "to glorify" is meant to unite the Divine Truth with the Divine Good in the Human. The Lord in the Father from eternity was the Divine Good and thence the Divine Truth, wherefore when He descended He was the Divine Truth from the Divine Good; a reciprocal union, or that of the Divine Truth with the Divine Good, was effected by the Lord in the Human while He was in the world; and it was accomplished successively, especially by redemption and by the fact that He did the will of the Father, and then fully by the last temptation, which was that of the cross, for temptation unites. Then was accomplished the reciprocal union of the Divine Truth with the Divine Good, thus the Father and Son are one, thus one Person like soul and body.

All Mine are Thine and Thine are Mine, but I am glorified in them (*John* xvii. 10).

I sanctify Myself, that they also may be sanctified in the truth (*John* xvii. 19).

That they may be one in Jesus as the Father is in Him (*John* xvii. 21–23).

Thomas said, my Lord and my God (*John* xx. 28).

From Daniel and the Prophets.

13. The Lord was represented before Daniel in a form almost like that in which He was presented before John (*Rev.* i. 14, 15). Before Daniel (*Dan.* x. 5, 6), and then almost like things happened (xii. 6, 7).

9 In that day, butter and honey shall every one eat that is left in the midst of the land (*Isa.* vii. 21, 22, 25). *The Church of the Lord.*

(Jehovah of hosts, Him shall ye sanctify, for *let* Him be your fear, and *let* Him be your dread. And He shall be for a sanctuary; but for a stone of stumbling and for a rock of offence, for a gin and a snare for the inhabitant of Jerusalem (*Isa.* viii. 13, 14; *Matt.* xxi. 42–44; *Luke* xx. 17, 18).)

(The people walking in darkness have seen a great light:
6 they that dwell in the land of the shadow of death, upon them hath the light shined. Unto us a Boy is born, unto us a Son is given, whose name is Wonderful, Counsellor, God, Hero, the Father of eternity, the Prince of Peace; to establish the Kingdom in judgment and justice from henceforth to eternity (*Isa.* ix. 1, 5, 6).)

In that day the remnant of Israel shall no more stay upon
9 him that smote them; but shall stay upon Jehovah, the Holy One of Israel, in truth (*Isa.* x. 20–22). Wherefore the wolf
9 shall dwell with the lamb, the leopard shall lie down with the kid, etc. They shall not do hurt in all the mountain of holi-

ness, for the earth shall be full of the knowledge of Jehovah. 9
It shall surely come to pass in that day that the Lord shall
again recover the remnant of His people (*Isa.* xi. 6–9, 11–16).

14. In that day thou shalt say, I will confess to Thee, O
Jehovah. Behold the God of my salvation, I will be confi- 9
dent. Then with joy shall ye draw water out of the wells of
salvation, for great is the Holy One of Israel in the midst of
thee (*Isa.* xii. 1–6).

In that day shall a man look to his Maker, and his eyes shall 9, 1
have respect to the Holy One of Israel (*Isa.* xvii. 4–7).

In that day shall five cities in the land of Egypt speak the
language of Canaan and swear to Jehovah of Hosts. In that
day shall there be an altar in the midst of the land of Egypt;
then Jehovah shall be known to Egypt and the Egyptians shall
know Jehovah in that day. In that day shall there be a highway out of Egypt into Assyria; in that day shall Israel be the 9
third with Egypt and with Assyria; and Jehovah shall bless,
saying, Blessed be Egypt, My people, and Assyria the work of
My hands, and Israel Mine inheritance (*Isa.* xix. 18–25). By
"Egypt" is signified the natural man, by "Assyria" the rational,
and by "Israel" the spiritual. *The Church of the Lord there
is treated of,* in which these three are.

O Jehovah, I have waited for Thee; the desire of *my* soul
is to Thy name and to the remembrance *of Thee.* With my
soul have I desired Thee in the night, yea with my spirit
within me I have waited for Thee in the morning: for when
Thy judgments are in the earth, the inhabitants of the world 7
will learn justice (*Isa.* xxvi. 8, 9).

In that day shall Jehovah of Hosts be for a crown of adornment, and for a diadem of beauty unto the residue of His
people, and for a spirit of judgment to him that sitteth in 7
judgment, and for strength to them that repel the battle before the gate (*Isa.* xxviii. 5, 6).

Therefore thus said the Lord Jehovah, Behold I lay in Zion
a stone, a tried stone, a precious corner stone of sure foundation: he that believeth shall not make haste. Then will I lay
judgment to the line, and justice to the plummet. Your
covenant with death shall be abolished, and your vision with 7
hell shall not stand (*Isa.* xxviii. 16–18).

15. (The voice of one that crieth in the wilderness, prepare ye the way of Jehovah, make straight in the desert a highway for our God: for the glory of Jehovah shall be revealed, and all flesh shall see *it* together (*Isa.* xl. 3–5).)

(O Zion that tellest good tidings, get thee up into the high mountain; O Jerusalem that tellest good tidings, lift up thy voice with strength, say, Behold your God! Behold the Lord Jehovih cometh with strength, and His arm shall rule for Him: behold, His reward is with Him and the recompense of His work before Him. He shall feed His flock like a shepherd; He shall gather the lambs into His arm, and carry *them* in His bosom, He shall gently lead those that give suck (*Is.* xl. 9–11).)

To whom will ye liken Me? to whom am I equal? saith the
9 Holy One. Lift up your eyes on high and behold who hath created these things, that bringeth out their host by number; He calleth them all by name (*Isa.* xl. 25, 26).

6, 9 Who hath raised up one from the east whom He calleth in justice to his following? He gave the nations before Him, and made Him to rule over kings (*Isa.* xli. 2).

I, Jehovah, the First, and with the last; I am the same (*Isa.* xli. 4).

Behold My servant, on whom I recline, Mine elect in whom My soul is well pleased; I have put My spirit upon Him: He shall bring forth judgment to the nations. A bruised reed
7 shall He not break, and the smoking flax shall He not quench: He shall bring forth judgment unto truth. He shall not quench nor break till He have set judgment in the earth (*Isa.* xlii. 1–4).

I, Jehovah, have called Thee in justice, and I will give Thee
9 for a covenant of the people, for a light of the nations; to open the blind eyes, to bring out the prisoner from the prison, and them that sit in darkness out of the prison house. I am Jehovah: that is My name, and My glory I will not give to another. Behold, the former things are come to pass, and new things do I declare: before they spring forth I cause you to hear them (*Isa.* xlii. 6–9).

Is there a God beside Me? I know no Rock (*Isa.* xliv. 8).
(Thus said Jehovah thy Redeemer, and He that formed thee

from the womb; I am Jehovah that maketh all things; that stretcheth forth the heavens alone; that spreadeth abroad the earth by Myself (*Isa.* xliv. 24).)

16. I will give thee the treasures of darkness, and hidden riches of secret places, that thou mayest know that I, Jehovah, which call thee by thy name am the God of Israel. I am Jehovah and there is none else, there is no God beside Me: that they may know from the rising and from the setting of the sun, that there is no God beside Me. I am Jehovah and there is none else (*Isa.* xlv. 3–6). 6, 9

(I have raised him up in justice: he shall build My city, not for price nor reward. Surely God is in Thee, and there is none else, there is no God. Verily Thou art a hidden God, O God of Israel, the Saviour (*Isa.* xlv. 13–15).) I am Jehovah; and there is none else (ver. 18). 6

(Am not I Jehovah? and there is no God else beside Me; a just God and a Saviour; there is none beside Me. Look unto Me, that ye may be saved, all the ends of the earth, for I am God and there is none else (*Isa.* xlv. 21, 22).)

I have sworn by myself, justice is gone out of My mouth, the word which shall not be recalled, that unto Me every knee shall bow, and every tongue shall swear (*Isa.* xlv. 23). 9

Remember the former things from eternity: For I am God, and there is no God else (*Isa.* xlvi. 9, 13).

My glory will I not give to another (*Isa.* xlviii. 11).

I am the First, I also am the Last (*Isa.* xlviii. 12).

(The voice of one that crieth in the wilderness, prepare ye the way of Jehovah, make straight in the desert a highway for our God. The glory of Jehovah shall be revealed, and all flesh shall see it together (*Isa.* xl. 3–5).)

(O Zion that tellest good tidings get thee up into the high mountain: O Jerusalem that tellest good tidings, lift up thy voice with strength; lift it up, be not afraid; say unto the cities of Judah, behold your God! Behold the Lord Jehovih cometh in strength, and His arm shall rule for Him: behold His reward is with Him, and the price of His work before Him. He shall feed His flock like a shepherd, He shall gather the lambs into His arm, and carry them in His bosom, He shall gently lead those that give suck (*Isa.* xl. 9–11).)

17. To whom will ye liken Me, to whom am I equal? saith the Holy One. Lift up your eyes on high, and behold, who hath created these things, etc. (*Isa.* xl. 25, 26).

(My judgment is with Jehovah, and the price of My work is with my God. Then shall I be precious in the eyes of Jehovah, and my God shall be my strength. Jehovah hath forsaken me, and the Lord hath forgotten me (*Isa.* xlix. 4, 5, 14). Because of Jehovah that is faithful and the Holy One of Israel who chooseth thee (7).)

I have given Thee for a light to the nations, that Thou mayest be My salvation unto the end of the earth. I have
7 given Thee for a covenant of the people, to restore the earth,
9 to divide the devastated heritages; to say to the prisoners, Go forth; to them that are in darkness, Reveal. They shall feed in the ways, and their pasture shall be on all hillsides; they shall not hunger nor thirst; by the springs of water shall He lead them (*Isa.* xlix. 6, 8–10).

(Let him trust in the name of Jehovah, and stay upon his God (*Isa.* l. 10).)

Look to me ye that follow after justice, ye that seek Jehovah; look unto the rock whence ye are hewn (*Isa.* li. 1).

7 Awake, awake, put on strength, O arm of Jehovah, awake as in the days of old (*Isa.* li. 9).

I will put my words in thy mouth, for the planting of the heavens, and laying the foundations of the earth (*Isa.* li. 16).

(My people shall know My name in that day, for I am He that doth speak: Behold, it is I. How delightful upon the mountains are the feet of Him that bringeth good tidings, that causeth to hear peace, that saith unto Zion, thy King reigneth. Watchmen shall lift up the voice; together shall they sing when they shall see eye to eye, that Jehovah returneth to Zion (*Isa.* lii. 6, 7).

7 Jehovah hath made bare the arm of His holiness in the eyes of all the nations; and all the ends of the earth have seen the salvation of our God (*Isa.* lii. 10).)

7 Who hath believed our word that is heard? and upon whom hath the arm of Jehovah been revealed (*Isa.* liii. 1)?

(The Lord is treated of throughout the chapter, and the state of His life is described here briefly in these words. That He had no form nor honor; that He was despised and not esteemed. That He was wounded on account of our transgressions, and bruised on account of our iniquities. That Jehovah hath made to light on Him the iniquity of us all. That He was brought as a lamb to the slaughter; that He was cut off from the land of the living. That because He offered His soul as a guilt offering His days were prolonged, and that the will of Jehovah prospered by His hand, in the fact that He bore their iniquities, and for them poured out His soul even unto death. That He was numbered with the transgressors, and interceded for the transgressors (*Isa.* liii. 1–12).)

18. Because of Jehovah thy God, and because of the Holy One of Israel (*Isa.* lv. 5).

Let the wicked return to Jehovah, and He will have mercy upon him, and to our God, for He will abundantly pardon (*Isa.* lv. 7).

Jehovah of Hosts is His name; and thy Redeemer the Holy One of Israel; the God of the whole earth shall He be called (*Isa.* liv. 5).

We have transgressed against Jehovah, and have departed from following our God (*Isa.* lix. 13).

They shall bring thy sons from far; silver and gold with them, for the name of Jehovah thy God, and for the Holy One of Israel (*Isa.* lx. 9).

Jehovah shall be to thee for an everlasting light, and thy God for thy glory (*Isa.* lx. 19).

(Ye shall be called priests of Jehovah, ministers of our God (*Isa.* lxi. 6).

In being glad I will be glad in Jehovah, my soul shall exult in my God (*Isa.* lxi. 10).

Arise and shine, for thy light is come, and the glory of Jehovah is risen upon thee. And nations shall walk to thy light, and kings to the brightness of thy rising (*Isa.* lx. 1–3). The Lord is treated of throughout the chapter. See the section on the consummation.

The Spirit of the Lord Jehovih is upon Me, because Jehovah hath anointed Me to tell good tidings to the poor. He hath sent Me to bind up the broken-hearted, to foretell liberty to the captives, and to those in bonds and to the blind; to proclaim the year of good pleasure, and the day of vengeance of God; to console all that mourn (*Isa.* lxi. 1, 2). Throughout that chapter the Lord's advent is treated of.

7 To proclaim the year of the good pleasure of Jehovah and the day of vengeance of our God (*Isa.* lxi. 2).

9 The Lord Jehovih will cause justice and praise to spring forth before all the nations (*Isa.* lxi. 11). Concerning the Lord.

7 Jehovah hath sworn by His right hand, and by the arm of His strength (*Isa.* lxii. 8).

7, 6 Say ye to the daughter of Zion, Behold thy salvation cometh; behold His reward is with Him, and the recompense of His work before Him (*Isa.* lxii. 11).

7 Who is this that cometh from Edom, with sprinkled garments from Bozrah, marching in the multitude of His strength, great to save (*Isa.* lxiii., *seq.*)? Concerning the battle of the Lord against the hells, and of their subjugation and thus the redemption of the faithful; wherefore it is said, the day of vengeance *is* in Mine heart, and the year of My redeemed is come. So He became a Saviour to them. Then the angel of the faces of Jehovah freed them, and He redeemed them (vers. 4, 8, 9).

19. Behold I am as a leader sheep (*dux ovis*) that is brought to the slaughter, saying, Let us destroy the wood in its sap with the fruit thereof, and let us cut it off from the land of the living, that his name may be no more remembered (*Jer.* xi. 19).

6 (Behold, the days come, saith Jehovah, when I will raise up unto David a righteous branch, who shall reign a King, and prosper, and do judgment and justice in the earth; and this is His name which they shall call Him, Jehovah our Justice (*Jer.* xxiii. 5, 6).)

Am I a God at hand and not a God afar off? can any man hide himself in secret places? Do not I fill heaven and earth (*Jer.* xxiii. 23, 24)?

6 (In that day they shall serve Jehovah their God, and David their king, whom I will raise up unto them (*Jer.* xxx. 8, 9).)

The land of Babylon was full of guilt against the Holy One of Israel (*Jer.* li. 5).

Jehovah of Hosts who makes the earth by His power, prepares the world by His wisdom, and stretches out the heavens by His intelligence (*Jer.* li. 15). 7

He is the former of all things, and of the rod of His inheritance: Jehovah of Hosts is His name, by whom He will do judgment upon all (*Jer.* li. 19–23).

20. (The Lord is described as to the Word appearing above the expanse of the cherubim (*Ezek.* i. 26–28), and is called the Lord Jehovih (*Ezek.* ii. 4; iii. 11, 27; iv. 14; v. 7, 8, 11; vi. 3, 11; vii. 2, 5; viii. 1, *seq.*). Then He is called the God of Israel (viii. 4, especially xi. 22, 23).)

I will raise up one shepherd over them, who shall feed them, My servant David. I, Jehovah, will be a God to them, and My servant David a prince in the midst of them. Then will I destroy for them the covenant of peace (*Ezek.* xxxiv. 23–25). 6, 9

My servant David shall be king over them, and they all shall have one shepherd. And I will make a covenant of peace with them; it shall be an everlasting covenant with them, and I will set My sanctuary in the midst of them to eternity. Thus shall My habitation be with them; and I will be God to them, moreover they shall be a people to Me (*Ezek.* xxxvii. 24, 25–28). Throughout the chapter the regeneration of man in the New Church is treated of, for this is meant by the dry bones, and by the two sticks which were one. 9

In that day will I make a covenant with the beast of the field and with the bird of the heavens, and I will break war from the earth, and make them to lie down securely. And I will betroth thee unto Me for ever, and I will betroth thee unto Me in justice and in judgment and in mercy, and I will betroth thee unto Me in faithfulness, and thou shalt know Jehovah. And it shall be in that day that I will hear the heavens, and they shall hear the earth (*Hos.* ii. 18–21). 9

I have consecrated their gain, and their wealth unto the Lord of the whole earth (*Mic.* iv. 13). 7

(Thou, Bethlehem Ephratah, though thou art little among the thousands of Judah, out of thee shall one come forth unto Me, that is to be ruler in Israel; whose goings forth *have been* from of old, from the days of eternity. Then shall he stand and feed in the strength of Jehovah, in the excellency of the 1

name of his God; and they shall abide; for now shall he increase unto the ends of the earth (*Mic.* v. 2–4). He will give
9 them until the time, until the remnant of his brethren shall return unto the sons of Israel (ver. 2). Concerning the New Church (iv. 5, *seq.*).)

21. Art thou not from old, Jehovah, my God, mine Holy One? let us not die. Jehovah, thou hast placed him for judg-
7 ment, and, O Rock, thou hast established him for correction (*Hab.* i. 12).

(The vision is yet for the appointed time; it shall not lie: wait for it, because in coming it will come, nor will it tarry (*Hab.* ii. 3).)

Jehovah, I have heard the report of Thee; I have revered Thy work; make that present in the midst of the years, in the midst of the years make [known]. God shall come out of Teman, and the Holy One from mount Paran. Selah. His
7, 9 honor covered the heavens, and the earth was full of His praise. His brightness will be as the light, rays coming forth from His hand, and there will be the hiding of His strength.
7 Thou wentest forth for the salvation of Thy people. I will be
5-12 glad in Jehovah, I will exult in the God of my salvation. Jehovah Lord is my strength, He will make me to walk upon mine high places (*Hab.* iii. 2–4, 13, 18, 19).

9 (Shout and be glad, O daughter of Zion; for, lo, I come that I may dwell in the midst of thee. Then many nations shall be joined to Jehovah in that day, they shall be to Me for a people, and I will dwell in thee (*Zech.* ii. 10, 11).)

(Exult greatly, O daughter of Zion; shout, O daughter of Jerusalem; behold, thy King cometh unto thee: He is just and saved, lowly, riding upon an ass, and upon the foal of asses. He shall speak peace unto the nations: and His dominion shall be from sea to sea, and from the river even unto the ends of
7 the earth.) Jehovah shall appear over them, and His weapon
14 shall go forth as the lightning, and the Lord Jehovih shall
16 sound with a trumpet, and shall go in the whirlwinds of the south. Jehovah their God shall save them in that day as the flock, His people (*Zech.* ix. 9, 10, 14, 16).

(Behold, I send Mine angel, who shall prepare the way before Me; and the Lord, whom ye seek, shall suddenly come to

His temple), and the messenger of the covenant whom ye seek. 7
Behold, He cometh, saith Jehovah of Hosts. Who may abide
His coming, and who may stand when He appeareth? (*Mal.*
iii. 1, 2.)

Behold, I send you Elijah the prophet before the great and
terrible day of Jehovah come, that he may turn the heart of 7
the fathers to the sons, and the heart of the sons to their
fathers, lest I come and smite the earth with a curse (*Mal.* iii.
23, 24).

22. (I have anointed my king upon Zion, the mountain of my 6
holiness. I will tell of the decree: Jehovah hath said unto me,
This day have I begotten thee. Ask of Me, and I will give
the nations for thine inheritance, and the bounds of the earth
for thy possession. Thou shalt break them with a rod of iron.
Kiss the Son, lest He be angry, and ye perish in the way, for
His anger will burn up quickly. Happy are all they that trust
in Him (*Ps.* ii. 6–12). "His anger will burn up quickly," signifies the Last Judgment from Himself.)

(Thou hast made him to be a little less than the angels, and
hast crowned him with glory and honor. Thou madest him to
have dominion over the works of Thy hands; Thou hast put
all things under his feet (*Ps.* viii. 5, 6, 7).)

(The rulers take counsel together against Jehovah and His
Christ. I have anointed my king over Zion. I will tell of
the decree: Jehovah hath said unto Me, Thou art My Son, this
day have I begotten thee. Ask of Me, and I will give the nations for Thine inheritance, and the bounds of the earth for
Thy possession. Kiss the Son, lest He be angry, and ye perish in the way, for His anger will burn up quickly. Blessed
are all they that trust in Him (*Ps.* ii. 2, 6, 7, 8, 12).)

(Jehovah, Thou hast made him to be a little less than
the angels, and hast crowned him with glory and honor.
Thou hast made him to have dominion over the works of Thy
hands; Thou hast put all things under his feet, etc. (*Ps.* viii.
6, 7 *seq.*).)

Lift up your heads, O gate, and be ye lift up, ye doors of 8
the world, that the King of glory may come in. Who is this 9
King of glory? Jehovah strong and mighty, Jehovah mighty
in battle (*Ps.* xxiv. 7–10).

23. Gird thy sword upon thy thigh, O mighty one, in thy glory and thine honor. In thine honor mount, ride upon the word of truth and of meekness and justice; thy right hand shall teach thee wonderful things. Thy weapons are sharp; the 7 people shall fall under thee, enemies of the King from their heart. Thy throne, O God, is for ever and ever, the sceptre of thine equity is the sceptre of thy kingdom. Thou hast loved justice, and held wickedness in hatred: therefore, O God, thy God hath anointed thee with the oil of gladness, all thy garments *smell* of myrrh and cassia. Kings' daughters were among thy precious ones; upon thy right hand did stand the queen in gold of Ophir. Then shall the king delight in thy beauty: for he is thy Lord. Therefore shall the people confess thee for ever and to eternity (*Ps.* xlv. 3 to end), where there are many additional statements.

(He shall have dominion from sea to sea, and from the river unto the ends of the earth. All kings shall bow down before Him, all nations shall serve Him, His Name shall be for ever, before the sun He shall have the name of Son; and all nations shall be blessed in Him, they shall call Him happy (*Ps.* lxxii. 8, 11, 17). Blessed be Jehovah God, the God of Israel, who doeth wonderful things, and blessed be His glorious name to eternity; and the whole earth shall be filled with His glory; Amen and Amen (vers. 18, 19).)

(I have made a covenant with My chosen, I have sworn unto 6 David My servant, thy seed will I establish to eternity and build up thy throne to generation and generation (*Ps.* lxxxix. 4–6).)

(Thou hast spoken in vision of thy holy one, and hast said, I have laid help upon the powerful one, I have exalted the chosen one, with whom my hand shall be established. I will set his hand in the sea, his right hand in the rivers. He shall call unto Me, Thou art my father. Also I will make him the first-born, his seed will I set for ever, and his throne as the days of the heavens. And his throne as the sun before Me, as the moon established to eternity, a faithful witness in the clouds (*Ps.* lxxxix. 19–38). These things are said of David, by whom the Lord is meant, for these things cannot refer to David, and of him it is said, In vision of thy holy one.)

(Sing unto Jehovah a new song; His right hand and the arm of His holiness hath made Him safe. Jehovah hath made known His salvation, His justice hath He revealed before the eyes of the nations. All the ends of the earth have seen the salvation of our God. Make a noise to Jehovah, all the earth; sound forth, shout and sing. For He cometh to judge the earth. He will judge the world in justice and the peoples with equity (*Ps.* xcviii. 1–9).)

(Jehovah said to my Lord, Sit Thou at My right hand, until I make Thine enemies Thy footstool. Jehovah shall send the sceptre of Thy strength out of Zion. Thou art a priest to eternity after the manner of Melchizedek (*Ps.* cx. 1, 2, 4).)

(David swore unto Jehovah, he vowed unto the mighty one of Jacob, I will not come into the tent of my house or go up upon my bed; I will not give sleep to mine eyes, until I find a place for Jehovah, a habitation for the mighty one of Jacob. 6 Lo, we heard of Him at Ephrathah. We will go into His habitation, we will bow down at His footstool. Arise, Jehovah, to Thy rest, Thou and the ark of Thy strength (*Ps.* cxxxii. 1–9).)

The Father loveth the Son, and hath given all things into His hand (*John* iii. 35).

I and the Father are one (*John* x. 30).

He that hath seen Me hath seen the Father   I am in the Father, and the Father in Me (*John* xiv. 6–17).

III. GOD, THE FATHER AND HOLY SPIRIT.

1. After Jesus gave commandment unto the disciples through the Holy Spirit (*Acts* i. 2).

Jesus said to the disciples that they should wait for the promise of the Father, which ye have heard of Me (*Acts* i. 4).

Then he said, ye shall receive the power of the Holy Spirit upon you (*Acts* i. 8).

A sound was heard as of a wind and there were seen cloven tongues like as of fire upon every apostle, and they were filled with the Holy Spirit, and they began to speak with other tongues as the Holy Spirit gave them utterance. Each one heard them speak with him in his own dialect; they spoke of the wonderful works of God, and Peter quoted to them from *Joel* ii. 1 to end (*Acts* ii. 1–18).

2. The Spirit of the Lord (*Acts* v. 9) is called the Holy Spirit (ver. 3).

They received the Holy Spirit by the laying on of the hands by the apostles (*Acts* viii. 17, 18; ix. 17).

The Holy Spirit spake. And they were sent out by the Holy Spirit (*Acts* xiii. 2–4).

Paul said to the Athenians, God giveth to everyone life, the spirit and all things. In Him we live and move and have our being (*Acts* xvii. 25, 28).

The invisible things of God from the creation of the world are clearly seen, understood by works, and His eternal power; so that they are without excuse (*Rom.* i. 20).

If any one hath not the Spirit of Christ he is none of His. He quickens your mortal bodies through the Spirit that dwelleth in you. The Spirit itself beareth witness with our spirit, that we are the sons of God (*Rom.* viii. 9–11, 14, 16).

What man hath known the things of a man, save the spirit of man which is in him? Even so the things of God knoweth no one, but the Spirit of God. The animal man receiveth not the things of the Spirit of God, for they are foolishness unto him, and he cannot know them (1 *Cor.* ii. 11, 14).

There are various gifts of the Spirit which are enumerated (1 *Cor.* xii. 7–21).

The Lord is the Spirit. Where the Spirit of the Lord is, there is liberty (2 *Cor.* iii. 17).

Because ye are sons, God sent forth the Spirit of His Son into your hearts, crying Abba, Father (*Gal.* iv. 6).

The ministration of the Spirit of Jesus Christ (*Phil.* i. 19; *Col.* i. 2; *Gal.* i. 3).

The Lord be with his spirit (2 *Tim.* iv. 22).

The Spirit of Christ, which testified (1 *Pet.* i. 11).

There are three that bear witness in heaven, the Father, the Word, and the Holy Spirit: and these three are one (1 *John* v. 7).

The Spirit is truth (1 *John* v. 6).

The Spirit of My Father speaketh in you (*Matt.* x. 20).

Jesus baptizeth you with the Holy Spirit (*Mark* i. 8).

It is not ye that speak, but the Holy Spirit (*Mark* xiii. 11).

John the Baptist was filled with the Holy Spirit in the womb of his mother (*Luke* i. 15, 41).

Jesus said, he that receiveth Me receiveth Him that sent Me (*Luke* ix. 48).

He spake this of the Spirit, which they that believe on Him should receive; the Holy Spirit was not yet; because Jesus was not yet glorified (*John* vii. 39).

The Holy Spirit is called the Spirit of truth (*John* xiv. 17). He is also called the Comforter, and Holy Spirit, whom the Father will send in My name (*John* xiv. 26).

If I went not away, the Comforter would not come unto you; if I go away I will send him unto you (*John* xvi. 7). By going away to the Father is meant to be united to the Father, as before, the Divine truth to the Divine. That the Spirit of truth from the Lord is about to receive, etc. (*John* xvi. 13–15).

From the Prophets.

3. (The Spirit of Jehovah breathed into it. Who hath directed the Spirit of Jehovah (*Isa.* xl. 7–13)?)

(It may perhaps be related concerning a divided Trinity, that this is taken from hell, "Divide and command." Are not all heresies concerning God from thence? It is otherwise if you conjoin the Trinity in one Person.)

(The words that Jehovah of Hosts sent in His spirit by the hand of the prophets (*Zech.* vii. 12).)

(Who is God save Jehovah? or who is a rock save our God? Jehovah liveth; blessed be my Rock; let the God of my salvation be exalted (*Ps.* xviii. 32, 47).)

(Jehovah answer thee, the name of the God of Jacob exalt thee (*Ps.* xx. 1).)

(Rulers take counsel together against Jehovah and His Christ (*Ps.* ii. 2).)

Arise, Jehovah; save me, O my God (*Ps.* iii. 7).

Who is God save Jehovah? and who is a rock save our God? (*Ps.* xviii. 31.)

Jehovah liveth; and blessed be my rock; and the God of my salvation shall be exalted (*Ps.* xviii. 47).

Jehovah answer thee in the day of trouble; the name of the God of Jacob exalt thee (*Ps.* xx. 2).

We will sing in thy salvation, and in the name of our God we will set up banners: Jehovah will fulfil all thy petitions (*Ps.* xx. 5).

He shall receive a blessing from Jehovah, and justice from the God of our salvation (*Ps.* xxiv. 5).

Jehovah of Hosts is with us; the God of Jacob is our refuge (*Ps.* xlvi. 12).

They tempted God, and censured the Holy One of Israel (*Ps.* lxxviii. 41).

Jehovah of Hosts, hear my prayers. Give ear, O God of Jacob (*Ps.* lxxxiv. 9).

Jehovah and the Holy One of Israel (*Ps.* lxxxix. 19).

(Jehovah and the mighty One of Jacob (*Ps.* cxxxii. 2, 5). Jehovah shall reign to eternity, thy God, O Zion, to generation and generation (*Ps.* cxlvi. 10).)

(Praise Jehovah, O Jerusalem; praise thy God, O Zion (*Ps.* cxlvii. 12).)

IV. THE COMING OF THE LORD.

THE CONSUMMATION. THE NEW CHURCH. CHRIST AND THE JUDGMENT.

5, 6 **1.** The sun shall be turned into darkness, and the moon into blood, before the great and notable day of the Lord come: and it shall come to pass that every one who shall call on the name of the Lord shall be saved (*Acts* ii. 19–21).

5, 9, 6 Ye, waiting for the revelation of our Lord Jesus Christ: Who shall confirm you even to the end, unreprovable in the day of our Lord Jesus Christ (1 *Cor.* i. 7, 8).

5, 6 When the fulness of time was come, God sent forth His Son, made of a woman, made under the law (*Gal.* iv. 4).

6, 7, 8 In the dispensation of the fulness of the times, that He might restore all things in Him both those which are in the heavens, and those which are on earth (*Ephes.* i. 10, 11, 13).

Until the day of Jesus Christ (*Phil.* i. 6, 10; ii. 26). 6
When Christ shall be manifested (*Col.* iii. 4). 6
In the presence of our Lord Jesus Christ at His coming 6
(1 *Thess.* ii. 19).
May he confirm your hearts at the coming of our Lord Jesus 6
Christ (1 *Thess.* iii. 13).
We shall be kept safe in the coming of the Lord. What 6
that coming will be, is described (1 *Thess.* iv. 15–17).
That day will come as a thief, etc. (1 *Thess.* v. 2–4). 6
That they may be unreprovable at the coming of our Lord 6
Jesus Christ (1 *Thess.* v. 23).
In the revelation of the Lord Jesus from heaven with angels, 6
and in a flame of fire (2 *Thess.* i. 7–10).
Concerning the coming of the Lord and the day; but 6
there will be a falling away first; but then shall iniquity 7
be revealed; His coming will be directly after the working
of Satan with signs and lying wonders. See generally (2
Thess. ii. 1–11). 9, 10
That in the last times they shall depart from the faith, giv- 4
ing heed to seducing spirits, hypocrisy, etc. (1 *Tim.* iv. 1, 2).
Be thou then blameless until the appearing of the Lord 6
Jesus Christ (1 *Tim.* vi. 14, 15).
That day (2 *Tim.* i. 12; iv. 8). 6
In the last days perilous times shall come; the covetous 5
boasters, blasphemers (2 *Tim.* iii. 1–6).
Jesus Christ shall judge the living and the dead at His ap- 7
pearing (2 *Tim.* iv. 1, 8).
Looking for the appearing of Jesus Christ (*Titus* ii. 13). 6
2. Be ye patient until the coming of the Lord: the coming 6
of the Lord is near (*James* v. 7, 8).
That we may be kept through faith unto salvation and glory, 6
in the last time, at the revelation of Jesus Christ (1 *Peter* i.
5, 7, 13).
The day of visitation (1 *Peter* ii. 12). 7
That ye may rejoice in the revelation of His glory (1 *Peter* 6
iv. 13).
I who *am* a partaker of the future revelation. When the 6 *seq.*
chief of the shepherds shall appear ye shall obtain a crown of
glory (1 *Peter* v. 1, 4).

6   That there shall come in the last of the days, scoffers, who will walk after their own lusts, and who will say, Where is the promise of His coming? etc. (2 *Peter* iii. 3, 4).

7   The heavens and the earth that now are, reserved unto fire in the day of judgment and perdition of the ungodly (2 *Peter* iii. 7).

6   The day of the Lord will come as a thief in the night: in which the heavens and the earth shall pass away; looking for and hastening the coming of the day of God, wherein the

8, 9 heavens, kindled with fire, shall be dissolved; nevertheless, we, according to His promise, look for new heavens and a new earth, wherein justice shall dwell (2 *Peter* iii. 10–14).

(*N.B.*—By "the fire" by which the world is to perish is meant wickedness; by the "world" is meant the church; by an "age" the period of the church, and by a "week" the state of the church. These things are confirmed by the angels of heaven.)

6   A thousand years with the Lord are as one day (2 *Peter* iii. 8; *Ps.* xc. 4).

5   **3.** Antichrist shall come in the last hour (1 *John* ii. 18).

6   We may not be ashamed of His coming, when He shall be manifested (1 *John* ii. 28; iii. 2).

7   The Lord cometh with ten thousands of saints to execute judgment upon all the ungodly, etc. (*Jude* 14, 15).

5   In the last time there will be mockers, etc. (*Jude* 18, 19).

6   Behold, He cometh with clouds, and every eye shall see Him, and all the tribes of the earth shall wail because of Him (*Rev.* i. 7).

6   He is, who is, and who was, and who is to come, the Almighty (*Rev.* i. 8).

6   Concerning the coming of the Lord, see *Acts* i. 4, 11; iii. 20, 21; xv. 16, 17; *Amos* ix. 11. Especially *Luke* xii. 35–48.

See above, passages concerning Christ.

6, 9 **4.** He who was and is to come, the Alpha and Omega, etc. (*Rev.* i. 4, 8, 11; ii. 8; iv. 8; xi. 17; xxi. 6; xxii. 13).

6   Behold He cometh with clouds, and all flesh shall see, etc. (*Rev.* i. 7).

6   That He will come as a thief (*Rev.* iii. 3).

6, 7 I will keep thee from the hour of temptation which shall come upon the whole world (*Rev.* iii. 10).

Behold I come quickly (*Rev.* iii. 11; ii. 5).

THE COMING OF THE LORD

He was dead, and yet alive unto the ages of ages (*Rev.* i. 18). 9
The Lamb standing, as it were slain (*Rev.* v. 6, 12).

The consummation in general is described by the four horses 1–5
going out from the Book, also by the souls seen of those who
had been slain for the Word of God, and by the great earthquake, and by heaven departing, and by the ungodly hiding
themselves in caves (*Rev.* vi. 1 to end).

Then the fulness of time is described, by the brethren who 5
should also be killed (*Rev.* vi. 11).

Because the great day of His wrath is come (*Rev.* vi. 17); 6, 8
also that the stars have fallen, and the heaven has departed
(*Rev.* vi. 13, 14).

The consummation in particular is described by various 5
things, and finally by locusts from the abyss (*Rev.* viii. and ix.).

The heresies in the last times are described by various things 4
(*Rev.* ix. 17–23).

That there shall be time no longer (*Rev.* x. 6). 5

There were voices from heaven, that the kingdoms are become 6
our Lord's and His Christ's; and He shall reign for ages of ages;
Thou hast taken Thy great power (*Rev.* xi. 15–17; xii. 10). 8, 9

The time is come for the judging of the dead (*Rev.* xi. 18). 7

The consummation is described by the dragon that wished
to devour the fœtus, and drew the third part of the stars from 5
heaven, also by the war between him and Michael, and that he
persecuted the woman and wished to destroy her with waters
(*Rev.* xii. 1 to end).

The earth was reaped, and the vintage or the vine was gathered (*Rev.* xiv. 15–19). 5

The last consummation is described by the seven plagues 5
sent down by the angels to the earth (*Rev.* xvi. 1 to end).

Behold, I come as a thief. Happy is he that watcheth, and 6
keepeth his garments, lest he walk naked (*Rev.* xvi. 15).

The battle of the great day of God Almighty (*Rev.* xvi. 14). 6

The invitation of all to the supper of the great God (*Rev.*
xix. 17, 18).

They cried Alleluia; for the Lord God omnipotent reigneth,
for the time of the marriage of the Lamb is come; and His 2
wife hath made herself ready; happy are they that are called
unto the marriage supper of the Lamb, etc. (*Rev.* xix. 6–9).

5   Smitten for the testimony of Jesus, and for the Word of God (*Rev.* xx. 4).

8, 9   They shall be priests of God and of Christ, and shall reign with Him a thousand years (*Rev.* xx. 6).

8, 9   A new heaven and a new earth; and the first heaven and the first earth were passed away (*Rev.* xxi. 1; *Isa.* lxvi. 22; *Ps.* cii. 26, 27).

9   Jerusalem descending from heaven prepared as a bride adorned for her husband: and the angel showed her as the bride, the Lamb's wife (*Rev.* xxi. 2, 9, 10).

9   Behold the tabernacle of God is with men, and He will dwell with them (*Rev.* xxi. 3). Behold He will make all things new (*Rev.* xxi. 5).

9   There shall not enter into the New Jerusalem any but they who are written in the Lamb's book of life (*Rev.* xxi. 26).

6   He would come quickly; and it is desired that He come (*Rev.* xxii. 7, 12, especially 16, 17).

7   **5.** John the Baptist said, Who hath warned you to flee from the wrath to come? (*Matt.* iii. 7.)

5   In the parable of the tares of the field, the Lord said, So shall it be in the consummation of the age; the reapers are the angels (*Matt.* xiii. 25–30, 37–43).

5   They gathered the good into vessels and cast out the evil; so shall it be in the consummation of the age (*Matt.* xiii. 47–50).

6   The Son of man shall sit upon the throne of His glory (*Matt.* xix. 28).

6, 7   David called the Messiah "Lord," Sit Thou on My right hand, till I make Thine enemies Thy footstool (*Matt.* xxii. 40–44; *Ps.* cx. 1; *Luke* xx. 41–44).

6, 7   Concerning the coming of the Lord and the consummation of the age (*Matt.* xxiv. 1 to end).

4   False Christs and false prophets shall arise; there shall be wars and rumors of wars, etc. (*Matt.* xxiv. 5–14, 23–25, 28). This signifies heresies in the early times.

4, 5   When ye shall see the abomination of desolation foretold by Daniel the prophet (*Matt.* xxiv. 15, 16, *seq.*).

5   There shall be affliction, such as was not from the beginning of the world (*Matt.* xxiv. 21).

Except those days should be shortened no flesh would be 5, 10
saved (*Matt.* xxiv. 22).

As the lightning cometh out of the east, so shall the coming 6
of the Son of man be (*Matt.* xxiv. 27). Thus was the Last
Judgment.

The sun shall be darkened, the moon shall not give [her 4
light], and the stars shall fall from heaven (*Matt.* xxiv. 29).

Then they shall see the Son of man coming in the clouds of 6
heaven, and He shall send the angels with the voice of a
trumpet (*Matt.* xxiv. 30, 31).

Of that hour My Father alone knoweth (*Matt.* xxiv. 36). 6

As the days of Noe, so shall the coming of the Son of man 6
be (*Matt.* xxiv. 37, 38).

So shall also the coming of the Son of man be (*Matt.* xxiv. 39). 6

Watch therefore, for ye know not what hour your Lord will 6
come, thus that it is not known in what hour the thief will
come; wherefore be ye ready; for in such an hour as ye think
not the Son of man will come (*Matt.* xxiv. 42–44).

Blessed is the servant whom the Lord shall find so doing. 6
But if the servant say in his heart, My Lord delayeth His
coming (*Matt.* xxiv. 46, 48).

The Lord of the servant shall come in an hour that he 6
knoweth not (*Matt.* xxiv. 50).

The parable of the ten virgins also describes the coming of
the Lord, and the state of heaven; that it is shut to those who 6, 7
have no oil, that is, charity, for it is said also there, Watch,
for ye know neither the day nor the hour wherein the Son of
man will come (*Matt.* xxv. 1–13).

The parable of the talents given to the servants also signifies
the coming of the Lord, and that every one shall return a 6 *seq.*
reckoning, for it is written (ver. 19): After a long time the
Lord cometh and reckoneth with them (*Matt.* xxv. 14–30).

So also the parable of the sheep and the goats (*Matt.* xxv. 6 *seq.*
31–46), for He says, When the Son of man shall come in the
glory of His Father (ver. 31).

Jesus said to the disciples, Behold I am with you all the 5
days even unto the consummation of the age (*Matt.* xxviii. 20).

6. Jesus said, concerning the temple, that there should not
be left a stone upon a stone, and the four disciples ask Jesus 6, 7

when it will be that all these things shall be fulfilled (*Mark* xiii. 1–4).

4 There would be wars and rumors, nation against nation; earthquakes (*Mark* xiii. 7, 8); these things signify heresies and schisms.

6 When ye shall see the abomination, the desolation foretold by Daniel the prophet, standing in the holy place (*Mark* xiii. 14).

5 Those shall be days of affliction, such as were not from the beginning of creation (*Mark* xiii. 19).

So that except the Lord had shortened those days, no flesh would be saved (ver. 20).

4 False Christs and false prophets arise, who will give signs (*Mark* xiii. 21–23).

4 The sun shall be darkened, the moon shall not give her light, and the stars shall fall from heaven (*Mark* xiii. 24, 25).

6 And then they shall see the Son of man coming in the clouds of heaven with much power and glory, who shall then send His angels, and shall gather together His elect (*Mark* xiii. 26, 27).

7 *seq.* Heaven and earth shall pass away; My words shall not pass away (*Mark* xiii. 31; *Matt.* xxiv. 35).

6 *seq.* Watch and pray; ye know not when the time shall be (*Mark* xiii. 33). For ye do not know when the lord of the house will come, at even, or at midnight, or at the cock-crowing, or in the morning (vers. 35–37).

7. Ye are like those who are waiting for the Lord, when He will return from the wedding, Blessed are the servants whom the Lord when He cometh findeth watching, whether He
6 cometh in the second watch, or in the third. Be ye ready, for the Son of man shall come in an hour when ye think not. If the servant say, The Lord delayeth His coming, He will come like a thief, etc. (*Luke* xii. 36–46).

Behold [your house] will be left unto you desolate. Ye
6 shall not see Me until [the time] come when ye shall say, Blessed is He that cometh in the name of the Lord (*Luke* xiii. 35).

The days will come when ye shall desire one day of the Son
6 of man, and ye shall not see, for as the lightning, so shall the Son of man be in His day. It shall be as it was in the days

of Noe and in the days of Lot. Even thus shall it be when
the Son of man shall be revealed (*Luke* xvii. 22–30).

That day is called night (*Luke* xvii. 34). 5

Remember Lot's wife, who looked back to Sodom (*Luke*
xvii. 32).

When the Son of man cometh, shall He find faith on the 6
earth (*Luke* xviii. 8)?

This is the stone which the builders rejected (*Luke* xx.
17, 18).

There shall not be left a stone upon a stone of the temple 5
(*Luke* xxi. 5, 6).

That there will be wars, rumors, earthquakes (*Luke* xxi. 4
9–11).

The powers of the heavens shall be shaken, and then shall 6
they see the Son of man coming in the clouds of heaven
(*Luke* xxi. 26, 27).

Take heed to yourselves lest that day come upon you suddenly, for as a snare it shall come upon all, therefore watch 6
ye all to stand before the Son of man (*Luke* xxi. 34–36).

8. The night shall come when no man shall be able to work 4
(*John* ix. 4).

In that day ye shall know that I am in My Father, and ye 2
in Me and I in you (*John* xiv. 20).

Christ said to Peter, When thou shalt be old, thou shalt 4
stretch forth thy hands, and another shall gird thee and lead
thee whither thou wouldst not (*John* xxi. 18).

Jesus said concerning John, If I will that he tarry till I 6
come, what is that to thee, Peter?—twice—(*John* xxi. 22, 23).

From the Old Testament.

9. God hath revealed what shall come to pass in the latter 5
days (*Dan.* ii. 28).

(The consummation of the church from its first foundation
to its end is described by the image seen by Nebuchadnezzar,
in like manner as the four ages by the ancients; the first,
which was before the flood, by gold; the second, after the flood,
by silver; the third, which was the Israelitish up to that time,
by brass; and the fourth, which was the Christian, by iron
mixed with clay (*Dan.* ii. 32, 33).

By "gold" is signified celestial good; by "silver" spiritual truth; by "brass" natural good; by "iron" natural truth; and by "iron mixed with clay" truth falsified, because it does not cleave together; by the seed of man the truth of the Word, which is also said of the feet of iron (*Dan.* ii. 34–43).)

(A stone which was not [made] by hands, which smote and ground up the image, and which became a great rock, signifies the Lord, who in the Word is meant by "a stone" and by "the rock" which filled all the earth, whose kingdom shall stand for ages of ages (*Dan.* ii. 34, 35, 44, 45).)

The fourth, seen in the furnace of fire, is said to be like the Son of man. It is not said man, because the Son of man signifies the Lord as to the Word; and this is also called an angel, whom God sent (*Dan.* iii. 25, 28).

The "Son of man" when said of another, and a "prophet," signify Him as the truth of the church from the Word.

2–9 The consummation is also described by the tree growing to the end of the earth seen by Nebuchadnezzar, in a dream; and the coming of the Lord, by the Watcher and the Holy One who descended and commanded to hew down the tree utterly; and that they left the stump of the roots in the earth in a band of iron and of brass, signifies the Word by which the church revived; this also happened in the time of Nebuchadnezzar (*Dan.* iv. 10–13, 17–31).

The consummation of the whole, or the destruction of all things of the church is described by the feast of Belshazzar in which with magnates and concubines he drinks the wine out of vessels of gold and silver from the temple of Jerusalem, and praised the gods of gold, of silver, etc., by which is signified the profanation of the holy things of the church, wherefore it was written on the wall that his kingdom was finished, and he was slain on that night (*Dan.* v. 1 to end).

(The consummation of the church is described by the four beasts out of the sea; also what the first was, what the second, third and fourth, which was terrible because it brake in pieces all things of good and truth. What they signify may be seen in *The Apocalypse Revealed*, n. 574. The complete consummation is meant by the slaying of the beast and the destruction of the body. That then the Lord will come and will reign unto ages of ages is evident from verses 13, 14, 22, 27. His church is meant by the holy people, because they are in Divine truths from the Lord (*Dan.* vii. 1 to end).)

10. The vastation of the good of charity by the falsities of faith is described by the ram and by the he-goat of the goats, by the former of which the good of charity is described (viii. 4), but that it was thrown down by the he-goat, wherefore it is said that he will cast the truth to the earth, and also take away the continual sacrifice and the habitation of the sanctuary (vers. 11, 12); that he will rise against the prince of the army and the princes, that is, against the Lord (vers. 10, 25); and that he destroys the holy people, that is, the church (vers. 24, 25) (*Dan.* viii. 1–end). 4, 5

That this prophecy treats of the Christian Church is clear, for it is said, that *at the time of the end shall be the vision.* That *it would take place in the end of his anger*, because *the vision was for many days* (vers. 17, 19, 26); and that it was the vision of the evening and the morning (*Dan.* viii. 1–end). 4, 5

In the ninth chapter the future state of the Christian Church is especially treated of, which the Lord the Saviour revealed to him; He Himself is there meant by the Lord God (vers. 3, 4, 7–9, 15–19): also by the Lord (*Ps.* cx. 1), and elsewhere; but by Jehovah God is meant God the Father (*Dan.* ix. 2, 13, 14, 20). 6

By "the destructions of Jerusalem" (*Dan.* ix. 2) is meant the devastation of the church in general; and afterwards by it (vers. 25–27) is meant the devastation of the Christian Church, as is clearly evident from the Lord's words (*Matt.* xxiv. 15). 4, 5

In verse 25, it treats of the first state of the Christian Church, while it was called Apostolic, thus until the Council of Nice, which was then in straitness of times on account of the heresies of that time. In verse 26 it treats of the second state of that church which was when the Papal power prevailed, in which all the Divine power of the Lord was transferred to the Pope; and the Word was almost buried, and with it all knowledge of the Lord, and all knowledge of the truth. This is meant by the Messiah or Christ being slain. It treats of the third state of that church which is called the Refor- 4, 5 mation in verse 27. In it the worship of the Lord ceased, because they departed from Him to three Gods from eternity, and thus relapsed into mere falsities, so that not one spiritual truth remains. Therefore it is there called the bird of abominations, desolation, consummation, destruction, and devastation (ver. 27); and by the Lord the abomination of desolation foretold by Daniel the prophet (*Matt.* xxiv. 15).

In the end of the days, for yet the vision is for days (*Dan.* x. 14).

4, 5 *For yet the end shall be at the time appointed* (*Dan.* xi. 27, 35, 45).

Seal the book until the time of the end (*Dan.* xii. 4, 9, 13).

8, 9 Michael shall rise up, but it shall be a time of trouble such as was not since there was a nation even unto this time; at that time thy people shall be delivered, every one that shall be found written in the book (*Dan.* xii. 1).

8, 9 The intelligent shall shine as the stars (*Dan.* xii. 3).

4, 5 At the appointed time of the stated times and the half time, all these things were to be consummated; and this is called the abomination that devastateth (*Dan.* xii. 7, 11).

These things have reference to the end of the Christian Church is evident from similar things which are said in
5 *Matthew* and in the *Apocalypse* (*Matt.* xii. 1, 2, 7, 10–12), besides other places; and that they are sealed until the time of the end.

11. (The solitude of Jerusalem is described in direful terms, that to the sole of the foot there is no soundness (*Isa.* i. 6–9).

(The worship of these things is vanity unless you have cleansed yourselves from evil (*Isa.* i. 11–18).)

9 The restoration of all things by the redemption, and then the salvation of the faithful and the condemnation of the unfaithful, is described (*Isa.* i. 25–31).

9 And it shall come to pass *in the last of the days* that the mountain of Jehovah shall be established because the Word of Jehovah shall be from Jerusalem (*Isa.* ii. 2–6). It treats of the restoration of all things through the New Church.

6, 8, 9 Jehovah alone shall be exalted in that day (*Isa.* ii. 11, 17).
7, 8 The restoration of all things through the New Church, which there is Jerusalem, where every one is written unto life; and it

is said, *In that day shall the branch of Jehovah* be for beauty and glory (*Isa.* iv. 1–end).

(That He would destroy the vine, because it did not bring forth grapes, but wild grapes; I will bring it to *desolation*, the house to *devastation*; because they regard not the work of Jehovah (*Isa.* v. 3–15).)

A curse upon them, because they call good evil and evil good, 7 and put darkness for light and light for darkness, since they have rejected the law of Jehovah, and despised the saying of the *Holy* One of Israel. He shall roar against him *in that day* like the roaring of the sea; and if *one* look unto the land, behold darkness, anxiety, and the light shall be darkened in the ruins thereof (*Isa.* v. 18–30).

That the Lord will appear in the Word; the Lord is meant 1 by "Adonai," and by "holy, holy, holy Jehovah of hosts," by "the Seraphim from above him" (*Isa.* vi. 1–8).

(Devastation is next treated of because they do not wish to understand the truth; that the cities therefore will be devastated, and the land will be brought back to solitude (*Isa.* vi. 9–13).)

(In that day Jehovah shall hiss for the fly that is in the uttermost part of the rivers of Egypt, and for the bee that is in the land of Assyria; and they shall come and shall rest in the *rivers of desolation* (*Isa.* vii. 18, 19).)

In that day shall the Lord shave the head and the hair of 7 Assyria; He shall also consume the beard (*Isa.* vii, 20). *The consummation.*

(In that day every place shall be for the brier and the thorn 7 (*Isa.* vii. 23, 24). *The consummation.*)

(What will ye do in the day of *visitation* and of *devastation* which shall come from far? to whom will ye flee for help? The devastation there is described by the pride of their own intelligence (*Isa.* x. 3–19), further (23–34). And it is said that Jehovah makes a *consummation* and decision in the whole earth (ver. 23).)

Howl ye; for *the day of Jehovah is at hand*, it will come as a devastation from Shaddai. Behold *the day of Jehovah com-* 7 *eth, cruel with indignation and with wrath* to lay thy land waste; and He shall destroy the sinners thereof out of it.

6 For the stars of the heavens and their constellations shine not with their light, the sun is darkened at his rising, and the moon shall not cause her light to shine (*Isa.* xiii. 6–10). Therefore I will shake heaven, and the earth will tremble in the *indignation* of Jehovah of Hosts, in the day of the wrath of anger (xiii. 13). There it treats of the vastation of Babylon.

12. Concerning the vastation of Babylon (*Isa.* xiv. 1–28),
4 which is there meant by Lucifer, and concerning the vastation of those who are meant by the dragon (xv. 2), who are there Philistia (vers. 29–32).

In that day shall the glory of Jacob be made thin, and gleaning grapes shall be left in it, as in the shaking of an olive tree (*Isa.* xvii. 4–6). In that day shall there be wasteness because thou hast forgotten the God of thy salvation. At eventide behold terror, and before the morning he is not (vers. 9–14).

(Calling to me out of Seir, Watchman, what of the night? Watchman, what of the night? The watchman said, The morning cometh and also the night (*Isa.* xxi. 11, 12).)

(Labor not to console Me, because of the *laying waste* of the daughter of My people. For it is a *day of tumult* and of treading down and of perplexity by the Lord Jehovih of hosts (*Isa.* xxii. 4–14).)

On the other hand *it shall come to pass in that day:* I will lay the key of the house of David upon His shoulder, and He shall open and none shall shut, and shut and none shall open (*Isa.* xxii. 20–24).

6 In this place, the coming of the Lord, after vastation, is
4 treated of. *In that day* the nail that is fastened in the sure place shall give way (verse 25); of the repeated vastation which is of the Christian Church.

(*In that day* shall the Lord Jehovih of Hosts call to weeping, and to mourning, and baldness (ver. 12), of the vastation (vers. 4–14). There the Lord is meant by the Lord Jehovih of Hosts.)

Howl, ye ships of Tarshish, for Tyre is devastated so that
4 there is no house. *It shall come to pass in that day* that Tyre shall be given over to oblivion for seventy years (*Isa.* xxiii. 1–

16). There the vastation of the church through no understanding of the Word is treated of. It shall be at the end of seventy years that Jehovah shall visit Tyre, that she may commit whoredom with all the kingdoms of the earth (ver. 17); of the repeated vastation of the church, which, after the Jewish Church, is Christian.

At length, her merchandise shall be holiness to Jehovah and her merchandise for them that dwell before Jehovah to eat to satiety (ver. 18). Concerning the coming of the Lord, and that there is then understanding of the Word. 9 6

13. Behold, Jehovah *making the earth void, and making it empty.* In the city is left wasteness and the gate will be crushed even to devastation (*Isa.* xxiv. 1–13). Of the full vastation of truth in the church, and in all its doctrine. A "city" is doctrine. Then follows the appearance of Jehovah, that is the coming of the Lord (vers. 14, 15). Concerning a second vastation which will be that of the Christian Church (vers. 16–20). After many days, however, Jehovah of Hosts shall reign in mount Zion and in Jerusalem (vers. 21–23). This is the second coming of the Lord, "mount Zion" is there the church as to the good of love, and "Jerusalem" is the church as to the truth of doctrine, as also in the *Apocalypse.* 6 8, 9

Jehovah of Hosts will make in this mountain unto all people a feast of fat things, a feast of wine on the lees, of fat things full of marrow, of wines on the lees well refined: and He will swallow up the face of the covering, the covering over all the peoples, and the veil that is spread over all the nations. He will swallow up death for ever (*Isa.* xxv. 6–8). Concerning the New Church, and its purity after the desolation. The coming of the Lord is described (ver. 9). 9

In that day shall this song be sung, salvation will He appoint for walls and bulwarks. Open ye the gates, that the just nation which keepeth faithfulness may enter in (*Isa.* xxvi. 1, 2). The coming of the Lord to the New Church. 9

Come, my people, enter thou into thy chambers and shut the door after thee; hide thyself as for a little moment until the anger be overpast. For, behold Jehovah cometh forth out of His place to visit the iniquity of the inhabitant of the earth: then the earths shall reveal her bloods and shall no more 7 cover her slain (vers. 20, 21). Concerning the coming of the Lord for the Last Judgment, after the desolation.

14. (We have conceived, we have been in travail, we have as it were brought forth wind; we have not wrought salvation in the earth (*Isa.* xxvi. 18). Desolation, and then mere falsities.)

In that day Jehovah with His hard and great and strong sword shall visit leviathan the long serpent, and leviathan the crooked serpent, and He shall slay the whales that are in the sea (*Isa.* xxvii. 1). A judgment upon those who are in faith separated from charity; also those who are only in natural faith and not in spiritual.

7 In that day Jehovah will cut off from the channel of the river unto the river of Egypt, and ye shall be gathered one by one, O ye sons of Israel. In that day ye shall sound with a great trumpet; and they shall come which were perishing in the land of Assyria, and they that were outcasts from the land 9 of Egypt, and they shall bow themselves in the mountain of 9 holiness at Jerusalem (vers. 12, 13). Concerning the advent of the Lord to gather the faithful to the new heaven and the New Church; by "Assyria" are meant those who are rational, 9 and by "Egypt" those who are natural; and that both would then become spiritual, because they would approach the Lord.

(Jehovah hath poured out upon you the spirit of deep sleep and hath closed your eyes, O prophets, and your heads, O seers, hath He covered. Therefore all vision is become unto you as the words of a book that is sealed, which if they give to one who knows letters, saying, Read this, I pray thee; he saith I cannot, for it is sealed; or if the book is delivered to him who knows not letters, saying, Read this, I pray thee; he saith I know not letters (*Isa.* xxix. 10–12). Concerning the desolation of truth.)

Is it yet a very little while and Lebanon shall be turned into 9 a fruitful field? Then *in that day* shall the deaf hear the words of the book, and the eyes of the blind shall see out of thick darkness and out of darkness (vers. 17, 18). After the destruction that the Lord would open the Word.

In that day shall thy cattle feed in a broad meadow; there shall be upon every lofty mountain and upon every high hill, rivers and streams of waters, in the day of the great slaughter, when the towers fall. For the light of the moon shall be as the light of the sun, and the light of the sun shall be sevenfold as the light of seven days, in the day that Jehovah shall bind up the breach of His people (*Isa.* xxx. 23, 25, 26). Concerning the church of the Lord after the completion of the Last Judgment.

15. Upon the land of my people shall come up the thorn and the brier, yea, upon all the houses of gladness in the joyous city; for the palace shall be a wilderness, the multitude of the city shall be forsaken, the hillside and the watch tower shall be above caves for ever, a joy of wild asses, a pasture for flocks: until the spirit be poured upon us from on high, then the wilderness shall be a fruitful field; judgment shall dwell in the wilderness and justice shall abide in the fruitful field. The work of justice shall be peace, and the labor of justice quietness and security for ever, so that My people shall dwell in a habitation of peace, and in tents of security, and in quiet resting-places (*Isa.* xxxii. 13–18). Concerning the vastation of the church and of its celestial state after redemption.

I will arise, saith Jehovah; now will I lift up Myself. He that walketh in justice and speaketh uprightly; that stoppeth the ear lest He hear blood, and shutteth the eyes lest He see evil; he shall dwell on high, his bread shall be given him, his waters shall be sure. Look upon Zion the city of our appointed feast: thine eyes shall see Jerusalem a quiet habitation, which shall not be dissipated, the stakes thereof shall never be removed; there Jehovah will be magnificent to us (*Isa.* xxxiii. 8–10, 15, 16, 20–22). Here concerning the vastation of the church, and afterwards the coming of the Lord to restore it.

All the host of the heavens shall waste away, and the heavens shall be rolled together as a scroll, and all their host shall fall. The spoonbill and the bittern shall possess it, and the owl and the raven shall dwell therein, and thorns shall grow over her palaces, the thistle and the brier in the fortresses thereof, so that it may be a habitation of dragons, a court for the daughters of the owl. And the zijim shall meet with the ijim, and the satyr shall meet his fellow; yea, the screech owl shall rest there, and shall find for herself a rest-

7 ing place. For it is the day of the vengeance of Jehovah, the year of the recompense for the controversy of Zion. Its fire shall not be quenched night nor day, from generation to generation *it shall lie waste* (*Isa.* xxxiv. 4, 8, 10, 11, 13–15). Concerning the complete vastation of the church as to charity or as to good; there follow the coming of the Lord and the restoration of the church in the following chapter; where are these words: Rejoice, O wilderness and dry place, in blossom-
6 ing let it blossom and exult: behold, your God will come with vengeance, He will come with the retribution of God. Then the eyes of the blind shall be opened, and the ears of the deaf shall be opened. Then shall the lame leap as a hind, and the
9 tongue of the dumb shall sing: yea, in the wilderness shall waters break out, and rivers in the plain of the wilderness. And the dry place shall become a pool and the thirsty place springs of water. An highway shall be there and a way,
10 which shall be called the way of holiness. Thus the *redeemed of Jehovah* shall return and come unto Zion with singing, and everlasting joy shall be upon their head; gladness and joy shall follow, sorrow and sighing shall flee away (*Isa.* xxxv. 1, 2, 4–8, 10). These words treat of the coming of the Lord and the state of heaven and the church after redemption.

16. (I will desolate and swallow up together. I will make waste mountains and hills and dry up all their herb; I will make the rivers islands and will dry up their pools; I will lead the blind by a way they knew not; I will make darkness light before them and the crooked places straight. Hear, ye deaf, and look, ye blind, that ye may see (*Isa.* xlii. 14–16, 18). Of the desolation and afterwards of the enlightenment in Divine truths.)

Fear not, for I am with thee: I will bring thy seed from the east, and gather thee from the west; I will say to the north, Give up; and to the south, Keep not back; bring My sons from far and My daughters from the end of the earth; every one that is called by My name, whom I have created for My glory; I have formed him; yea, I have made him. Bring forth the
7, 8, 9 blind people that have eyes and the deaf that have ears (*Isa.* xliii. 5–8). Concerning the New Church of the Lord after the redemption.

Behold I will do a new thing; now shall it spring forth; I will even make a way in the wilderness, and rivers in the desert; the wild beasts of the field shall honor Me, the dragons and the owls, for I have given waters in the wilderness, rivers in the desert to give drink to My people, My chosen (*Isa.* xliii. 19, 20). Concerning the New Church after the completion of the redemption.

He will say to Jerusalem, Thou shalt be inhabited, and to the cities of Judah, Ye shall be built, and I will raise up the *waste places* thereof, saying to Jerusalem, Be thou built; and to the temple, Be thy foundation laid (*Isa.* xliv. 26–28). 9

(Thy destroyers, and thy devastators shall go forth from thee. For as for thy waste and thy desolate places, they that swallow thee up shall be far away (*Isa.* xlix. 17, 19).

These two things have befallen thee, devastation and breaking; thy sons have fainted, they have lain at the head of all the streets (*Isa.* li. 19, 20).)

Jehovah will console all the waste places of Zion, so that He maketh her wilderness like Eden, and her desert like the garden of Jehovah, joy and gladness shall be found therein, confession and the voice of singing (*Isa.* li. 3). 9

The heavens shall vanish away like smoke, and the earth 7, 8, 9 shall grow old like a garment, but My salvation shall be for ever, and My righteousness shall not be broken (*Isa.* li. 6).

Behold I will set thy stones with antimony, and lay thy foundations in sapphires. I will make thy suns of rubies, and thy gates of the stones of carbuncle, and all thy border of pleasant stones: all thy sons shall be taught of Jehovah, great (*multa*) shall be the peace of thy sons. In justice shalt thou be established (*Isa.* liv. 11–14). Concerning the New Church of the Lord: almost as the New Jerusalem after the redemption, is described in the *Apocalypse* such as it would be. This is treated of in the preceding verses 5–8. 9

Thus said Jehovah, Keep ye judgment and do justice, for My salvation is near to come and My justice to be revealed 7, 4, 9 (*Isa.* lvi. 1). Concerning the coming of the Lord.

17. The vastation of good and truth and thence their change into evil and falsity in the church are treated of as described in *Isa.* lix. 1–16; and it is said that vastation and breaking are in their paths (ver. 7). Afterwards in the same chapter the 7 coming of the Lord and the redemption are treated of from vers. 16–21, where it is also said, Jehovah saw that there was no man, He wondered that there was no intercessor; therefore His own arm brought salvation unto Him, and His justice upheld Him. And He put on justice as a breastplate, and a helmet of salvation upon His head: He also put on garments of vengeance, and covered Himself with zeal as with a cloak; anger to His enemies, retribution to His adversaries. So shall they fear the name of Jehovah from the west and His glory from the rising of the sun. Although he shall come as a rushing stream, the spirit of Jehovah shall bring in an ensign against him; then the Redeemer shall come to Zion. This is My covenant with them, saith Jehovah, My spirit that is upon thee, and My words, which I have put in thy mouth, shall not depart out of thy mouth, nor out of the mouth of thy seed, from henceforth and for ever (vers. 16–21). In the following chapter (lx.) the church of the Lord is treated of, after the judgment upon the evil, thus after the act of redemption, concerning which we read as follows:—Arise, shine; for thy light is come, and the glory of Jehovah is risen upon thee. For, behold, darkness covers the earth, and thick darkness the peoples; but Jehovah shall rise upon thee, and His glory shall be seen upon thee. And the nations shall come to thy light, and kings to the brightness of thy rising. Lift up thine eyes round about and see: they all gather together and come to thee. All from Sheba shall come, they shall bring gold and frankincense, and shall proclaim the praises of Jehovah. Thy gates also shall be open continually, they shall not be shut day nor night; to bring to thee the host of the nations. For the nation or kingdom that will not serve thee shall perish. Thou shalt suck the milk of the nations, and shalt suck the breasts of kings, that thou mayest know that I Jehovah am thy Saviour and thy Redeemer, the Powerful One of Jacob. Violence shall no more be heard in thy land, vastation nor breaking within thy borders, but thou shalt call thy walls Salvation, and thy gates Praise. The sun shall no more be for a light by day, nor shall the moon shine for brightness unto thee, but Jehovah shall be for the light of eternity, and thy God, thy adornment (*Isa.* lx. 1–22). Concerning the New Church of the Lord.

18. The state of the church is continued by the Lord (*Isa.* lxi.) because He will restore all things: as follows—Then shall they build the wastes of eternity, they shall raise up the former desolations, and they shall renovate the waste cities, the desolation of a generation. And ye shall be called the priests of Jehovah, the ministers of our God. I will give them the reward of their work in truth, and I will make a covenant of eternity with them (*Isa.* lxi. 1-11).   9, 10

Afterwards the state of the church is treated of after the second coming and after the redemption at that time. This church is the New Jerusalem treated of in the *Apocalypse*. Concerning it we read these words in *Isaiah*:—For Zion's sake I will not be silent, and for Jerusalem's sake I will not rest until her justice go forth as brightness, and her salvation shall burn as a lamp. Then shall the nations see thy justice, and all kings thy glory; and thou shalt be called a new name, which the mouth of Jehovah shall name. Thou shalt also be *a crown of beauty* in the hand of Jehovah, and a royal tiara in the hand of thy God. Thou shalt no more be called forsaken, and thy land shall no more be called a waste, but thou shalt be called My good pleasure is in her, and thy land shall be married. For Jehovah shall be well pleased in thee, and thy land shall be married. As the joy of the bridegroom over the bride, so shall thy God rejoice over thee. I have set watchmen upon thy walls, O Jerusalem: they shall not be silent day nor night continually; ye that make mention of Jehovah, keep not silence, till He repair and make Jerusalem a praise in the earth. Jehovah hath sworn by His right hand, and by the arm of His strength, I will no more give thy corn to be food for thine adversaries; but they that have collected it shall eat it and praise Jehovah. Go through, go through the gates, prepare ye the way of the people. Behold, Jehovah hath made it to be heard to the end of the earth, Say to the daughter of Zion, Behold thy salvation shall come, behold his reward is with him, and the price of his work before him. They shall call them, the people of holiness, the redeemed of Jehovah; and thou shalt be called, A city sought out, not deserted (*Isa.* lxii. 1-12).   6

   7

   9, 10

19. In the following chapter (lxiii.), the combat of the Lord with the hells and their subjugation is treated of, where we   7, 8 read these words: Who is this that cometh from Edom, with sprinkled garments from Bozra? this that is honorable in His apparel marching in the multitude of His strength. I that speak in justice, great to save. Wherefore art Thou red as to Thy garments and Thy garments like him that treadeth in the wine-press? I have trodden the wine-press alone, and of the peoples there was no man with Me: therefore I trod them in Mine anger and trampled them in My wrath, whence their victory is sprinkled upon My garments and I have stained all My raiment. For the day of vengeance is in Mine heart and the year of My redeemed is come. I had looked round, but there was none to help, and I was astonished, but there was none to uphold: therefore Mine own arm brought salvation unto Me. And I trod down the peoples in Mine anger and I made their victory to descend upon the earth. He said, surely they are My people, so He became their Saviour. In all their straitness, there was straitness for Him, and the angel of His faces freed them. On account of His love and His pity He redeemed them; and He bare them, and carried them all the days of old (*Isa.* lxiii. 1-9). The supplication of the faithful to the Lord, that then they might be liberated from the hells (vers. 15-19), where we read these words: Look down from heaven and behold from the habitation of Thy holiness and Thy beauty: where are Thy zeal and Thy powers? the yearning of Thy bowels and Thy compassions are restrained towards me. For Thou art our Father; Abraham knoweth us not, and Israel doth not acknowledge us: Thou Jehovah art our Father, our Redeemer, from everlasting is Thy name; why wilt Thou make us to err from Thy ways, and harden our heart from Thy fear? Return for Thy servants' sake. They almost possessed the people of Thy holiness: our adversaries have trampled Thy sanctuary. O that Thou wouldst rend the heavens and come down, that the mountains might flow down at Thy presence (*Isa.* lxiii. 15-19). The lamentation of the faithful that the church was laid waste, and supplication that He would bring help (*Isa.* lxiv. 1-11, where are several things which can be taken therefrom). The reply of the Lord to their supplication (*Isa.* lxv.), where first the evil who have not worshiped God but have gone away to the worship of other gods, are treated of (vers. 1–15), and afterwards the restoration of the New Church, which is meant by Jerusalem, and its happy state (vers. 17–25), where are these words: Behold I create new heavens and a new earth, so that the former shall not be remembered. But be glad and exult in that which I create, behold I will create Jerusalem an exultation and her people a gladness. They shall not labor in vain nor bring forth in terror, for they are the seed of the blessed of Jehovah. The 9 wolf and the lamb shall feed together, and the lion shall eat straw like the ox. They shall not do evil, nor destroy in all the mountain of holiness (*Isa.* lxv. 17–25).

20. For the nation and kingdom that will not serve Thee 9 shall perish, and the nations shall be utterly wasted (*Isa.* lx. 12). Of the Lord.

Then shall they build the wastes of eternity, they shall raise up the former desolations, and they shall renew the waste 9 cities, the desolations of a generation (*Isa.* lxi. 4). There throughout the whole chapter the coming of the Lord is treated of.

The whole of *Isaiah*, Chap. lxii., treats of the New Church, *N.B.* 9 which is called Jerusalem.

Thou shalt no more be termed forsaken; and thy lands shall 9 not be termed a waste (*Isa.* lxii. 4). The New Jerusalem is treated of throughout the chapter.

(The cities of thy holiness are become a wilderness, Zion is become a wilderness, and Jerusalem a waste, and all our desirable things are become a waste (*Isa.* lxiv. 9, 10).)

Behold I create new heavens and a new earth so that the 8, 9 former things shall not be remembered nor come upon the heart. But be ye glad and exult forever in that which I create: behold I will create Jerusalem an exultation and her people a gladness, so that I will exult over Jerusalem and be glad over My people. The wolf and the lamb shall feed together, but dust shall be the serpent's bread. They shall not do evil, nor destroy in all the mountain of My holiness (*Isa.* lxv. 17–25). Concerning the New Church.

Rejoice ye with Jerusalem, and exult in her all ye that love her; be glad with gladness for her, that ye may suck and be satisfied from the breast of her consolations, that ye may press

out and be delighted from the splendor of her glory. For as
9 the new heavens and the new earth which I will make, shall
stand before Me, so shall stand your name and your seed (*Isa.*
lxvi. 10, 11, *seq.*, 22).

21. (The young lions roar, they give out their voice, they
reduce the land to wasteness (*Jer.* ii. 15).)

At that time they shall call Jerusalem the throne of Jeho-
9 vah, and all the nations shall be gathered on account of the
name of Jehovah to Jerusalem (*Jer.* iii. 17). Concerning the
New Church.

(A lion has gone up from his thicket and a destroyer of nations has set out; he is gone forth from his place to reduce thy
land to wasteness. It shall come to pass in that day that the
heart of the king shall perish and the heart of the princes, and
the priests shall be astonished, and the prophets shall wonder
(*Jer.* iv. 7, 9).)

Breaking upon breaking is cried, for the whole land is devastated; suddenly are my tents devastated. I beheld, when lo,
Carmel was a wilderness, and all the cities were desolated at
the presence of Jehovah, for thus saith Jehovah the whole land
shall be a waste; nevertheless I will not make a full end (*Jer.*
iv. 20, 26–28; v. 10, 18).

7 Shall I not visit for this, and shall not my soul take vengeance on such a nation as this? (*Jer.* v. 9, 29.)

(As a fountain causeth its waters to be cast forth, so Jerusalem causeth her wickedness to be cast forth; violence and
vastation is heard in her. Receive reproof, lest my soul be
alienated from thee; lest I reduce thee to a waste, a land not
inhabited (*Jer.* vi. 7, 8).)

7 At [that] time I will visit them (*Jer.* vi. 15).

(Daughter of my people, make thee mourning for an only
begotten, for the waster shall suddenly come upon you (*Jer.*
vi. 26).

(Behold the days come. The carcase of this people shall
be for food for the bird of the heavens, and for the beast of
the earth, none frightening them away. I will cause to cease
from the streets of Jerusalem the voice of the bridegroom, and
the voice of the bride: for the land shall become a waste (*Jer.*
vii. 32–34; *Gen.* xv. 11, 17).)

22. They shall fall among them that fall: in the time of their 7
visitation they shall fall down. In consuming I will consume
them: there shall be no grapes on the vine, nor figs on the
fig tree (*Jer.* viii. 12, 13).

Shall I not visit them for this? shall I not take vengeance 7
on such a nation as this (*Jer.* ix. 8)?

(I will take up a lamentation for the habitations of the wilderness, because they are laid waste. Moreover I will make Jerusalem heaps, a habitation of dragons; I will reduce the cities of Judah to a waste. Therefore the land is perished and devastated like a wilderness (*Jer.* ix. 9–11).)

In the time of their visitation they will perish (*Jer.* x. 15). 7

(My tent is devastated, and all my cords are torn out (*Jer.* x. 20).)

(The voice of a noise, and a great commotion out of the land of the north, to reduce the cities of Judah to a waste, a habitation of dragons. The nations have consumed him and have devastated his habitation (*Jer.* x. 22, 25).)

Jehovah of Hosts said, Behold I am visiting upon them, I 7
will bring evil in the year of their visitation (*Jer.* xi. 22, 23).

Determine them for the day of slaughter (*Jer.* xii. 3). 7

(Many shepherds have destroyed My vineyard, they have trampled My field, they have made My desirable field into a wilderness of solitude. He hath made it a solitude; it mourned unto me, O desolate one; the whole land is desolate because no man layeth it to heart (*Jer.* xii. 10, 11).)

What wilt thou say when Jehovah shall visit upon thee 7
(*Jer.* xiii. 21).

Behold the days come in which it shall be said, Jehovah 9
liveth that caused the sons of Israel to come up from the land
of the north (*Jer.* xvi. 14, 15; xxiii. 7, 8).

I will bring evil upon them in the year of their visitation 7
(*Jer.* xxiii. 12).

(A voice of the cry of the shepherds, for Jehovah layeth waste their pasture. Whence the sheepfolds of peace are laid waste on account of the heat of the anger of Jehovah. As a young lion he hath forsaken his tabernacle; for their land is brought to desolation (*Jer.* xxv. 36–38).)

23. (This city (Jerusalem) shall be devastated so that there is no inhabitant (*Jer.* xxvi. 9). This city shall become a devastation (*Jer.* xxvii. 17).)

That great day there is none like it, a time of trouble (*Jer.* xxx. 7).

Behold the tempest of the anger of Jehovah shall go forth, a tempest rushing upon the head of the impious. In the latter days ye shall understand it (*Jer.* xxx. 23, 24).

(Jerusalem and the cities of Judah are a desolation, nor is there an inhabitant in them (*Jer.* xliv. 2, 6, 22).)

(Because of the day that cometh to lay waste all the Philistines (*Jer.* xlvii. 4). Throughout the chapter the vastation of the Philistines is treated of, who are those that are in some understanding of truth but not in the will of good, whence there is profanation of the truth by falsities, as with those who are in faith alone.)

(Of the vastation of those who adulterate the goods of the Word and the church, who are described by Moab: of their vastation the whole chapter treats (*Jer.* xlviii.). And there vastation, desolation and visitation are mentioned (vers. 1, 3, 8, 9, 15, 20, 32, 34), visitation (ver. 44). Again, of the desolation of those who adulterate the truths of the church; who is the man of Edom (xlix. 7–22). Vastation and desolation are named (xlix. 10, 13, 17, 20). Moreover, of those who falsify truths, who are the sons of Ammon, Damascus and Elam (*Jer.* xlix., particularly verses 2, 3, *seq.*).)

(Of those who vastate the church by the love of self and the love of dominion, who are Babel (*Jer.* l. 1–end), where in particular vastation and desolation are named (vers. 3, 13, 23, 27, 45).)

(Of the vastation of the Word and the church by Babel, throughout the chapter (*Jer.* li.) where vastation and desolation in particular are named and described (vers. 26, 29, 41, 43, 48, 53, 55, 56, 62).)

Everywhere in the prophets vastation and desolation are described by the sword, famine and pestilence. By the "sword" is meant falsity, by "famine" the loss of truth and good, by "pestilence" the evil of that life; they are also called the "slain" and many times it is said they are without bread and water, as in *Ezek.* xi. 6, 7, and elsewhere.

24. (The Lord is described as to the Word, appearing above the expanse of the cherubim (*Ezek.* i. 26–28); and is called Lord Jehovih (ii. 4; iii. 11, 27; iv. 14; v. 5, 7, 8, 11; vi. 3. 11; vii. 2, 5; viii. 1, *seq.*; also the God of Israel (viii. 4).)

(That they may want bread and water; and a man and his brother be desolated; and fade away on account of their iniquity (*Ezek.* iv. 17).)

In all your habitations the cities shall be devastated, also the high places (*Ezek.* vi. 6).

The end is come, the end upon the four corners of the land; I will send My anger upon thee, and I will judge thee according to thy ways. The end is come, the end is come, the morning is come upon thee, O inhabitant of the earth, the time is come, the day of tumult is near (*Ezek.* vii. 2–12).

(They shall eat their bread with solicitude, and drink their waters with astonishment, that her land may be devastated from the fulness thereof; the cities that are inhabited shall be devastated, and the land shall be a desolation (*Ezek.* xii. 19, 20).)

The vision which the prophet seeth after many days, and prophesying *it in times that are far off* (*Ezek.* xii. 27).   *N.B.*

That [he is against] the pillows under the hands, through 4 lies, etc. (*Ezek.* xiii. 20–23).

(Let the land of Egypt be a solitude and a waste; it shall be made an utter waste and desolation; a solitude in the midst of desolate lands, and its cities shall be a solitude in the midst of cities that have been devastated (*Ezek.* xxix. 9, 10, 12, concerning *Egypt*).)

(They shall be devastated in the midst of the lands that are devastated, and her cities in the midst of the cities that are desolate; I will lay waste the land and the fullness thereof (*Ezek.* xxx. 7, 12).)

(When I shall extinguish thee I will cover the heavens, and will make the stars thereof black; I will cover the sun with a cloud; I will make black all the luminaries of light in the heavens above thee, and will set darkness upon the land (*Ezek.* xxxii. 7, 8).)

(The violent of the nations shall devastate the pride of Egypt, so that all the multitude thereof may be destroyed. I will 5 make the land of Egypt a waste, so that it is a land desolated of that whereof it was full (*Ezek.* xxxii. 12, 15).)

25. A day of cloud and thick darkness (*Ezek.* xxxiv. 12).

7

(I will make mount Seir and the cities thereof into a waste and devastation, into a waste of eternity (*Ezek.* xxxv. 3, 4, 7, 9, 12, 14, 15).)

9 Then the cities shall be inhabited, and the wastes shall be built (*Ezek.* xxxvi. 10).

When I shall sanctify Myself among you, then I will give
9 you a new heart, and I will give a new spirit in the midst of you and I will take away the heart of stone, and will give you a heart of flesh, and I will give a new spirit in your midst, and ye shall be My people, and I will be your God (*Ezek.* xxxvi. 23, 26–28).

In the day that I have cleansed you from all your iniquities,
9 I will make you to dwell in cities, and the waste places shall be built; they shall say, This land that was devastated is become as the garden of Eden, and the desolate and devastated cities are fortified and inhabited (*Ezek.* xxxvi. 33–38).

Behold I will open your graves and cause you to come up out of your graves, O my people, and I will lead you upon the
9 land of Israel, and I will put my spirit in you that ye may live (*Ezek.* xxxvii. 12–14). Concerning the dry bones: by the inflowing of the breath among them, and their living again, regeneration is described.

7 After many days thou shalt be visited, and in the latter days they shall come upon the land that was made a waste (*Ezek.* xxxviii. 8, 16).

7 They shall bury Gog in the day in which I shall be glorified (*Ezek.* xxxix. 11, 12, 13). Gog is one who is in external worship, but not in internal.

9 Of the great sacrifices upon the mountains of Israel, and that thus He will set His glory among the nations that they may know that Jehovah is their God from that day, and henceforward (*Ezek.* xxxix. 17–22).

Of the New Church which is described by many things in
9 *Ezek.* xl.–xlviii.: of the city which is the New Jerusalem, and of its gates (xl.): of the temple, etc. (xli.): of the court and of the chambers there (xlii.): of the eastern gate where the glory of the God of Israel is seen, and of His worship (xliii.): next of His worship and of ministration (xliv.): of the statutes for the

prince (xlv., xlvi.): of waters from the house (xlvii.): of the allotment of the land according to tribes (xlvii., xlviii.). That the name of the city is, Jehovah there (xlviii. 35).

26. (In *Hosea* from beginning to end falsification is treated of, which is described by whoredom and Ephraim.)

[The sons of Israel shall abide many days: there shall be no king, no prince, no sacrifice, no image, no ephod, and no teraphim.] Then shall the sons of Israel return and seek Jehovah their God, and David their king, and come with fear to Jehovah, and to His goodness, in the last days (*Hos.* iii. 4, 5).

(I will return to my place, and they will seek Me in the morning (*Hos.* v. 15). Jehovah will revive us after three days, in the third day He will raise us up so that we shall live before Him; His going forth is prepared as the dawn (*Hos.* vi. 2, 3).)

. (Woe unto them because they have wandered away from Me! destruction unto them! because they have transgressed, and I have redeemed them (*Hos.* vii. 13).

Devastation shall stand among thy people, there shall be laying waste, as in the day of battle (*Hos.* x. 14).

Ephraim feedeth on wind and followeth after the east wind, every day he increaseth lies and desolation, they make a covenant with the Assyrians, and oil is carried into Egypt (*Hos.* xii. 2).

27. A nation is come up upon my land and hath laid waste my vine (*Joel* i. 6, 7).)

(Alas for the day! for the day of Jehovah is at hand, as vastation from the thunderer shall it come. The storehouses are devastated, the garners are destroyed, even the flocks of sheep are made desolate, the fire hath devoured the habitations of the wilderness (*Joel* i. 15–20).)

Before Him the earth was moved, the heavens trembled, the sun and moon were blackened, and the stars withdrew their shining. Jehovah uttered His voice before His army, for the day of Jehovah is great and very terrible; who shall abide it? (*Joel* ii. 10, 11.)

Afterwards the great and terrible day is treated of (*Joel* ii. 1–11). The coming of Jehovah and then the New Church, is treated of (12–27) and it is said that it shall come to pass

~7~ afterwards, I will pour out my spirit upon all flesh so that your sons and your daughters shall prophesy, etc. (ii. 28) and it is said, the sun shall be turned into darkness, and the moon into blood, before the great and terrible day of Jehovah come. But ~9~ it shall come to pass that every one who shall call upon the name of Jehovah shall be delivered, for in mount Zion and in Jerusalem shall be escape (ii. 31, 32).

Heaps, heaps in the valley of decision, for the day of Jehovah is near in the valley of decision. The sun and the moon ~6, 7~ were blackened and the stars withdrew their shining. Jehovah shall roar out of Zion, and utter His voice from Jerusalem so that the heavens and the earth shall shake, but Jehovah will be the refuge of His people; then will Jerusalem be holiness. It shall come to pass *in that day* that the mountains shall drop ~9~ down must, and the hills shall flow with milk. Judah shall dwell for ever and Jerusalem to the generation of generations (*Joel* iii. 14–20).

28. (He who turneth the dawn into the shadow of death and day into night (*Amos* v. 8).)

(And it shall come to pass in that day that I will cause the sun to set at noon, and I will darken the earth in the day of light (*Amos* viii. 9).)

Behold the days will come in which I will send a famine in the land, not a famine of bread, nor a thirst for waters, but for hearing the words of Jehovah (*Amos* viii. 11). In that day they shall run to and fro to seek the word of Jehovah and shall not find it. In that day shall the beautiful virgins and the young men faint for thirst (vers. 12, 13).

In that day will I raise up the tent of David that is fallen, and close up the breaches thereof, and I will raise up his ruins, ~9~ and I will build it as in the days of old; behold the days come that the mountains shall distil must, and all the hills shall melt; they shall build the devastated cities, then will I plant them upon their land nor shall they be pulled up any more out of their land (*Amos* ix. 11–15).

~9~ **29.** Jerusalem is called the gate of the people (*Mic.* i. 9).

(Thus said Jehovah against the prophets that seduce my people, Whosoever does not fondly kiss their mouth, against him they sanctify war. Therefore it shall be night unto you instead of vision, and darkness shall arise upon you instead of divining, and the sun shall set over the prophets, and the day shall grow black over them (*Mic.* iii. 5, 6). The "prophets" are those who teach the things of the church.)

In the *last days* it shall come to pass that the mountains of *N.B.* the house of Jehovah shall be established in the top of the mountains, and people shall flow into it. Many nations shall come and say, Come, and we will go up to the mountain of Jehovah that He may teach us of His ways, and we may walk in His paths, for out of Zion shall go forth doctrine, and the Word 9 of Jehovah from Jerusalem. Then they shall sit every man under his vine and under his fig tree, none making them afraid. All peoples will walk in the name of their God, and we will *N.B.* walk in the name of Jehovah our God for ever and to eternity. In that day Jehovah, shall reign over them in mount Zion from henceforth and for ever. Thou hillside of the daughter of Zion, the former kingdom shall come unto thee, the kingdom of the daughter of Jerusalem (*Mic.* iv. 1–8).

The day for building thy walls; this day the statute shall be 9 far removed; this day when they shall come thence to thee from Assyria, to the cities of Egypt, from sea to sea, from mountain to mountain (*Mic.* vii. 11, 12).

30. (Behold upon the mountains the feet of Him that bringeth good tidings, that publisheth peace! O Judah keep thy feasts, for Belial shall no longer pass through thee; everyone shall be cut off (*Nahum* i. 15).)

It is called the day of cold (*Nahum* iii. 17). 7

(I will utterly consume all things from off the surface of the earth; I will consume man and beast; I will consume the bird of the heavens, and the fishes of the sea; I will cut off man from the surface of the earth (*Zeph.* i. 2, 3).)

Whilst the fierce anger of Jehovah come not yet upon you; whilst the day of the anger of Jehovah come not yet upon you; 7 it may be ye shall be hid in the day of the anger of Jehovah. Gaza shall be forsaken and Ashkelon a waste, when Jehovah their God shall visit them (*Zeph.* ii. 2–4, 7).

(Moab shall be as Sodom, the sons of Ammon as Gomorrah, a place left for the nettle, and a pit of salt, and a waste to eternity (*Zeph.* ii. 9).)

After the vastation and the Last Judgment which are treated of in the preceding passages, these words follow: Then at last will I turn to the peoples with a pure language, that they may all call upon the name of Jehovah to serve Him with one shoulder. The remnant of Israel shall not do perversity, nor speak a lie, nor shall the tongue of deceit be found in their mouth. Shout, be glad, and exult with all the heart, O daughter of Jerusalem. The King of Israel, Jehovah, is in the midst of thee, thou shalt not fear evil any more. In that day it shall
9 be said to Jerusalem, fear thou not. Jehovah God is in the midst of thee; He, mighty, will save, He will be glad over thee with joy, He will rest in His love, He will exult over thee with shouting. At that time I will bring you, in it I will gather you, for I will make you a name and a praise among all the peoples of the earth (*Zeph.* iii. 9–20).

Yet once a little while, when I will shake the heavens and
7 the earth, the sea and the dry land; then will I shake all nations that the choice of all nations may come, that I may fill this house with glory. The glory of this latter house shall be greater than that of the former, for in this place He will give peace (*Hag.* ii. 6–9).

6   **31.** I am returned to Jerusalem with mercies: my house shall
9 be built in it. Jehovah of Hosts shall yet choose Jerusalem (*Zech.* i. 16, 17).

I saw a man with a measuring line in his hand. He said, I go to measure Jerusalem to see what is the breadth thereof and what is the length thereof. For I, saith Jehovah, will be
6, 9 unto Jerusalem a wall of fire round about, and I will be the glory in the midst of her. Jehovah shall choose Jerusalem again (*Zech.* ii. 1–12).

6, 9   Jehovah chooseth Jerusalem; is not this a brand snatched from the fire? (*Zech.* iii. 2.)

9   Jehovah said, I will remove the iniquity of the land in one day. In that day shall ye call, a man to his neighbor, under the vine and under the fig tree (*Zech.* iii. 9, 10).

Thus said Jehovah; I will return to Zion and dwell in the midst of Jerusalem; therefore Jerusalem shall be called a city
6 of truth, and the mountain of Jehovah of Hosts the mountain of holiness. The streets of the city shall yet be filled with

boys and girls playing in the streets thereof. I will bring them that they may dwell in the midst of Jerusalem, that they may be My people, and I may be their God, in truth and justice. Thus many people shall come to seek Jehovah of Hosts in Jerusalem, to intreat the faces of Jehovah (*Zech.* viii. 2–5, 8, 12, 15, 20–22).

In that day all the nations of the earth shall be gathered together against Jerusalem. In that day shall Jehovah protect the inhabitant of Jerusalem. The house of David shall be as God, as the angel of Jehovah before them. In that day I will seek to destroy all the nations that come against Jerusalem. But I will pour upon the house of David, and upon the inhabitant of Jerusalem the spirit of grace and of prayers, that they may look upon Me whom they pierced (*Zech.* xii. 3, 8–10).

In that day there shall be a fountain opened to the house of David, and to the inhabitants of Jerusalem. In that day I will cut off the names of the idols out of the land, and I will cause the unclean spirit to pass out of the land (*Zech.* xiii. 1, 2).

It shall be one day which is known unto Jehovah, not day nor night, for about evening time it shall be light. And it shall be in that day that living waters shall go out from Jerusalem, in summer and in winter. And Jehovah shall be King over all the earth: in that day shall Jehovah be one, and His name one. There shall be no more curse upon the earth, but Jerusalem shall dwell securely (*Zech.* xiv. 6–9, 11). In that day there shall be no more the Canaanite in the house of Jehovah (verse 21).

(All the gates of Zion are devastated (*Lam.* i. 4). Jehovah hath turned me back, He laid me waste (ver. 13). My sons are devastated (ver. 16). Devastation and breaking are come upon us (*Lam.* iii. 47).)

Thine iniquity is consummated, He will visit thine iniquity. He will manifest thy sins (*Lam.* iv. 22).

32. (Let destruction come upon him before he knows, and into that devastation let him fall. Lord, rescue my soul from the devastators (*Ps.* xxxv. 8, 17).)

A day of famine and a time of evil (*Ps.* xxxvii. 19).

(I understood their end, thou hast cast them down to wasteness, and they are brought into wasteness suddenly, they are consummated (*Ps.* lxxiii. 17–19).)

For a thousand years in Thy sight are as yesterday when it is past (*Ps.* xc. 4).

Thou hast laid the foundation of the earth, and the heavens are the work of Thy hands. They shall perish, but Thou shalt endure, and all shall grow old like a garment; as a garment shalt Thou change them and they shall be changed: but Thou art the same, Thy years are not consumed; the sons of Thy servants shall dwell, and their seed shall be established before Thee (*Ps.* cii. 26–29).

Our feet were standing within thy gates, O Jerusalem. Jerusalem is builded as a city that is compact together. There are set thrones for judgment. Seek the peace of Jerusalem, let them be quiet that love thee (*Ps.* cxxii. 1–9).

A song of Jehovah. If I forget thee, Jerusalem, let my right hand forget. Let my tongue cleave to the roof of my mouth, if I remember thee not, if I do not set Jerusalem above the beginning of my joy (*Ps.* cxxxvii. 5, 6).

(A full consummation was made, that is, was completed, when the Lord exclaimed upon the cross, It is finished (*John* xix. 28–30; *Ps.* xxxv. 7, 8, 17).)

V. FAITH.

1. Faith which is in Christ hath given him soundness before you all; of the lame man healed by Peter and John (*Acts* iii. 16).

The eunuch before he was baptized by Philip said that the Son of God was Jesus Christ (*Acts* viii. 37).

Believing in the Lord Jesus Christ (*Acts* xi. 17).

Paul said to the keeper of the prisoners who asked what he should do to be saved, Believe in the Lord Jesus Christ, so thou shalt be saved, and thy house (*Acts* xvi. 30, 31).

Paul testified both to the Jews and Greeks repentance towards God and faith in our Lord Jesus Christ (*Acts* xx. 21).

Felix the governor heard Paul concerning faith in Christ (*Acts* xxiv. 24).

The Lord said to Paul that He would deliver him from the people, to open their eyes, and to receive remission of sins by faith in Me (*Acts* xxvi. 17, 18).

God presents faith to all men (*Acts* xvii. 31).

2. The just lives by faith (*Rom.* i. 17).

The justice of God by faith of Jesus Christ unto all and upon all them that believe (*Rom.* iii. 22). He who through faith is in Jesus (ver. 26).

God hath set forth Jesus Christ, a propitiation through faith in His blood, to show His justice (*Rom.* iii. 25).

Where is then the glorying? It is excluded. By what law? of works? Nay: but by the law of faith (*Rom.* iii. 27).

Therefore we conclude that a man is justified by faith without the deeds of the law (*Rom.* iii. 28).

God justifies circumcision (that is the Jews) out of faith, and uncircumcision (that is the nations) through faith (*Rom.* iii. 30).

Do we then make void the law? Not so: but we establish the law (*Rom.* iii. 31).

Abraham believed God, and it was imputed to him for justice (*Rom.* iv. 3, 9).

To him that worketh not, but believeth in Him that maketh just the ungodly, faith is imputed for justice (*Rom.* iv. 5).

Abraham was made heir of the world by the justice of faith, but not by the law (*Rom.* iv. 13, 14).

That not through works but through faith is justice imputed (*Rom.* iv. 2–24). See *Works*.

Through Christ we have access to God and grace by faith (*Rom.* v. 2).

The nations attained to justice, justice which is from faith. Whosoever believeth in Christ suffers [not] from shame (*Rom.* ix. 30, 33).

The Scripture saith, Every one that believeth in Him shall be saved (*Rom.* x. 11).

Faith cometh by hearing, and hearing by the Word of God (*Rom.* x. 17).

Let every one be prudently wise, as God hath dealt a measure of faith (*Rom.* xii. 3).

Everything that is not from faith is sin (*Rom.* xiv. 23). He understands the faith of eating this or that.

Since we have the same spirit of faith (2 *Cor.* iv. 13).

That he reproved Peter because he Judaized, although knowing that a man is justified by the faith of Jesus Christ and not by the works of the law (*Gal.* ii. 11–16).

I live in the faith which is in the Son of God (*Gal.* ii. 20).

This I wish to hear, whether you have received the spirit by the works of the law or by the hearing of faith? (*Gal.* iii. 2, 5.)

Ye shall know that they which be of faith are the sons of Abraham: that God justifies the nations by faith. That no man shall be justified by the law in the sight of God is evident: for the just shall live by faith. Now indeed the law is not of faith: but the man that doeth them shall live by them. The law was our schoolmaster unto Christ, that we might be justified by faith: *for ye are all the sons of God by faith in Jesus Christ*, etc. (*Gal.* iii. 5–26).

In Jesus Christ neither circumcision nor uncircumcision availeth anything, but faith working by love (*Gal.* v. 3–6; vi. 15).

3. That Christ may dwell in your hearts by faith, that ye may be rooted and grounded in love (*Eph.* iii. 17, 18).

To believe in Christ (*Phil.* i. 29).

I have not justice which is of the law, but that which is from the faith of Christ, justice which is of faith from God (*Phil.* iii. 9).

Faith in Jesus Christ and love (*Col.* i. 4).

Faith in Christ (*Col.* ii. 5).

Faith and charity (1 *Thess.* iii. 6; 1 *Tim.* i. 5, 14; 2 *Tim.* i. 13; *Titus* ii. 2).

The faith of the truth (2 Thess. ii. 13).

By faith which is in Jesus Christ (2 *Tim.* iii. 15).

Without faith it is impossible to please God (*Heb.* xi. 6–end). Faith means to believe what God has said.

Jesus the leader and perfecter of faith (*Heb.* xii. 2).

Faith without works is dead. Show me thy faith without works, and I will show thee my faith by works; that faith must coöperate with works; wherefore a man is justified by works and not by faith alone (*James* ii. 14–26).

Demons believe but shudder (*James* ii. 19).

Have the faith of our Lord Jesus Christ, of glory (*James* ii. 1).

4. These are they that keep the commandments, and the faith of Jesus (*Rev.* xiv. 12).

Christ says, He that loseth his soul for My sake shall save it. Beside many other passages (*Mark* viii. 34–38; *Matt.* x. 37–39; *Luke* ix. 23, 24).

He that believeth and is baptized shall be saved, but he that believeth not shall be condemned, that is to say, that He rose again and was the Son of God. It is said, " baptized," because the apostles did not baptize any one unless they received the Holy Spirit; and these are regenerated (*Mark* xvi. 16).

No one having drunk the old straightway desireth the new; for he saith, the old is more useful (*Luke* v. 39). But that they do not agree together (ver. 36–38).

He says to the woman, Thy sins are forgiven, thy faith hath saved thee (*Luke* vii. 49, 50; viii. 48, 50; xvii. 19; xviii. 42).

When the Son of man cometh shall he find faith in the earth? (*Luke* xviii. 8.)

Jesus said, believe in God, believe also in Me (*John* xiv. 1).

Jesus said, they who believe in Me through the word of the apostles (*John* xvii. 20).

That believing they may have life in His name (*John* xx. 31).

VI. CHARITY AND GOOD WORKS.

1. They had all things in common, and divided them with all, and broke bread (*Acts* ii. 42, 44, 45; iv. 32–37).

The charity of the Primitive Church, afterwards described in a few words (*Acts* xi. 28–30).

Bless them that persecute you, curse not, being of the same mind one toward another, not minding high things, recompensing to no one evil for evil, providing things honest in the sight of all men. If thine enemy hunger, feed him; if thou doest this thou shalt heap coals of fire upon his head. Be not overcome by evil, but overcome evil by good (*Rom.* xii. 14–21).

Render to all their dues, tribute to whom tribute; custom to whom custom; fear to whom fear; honor to whom honor. Owe no man anything except to love (*Rom.* xiii. 7, 8).

He that loveth another hath fulfilled the law. For this, Thou shalt not commit adultery; Thou shalt not kill; Thou shalt not steal; Thou shalt not be a false witness; Thou shalt not covet; and if there be any other commandment it is comprehended in this word, Thou shalt love thy neighbor as thyself. Love worketh no ill to the neighbor; therefore love is the fulfilling of the law (*Rom.* xiii. 8–10).

Let us lay aside the works of darkness, and let us put on the arms of light (*Rom.* xiii. 12).

Let every one of us please his neighbor in good to edification (*Rom.* xv. 2).

2. If I have all things (which are enumerated), and have not charity, I am nothing (1 *Cor.* xiii. 1–3).

What charity is, is described (1 *Cor.* xiii. 4–7).

But now abideth faith, hope, charity, these three, but the greatest of these is charity (1 *Cor.* xiii. 13).

In Jesus Christ neither circumcision availeth anything, nor uncircumcision, but faith which worketh by charity. The law is fulfilled in one word, in this, Thou shalt love thy neighbor as thyself (*Gal.* v. 6, 14).

Of love through faith in Jesus Christ (*Eph.* iii. 18; v. 2).

Whatsoever things are true, weighty, just, lovely, of good report, virtue, think these things (*Phil.* iv. 8).

That they may walk being fruitful in every good work (*Col.* i. 10, 11).

That they may put on the new man, and love, and the things that belong to it (*Col.* iii. 10, 12, 14).

That they may be rich in good works, laying up a store of good for themselves (1 *Tim.* vi. 17, 18).

Concerning charity (1 *Thess.* v. 13; 2 *Thess.* i. 3).

3. That from good works that may glorify God in the day of visitation (1 *Peter* ii. 12).

Charity is described in various ways (1 *Peter* iii. 8, 9, 11).

Charity covers a multitude of sins (1 *Peter* iv. 8).

Whoso shall keep His Word and His commands, in him is the love of God; hereby we know that we are in Him (1 *John* ii. 4–6).

He that loveth his brother abideth in the light, and he that hateth his brother is in darkness (1 *John* ii. 9–11). Similar is the case of him who loves the world (vers. 15, 16).

Whosoever doeth not justice, and loveth not his brother is not of God (1 *John* iii. 10, 11, 14, 15).

Let us not love in word and tongue, but in deed and in truth (1 *John* iii. 18).

Let us love one another, for love is of God, for God is love, etc. (1 *John* iv. 7–9).

No one hath seen God at any time. If we love another, God abideth in us (1 *John* iv. 12).

If any one say I love God, but hateth his brother, he is a liar, for he who loves God loves his brother also (1 *John* iv. 19–21).

Every one that loveth Him that begat him loveth Him that is born from Him (1 *John* v. 1, 2).

By this we know that we love the sons of God, when we keep the commandments of God; and he loves God (1 *John* v. 2, 3).

This is love, that we walk according to His commandments (2 *John* 5, 6; 1 *John* v. 2).

He that doeth good is of God: he that doeth evil hath not seen God (3 *John* 11).

If God so loved us, we ought to love one another (1 *John* iv. 11).

4. Various things concerning charity and good works (*Rev.* ii. 4, 5, 19, 26; iii. 15).

Their works follow with them (*Rev.* xiv. 13).

That all are judged according to their works (*Rev.* xx. 12, 13).

The works of charity are taught in fullness by the Lord (*Matt.* v., vi., vii.).

That the Son shall come in the glory of the Father, and He shall render to every one according to his works (*Matt.* xvi. 27).

Thou shalt love God with the whole heart and the neighbor as thyself (*Matt.* xxii. 35–39).

Iniquity shall be multiplied and the love of many shall grow cold (*Matt.* xxiv. 12).

Charity is to do rightly in every work, and no more, is clear from the teaching of John to those who asked questions (*Luke* iii. 10–14).

They asked, What shall we do that we may work the works of God? He answered, It is the work of God that ye believe in Him whom the Father hath sent (*John* vi. 28, 29).

A commandment of the Lord that they should love one another (*John* xiii. 34, 35).

The Father is the husbandman, Jesus the vine. Everyone not bearing fruit in Me, He taketh him away, etc.; and thus that as branches in the vine they should abide in the Lord, and the Lord in them. Otherwise they shall be cast out (*John* xv. 1-6).

Continue ye in my love: he who keeps My commandments abides in My love (*John* xv. 9, 10, 12, 14, 17).

That the love wherewith Thou hast loved Me may be in them and I in them (*John* xvii. 26).

That the Lord gave the mother to John, and he took her unto his own (*John* xix. 26, 27), signifies that the church is where the goods of charity are. Mary signifies the church, and John the works of charity.

That John followed Jesus, and Jesus said, If I will that he tarry till I come (*John* xxi. 20, 22, 23) signifies if the works of charity remain till the coming of the Lord.

Jehovah, Thou hast wrought all our works in us (*Isa.* xxvi. 12).

VII. LAW AND WORKS.

1. Every one will be judged according to works (*Rom.* ii. 5-10, 12). See *Judgment*.

As many as have sinned without the law shall perish without the law; and as many as have sinned in the law shall be judged by the law. For not the hearers of the law shall be justified by God, but the doers of the law shall be justified (*Rom.* ii. 12, 13).

The nations, which have not the law, do by nature the things of the law; these are the law unto themselves; which show the work of the law written in their hearts, their conscience bears witness for them (*Rom.* ii. 14, 15).

By the deeds of the law there shall no flesh be justified before God (*Rom.* iii. 20). The reason why all are sinners is given in the preceding verse.

Boasting is excluded. By what law? of works? Nay: but by the law of faith. Therefore we conclude that a man is justified by faith without the deeds of the law. Do we then make void the law through faith? Not so, but we establish the law (***Rom.*** iii. 27, 28, 31).

If Abraham was justified by works, he hath glory, and not from God. The Scripture saith, Abraham believed in God, and it was imputed to him for justice. Now to him that worketh, the reward is not imputed of grace but of debt. But to him that worketh not but believeth, on him that justifies the ungodly, faith is imputed for justice. David says, Happy is the man to whom God imputeth justice without works: Happy are they whose iniquities are remitted, and whose sins are hidden; happy is the man to whom the Lord imputeth not sin (*Rom.* iv. 2–9, 13, 22).

How we are to understand that we are not under the law, but under grace (*Rom.* vi). See *Regeneration*.

The law has revealed what sin and lust are (*Rom.* vii. 7–11, 13, *seq.*).

The law is spiritual, man is carnal. Not what I wish I do, but what I hate, that I do. I see another law in my members which wars against the law of my mind; I consent to the law of God according to the internal man. For with my mind I serve the law of God; but with the flesh the law of sin (*Rom.* vii. 14–25).

If by grace, then it is no more of works, since grace is no more grace; but if it be of works, then it is no more grace, since work is no more work (*Rom.* xi. 6).

Charity is the fulfilling of the law (*Rom.* xiii. 8–10). See *Charity*.

He that soweth sparingly shall reap also sparingly: but he that soweth with blessings shall also reap with blessings (2 *Cor.* ix. 6).

2. Be ye doers of the Word, and not hearers only. The state of him who is a hearer only is described (*James* i. 22–25).

Of faith without works, what it is, from *James*. See *Faith*.

Whosoever shall keep the whole law and yet fall away in one matter, is made guilty of all (*James* ii. 10, 11).

What the works done by the Scribes and Pharisees are, and yet they impose them upon men to do them (*Matt.* xxiii. 2–7).

Every one who doeth evil deeds hateth the light, lest his deeds should be reproved (*John* iii. 19–21).

They that have done good shall come forth unto the resurrection of life; they who have done evil unto the resurrection of judgment (*John* v. 29).

VIII. THE GOSPEL.

The gospel of the Son of God (*Rom.* i. 9). The gospel of Christ (1 *Cor.* ix. 12, 18).

IX. THE LAST JUDGMENT.

See. also *Consummation* and *Redemption*.

1. (*Luke* xvii. 22–33.)

Impenitent heart thou treasurest up unto thyself anger against the day of anger and revelation of the just judgment of God, who will render to every man according to his deeds: to them who by patience in good works, eternal life: and affliction and anguish to every one that doeth evil, both Jew and Greek: for as many have sinned without the law shall perish without the law, and as many as have sinned under the law shall be judged by the law (*Rom.* ii. 5–10, 12).

In the day when God shall judge the hidden things of men by Jesus Christ, according to my gospel, through Jesus Christ (*Rom.* ii. 16).

God hath appointed a day in which He will judge the world in justice (*Acts* xvii. 31).

We shall all stand before the judgment seat of Christ, wherefore every one of us shall give an account of himself to God (*Rom.* xiv. 10, 12).

Do not judge anything before the time, until the Lord come, who will throw light on the hidden things of darkness, and will make manifest the counsels of the hearts, and each one shall have praise of God (1 *Cor.* iv. 5).

The saints shall judge the world, and they shall judge the angels also (1 *Cor.* vi. 2, 3).

We must all be made manifest before the judgment seat of Christ, that every one may receive the things [done] in the body, according to that he hath done, whether it be good or evil (2 *Cor.* v. 10).

Whatsoever good thing any man doeth, that shall he receive from the Lord, whether he be bond or free (*Eph.* vi. 8).

God who judges according to the work of each one (1 *Pet.* i.17). 7

That the world will perish by fire (2 *Pet.* iii. 7, 10). See *Consummation*. 7

The Lord cometh with ten thousands of saints to do judgment upon all the impious (*Jude* 14, 15). 7

Of the Last Judgment (*Rev.* vi. 13–17). See *Consummation*. 7

The time of judging the dead (*Rev.* xi. 18). 7

Adore God, for the hour of His judgment is come (*Rev.* xiv. 7). 7

Of the Last Judgment. That they are judged according to their works, and are cast into the lake of fire and brimstone (*Rev.* xx. 10–15). 7

He will raise up the good in the last day (*John* vi. 39, 40, 44, 54), because before that the heaven of Christians was not in order (*John* xii. 48). 7

From the Prophets.

2. *The day of Jehovah of Hosts* shall be upon every one that is proud and haughty. *In that day shall a man cast away* his idols; when He arises to terrify the earth (*Isa.* ii. 12–21). *Concerning the Last Judgment.* 7

Jehovah of Hosts shall be exalted in judgment, and God that is holy shall be sanctified in justice (*Isa.* v. 16, 17). In the first part desolation is treated of (vers. 3–15), afterwards the curse upon the evil (vers. 18–30).

When thou shalt be visited of Jehovah God with thunder and with earthquake, and a great voice, with storm and tempest, and the flame of devouring fire (*Isa.* xxix. 6). 7

It is called a day of vengeance (*Isa.* lxi. 2). 7

Of the Lord's battle with the hells and of their subjugation, and thus of the redemption of the faithful (*Isa.* lxiii. 1–14). 7

As an east wind will I scatter them: I will regard them from the back and not from the face in the day of their calamity (*Jer.* xviii. 17). 7

They have been driven before thee; in the time of thine anger deal with them (*Jer.* xviii. 23). 7

Concerning the day of judgment, which is called the day of revenge, of vengeance, of ruin, of anger. See many places in the section on *Redemption*. 7 *N.B.*

7 **3.** That the Lord Jehovih would pour out His anger against them to consume them (*Ezek.* xx. 8–13).

7 That Jehovah will execute great vengeance, and take vengeance in wrath (*Ezek.* xxv. 12, 14, 15, 17).

7 I will make thee a desolate city, and I will cause thee to go down into the pit, to the people of old time, and cause thee to dwell in the land of the lower places, in the desolation of old, with them that go down to the pit, that thou mayest not dwell; then *will I set glory in the land of the living* (*Ezek.* xxvi. 19, 20). Concerning *Tyre.*

7 The day of its fall (*Ezek.* xxvi. 18). Concerning *Tyre.*

7 Howl ye, alas the day! for the day is near, the day of Jehovah is near, a day of cloud (*Ezek.* xxx. 2, 3). Concerning *Egypt.*

7 In the day when Pharaoh shall go down into hell, I will cover the deep upon him; when I shall cause him to go down into hell with them that go down into the pit, and into the lower earth (*Ezek.* xxxi. 15–18; xxxii. 18, 27, 29). Hell in this place is called a grave where they lie (xxxii. 22, 23, 25, 26), and a pit.

7 That they will cause terror in the land of the living (*Ezek.* xxxii. 24, 25).

7 After many days thou shalt be visited, and in the latter years thou shalt come upon the land (*Ezek.* xxxviii. 8, 16).

7 In that day there shall be a great earthquake in the land of Israel (*Ezek.* xxxviii. 19).

7 **4.** In that day I will visit, and make an end of the kingdom of Israel (*Hos.* i. 4, 5).

7 The days of visitation will come, the days of retribution will come, He will visit their sins (*Hos.* ix. 7, 9).

7 They shall say to the mountains, Cover us; and to the hills, Fall on us (*Hos.* x. 8).

7 They shall be laid waste as in the day of battle (*Hos.* x. 14).

7 The controversy of Jehovah with Judah, to visit upon Jacob, according to his ways, according to his doings will He recompense him (*Hos.* xii. 3).

7 The day of Jehovah is great and very terrible, who then shall sustain it (*Joel* ii. 11; iii. 4)?

7 A day of battle and a day of tempest (*Amos* i. 14).

Then the powerful one shall not deliver his soul, and the 7
strong of heart among the heroes shall flee away naked in that
day (*Amos* ii. 14, 16).

He will visit upon them all their iniquities, in that day 7
(*Amos* iii. 2, 14).

If they dig into hell, if they ascend to the heavens or in 7
the depth of the sea, etc., thence will I draw them out (*Amos*
ix. 2–6).

Woe unto you that desire the day of Jehovah; to what end 7
is the day of Jehovah for you? it is a day of darkness and not
of light. Shall not the day of Jehovah be darkness and not
light? and thick darkness and no brightness in it? (*Amos*
v. 18, 20.)

The end is come upon my people Israel. Wherefore the 7
songs of the temple shall be howlings in that day: there shall
be many a dead body (*Amos* viii. 2, 3).

It is called the day of destruction, the day of straitness 7
(*Obad.* 12–14, 18).

The day of Jehovah is near upon all the nations; as thou 7
hast done, it shall be done unto thee: thy retribution shall return upon thy head. But upon mount Zion shall be deliverance,
and there shall be holiness (*Obad.* 14, 15, 17).

5. Thine hand shall be lifted up upon thine adversaries, all
thine enemies shall be cut off. It shall come to pass in that day
that I will cut off the horses, I will destroy the chariots, I will 7
cut off the cities, also juggling tricks from thine hand, graven
images, statues, groves, and cities. And I will execute vengeance in anger and wrath upon the nations, who have not obeyed
(*Micah* v. 9–14). He who is from Bethlehem Ephratah will do
this, etc. (vers. 1–7).

The day of thy watchmen, thy visitation cometh (*Micah* vii. 4). 7

The mountains shall quake before Him, and the hills shall 7
melt, and the earth shall be burned before Him. Who shall
stand up before His indignation, or who shall stand in the
wrath of His anger? (*Nahum* i. 5, 6.)

Behold upon the mountains the feet of Him that bringeth
good tidings, that publisheth peace! O Judah, keep thy feasts,
perform thy vows, for belial shall no more pass through thee; 7
everyone shall be cut off. The shield of his mighty men is

made red, the men of might are in purple; the chariots shall be in the fire of torches in the day in which he hath prepared himself (*Nahum* i. 15; ii. 1–3).

7 **6.** He stood and measured the earth: He beheld and drove asunder the nations; aye, the mountains of eternity were scattered, and the hills of an age did bow themselves. The sun and moon stood still in their seat; at the light Thine arrows went, at the splendor the shining of Thy spear: in anger the earth will go away, Thou shalt thresh the nations in the nostrils.

7 Thou wentest forth for the salvation of Thy people, for saving Thine anointed; Thou didst strike off the head from the house of the impious; I will rest in the day of trouble; when He shall come up against the people who plunder him (*Hab.* iii. 6, 11–13, 16).

7 Hold thy peace at the presence of the Lord Jehovih, for the day of Jehovah is at hand. It shall come to pass in the day of the sacrifice of Jehovah I will visit the princes, I will visit them that fill their masters' houses with violence and deceit. Whence there shall be in that day a noise of a cry, howling and a great breaking (*Zeph.* i. 7–10).

It shall come to pass in that time that I will search Jerusalem with lamps, and I will visit the men that are settled upon their lees. Then shall their wealth be for a prey, and their houses a devastation. The great day of Jehovah is near, it is near, it hasteneth greatly, the voice of the day of Jehovah crying out bitterly, a day of wrath is this day, a day of trouble and distress, a day of waste and devastation, a day of darkness and thick darkness, a day of cloud and cloudiness, a day of trumpet and alarm upon the fenced cities. Their silver and gold shall not be able to deliver them in the day of the wrath of the anger of Jehovah; and the whole land shall be devoured by the fire of His zeal: for He shall make a speedy consummation of all them that dwell in the land (*Zeph.* i. 12–18).

N.B. Jehovah in the morning, in the morning will He bring judgment to light, nor will He fail. Therefore wait ye upon Me, saith Jehovah, until the day that I rise up to the prey, to pour upon them Mine indignation, all the wrath of Mine anger, for the whole land shall be devoured in the fire of My zeal (*Zeph.* iii. 5, 8).

Of the city their corners shall be devastated, I will desolate 7
their streets, their cities shall be devastated, so that there is
no man, nor an inhabitant (*Zeph.* iii. 6).

It shall come to pass in all the land, two parts in it shall be 7
cut off, they shall expire, but the third shall be left therein
(*Zech.* xiii. 8, 9).

7. Behold the day of Jehovah cometh. I will gather all the 7
nations against Jerusalem to battle. Then shall Jehovah go
forth, and fight against those nations. His feet shall stand in
that day upon the mount of Olives, which is in front of Jerusalem on the east; and the mount of Olives shall be cleft, part
of it toward the east and toward the sea, with a very great
valley, and part of the mountain shall remove toward the
north and part toward the south. It shall come to pass in that
day, there shall not be light, brightness nor condensation.
And there shall be one day which shall be known to Jehovah, 7
not day nor night: for at evening time there shall be light
(*Zech.* xiv. 1–7; especially *Ps.* ix. 5–9, 18).

A day of anger (*Lam.* i. 12; ii. 1). A time of anger (*Ps.* 7
xxi. 10). For His anger shall burn up quickly: spoken of the
Lord (*Ps.* ii. 12). Of the Last Judgment (*Ps.* ix. 5–9, 18).

The earth shook, and the earth trembled, and the foundations 7
of the mountains were shaken when He was wroth. There went
up a smoke in His nostrils. He bowed the heaven, He came
down: and thick darkness was under His feet (*Ps.* xviii. 7–11,
seq.). By all these things the Last Judgment is described.

The judgment is described (*Ps.* ix. 5–9, 18, also *Ps.* xviii. 7
8–20). Here are described the destruction of the impious, and
the salvation of the faithful.

Of the judgment wrought by the Lord (*Ps.* xlv. 4–6), and then 7
His kingdom (ver. 7, *seq.*). See article concerning *Desolation.*

Out of Zion God shall shine. Our God shall come and shall 7
not keep silence: a fire shall devour before Him, and about
Him a storm shall rage vehemently. He shall call to the
heaven above, and to the earth, to judge His people. Gather
to Me My saints. The heavens shall declare His justice. God
is judge (*Ps.* l. 2–6).

Thou, Jehovah, God of armies, the God of Israel, awake to 7
visit all nations (*Ps.* lix. 5).

7, 9   Concerning the judgment, and, after it, concerning the kingdom of the Lord (*Ps.* lxxii. 1–17).

7   The day of battle (*Ps.* lxxviii. 9).

7   Jehovah cometh, He cometh to judge the earth; He shall judge the peoples in uprightness, and the world in justice (*Ps.* xcvi. 10, 13; also xcviii. 9). In this Psalm the coming of the Lord is treated of.

7   In the dawn Jehovah will cut off all the impious of the earth; He will cut off from the city of Jehovah all that do iniquity (*Ps.* ci. 8).

7   The saying of Jehovah to my Lord, Sit thou at My right hand, until I make thine enemies thy footstool. Jehovah shall send the rod of thy strength out of Zion: rule thou in the midst of thine enemies. Thy people shall be willing in the day of thy power. The Lord at thy right hand hath struck down kings in the day of His anger. He shall judge among, He hath filled with dead bodies; He hath stricken down the head over many lands (*Ps.* cx. 1–7).

7   That there will be a judgment as of Sodom upon all when the Son of man shall be revealed (*Luke* xvii. 22–37).

X. [BAPTISM.*

Something concerning baptism (1 *Peter* iii. 20, 21).]

[See *Acts* i. 5; ii. 38, 41; viii. 16, 36, 37; x. 48; xiii. 24; xix. 4–6; *Gal.* iii. 27; 1 *Peter* iii. 20, 21; *John* xiii. 8, 12). Jesus said to Peter, If I wash thee not, thou hast no part with Me. He washed the feet of the Apostles.]

XI. THE HOLY SUPPER.

The cup of blessing which we bless, is it not the communion of the blood of Christ? The bread which we break, is it not the communion of the body of Christ? For we being many are one bread, one body; for we are all partakers of one bread (1 *Cor.* x. 16, 17).

---

*In this section on Baptism all after the first sentence is in another handwriting, with the observation that it is "copied from a leaf presented to Mr. Clover of Norwich."—*Tr.*

Many things are said of the Holy Supper; of those who approach it worthily and unworthily (1 *Cor.* xi. 23–29).

XII. PREDESTINATION.

We know that to them that love God all things work together for good, to them who are called of God according to His purpose. For whom He foreknew, He also predestined to be conformed to the image of His Son. Moreover, whom He predestined and whom He called, them He also justified: and whom He justified, them He also glorified. Who shall accuse God's elect? It is God that justifieth (*Rom.* viii. 28–30, 33).

Concerning predestination. Shall the thing formed say to the Former, Why hast thou made me thus? Many other things in addition (*Rom.* ix. 8, 11, 15, 18–23; xi. 7–10, 32, 33).

That the elect are in Christ before the foundation of the world, according to the good pleasure of His will (*Eph.* i. 3–13). A universal election of those who believe in Christ is meant, as is clear from verses 10, 11, 13.

According to the purposes of the ages which God hath accomplished in Christ Jesus our Lord (*Eph.* iii. 11).

Something concerning what was purposed by God before the ages (2 *Tim.* i. 9, 10).

Foreknown before the foundation of the world (1 *Peter* i. 20).

God hath called us to eternal glory in Jesus Christ (1 *Peter* v. 10).

Give diligence to make your calling and election sure: thus shall be richly supplied unto you the entrance into the eternal kingdom of our Lord and Saviour Jesus Christ (2 *Peter* i. 10, 11).

If we confess our sins, the Lord remits them for us and cleanses us from unrighteousness (1 *John* i. 9).

From the Prophets.

The elect are said to be those who, after the separation has been made between the good and the evil, are raised up; the rejected, those who have done evil, the elect, those who have done good. In this sense they are called the elect (*Isa.* lxv. 9, 15, 22).

XIII. REPENTANCE.

Do repentance and be baptized (*Acts* ii. 38).

Do repentance and be converted that your sins may be blotted out for you (*Acts* iii. 19).

To give repentance to Israel and the remission of sins (*Acts* v. 31).

Paul said to the Athenians that God commanded all men everywhere to repent (*Acts* xvii. 30).

That those who have once earnestly repented and tasted of the heavenly gift, etc., and then fall away again, cannot again be renewed unto repentance (*Heb.* vi. 4–8).

Various things about repentance (*Rev.* ii. 5, 16; 22; iii. 3, 19).

Except ye repent ye shall all perish (*Luke* xiii. 3, 5).

The joy of the angels over one that repents (*Luke* xv. 7, 10): and of the lost son who repented (vers. 11 to end).

From the Prophets.

That worship and prayer are vanity unless they purify themselves from evils, and what they are when purified (*Isa.* i. 11–20).

Is not this the fast? to loose the bands of wickedness? Then shall thy light break forth as the morning, and thine health shall spring forth speedily: thy justice shall go before thee; the glory of Jehovah shall gather thee. Thy light shall rise in darkness, and thy thick darkness be as noonday. Jehovah shall lead thee continually, and satisfy thy soul in drought, so that thou shalt be as a watered garden, and as a spring of waters. And thou shalt delight thyself in Jehovah (*Isa.* lviii. 6, 10, 11, 14).

XIV. JUSTIFICATION. REGENERATION. THE CHURCH.

1. Of justification and regeneration; see *Faith, Charity, Works, Law.*

Since we are not under the law, but under grace, is it permitted to sin? Be it far from us. Since we are dead to sin, how shall we live in sin? but in newness of life. Wherefore sin shall not reign in your mortal body, that ye should obey the lusts thereof; but present your members servants of justice unto holiness (*Rom.* vi. 1, 2, 4, 10–16, 19, 20, 22; vii. 4–7). See also *Law*.

That there is another law in the members, or in the body, which wars against the law of the mind (*Rom.* vii. 12–25). See *Law*.

There is no condemnation to them which are in Christ Jesus, who walk not after the flesh, but after the spirit. God sent the Son that the justification of the law might be fulfilled in those who walk not after the flesh but after the spirit. To be carnally minded is death, but to be spiritually minded is life and peace. For if ye live after the flesh ye shall die, but if ye through the Spirit mortify the deeds of the body, ye shall live. For as many as are led by the Spirit of God, these are the sons of God. The Spirit itself beareth witness with our spirit that we are the sons of God (*Rom.* viii. 1–6, 13, 14, 16).

The nations have attained to justice, justice which is of faith (*Rom.* ix. 30).

2. The animal man receiveth not the things of the Spirit of God, for they are foolishness unto him, and he cannot know them (1 *Cor.* ii. 14).

The wisdom of this world is foolishness with God (1 *Cor.* iii. 19).

Know ye not that ye are a temple of God, and the Spirit of God dwelleth in you (1 *Cor.* iii. 16; vi. 19, 20).

Ye are washed, sanctified and justified in the name of the Lord Jesus by the Spirit of our God (1 *Cor.* vi. 11).

God doth not suffer you to be tempted above that ye are able, but will with the temptation make also a way of escape, that ye may be able to endure it (1 *Cor.* x. 13).

Not that we are sufficient of ourselves to think anything as of ourselves; but that we are sufficient is from God, who hath made us sufficient as ministers of the New Testament; not of the letter but of the spirit: for the letter killeth but the spirit giveth life (2 *Cor.* iii. 5, 6).

The god of this age hath blinded the sense of the unbelieving that the light of the glorious gospel of Christ, who is the image of God, should not shine unto them (2 *Cor* iv. 4).

If any man be in Christ, he is a new creature: old things are passed away; behold, all things are become new (2 *Cor.* v. 17).

Ye are a temple of the living God; as God hath said, for I will dwell in them and walk around in them; and I will be their God, and they shall be My people (2 *Cor.* vi. 16).

I have espoused you to one man, that I might present a pure virgin to Christ (2 *Cor.* xi. 2).

3. That we are the sons of God through Christ, and thus heirs (*Gal.* iv. 4–7).

Exult, O barren, thou that didst not bear (*Isa.* liv. 1; *Gal.* iv. 19, 27).

The flesh lusteth against the spirit, and the spirit against the flesh (*Gal.* v. 16, 17).

The works of the flesh and the works of the spirit are enumerated (*Gal.* v. 17–23).

They that are Christ's have crucified the flesh with the passions and lusts. If we live in the spirit, let us also walk in the spirit (*Gal.* v. 24, 25).

Bear ye one another's burdens, and so fulfil the law of Christ (*Gal.* vi. 2). In Jesus Christ neither circumcision availeth anything, nor uncircumcision, but a new creature (*Gal.* vi. 15).

As any man soweth, so shall he reap (*Gal.* vi. 7–10).

Ye are saved through faith, not by works, lest any one should boast. For we are his workmanship, created in Jesus Christ unto good works, which God hath prepared that we should walk in them (*Eph.* ii. 8–10).

Through Christ [all the building] groweth into a holy temple in the Lord: and is builded for a habitation of God in the Spirit (*Eph.* ii. 20–22).

Ye ought to put off the old man and put on the new (*Eph.* iv. 22, 24).

Ye were once darkness, but now are ye light in the Lord, walk as sons of light (*Eph.* v. 8).

Be ye strong in the Lord and in the power of His might. Put on the armor of God for this, that ye may be able to stand against the wiles of the devil. For us the contest is not against flesh and blood, but against principalities, etc. And take the helmet of salvation, and the sword of the Spirit, which is the Word of God (*Eph.* vi. 10–13, 17).

They profess to know God, but in works they deny Him (*Titus* i. 16).

God saves us by the washing of regeneration and the renewing of the Holy Spirit; which He poured out on us through Jesus Christ; that being justified by His grace, we might be heirs according to the hope of eternal life (*Titus* iii. 5–7).

That they who are fully regenerated, if they shall fall away, cannot again be regenerated (*Heb.* vi. 4–8).

That He will inscribe the law in their heart, etc. (*Heb.* viii. 10, 11; x. 16).

The heavenly Jerusalem, the city of the living God (*Heb.* xii. 22, 23).

4. The state of him who is not in faith but in doubt, is described; that he is double minded, unstable (*James* i. 6–8).

Happy is the man that endureth temptation; for it is such that no one is tempted of God, but by his own lust (*James* i. 12–14).

It pleased God to beget you by the word of truth (*James* i. 18).

Draw nigh to God, then He will draw nigh (*James* iv. 8).

Cleanse your hands and purify your hearts, men of double mind (*James* iv. 8).

He who knoweth to do good, and doeth it not, to him it is sin (*James* iv. 17).

Regenerated through the living Word of God (1 *Peter* i. 23).

The Lord is a living stone; that ye as living stones may be built up into a spiritual house (1 *Peter* ii. 4, 5).

Whosoever is born of God, doth not sin, for His seed remaineth in him (1 *John* iii. 9, 10; v. 18).

Whosoever believeth that Jesus is the Christ is born of God, and every one that loveth Him that begat, loveth him that is born of Him (1 *John* v. 1).

Look ye that we lose not, but receive a full reward (2 *John* 8).

Whosoever abideth not in the doctrine of Christ, hath not God. He that abideth hath both the Father and the Son (2 *John* 8–10).

5. Ask, and it shall be given you; seek, and ye shall find; knock, and it shall be opened unto you (*Matt.* vii. 7, 8).

Of the sower also this; he who received the seed on stony places, the same is he that heareth the Word and straightway with joy receiveth it. He hath no root, but dureth for a while (*Matt.* xiii. 20, 21; *Mark* iv. 5, 16; *Luke* viii. 13).

Jesus said to the disciples, Ye are they who have followed Me in the regeneration (*Matt.* xix. 28).

6. A man is regenerated as he is born, and grows up, compared with the seed which grows gradually into an ear (*Mark* iv. 26-29). Also with a grain of mustard seed (vers. 30-32).

Unless a man believes in God, God cannot give him faith, and contrariwise; this is confirmed by what the Lord says, If thou believest, thou shalt be saved; and He could not do miracles in His own country because they did not believe (*Mark* vi. 4, 5); besides many other places where reciprocal faith is treated of.

Whosoever hath, to him shall be given; whosoever hath not, from him shall be taken that which he thinketh that he hath (*Luke* viii. 18). Many other places in the margin. Of those who from the external man know many things, and yet are not internal men.

No man looking back is fit for the kingdom of God (*Luke* ix. 62).

He that is not with Me is against Me; and he that gathereth not with Me scattereth (*Luke* xi. 23; *Matt.* xii. 30).

As many as received Him to them gave He power to become the sons of God, to them that believe on His name (*John* i. 12, 13).

Of His fullness have we all received (*John* i. 16).

Behold the Lamb of God who taketh away the sin of the world! (*John* i. 29) who baptizeth with the Holy Spirit (ver. 33).

Hereafter ye shall see heaven opening itself, and the angels ascending upon the Son of man (*John* i. 51).

Man must be born again of water and the Spirit that he may enter into the kingdom (*John* iii. 5).

Jesus gives living water; that water will become a fountain of water springing up unto eternal life (*John* iv. 10-14).

Jesus saith, Ye will not come to Me that ye may have life (*John* v. 40).

Jesus said, I am come into the world that they which see not may see, but they which see may become blind (*John* ix. 39). Of him that was born blind.

Jesus is the good shepherd, and the sheep hear His voice; and He is the door (*John* x. 1–17, 27, 28).

They should abide in Christ, and Christ in them (*John* xv. 1–6). See *Charity*.

From the Prophets. See also *Redemption*.

7. Thus said Jehovah, thy Maker and thy Former from the womb, For I will pour waters upon the thirsty and streams upon the dry land: I will pour out My spirit upon thy seed and My blessing upon thine offspring: and they shall spring up among the grass, and as willows by the rivers of waters (*Isa.* xliv. 2, 3, 4).

I have formed thee; thus said thy Redeemer and thy Former from the womb, I am Jehovah that maketh all things; that stretcheth forth the heavens alone; and spreadeth abroad the earth by Myself. I will blot out as a cloud, thy transgressions and, as a cloud, thy sins: return unto Me; for I have redeemed thee (*Isa.* xliv. 21–24).

Drop down, ye heavens, from above, and let the clouds flow down with justice: let the earth open that they may bring forth salvation, and let justice spring forth together. Thus said Jehovah, the Holy One of Israel, and His Former, I have made the earth, and I have created man upon it: My hands have stretched out the heavens, and all their hosts have I commanded (*Isa.* xlv. 8, 11, 12).

Jehovah said, my Former from the womb (*Isa.* xlix. 5).

That regeneration, which will take place in the New Church, is described by dry bones (*Ezek.* xxxvii. 1–15), and also by the two sticks of Judah and Joseph, which were to become one stick (vers. 15–20). That this is done by the Lord, who is there meant by David (vers. 24–28).

Create in me a clean heart, O God; and renew a steadfast spirit in the midst of me. And take not the spirit of holiness from me. Restore unto me the joy of Thy salvation; and let Thy free spirit uphold me (*Ps.* li. 10–12).

Jehovah is nigh unto all them that call upon Him, and He will hear their cry (*Ps.* cxlv. 13, 19).

XV. FREE WILL.

[See *The True Christian Religion*, n. 466–500.]

XVI. IMPUTATION.

See *Faith and Works*, especially *Judgment*.

Each one shall receive his own reward, according to his own labor (1 *Cor.* iii. 8).

XVII. [HEAVEN AND SALVATION.

After the resurrection Jesus spake to the disciples of the kingdom of God (*Acts* i. 3).

The Sadducees say that there is no resurrection, neither angel, nor spirit: but the Pharisees confess both (*Acts* xxiii. 8).

The kingdom of God is not food and drink, but justice, and peace, and joy in the Holy Spirit. Let us therefore follow the things of peace, and the things whereby we may edify one another (*Rom.* xiv. 17–19).

Some things concerning the resurrection (1 *Cor.* xv. 49–53).]*

XVIII. CONDEMNATION AND HELL.

That no whoremonger, nor unclean, nor covetous man hath any inheritance in the kingdom of Christ and of God (*Eph.* v. 5).

XIX. REDEMPTION.

See *Judgment* and *Regeneration*.

1. We are justified freely by His grace through the redemption that is in Christ Jesus. The justice of God by faith of Jesus Christ in all and upon all that believe (*Rom.* iii. 22, 24, 25).

---

* In the original manuscript this section is in the handwriting of the Rev. M. Sibly.—*Tr.*

To be justified by law, by works, by faith. See *Law, Works, Faith.*

To this end was the Son of God manifested, that He might destroy the works of the devil (1 *John* iii. 8).

Now is the judgment of this world: now is the prince of this world cast out (*John* xii. 31).

The Comforter will reprove the world of judgment, because the prince of this world is judged (*John* xvi. 8, 11).

Be of good cheer; I have overcome the world (*John* xvi. 33, 34).

From the Prophets.

2. Like as the lion roareth and the young lion over his prey; so shall Jehovah of Hosts come down to fight upon mount Zion and upon the hill thereof. As birds flying, so will Jehovah of Hosts protect Jerusalem; in protecting also He will deliver it; and in passing over He will free it (*Isa.* xxxi. 4, 5).

Fear not, thou worm, Jacob, and ye men of Israel about to perish, saith Jehovah, and thy Redeemer, the Holy One of Israel. Behold, I have made thee a new sharp threshing instrument having teeth; thou shalt thresh the mountains and beat them small, and make the hills as chaff. Thou shalt disperse that the wind may carry them away; but thou shalt exult in Jehovah, thou shalt glory in the Holy One of Israel (*Isa.* xli. 14–16). Concerning the Last Judgment and the subjugation of the hells. I will open rivers upon the hillsides and place fountains in the midst of the valleys; the wilderness I will make a pool of waters, and the dry land springs of water. I will place in the desert the cedar of Shittah; that they may see and know and attend, and understand together, that the hand of Jehovah hath done this, and the Holy One of Israel hath created it (*Isa.* xli. 18–20). Concerning the New Church and the understanding of truth after that time.

Jehovah shall go forth as a mighty man; as a man of wars He shall stir up zeal: He shall cry, yea, He shall shout aloud; over His enemies He shall prevail (*Isa.* xlii. 13).

3. Thus said Jehovah thy Creator, O Jacob, and thy Former, O Israel: Fear not, for I have redeemed thee, and I have called thee by thy name; thou art Mine (*Isa.* xliii. 1).

I am Jehovah thy God, the Holy One of Israel, thy Saviour (*Isa.* xliii. 3).

I, I am Jehovah; and beside Me there is no Saviour (*Isa.* xliii. 11).

Thus said Jehovah, your Redeemer, the Holy One of Israel (*Isa.* xliii. 14).

I Jehovah am your Holy One, the Creator of Israel, your King (*Isa.* xliii. 15).

The people which I have formed for Myself: they shall set forth My praise (*Isa.* xliii. 21).

Thus said Jehovah, the King of Israel and his Redeemer, Jehovah of Hosts; I am the First and I am the Last: and beside Me there is no God (*Isa.* xliv. 6).

Break forth into singing, ye mountains; for Jehovah hath redeemed Jacob, and will glorify Himself in Israel. Thus said Jehovah thy Redeemer, and thy Former from the womb: I am Jehovah that maketh all things; that stretcheth forth the heavens alone, that spreadeth forth the earth by Myself (*Isa.* xliv. 23, 24).

I will blot out as a cloud thy transgressions, and, as a cloud, thy sins; return unto Me; for I have redeemed thee (*Isa.* xliv. 22).

Surely God is in thee, and there is none else. Verily Thou art a hidden God, O God of Israel, the Saviour. Israel is saved by Jehovah with an everlasting salvation: ye shall not be touched by shame even to the eternities of eternity (*Isa.* xlv. 14, 15, 17).

Am not I Jehovah? and there is no God else beside Me; a just God and a Saviour; there is none beside Me. Look unto Me that ye may be saved, all the ends of the earth, for I am God, and there is none else (*Isa.* xlv. 21, 22).

As to our Redeemer, Jehovah of hosts is His name, the Holy One of Israel (*Isa.* xlvii. 4).

Thus said Jehovah thy Redeemer, the Holy One of Israel; I am Jehovah thy God which teacheth thee to profit, which leadeth thee in the way that thou shouldest go. O that thou hadst hearkened to My precepts, for then thy peace would have been as a river, and thy justice as the waves of the sea (*Isa.* xlviii. 17, 18).

4. Make this to be heard, utter it even to the end of the earth: Jehovah hath redeemed His servant Jacob. Then they will not thirst; He will lead them in the waste places; He will make the waters to flow out from the rock for them; then He will cleave the rock, that the waters may flow out (*Isa.* xlviii. 20, 21).

Thus said Jehovah, the Redeemer of Israel, His Holy One (*Isa.* xlix. 7).

That all flesh may know that I Jehovah am thy Saviour and Redeemer, the Mighty One of Jacob (*Isa.* xlix. 26).

Jehovah said, Is My hand shortened at all that there is no *redemption?* or is there no power in Me to deliver? I clothe the heavens with blackness, and I make sackcloth their covering (*Isa.* l. 2, 3). Redemption is to snatch the good from the evil, and to separate the evil from the good, otherwise the evil would destroy the good.

Art not Thou He who hath made the depth of the sea a way for the *redeemed* to pass over? So shall *the redeemed of Jehovah* return, and they shall come with singing unto Zion, so that the joy of eternity shall be upon their head: they shall obtain gladness and joy; and sorrow and mourning shall flee away (*Isa.* li. 10, 11). Redemption is represented by the crossing of the Egyptians through the Red Sea against the children of Israel.

Ye have sold yourselves for naught; so that ye shall not be redeemed by silver (*Isa.* lii. 3).

Sound ye forth, sing together, ye waste places of Jerusalem; for Jehovah hath consoled His people, He hath redeemed Jerusalem (*Isa.* lii. 9).

Jehovah of Hosts is His name; and thy Redeemer the Holy One of Israel; the God of the whole earth shall He be called (*Isa.* liv. 5).

With the mercy of eternity will I have mercy on thee, said thy Redeemer, Jehovah (*Isa.* liv. 8).

Then He shall come the Redeemer of Zion (*Isa.* lix. 20). The combat of the Lord with the hells is treated of (vers. 16–19).

That thou mayest know that I, Jehovah, am thy Saviour and thy Redeemer, the Mighty One of Jacob (*Isa.* lx. 16).

They shall call them the people of holiness, the redeemed of Jehovah (*Isa.* lxii. 12). Concerning the New Jerusalem or Church, throughout the chapter.

The combat of the Lord with the hells, and thus the Last Judgment upon the evil who had vastated the church, and thus redemption, is described in *Isaiah* (lxiii. 1–10). Wherefore it is there said, For the day of vengeance is in Mine heart, and the year of My redeemed is come (ver. 4). And concerning the redeemed, Surely, they are My people so that He became a Saviour for them. Also, The angel of the faces of Jehovah hath freed them, for the sake of His love He hath redeemed them, and carried them all the days of eternity (vers. 8, 9). Here it is clear that redemption is to subjugate the hells, by fighting with them, and thus the faithful are to be saved, from whom are formed the new heaven and the New Church.

Thou art our Father, Abraham knoweth us not, and Israel doth not acknowledge us; Thou, O Jehovah, art our Father, our Redeemer; from everlasting is Thy name (*Isa.* lxiii. 16).

5. I will deliver thee out of the hand of the evil, and I will redeem thee out of the hand of the violent (*Jer.* xv. 21).

Jehovah will gather Israel, and keep him, as a shepherd doth his flock. For Jehovah hath redeemed Jacob, and freed him from the hand of him that was stronger than he (*Jer.* xxxi. 10, 11). Throughout the whole of this chapter, and also Chapter xxxiii., the redemption and liberation of men of the church is treated of. But in the former chapters from the first up to this one the vastation of the church is treated of.

Behold the days come in which I will make a new covenant; not according to the covenant that I have made, for they have made void this covenant. But this shall be the covenant that I will make after those days, I will put My law in their midst, and I will write it upon their hearts, and I will be their God, and they shall be My people. Nor shall they teach, a man his companion, nor a man his brother; Know Jehovah: for they shall all know Me, from the least of them unto the greatest of them (*Jer.* xxxi. 31–34, 38). This is said of the New Church after redemption.

N. B.—That is the day of the Lord Jehovih of Hosts, a day of vengeance, that he may take vengeance on His adversaries (*Jer.* xlvi. 10).

Because the day of calamity shall come upon Egypt, the time of their visitation (*Jer.* xlvi. 21).

Their Redeemer is strong, Jehovah of Hosts is His name (*Jer.* l. 34).

Concerning the day of the visitation upon Babylon, in which vengeance must be taken upon it (*Jer.* l. 18, 27, 28, 31).

The time of the vengeance of Jehovah, and of retribution (*Jer.* li. 6).

Jehovah of Hosts is the Former of all things, and of the rod of His inheritance by which He will do judgment (*Jer.* li. 19–23).

It is also called the time of the harvest of Jehovah of Hosts, the God of Israel (*Jer.* li. 33).

The day of the vengeance of Jehovah, the vengeance of His temple (*Jer.* li. 11).

The days in which He will visit upon Babylon (*Jer.* li. 44, 47, 52).

It is called the day of evil (*Jer.* li. 2).

6. Concerning the Last Judgment (*Ezek.* vii. 2–12). See *Desolation*.

A day of tumult (*Ezek.* vii. 7), a day of anger (ver. 19).

The visitations of the city draw near (*Ezek.* ix. 1).

To stand in the battle in the day of Jehovah (*Ezek.* xiii. 5).

That Jehovah hath redeemed them, and yet they have gone astray (*Hos.* vii. 13).

I am Jehovah thy God, thou shalt not acknowledge any god beside Me, and there is no Saviour beside Me (*Hos.* xiii. 4).

I will redeem them from the hand of hell: I will free them from death; I will be thy plague, O death: O hell, I will be thy destruction (*Hos.* xiii. 14).

There shalt thou be delivered; there Jehovah shall redeem thee from the hand of thine adversaries (*Micah* iv. 10).

I caused thee to go up out of the land of Egypt; and out of the house of bondage have I redeemed thee (*Micah* vi. 4).

I will gather them, for I will redeem them (*Zech.* x. 8).

7. Jehovah my rock, and my Redeemer (*Ps.* xix. 14).

Let the meditation of my heart be before Thee, O Jehovah, my rock and my Redeemer (*Ps.* xix. 14).

O Jehovah, redeem me and pity me (*Ps.* xxvi. 11).

Thou hast redeemed me, Jehovah, God of truth (*Ps.* xxxi. 5).

Jehovah will redeem the soul of His servants (*Ps.* xxxiv. 22).

Arise for our help, redeem us for Thy mercy's sake (*Ps.* xliv. 26).

A brother shall by no means redeem a man: but God will redeem my soul from the hand of hell (*Ps.* xlix. 7, 15).

Jehovah shall redeem my soul with peace (*Ps.* lv. 18).

Jehovah, draw nigh unto my soul, deliver it, redeem me from mine enemies (*Ps.* lxix. 18).

I will sing to thee, and my soul, which Thou hast redeemed (*Ps.* lxxi. 23).

Thou hast redeemed the tribe of Thine inheritance (*Ps.* lxxiv. 2).

Thou hast with Thine arm redeemed Thy people (*Ps.* lxxvii. 15). Here, and in what follows, judgment upon the evil is treated of.

They remembered not that God was their rock, and the High God their Redeemer (*Ps.* lxxviii. 35).

Jehovah, who redeemeth thy life from the pit (*Ps.* ciii. 4).

He redeemed them from the hand of the enemy (*Ps.* cvi.). Here the destruction of the Egyptians in the Red Sea is treated of.

The redeemed of Jehovah whom He hath redeemed from the hand of the adversary (*Ps.* cvii. 2).

Jehovah sent redemption to His people (*Ps.* cxi. 9).

Let Israel hope in Jehovah, for with Him there is plenteous redemption. And He shall redeem Israel from all his iniquities (*Ps.* cxxx. 7, 8).

For more from the prophets concerning redemption, see *Regeneration.*

XX. SIN; ALSO ORIGINAL SIN.

The Apostles commanded that they should abstain from idol-sacrifices, blood, a thing strangled, and whoredom (*Acts* xv. 20-29). By these four things are signified the falsities of evil and things falsified. Similarly in xxi. 25.

Many crimes and sins are enumerated of which they who do not know God, and do not believe in Him, are full (*Rom.* i. 28-32).

There is none just, not even one. There is none that is intelligent; none that seeketh God. They have all turned aside, at the same time they have become useless; there is none that doeth good, not even one (*Rom.* iii. 10-12, *seq.*).

They are called the dead who are in sins (*Rom.* v. 17; vi. 2, 10-13; vii. 10).

Sins are enumerated (1 *Cor.* vi. 9, 10).

The works of the flesh are enumerated (*Gal.* v. 19-21; 1 *Tim.* i. 9, 10).

The dead in sins (*Eph.* ii. 1, 5). Awake, arise from the dead (*Eph.* v. 14; *Col.* ii. 13).

Ye are dead, and your life is hid with Christ in God (*Col.* iii. 3).

That they were to put off all things unclean, and the old man, and put on the new (*Col.* iii. 5-10, 12).

Avarice is the root of all evils (1 *Tim.* vi. 9, 10).

They profess to know God, but deny Him by works (*Titus* i. 16).

Repentance from dead works (*Heb.* vi. 1; ix. 14).

To judge the living and the dead (1 *Peter* iv. 5, 6).

Watch: because the devil as a roaring lion goeth about (1 *Peter* v. 8).

That he is dead; and that the things about to die should be strengthened (*Rev.* iii. 1, 2).

The dead are judged (*Rev.* xx. 12, 13).

Evils proceeding out of man, enumerated by the Lord (*Mark* vii. 21, 22).

INDEX OF SCRIPTURE PASSAGES.

GENESIS

Chap.	Verses.	Section.	Chap.	Verses.	Section.
XV.	11, 17	iv. 21			

DEUTERONOMY

Chap.	Verses.	Section.	Chap.	Verses.	Section.
XVIII.	15–19	ii. 1	..	..	..

PSALMS

Psalm.	Verses.	Section.	Psalm.	Verses.	Section.
II.	2	iii. 3	LIX.	7, 15	xix. 7
	2–12	ii. 22	LXIX.	18	xix. 7
	6–12	ii. 22	LXXI.	23	xix. 7
	7	ii. 6, iii. 3	LXXII.	1–17	ix. 7
	12	ix. 7		8, 11, 17	ii. 23
III.	7	iii. 3		18, 19	ii. 23
VIII.	5, 6, 7	ii. 22	LXXIII.	17, 18, 19	iv. 32
	6, 7	ii. 10	LXXIV.	2	xix. 7
	6, 7 seq.	ii. 22	LXXVII.	15	xix. 7
IX.	5–9, 18	ix. 7, ix. 7	LXXVIII.	9	ix. 7
XVI.	10	ii. 1		35	xix. 7
XVIII.	7–11	ix. 7		41	iii. 3
	8–20	ix. 7	LXXXIV.	9	iii. 3
	31	iii. 3	LXXXIX.	4, 5, 6	ii. 23
	32, 47	iii. 3		19	iii. 3
	47	iii. 3		19–38	ii. 23
XIX.	14	xix. 7	XC.	4	iv. 2, 32
XX.	1	iii. 3	XCVI.	10, 13	ix. 7
	2	iii. 3	XCVII.	7	ii. 6
	5	iii. 5	XCVIII.	1–9	ii. 23
XXI.	10	ix. 7		9	ix. 7
XXIV.	5	iii. 5	CI.	8	ix. 7
	7–10	ii. 22	CII.	26, 27	iv. 4
XXVI.	11	xix. 7		26–29	iv. 32
XXXI.	5	xix. 7	CIII.	4	xix. 7
XXXIV.	22	xix. 7	CVI.	cited	xix. 7
XXXV.	7, 8, 17	iv. 32	CVII.	2	xix. 7
	8, 17	iv. 32	CX.	1	ii. 1, iv. 5, iv. 10
XXXVII.	19	iv. 32		1–7	ix. 7
XLIV.	26	xix. 7		1, 2, 4	ii. 23
XLV.	3 to end	ii. 23	CXI.	9	xix. 7
	4, 5, 6	ix. 7	CXXII.	1–9	iv. 32
	7 seq.	ix. 7	CXXX.	7, 8	xix 7
XLVI.	12	iii. 3	CXXXII.	1–9	ii. 23, iv. 32
XLIX.	7, 15	xix. 7		2–5	iii. 3
L.	2–6	ix. 7	CXXXVII.	5, 6	iv. 32
LI.	10, 11, 12	xiv. 7	CXLV.	18, 19	xiv. 7
LV.	18	xix. 7	CXLVI.	10	iii. 3
LIX.	5	ix. 7	CXLVII.	12	iii. 3

413

ISAIAH

Chap.	Verses.	Section.	Chap.	Verses.	Section.
I.	6–9	iv. 11	XXX.	23, 25, 26	iv. 14
	11–18	iv. 11	XXXI.	4, 5	xix. 2
	11–20	xiii.	XXXII.	13–18	iv. 15
	25–31	iv. 11	XXXIII.	8, 9, 10, 15,	
II.	2–6	iv. 11		16, 20, 21,	iv. 15
	11, 17	iv. 11		22	
	12–21	ix. 2	XXXIV.	4, 8, 10, 11,	iv. 15
IV.	1 to end	iv. 11		13, 14, 15	
V.	3–15	iv. 11, ix. 2	XXXV.	1–10	iv. 15
	16, 17	ix. 2	XL.	3, 4, 5	ii. 15, ii. 16
	18–30	iv. 11, ix. 2		7–13	iii. 3
VI.	1–8	iv. 11		9, 10, 11	ii. 15, ii. 16
	9–13	iv. 11		25, 26	ii. 15, ii. 16
VII.	18, 19	iv. 11	XLI.	2	ii. 15
	20	iv. 11		4	ii. 15
	21, 22, 25	ii. 13		14, 15, 16	xix. 2
	23, 24	iv. 11		18, 19, 20	xix. 2
VIII.	13, 14	ii. 13	XLII.	1–4	ii. 15
IX.	1, 5, 6	ii. 13		6–9	ii. 15
X.	3–19	iv. 11		13	xix. 2
	20–22	ii. 13		14–18	iv. 16
	23–34	iv. 11	XLIII.	1	xix. 3
XI.	6–9, 11–16	ii. 13		3	xix. 3
XII.	1–6	ii. 14		5–8	iv. 16
XIII.	6–10	iv. 11		11	xix. 3
	13	iv. 11		14	xix. 3
XIV.	1–28	iv. 12		15	xix. 3
XV.	2	iv. 12		19, 20	iv. 16
	29–32	iv. 12		21	xix. 3
XVII.	4, 5, 6	iv. 12	XLIV.	2, 3, 4	xiv. 7
	4–7	ii. 14		6	xix. 3
	9–14	iv. 12		8	ii. 15
XIX.	18–25	ii. 14		24	ii. 15
XXI.	11, 12	iv. 12		22	xix. 3
XXII.	4–14	iv. 12		23, 24	xix. 3
	12	iv. 12		24	ii. 15
	20–24	iv. 12		26, 27, 28	iv. 16
	25	iv. 12	XLV.	3–6	ii. 16
XXIII.	1–16	iv. 12		8, 11, 12	xiv. 7
	17	iv. 12		13, 14, 15	ii. 16
	18	iv. 12		14, 15, 17	xix. 3
XXIV.	1–13	iv. 13		18	ii. 16
	14, 15	iv. 13		21, 22	ii. 16, xix. 3
	16–20	iv. 13		23	ii. 16
	21–23	iv. 13	XLVI.	9, 13	ii. 16
XXV.	6, 7, 8, 9	iv. 13	XLVII.	4	xix. 3
XXVI.	1, 2	iv. 13	XLVIII.	11	ii. 16
	8, 9	ii. 14		12	ii. 16
	12	vi. 4		17, 18	xix. 3
	18	iv. 14		20, 21	xix. 4
	20, 21	iv. 13	XLIX.	4, 5, 14	ii. 17
XXVII.	1	iv. 14		5	xiv. 7
	12, 13	iv. 14		6	ii. 1
XXVIII.	5, 6	ii. 14		6, 8–10	ii. 17
	16–18	ii. 14		7	xix. 4
XXIX.	6	ix. 1		17, 19	iv. 16
	10–12	iv. 14		26	xix. 4
	17, 18	iv. 14			

INDEX OF SCRIPTURE PASSAGES

ISAIAH (Continued)

Chap.	Verses.	Section.	Chap.	Verses.	Section.
L.	2, 3	xix. 4	LX.	1, 3	ii. 18
	10	ii. 17		9	ii. 18
LI.	1	ii. 17		12	iv. 20
	3	iv. 16		16	xix. 4
	6	iv. 16		19	ii. 18
	9	ii. 17	LXI.	2	ii. 18, ix. 2
	10, 11	xix. 4		1–11	iv. 18
	16	ii. 16		2	ii. 18
	19, 20	iv. 16		4	iv. 20
LII.	3	xix. 4		6	ii. 18
	6, 7	ii. 17		10	ii. 18
	9	xix. 4		11	ii. 18
	10	ii. 17	LXII.	cited	iv. 20
LIII.	1	ii. 17		1–12	iv. 19
	1–12	ii. 17		4	iv. 20
	7, 8, 9	ii. 1		8	ii. 18
LIV.	1	xiv. 3		11	ii. 18
	5	ii. 18, xix. 4		12	xix. 4
	5, 8	iv. 16	LXIII.	cited	ii. 18
	8	xix. 4		1–9	iv. 19
	11–14	iv. 16		1–10	xix. 4
LV.	5	ii. 18		1–14	ix. 2
	7	ii. 18		4, 8, 9	ii. 18
LVI.	1	iv. 16		15–19	iv. 19
LVIII.	6, 10, 11, 14	xiii.		16	xix. 4
LIX.	1–16	iv. 17	LXIV.	1–11	iv. 19
	7	iv. 17		9, 10	iv. 20
	13	ii. 18	LXV.	1–15	iv. 19
	16–21	iv. 17		9, 15, 22	xii.
	16–19	xix. 4		17–25	iv. 19, 20
	20	xix. 4	LXVI.	10, 11, seq. 22	iv. 20
LX.	1–22	iv. 17		22	iv. 4

JEREMIAH

Chap.	Verses.	Section.	Chap.	Verses.	Section.
II.	15	iv. 21	XVIII.	23	ix. 2
III.	17	iv. 21	XXIII.	5, 6	ii. 19
IV.	7, 9	iv. 21		7, 8	iv. 22
	20, 26, 27	iv. 21		12	iv. 22
V.	9, 29	iv. 21		23, 24	ii. 19
	10, 18	iv. 21	XXV.	36, 37, 38	iv. 22
VI.	7, 8	iv. 21	XXVI.	9	iv. 23
	15	iv. 21	XXVII.	17	iv. 23
	26	iv. 21	XXX.	7	iv. 23
VII.	32, 33, 34	iv. 21		8, 9	ii. 19
VIII.	12, 13	iv. 22		23, 24	iv. 23
IX.	8	iv. 22	XXXI.	10, 11	ii. 6, xix. 5
	9, 10, 11	iv. 22		31–34, 38	xix. 5
X.	15	iv. 22	XXXIII.	cited	xix. 5
	20	iv. 22	XLIV.	2, 6, 22	iv. 23
	22, 25	iv. 22	XLVI.	10	xix. 5
XI.	19	ii. 19		21	xix. 5
	22, 23	iv. 22	XLVII.	4	iv. 23
XII.	3	iv. 22	XLVIII.	1, 3, 8, 9 ⎫	
	10, 11	iv. 22		15, 20, 32, ⎬ iv. 23	
XIII.	21	iv. 22		34, 44 ⎭	
XV.	21	xix. 5	XLIX.	2, 3 seq.	iv. 23
XVI.	14, 15	iv. 22		7 to 22	iv. 23
XVIII.	17	ix. 2		10, 13, 17, 20	iv. 23

JEREMIAH (Continued)

Chap.	Verses.	Section.	Chap.	Verses.	Section.
L.	1 to end	iv. 23	LI.	6	xix. 5
	3, 13, 23, 27, 45	iv. 23		11	xix. 5
	18, 27, 28, 31	xix. 5		15	ii. 19
LI.	26, 29, 41,			19 to 23	ii. 19, xix. 5
	48, 53, 55,	iv. 23		26, 29, 41,	
	56, 62			43, 48, 53,	iv. 23
	34	xix. 5		55, 56, 62	
	2	xix. 5		33	xix. 5
	5	ii. 19		44, 47, 52	xix. 5

LAMENTATIONS

I.	4	iv. 31	II.	1	ix. 7
	12	ix. 7	III.	47	iv. 31
	13	iv. 31	IV.	22	iv. 31
	16	iv. 31			

EZEKIEL

I.	26, 27, 28	ii. 20, iv. 24	XXX.	2, 3	ix. 3
II.	4	ii. 20, iv. 24		7, 12	iv. 24
III.	11, 27	ii. 20, iv. 24	XXXI.	15 to 18	ix. 3
IV.	14	ii. 20, iv. 24	XXXII.	7, 8	iv. 24
	17	iv. 24		12, 15	iv. 24
V.	7, 8, 11	ii. 20. iv. 24		18, 27, 29	ix. 3
VI.	3, 11	ii. 20, iv. 24		22, 23, 25, 26	ix. 3
	6	iv. 24		24, 25	ix. 3
VII.	2, 5	ii. 20, iv. 24	XXXIV.	12	iv. 25
	2 to 12	xix. 6		23, 24, 25	ii. 20
	7	xix. 6	XXXV.	3, 4, 7, 9, 12,	iv. 25
	19	xix. 6		14, 15	
VIII.	1 seq.	ii. 20, iv. 24	XXXVI.	10	iv. 25
	4	iv. 24		23, 26, 27, 38	iv. 25
IX.	1	xix. 6		33–38	iv. 25
XI.	6, 7	iv. 23	XXXVII.	1–15	xiv. 7
	22, 23	ii. 20		12, 13, 14	iv. 25
XII.	19, 20	iv. 24		15–20, 24–28	xiv. 7
	27	iv. 24		24–28	ii. 20, xiv. 7
XIII.	5	xix. 6	XXXVIII.	8, 16	iv. 25, ix. 3
	20 to 23	iv. 24		19	ix. 3
XX.	8, 13	ix. 3	XXXIX.	11, 12, 13	iv. 25
XXV.	12, 14, 15, 17,	ix. 3		17–22	iv. 25
XXVI.	18	ix. 3	XL. to	} cited	iv. 25
	19, 20,	ix. 3	XLVIII.		
XXIX.	9, 10, 12	iv. 24	XLVIII.	35	iv. 25

DANIEL

II.	28	iv. 9	VIII.	1 to end	iv. 10
	32, 33	iv. 9		4	iv. 10
	34–43	iv. 9		10, 25	iv. 10
	34–45	iv. 9		11, 12	iv. 10
III.	25, 28	iv. 9		17, 19, 26	iv. 10
IV.	10–13	iv. 9		24, 25	iv. 10
	17–21	iv. 9	IX.	2, 13, 14, 20	iv. 10
V.	1 to end	iv. 9		2, 25, 26, 27	iv. 10
VII.	1 to end	iv. 9		3, 4, 7, 8, 9,	iv. 10
	13, 14, 22, 27	iv. 9		15–19	

INDEX OF SCRIPTURE PASSAGES

DANIEL (Continued)

Chap.	Verses.	Section.	Chap.	Verses.	Section.
IX.	25	iv. 10	XII.	1	iv. 10
	26	iv. 10		3	iv. 10
	27	iv. 10		4, 9, 13	iv. 10
X.	5, 6,	ii. 13		6, 7	ii. 13
	14	iv. 10		7–11	iv. 10
XI.	27, 35, 45	iv. 10			

HOSEA

Chap.	Verses.	Section.	Chap.	Verses.	Section.
I.	4, 5	ix. 4	X.	8	ix. 4
II.	18–21	ii. 20		14	iv. 26, ix. 4
III.	4, 5	iv. 26	XII.	2	iv. 26
V.	15	iv. 26		3	ix. 4
VI.	2, 3	iv. 26	XIII.	4	xix. 6
VII.	13	iv. 26, xix. 6		14	xix. 6
IX.	7, 9	ix. 4			

JOEL

Chap.	Verses.	Section.	Chap.	Verses.	Section.
I.	6, 7	iv. 27	II.	12–27	iv. 27
	15–20	iv. 27		28	iv. 27
II.	1–11	iii. 1, iv. 27		31, 32	iv. 27
	10, 11	iv. 27	III.	4	ix. 4
	11	ix. 4		14–20	iv. 27

AMOS

Chap.	Verses.	Section.	Chap.	Verses.	Section.
I.	14	ix. 4	VIII.	9	iv. 28
II.	14, 16	ix. 4		11	iv. 28
III.	2, 14	ix. 4		12, 13	iv. 28
V.	8	iv. 28	IX.	2–6	ix. 4
	18, 20	ix. 4		11	ii. 1, iv. 3
VIII.	2, 3	ix. 4		11–15	iv. 28

OBADIAH

	12, 13, 14, 18,	ix. 4		14, 15, 17	ix. 4

MICAH

Chap.	Verses.	Section.	Chap.	Verses.	Section.
I	9	iv. 29	V.	1–7	ix. 5
III.	5, 6	iv. 29		5 seq.	ii. 20
IV.	1–8	iv. 29		9–14	ix. 5
	5, seq.	ii. 20	VI.	4	xix. 6
	10	xix. 6	VII.	4	ix. 5
	13	ii. 20		11, 12	iv. 29
V.	2, 3, 4	ii. 20			

NAHUM

Chap.	Verses.	Section.	Chap.	Verses.	Section.
I.	5, 6	ix. 5	II.	1–3	ix. 5
	15	iv. 30, ix. 5	III.	17	iv. 30

HABBAKUK

Chap.	Verses.	Section.	Chap.	Verses.	Section.
I	12	ii. 21	III.	18, 19	ii. 21
II	3	ii. 21		6, 11, 12, 13, 16	ix. 6
III.	2, 3, 4, 13,	ii. 21			

ZEPHANIAH

Chap.	Verses.	Section.	Chap.	Verses.	Section.
I.	2, 3	iv. 30	II.	9	iv. 30
	7–10	ix. 6	III.	5, 8	ix. 6
	12–18	ix. 6		6	ix. 6
II.	2, 3, 4, 7	iv. 30		9–20	iv. 30

HAGGAI

II.	6–9	iv. 30

ZECHARIAH

I.	16, 17	iv. 31	X.	8	xix. 6
II.	1–12	iv. 31	XII.	3, 8, 10	iv. 31
	10, 11	ii. 21	XIII.	1, 2	iv. 31
III.	2	iv. 31		8, 9	ix. 6
	9, 10	iv. 31	XIV.	1–7	ix. 7
VII.	12	iii. 3		6–9, 11	iv. 31
VIII.	2–5, 8, 12, 15, 20–22	iv. 31		21	iv. 21
IX.	9, 10, 14, 16	ii. 21			

MALACHI

III.	1, 2	ii. 21	III.	23, 24	ii. 21

MATTHEW

I.	21	ii. 10	XXII.	40–44	iv. 5
II.	1–6	ii. 10	XXIII.	2–7	vii. 2
	11	ii. 10		8, 10	ii. 10
III.	7	iv. 5	XXIV.	1 to end	ii. 10, iv. 5
	11	ii. 11		5–14	ii. 10
	15	ii. 10		5–14, 22–25, 28	iv. 5
IV.	7–10	ii. 10		12	vi. 4
V.	cited	vi. 4		15	iv. 10
VI.	cited	vi. 4		15, 16, *seq.*	iv. 5
VII.	cited	vi. 4		21	iv. 5
	7, 8	xiv. 5		22	iv. 5
IX.	18	ii. 10		24, 25	i. 2
X.	20	iii. 2		27	iv. 5
	37, 38, 39	v. 4		29	iv. 5
	40	ii. 10		30, 31	iv. 5
XI.	27, 28	ii. 10		35	iv. 6
XII.	1, 2, 7, 10, 11, 12	iv. 10		36	iv. 5
	30	ii. 11, xiv. 6		37, 38	iv. 5
XIII.	20, 21	xiv. 5		39	iv. 5
	25–30, 37–43	iv. 5		42, 43, 44	iv. 5
	47–50	iv. 5		46, 48	iv. 5
XIV.	33	ii. 10		50	iv. 5
XV.	25	ii. 10	XXV.	1–13	iv. 5
	31	ii. 10		19	iv. 5
XVI.	27	vi. 4		14–30	iv. 5
XIX.	28	xiv. 5		31–46	iv. 5
	28	iv. 5	XXVIII.	9	ii. 10
XXI.	42–44	ii. 13		18	ii. 10
XXII.	35–39	vi. 4		20	iv. 5

INDEX OF SCRIPTURE PASSAGES

MARK

Chap.	Verses.	Section.	Chap.	Verses.	Section.
I.	7	ii. 11	XIII.	7, 8	iv. 6
	8	iii. 2		11	iii. 2
	24	ii. 11		14	iv. 6
II.	19, 20	ii. 11		19, 20	iv. 6
III.	22	i. 2		21, 22, 23	iv. 6
IV.	5, 16	xiv. 5		22	i. 2
	26–29	xiv. 6		24, 25	iv. 6
	30, 32	xiv. 6		26, 27	iv. 6
VI.	4, 5	xiv. 6		31	iv. 6
VII.	21, 22	xx.		33	iv. 6
VIII.	34–38	v. 4		35–37	iv. 6
XIII.	1–4	iv. 6	XVI.	16	v. 4

LUKE

Chap.	Verses.	Section.	Chap.	Verses.	Section.
I.	15, 41	iii. 2	XII.	35–48	iv. 3
	16, 17	ii. 11		36–46	iv. 7
	31, 32, 33	ii. 11	XIII.	3, 5	xiii.
	35	ii. 11		35	iv. 7
	47	ii. 11	XV.	7–10	xiii.
	68	ii. 11		11 to end	xiii.
	78	ii. 11	XVI.	29–31	i. 2
II.	26	ii. 11	XVII.	19	v. 4
III.	10–14	vi. 4		22–30	iv. 7
IV.	12	ii. 11		22–33	ix. 1
V.	35	ii. 11		22–39	ix. 7
	36–38	v. 4		32	iv. 7
	39	v. 4		34	iv. 7
VII.	49, 50	v. 4	XVIII.	8	iv. 7, v. 4
VIII.	13	xiv. 5		42	v. 4
	18	xiv. 6	XIX.	38	ii. 11
	48, 50	v. 4	XX.	17, 18	ii. 13, iv. 7
IX.	20	ii. 11		41–44	iv. 5
	23, 24	v. 4	XXI.	5, 6	iv. 7
	48	iii. 2		9, 10, 11	iv. 7
	62	xiv. 6		26, 27	iv. 7
XI.	15, 17, 19	i. 2		34, 35, 36	iv. 7
	23	xiv. 6	XXII.	69	ii. 11
	23	ii. 11	XXIV.	52	ii. 10

JOHN

Chap.	Verses.	Section.	Chap.	Verses.	Section.
I.	1–14	ii. 12	III.	35	ii. 23
	12, 13	xiv. 6	IV.	10–14	xiv. 6
	15, 16, 27, 30	ii. 12	V.	18–23	ii. 12
	16	xiv. 6		21, 26, 27	ii. 12
	18	ii. 12		29	vii. 2
	27	ii. 12		40	xiv. 6
	29, 33	xiv. 6	VI.	28, 29	vi. 4
	51	xiv. 6		33	ii. 12
III.	5	xiv. 6		35, 50, 51	ii. 12
	13, 14	ii. 12		39, 40, 44, 54	ix. 1
	19, 20	ii. 12, vii. 2		46	ii. 12
	19, 20, 21	vii. 2	VII.	39	iii. 2
	29	ii. 12	VIII.	12	ii. 12
	31	ii. 12		56, 58	ii. 12
	34, 35	ii. 12			

JOHN (Continued)

Chap.	Verses.	Section.	Chap.	Verses.	Section.
IX.	4	iv. 8	XV.	1–6	vi. 4, xiv. 6
	5, 39	ii. 12		9, 10, 12, 14, 17	vi. 4
	38	ii. 10			
	39	ii. 12, xiv. 6		23, 24	ii. 12
	1–17, 27, 28	xiv. 6	XVI.	5, 6, 7, 16, 17, 29	ii. 12
X.	30	ii. 12			
	38	ii. 12		7	iii. 2
XII.	13, 15	ii. 11		8, 11	xix. 1
	31	xix. 1		13, 14, 15	iii. 2
	35, 36, 46	ii. 12		15	ii. 12
	48	ix. 1		26, 27, 28	ii. 12
XIII.	8, 12	x.		28, 29, 30, 31	ii. 12
	20	ii. 12		33, 34	xix. 1
	34, 35	vi. 4	XVII.	1, 5	ii. 12
XIV.	1	ii. 12, v. 4		2	ii. 12
	4, 5, 6	ii. 12		3	ii. 12
	6	ii. 12		10	ii. 12
	6–17	ii. 23		19	ii. 12
	7, 8, 9	ii. 12		20	v. 4
	10, 11	ii. 12		21, 22, 23	ii. 12
	10, 41	ii. 12		26	vi. 4
	13, 14	ii. 12	XIX.	26, 27	vi. 4
	17	iii. 2		28–30	iv. 32
	19	ii. 12	XX.	28	ii. 12
	20	iv. 8		31	v. 4
	21, 23	ii. 12	XXI.	18	iv. 8
	23	ii. 12		20, 22, 23	vi. 4
	26	iii. 2		22, 23	iv. 8

ACTS

Chap.	Verses.	Section.	Chap.	Verses.	Section.
I.	2	iii. 1	V.	29–40	i. 1
	3	xvii.		31	xiii.
	4	iii. 1	VI.	8	i. 1
	4, 11	iv. 3	VIII.	6, 7, 13	i. 1
	5	x.		9, 10, 20–24	i. 1
	8	iii. 1		16, 36, 37	x.
	9, 11	ii. 1		17, 18	iii. 2
	13, 26	i. 1		32, 33	ii. 1
	16–19	i. 1		37	ii. 1, v. 1
II.	1–18	iii. 1	IX.	17	iii. 2
	19, 20, 21	iv. 1		20	ii. 1
	27, 28, 29, 31	ii. 1		33, 34, 36–42	i. 1
	34, 35	ii. 1	X.	36	ii. 1
	38	xiii.		42	ii. 1
	38, 41	x.		48	x.
	39	ii. 1	XI.	17	v. 1
	42, 44, 45	iv. 1		26	ii. 1
	43	i. 1		28, 29, 30	vi. 1
III.	1–20	i. 1	XIII.	2, 3, 4	iii. 2
	15	ii. 1		11	i. 1
	16	v. 1		24	x.
	19	xiii.		33	ii. 1
	20, 21	ii. 1, iv. 3		24–37	ii. 1
	22–24	ii. 1		47	ii. 1
IV.	10, 30	i. 1	XIV.	3, 8, 9, 10, 19, 20	i. 1
	32–37	vi. 1			
V.	3, 9	iii. 2	XV.	16, 17	ii. 1, iv. 3
	12, 15, 16	i. 1			

INDEX OF SCRIPTURE PASSAGES

ACTS (Continued)

Chap.	Verses.	Section.	Chap.	Verses.	Section.
XV.	20, 29	xx.	XX.	21	v. 1
XVI.	25, 26, seq.	i. 1	XXI.	13	ii. 1
	30, 31	v. 1		25	xx.
XVII.	25, 28	iii. 2	XXIII.	8	xvii.
	30	xiii.	XXIV.	24	v. 1
	31	v. 1, ix. 1	XXVI.	17, 18	v. 1
	4, 5, 6	x.	XXVIII.	3, seq. 8	i. 1
XIX.	11, 12	i. 1		31	ii. 1
XX.	9	i. 1			

ROMANS

Chap.	Verses.	Section.	Chap.	Verses.	Section.
I.	3, 4	ii. 2	VII.	10	xx.
	6	ii. 2		12–25	xiv. 1
	9	viii.		14–25	vii. 1
	17	v. 2		1, 4	ii. 2
	20	iii. 2	VIII.	1–6, 13, 14, 15	xiv. 1
	28–32	xx.		9, 10, 11, 14, 16	iii. 2
II.	5–10, 12	vii. 1, ix. 1		28, 29, 30, 33	xii.
	12, 13	vii. 1		34	ii. 2
	14, 15	vii. 1		35–39	ii. 2
	16	ix. 1	IX.	5	ii. 2
III.	10 seq.	xx.		8, 11, 15, 18–23	xii.
	20	vii. 1		30	xiv. 1
	22	ii. 2		30, 33	v. 2
	22, 24, 25	xix. 1	X.	11	v. 2
	22, 26	v. 2		13	ii. 2
	25	v. 2		17	v. 2
	27	v. 2	XI.	6	vii. 1
	27, 28, 31	vii. 1		7–10, 32, 33	xii.
	28	v. 2	XII.	3	v. 2
	30	v. 2		5, 6	ii. 2 !
	31	v. 2		6–13	ii. 2
IV.	2–24	v. 2		14–21	vi. 1
	2–9, 13, 22	vii. 1	XIII.	7, 8	vi. 1
	3, 9	v. 2		8, 9, 10	vi. 1, vii. 1
	5	v. 2		12	vi. 1
	13, 14	v. 2		14	ii. 2
V.	1, 2,	ii. 2	XIV.	8, 9	ii. 2
	2	v. 2		10, 12	ix. 1
	10, 11	ii. 2		11	ii. 2
	12, 13, 15, 18, 19	ii. 2		17, 18, 19	xvii.
	17	xx.		23	v. 2
VI.	cited	vii. 1	XV.	2	vi. 1
	1, 2, 4, 10–16, 19, 20, 22	xiv. 1		12	ii. 2
	2, 10–13	xx.		19, 20, 21	ii. 2
VII.	4–7	xiv. 1	XVI.	8–13	ii. 2
	7–11, 13 seq.	vii. 1			

1 CORINTHIANS

Chap.	Verses.	Section.	Chap.	Verses.	Section.
I.	3	ii. 12	II.	14	xiv. 2
	7, 8	iv. 1	III.	8	xvi.
	30, 31	ii. 3		11, 12 seq.	ii. 3
II.	2	ii. 3		16	xiv. 2
	11, 12	ii. 3		19	xiv. 2
	11, 14	iii. 2		22, 23	ii. 3

CORINTHIANS (Continued)

Chap.	Verses.	Section.	Chap.	Verses.	Section.
IV.	5	ix. 1	XI.	23–29	xi.
VI.	2, 3	ix. 1		26	ii. 3
	9, 10	xx.	XII.	3	ii. 3
	11	xiv. 2		7–21	iii. 2
	19, 20	xiv. 2		27	ii. 3
VIII.	4, 5, 6	ii. 3	XIII.	1, 2, 3	vi. 2
IX.	12, 18	viii.		4–7	vi. 2
X.	4	ii. 3		13	vi. 2
	13	xiv. 2		4–7	vi. 2
	16, 17	xi.	XV.	49–53	xvii.
XI.	3	ii. 3			

2 CORINTHIANS

Chap.	Verses.	Section.	Chap.	Verses.	Section.
III.	5, 6	xiv. 2	VI.	16	xiv. 2
	17	iii. 2	IX.	6	vii. 1
IV.	4	xiv. 2	XI.	2	xiv. 2
	6	ii. 3		13, 14, 15	i. 2
	13	v. 2		24–27, 32, 33	i. 2
V.	10	ix. 1	XII.	2, 3, 4	i. 2
	17	xiv. 2		7, 8, 9	i. 2
	18–21	xx.	XIII.	5	ii. 3

GALATIANS

Chap.	Verses.	Section.	Chap.	Verses.	Section.
I.	3	iii. 2	IV.	19, 27	xiv. 3
	8, 9	ii. 4	V.	3–6	v. 2
II.	11–16	v. 2		6, 14	vi. 2
	20	ii. 4, v. 2		16, 17	xiv. 3
III.	2, 5	v. 2		17–23	xiv. 3
	5–26	v. 2		19, 20, 21	xx.
	27	x.		24–25	xiv. 3
IV.	4	iv. 1	VI.	2	xiv. 3
	4–7	xiv. 3		7–10	xiv. 3
	6	iii. 2		15	xiv. 3

EPHESIANS

Chap.	Verses.	Section.	Chap.	Verses.	Section.
I.	3–13	xii.	IV.	4–7	ii. 4
	10, 11, 13	iv. 1, xii.		10	ii. 4
	20–23	ii. 4		12, 15, 16	ii. 4
II.	1, 5	xx.		22, 24	xiv. 3
	8, 9, 10,	xiv. 3	V.	2	vi. 2
	18, 20, 21, 22	ii. 4		5	xviii.
	20, 21, 22	xiv. 3		8	xiv. 3
III.	9	ii. 4		14	xx.
	11	xii.		23	ii. 4
	12	ii. 4		30	ii. 4
	17, 18	v. 3	VI.	8	ix. 1
	18	vi. 2		10–13, 17	xiv. 3

PHILIPPIANS

Chap.	Verses.	Section.	Chap.	Verses.	Section.
I.	1, 4	ii. 12	II.	7–11	ii. 5
	6, 10	iv. 1		26	iv. 1
	8	ii. 5	III.	9	ii. 5, v. 3
	19	iii. 19	IV.	8	vi. 2
	29	v. 3			

INDEX OF SCRIPTURE PASSAGES

COLOSSIANS

Chap.	Verses.	Section.	Chap.	Verses.	Section.
I.	2	iii. 2	II.	19	ii. 5
	4	v. 3	III.	1	ii. 5
	10, 11	vi. 2		3	ii. 5, xx
	15, 16	ii. 5		4	iv. 1
	17, 18, 24	ii. 5		5–10, 12	xx.
	18, 19, 20	ii. 5		10, 12, 14	vi. 2
II.	3	ii. 3		11	ii. 5
	5	v. 3		15	ii. 5
	9	ii. 5		17	ii. 5
	13	xx.		24	ii. 5

1 THESSALONIANS

II.	19	i. 2, iv. 1	V.	2, 3, 4	iv. 1
III.	6	v. 3		13	vi. 2
	13	iv. 1		23	iv. 1
IV.	15, 16, 17	iv. 1			

2 THESSALONIANS

I.	3	vi. 2	II.	9	i. 2
	1–11	iv. 1		13	v. 3
II.	1–11	i. 2, iv. 1			
	7–10	iv. 1			

1 TIMOTHY

I.	5, 14	v. 3	IV.	1, 2	iv. 1
	9, 10	xx.	VI.	9, 10	xx.
II.	5, 6	ii. 6		14, 15	iv. 1
III.	16	ii. 6		17, 18	vi. 2

2 TIMOTHY

I.	9, 10	xii.	III.	15	v. 3
	12	iv. 1		1–6	iv. 1
	13	v. 3	IV.	1, 8	iv. 1
II.	13	ii. 6		8	iv. 1
III.	1–6	iv. 1		22	iii. 2

TITUS

I.	16	ii. 6, xiv. 3, xx.	II.	13	iv. 1
II.	2	v. 3	III.	5. 6, 7	xiv. 3

HEBREWS

I.	1, 2–9, 13	ii. 6	VII.	11, 15, 21	ii. 6
II.	7, 8, 10	ii. 6	VIII.	1	ii. 5
	17	ii 6		10, 11	xiv. 3
III.	1	ii. 6	IX.	14	xx.
IV.	14	ii. 6	X.	12	ii. 5
V.	10	ii. 6		16	xiv. 3
VI.	1	xx.	XI.	6 to end	v. 3
	4–8	xiii., xiv. 3	XII.	2	ii. 5, v. 3
	20	ii. 6		22, 23	xiv. 3
VII.	1, 2, 3, 10	ii. 6			

JAMES

Chap.	Verses.	Section.	Chap.	Verses.	Section.
I.	1	ii. 7	II.	10, 11	vii. 2
	6, 7, 8	xiv. 4		14–26	v. 3
	12, 13, 14	xiv. 4		19	v. 3
	18	xiv. 4	IV.	8	xiv. 4
	22–25	vii. 2		17	xiv. 4
II.	1	v. 3	V.	7, 8	iv. 2

1 PETER

Chap.	Verses.	Section.	Chap.	Verses.	Section.
I.	2	ii. 7	III.	8, 9, 11	vi. 3
	5, 7, 13	iv. 2		20, 21	x.
	11	iii. 2		22	ii. 7
	17,	ix. 1	IV.	5, 6	xx.
	20	xii.		8	vi. 3
	23	xiv. 4		11	ii. 7
II.	4, 5	xiv. 4		13	iv. 2
	4–8	ii. 7	V.	1, 4	iv. 2
	5	ii. 7		8	xx.
	12	iv. 2, vi. 3		10	xii.
	25	ii. 7			

2 PETER

Chap.	Verses.	Section.	Chap.	Verses.	Section.
I.	1	ii. 7	III.	2	ii. 7
	8	ii. 7		3, 4	iv. 2
	10, 11	xii.		7	iv. 2
	11	ii. 7		7, 10	ix. 1
	17, 18	ii. 7		8	iv. 2
II.	20	ii. 7		10 to 14	iv. 2

1 JOHN

Chap.	Verses.	Section.	Chap.	Verses.	Section.
I.	2, 5	ii. 8	III.	24	ii. 8
	3,	ii. 8	IV.	2, 3	ii. 8
	9	xii.		7, 8, 9	vi. 3
II.	1	ii. 8		10	ii. 8
	2	ii. 8		11	vi. 3
	4, 5, 6	vi. 3		12	vi. 3
	5, 6, 24	ii. 8		13, 15, 16	ii. 8
	9, 10, 11	vi. 3		19, 20, 21	vi. 3
	15, 16	vi. 3	V.	1	ii. 8, xiv. 4
	18	iv. 3		1, 2	vi. 3
	22, 23	ii. 8		2	vi. 3
	28	iv. 3		2, 3	vi. 3
III.	2	iv. 3		5	ii. 8
	6	ii. 8		6	iii. 2
	8	ii. 8		7	iii. 2
	8	xix. 1		10–13	ii. 8
	9, 10	xiv. 4		18	xiv. 4
	10, 11, 14, 15,	vi. 3		20, 21	ii. 8
	18	vi. 3			

2 JOHN

	3	ii. 8		8	xiv. 4
	5, 6	vi. 3		8–10	xiv. 4

3 JOHN

Chap.	Verses.	Section.	Chap.	Verses.	Section.
	11	vi. 3			

JUDE

	4	ii. 8		18, 19	iv. 3
	14, 15	iv. 3, ix. 1		25	ii. 8

REVELATION

Chap.	Verses.	Section.	Chap.	Verses.	Section.
I.	4, 8, 11	ii. 9, iv. 4	XI.	18	iv. 4, ix. 1
	5	ii. 9	XII.	1 to end	iv. 4
	7	iv. 3, iv. 4		10	iv. 4
	8	iv. 3, iv. 4	XIV.	4	ii. 9
	13–18	ii. 9		6	ii. 9
	14, 15	ii. 13		7	ix. 1
	16	ii. 9		12	v. 4
	18	iv. 4		13	ii. 9, vi. 4
II.	4, 5, 19, 26	vi. 4		14	ii. 9
	5	iv. 4		15–19	iv. 4
	5, 16, 22	xiii.	XV.	3, 4	ii. 9
	8	ii. 9	XVI.	1 to end	iv. 4
III.	1, 2	xx., iv. 4		14	iv. 4
	3	iv. 4		15	iv. 4
	3, 19	xiii.	XVII.	14	ii. 9
	10	iv. 4	XIX.	6–9	iv. 4
	11	iv. 4		10	ii. 9
	15	vi. 4		10–16	ii. 9
	20	ii. 9		16	ii. 9
IV.	8	iv. 4		17, 18	iv. 4
V.	1 seq.	ii. 9	XX.	4	iv. 4
	6, 12	iv. 4		6	iv. 4
	9–14	ii. 9		10–15	ix. 1
VI.	1 to end	ii. 9, iv. 4		12, 13	vi. 4, xx.
	11	iv. 4	XXI.	1	iv. 4
	13, 14	iv. 4		2, 9, 10	iv. 4
	13–17	ix. 1		3	ii. 9, iv. 4
	17	iv. 4		5	iv. 4
VII.	10, 16, 17	ii. 9		6	ii. 9, iv. 4
VIII.	cited	iv. 4		22, 23	ii. 9
IX.	cited	iv. 4		26	iv. 4
	17–23	iv. 4	XXII.	3	ii. 3
X.	6	iv. 4		5	ii. 9
XI.	15, 16, 17	iv. 4		7, 12, 16, 17	iv. 4
	17	ii. 9, iv. 4		13	ii. 9, iv. 4

THE PRECEPTS OF THE DECALOGUE.

I.

AFTER THE LAST JUDGMENT WAS ACCOMPLISHED, A NEW CHURCH WAS PROMISED, WHICH IS MEANT BY THE NEW JERUSALEM IN THE APOCALYPSE.

1. Explain Chap. xxi. from verse 1 to the end. Also Chap. xxii. 1–5.

2. From other parts of the Word, that by Jerusalem is meant the Church; as in the following passages:—

Isa. i. 1; iv. 4; ix. 1; ii. 1; iii. 8; v. 4; vii. 1; x. 10–12, 32; xxii. 10; xxxi. 5; xxxiii. 20; xxxvi. 2, 7, 20; xxxvii. 10, 22, 32; xl. 2; xli. 27; xliv. 26, 28; lxii. 1, 7; lxiv. 10; lxv. 18; lxvi. 10, 20; xxvii. 13; xxx. 19; ii. 3; iii. 1; iv. 3, 4; xxiv. 23; xxviii. 14; xxxi. 9; lxv. 19; lxvi. 13; v. 3; viii. 14; xxii. 21; xi. 9; li. 17; lii. 1, 2, 9; lvii. 6.

The daughter of *Jerusalem, Lam.* ii. 13, 15; *Micah* iv. 8; Zeph. iii. 14; Zech. ix. 9.

Jer. i. 3, 15; ii. 2; iii. 17; iv. 3, 10, 11; v. 1; vi. 1; vii. 17, 34; viii. 5; ix. 10, 11; xi. 6, 13; xiii. 9; xiv. 2, 16; xvii. 19, 21, 26, 27; xix. 7, 13; xxii. 19; xxiii. 14, 15; xxv. 18; xxvi. 18; xxvii. 3, 20, 21; xxix. 2; xxxii. 2, 44; xxxiii. 10, 13, 16; xxxiv. 19; xxxv. 11; xxxvi. 9, 31; xxxvii. 5, 11, 12; xxxviii. 28; xxxix. 1, 8; xl. 1; xliv. 2, 6, 9, 13, 17, 21; li. 35, 50; lii. 12–14; iv. 16; vi. 6; xxxiv. 1, 7, 19; lii. 4; xxvii. 18; xxix. 25; xxxiv. 8; xxxv. 11; xxiv. 1, 8; xxvii. 20; xxix. 1, 2, 4, 20; iv. 5; xv. 4; xxxiv. 6; lii. 1, 3; iv. 4; viii. 1; xi. 2, 9, 12; xiii. 13; xvii. 20, 25; xviii. 11; xix. 3; xxv. 2; xxxii. 32; xxxv. 13, 17; xlii. 18; iv. 14; vi. 8; lii. 29; xiii. 27; xv. 5.

Lam. i. 7, 8, 17; ii. 10; iv. 12.

Ezek. iv. 1, 7; v. 5; viii. 3; ix. 4, 8; xiii. 16; xiv. 21, 22; xvi. 2, 3; xvii. 12; xxi. 2, 20, 22; xxii. 19; xxiii. 4; xxxiii. 21; xxxvi. 38; xxiv. 2; xxvi. 2; iv. 16; xii. 10; xi. 15; xii. 19; xv. 6.

427

Dan. i. 1; vi. 10; ix. 2, 12, 16, 25; v. 2, 3; ix. 7.
Joel iii. 1, 5, 6, 16, 17, 20.
Amos ii. 5; i. 2.
Obad. 11, 20.
Micah i. 1, 5, 9, 12; iii. 10, 12; iv. 2.
Zech. i. 12, 14, 16, 17, 19; ii. 2, 4, 12; iii. 2; vii. 7; viii. 3, 4, 8, 15; xii. 2, 3, 6; xiv. 4, 10, 11, 17; xii. 2, 9; xiv. 2, 12, 16; xiv. 8, 14; ix. 10; viii. 22; xii. 6, 11; xiv. 21; xii. 5, 7, 8, 10; xiii. 1.
Mal. iii. 4; ii. 11.
Zeph. i. 4, 12; iii. 16.
David, Ps. li. 18; lxxix. 1, 3; cxxii. 3, 6; cxxv. 2; cxxviii. 5; cxxxvii. 6, 7; cxlvii. 2; lxviii. 29; cxxxv. 21; cii. 21; cxvi. 19; cxxii. 2; cxxxvii. 5; cxlvii. 12.

3. Something concerning the things that precede in the *Apocalypse;* as concerning the dragon and the scarlet beast, and concerning their destruction.

4. Concerning the Last Judgment; it has been described, and is further to be described.

5. Why a New Church is established, when the Last Judgment is accomplished.

6. It was not done before, lest holy things should be profaned.

7. It was then promised, that the spiritual sense of the Word was to be disclosed; and that the Lord alone is the Word.

8. Concerning His coming at that time.

9. On this account heaven has been opened to me.

II.

Now Is the End of Church, and with Few at this Day Is There Any Religion.

1. It is not known concerning the Lord, that He is the only God, who governs heaven and earth; thus that God is one in Person and Essence, in whom is a Trinity: when yet all religion is founded upon a knowledge of God, and upon the adoration and worship of Him.

2. It is not known that faith is nothing else but truth; and it is not known whether that which they call faith is truth, or not. Take certain things from the small work concerning the Lord.

3. There is a faith at this day; and tell what it is; . . . also there are degrees of justification: whether they are truths may be concluded from the following:

4. If this is faith, there is no need of truths, nor any need of charity, nor indeed of the knowledge of them.

5. It is not known what charity is.

6. Neither are evil and good known.

III.

EVERY MAN IS A MAN AFTER DEATH, AND THEN HE IS HIS LOVE; AND HIS LOVE IS HIS LIFE, WHICH REMAINS TO EVERY ONE TO ETERNITY.

1. Every one is examined after death as to what his love is.

2. Every spirit is his affection.

3. The whole heaven is distinguished into societies according to the varieties of the affections, and the whole hell according to the varieties of the lusts.

4. Such as a man's affection is, such is his thought.

IV.

THE DEVIL DWELLS WITH MAN IN THE EVILS OF HIS LIFE, AND THE LORD IN THE GOODS OF HIS LIFE.

V.

TO SHUN EVILS IS TO DO GOOD, AND THIS IS RELIGION ITSELF.

1. Some things concerning combats and temptations.

2. To shun evils is nothing else but to shun the devil; and as far as a man does this, he is conjoined to the Lord, and heaven is opened; and until then he is in hell.

VI.

The Man Who Shuns Evils Because They Are Sins Has Faith, and so Much of Faith as He Shuns Them.

1. There are truths of faith and truths of life. As far as the truths of life are made to be of one's life, so far the truths of faith are made to be of one's faith, and not in the least more or less.

2. Enumerate the truths of faith, which otherwise are science, and not faith.

3. On the exhortation of the English before the Holy Supper, and also that of the Swedes, also from obotfärdigas förhinder

4. Therefore there are two tables, and they are called a covenant: as far as the one is done by man, so far the other is opened.

VII.

The Ten Precepts of the Decalogue Contain All the Things of Religion in a Summary.

1. Many things concerning the sanctity of the Decalogue.

Recapitulation.

A recapitulation of the seven articles, and that it can be denied by no one, but that they are religion itself.

MARRIAGE

MARRIAGE

(DE CONJUGIO)

A POSTHUMOUS WORK OF

EMANUEL SWEDENBORG

MARRIAGE.

THE REPRESENTATION OF CONJUGIAL LOVE BY MOST BEAUTIFUL THINGS.

1. Love truly conjugial is represented in heaven by various things. It is represented by adamantine auras; sparkling as if from rubies and carbuncles; also by most beautiful rainbows and golden rains, which, when they are beheld, fill the bystanders with such pleasurableness and such delights, that they affect the inmosts of the mind. I have heard the angels, when conjugial love was so represented in the paradises of heaven, say that they were filled with such delight, that they could not express it otherwise than that it was delight itself, from which, as from their origin, all the rest of delights arise; and this delight was said to be a pure delight of the mind without any excitation of lust, for such is conjugial love in its origin.

2. Since love truly conjugial is in its origin pure delight itself of the mind, and that love is the fundamental of all loves, and from love is all the beauty of the angels in heaven, for love or the affection of love forms every one, wherefore every angel is as to his face the image of his love or affection, hence it is that all the beauty of the angels in heaven is from their conjugial love; for the inmost of their life which shines through is thence. An angel was seen by me, who was in pure conjugial love (he was from the third heaven); such was his beauty that the bystanders were carried away with admiration, saying that it was beauty itself in its essence.

3. That love truly conjugial is such beauty, and also such delight, is from its first origin, which is the union of the Divine love of the Lord with His Divine wisdom; then the marriage of the Lord with heaven, and with the church, and thence with every one the marriage of good and truth, concerning which origins of love truly conjugial it shall be spoken in their places.

In Love Truly Conjugial there Is Nothing Whatever of Lasciviousness.

4. Those who do not know what love truly conjugial is, and who are not in it, may think that it is not given without lasciviousness, but yet the difference is such as is between heaven and hell; for their delight appears in externals as if the same, but every external derives its quality and its essential nature from internals. The internal of conjugial love is from the Lord, and thence from heaven, and from everything auspicious and happy there; but the internal of lasciviousness or of adultery is from the devil, thus from hell and from everything inauspicious and unhappy. Every external derives its essence from internals; therefore neither are the external of conjugial love and the external of adultery alike. The external of conjugial love is filled with all the delights of heaven, and the enjoyment of heaven which is in that love expels all the enjoyment of hell; hence those two enjoyments in external form are, because of their internals, altogether dissimilar. The angels also clearly perceive from the sphere of the love of two consorts whether what is lascivious is in it, and its quality and quantity, and so far remove themselves from them. The reason that the angels so far remove themselves is, that the lasciviousness of adultery communicates with the hells, but the chastity of marriage with heaven.

Love Truly Conjugial Is Chastity Itself.

5. Celibacy is not called chastity in the heavens, nor is a girl called chaste, neither is an unmarried woman, nor a virgin, but a wife who turns away from adultery is called chaste; likewise a husband who turns away from it, because love truly conjugial is what is called in heaven chastity.

Conjugial Love Is Innocence Itself.

6. Consorts who are in conjugial love appear in heaven like the innocent.

Conjugial Love Is Love to the Lord.

7. All who are in love truly conjugial are in love to the Lord, because it descends from the marriage of the Lord with the church; hence it is that they who are in the third heaven, who are all in love to the Lord, are in love truly conjugial. Love truly conjugial cannot be given except by the Lord.

Two Consorts in Heaven Make One Angel.

8. There is between two consorts in heaven a similar conjunction as there is in every man between the will and the understanding, or between the good which is of the will and the truth which is of the understanding; because the female by nature is affection, which is of the will, and the male is by nature thought, which is of the understanding; more concerning these in the work on *Heaven and Hell*.

Those Who Have for an End in Marriages Lasciviousness Such As Is of Adultery.

9. There appeared to me as if in a kitchen, wherein was a dark fire-place, without fire on the hearth, [women] with knives in their hands with which they, as it were, wished to slay infants; they were crafty, cunning, and malicious, all harlots, secretly alluring men to themselves from every quarter. These being inspected by the angels, appeared like intestines in pairs of balls, one of which was filthily bloody, the other foully yellow; thus were represented their lusts when they were inspected by angels. All were such women as seek matrimony solely for the sake of adultery with others, because then they do not fear scandal on account of illegitimate offspring, which they attribute to the husband; their lot is most cruel; all things there are filthy; they dwell in caves, and on account of their ugliness and deformity they fear to be seen, nor can they longer allure any adulterer because they are deformed and have a foul smell; men, also, with whom adulteries are the end of matrimony, and afterward have lived with adulteresses, acquire such a nausea for a wife that they fly from them. They become at length impotences, and with them the life of thought and speech perishes in the society of wives, and especially in the society of their own wives.

Mice.

10. Lascivious wives, and also unmarried women who make light of whoredoms, dwell in two kinds of places, some in the western region in front, and some behind. All that are there knew how to insinuate themselves with men by simulated affections, by which they acquired the lascivious love of some male, caring nothing whether they were good affections or whether evil affections. Those who dwell in front were crafty and cunning, and of such a genius that they could perceive of what nature, disposition, inclination and cupidity were the men whom they wished to allure, especially in depriving a man of his wealth, and in the meantime that they may live luxuriously. They dwell there in caves wherein all things are fetid, and the places where they dwell smell like the smell where mice are; they even appear when seen by angels like great mice. I have heard certain ones, who had been in their caves, saying that the smell was that of mice, and that their places were fetid and filthy; but that they knew how, by phantasies, to render themselves beautiful, and also to decorate these places with various articles, but this only for some moments; for when the phantasies cease the appearances cease, and then all things are foul. It is said even that they delight in those foul and filthy things, the more so the more interiorly they are in them. That they are thus delighted is from correspondences with such a life. They were often seen by me, sometimes when by phantasies they had assumed beauty, appearing then magnificent in dress and charming in countenance; but as soon as fantastic thought was removed from them, which is done by a good spirit and by an angel, they appear deformed altogether like devils, some black, some horribly flamy, some like corpses, and also they were often seen by me like great mice with long tails. Their concupiscences appeared thus. What is wonderful, there are some spirits of both sexes who in the appearance of their passions appear like cats, and those mice fear them just as mice fear cats on earth; they appear like cats because they cared nothing for religious things, except that they heard them but retained nothing of them. I saw that in those caves are noble wives, yea, of such men as were of the first nobility;

but all there are compelled to labor, but no one of them can go out, nor is it permitted to let them out, because they are cunning beyond the rest of spirits, and enter the affections of men secretly and draw away their minds; in this they are more skilful than the rest, and so they are shut up, that at last they do not open a finger to let them out.

11. They, however, who dwell below in the western region are similar and in greater number. They are unmarried females who have given themselves to whoredom and passed their whole life in whoredom; there is a similar smell of mice there, not so strong, and they also appear like mice, but smaller. The caverns where they are appear winding and subterranean, one cavern below another, and a great multitude is there.

12. I have seen the larger mice, when a preacher came to them, hold by phantasy a book of psalms in their hand, and look towards certain from whom they draw what to answer, and answer as from themselves; this by cunning, and then they feign devotion, when yet they have no devotion at all; so they deceive the preachers, but they do this in the gates; but within in the caverns they answer nothing, because they cannot look to those from whom they draw the answers.

VARIOUS THINGS CONCERNING MARRIAGE AND ADULTERIES.

13. (1) Heaven is marriage and adultery is hell.

14. (2) Marriage descends from the marriage of good and truth, and adultery from the marriage of evil and falsity.

15. (3) Therefore there is given priestly adultery which in external appearance is similar.

16. (4) In heaven they abhor adulteries, and therefore heaven is closed to adulterers; and hell is opened wide according to the quality and quantity of the adultery.

17. (5) A man by conjugial love receives the form of love in the mind, and therefrom in the body, thus the form of heaven.

18. And a man by adulteries receives the form of adultery, thus the form of hell.

19. (6) Conjugial love is the fundamental love of all heavenly loves, and it is the image of heaven, thus of the Lord.

20. (7) Heavenly joy is founded upon conjugial love.

21. (8) Hence the heavenly joys which the angels have solely from thence are innumerable; and scarcely one of those innumerable joys is known in the world, because at this day adultery reigns there even from falsity of doctrine, but that they were known in part to the ancients.

22. (9) Angelic wisdom grows by marriages, and it is in the place of procreation to them; for which reason it is a procreation of wisdom, whence daughters, sons, father and mother in the Word signify such things as are of good and truth, thus which are of wisdom; passages may be adduced from the Word.

23. (10) From adulteries all ignorance and stupidity in spiritual things grow, because it is the marriage of falsity and evil. The falsification and adulteration of the truth and good of the Word is signified by whoredoms there, may be proved from the Word.

24. (11) To love the consort is to do good before the Lord, because this is chastity itself; and the church itself is called virgin and daughter, as the daughter and the virgin of Zion and Jerusalem. Passages may be quoted.

25. (12) Conjugial love has communication with heaven, and the organs of generation have correspondence with the third heaven; especially the womb, concerning which correspondence.

26. Even intercourse from conjugial love communicates.

27. (13) That love arises from the Lord's influx alone through the third heaven.

28. (13) (a) The third heaven is the conjugial of heaven; thus marriages are held as most holy in heaven, and adulteries profane.

29. (14) What adulteries are, considered.

30. (15) Conjugial love increases in potency and effect to eternity, insomuch that it is love as to all power and effect, thence is the life of their souls; but with adulteries love decreases as to power and effect, even so that it becomes impotence and a stock, and scarce of any life.

31. (16) No one can be in conjugial love unless he be spiritual by combat against evils and their falsities, and unless he acknowledges the Lord and His Divine.

32. (17) The wife and husband are consociated as to mind as one flesh.

It is my bone and my flesh, as Adam said.

33. (18) Conjugial love continually unites, that they be (one man).

34. (19) Conjugial love depends on the love of the wife, and such is the love of the husband in reciprocation, and the love of the wife does not depend on the love of the husband; the reason is, because like as the will actuates the understanding, good actuates truth, hence it is that it is said that the husband ought to cleave to the wife; the contrary is the case with those who are not in conjugial love.

35. (20) The wife wills to think and will as the husband, and the husband as the wife, and because each wills this, each is led by the Lord as one, and the two are one angel; for when the will and the understanding are not one's own, but the others, and this mutually and reciprocally, it cannot be otherwise than that they be led by the Lord as one.

36. (21) Hereditary evil becomes by adulteries continually more malignant, which is on account of adulteries which are considered allowable.

37. (22) Adulteries are most filthy may appear only from this, that the seed of the man as to its spiritual, and also as to its interior natural, adds itself to the body of the woman, for the man's life is in it; what, then, can it be, when the lives of several men are introduced at the same time, but filthiness and interior putridity.

38. (23) An example that one acquires such a nausea and disgust against his wife, as not to be able to look at her, merely when he doubted about God and the Word, was the priest, i. . . . .

39. (24) Conjugial love is such love, such delight, and such wisdom to those, that heaven is in it; that so far they are men, is confirmed by angels of heaven by a living voice. Afterwards they looked into hell, and said that there was all filthiness, and that especially adulterers and adulteresses appear like swine and hogs, and those who are like swine and hogs delight in ordure; and they said that one of them delighted in it so much that he wished to eat it. This coincides with the prophet who was ordered to make for himself a cake with dung.

40. (25) By conjugial love the interiors of the mind are opened, because the influx into it is from the Lord through the third heaven; thence a man becomes receptive of all celestial loves and likewise of truths.

41. (26) In conjugial love is the inmost of conscience.

Conjugial Love with the Angels.

42. I have spoken concerning conjugial love with angels, and they said that it is the inmost of all loves, and that it is such that a consort sees his consort in his soul and in his mind, so that his spiritual image is there; and thus that a consort has the consort as if in himself, and this is cohabitation in the spiritual sense. This also was represented by angelic ideas which cannot be expressed. Hence their conjunctions are delicious.

To One Man One Wife.

43. In the Christian world, where interior things of the church are revealed, and where the Lord is worshiped, and it is known that from Him is heaven and the church, and the church is conjoined with Him, as a wife with a husband, and that there is but one church, and that with those who are of that church there will be the conjunction of good and truth, it is not allowed to take several wives, for this would be to pervert the spiritual which is, or can be in marriage. Wherefore, if a Christian man should take several wives, it would be as if he had with himself two churches; also as if truth should take its essence from two goods, with which marriage is not given; for good is the *esse* of truth, and the *esse* or essence of one truth from two goods is not given. Whence it is that love truly conjugial can by no means be given in the case of one man with several wives, for thus it would be lasciviousness that would enter; besides, love cannot be divided, since it is from the affection of one, which is of the will, concordant with the thought of another, which is of the understanding, and this unanimity and cohabitation, which makes the essence of conjugial love, cannot be given (in the case of several wives). In a word, with them there is not the Christian Church, wherefore when an angel in heaven only thinks of several wives, the celestial and angelic perishes, and joy as well as wisdom with him, and he falls from heaven.

44. There have been seen those from Christians who have confirmed themselves about polygamy, they were several thousands in one society; for those who are alike as to love form a society, and conjugial love is the fundamental of all, and when the Last Judgment took place, that region appeared as if swallowed up by hell, and afterwards it was said that they knew nothing about their members of generation, just as if they had been without them; they had confirmed themselves in this from the Judaism of the Old Testament, because it was then lawful to take several wives; but it is lawful in Mohammedanism everywhere. It was permitted to the Jews because the Jews were external men, inwardly idolaters, with whom the interiors of the church were not, nor were opened; wherefore they did not recognize the Lord. What it is with Mohammedans shall be told hereafter.

45. In a word, several consorts and one husband cannot become one flesh, that is, one mind, which consists of will and understanding, the marriage of which, as far as relates to the mind in its existence, presents a marriage; for all things in the universe relate to the marriage of good and truth; thus to marriage, in order that they may be anything, and produce any thing, and marriage itself in its very form and its very essence, is presented in man with his compeer; likewise in an angel.

A PLURALITY OF WIVES AMONG MOHAMMEDANS.

46. I have spoken with Mohammedans about the spiritual marriage, that it is the marriage of good and truth, and that good loves truth, like two consorts, and that they desire to be conjoined, and to produce goods and truths, like daughters and sons, and to procreate families as it were. This they understood well, and also that conjugial love descends from that spiritual origin, and that all the spiritual with man undergoes a change, so that it may scarcely be recognized when it descends into the natural, but is known only by correspondences. From which it appears that those who have several wives conceded to them from their religion, cannot have love truly conjugial; and it is said that a plurality of wives was conceded to them, or polygamy was permitted, because those who are in warm countries, more than those who are in cold countries, burn with libidinous heat; therefore if polygamy had not been permitted them, many of them would rush into adulteries more than Europeans, and would thus act contrary to their religious persuasion, and to act contrary to that is to profane what is holy. It was shown further that all their love of marriage is lascivious, thus not spiritual, and cannot become spiritual unless they acknowledge the Lord.

47. The lot of those in the other life is such, that first, as in the world they there take several wives besides concubines (*pellices*); but because in the spiritual world the conjunction is of souls, and they are of different souls, they cannot be together, but separate from each other spontaneously, and are finally conjoined to a woman who is of similar soul; thus gradually they separate from their women, and thus finally are united with one with whom their soul accords; moreover, they who persist in polygamy, in the course of time become so feeble and impotent that they are disgusted with marriage, for lasciviousness brings this with itself.

48. Those of them who are in their heaven have but one wife, and have rejected more, for there is a Mohammedan heaven distinct from the Christian heaven; but they who at last, as do many, acknowledge the Lord as one with the Father, are separated into heavens, which communicate with the Christian heavens, and with them there is conjugial love.

49. They have heard from the angels conjugial love described as to its delights and pleasantnesses, and that it endures to eternity with an infinite variety of delights and pleasantnesses, and they wondered, many of them therefore received faith in the Lord, and were sent among the angels of the Christian heavens, and instructed concerning the Lord and in the doctrine of love and faith towards Him

The State of Consorts After Death.

50. Almost every one who has lived in marriage in the world, after death either meets with his wife, if she died first, or awaits her. When they meet, they mutually explore each other as to what their mutual affection was; and if there had not been mutual affection, they separate spontaneously, for two dissimilar affections and thoughts cannot consociate, for there is a communication of all affections and thence of thoughts; if there is not a concordance, a great uneasiness begins, then difficult breathing, like a discordant panting, so that they cannot but be separated, and then they are conjoined with others according to similitude.

51. They who have lived in celibacy, live also in celibacy for a long time; but, if they have desired marriage in the world, they also at length enter into marriage.

52. Those who cannot await the other consort, whether male or female, are conjoined in the meanwhile to another similar one; but then there is given them a perception that it is the same consort they had in the world, but this is dissolved, because there were no betrothing and nuptials, when the true consort arrives, for then from cohabitation in the world they know each other well, and they who wish remain with their own, as was said before.

53. The marriages of the angels of heaven are all provided by the Lord, who alone knows the similitude of souls which is to endure to eternity; and then a consort from the first glance recognizes his consort, which is because the similitude of souls conjoins

54. But in hell there are not marriages, but there are adulteries; in infernal societies there the men are separated from the women, and when they think that they are to speak with a wife, from a habit acquired in the world, he goes to the women and a persuasion is given him then that this or that one is his woman, with whom he then consociates himself; but that persuasion is varied, because it makes no difference, since in hell there is no marriage but adultery.

Those Who Live Modestly and Chastely in Outward Form, but Think Lasciviously.

55. Afar off were seen women concerning whom it was said that they had lived in the world as virgins, and had avoided matrimony for the sake of chastity, saying that matrimonies were in themselves unchaste, comparing them to allowed whoredoms; it was said also that many of them were from convents, professing chastity for the sake of heaven or eternal salvation. They appeared from afar as naked, because chastity and innocence is represented in the spiritual world by nakedness, which also signifies a life blameless and free from whoredom; but it was perceived that from afar off, in a secret place, they dealt, after death, with men, adulterers, taking care sagaciously not to be seen; but when they were manifestly infested, then they escaped with mocking and fled away. Then was felt the ardor of the men who desired them for wives, because they thought them more chaste and innocent than others. It was said that they were more obscene than others, having delighted in heinous lascivicusness; they were such women as had thought lasciviously within themselves.

56. It was said of them that after a space of time they acquire such an aversion for matrimony that nothing can exceed it, and conjugial love perishes, and they become disgusting, and this after they have been for some time foul prostitutes, having cast aside all shame, because the external being removed, the internal acts, and their internal without the external is then without any bond from shame.

57. Those who have affected external sanctity, and also have been given to devotion, and thus are religious, because they become profane and have mingled adulteries with the delight of sanctity, whence comes profanation, appear at length like bony skeletons.

To Command in Marriages Takes Away Conjugial Love, and Concerning the Dutch Women.

58. Concerning the love of commanding in marriages, that it takes away all love truly conjugial, since conjugial love is such that the one wills to think and will as the other, and thus mutually and reciprocally, so neither one commands, but the Lord; thence is the delight of conjugial love

59. That wives may not command over husbands is taken care of there in societies; there the men dwell on one side and the women or wives on the other, and when the men desire they send to them and summon them, and then they are separated, or live separately; if the wives are indignant and become angry on account of it, and infest the men because of serving and obeying when they are called; then they are sent forth from the society and wander over various places, and a desire is given to them of going away and deserting the husband; then when they wander, everywhere they encounter an inclosure or obstacle, as it were a marsh, water, or a wall, and so forth; and while this lasts the desire of going away diminishes, and they do this until they are tired out, and then they return to the society and to the mansion there where they had been before; thus the Dutch women are amended.

The Torment of Those Who are of Hell, from the Influx of Conjugial Love.

60. All influx from heaven torments the infernals, wherefore hell is removed from heaven and is also everywhere shut up, so that influx may not at all be felt; the reason is, that they are in contrary love, and just as infernal love torments the celestials, so celestial love torments the infernals; but the celestial prevails, wherefore hell is removed as far as possible; this is meant in the Evangelist, in Abraham's saying that there is a gulf, so that there is no passing over.

61. But the influx of conjugial love from heaven especially torments the infernals; I have seen spirits in hell brought even into the world of spirits, which is the middle, when these perceive the influx of conjugial love, they come into fury so as to act like furies, and also as if they were tormented like serpents in tamarisks [*myrica*], twisting hither and thither their bodies and intestines like one who is twisted miserably by torment within; they compared their suffering with the greatest sufferings; the reason is that the love of marriage and the love of adultery are altogether opposite, and conjugial love itself is heaven, and the love of adultery is hell. The love flows into their externals and torments their internals.

The Infernal Marriage.

62. The infernal marriage is when one wills to command and the other wills not to serve; thence is deadly hatred interiorly. This was represented by the most direful things, which on account of direfulness cannot be described. They breathe nothing else than slaughter, and also torment of each other; wherefore they are separated and live separated in hell and adultery, concerning which above, concerning Charles XII.

Those Who Plot Against Conjugial Love.

63. I have heard from such, many plots and secret arts of alluring chaste wives to adultery. I have seen more arts than in the world, gaining the favor of them as well as of the husband, by flattering both, and especially the husband; putting on the appearance of interior friendship, exploring the desires and cupidities of the wife, whether she wishes openly or unwillingly, besides a thousand other things. But such are sent not long after death into a hell, situated under the hinder part of the province of the knee, and are there very deep and altogether shut up, that there may be no aperture whatever to look out of that prison, for they are dangerous against conjugial love, which is most holy, and there they are compelled to labor, and have a harlot in place of a wife.

64. But they who have the rage of violation, and perceive a delight in violation, are let down into a cadaverous hell whence exhales a smell as from corpses, which excites vomiting; it excites it with me.

65. They plot by means of love towards infants; they were seen to rise from the earth over in front of Gehenna, almost invisible, continually removing obstacles, so that they might come into chaste homes; these they love, but not unchaste ones. They can put on various countenances, and also by arts send themselves forth through thoughts as if they were elsewhere, and thus enter. They put on also a countenance of innocence, and preach chastity; they extol it with praises; they enter into friendships in various ways, even so that they are praised and loved, and if the wife is conscious and desirous, she is praised. They spoke with me, saying, that they wondered that there could be any so conscientious as to say that this is against conscience, charity, and religion; they were in such persuasion, that they saw no evil in it, much less anything filthy. They also spoke sanely concerning marriage; their hell also is under the buttocks, in front, in the foul excrementitious smell there; and because they are crafty, feigning chastity, innocence, and friendships, and many other things, therefore when they come to their internals, which are adulteries, they are vastated until they appear deformed devils; as to internals little of the human remains. They become stupid because they are against the holiness of heaven. They mock and laugh at those who call marriages holy, and adulteries profane or even unlawful.

LOVE TRULY CONJUGIAL IS NAKED.

66. The angels of the third heaven are those who are in celestial marriage more than others, for they are in love to the Lord, and thence in the marriage of good and truth; whence also they are in conjugial love more than other angels, and in innocence and chastity. These walk with a cincture around the loins when abroad, and without the cincture when at home; and yet in their nakedness, they look upon the consort as a consort, nor is there anything lascivious therein. They say that to look at a consort clothed detracts from the idea of marriage, and what is wonderful, nakedness does not excite or stimulate; it is, however, as an internal bond of conjugial love. In bed they lie conjoined as they were created, and sleep so. They say that they cannot do otherwise, because conjugial love itself, which is perpetual, conjoins; thus also the life of the one is communicated with the life of the other, and the life of the husband becomes appropriated to the wife; that it may be as we read of Adam when he saw Eve his wife: "Behold my bone and my flesh," and also that "they were naked and not ashamed," that is not lascivious; but as soon as Adam through his wife receded from love to the Lord, which is meant by "the tree of life" in Paradise (of which there, and *Rev.* ii. 7), which happened because they acted from themselves and their own proprium, namely, from the science and delight of the natural man, then the marriage of good and truth perished, then nakedness became lascivious, and the chastity of marriage failing, they were ashamed of nakedness, and were clothed with fig-leaves, and afterwards with woollen garments; thence by nakedness in the Word is meant lasciviousness, like that of adultery.

67. In the other heavens under the third, all appear clothed, and also blush at nakedness before the eyes of others, because it excites lasciviousness; to them marriage is not such a delight as in the third heaven; in the lowest heaven there is also something of cold but not indeed as in the world.

68. I was carried by the Lord through changes of state towards the left to a certain mountain, where all were naked, wives and husbands, at a distance I spoke with them, and they said that all are naked there, and nevertheless no lascivious appetite or desire was caused to any one from seeing nakedness, and that each consort loved the consort tenderly; also that they could not be united with them clothed; they told the reason, that all were chaste in mind, because they were such in the world. When any new comer of such a nature arrives from the world, they explore him, which is done by his putting off his garments and stripping himself; then they perceive immediately whether he has a genuine conjugial; if not, he is driven away with punishment; they drive him with blows until he appears no more, and this to the depth. There was a certain one who thought he was in like conjugial love, because in the world he had lived chastely with his wife, nor had he ever had anything in common with harlots; he at first could look upon naked women without any emotion of mind, but when his sight had been fixed for some time he was deprived of his senses at the sight, and finally at the touch of nakedness, and stood without speech as if half dead, wherefore, he was driven away; the reason was that he was not in love to the Lord nor in the marriage of good and truth. They said that few could approach, because the sphere of conjugial love is such, that others cannot bear it;—they said that they live in houses with menservants and maid-servants who are all in marriage.

69. The angels of the third heaven dwell upon mountains, not rocky but of earth, upon which are paradises and gardens with trees; the mountains appear elevated to a point, in the highest part of the mountains are the best and most chaste; below, according to degree in marriage, are the spiritual and the spiritual natural; also their distinctions are according to the quarters, the eastern quarter where they are in love, the south where they are in wisdom.

Conjugial Love Descends from the Marriage of Good and Truth.

70. From much experience it has become known to me that no one has conjugial love unless he be in the love of truth from good, and in the love of good through truth, that is, in celestial marriage; and that no one can be in any mutual love of good and truth except they who shun adultery and are averse to it as infernal; and this although they may have lived in marriage in the world, and loved their consort on account of cohabitation and the delight of earthly life, and for the sake of children. For celestial things ought to flow into conjugial love, and man after death comes into his celestial or spiritual things, and then becomes such altogether as he was with regard to them, nor can it be otherwise.

Conjugial Love Causes a Man To Be Love.

71. Man was created to be love and thence wisdom, since the Lord is Divine love and Divine wisdom, and it is from creation that a man is the image and likeness of the Lord (*Gen.* i. 26, 27). And this cannot be without genuine conjugial love. From that everything of man can be turned into love, for in marriage it is lawful for each to love even the body from the heart, and thus to dispose the soul and all things thence to the form of love, which otherwise is not possible. The inmost and outermost there make one, and induce that form, and that form is a form of heaven.

The Exploration of Spirits by Conjugial Love.

72. Spirits who have recently come into the spiritual world are explored, first of all, as to whether they are against conjugial love; they are led to places where the sphere of conjugial love passes by, or to chaste consorts; if then they change countenance and indignation appears, and more, if they then think lasciviously, and still more if they speak so, it is a sign that they are of infernal mind; but if they then rejoice and are exhilarated, that they are of a celestial mind; it is a test whether they are of heaven or of hell; those who are against conjugial love are of hell; they who are with it are of heaven.

ADULTERIES FROM FAITH SEPARATED FROM CHARITY.

73. I was with those who had confirmed themselves in faith separated from charity, not only in doctrine but also in life, believing that they were to be saved by faith alone even in the hour of death, howsoever they had lived; and thus that all evils were either not regarded by God the Father, or excused on account of the infirmity of man, or remitted, and that when remitted, they were also washed away; they looking to the merit of the Lord from the fulfilment of the law, and that by the passion of the cross He had taken away the sins of the world, and the condemnation of the law, and various things which their doctrine teaches. I perceived when they were in the company of those, or among those with whom they communicated, when we were speaking of that faith, there existed the most obscene representations of heinous adultery, such as that of a son with a mother.* The sphere itself was such that it could be perceived by spiritual communication. They act into the occiput, and thus enter into the thought. From their presence also comes pain in the left knee.

74. The reason that such adultery is perceived from them is that they think of God, of the Lord, of salvation and of eternal life, and they confirm those things from the Word, which thence are spiritual, and because there can be nothing of faith unless it be conjoined with some love, and with them this is conjoined with love merely natural and with its cupidities, and the conjunction of faith with evil love makes that adultery. They think concerning faith from an evil life, and when they are in the delights of terrestrial and corporeal love, thence is the conjunction of faith or truth with evil. The spiritual which is of faith is as a mother, and the son is evil.

75. I have seen cohorts of them cast out into the hells, and many of them into deserts, where everything of faith is taken away from them, and there they live like wild beasts, and when everything of faith is taken away from them, they are almost deprived of rationality.

Why in the Christian World, more than Elsewhere, Adulteries Are Not Abhorred.

76. The Gentiles wonder why in the Christian world adulteries and whoredoms are accounted allowable by many and even by most, when yet their religion from the Word of both Testaments condemns them to hell; but the reason was told, that few live according to their religion, but have embraced the doctrine that faith saves; that is, that thinking and not living (saves); and because thus truth is conjoined with evil, thence from the influx from hell adulteries are loved and received, and also they excuse them. For the influx of hell prevails with them over the influx of heaven. The sphere of adultery also closes heaven, and when heaven is closed, hell is opened: hence its origin comes from the falsity of religions. It is otherwise with those who place religion in life and doctrine at the same time.

The Sphere of Adultery.

77. When they speak against the truths and goods of faith and charity, a sphere of whoredom and adultery is produced, and then adulterers rush thither as crows to a carcass, and delight in that stench; thence the sphere is filled with such and other obscene things, that a good person would be horrified.

Adulterers and Their Hells.

78. Their hells are under the buttocks, which are excrementitious; they desire to emerge thence and come into the world, but in vain, because they had loved terrestrial and corporeal things. Thence appeared, as it were, a vomiting and heaving, in such an effort are they.

Adulteries in the Christian World.

79. There are many there of family and of illustrious condition, and thus not of the common people, because they adopted the principle that marriages are for the sake of offspring, and it matters not whether they are violated by others; and they laugh at the sanctity of marriage, calling them silly.

Such were brought up out of the hells in great numbers, and being let into the state in which they were in the world, they inquired where there were beautiful wives, and when it was pointed out, they rushed like insane persons and like furies, wishing to enter into houses; but in their blind heat they were carried away to a place where the earth opened, and the crowd was cast into a hell which was behind the back.

THE INFLUX OF ADULTERY FROM GENII.

80. I have passed through the hell where were crafty and interiorly vastated adulterers, and then it was permitted them to flow into the affections of my will, and with such subtlety and art and skill to invert, pervert, and extinguish my thoughts in favor of chastity, and to induce the enjoyment and lust of adultery. They turned themselves to every particle of thought from affection, persuading silently: this was done with me, that I might know that man of himself could in no way resist the delight of adultery except from the Lord; for they act into the hereditary life within the thought, insomuch that man can in no wise observe it; but there was then given me by the Lord an interior perception of their effort.

PRIESTLY WHOREDOM.

81. This is especially committed by those who have confirmed the falsities of doctrine from the Word, and thus have falsified and adulterated it; the reason is that the Word is marriage, corresponds to marriage, and in itself is spiritual; and the delight of natural love falsifies it, especially in preachers.

82. They who read the Word without doctrine cannot but fall into many fallacies from the sense of the letter which is according to appearances with man, and at the same time they have acquired many falsities and confirmed themselves in them, and at the same time are thence in the pride of their own intelligence; these produce adulteries as of a father with a daughter-in-law.

83. They who confirm themselves that all evils are remitted by the Holy Supper, without other repentance and without conversion of life, and who do evils, and are in the belief that afterwards evil or sins are taken away by the Holy Supper, their adultery is with the maternal aunt.

84. Because the Jewish nation had by traditions falsified all things of the Word, it is called by the Lord an adulterous nation.

85. When charity is acknowledged and not faith, and yet the life of charity is not lived, and they still read the Word, it is the adultery of sister and brother. There are those who frequent the temple, and then pray devoutly and care nothing for evils of life, as thefts, secret robberies, adulteries, hatreds, revenges, cursings of enemies and those who do no favor them. This is with a sister.

86. The love of self, especially of ruling and yet thinking from the Word, is such as that of Sodom, wherefore they demanded the angels from the house of Lot.

87. Those who speak much concerning God, and yet care nothing about deceiving men and depriving them of their goods, commit adultery with maid-servants, whom they change frequently.

THE HELLS OF ADULTERERS.

88. There are many hells of these, according to the kinds of adultery, which are various.

89. I have seen harlots who hid themselves in the western region and obstructed the roads, that none might approach except they were willing; I was taken thither; and they were harlots who were all cast into a marshy pool, remote at the back, in the west; they were such as were openly harlots.

90. Those who had exercised whoredom secretly, without the knowledge of others, and were such to the end of life, were cast into a dark cavern in the west.

91. Some harlots of noble family who excelled in genius, and also could reason about God, are cast into a marshy pool in the southern region.

92. Other harlots who were able to steal men by arts not known in the world, compelling them into their proprium by praises and by the immersion of their mind into themselves, and because then being without protection from the Lord, they were delivered over to them, such women are cast into a place burning as it were with sulphur and fire, according to appearance. They dwell in the southwestern quarter, and similar men are cast into a dark abyss sloping under the pool of the women. Women fascinate men, and men women, by diabolical arts, which are many and which it is not allowed to recount.

93. Those who are adulterers spiritually are distinguished from adulterers naturally; the latter, if they perceive delight in adulteries, and no delight in marriages, are excluded from heaven, and are all sent into hells; but the adulterers spiritually, although they perceive nothing unlawful in adulteries, are yet explored and even amended, and others are allotted places according to life.

94. There are some in excrementitious hells who are addicted to variety, and by it have extinguished the conjugial; and at the same time are voluptuous; they are in the province of the intestines, under the former, where are everywhere sinks and a foul odor; and everywhere there are caverns from which such an odor exhales.

95. Those who had a communion of wives are bound as it were into a bundle, and the bundle is tied together by a stretched-out serpent and they are cast into a whirlpool which is beyond the spiritual world of this earth.

96. They who seduced by the appearance of piety, and thence persuade themselves that adulteries are not contrary to the Christian life, are sent into Gehenna, whence is perceived a stench as of burnt bones and hair, and are there in the fantasy that they are bitten by serpents; when in heat they are on fire, and when they approach heaven they become frozen like ice, and are miserably tortured.

97. Monks and Jesuits who have acted thus under the pretext of piety, and on account of pity towards them, with the promise that they would remit sins, are also committed to Gehenna.

THE CORRESPONDENCE OF THE MEMBERS DEDICATED TO GENERATION IN BOTH SEXES.

98. Those societies which correspond to the genitals are distinct from others, because that region in the body is also distinct.

99. Those who love infants, and educate them in heaven, constitute the province of the genital members, especially of the testicles and the neck of the womb, and live the most sweet and happy life.

100. There are societies of the third heaven, which especially correspond to those members, because they have conjugial love.

101. In general it is to be held that the loins, and the members appertaining thereto, correspond to genuine conjugial love, consequently to those societies where there is such love; the angels there are more celestial than others, and more than others live in a state of innocence and peace, and in its delights which are inmost.

102. There appeared to me trees planted in a nursery, one of which was taller, the other lower, and two small ones. The lower tree delighted me greatly; and at the same time the most pleasant quiet, which I cannot express, affected my mind. The angelic spirits interpreted this sight, saying, that conjugial love was represented, the quiet and peace of which were also felt in the mind. By the higher tree was signified the husband, by the lower one the wife, and by the two small ones children. They added that in such pleasantness of peace were those who belong to the province of the loins.

103. There appeared to me a great dog, such as he who is called Cerberus among the most ancient writers; he had terrible jaws. It was said that such a dog signifies a guard, that man may not pass from celestial conjugial love to the infernal love of adultery. When there is a passing from that love to this opposite one, the delight appearing almost similar, then there is set such a keeper, as it were, that opposite delights may not communicate.

104. The inmost heaven through which the Lord insinuates conjugial love, consists of those there who are in greater peace than others. Peace in the heavens is comparatively like spring in the world, which delights and vivifies all things; it is celestial delight itself in its essence. The angels who are there are the wisest of all, and from innocence appear to the others like infants; they love infants even more than their fathers and mothers have loved them. They also preside over those who are with young.

105. There are celestial societies with which each and all the members and organs dedicated to generation in either sex correspond. Those societies are distinguished from others, just as that province in man is altogether distinct from the rest. Those who have loved infants most tenderly, as such mothers, are in the province of the womb and the surrounding organs, namely, in the neck of the womb and the ovaries; and those who are there are in a most sweet and tranquil life, and in celestial joy more than others.

106. But what and of what quality those societies are which belong to each organ of generation, is not given to know, for they are interior. They refer also to the uses of those organs which are hidden and also removed from knowledge; for the reason, which is providential, that such things which are in themselves most celestial may not be injured by filthy thoughts, which are of lasciviousness, whoredom, and adultery, which thoughts are excited with many when those organs are only named. From the *Arcana Cœlestia* [n. 5055].

107. It is enough to know that love truly conjugial has immediate communication with the third heaven, and also that love itself with its celestial delight is there preserved in all its variety, and also its acts, such as kisses, embraces, and many other things which delight that heaven, for that heaven is in the communication of good affections, when the spiritual heaven is in the communication of the thoughts of truth; hence it is evident that filthy affections and thoughts altogether close both heavens.

108. A triturating vessel was seen by me, and by it stood a man with an iron instrument, who from his phantasy seemed to himself to triturate men in the vessel, torturing them in direful ways; the man did this with great delight. The delight itself was communicated, that I might know what and how great was the highest infernal delight with those who were such. It was told me that such a delight reigned with the posterity of Jacob, and that they perceived nothing more delightful than to treat the Gentiles cruelly, to expose them when killed to the wild beasts and birds to be devoured, to cut them while living with saws and axes, to cast them into a brick furnace (2 *Samuel*, 12: 31), to dash to pieces and cast forth infants. Such things were never commanded nor ever permitted, excepting to those the sinew of whose thigh was out of joint, as Jacob's when he wrestled with the angel (*Gen.* xxxii. 26, 32, 33). Such dwell under the right heel, where are adulterers who are also cruel. Among the adulterers who are both cruel and the most unmerciful, are many of the Jesuits and monks who were adulterers; their delight is similar when they behold the punishment of death, especially on those who derogate from their despotic power over the church and heaven, and over the souls of men, and also who infringe on their privileges.

109. Those who have lived in things contrary to conjugial love, namely, in adulteries, when they approached me, infused a pain into the loins, severe according to the life of adulteries which they had led, from which it appears that the loins correspond to conjugial love; their hell also is under the hinder parts of the loins, under the buttocks, where they live in filthy and excrementitious things; these also are delightful to them, for such things in the spiritual world correspond to their pleasures.

110. Those who are in things contrary to conjugial love, strike pain also into the testicles; they are those who lay an ambush by love, friendship, and good offices, concerning which the following: There arose from the region of Gehenna, as it were, a certain inconspicuous air; it was a band of such spirits, but it appeared then to me as one only, although they were many; against whom were interposed, as it were, bundles, which nevertheless they seemed to themselves to remove, by which was signified that they desire to remove obstacles, for in such manner do the thoughts and efforts of the mind appear representatively in the world of spirits, and when they appear, it is immediately perceived there what they signify; afterwards it seemed as if there proceeded from that body someone small and snow-white, who came to me, by which was signified their thought and intention, that they wished to put on the state of innocence, that no one should suspect anything of their quality; when he came to me he let himself down towards the loins and seemed to bend himself, as it were, around both of them, by which it was represented that they were in chaste conjugial love; then around the feet by spiral turns, by which was signified insinuation by such things as are in their nature delightful; finally that little one became almost invisible, by which was signified that he wished to be altogether hidden; it was told me that such was the insinuation of those who plotted against conjugial love: namely, who in the world had insinuated themselves for the end of committing adultery with wives, talking chastely and sanely concerning conjugial love, caressing infants, praising the husband in every manner of speech, so that they might be thought friendly and innocent, when yet they were cunning adulterers; it was shown me what such become, for after these things were done, that little snow-white person who represented the band arising from Gehenna was made conspicuous, and appeared dusky and very black, and very much deformed besides, and was cast forth into a deep hell under the middle part of the loins, where they live in excrements. I afterwards spoke with similar ones, and they wondered that any one should have conscience about adulteries, and on account of conscience should not lie with the wife of another when it was allowed; and when I spoke with them about conscience, they denied that any one had conscience. It was told me that such were mostly from the Christian world, and rarely any from other parts.

MARRIAGES.

111. What genuine conjugial love is, and whence is its origin, few at this day know, because few are in it; nearly all believe that it is inborn, and thus flows from a certain instinct, as they say, and the more so because the conjugial exists also with animals; when yet there is such a difference between conjugial love with men and the conjugial with beasts as there is between the state of a man and the state of a brute animal.

112. Conjugial love takes its origin from the marriage of the Lord with heaven and with the church, and thence from the marriage of good and truth. That conjugial love draws its inmost essence from thence, does not appear to the sense and comprehension, but yet can be proved from influx and from correspondence, and besides from the Word; from influx, because heaven is from the union of good and truth which inflows from the Lord, and is compared to marriage and called marriage; from correspondence, because when good united with truth flows down into a lower sphere, it presents there a union of minds, and when into one still lower, it presents a marriage; wherefore the union of minds from good united to truth from the Lord is conjugial love itself.

113. That genuine conjugial love is from thence may also be proved from this, that no one can be in it unless he be in good through truth, and in truth from good from the Lord; also from this, that celestial blessedness and happiness are in that love, and all they who are in it come into heaven or into celestial marriage; also from this, that when there is speech with the angels concerning the union of good and truth, there is presented in the lower region among good spirits a representative of marriage, and among the evil spirits is presented a representative of adultery; hence it is that the adulteration of good and the falsification of truth is called adultery and whoredom.

114. The men of the Most Ancient Church more than others on this earth lived in genuine conjugial love; they are those who were described by the ancients by those who lived in the golden age where innocence, love, and justice reigned. In that love there was heaven to them, but later, after the knowledge of the Lord, and thence love towards Him, perished, conjugial love perished, love towards children remaining; but children can be loved by the evil, but a consort cannot be loved except by the good.

115. I have heard from the most ancient people that conjugial love is such, that each one wishes to be altogether the other's, and this reciprocally, thus mutually and interchangeably, and then that the conjunction of two minds is such, that this mutual and interchangeable is in all and everything of the thought.

116. I have spoken with the angels concerning this mutual and reciprocal, and it was described that the image of one is in the mind of the other, and that thus they cohabit, not only in the single things but also in the inmosts of life; and that the Divine love of the Lord can flow into such a one with what is happy and blessed. They said also that they who have lived in such conjugial love in the world, are together, and cohabit in heaven as angels, also together with their children; but that very few are from Christendom at the present day, but all from the Most Ancient Church which was celestial, and many from the Ancient Church which was spiritual.

117. It was told me that the kinds of celestial and spiritual happinesses that is, only their universals, are indefinite in number and ineffable, and scarcely any one of them is known in the Christian world, because they are not in the marriage of good and truth, nor in love to the Lord; they know not whence is good, and thus what is truth, and they know not that the Lord alone is the God of the universe.

118. With those who live in conjugial love, the interiors of the mind are open through heaven, even to the Lord, for that love inflows from the Lord through the inmost of man; they thence have the kingdom of the Lord in themselves, and thence genuine love towards infants, which is for the sake of the Lord's kingdom, and thence they are more receptive of celestial loves than others, and are in mutual love more than all, for this comes thence as a stream from its fountain; for from the marriage of good and truth descend and are derived all loves, which are like the love of parents towards children, the love of brothers between themselves, and love towards relatives, thus according to degrees in their order, which loves are only from the marriage of good and truth; from this marriage are formed all celestial societies, according to all their consanguinities and affinities, and at the same time in each society, whence heaven is called a marriage.

119. Genuine conjugial love is not possible except between pairs, that is, in the marriage of one man with one wife, but not with many; because conjugial love is mutual and reciprocal, and the life of one interchangeably in that of the other, so that they are as one. Such a union is given between pairs, but not between many, for many destroy that love. The men of the Most Ancient Church, who were celestial and in the perception of the union of good and truth like angels, had one wife only; they said that they perceived with one wife celestial delights and happinesses, and when marriage with several was only named, they were horrified. That the marriage of one wife and husband descends from the marriage of good and truth is evident from the words of the Lord in *Matthew* xix. 3–12, which may be seen and adduced; also from the words of Adam concerning his wife. By " Adam and his wife" there is signified in the internal representative sense the Most Ancient Church, which was the golden age, the age of Saturn, concerning which the ancient authors wrote.

120. I have perceived the contrary with adulterers, that they are nauseated at marriage and all things which are of marriage, so that they see a wife but do not speak with her from any life; they are averse to all things of it which consorts formerly loved with delights. But as soon as they see the beautiful wife of another as the wife of another, they burn with cupidity; a fiery life kindles the countenance and eyes, and they take delight in everything of her which the husband is averse to, and thus he does when he sees other women.

121. There was a certain spirit in middle altitude, who in the life of the body had lived lasciviously, being delighted with variety, so that he had loved no one woman constantly, but in brothels, and thus had committed whoredom with many and afterwards rejected each one, whence it happened that he had extinguished the desire for marriage, and had contracted an unnatural nature; all these things were disclosed, and when he attempted a like thing in the spiritual world he was miserably punished, and this in sight of the angels, and then cast into a hell, which is such that they appear there like scum such as is on the surface of the sea; they are the mucus of the nostrils and almost without life, because they have lost everything human, because everything of heaven, which is founded upon conjugial love.

122. That they cannot be in heaven is evident, for they are as it were contrary to the love of marriage, thus they are contrary to the affections of good and truth from which heaven originates; for when marriage is mentioned there, filthy ideas immediately come in from influx into the contrary. In their ideas are obscene, yea heinous things. They are also in the purpose of destroying heavenly societies. Their religion is to say that they acknowledge the Creator of the universe, Providence only universal, and salvation from faith alone, and that it cannot be worse with them than with others; but when they are explored as to what they are in heart, which is done in the other life, they do not believe those things at all, but in nature instead of the Creator of the universe; and instead of a universal Providence, in none at all; religion they believe to be for a restraint on the common people to make them live morally. With those who by adulteries have acquired a disgust and nausea for marriages, when anything pleasant, blessed, and happy flows down from heaven, it is turned into what is nauseous and loathsome, then into what is painful, and finally into what is noisome; with others into what is obscene.

123. They desire to obsess man, and with man to return into the world; but they are shut up that they may not speak with man.

124. The conjugial is represented everywhere in the kingdoms of nature, as from the transformation of worms into nymphs and chrysalises, and thus into winged insects; for when the time of their marriages arrives, which is when they put off earthly forms, which is their worm form, they are distinguished with wings and become flying insects; then they are elevated into the atmosphere as into a certain heaven of theirs, and there they sport among themselves, transact marriages, lay their eggs on leaves, and are nourished with the juice of flowers. They are then also in their beauty, for they have wings of golden, silvery, blue, and shining white colors, and some beautifully distinguished and variegated. Such things does the conjugial produce with such lowly small animals.

125. There are those who have the cupidity of deflowering young virgins, or to whom virginities and thefts of virginities are the greatest pleasures, without the end of marriage, and when they have stolen the flower of virginity, they afterwards desert them. Those who have led such a life, because it is contrary to their spiritual and celestial nature, and because they destroy the conjugial, are interior murderers, who undergo the most grievous punishment in the other life, for they regard this only from the flower of virginity, which being bereft, they love them no longer, and because it is contrary to innocence, which they wound and kill by leading into a life of harlotry innocent women who otherwise would be chaste, who might be imbued with conjugial love, and thus are destroyers of marriages. It is known that it is the first flower of love which initiates virgins into chaste conjugial love and conjoins the souls of consorts, and because the sanctity of heaven is founded upon conjugial love, thus upon innocence. They are led into phantasies, the actions in which appear as it were real and sensible, and they seem to themselves to sit upon a furious horse which throws them upwards, so that they are thrown down from the horse as if with risk of life, such a terror is struck into them; afterwards they appear to themselves to be under the belly of a furious horse, and shortly it seems to them as if they went through the posteriors of a horse into his belly, and then it appears to them as if they were in the belly of a filthy harlot, which harlot is changed into a great dragon, and there they remain wrapped up in torments; this punishment returns as often as they are in that cupidity, and approach young virgins with their craft. Others are punished by disjointings and unjointings, or by contortions and retortions, from which punishments they are so torn to pieces that they seem to themselves as if cut into bits or fragments with cruel pain, and if then they do not desist, they are cast into a hell of foul-smelling odor.

126. Those who in the life of the body think lasciviously, and whatsoever others speak convert it into lasciviousness, even holy things, do not cease to think and speak thus in the other life; and there, because their thoughts are communicated, those things come out into obscene representations, whence are scandals. Their punishment is to be stretched out horizontally in the presence of the spirits whom they have injured and whirled around like a roller from left to right rapidly, and then in a reverse direction in another position, and then in another, and so naked in the presence of all, or half naked according to the quality of their lasciviousness, and at the same time they are struck with shame. Then they are whirled around by the head and feet transversely like a wheel;

resistance is caused, and at the same time pain, and again resistance and at the same time pain, for two forces act, one around, the other back, and so with the drawing apart pain is caused.

N. B.   N. B.

More concerning these subjects may be seen in the first extracts: in ADULTERY, HARLOT, LASCIVIOUSNESS, MARRIAGE; also in Notes from the ARCANA CŒLESTIA. *Especially from Notes upon the Apocalypse, and in extracts from the work on " Heaven and Hell," and also from other places.*

Angelic Wisdom Concerning Marriage

INDEXES

TO "THE MISSING TREATISE"

ANGELIC WISDOM

CONCERNING

MARRIAGE

POSTHUMOUS WORKS OF

EMANUEL SWEDENBORG

EDITOR'S NOTE.

The two indexes which follow belong to a work usually referred to as the Missing Treatise on Conjugial Love. The manuscript of this work has not been found. It was probably the first draught of the work on *Conjugial Love*, published by Swedenborg. There was in it about 2,050 short paragraphs. It was divided into two parts, with sixteen chapters in the first and ten chapters in the second part. The subjects and wording of the indexes closely agree with those in the work on *Conjugial Love*.

The Latin text prepared from the Photolithograph Manuscript by Dr. Samuel Howard Worcester has been compared with the Photolithograph Manuscript, and a number of corrections have been made. The changes are noted in the critical notes. We desire to acknowledge our indebtedness to the Rev. Alfred Acton for a list of corrections of the Latin text of these indexes, and of the *Last Judgment* (*Posthumous*), published in Vol. I.

Some references to paragraphs in the indexes do not agree; but as the original work is not extant, we have retained the figures as they are given in the original manuscript.

JOHN WHITEHEAD,
Editor and Translator.

Angelic Wisdom Concerning Marriage.

Order of the Chapters.

Part First.

I.—Marriages in Heaven [(*See the same subject treated of in the published work concerning Conjugial Love*, n. 27–41)].

II.—The State of Consorts After Death [(*C. L.*, n. 45–54)].

III.—Love Truly Conjugial [(*C. L.*, n. 57–73)].

IV.—The Origin of Love Truly Conjugial, from the Marriage of Good and Truth [(*C. L.*, n. 83–102)].

V.—The Marriage of the Lord and the Church, and Correspondence with It [(*C. L.*, n. 116–131)].

VI.—The Chaste and the Unchaste [(*C. L.*, n. 138–150)].

VII.—Universals Concerning Conjugial Love [(*C. L.*, n. 209–230)].*

VIII.—The Causes of Coldnesses, of Separations, and of Divorces, with Consorts [(*C. L.*, n. 234–260)].

IX.—The Causes of Apparent Love, Friendship and Favor with Consorts [(*C. L.*, n. 271–292)].

X.—The Change of the State of Life with Man and with Woman by Marriage, from which the Young Man Becomes a Husband, and the Virgin Becomes a Wife [(*C. L.*, n. 184–206)].

[AUTHOR'S MARGINAL NOTES, FROM THE PHOTOLITHOGRAPH, p. 20.—VII.]

* Universals:—The conjugial sphere from heaven inflows into the wife only, and through her into the husband, and is received by the husband according to his wisdom [(*C. L.*, n. 225)].

The delight of conjugial love is holy and chaste [(*C. L.*, n. 144, 346)].

Conjugial love regards the eternal [(*C. L.*, n. 38, 44, 200, 216)].

XI.—CONJUNCTION OF SOULS AND MINDS BY MARRIAGE; WHICH CONJUNCTION IS MEANT BY THE WORDS OF THE LORD, THAT THEY ARE NO LONGER TWO, BUT ONE FLESH [(*C. L.*, n. 156[*]–181)].*

XII.—BETROTHALS AND NUPTIALS [(*C. L.*, n. 295–314)].

XIII.—REPEATED MARRIAGES [(*C. L.*, n. 317–325)].

XIV.—POLYGAMY [(*C. L.*, n. 332–352)].

XV.—JEALOUSY [(*C. L.*, n. 357–379)].

XVI.—THE LOVE OF INFANTS, OR PARENTAL LOVE, AND ITS CONJUNCTION WITH CONJUGIAL LOVE [(*C. L.*, n. 385–414)].

PART SECOND.

I.—THE OPPOSITION OF CONJUGIAL LOVE AND SCORTATORY LOVE [(*C. L.*, n. 423–443)].

II.—FORNICATION; ALSO CONCERNING KEEPING A MISTRESS [(*C. L.*, n. 444[*]–460)].

III.—CONCUBINAGE [(*C. L.*, n. 462–476)].

IV.—ADULTERIES AND THEIR DEGREES [(*C. L.*, n. 478–499)].

V.—THE LUST OF VARIETIES [(*C. L.*, n. 506–510)].

VI.—THE LUST OF DEFLORATION [(*C. L.*, n. 501–505)].

VII.—THE LUST OF VIOLATION [(*C. L.*, n. 511, 512)].

VIII.—THE LUST OF SEDUCING INNOCENCIES [(*C. L.*, n. 513, 514)].

IX.—THE CORRESPONDENCE OF SCORTATIONS AND ADULTERIES WITH THE VIOLATION OF SPIRITUAL MARRIAGE, WHICH IS THE MARRIAGE OF GOOD AND TRUTH [(*C. L.*, n. 515–520)].

X.—THE IMPUTATION OF EACH LOVE, SCORTATORY AND CONJUGIAL [(*C. L.*, n. 523–531)].

[MARGINAL NOTES.]

*They are conjoined as to minds, and at length as to souls; which conjunction is this:—

They are conjoined as to duties [*officia*] [(*C. L.*, n. 174–176)].

They are conjoined as to internals more and more, even so that they wish to be one [(*C. L.*, n. 185, 196)].

This union was inscribed on them by creation [(*C. L.*, n. 66)].

The more they are united, the more do they become sensible of the state of blessedness, through the delights of peace (*see also* n. 854, iii., iv.; n. 2007, 2023, 2036, 2047, 2048).

At the same time rational wisdom and moral wisdom are conjoined. *What each of these is* [(*C. L.*, n. 102, 163, 168, 293)].

GENERAL CONTENTS.

1. *Marriages in heaven* (n. 2–30 [*C. L.*, n. 27–41]).
2. *The origin of conjugial love* (n. 31–76 [*C. L.*, n. 83–102]).
3. *The delights of love truly conjugial* (n. 77–146 [*C. L.*, n. 183; see also n. 69, 144, 155, 293, 294]).
4. *The connection of conjugial love with all the loves of heaven* (n. 147–222 [*C. L.*, n. 388–390]).
5. *Masculine and feminine conjugial love, specifically; and the intelligence of each* (n. 223–303 [*C. L.*, n. 218; see also n. 32, 61, 88, 90, 168]).
6. *The marriage of good and truth* (n. 304–407 [*C. L.*, n. 83–102, 122, 123]).
7. *The differences and the variety of conjugial love, according to the states of the church with men* (n. 408–568 [*C. L.*, n. 130]).
8. *The increments of love truly conjugial, and the decrease of love not truly conjugial* (n. 769–763[1] [*C. L.*, n. 162, 184–200, 213, 214, 432, 433]).*
9. *Conjugial similitude and dissimilitude* (n. 564–852[2] [*C. L.*, n. 227–229, 246]).
10. *The causes of coldnesses, separations, and divorces, with consorts* (n. 853–1018 [*C. L.*, n. 234–260]).
11. *Polygamy, or plurality of wives* (n. 1019–1110 [*C. L.*, n. 332–352]).
12. *Betrothals and nuptials* (n. 1111–1193 [*C. L.*, n. 295–314]).
13. *The difference between the love of the sex with beasts and the love of the sex with men* (n. 1194–1251 [*C. L.*, n. 94, 137, 230, 416; see also the posthumous treatise, Concerning Divine Love, xxi.]).
14. *The change of state of woman and of man by marriage; from which change the virgin becomes a wife, and the young man a husband* (n. 1252–1286 [*C. L.*, n. 184–200]).
15. *The state of widowers and of widows; also concerning repeated marriages* (n. 1287–1300 [*C. L.*, n. 317–325]).
16. *The marriage of the Lord with the church* (n. 1301–1344 [*C. L.*, n. 116–131]).
17. *Correspondence of the marriage of the Lord and the church with things relating to marriage with angels and men* (n. 1345–1457 [*C. L.*, n. 125–127]).
18. *Natural conjugial potency and spiritual conjugial potency* (n. 1459–1585 [*C. L.*, n. 220, 221]).
19. *The causes of love, friendship, and favor, between consorts* (n. 1586–1641 [*C. L.*, n. 180, 214. 290]).
20. *The love of infants, or parental love* (n. 1642–1700 [*C. L.*, n. 176, 211]).
21. *The conjunction of conjugial love with love of infants or parental love* (n. 1701–1718 [*C. L.*, n. 385–414]).
22. *The state of two consorts after death* (n. 1719–1737 [*C. L.*, n. 45–54]).

[MARGINAL NOTE].

*See the UNIVERSALS concerning conjugial love, n. 569–763; especially the last part of n. 723, concerning masculine love and feminine; also n. 564–852.

SCORTATORY LOVE (n. 1738. seq.).

1. *Jealousy* (n. 1739–1791 [*C. L.*, n. 357–379]).
2. *Fornication* (n. 1792–1848 [*C. L.*, n. 444[*]–460]).
    It there treats:—
    (1) *Concerning keeping a mistress* (n. 1806, seq. [*C. L.*, n. 459, 460]):
    (2) *Concerning the lust of varieties* (n. 1811 [*C. L.*, n. 506–510]):
    (3) *Concerning the lust of defloration* (n. 1814 [*C. L.*, n. 501–505]):
    (4) *Concerning the lust of violation* (n. 1419[1] [*C. L.*, n. 511, 512]):
    (5) *Concerning the lust of seducing innocencies* (n. 1823 [*C. L.*, n. 513, 514]).
3. *Concubinage* (n. 1849–1873 [*C. L.*, n. 462–467]).
4. *Adulteries* (n. 1874–1909 [*C. L.*, n. 478–499]).
5. *The opposition of conjugial love and scortatory love* (n. 1910-1949 [*C. L.*, n. 423–443]).
6. *The correspondence of whoredoms and adulteries with the violation of spiritual marriage, which is the marriage of good and truth* (n.) 1950–2001 [*C. L.*, 515–520]).

CONTENTS OF THE REMAINING ARTICLES.

1. *The perception and the wisdom proper to man and proper to woman, also the conjunction of man and woman by them* (n. 2007 [*C. L.*, n. 163–173]).
2. *Duties proper to man and proper to woman; also the conjunction of man and woman by them* (n. 2023 [*C. L.*, n. 174–176]).
3. *The transcription of the love of his own (proprii) with the man, into conjugial love with the wife* (n. 2036 [*C. L.*, n. 32, 88, 156[*], 193, 293, 353]).
4. *The faculties, inclinations, affections and qualities of men and of women, and their conjunction by marriage* (n. 2047 [*C. L.*, n. 163–180]).
5. *Proprium in man, and proprium in woman; and their transcription into conjugial love* (n. 2048 [*C. L.*, n. 32, 156, 163–173]).
6. *Coldnesses in marriages* (n. 2049 [*C. L.*, n. 234–260]).
7. *Difficulties in understanding the conjunctions of consorts, and the varieties therefrom* (n. 2050).

MEMORABILIA.

Consorts from the third heaven were seen, borne in a chariot, and descending; described as to face and as to garments; having spoken with me, they let down a parchment on which were inscribed arcana of conjugial love (n. 1, p. 16 [*C. L.*, n. 42, 43]).

The correspondence of conjugial love with fire, with the colors of the rainbow, with fragrant things, with rose-gardens and arbors, with winged things and animals, represented by angels (n. 29, p. 42½, 43 [*C. L.*, n. 76, 293, 294, 316]).

The nuptial garden which appears round about the houses while nuptials are celebrated; and the Divine Providence which encompasses marriages: from the discourse of a certain wise person in the garden (n. 76, p. 49 [*C. L.*, n. 316]).

There were seen consorts from the third heaven; at first appearing as infants decked with garlands, afterwards of their proper stature. They had lived a thousand years in conjugial blessedness. Conjugial love, as it is in that heaven, is described; it is from wisdom and from the love of wisdom, and it is with those who do uses, etc. (n. 146, p. 50 [*C. L.*, n. 137]).

Something about the magnificent and splendid things in heaven: next it is told whence angels have perpetual potency: confirmed by reasons, given by an angel (n. 222, p. 46½, 47 [*C. L.*, n. 12–20, 355, 356]).

A paper on which was inscribed, "The Marriage of Good and Truth;"—how it appeared on the way, when let down to the earth by an angel, and how it was changed: also many things about that marriage, in the whole heaven and in the church (n. 301, p. 46 [*C. L.*, n. 115]).

Adulterers seen like satyrs, in the company of harlots, in a wood and in a cavern[1] there; afterwards in a house: where they were speaking heinous things about marriages, nature, and **religion** (n. 407 [*C. L.* n. 521]).

A discussion concerning God and nature,—(1) **Whether nature is of life, or life of nature**: (2) Whether the centre is of the expanse, or the expanse of the centre: (3) Concerning the centre and the expanse of nature and of life (n. 568, p. 79 [*C. L.*, n. 380]).

Concerning a certain garden, in which there were several married pairs; also conversations there respecting love, wisdom and use; that the three proceed from the Lord, and that hence are conjugial love and its ineffable delights: much concerning these and their origin (n. 763, p. 41 [*C. L.*, n. 183].)

Concerning a young man who boasted of his whoredom; he was conducted into heaven, and there he was held by turns in his externals and his internals: while in externals he saw heavenly things, but while in internals he saw the opposite (*concerning which see* n. 852, p. 77 [*C. L.*, n. 477]).

While following the light, I came to the Temple of Wisdom, around which there dwelt those who were wise; there I conversed with them concerning the cause of the beauty of the female sex (n. 1018, p. 45 [*C. L.*, n. 56]).

Of the new things revealed by the Lord: as concerning the spiritual sense of the Word, and concerning correspondences, concerning heaven and hell, concerning the spiritual world and the sun there; also concerning conjugial love, as being according to religion: but that these things are not received in the world was testified by experience (n. 1108, p. 48, also 50 [*C. L.*, n. 532–534]).

Discussions, by the wise, of the following subjects:—(1) What the image of God is, and what the likeness of God: (2) That man is not born into love and into knowledge, as the beasts are, but only into capacity to know and inclination to love: (3) Concerning the tree of life, and the tree of the knowledge of good and evil (n. 1193, p. 60 [*C. L.*, n. 132–136]).

Concerning Athenæum, Parnassium, and Heliconeum: conversation with ancient wise men, and with two newly come from the earth, about men who had been found in the forest; also concerning things that were said in favor of nature and the life of beasts, compared with the life of men (n. 1251, p. 64 [*C. L.*, n. 151[*]–154[*]]).

Again three new-comers were conducted to Athenæum,—a priest, a politician, and a philosopher; who reported, as news from the earth, that a certain person had written various things[1] about the life of men after death and about the spiritual world; and they told how these subjects were discussed on earth (n. 1286, p. 66 [*C. L.*, n. 182]).

A tumult against three priests, who preached that with adulterers there is no acknowledgment of God, and consequently that they have not heaven; also what happened to them, out of heaven (n. 1300, p. 75 [*C. L.*, n. 500]).

Concerning a novitiate who meditated about heaven and hell, and who was told to make inquiry, and to learn what delight is: he was led to three assemblies,[2] in which he learned what the delight of heaven is, and what the delight of hell (n. 1344, p. 54 [*C. L.*, n. 461]).

A disputation by spirits concerning God and concerning nature; in favor of nature from devils, and in favor of God from angels: also that man may confirm himself in favor of God, more than for nature, from the things that he can see: those things are adduced which were written on this subject in *Angelic Wisdom concerning Divine Love and Divine Wisdom* (n. 1458, p. 62 [*C. L.*, n. 415–422]).

A melody was heard concerning chaste love of the sex; and that they have that love who are in love truly conjugial, and thence in fullest potency (n. 1585, p. 64 [*C. L.*, n. 55]).

Various reasonings about the soul; and finally that the soul is the man living after death, because it is the form of all the affections of love, and of all the perceptions of wisdom, and is their receptacle (n. 1641,[3] p. 70 [*C. L.*, n. 315]).

After this there was a conversation about the spiritual and the natural; and it was shown what differences there are between them, as to languages, writings, and thoughts: the conversation was renewed when looking at a moth,[4] and observing that when divided it was more and more multiform, and not more and more simple (n. 1699, p. 72 [*C. L.*, n. 326–329]).

Wise men were called together from nine kingdoms of Europe, to give their opinion concerning the origin of conjugial love, and concerning its virtue and potency; and at last the prize, which was a turban, was given to an African (n. 1718, p. 30 [*C. L.*, n. 103–114]).

Three orators from France discoursed concerning the origin of the beauty of the female sex; one said that it was from love, another from wisdom, and the third from the conjunction of love and wisdom (n. 1737, p. 57½, 58 [*C. L.*, n. 381–384]).

Concerning two angels, who had died in infancy, and who could not perceive what whoredom is, because it is not from creation. Conversation about it, and concerning evil; how evil exists, when from creation there is only good (n. 1738, p. 86 [*C. L.*, n. 444]).

Exclamations were heard, "O how just," "O how learned," "O how wise;" and it is here said of those called just, that they were those who gave judgment from friendship, and were able skilfully to pervert all things; they had no understanding of things that were just: their assemblage is described (n. 1791, p. 37 [*C. L.*, n. 231]).

Preliminary statements concerning the joys of heaven, and concerning nuptials there (n. 1826–1848, p. 1 [*C. L.*, n. 1–25]).

Concerning the love of dominion from the love of self; with politicians, that they wish to be kings and emperors; with canons, that they wish to be gods. Concerning devils that were seen, who had been in such love; also concerning two popes (n. 1873, p. 56 [*C. L.*, n. 261–266]).

Again in Athenæum; where three new-comers were heard to say that they had believed that in heaven there were no administrations and works, because there was eternal rest; and it was shown that doing uses is that rest; there was also mention of books and writings; and it was said that there are these also in heaven, for all substantial things which are called spiritual are there (n. 1909, p. 68 [*C. L.*, n. 207]).

Of those concerning whom was the exclamation, "O how learned:" they were those who go no farther in their reasoning than to question whether a thing is so, and who are called reasoners (n. 1948, p. 38 [*C. L.*, n. 232]).

Of those concerning whom was the exclamation, "O how wise:" they were those who were able to make whatever they pleased to be true, and were called confirmers (n. 1949, p. 30 [*C. L.*, n. 233]).

A conversation of angels with three novitiates concerning nuptials in heaven (*various things*, n. 2001, p. 17 [*C. L.*, n. 44]).

Golden rain was seen: I was conducted to a hall where husbands and wives instructed me concerning conjugial love; also concerning its delights, from the wives there (n. 2002, p. 34 [*C. L.*, n. 155 [*]]).

Conversation with those who lived in the golden age, concerning conjugial love, and in regard to their marriages (n. 2003, p. 20, *seq*.[1] [*C. L.*, n. 75]).

Conversation with those who lived in the silver age; this, too, concerning conjugial love (n. 2004 [*C. L.*, n. 76]).

Conversation with those who lived in the copper age (n. 2005 [*C. L.*, n. 77]).

Conversation with those who lived in the iron age; they were polygamists (n. 2006 [*C. L.*, n 78]).

Conversation with those who lived after those four ages; they were whoremongers and adulterers (n. 2034 [*C. L.*, n. 79, 80]).

Of the conversion of this age into a golden age by the Lord; concerning which the angels glorified the Lord (n. 2035 [*C. L.*, n. 81]).

Concerning one's own intelligence or prudence, that it is not [anything] n. 2051, p. 59 [*C. L.*, n. 353]).

Whether conjugial love and love of [their own] beauty coexist in women; and whether conjugial love and the love of their own intelligence coexist in men (n. 2052, p. 52 [*C. L.*, n. 330, 331]).

Again the golden rain was seen, and some arcana respecting conjugial love in women were disclosed (n. 2053, p. 35 [C. L., n. 208]).

Spiritual coldness has its seat in the highest region (n. 2054, p. 51 [C. L., n. 270]).

Concerning those who are in the love of the world (p.[1] 90 [C. L., n. 267-269]).

The delights of conjugial love are delights of wisdom (p.[2] 91 [C. L., n. 293]).

And the pleasures of scortatory love are pleasures of insanity (p.[3] 92 [C. L., n. 294]).*

---

* [A memorandum of the Author here follows:—] Concerning adulterers as satyrs; this has not been written out, see before n. 407,—and let it be allowed[4].

FIRST INDEX.

ADULTERIES (*Adulteria*).—(*See also* LASCIVIOUSNESS.)
Concerning the three degrees of adulteries (n. 386-388 [*C. L.*, n. 432, 485-499]). (*See* DEGREES.)
Concerning adulterers seen as satyrs, in company with harlots, in a wood, and in a cavern there; and afterwards in a house, where they were conversing together about marriage, nature, and religion (*Memorab.*, n. 407 [*C. L.*, n. 521]).
They who have no religion have not conjugial love; but lust which is worse than the lust of a wild beast (n. 439¹-445 *C. L.*, n. 79, 239, 240).
Of the closure of the mind with adulterers and the evil (*various things*, n. 562-565 [*C. L.*, n. 203]).
Conjugial similitude and dissimilitude are not regarded with those who are in scortatory love (n. 818-822).²
Conjugial love and scortatory love are altogether opposite to each other (n. 847-851 [*C. L.*, n. 423-429]).
Concerning a young man who boasted of his whoredom; he was conducted into heaven; he was held by turns in externals and internals; and thus he saw opposite things (*Memorab.*, n. 852 [*C. L.*, n. 477]).
An internal cause of coldness between consorts is, that the evil of whoredom is not believed to be sin; still more, if it is confirmed that it is not sin (n. 913-917 [*C. L.*, n. 240]).
A cause of coldness is, whoredom before marriage with the wives of others; also meretricious love and concubinage after marriage: in general, all libidinousness by which the conjugial perishes (n. 918-928).
A cause of coldness between consorts is, that conjugial love is believed to be one with scortatory love (n. 958-961 [*C. L.*, n. 247]).
Whoredom is the genuine cause of divorce (n. 985-993 [*C. L.*, n. 255]).
Adulterers do not acknowledge God (*Memorab.*, n. 1300 [*C. L.*, n. 500]).

Whoredoms in general correspond to falsifications of truth and profanations of good, by means of the Word (n. 1399–1403 [*C. L.*, n. 77, 80, 517, 518]).

Heinous adulteries within the prohibited degrees correspond to certain heresies confirmed by the Word (n. 1405–1407 [*C. L.*, n. 519]).

The internal and spiritual cause of conjugial love is to shun adulteries from religion (n. 1602–1606 [*C. L.*, n. 147–149]).

An external or natural cause of love and friendship between consorts, is abstinence from whoredom from any cause, excepting impotence only (n. 1611–1614).

Concerning angels of innocence, who did not understand what scortatory love[1] is (*Memorab.*, n. 1738 [*C. L.*, n. 444]).

Concerning fornication (*see* FORNICATION, MISTRESS).

There are several kinds of adulteries; there are those that are mild, those that are grievous, and those that are most grievous (n. 1876 [*C. L.*, n. 479, 487, 491, 493]).

Simple adultery is that of an unmarried man with the wife of another, or of an unmarried woman with another's husband (n. 1877–1879 [*C. L.*, n. 480]).

It can be seen from reason that adultery is unjust (*various things*, n. 1778[2] [*C. L.*, n. 481]).

Duplicate adultery is the adultery of a husband with the wife of another, or of a wife with another's husband (n. 1880–1885 [*C. L.*, n. 482]).

With whom there is such adultery (*various things*, n. 1882 [*C. L.*, n. 483]).

There is such in England (n. 1883 [*C. L.*, n. 483]).

Triplicate adultery is with blood-relations (n. 1884, **1885** [*C. L.*, n. 484]).

There are adulteries of will, and there are adulteries of deed; and adulteries of the will in themselves are like those that are actual when opportunity offers and various fears do not prevent (n. 1886, 1887 [*C. L.*, n. 490]).

There are actual adulteries which are of the will, and there are adulteries which are not thus of the will; the latter are mild, but the former grievous (n. 1889–1892 [*C. L.*, n. 486, 491–494]).

Causes that certain adulteries are not committed in man's interior will (n. 1892 [*C. L.*, n. 486]).

Adulteries that are actual and of the will make man natural, sensual, and corporeal, as to the will, its inclinations and affections (n. 1894–1896 [*C. L.*, n. 495, 496]).

Their effect is, that man does not acknowledge God, the Divinity of the Lord, the holiness of the Word, and consequently the other things that belong to the church and to religion (n. 1897–1903 [*C. L.*, n. 497]).

Adulterers have the capacity to understand, equally with those who are not adulterers; but they abuse their rationality to confirm their adulteries (n. 1904–1908 [*C. L.*, n, 498, 499]).

How adulterers converse in favor of adulteries and against marriages (n. 1908 [*C. L.*, n. 500]).

The opposition of conjugial love and scortatory love (n. 1910–1947 [*C. L.*, n. 423–443]).

Scortatory love is opposite to celestial love, because scortatory love is infernal, and conjugial love is heavenly (n. 1911–1914 [*C. L.*, n. 429]).

Scortatory love is in the enjoyment of evil and falsity, but conjugial love in the enjoyment of good and truth (n. 1915–1919 [*C. L.*, n. 427]).

The uncleanness of hell is from scortatory love, and the cleanness of heaven is from conjugial love (n. 1920–1924 [*C. C.*, n. 430]).

So with what is unclean and what is clean, in the church (n. 1925–1931 [*C. L.*, n. 431]).

Scortatory love begins from the flesh, but conjugial love from the spirit (n. 1932–1938 [*C. L.*, n. 440, 441]).

Scortatory love makes a man (*homo*) not man; yea, the man not a man: but conjugial love makes a man (*vir*) more and more a man; yea, the man more and more a man (n. 1939–1942 [*C. L.*, n. 432, 433]).

The delights of scortatory love are pleasures of insanity, and the delights of conjugial love are enjoyments of wisdom (n. 1943–1947 [.*C L.*, n. 442, 443).

Correspondence of whoredoms and adulteries with the violation of spiritual marriage, which is that of good and truth

(n. 1950-2000 [*C. L.*, n. 515-520]). (*See* Correspondence.)

Adulteries are infernal (*various things*, n. 1999 [*C. L.*, n. 356, 477, 483]). (*See* Correspondence.)

Some things respecting adulterers and adulteries in hell (n. 2000 [*C. L.*, n. 500, 520]).

Concerning those who lived after the four ancient ages; they were whoremongers and adulterers (*Memorab.*, n. 2034 [*C. L.*, n. 79, 80]).

Concerning the hells of adulterers, in the west; where they appear like lakes of fire and brimstone (*Memorab.*, n. 2035 [*C. L.*, n. 79, 80]).

Affection (*Affectio*).—(*See* Love in general.)

The affections of the love of good are infinite in number; so too the affections of the love of evil, which are called[1] lusts (n. 766 [*C. L.*, n. 427]).

Affections which are of love distinguish men from each other; affections of good distinguish the good, and affections of evil distinguish the evil (n. 773-779 [*C. L.*, n. 427]).

The affections of the love of good and the affections of the love of evil are internal and external (n. 780-784 [*C. L.*, n. 272]).

With some the internal and the external affections of love are concordant and act as one, and with others they are discordant (n. 785-802 [*C. L.*, n. 272]).

Nearly all in the natural world can be conjoined as friends as to external affections, but few as to internal affections (n. 803-813 [*C. L.*, n. 272]).

In the spiritual world, however, all are conjoined as to the internal affections of love (n. 814-823 [*C. L.*, n. 273]).

With men there are internal affections, and with women external affections (n. 824-832 [*C. L.*, n. 32, 88, 89]).

There is an infinite variety of internal affections with men, and an infinite variety of external affections with women (n. 833-840 [*C. L.*, n. 36]).

There is given a similarity and a dissimilarity between the internal affections of men and the external affections of women (n. 841-844 [*C. L.*, n. 195, 227]).

Several articles concerning the inclinations and affections, or the qualities of men and of women, and concerning the conjunction of these by marriage (n. 2047 [*C. L.*, n. 88-91, 218]).

ANGEL (*Angelus*).—(*See the other Index.*)

BEAST (*Bestia*).—(*See the other Index also.*)
Various things concerning the state of beasts (n. 576 [*C. L.*, n. 94-96, 133, 134]).
Love of the sex with men and with beasts (n. 1194-1251 [*C. L.*, n. 48, 94-96]).
Differences between beasts and men (n. 1194, 1197, 1198 [*C. L.*, n. 48, 94-96, 133, 134]).
Man acts from the will and from its freedom, and from the understanding and according to its reason: but the beast acts not from a will, thus not from freedom, neither from an understanding, thus not according to its reason; but from connate loves, through knowledges that promote them (n. 1196-1199 [*C. L.*, n. 133, 134]).
Because man has will and understanding, he knows the order according to which he ought to live; he knows this from the Divine laws which are those of the church, from the civil laws which are those of society, and from the laws of reason; but the beasts know not any order from those laws, but are carried along by knowledges that are born to their loves, and of which they are wholly ignorant, to do what they do (n. 1200-1211 [*C. L.*, n. 133, 134]).
The influx into men and into beasts (n. 1200 [*C. L.*, n. 94, 137]).
Man is born with the faculty to become rational and spiritual, and the beast is born with no faculty for these things (n. 1212-1218 [*C. L.*, n. 96, 151-153]).
From these three considerations it follows, that in all which a man thinks, speaks, wills, and does, there is the rational and the spiritual, in their own way; but that in all that a beast expresses by sound or by act, there is not the rational nor the spiritual in any way (n. 1219-1221 [*C. L.*, n. 94, 133, 134]).

In the love of the sex with men there consequently is the rational and the spiritual,[1] and thence imputation; but in the love of the sex with beasts there are not those (n. 1220–1235).

In everything that man does, there is imputation; but there is no imputation in anything done by a beast (n. 1222–1227 [*C. L.*, n. 96]).

Therefore if the love of the sex with men were as it is with beasts, man would not from this be as a beast, but viler than a beast (n. 1234, 1235).

There are many other distinctions between the love of the sex with men and with beasts; but they can be seen by those only who are familiar with the differences between man and beast (n. 1236–1238).

Man is not born into the knowledge that pertains to love of the sex, but the beast is born into it all; but this knowledge is knowledge to man, but to the beast it is not knowledge (n. 1239–1242 [*C. L.*, n. 133, 134]).

Since the knowledge into which the beast is born is void of reason, a beast cannot be said to have any love for the sex; but only something analogous thereto, which is nothing else than desire from the heat of the flesh (n. 1243–1246).

All things that have been said of marriages and whoredoms, have been said concerning men: they cannot be said of beasts, for these have neither marriages nor whoredoms (n. 1247–1250).

Conversation with ancient wise men about men found in the forest, and concerning the state of men in comparison with the state of beasts (*Memorab.*, n. 1251 [*C. L.*, n. 151[*], 154[*]]).

BEAUTY (*Pulchritudo*).—Discourse of the wise concerning the beauty of the female sex (*Memorab.*, n. 1018 [*C. L.*, n. 56]).

Three orators from France, on the beauty of the female sex (*Memorab.*, n. 1737 [*C. L.*, n. 381–384]).

Whether conjugial love and love of one's own beauty[1] can exist together; also whether conjugial love and love of one's own intelligence can exist together (*Memorab.*, n. 2052 [*C. L.*, n. 330, 331]).

BETROTHAL (*Desponsatio*).—(*See* BRIDEGROOM.)

BIRTH (*Nativitas*).
NATIVITY (*Nativitas*).
{ —Spiritual births are meant in the Word by the many names of generation (n. 1335–1337, 1338–1341 [*C. L.*, n. 120]).

BRIDEGROOM (*Sponsus*).
BRIDE (*Sponsa*).
BETROTHALS (*Desponsatio*).
{ —Be'rothals and nuptials (n. 1111–1192 [*C. L.*, n. 295–314]).

Selective choice belongs to the man, and not to the woman (n. 1113–1117 [*C. L.*, n. 296]).

The man ought to court and to solicit the woman respecting marriage with himself, and not the woman the man (n. 1118–1121 [*C. L.*, n. 297]).

The woman ought to consult her parents, or those who are in place of parents, and deliberate with herself, before she consents (n. 1122–1125 [*C. L.*, n. 298, 299]).

After a declaration of consent, pledges are to be given (n. 1126–1128 [*C. L.*, n. 300]).

Consent is to be confirmed and established by solemn betrothal (n. 1129–1136 [*C. L.*, n. 301]).

By betrothal the internal man of each is formed for conjugial love (n. 1136–1140 [*C. L.*, n. 301, 302]).

Causes (n. 1139 [*C. L.*, n. 301, 302]).

By betrothal the mind of one is conjoined to the mind of the other, so that a spiritual marriage takes place before the natural and bodily (n. 1141–1150 [*C. L.*, n. 303]).

This is the case with those who think chastely concerning marriage; it is otherwise with those who think unchastely (n. 1150, 1151 [*C. L.*, n. 304]).

Within the time of betrothal it is not allowable to be joined corporeally (n. 1151–1156 [*C. L.*, n. 305]).

After the completion of the period of betrothal nuptials ought to take place (n. 1157–1160 [*C. L.*, n. 306]). (*See* NUPTIALS.)

CAUSE (*Causa*).—(*See also the other Index.*)

How the end progresses through causes to effects, acts reciprocally, and accomplishes its circle (*various things,* n. 79–81 [*C. L.*, n. 387, 400, 401]).

In every created thing there are end, cause and effect, also progression through them (n. 82–84 [*C. L.*, n. 400]).

End, cause and effect act as one (n. 85, 86 [*C. L.*, n. 387, 401]).

Illustrated by soul, spirit and body (n. 86).

The love is the end, the mediate form of the love is the cause, and the ultimate form of the love is the effect (n. 87, 88 [*C. L.*, n. 387]).

In the Lord is the one only end which is love, the one only cause which is wisdom, and the one only effect which is use (n. 89–96 [*C. L.*, n. 400]).

These three proceed from the Lord as a one (n. 97–100 (n. *C. L.*, n. 400]).

All who are in love truly conjugial become angels after death; the converse also is true (n. 743–752 [*C. L.*, n. 48–53]).

CENTRE (*Centrum*).—Whether the centre is of the expanse, or the expanse of the centre (*Memorab.*, n. 568 [*C. L.*, n. 380]).

CHASTITY (*Castitas*).—Many things concerning chastity (n. 254–257 [*C. L.*, n. 44, 138, 139, 143, 149, 302, 503]). (*See also* LASCIVIOUSNESS.)

Articles on the chaste and the unchaste (n. 2046 [*C. L.*, n. 138–156]).

CHURCH (*Ecclesia*).—*See also* SPIRITUAL, MARRIAGE, (RELIGION).

The marriage of the Lord with the church (n. 1301–1344 [*C. L.*, n. 115–131]).

In the Word the Lord is called "the Bridegroom" and "Husband," and the church is called "the Bride" and "Wife;" the conjunction of the Lord with the church, and of the church with the Lord, is called "the marriage" (n. 1304, 1305 [*C. L.*, n. 117]).

The Lord is called "Husband" from the Divine good and the Divine truth united; and the church is called "Wife" from the reception of the Divine good in the Divine truth (n. 1306–1310 [*C. L.*, n. 116–126]).

- This marriage is with the Divine Human of the Lord, and through this with the Divine that is called the Father (n. 1311–1317 [*C. L.*, n. 129]).
- They make the church, with whom there is that marriage, who go immediately to the Lord and live according to His precepts (n. 1318, 1319 [*C. L.*, n. 129]).
- They are in this marriage who are and who will be of the church which is meant by "the New Jerusalem" (n. 1320–1323 [*C. L.*, n. 43, 534]).
- They who are in this marriage are in consociation with angels (n. 1304–1328).
- All are in this marriage who are being reformed and regenerated by the Lord (n. 1329–1331).
- There is Divine celestial marriage, Divine spiritual marriage, and Divine natural marriage; and still the three make one marriage (n. 1332–1334).
- Whereas offspring are born from that marriage, which are goods and truths, therefore the Lord is called "Father," and the church is called "Mother" (n. 1335–1337 [*C. L.*, n. 118–120]).
- Births from the Lord as Father through the church as Mother are all spiritual, and they are meant in the spiritual sense of the Word by "sons," "daughters," "brothers," "sisters," "sons-in-law," "daughters-in-law," and by other names designating descent from one father (n. 1338–1341 [*C. L.*, n. 120]).
- The means of the Lord's conjunction with the church, and of the church with the Lord, is the Word; for this is from the Lord, and is the Lord (n. 1342 [*C. L.*, n. 128]).
- The Word is the means of conjunction to those who read it for the end that they may learn truths and live according to them (n. 1343 [*C. L.*, n. 129]).
- Correspondence of the spiritual marriage, which is that of the Lord and the church, with marriages in the heavens and on earth (n. 1345–1458 [*C. L.*, n. 125–127]). (*See* CORRESPONDENCE.)
- Glorification from the Word by the angels of heaven, because of the advent of the Lord (*Memorab.*, n. 2035 [*C. L.*, n. 81]).

COLDNESS (*Frigus*).—Causes of coldnesses, separations and divorces, with consorts (n. 853–1018 [*C. L.*, n. 234–260]).

Spiritual heat is love, and spiritual cold is no love (n. 855–857 [*C. L.*, 235]).

Spiritual celestial heat is the love of good and truth, and infernal spiritual heat is spiritual cold (n. 858–864 [*C. L.*, n. 235]).

There is spiritual coldness between consorts when there is not love, because there is not union of souls and is not conjunction of minds; whence there is indifference, contempt, disgust, aversion, enmity, hatred; from which at length with many there is separation as to bed, bedchamber and house (n. 867–869 [*C. L.*, n. 236]).

The causes of coldness are interior, exterior, and accidental (n. 870–874 [*C. L.*, n. 237]).

Of the interior causes of coldness, the *first* is the rejection of all things of the church (n. 875–891 [*C. L.*, n. 240]):

The *second* cause is, that one has religion, and not the other (n. 892–897 [*C. L.*, n. 241]):

The *third*, diversity of religion, or that one has one religion and the other another (n. 898–905 [*C. L.*, n. 242]):

The *fourth*, falsity of religion imbued (n. 906–912 [*C. L.*, n. 243]):

The *fifth*, that the evil of whoredom is not believed to be sin; and more if it is confirmed that it is not sin (n. 913–916 [*C. L.*, n. 243]):

The *universal* interior cause of coldness is, all love of evil, especially the love of whoredom, of which there is variety; there is whoredom before marriage, with the wives of other men, there is meretricious love or love of concubinage after marriage, also the desire of defloration, the lust for varieties, the enticement of violation, and in general all that is lustful, from which the human conjugial perishes (n. 918–928 [*C. L.*, n. 244, 245]).

Of the exterior causes of coldness between consorts, the *first* is, dissimilitude of external minds (*animorum*) and manners (n. 929–934 [*C. L.*, n. 246]);

The *second*, inequality of state and condition in externals (n. 935–933 [*C. L.*, n. 246, 250]).

The *third*, every cupidity of evil, especially that of having dominion on the part of one, and more when there is this desire in both (n. 939-945 [*C. L.*, n. 248]):

The *fourth*, that cohabitation with a wife from covenant and law seems forced, and not free; and thus a debt, and not free will (n. 946-950 [*C. L.*, n. 257]):

The *fifth*, that there is no determination to any pursuit; whence comes either stupid slothfulness or wandering cupidity (n. 951-953 [*C. L.*, n. 249]):

The *sixth*, that conjugial love is believed to be one with scortatory love (n. 958-961 [*C. L.*, n. 247]).

Of the external causes of coldness between consorts the *first* is a vitiated condition of the mind (n. 962-966 [*C. L.*, n. 252]):

The *second*, a vitiated condition of the body (n. 967-971 [*C. L.*, n. 253]):

The *third*, impotence (n. 972-978 [*C. L.*, n. 254]).

Of accidental causes of cold between consorts, the *first* is the commonness, from being continually allowable (n. 994-1000 [*C. L.*, n. 256]):

The *second* is, unseasonable solicitation by the wife, and immodest discourse by her respecting love (n. 1001-1006 [*C. L.*, n. 258]):

The *third* is, the thought of the husband at the side of his wife by night, and at the sight of her by day, that she is willing and he not yet able (n. 1007-1012 [*C. L.*, n. 259]);

A cause of coldness on the part of the wife, that she knows, hears or thinks that the husband is able but not willing (n. 1013-1017 [*C. L.*, n. 259]).

Man does not know of this coldness before the nuptials (n. 1017, *end*).

Articles concerning coldness (n. 2049 [*C. L.*, n. 234]).

Some causes of coldness (*Memorab.*, n. 2053 *at end* [*C. L.*, (n. 208]).

Conjugial cold has its seat in the highest region of the mind (*Memorab.*, n. 2054 [*C. L.*, n. 270]).

CONCUBINAGE.—Concerning concubinage (n. 1849-1872 [*C. L.*, n. 462-476]).

Concubinage is the adjunction of a concubine to a wife (n. 1851 [*C. L.*, n. 462]).

The adjunction of a concubine to a wife, or simultaneous concubinage, is altogether unlawful to Christians, and is detestable (n. 1852–1857 [*C. L.*, n. 464]).

It is polygamy, which has been condemned in the Christian world, and is to be condemned (n. 1858, 1859 [*C. L.*, n. 465]).

It is whoredom, by which the conjugial, which is the jewel of Christian life, is destroyed (n. 1860-1862 [*C. L.*, n. 466]).

There are two kinds of concubinage, which differ very greatly from each other: one kind is simultaneous, or conjointly with a wife; the other is substitutional, and is apart from a wife; and there are causes legitimate, just and excusatory, which concede this second kind of concubinage (n. 1863 [*C. L.*, 463, 467]).

Legitimate causes which concede concubinage that is substitutional and apart from the wife, are the legitimate causes of divorce (n. 1864–1866 [*C. L.*, n. 468, 469]).

Just causes are all the just causes of separation as to bed (n. 1867 [*C. L.*, n. 470]).

The excusatory causes are real and are not real. Excusatory causes that are real, are those which are drawn from what is just; excusatory causes which are not real, are those which are not drawn from what is just, although from an appearance of it (n. 1868, 1869 [*C. L.*, n. 471–474]).

The love of concubinage and conjugial love are diverse (n. 1870 [*C. .L*, n. 466]).

They who, from causes legitimate, just, and really excusatory, are in the love of this concubinage, may be at the same time in conjugial love; but they who are in the love of concubinage, and not from these causes, are in no conjugial love (n. 1871, 1872 [*C. L.*, n. 475]).

CONFIRMATION (*Confirmatio*).—Concerning confirmers who confirm all things, and who do not know whether truth is truth (*Memorab.*, n. 1949 [*C. L.*, n. 233]).

CONJUGIAL (*Conjugiale*).—The conjugial is chief among the essentials of human life, and it distinguishes man from common animal life: according to it, therefore, man is man (n. 834–838 [*C. L.*, n. 140, 148, 203, 230]).

According to the loss and deficiency of the conjugial, man approaches the nature of the beast (n. 840–846).

Certain causes from which the conjugial perishes (n. 922 [*C. L.*, n. 80]).

Some things regarding the conjugial, and the things which destroy it (n. 1734, 1735 [*C. L.*, n. 238–243]).

The conjugial is the very jewel of human life, and the repository of the Christian religion; it is therefore to be preserved in every possible way (n. 1804, 1805 [*C. L.*, n. 456–458, 466, 531]).

Also, what the conjugial is (n. 1805 [*C. L.*, n. 457]).

The conjugial may be conserved by keeping a mistress (n. 1806, 1807 [*C. L.*, n. 459]).

The conjugial is destroyed by the excessive lusts of varieties (n. 1810–1813 [*C. L.*, n. 456]);

By the lust of defloration (n. 1814–1817 [*C. L.*, n. 504]).

So, too, by the lust of violation (n. 1819–1822 [*C. L.*, n. 511]).

And also by the lust of seducing innocencies (n. 1823–1825 [*C. L.*, n. 513, 514]).

CONJUGIAL LOVE (*Amor conjugialis*).—(*See the second Index.*)

There is a universal sphere of conjugial love, filling both worlds (n. 2 [*C. L.*, n. 90, 222, 225]).

Man after death is his own love and the wisdom therefrom (n. 9–12 [*C. L.*, n. 34, 36]).

Man is his own love, and love is the man (n. 9 [*C. E.*, n. 35, 39]).

The love of the spirit, or of the internal man, remains after death (n. 10 [*C. L.*, n. 34–36, 46]);

But not the external (n. 11 [*C. L.*, n. 35]).

There is not love without knowledge, intelligence, and wisdom (n. 12 [*C. L.*, n. 134]).

Something about the love of heaven and the love of hell (n. 13).

(*Concerning the love of the sex, see* SEX.)

Love in general is an image of the one in the other, from agreement (n. 18 [*C. L.*, n. 172, 173]).

This is still more the case with conjugial love, which is described as to its quality (n. 19, 20 [*C. L.*, n. 172, 173]).

Conjugial love represented by fire, colors, fragrances, rose-gardens, arbors, flying things, animals (*Memorab.*, n. 29 [*C. L.*, n. 76, 293, 294, 316]).

Conjugial love has been destroyed on earth, but it can be raised up by the Lord (n. 31 [*C. L.*, n. 69, 81]).

The origin of conjugial love (n. 31–76 [*C. L.*, n. 60, 61, 75, 83, 102, 103, 143]).

Conjugial love is from the Lord, because all the good of love and the truth of wisdom are from Him (n. 34–35 [*C. L.*, n. 60, 84–86]).

How conjugial love flows in with man (n. 51 [*C. L.*, 92, 93]).

Conjugial love again described as to its quality, as to its conjunction and its reciprocation with male and with female: also illustrated from the Word (n. 52–55 [*C. L.*, n. 33, 37, 61, 132, 316]).

The spiritual love of minds internal and external (*mentium et animorum*) descends from the highest[1] origin (*illustrated*, n. 57–59 [*C. L.*, n. 61, 68, 69]).

Through spiritual conjugial love exists natural conjugial love, which belongs to all things of the body (n. 60–62 [*C. L.*, n. 69]).

The quality of the influx (*illustrated*, n. 60–62 [*C. L.*, n. 86, 183, 208, 304, 313, 355, 461]).

Hence conjugial love is made full (n. 63–66 [*C. L.*, n. 310]).

Concerning love in the body; in the breast, and in the loins (n. 64, 65, 67, 68 [*C. L.*, n. 76, 171, 179, 183, 224, 305, 310]).

Connected series of causes as to conjugial love, from the first to the last (n. 63–65).

They have conjugial love who go to the Lord, and who are in the marriage of good and truth; thus conjugial love is with those who are in true religion (*illustrated*, n. 67, 68 [*C. L.*, n. 67, 68, 70, 81, 98]).

(*Concerning the delights of conjugial love, see* DELIGHTS.)

The delights of conjugal love belong to the sense of touch (n. 116–119 [*C. L.*, n. 210, 396]).

The most exalted use is from conjugal love (n. 128–130 [*C. L.*, n. 68]).

Conjugal love is according to conjunction with the Lord (n. 131–135 [*C. L.*, n. 71, 72]).

It is according to religion, and there is none where there is not religion (n. 140–144 [*C. L.*, n. 531]).

Conjugal love is from wisdom and its love, conjoined (*Memorab.*, n. 146 [*C. L.*, n. 137]).

Conjugal love is according to uses (*Memorab.*, n. 146 [*C. L.*, n. 137]).

They [who have mutually loved each other, and from religion have shunned adulteries as enormous sins,] come into the flower of their life (*Memorab.*, n. 146 [*C. .L*, n. 137]).

The connection of conjugal love with all the loves of heaven (n. 147–222 [*C. L.*, n. 65–67]).

The more one shuns adultery, the more he loves the consort (n. 185–188).

They become one form (n. 189–197 [*C. L.*, n. 195–201]).

Many things from the angels concerning conjugal love; what the husband has therefrom, and what the wife (n. 193).

Various things from the angels concerning the chasteness of marriage; examination is made as to quality in respect to it (n. 206).

The one form, which husband and wife become, conjoins itself with all of that[1] society (n. 212–216).

Concerning masculine conjugial love and feminine, specifically; also concerning the intelligence of each (n. 223–301 [*C. L.*, n. 184–199, 218]). (*See* SEX.)

Whence are the delights (*deliciae*) of conjugal love, many things (n. 258–262 [*C. L.*, n. 198]). (*See* SEX.)

Communication of delights from wives with their husbands (n. 263–265 [*C. L.*, n. 188, 189]). (*See* SEX.)

From these things may be seen the difference between conjugial love and the love of the sex. The latter is natural, and common to all animals; the former is spiritual, and is peculiar to man (n. 294–300 [*C. L.*, n. 94–100]).

(*Concerning the degrees of conjugial love, see* DEGREES.)

Conjugial love makes one with the church and religion with them (n. 393–406 [*C. L.*, n. 129–131]). (*See* RELIGION.)

Conjugial love makes one with the state of the church and of religion with man, and such is heaven to him (n. 393–406 [*C. L.*, n. 129–131, 238, 458]). (*See* RELIGION.)

The differences and variety of conjugial love, according to the states of the church with men (n. 408–568 [*C. L.*, n. 130, 434]).

Conjugial love is internal and is external (n. 409–412 [*C. L.*, n. 534]).

That internal love is twofold, spiritual and celestial (n. 413–416 [*C. L.*, n. 305]).

The external also is twofold, rational and natural (n. 417–421 [*C. L.*, n. 305, 310]).

The internal is angelic, and can be given with men (n. 422–425).

The external properly is human (n. 426, 427).

Natural conjugial love, separate from rational conjugial love, properly is ferine (n. 427–430 [*C. L.*, n, 230]).

Internal conjugial love, celestial and spiritual, cannot be separated from external conjugial love, rational and natural; but they are together, and thus act as one (n. 430–434).

Conjugial love in its first origin is the love of good and truth (n. 562–572 [*C. L.*, n. 83–102]).

They have love truly conjugial who are in truths and love to propagate them (n. 513–515 [*C. L.*, n. 220]).

The increments and the decrements of conjugial love (n. 569–763 [*C. L.*, n. 157–181, 211–214]).

Man is man according to the quality of conjugial love with him (*various things*, n. 575–592 [*.C L.*, n. 140, 432]).

He is man so far as spiritual conjugial love makes one with natural conjugial love (n. 593–597 [*C. L.*, n. 230]).

In love truly conjugial there is the eternal; and conversely (n. 622–629 [*C. L.*, n. 38, 44, 200, 216]).

How spiritual love proceeds from firsts to ultimates (n. 630–638 [*C. L.*, n. 101, 183, 400, 401, 440, 441, 447]).

Conjugial love is without any lasciviousness (n. 630–638 [*C. L.*, n. 143–146]).

Spiritual celestial love between consorts is love truly conjugial; which regarded in itself is union of souls, conjunction of minds, and endeavor in all things of the body to conjunctions in the breast, and delightful conjunction from these (n. 865-870 [*C. L.*, n. 179]).

The states of this love are innocence, peace, tranquillity, inmost friendship, desire of soul and heart to do all good to the other, full trust in each other; in which and in all of which, there is blessedness, satisfaction, delight and pleasure; and from the eternal fruition of these, there is felicity of life (n. 871-886 [*C. L.*, n. 180]).

Conjugial love seems a debt and not free will; thus forced and not free (n. 946-950 [*C. L.*, n. 257, 466]).

Where conjugial love has its seat (n. 1024 [*C. L.*, n. 238, 270, 457, 466]).

Man is in the state of creation when in that love (n. 1025 [*C. L.*, n. 66, 84-86]).

He is in conjunction with the Lord, and in the reception of all things of good and truth (n. 1026, 1027 [*C. L.*, n. 113, 341]).

He is in potency (n. 1028, 1029 [*C. L.*, n. 55, 113, 207, 355]).

Experience, showing that love truly conjugial flows in through the wife into the husband; also that if the consort is not loved, the wife's love flowing in causes nausea (n. 1178 [*C. L.*, n. 161]).

The quality of conjugial love with the most ancient people is described (n. 1187 [*C. L.*, n. 73, 75]).

Love truly conjugial is reciprocal, the love of the one with the other's love (*some things from the angels*, n. 1264 [*C. L.*, n. 132]).

Natural and spiritual conjugial love and potency (n. 1459-1585 [*C. L.*, n. 220, 221]). (*See* POTENCY.)

Causes of love, of friendship and of favor between consorts (n. 1586-1640 [*C. L.*, n. 180, 214, 271-292]). (*See* FRIENDSHIP.)

Supereminent conjugial love, that it is to regard the good of the consort as one's own (n. 1625).

The conjunction of conjugial love with love of infants (n. 1707-1716 [*C. L.*, n. 385-404]). (*See* PARENTAL LOVE.)

Judgments of wise men from the kingdoms of Europe respecting the origin of conjugial love, and concerning its virtue and potency (*Memorab.*, n. 1718 [*C. L.*, n. 103–114]).

The state of married partners after death (n. 1719–1736 [*C. L.*, n. 45–54]). (*See* MARRIAGE.)

The opposition of conjugial love and scortatory love (n. 1910–1947 [*C. L.*, n. 423–433]). (*See* ADULTERY.)

They who are in the pride of their own intelligence are wholly unable to love the wife (*many and various things*, n. 2042–2045 [*C. L.*, n. 88, 193, 331, 353]).

The transcription of the love of proprium with the man into conjugial love with the wife (*articles*, n. 2036, *seq.* [*C. L.*, n. 32, 88, 156[*], 193, 293, 353]).

Inclinations, affections and qualities of men and women, by which conjunction is effected (*articles*, n. 2047 [*C. L.*, n. 156[*]–181]).

The difficulties in knowing the conjunctions of consorts (*articles*, n. 2050).

Again was seen the golden rain; and some arcana were disclosed respecting conjugial love with women (*Memorab.*, n. 2053 [*C. L.*, n. 208]).

Concerning love truly conjugial (*articles*, n. 2055 [*C. L.*, n. 57–73]).

CONVERSION.—(*See the second Index, s. v.* TURNING.)

CORRESPONDENCE (*Correspondentia*).—Correspondences in the Word (n. 1345 [*C. L.*, n. 127, 515, 532]).

Respecting the correspondence of the marriage of the Lord and the church with marriages in the heavens and on earth (n. 1345–1358 [*C. L.*, n. 125–127]).

There is not any correspondence of the marriage of the Lord and the church with the marriages of the angels and of men (n. 1347 [*C. L.*, n. 125, 126]).

There is a correspondence of conjugial things in angels and men [which are conjugial love, chastity, seminal potency, prolification, parental love, and the things pertaining to these], with the truths and goods of the church (n. 1348–1350 [*C. L.*, n. 127]).

There is correspondence of conjugial love with the marriage of good and truth, from which marriage the church is the church (n. 1351-1353 [*C. L.*, n. 62, 122-124, 127, 518]).

There is correspondence of conjugial chastity with genuine truths from the Word (n. 1354-1356 [*C. L.*, n. 127]).

There is correspondence of seminal potency with the reception of spiritual truths from the Lord through the Word, and with the affection for propagating them; thus with the spiritual affection of truth and at the same time with use (n. 1357-1360 [*C. L.*, n. 127, 220, 433]).

The correspondence of spiritual prolification is with the love of producing, and in the state of creation of conserving the truths and goods of the church (n. 1361, 1362 [*C. L.*, n. 115, 127]).

The correspondence of parental love is with the love of innocence and of protecting it from evils and falsities (n. 1363 [*C. L.*, n. 127, 395 *at end*]).

There is the correspondence of these conjugial things in marriages of one man with one wife, thus with those who are in the marriage of good and truth from the Lord (n. 1364).

With those who are polygamists from religion, the correspondence of these conjugial things is a remote correspondence; but with polygamists in Christendom the correspondence is with the falsities and evils of hell (n. 1365, 1366).

The correspondence of these conjugial things with those who have confirmed falsities of faith, is with the evils and falsities of hell (n. 1367, 1368).

So, too, with those who are in evils of life (n. 1389-1393).

With those who are in diverse religions, there is not correspondence with goods and truths (n. 1394, 1395).

The correspondence of good and truth cannot be given with those who are in the love of self and in the pride of their own intelligence (n. 1396-1398).

Whoredoms in general correspond to the falsifications of the truth and the profanations of the good of the church from the Word (n. 1399-1403 [*C. L.*, n. 515-520]).

Heinous adulteries within the prohibited degrees correspond to certain heresies confirmed by the Word (n. 1405-1457 [*C. L.*, n. 519]).

There is a correspondence of spiritual marriage, or that of truth and good, with the actual marriage of men, that is, of husband and wife (n. 1952-1954 [*C. L.*, 520]).

Violation of spiritual marriage therefore corresponds to violation of the marriages of men (n. 1955-1958 [*C. L.*, n. 515-520]).

Hence it follows that to violate the truths of the Word and the church by falsifying them, is to commit whoredom spiritually; and that to violate the goods of the Word and the church by perverting them, is to commit adultery spiritually (n. 1959-1962 [*C. L.*, n. 518]).

They, therefore, who are in spiritual whoredom and adultery are also in actual natural whoredom and adultery; the converse also is true (n. 1963-1969 [*C. L.*, n. 520]).

Spiritual marriage is violated when the truth of the church is separated from its good, and when its good is separated from its truth (n. 1970-1976 [*C. L.*, n. 519]).

Spiritual marriage is violated when appearances of truth, in the Word, are taken for genuine truths and are confirmed (n. 1977-1979).

Spiritual marriage is violated by those who with the lips make profession of another church than that which they acknowledge in heart; and it is very greatly violated by those who in heart acknowledge no church (n. 1980-1982).

Spiritual marriage is violated by those who learn the truths of doctrine from the Word but live wickedly; also by those who are devout in worship but do not reflect at all on their lives (n. 1983-1987).

Spiritual marriage is violated by those who study the sense of the letter alone, without doctrine (n. 1988-1991).

The marriage of good and truth is violated when the Word is read for various ends, and not at the same time read for the sake of the knowledges of good and truth (n. 1992-1994).

There are as many genera and species of spiritual whoredoms as there are of natural, for so many are the correspondences (n. 1995-1997).

From these things also it may be seen that marriages are heavenly, and that adulteries are infernal (n. 1998–2000).

DEFLORATION (*Defloratio*).—(*See* VIRGINITY.)

DEGREES (*Gradus*).—There are three degrees [of life], and the three degrees of life are in every man (n. 149–153).

There are three degrees of love and wisdom (n. 154–158).

There are three degrees of substances and forms (n. 154–158).

These three degrees can be opened with man; and they are opened as man receives truths in the understanding and does them in will (n. 159–162).

Differences between those with whom the natural degree has been opened, and those with whom the spiritual degree, and the celestial degree, has been opened (n. 202–207).

The marriage of good and truth descends from the Lord through three degrees, and in each degree it goes on from greatest to least; hence there is infinite variety in that marriage (n. 373–375).

Marriages of the highest degree, which are called celestial, are infinitely more perfect than marriages of the lower degree which are called spiritual, and these are infinitely more perfect than marriages of the lowest degree which are called natural (n. 376–378).

Marriages of the lowest degree are perfect in the measure of the reception of the influx of the conjugial sphere from the two higher degrees (n. 379–381).

These marriages without the reception of influx from the two prior, do not draw their origin from the marriages of good and truth, but from the connubial relations of evil and falsity, which are adulteries (n. 382–385).

Adulteries also are of three degrees (n. 386–388).

Degrees, and influx according to degrees (n. 433, 434).

Man is a form of the three degrees; celestial, spiritual, and natural (n. 699).

Substance, because it is form, is a subject (n. 700–708).

DELIGHTS (*Deliciae*), (*jucundum*). (*See the other Index also.*)
The delights of conjugial love (n. 77–146 [*C. L.*, n. 183; *compare* n. 69, 144, 155, 198, 293, 294, 443]).

All things of joy and of gladness are meant by delights (*enumerated*, n. 77).

Love through wisdom makes them to be felt (n. 77 [*C. L.*, n. 8 *end*, 461]).

All delights are from love and its effect (n. 78 [*C. L.*, n. 8 *end*]).

The delights of love are all in the effect, and by this they are in the means (n. 78 [*C. L.*, n. 8 *end*]).

Delights follow in order, as end, cause, and effect (n. 82, *etc.*).

In conjugial love, by it and from it, all delights are in their fulness (n. 104, 105 [*C. L.*, n. 68, 69]).

The highest and inmost delights, which are of peace and innocence, are imperceptible; but they become perceptible as they descend; and at length in ultimates they become a delight that is sensible to the highest degree (n. 106–109 [*C. L.*, n. 69, 183]).

The *first* reason why delights become in the highest measure perceptible in ultimates, is, that they descend in order from those which are imperceptible, and in ultimates all are together (n. 110–120 [*C. L.*, n. 68, 69]).

The *second* reason is, that conjugial love affects the most minute particulars of both mind and body (n. 120–123 [*C. L.*, n. 68, 69]).

The *third* reason is, that there is communication of that love and its delights with the heavens (n. 124–128 [*C. L.*, n. 144]).

The *fourth* reason is, that those delights are according to use, and the use of conjugial love is the most excellent of all (n. 128–131 [*C. L.*, n 183]).

The *fifth* reason is, that they have conjugial love who are in conjunction with the Lord (n. 131–136).

Hence the delights of this love are ineffable and beyond number (n. 136–140).

This is unknown in the world, for the reason that there is not religion (n. 140–145 [*C. L.*, n. 534]).

From this come the delight (*jucundum*), satisfaction and bliss of consorts (n. 217–221 [*C. L.*, n. 69, 180, 213]).

Some arcana from angels respecting the delights of conjugial love (n. 221 [*C. L.*, n. 69]).

Whence come the delights of conjugial love (n. 258–262 [*C. L.*, n. 180, 198, 221]). (*See* SEX.)

Principally (n. 261):

Their communication, with husbands (n. 263–265 [*C. L.*, n. 210–225, 294]). (*See* SEX.)

As conjugial love becomes more interior, it is the more full of delights (n. 522–526).

And thus it is enduring in delights, and they continually increase (n. 527–548).

In respect to its delights and to their exaltations and constancy, conjugial love is according to its origins in minds (n. 549–560).

Various things regarding the delights of conjugial love (n. 560).

In accordance with its origin, conjugial love becomes more or less perceptible to the senses (n. 598–605 [*C. L.*, n. 213]).

With every one, internal happiness is according to conjugial love (n. 664–676 [*C. L.*, n. 180]).

All who are in love truly conjugial become angels (n. 752 [*C. L.*, n. 48–53]).

Some things respecting the delights of conjugial love (*Memorab.*, n. 763 [*C. L.*, n. 183]).

The celestial beatitudes, the spiritual satisfactions, and the natural delights (*jucunditates*) which have been provided from the beginning for those who are in love truly conjugial, can be given only with one wife (n. 1030–1034 [*C. L.*, n. 335]).

They can be given only by the Lord (n. 1035–1041 [*C. L.*, n. 336]).

The delights of love truly conjugial, even its ultimate delight, are without any lasciviousness (n. 1085 [*C. L.*, n. 144, 346]).

Concerning a spirit who wished to know what heaven and hell are, and to whom it was said, "Inquire what delight (*jucundum*) is, and you will know;" and he made inquiry (*Memorab.*, n. 1344 [*C. L.*, n. 461]).

Various things respecting the delights of conjugial love (n. 1731 [*C. L.*, n. 51, 52]).

The joys of heaven, and nuptials there (n. 1826–1848 [*C. L.*, n. 1–25]).

Something respecting conjunction by means of delights (*jucunda*), with the evil (n. 1919).

Concerning the delights of conjugial love, from certain wives in heaven (*Memorab.*, n. 2002 [*C. L.*, n. 155[*]]).

DISEASE (*Morbus*).—A vitiated state[1] of the mind is a cause of coldness between consorts (n. 962[2] [*C. L.*, n. 252]).

These are enumerated (n. 962–966 [*C. L.*, n. 252]).

A vitiated condition of the body, and diseases which are enumerated, are also a cause (n. 967–971 [*C. L.*, n. 253]).

The two are also causes of separation (n. 979–984 [*C. L.*, n. 252, 253]).

Jealousy with some persons comes from various sicknesses of the mind (n. 1779–1785 [*C. L.*, n. 373–375]).

Ill consequences that arise from excessive restraint of venereal heat (n. 1802 [*C. L.*, n. 450]).

DIVORCE (*Divortium*).—Causes of coldnesses, separations, and divorces, with consorts (n. 853–1018 [*C. L.*, n. 234–260]). (*Also see* COLDNESS.)

Vitiated conditions of mind, vitiated conditions of body, and also impotence are causes of separation as to bed (n. 979–984 [*C. L.*, n. 252–254]).

Whoredom is the genuine cause of divorce (n. 985–993 [*C. L.*, n. 255]).

DUTIES (*Officia*).
OFFICES (*Officia*). —The proper duties of men and of women, and conjunction by means of them (*articles*, n. 2023, etc. [*C. L.*, n. 174–176]).

EFFECT (*Effectus*).—(*See the other Index.*) (*See* END.)

END (*Finis*).—(*See* CAUSE.) (*See the other Index.*)

ERUDITION (*Eruditio*).—(*See* WISDOM, UNDERSTANDING.)

ETERNAL (*Aeternum*).—In love truly conjugial there is the eternal (n. 622–628 [*C. L.*, n. 38, 44, 200, 216]).

EVIL (*Malum*).—(*See the other Index also.*)
  Man does truths from the will so far as he shuns evils as sins (n. 163–167 [*C. L*, n. 147]).

EXTERNAL (*Externum*). ⎫ —(*See the other Index also.*)
EXTREME (*Extremum*). ⎭ New creations, propagations and procreations are effected from firsts by ultimates (*illustrated*, n. 75).
  The state of the mind depends on the state of the outmost in the body (*various things*, n. 528–538 [*C. L.*, n. 221]).
  So with conjugial love (n. 528–538 [*C. L.*, n. 221]).
  Influx of the soul into its ultimates, thus into the organs of generation (n. 539–548);
  And the formation of seed, etc. (n. 549–560 [*C. L.*, n. 220]).
  How conjugial love progresses from firsts to ultimates (n. 630–638 [*C. L.*, n. 101, 183, 441]).
  The internal and the external man (n. 766–844 [*C. L.*, n. 148, 185, 427]). (*See* AFFECTION.)

FAVOR (*Favor*).—Causes of love, of friendship, and of favor between consorts (n. 1586–1640 [*C. L.*, n. 180, 214, 271–292]). (*See* FRIENDSHIP.)

FEMALE AND MALE (*Femina et Masculus*).—Various things (n. 6). (*See* SEX.) (*See also the other Index.*)

FORM (*Forma.*)—(*See* SUBSTANCE.)

FORNICATION (*Fornicatio*).—Concerning fornication (n. 1792–1810 [*C. L.*, n. 444[*]–460]).
  With every man the love of the sex is inborn; and inwardly therein, conjugial love; fornication is the love of the sex that precedes conjugial love, and thus it is lust before marriage (n. 1794–1796 [*C. L.*, n. 445]).
  The love of the sex, which is what fornicates, has its beginning together with seminal potency: its commencement is when the understanding lifts itself up, and thence man begins to think from himself, and when the voice of the boy is changed to that of the young man (n. **1797–1799** [*C. L.*, n. **446**]).

The love of the sex grows and strengthens itself earlier and more strongly with one than with another (n. 1800 [*C. L.*, n. 450]).

The love of the sex, with those in whom it strengthens itself earlier and to a greater degree than with others, cannot be totally suppressed without harm (n. 1801, 1802 [*C. L.*, n. 450]).

For this reason brothels are tolerated in large cities[1] in the European world (n. 1803 [*C. L.*, n. 451]).

The greatest care should be taken lest the human conjugial be destroyed by inordinate and immoderate fornications: care must be taken, in every way, that this be preserved; since the conjugial is the very jewel of human life, and the repository of the Christian religion (n. 1804, 1805 [*C. L.*, n. 456–458]). (*See, further, the article* MISTRESS.)

FRIENDSHIP (*Amicitia*).—Causes of love, of friendship, and of favor between consorts (n. 1586–1640 [*C. L.*, 180, 214, 290]).

While there is love between consorts, there is also friendship and favor (n. 1588–1590 [*C. L.*, n. 180, 214, 290]).

If between consorts there be not spiritual conjugial love, there still may be friendship and favor: and if there be not friendship between them, there still may be favor, that is, the civility of moral life (n. 1591–1594 [*C. L.*, n. 278, 287–293]).

An internal or spiritual cause of conjugial love and friendship is true religion (n. 1595–1597 [*C. L.*, n. 238, 239, 531]).

And that both have the same religion (n. 1598–1601 [*C. L.*, n. 242]).

Also that from religion adulteries be shunned (n. 1602–1606 [*C. L.*, n. 147–149]).

An internal and spiritual cause of conjugial love is similitude of souls and of minds; and an external or natural cause is similitude of manners and of state and condition in society (n. 1606–1608 [*C. L.*, n. 246, 250]).

An external or natural cause of love or friendship between consorts is potency (n. 1609, 1610):

Also abstinence from whoredom, from any cause excepting impotency (n. 1611–1614).

There is also indifference on the part of the wife to the acts of Venus; and from this, and sometimes from a turning of the back, the husband is persuaded that his wife is without any desire for those acts (n. 1615–1617 [*C. L.*, n. 259, 294]).

There is also the love of infants and children, common to both (n. 1618–1622 [*C. L.*, n. 284, 404, 409]).

There are with each partner, industry, assiduity and intelligence, in their duties; and in some of these there is mutual assistance (n. 1622–1624 [*C. L.*, n. 164, 165, 176, 283]).

There is also prudence in conforming to the nature and genius of the other (n. 1625–1627 [*C. L.*, n. 282, 294]).

Inequality in worldly things that are loved, sometimes conduces to love or to friendship between partners (n. 1628–1633 [*C. L.*, n. 287]).

A cause of apparent favor, as friendship or as love, is the love of peace in the house, and a love for reputation outside of the house (n. 1634–1637 [*C. L.*, n. 285, 286]).

A cause of apparent favor, as friendship or love, is, that the wife does not cease to favor her husband when his potency ceases. This favor may become love when they grow old together (n. 1637–1640 [*C. L.*, n. 290]).

Concerning the state of familiarity between consorts; whence that familiarity comes, and what its quality (n. 1639).

GARDEN (*Hortus*).—(*See the other Index.*)

GENERATION (*Generatio*).—(*See* BIRTH.) (*See the other Index.*)

GOOD (*Bonum*).—Good and truth are most universal, thence[1] they are in each and all things in heaven and in earth (n. 306–311 [*C. L.*, n. 84–86]).

Good by itself alone is not given, nor truth by itself alone; but where good is, there is truth; and the converse: wherefore the one without the other is but a thing of reasoning (n. 312–314 [*C. L.*, n. 87]).

There is truth of good and good of truth, which are two distinct things because one is from the other (n. 315–319 [*C. L.*, n. 88, 89]).

Truth of good is masculine, and good of truth is feminine (n. 319 [*C. L.*, n. 90, 91]).

Between these two is the marriage which is properly meant by the marriage of good and truth (n. 324, 325 [*C. L.*, n. 93, 100]).

Between the two there is love, which is called conjugial love (n. 326–329 (*C. L.*, n. 65, 92, 93]).

In that marriage there are reciprocal action and reaction, from which one becomes the other's; whence there is mutuality (n. 341 [*C. L.*, n. 293]).

(*See* SPIRITUAL MARRIAGE, MARRIAGE, CONJUGIAL LOVE, SEX.)

Good and truth are not given abstracted from substances; neither are substances given abstracted from forms (n. 341–343 [*C. L.*, n. 66, 186]). (*See* SUBSTANCE.)

HEAVEN (*Cœlum*).—(*See the other Index also.*)

Consorts were seen in heaven who lived in love truly conjugial; by whom truly conjugial love was represented, in its own form (*Memorab.*, n. 1 [*C. L.*, n. 42, 43]).

Concerning marriages in heaven (*articles*, n. 2–28 [*C L.*, n. 27–41]).

Some things respecting conjugial love in heaven (n. 19, 20 [*C. L.*, n. 37, 38, 64, 430]).

From what is there said, it follows that there are marriages in the heavens; reasons (n. 22 [*C. L.*, n. 40]).

Heaven is not from angels created such, but from men; reasons why this is unknown (n. 23 [*C. L.*, n. 28, 156[*]]).

Man is man after death, and there are full marriages between males and females from personal observation (25 [*C. L.*, n. 39, 51]).

There are spiritual offspring therefrom (n. 26, 27 [*C. L.*, n. 51, 52, 65, 211]).

With the angels, wisdom and its love conjoin themselves; consequently conjugial love is there perfect (n. 27, 28).

Conjugial love is in the heavens, and is communicated[1] (n. 124–127).

Something concerning the magnificent and splendid things in heaven (*Memorab.*, n. 222 [*C. L.*, n. 12–20]).

Various things concerning marriages after death (n. 1719–1736 [*C. L.*, n. 45–54]). (*See* MARRIAGE.)

The Lord's words explained, that there is not given a wife to a man (n. 1727 [*C. L.*, n. 41]).

Many other things concerning marriages in heaven (n. 1719–1736 [*C. L.*, n. 27–41, 45–54]). (*See* MARRIAGE.)

Preliminary observations respecting the joys of heaven and nuptials there (n. 1826–1848 [*C. L.*, n. 2–25]).

There are ministries, functions and works in heaven (*Memorab.*, n. 1909 [*C. L.*, n. 207]).

Other things concerning conjugial love in the heavens (*Memorab.*, n. 2001 [*C. L.*, n. 44]).

Marriages in the golden age, in the silver, in the copper, and in the iron (*Memorab.*, n. 2003–2006 [*C. L.*, n. 75–78]).

How marriages are provided in heaven (n. 2038 *C. L.*, n. 229, 316, 411]).

HELL (*Infernum*).—Various things respecting the unclean things of hell (n. 1922 [*C. L.*, n. 430, 495, 500]).

The hells of adulterers, in the west, appear like lakes of fire and brimstone (*Memorab.*, n. 2035 [*C. L.*, n. 80]).

IMAGE OF GOD (*Imago Dei*).—(*See also the other Index.*)

Some things in regard to the image of God in marriages (n. 46–50, 51–56). (*See* CONJUGIAL LOVE.)

What is signified by "the image of God" and "the likeness of God," and "eating of the tree of life" (*Memorab.*, n. 1193 [*C. L.*, n. 132–136]).

IMMORTALITY (*Immortalitas*).—(*See also the other Index.*)

A man lives a man after death (n. 3–5 [*C. L.*, n. 28–31, 44]). (*See* MAN.)

The life of man after death; reasonings by a priest, a politician and a philosopher, with the ancient wise men (*Memorab.*, n. 1286 [*C. L.*, n. 182]).

IMPOTENCY (*Impotentia*).—(*See* POTENCY.)

INCLINATION (*Inclinatio*).—(*See* AFFECTION.)

INFANTS (*Infantes*).—(Love of infants, see PARENTAL LOVE.)

INFINITE (*Infinitum*).—Propagations are an image of the infinite and eternal (n. 353, *seq*. [*C. L.*, n. 220]).
Other things from which there exists an image of the infinite and the eternal (353–360, 361–371[1]).

INFLUX (*Influxus*).—(*See the other Index also.*)
The quality of the influx of the mind into the body (*illustrated*, n. 58, 60–62).
How man receives influx from the Lord; how he receives it with the understanding, and love thereby (*illustrated*, n. 75).
Much concerning degrees, and influx according to them (n. 433, 434).
Influx of the soul into the organs of generation (n. 539–548 [*C. L.*, n. 183]).
Various things concerning the influx of the spiritual world into the natural world (n. 578 [*C. L.*, n. 380]).
Influx into men and into beasts (n. 1200 [*C. L.*, n. 183]).
How man is led by the Lord in freedom (n. 1227 [*C. L.*, n. 444]).
Influx of the marriage of love and wisdom, and its reception by men (n. 2038 [*C. L.*, n. 122, 123, 188]).
Also various things concerning it as it is with women, and concerning its reception (n. 2041 [*C. L.*, n. 122, 123]).

INNOCENCE (*Innocentia*).—Various things in regard to the sphere of the love of innocence from the Lord, and of its protection by the Lord (n. 1363 [*C. L.*, n. 127]).
The state and sphere of innocence and peace with parents and with infants, while these are loved (*various things*, n. 1678, 1679 [*C. L.*, n. 395–397]).
Angels of innocency, who did not understand what scortatory love was (*Memorab.*, n. 1738 [*C. L.*, n. 444]).
The cupidity for seducing innocencies, and the lot after death of those who are in it (n. 1823–1825 [*C. L.*, n. 513, 514]).

INTELLIGENCE (*Intelligentia*).—(*See* UNDERSTANDING.)

JEALOUSY.—(*See* ZEAL.)

JUDGE (*Judex*).
JUDGMENT (*Judicium*).
{ —Judges of friendship, concerning whom was the exclamation, "O how wise" (*Memorab.*, n. 1791 [*C. L.*, n. 233]). }

LASCIVIOUSNESS (*Lascivia*).—Conjugial love is without any lasciviousness (n. 630–638 [*C. L.*, n. 148]).

Love truly conjugial is without lasciviousness (*various things*, n. 1045).

The chaste and the unchaste (*many articles*, n. 2046 [*C. L.*, n. 138–156]).

LAST (*Ultimum*).
OUTMOST (*Ultimum*).
ULTIMATE (*Ultimum*).
} —(*See* EXTREME.)

LUST (*Libido*).—(*See* LASCIVIOUSNESS.)

LIFE (*Vita*).—(*See the other Index.*)
What is signified by "eating of the tree of life" (*Memorab.*, n. 1193 [*C. L.*, n. 135]).

LORD (*Dominus*).—(*See the other Index also.*)
Glorification of the Lord in the heavens on account of His advent, from the Word (*Memorab.*, n. 2035 [*C. L.*, n. 81]).

LOVE IN GENERAL (*Amor in genere*).—(*See the second Index,* s. v. LOVE.) (*See also* AFFECTION, LOVE OF SELF AND THE WORLD.)

All the good of love is from the Lord (n. 33–35 [*C. L.*, n. 84]).

There is love in which the man is, in which the world is, and in which is God (*concerning which*, n. 34).

(*On the union of love and wisdom, or of good and truth, see* SPIRITUAL MARRIAGE.)

Man cannot love the Lord [as He is in Himself], but he can love what is from the Lord (*illustr.*, n. 70, 71).

And he can love what is from the Lord, as from himself (*illustr.*, n. 71–73).

From the Lord there is masculine love, and there is feminine; but nevertheless love is not made full except by both together (n. 74 [*C. L.*, n. 32, 33, 90]).

On the progression of love, as end, cause, and effect; or as love, wisdom, and use (n. 79-100 [*C. L.*, n. 400, 401]). (*See* CAUSE.)

Concerning the connection of conjugial love with the loves of heaven (n. 147-222 [*C. L.*, n. 65-69]).

Perceptions are formed from affections, and affections are of love (n. 147 [*C. L.*, n. 197]).

The form of love in which a man is when in the world, remains after death, and makes a one with the form of the society into which he comes (n. 208, *seq.* [*C. L.*, n. 34-36]).

Various things respecting love towards the neighbor (n. 514 [*C. L.*, n. 269]).

Love is will in the mind, it is endeavor in the body, and it becomes act when it is brought to its termination (n. 528, 529 [*C. L.*, n. 215]).

Man is a form of love, wisdom and use ([n. 683-690] [*C. L.*, n. 361]). (*See* MAN, USE.)

The love of his own wisdom sinks man down (n. 734-739 [*C. L.*, n. 88, 193, 353]).

An exterior cause of coldness between married partners is the love of exercising domination on the part of one; still more, if they both have it (n. 939-945 [*C. L.*, n. 248]).

The love of domination cleaves conjugial love asunder (*various things concerning this*, n. 945 [*C. L.*, n. 248]).

Concerning the love of dominion that comes from the love of self, with the laity, that they wish to be kings and emperors; and with the clergy that they wish to be deities and gods (*Memorab.*, n. 1873 [*C. L.*, n. 261-266]).

Concerning the love of dominion that comes from the love of uses (n. 1873 [*C. L.*, n. 261-266]).

The love of himself that is with the man, and pride in his own intelligence, have been transferred into the wife (*various things concerning this*, n. 725-742 [*C. L.*, 32, 156]).

Various things concerning the love of self (n. 725-742).

LOVE OF CHILDREN.—(*See* PARENTAL LOVE.)

LOVE OF THE SEX (*Amor sexus*).—Distinction between the love of the sex that is with men, and the love of the sex in beasts (n. 1194-1251 [*C. L.*, n. 94-96]). (*See* BEAST.)

The chaste love of the sex, which is with those who are in love truly conjugial and hence of fullest potency (*Memorab.*, n. 1585 [*C. L.*, n. 55]).

Some things in regard to the love of the sex (n. 1793–1803 [*C. L.*, n. 46, 48, 94, 98, 444[*]–450]). (*See* FORNICATION.)

The beginning of the love of the sex; when it takes place (n. 1797–1799 [*C. L.*, n. 141, 446]).

Harm that arises from an excessive restraint of the venereal heat (n. 1801, 1802 [*C. L.*, n. 450]).

LUST.—(*See* LASCIVIOUSNESS.)

MALE (*Masculus*).—(*See* SEX.) (*See the other Index.*)

Various things concerning the male and the female (n. 6–8 [*C. L.*, n. 32, 33, 61, 100, *etc.*, 218, 220–230]). (*See* SEX.)

The man was created a form of wisdom from love; the woman, a form of love from wisdom (n. 168 [*C. L.*, n. 32]).

Masculine conjugial love, and feminine, specifically; and the intelligence of each (n. 223–301 [*C. L.*, n. 216–218]). (*See* SEX.)

MAN (*Homo*).—(*See the other Index.*)

A man lives a man after death (n. 2–5 [*C. L.*, n. 28–31, 44]).

This is not known in the world, and yet it is of common perception (*concerning which see* n. 3 [*C. L.*, n. 28]);

From angels seen as men (n. 4 [*C. L.*, n. 28, 30]);

From the soul, as being the man (n. 5 [*C. L.*, n. 29, 31]).

The male after death is a male, and the female is a female (*illustr.*, n. 6–8 [*C. L.*, n. 32, 33]). (*See* SEX.)

A man after death is not a mere breath, but a real man (*illustr.*, n. 24, 25 [*C. L.*, n. 29]).

How man receives love and wisdom from the Lord; that he receives wisdom with the understanding; and how the will successively adjoins itself (*illustr.*, n. 75 [*C. L.*, n. 122–124]).

In man there are three things which are one,—soul, spirit and body; these are as end, cause, and effect (n. 85, 86 [*C. L.*, 101, 158]).

(*For various things concerning the degrees of life with man, see* DEGREES.)

Man consists of soul, spirit, and body (n. 474-476 [*C. L.*, n. 101, 158]).

A man is a man according to the quality of the conjugial love with him (*various things*, n. 575¹-592 [*C. L.*, n. 96, 230, 432]).

He is a man so far as spiritual conjugial love makes one with natural conjugial love (n. 593-597).

They who are in love truly conjugial are forms of celestial love, of spiritual, and of natural (n. 677-682, *seq*).

Man was created a form of love and wisdom (n. 683-685 [*C. L.*, n. 16, 183, 361]).

All things in man are actually effects of love and wisdom, which are uses (n. 686-693 [*C. L.*, n. 16, 183]). (*See* USES.)

Man was created a form of love and wisdom (n. 683).

For man to be that form in perfection, there could be nothing lacking (n. 684, 685).

All things in man are uses from love by wisdom (n. 689-690 [*C. L.*, n. 183]).

Man is a single series of all the uses in the universe (n. 691-693). (*See* USE.)

Man is a form of the three degrees, celestial, spiritual and natural (n. 699, 709, 719 [*C. L.*, n. 67, 532]).

How man becomes such a form, and that conjugial love is the medium (n. 717-721).

From the form in which a man is, only that which is similar can proceed (n. 722 [*C. L.*, n. 85]).

Every man has an internal will and an internal understanding (n. 780-784 [*C. L.*, n. 185]).

Many things concerning the internal and the external man (n. 766-844 [*C. L.*, n. 148, 185, 269, 427]). (*See* AFFECTION.)

Man is not born into any knowledge, but only into the capacity and inclination (*Memorab.*, n. 1193 [*C. L.*, n. 132-136]).

Love of the sex with men and with beasts (n. 1194-1251 [*C. L.*, n. 94-96, 133]). (*See* BEAST.)

The state of men and their various and successive changes of state, compared with beasts (n. 1194-1217² [*C. L.*, n. 94-96]). (*See* BEAST.)

How man is led by the Lord in freedom (n. 1227 [*C. L.*, n. 444]).

FIRST INDEX 515

Men found in forests (*Memorab.*, n. 1251 [*C. L.*, n. 151[*]–154[*]]).
Changes of state with man and with woman (n. 1252–1285 [*C. L.*, 184–206]). (*See* STATE.)
Reasonings concerning the life after death; by a priest, a politician and a philosopher, with the ancient wise men (*Memorab.*, n. 1286 [*C. L.*, n. 182]).

MARRIAGE (*Conjugium*).—(*See also the other Index.*)
A universal sphere of conjugial love proceeds from the Lord and fills the universe, or both worlds (n. 2 [*C. L.*, n. 92, 115, 220, 222, 355]).
(*Concerning love of the sex, see* SEX.)
(*Concerning spiritual marriage, which is the marriage of good and truth, see below.*)
Marriages are of the Divine providence; and they are in the most minute particulars with male and with female (*Memorab.*, n. 76 [*C L.*, n. 316]).
Whence is the conjugial, in its first origin (n. 101–103 [*C. L.*, n. 60, 61, 83, 103–114, 183, 238]).
Two consorts make one form of wisdom and love (n. 189–193 [*C. L.*, n. 100–102, 201]).
All things that are born from that form derive a likeness therefrom; thus they are in the marriage of wisdom and love (n. 194–198 [*C. L.*, n. 202–205]).
All affections of the will and perceptions of the understanding with them are in like form (n. 199–201).
That form conjoins itself with all the loves of a society (n. 212–216).
Various things from angels concerning the chastity of marriage (n. 216).
Masculine and feminine conjugial love specifically, and the intelligence of each (n. 223–301 [*C. L.*, n. 218]). (*See* SEX.)
How a virgin becomes a wife (*various things*, n. 279–281 [*C. L.*, n. 173, 198, 199]). (*See* SEX.)
Various things on this subject (n. 281). (*See* SEX.)
Still others (n. 282–284). (*See* SEX.)
Three degrees of marriages and adulteries (n. 373–384 [*C. L.*, n. 270]).

Conversation of adulterers about marriages (*Memorab.*, n. 407 [*C. L.*, n. 521, 522]).

Consorts who are in love truly conjugial wish to be one; and consorts who are not, wish to be two (*many things*, n. 606–621 [*C. L.*, n. 215]).

Conjugial love is chiefly dependent on husbands (n. 753–757 [*C. L.*, n. 216]).

Arcana concerning the communication of love between consorts (n. 758–762 [*C. L.*, n. 217]).

Conjugial similitude and dissimilitude (n. 765–882 [*C. L.*, n. 227–229]). (*See* SIMILITUDE.)

Causes of coldnesses, separations and divorces, with consorts (n. 853–1018 [*C. L.*, n. 234–260]). (*See* COLDNESS, DIVORCE.)

After the nuptials a man is to leave his father and mother, and of the sex he is to love his wife only (n. 1181–1187 [*C. L.*, n. 194, 411]).

Changes of state with man and woman, especially through marriage (n. 1252–1285 [*C. L.*, n. 184–206]).

Signs that consorts wish to be one (*various things*, n. 1262, 1278).

Repeated marriages (n. 1287–1300 [*C. L.*, n. 317–325]). (*See* WIDOW.)

The state of consorts after death (n. 1719–1736 [*C. L.*, n. 45–54]).

The love of the sex remains with man after death such as it was in the world interiorly, that is, in his interior will and the thought from it (n. 1721–1723 [*C. L.*, 46, 47]).

So, too, conjugial love remains such as it was interiorly (n. 1724, 1725 [*C. L.*, n. 48]).

Two consorts for the most part meet after death, recognize each other, consociate, and for some time live together; this takes place in their first state, thus while they are in externals as they were in the world (n. 1726, 1727, [*C. L.*, n. 37, 46, 47]).

Various circumstances about these things (n. 1725, 1728).

The Lord's words explained, that a wife is not given to a man (n. 1727 [*C. L.*, n. 41]).

- Successively, as they put off externals and enter into their internals, they have a perception of the quality of the inclination that they have had for each other; and so whether they can live together as one or not (1728, 1729, [*C. L.*, n. 48]).
- If they are unable to live together as one they separate; the man from the wife, the wife from the man, or each from the other (n. 1728, 1729 [*C. L.*, n. 49]).
- Then there is given to the man a suitable wife, and to the woman a suitable husband (n. 1728, 1729 [*C. L.*, n. 50, 54]).
- In their relation to each other, consorts enjoy conjugial delight similar to those in the world, but more happy; but without prolification; instead of which, or in its place, there is spiritual prolification, which is that of good and truth (n. 1730–1732 [*C. L.*, n. 51, 52]).
- Such is the case with those who come into heaven; but it is otherwise with those who go into hell (n. 1733–1736 [*C. L.*, n. 53, 54]).
- Various things about infernal marriages (n. 1736 [*C. L.*, n. 54]).
- Causes that prevent marriages from being contracted until advanced age (n. 1795 [*C. L.*, n. 450]).
- Preliminary observations respecting the joys of heaven and nuptials there (n. 1826–1848 [*C. L.*, n. 1–25]).
- Marriages in the golden age, the silver, and the copper (*Memorab.*, n. 2003–2006 [*C. L.*, n. 74–77]).
- Marriages in the iron age, when they had become polygamic (*Memorab.*, n. 2006 [*C. L.*, n. 78]).
- Transcription of the love of proprium with the man into conjugial love with the wife (*articles*, n. 2036, *seq.* [*C. L.*, n. 32, 88, 156,[*], 193, 293, 353]).
- The inclinations, affections and qualities of men and of women, through which conjunction is effected (*many articles*, n. 2047 [*C. L.*, n. 156[*]–181]).
- Difficulties in understanding the conjunctions of consorts (*articles*, n. 2050).

MARRIAGES IN THE HEAVENS (*Conjugia in caelis*).—(*See* HEAVEN.)

MARRIAGE, SPIRITUAL.—(*See* SPIRITUAL MARRIAGE.)

MIND (*Mens*).—(*See the other Index.*)
  The mind of man is not only in the head, but everywhere throughout the body (*illustr.*, n. 58–60 [*C. L.*, n. 178, 260]).
  The opening of the mind, and the consequent perfection of conjugial[1] love, and of the delights therefrom (n. 539–548, 549–560 [*C. L.*, n. 94]).
  Various things concerning the opening and the closing of the mind (n. 561–563 [*C. L.*, n. 188, 189, 203]).

MISTRESS, KEEPING A (*Pellicatus*).—(*See also* FORNICATION.)
  The greatest care should be taken lest the human conjugial be destroyed by inordinate and immoderate fornications: care must be taken, in every way, that this be preserved, since the conjugial is the very jewel of human life, and the repository of the Christian religion (n. 1804–1806 [*C. L.*, n. 456–458]).
  With those who for various reasons cannot yet enter into marriage, and who on account of salacity are unable to govern their lust, that conjugial is kept in existence by taking a mistress (n. 1806, 1807 [*C. L.*, n. 459]);
  Provided that this relation is not formed with a virgin or maiden, nor with a married woman, and is kept apart from conjugial love (n. 1808–1810 [*C. L.*, n. 460]).

MOHAMMEDANS (*Mahumedani*).—Why polygamy was permitted to the Mohammedans (1065–1070 [*C. L.*, n. 341]).
  Concerning the Mohammedan heavens, and that they come into the second heaven who give up their mistresses (n. 1071–1077 [*C. L.*, n. 342–344]).

NATIVITY (*Nativitas*).—(*See* BIRTH.)

NATURE (*Natura*).
NATURAL (*Naturale*).
  —Conversation of adulterers concerning nature and religion (*Memorab.*, n. 407 [*C. L.*, n. 521, 522]).
  The highest natural, the middle, and the lowest (n. 482 [*C. L.*, n. 442, 496]).

The centre and the expanse of nature and of life (*Memorab.*, n. 568 [*C. L.*, n. 380]).

Various things respecting the spiritual and the natural, the difference between them, and their conjunction (n. 575 [*C. L.*, n. 31, 326–329]).

Various things in regard to the spiritual world and its influx into the natural world (n. 577, 578 [*C. L.*, n. 380]).

From the things which may be seen in the world, man may confirm himself in favor of God more than for nature (*Memorab.*, n. 1458 [*C. L.*, n. 415–422]).

Difference between the spiritual and the natural as to writings, languages, and thoughts (*Memorab.*, n. 1699 [*C. L.*, n. 326–329]).

NUPTIALS (*Nuptiae*).—(*See* BRIDEGROOM.)

Betrothals and nuptials (n. 1111–1192 [*C. L.*, n. 295–314]).

When the period of betrothal is completed, nuptials ought to take place (n. 1157–1160 [*C. L.*, n. 306]).

Before the nuptials the marriage covenant is to be made in the presence of witnesses (n. 1161–1165 [*C. L.*, n. 301, 307]).

Because marriage regarded in itself is spiritual and consequently holy, it ought to be consecrated and confirmed by a priest (n. 1166–1173 [*C. L.*, n. 308]).

After the nuptials the spiritual marriage, which is of the internal man, becomes also natural, which is of the external man, and thus at last full (n. 1173–1180 [*C. L.*, n. 310]).

The man after the nuptials is to leave father and mother, and of the sex he is to love his wife alone (n. 1181–1187 [*C. L.*, n. 112, 194, 411]).

OFFICES.—(*See* DUTIES.)

OFFSPRING.—(*See* PROCREATION.)

[ONE (*Unum*).—(*See the other Index.*)]

ORGANS OF GENERATION.—(*See* SEED.) (*See also the other Index.*)

OUTMOST (*Ultimum*).
LAST (*Ultimum*).   }—(*See* EXTREME.)
ULTIMATE (*Ultimum*).

OWN.—(*See* PROPRIUM.)

PARENTAL LOVE, *or* THE LOVE BETWEEN PARENTS AND CHILDREN (*Storge*).—Various things respecting the sphere of innocence, and of its protection from evils and falsities (n. 1363 [*C. L.*, n. 127, 391, 394, 395, 399]).

The love of infants and of children is an external or natural cause of love or friendship between consorts (n. 1618–1621 [*C. L.*, n. 284, 387, 404]).

Concerning the love of infants or parental love (n. 1642–1699 [*C. L.*, n. 385–414]).

From the Divine providence proceed two universal spheres; one, that of conjugial love; and the other, that of the love of infants (*much concerning these spheres*, n. 1644–1657 [*C. L.*, n. 386–397]). (*See* SPHERE.)

The sphere of the love of infants is the sphere of protecting and supporting those who are unable to protect and support themselves (n. 1658–1662 [*C. L.*, n. 391]).

The sphere of the love of infants inflows into all living and animate things in the universe, and fills them with the love of innocence and peace, which love is received by them in their own way (n. 1663–1666 [*C. L.*, n. 388, 394]):

And it induces upon them a new and wonderful state; one that is full of the love of supporting and protecting their own offspring (n. 1667, 1668 [*C. L.*, n. 392]).

Every one living and animate receives this state into himself or herself after a birth; nor is there knowledge that it inflows, because the influx is not felt (n. 1669 [*C. L.*, n. 391, 392]).

The sphere of this love affects the female sex more than the male; thus mothers more than fathers (n. 1670, 1671 [*C. L.*, n. 393]).

It affects fathers and mothers variously, each according to the state of the mind (n. 1672–1674 [*C. L.*, n. 405, 408]).

It affects the evil and the good equally, and gives each the disposition to love and protect his own offspring, from his own affection (n. 1675-1677 [*C. L.*, n. 392]).

The sphere of this love of innocence and peace inflows into the external minds (*animos*) of parents and also into infants, and it conjoins itself in their outmost parts, especially by the touch (n. 1678, 1679 [*C. L.*, n. 396]).

In the degree in which innocence and peace recede with infants, there is a relaxation of that conjunction or that love; this is accomplished successively even to separation (n. 1681-1684 [*C. L.*, n. 398]).

The state of innocence and peace with infants is, that they know nothing and can do nothing from themselves, but from others, especially from the father and mother; and this state successively recedes as they know and become able to act from themselves, and not from others (n. 1685-1689 [*C. L.*, n. 399]).

The sphere of the love of infants progresses in a certain series, from and through causes into effects, and it makes periods, by means of which creation is preserved and continued in the state foreseen and provided (n. 1690-1692 [*C. L.* n. 400]).

The love between parents and children descends and does not ascend, and for this there are many reasons (n. 1693-1698 [*C. L.*, n. 402]).

The conjunction of conjugial love with the love of infants or parental love (n. 1701-1717 [*C. L.*, n. 404]).

In legitimate marriages infants are loved as legitimate and heirs (n. 1703, 1704).

With consorts who love each other, conjugial love is conjoined with parental love through spiritual and rational causes, and natural causes from these, which are with them from the Lord (n. 1707-1709 [*C. L.*, n. 404]).

In the case of such consorts, there is parental love through the husband with the wife, and on the other hand there is parental love with the husband from the Lord through the wife; in consequence, the love of the one is also conjoined mutually and in its turn with the love of the other (n. 1710, 1711).

With consorts who do not love each other, although there is not conjunction of those two loves from what is higher, interior, or prior, still there is a conjunction from what is lower, exterior, or posterior; but such conjunction is inverted, and consequently is light and wandering (n. 1712, 1713 [*C. L.*, n. 408]).

The love of parents towards their children remains after death, in the case of consorts who have loved each other; it is otherwise with those who have not loved each other (n. 1714–1717 [*C. L.*, n. 410]).

PELLICACY.—(*See* MISTRESS.)

[PERCEPTION.— (*See the other Index.*)]

POLYGAMY (*Polygamia*).—Concerning polygamy (n. 1019–1108 [*C. L.*, n. 332–352]).

Only with one wife can there be given love truly conjugial, potency, friendship, confidence, and such conjunction of minds that two are one flesh (n. 1021–1029 [*C. L.*, n. 333, 334]).

Only with one wife can there be given the celestial beatitudes, spiritual satisfactions and natural enjoyments, which have from the beginning been provided for those who are in love truly conjugial (n. 1030–1034 [*C. L.*, n. 335]).

Love truly conjugial is not given except to those who are of the Christian Church (n. 1042–1046 [*C. L.*, n. 337]).

Hence it is not lawful for Christians to marry more than one wife (n. 1047 [*C. L.*, n. 338]).

If a Christian were to marry more than one wife, he would commit not only natural but also spiritual adultery (n. 1051–1058 [*C. L.*, n. 339]).

The sons of Jacob were permitted to marry more wives, because the Christian Church was not with them, and therefore love truly conjugial could not be given (n. 1059–1064 [*C. L.*, n. 340]).

Why polygamy was permitted to the Mohammedans (n. 1059–1064 [*C. L.*, n. 341]).

FIRST INDEX

Concerning the heavens of the Mohammedans, and that they who give up their mistresses enter into the second heaven (n. 1065–1077 [*C. L.*, n. 342, 343]).

Polygamy is lasciviousness (n. 1079–1082 [*C. L.*, n. 345]).

With polygamists there cannot be given conjugial chastity, purity and holiness (n. 1083–1086 [*C. L.*, n. 141, 346]).

Polygamy is not sin to those with whom it is from religion (n. 1090–1094 [*C. L.*, n. 348]).

Polygamy is not sin with those who are in ignorance concerning the Lord (n. 1095–1098 [*C. L.*, n. 349, 350]).

So long as polygamists remain polygamists, they cannot become spiritual (n. 1087–1089 [*C. L.*, n. 347]).

Those polygamists are saved who live according to the civil laws of justice (n. 1099–1102 [*C. L.*, n. 351]);

But they cannot be consociated with angels in the Christian heavens (n. 1103–1107 [*C. L.*, n. 352]).

The difference between polygamists from religion and polygamists in Christendom (n. 1365, 1366 [*C. L.*, n. 338–350]).

Concerning those who lived in the iron age; that they were polygamists (*Memorab.*, n. 2006 [*C. L.*, n. 78]).

POTENCY (*Potentia*).—Angels have perpetual potency, because they are in perpetual love (*illustrated*, n. 68 [*C. L.*, n. 207, 355, 356, 433]).

Whence angels have perpetual potency, confirmed by reasons presented by an angel (*Memorab.*, n. 222 [*C. L.*, n. 355, 356]).

Determinations to the ultimate delight are in the good pleasure of the husband (n. 258–262 [*C. L.*, n. 221]).

Wives cannot bear to hear their husbands say that they are able but not willing; they can, however, bear to hear it said that they are willing but not able: the latter perpetuates love, but the former dissolves it (n. 266–268 [*C. L.*, n. 219]).

Increase of potency according to the opening of the interiors of the mind (n. 539–548, 549–560 [*C. L.*, n. 220]).

Conjugial love, according to its spiritual state, produces potency; nine reasons (n. 639–663).

Impotence is a cause of coldness and separation between consorts (n. 972–978 [*C. L.*, n. 254]).

Various causes and species of impotence (n. 972–978 [*C. L.*, n. 221]).

He who is in love truly conjugial is in its virtue and its potency (n. 1024–1028 [*C. L.*, n. 55, 355, 433]).

Correspondence of seminal potency with reception of spiritual truths through the Word (*various things*, n. 1458 [*C. L.*, n. 127, 220]).

Also various things concerning natural and spiritual conjugial potency (n. 1360 *C. L.*, n. 355, 433]).

Natural and spiritual conjugial love and potency (n. 1459–1652 [*C. L.*, n. 44, 55, 207, 220, 221, 355, 433]).

Various causes of potency (n. 1562, 1564).

By spiritual conjugial potency is meant potency such as those have who are in the truths and goods of the church (n. 1563–1565).

Various things concerning natural potency from spiritual (n. 1564).

There is natural conjugial potency from the love of the sex, which when not limited to the wife is lewdness; and the potency of this is lasciviousness (n. 1566).

Spiritual conjugial potency is from conjugial love, with one wife: when this [potency] becomes conjugial it is chastity, and its potency is without lasciviousness (n. 1567).

Natural conjugial potency successively decreases, as its love, which is lewdness, is not limited (n. 1568–1573).

But spiritual conjugial love successively increases, as its love, which is heavenly, is purified from lascivious love of the sex (n. 1574).

Natural conjugial potency decreases even till it becomes nought; but that which is spiritual increases even till it becomes constant (n. 1574–1577).

Natural conjugial potency successively extinguishes the interior fire of man's life, and dims its light; but that which is spiritual successively kindles the fire of man's life and exalts its light (n. 1579).

Natural conjugial potency deprives the soul and the spirit of their own beatitudes and delights; the contrary is the case with that which is spiritual (n. 1580–1582).

The man who is in spiritual conjugial potency, from chaste love becomes a more and more internal and perfect man; the opposite is the case with him who is in natural potency (n. 1583, 1584).

Potency is an external or natural cause of love or of friendship between consorts (n. 1609, 1610 [*C. L.*, n. 49, 274, 290]).

Judgments of the wise from the kingdoms of Europe, concerning the origin of conjugial love, and concerning its virtue and potency (*Memorab.*, n. 1718 [*C. L.*, n. 103-114]).

Concerning seminal potency,—when it begins (n. 1799 [*C. L.*, n. 446]).

PROCREATION (*Procreatio*).
OFFSPRING (*Proles*).
PROLIFICATION (*Prolificatio*).
PROLIFIC (*Prolificum*).

—(*See also* SEED.)
Procreations take place on earth, because they are from firsts by ultimates (*illustr.*, n. 75).

The angels were once men (n. 75 [*C. L.*, n. 28–30]).

Offspring born of two who are in love truly conjugial derive from their parents the conjugial good and truth; from which they have the inclination and capacity, if sons to perceive the things that belong to wisdom, if daughters to love the things which wisdom teaches (n. 285–290 [*C. L.*, n. 202–204]).

This is the case for the reason that the soul of the offspring is from the father, and the clothing corresponding to the soul is from the mother (n. 291–293 [*C. L.*, n. 206]).

How man (*homo*) comes into the seed, and the quality of the seed (*various things*, n. 293 [*C. L.*, n. 183, 220, 245]).

In the marriage of good and truth there is what is generative and prolific, whence are the propagations of all things in the universe, through which there is a continuance of creation (n. 330–336 [*C. L.*, n. 92, 115]).

Because goods and truths are in forms, therefore all things propagate themselves substantially and materially (n. 344–352).

Propagations are continuations of creation; and in them there is the image of the infinite and eternal, from the Lord the Creator, who is infinite and eternal (n. 353 *etc.*, to 372 [*C. L.*, n. 183, 220]).

The soul is in a state of perpetual fructification[1] and propagation (n. 498-501 [*C. L.*, n. 220]).

Conjugial love in its origin is the love of the propagation of good and truth (n. 502-511).

(*Concerning the organs of prolification, see* SEED.)

The influx of the soul into the organs of generation, and the formation of the seed, thus of man (n. 539-548, 549-560 [*C. L.*, n. 183, 220, 245]).

What is prolific in living things and in things not living (n. 581, 582 [*C. L.*, n. 183]).

Spiritual conjugial love is that from which, in which, and thus for which, there is conception, growth and formation (n. 579-584 [*C. L.*, n. 66]).

How conjugial love progresses from firsts through mediates to ultimates (n. 630-638 [*C. L.*, n. 101, 183, 400, 401, 440, 441, 447]).

From the form in which man is, there can proceed only that which is similar (n. 722-752 [*C. L.*, n. 85]).

Love and wisdom increase with those who are in conjugial love (n. 723, 724, 740-742 [*C. L.*, n. 93, 95, 98, 130, 211]).

Prolification corresponds to the love of producing and preserving the truths and goods of the church (n. 1361, 1362 [*C. L.*, n. 127, 389, 390]).

In the heavens there is spiritual prolification, but not natural (*various things*, n. 1732 [*C. L.*, n. 49, 51-53, 65]).

PROPRIUM (*Proprium*).—Propriums of the understanding and propriums of the will, which are transcribed into conjugial love (*articles*, n. 2036, 2048 [*C. L.*, n. 32, 156, 163-173]).

PROVIDENCE (*Providentia*).—(*See the other Index also.*)

Marriages are of the Divine providence (*Memorab.*, n. 76 [*C. L.*, n. 316]).

Those who look to the Lord and love chaste marriage, marriages and their felicities[1] are provided (n. 1188-1192 [*C. L.*, n. 49, 98, 229, 411, 444]).

From the Lord goes forth the Divine providence for the preservation of the created universe and for its continuance to eternity (n. 1644-1647 [*C. L.*, n. 386, 391, 392]).

From this are the two universal spheres (n. 1648-1652 [*C. L.*, n. 386-393]). (*See* SPHERE, PARENTAL LOVE.)

QUALITIES (*Qualitates*).—Qualities or inclinations and affections of men and of women, by means of which is conjunction (*articles*, n. 2047 [*C. L.*, n. 88, 89]).

RATIONAL (*Rationale*).—(*See* UNDERSTANDING.)

Reasoners who think no further than whether a thing is so (*Memorab.*, n. 1948 [*C. L.*, n. 232]).

RELIGION (*Religio*).—Conjugial love is according to the religion (n. 131-135, 140-144 [*C. L.*, n. 130, 238-243, 531]).

It is from religion (*see above*, CONJUGIAL LOVE, *and* MARRIAGE OF GOOD AND TRUTH, OR SPIRITUAL MARRIAGE).

The marriage of good and truth is in each single thing of the Word, the church, and religion; wherefore that marriage makes one with the church and religion with men (n. 393-397 [*C. L.*, n. 128-130, 516]).

Hence it follows that conjugial love with men is altogether according to the states of the church and of religion with them (n. 398-401 [*C. L.*, n. 130-142, 238]).

Therefore everyone has heaven according to his conjugial love (n. 402-406 [*C. L.*, n. 77]).

Conversation of adulterers concerning nature and concerning religion (*Memorab.*, n. 407 [*C. L.*, n. 521, 522]).

Variety of conjugial love according to the states of the church with man (n. 408-568 [*C. L.*, n. 324]).

Love truly conjugial is according to the states of the church with men (n. 435-437 [*C. L.*, n. 130, 149]).

They who have no religion have not conjugial love; but they have lust which is worse than the lust of a wild beast (n. 439-445 [*C. L.*, n. 239]).

To every one the state of the church is according to his acknowledgment of God, and at the same time according to the life of his religion (n. 446–449 [*C. L.*, n. 129]).

The state of the church is interior[1] according to the acknowledgment of the one God, and at the same time to a life of love (n. 450–453).

The state of the church is internal with those who go to the Lord, and shun evils as sins (*shown*, 454–463).

They alone have love truly conjugial who are being received into the Lord's New Church or the New Jerusalem (n. 464–526; *especially* n. 516–521 [*C. L.*, n. 43, 534]).

They have conjugial love who are in truths by means of the Word, and who wish to propagate them (n. 513–515 [*C. L.*, n. 128]).

Various things concerning the opening and the closing of the mind (n. 561, 563, 565 [*C. L.*, n. 188, 189]).

Conjugial love is according to the states of the church (*various things*, n. 566 [*C. L.*, n. 130, 142, 238]).

Why this is not known in the world (n. 567 [*C. L.*, n. 240]).

Love truly conjugial is with those who from religion love chastity; and its opposite is with those who do not love chastity from religion (n. 571–574 [*C. L.*, n. 147–149]).

Conjugial love becomes interior by religion; and it becomes exterior without it (n. 598–605).

The origin of conjugial love from the Lord (*Memorab.*, n. 763 [*C. L.*, n. 183]).

Conjugial similitudes are provided by the Lord in the case of those who go to Him and desire love truly conjugial (n. 810–817 [*C. L.*, n. 49, 229]).

Of the internal causes of coldness between consorts, the *first* is the rejection of all things of the church and of religion (n. 875–894 [*C. L.*, n. 240]):

The *second*, that one has religion, and not the other (n. 892–897 [*C. L.*, n. 241]):

The *third*, that one has one religion and the other another (n. 898–905 [*C. L.*, n. 242]):

The *fourth*, imbued falsity of religion (n. 906–912 [*C. L.*, n. 243]).

He who is in love truly conjugial is in the state of creation, in conjunction with the Lord, and in the reception of all things of good and truth (n. 1024–1028 [*C. L.*, n. 66, 84–86]).

Conjugial beatitudes, satisfaction and delights can be given only by the Lord, and to those who go to Him (n. 1030–1041 [*C. L.*, n. 335, 336]).

Consequently they can be given to those only who are of the Christian Church; and it is in consequence of this that it is not allowable for Christians to marry more than one wife (n. 1042–1050 [*C. L.*, n. 337, 338]).

Conversation with angels concerning arcana revealed by the Lord, concerning the Word, heaven, religion, and concerning conjugial love as being from religion; and grief that these things are not esteemed as of any value in the world (*Memorab.*, n. 1108, 1109 [*C. L.*, n. 532–534]).

For those who look to the Lord and love chaste marriage, marriages and their felicities are provided (n. 1188–1192 [*C. L.*, n. 49, 229]).

The marriage of the Lord with the church (n. 1301–1344 [*C. L.*, n. 116–131]). (*See* CHURCH.)

Concerning the correspondence of the marriage of the Lord and the church with marriages in the heavens and on earth (n. 1345–1458 [*C. L.*, n. 125–127]).

Conjugial love is according to the religion (*various things*, n. 1595–1597, 1598–1601, 1602, *seq.* [*C. L.*, n. 130, 142, 238]).

Adulteries produce the effect that the man does not acknowledge God, the Divinity of the Lord, the holiness of the Word, and consequently the other things that pertain to the church and religion (n. 1897–1903 [*C. L.*, n. 497]).

(*For other things concerning the marriage of good and truth, see* SPIRITUAL MARRIAGE *and* CORRESPONDENCE.)

Spiritual marriage is violated when the truth of the church is separated from its good, and when its good is separated from its truth (n. 1970–1979 [*C. L.*, n. 519]). (*See* CORRESPONDENCE.)

[REPENTANCE.—(*See the other Index.*)]

SEED (*Semen*).—Various things respecting procreation by seed (n. 291–294 [*C. L.*, n. 220, 245]).

The state of the extreme parts in the body is dependent on the state of the mind (n. 528–538 [*C. L.*, n. 221, 355]).

The ultimate region where the organs of generation are. The soul and the mind are there in their ultimates. Various things respecting influx and operation (n. 539–548 *C. L.*, n. 183, 310]).

Formation of the seed, and thus of man (n. 539–548, 549–560 [*C. L.*, n. 183, 220, 245]).

Whence the seed (n. 659–662 [*C. L.*, n. 127, 245]).

SEMEN.—(*See* SEED.)

SEPARATION BETWEEN CONSORTS (*Separatio inter conjuges*).—(*See* DIVORCE.)

SEX (*Sexus*).—A male is a male, and a female is a female, after death (n. 6–8 [*C. L.*, n. 32, 33]).

In what the masculine consists, and in what the feminine; also in what consists the conjunction of the two (n. 6 [*C. L.*, n. 32, 56, 61]).

Differences of the two in internal and in external form (n. 7, 8 [*C. L.*, n. 32, 33]).

The sex and its love are in the whole and in every part; and this love especially remains after death (n. 14–17 [*C. L.*, n. 37, 46, 47]);

Because this love is the universal of all loves (n. 14–16 [*C. L.*, n. 46]).

The male is wisdom and understanding; the wife is the love of the man's wisdom and understanding (n. 52–56 [*C. L.*, n. 32, 33, 88, 90]).

There is masculine love to the Lord, and there is feminine; and the love is not full unless these are together (n. 74).

The man is a form of wisdom from love, and the woman is a form of love from wisdom (n. 168–171 [*C. L.*, n. 187]).

They have fallen into the opposite form through evils (n. 172–175).

But still man can be led back into the form into which he was created, if he goes to the Lord and shuns evils as sins (n. 176–180, 181–184 [*C. L.*, n. 81]).

- Concerning masculine and feminine conjugial love specifically, and concerning the intelligence of each (n. 223–301 [*C. L.*, n. 184–199, 218]).
- Husbands are from creation forms of wisdom, of intelligence and of knowledge; and wives are from creation forms of the love of these (n. 225–227 [*C. L.*, n. 187]).
- Wives do not enter into the wisdom, intelligence and knowledge proper to the husbands; but they are affected by them, and[1] they love their husbands on account of them (n. 228–230 [*C. L.*, n. 168, 170–175]).
- Various arcana respecting the state of men and the state of women (n. 230 [*C. L.*, n. 187–191]).
- With husbands there is an elevation of the interiors of the mind into higher light, and with wives there is an elevation of the mind into superior heat; and a wife is sensible of the delights of her heat together with the light of her husband (n. 231–233 [*C. L.*, 188, 189]).
- Various things from angels concerning this also (n. 233 [*C. L.*, n. 293]).
- The wife wishes to be united to the husband as to his internal will, and the husband wishes to be united to the wife as to her external will; and thus the will of the two, internal and external, is made one (n. 234–238 [*C. L.*, n. 163–165]).
- Various things in regard to this from conversation with angels (n. 238 [*C. L.*, n. 293]).
- With the wife there is in the highest measure clear-sightedness for knowing the affections of the husband, and the greatest tact in regulating them; and with every sense wives have a perception of the inclination of the husband towards them, especially with the sense of touch in the palms of their hands (n. 239–242 [*C. L.*, n. 166]).
- Various things concerning this clear-sightedness of wives (n. 241 [*C. L.*, n. 208]).
- Wives have an inborn prudence in concealing their love and also this clear-sightedness from their husbands (n. 243–246 [*C. L.*, n. 167]).
- Various things from angels concerning this, and concerning the opposite state (n. 248, 249 [*C. L.*, n. 208]).

Conjugial love principally has its seat with wives, and husbands receive it from their wives (n. 250-253 [*C. L.*, n. 161, 216[*], 224]).

The chasteness of conjugial love has its seat principally with wives, and not in like manner with husbands unless wisdom effects it (n. 254-257).

Wives are sensible of the delights of conjugial love from the bosom love which is inmost friendship; the determinations of this love to the ultimate delight are in the good pleasure of the husband (n. 258-262 [*C. L.*, n. 221]).

Various things respecting the delights of that love, and whence they are (n. 261 [*C. L.*, n. 188, 189, 198]).

As husbands from wisdom love conjugial chastity and friendship, so they are sensible of the delights of conjugial love communicated to them by their wives (n. 263-265).

The intelligence of women in itself is tender, pacific, yielding, soft, beautiful, modest, lovely, like themselves; and the intelligence of men in itself is grave, harsh, hard, tenacious, high-spirited, wandering with license (n. 269-273 [*C. L.*, n. 218]).

The intelligence of the wife is connected with the external matters called economical and domestic; as to internal things and public matters, she depends on the intelligence of her husband; if a widow, she is dependent on the intelligence of men, except for those things which she has derived from her husband by remembrance (n. 274-278 [*C. L.*, n. 90, 91, 325]).

A wife is actually formed into the love of her husband's wisdom; and this is done by[1] the reception of the offshoots of his soul, together with the delight that arises from her desire to be the love of her husband's wisdom: thus from being a virgin she becomes a wife; thus she becomes a similitude (n. 279-281 [*C. L.*, n. 172, 173, 198, 199]).

Various things concerning this, from the conversation of angels (n. 281).

Thus the wisdom of the husband is given to his wife, is appropriated, and becomes implanted in her life; whence the love of her husband's wisdom exists in the wife, and grows (n. 282-284 [*C. L.*, n. 173]).

The truth of good is masculine, and the good of truth is feminine (n. 319-323 [*C. L.*, n. 90, 91]).

The male was created to become wisdom, and the female to become the love of the wisdom of the man (n. 725-731, 732-742 [*C. L.*, n. 32, 33]).

Conjugial love chiefly depends on husbands (n. 753-757 [*C. L.*, n. 216[*]]).

Certain arcana concerning the communication of love between consorts (n. 758-762).

The affections of men and of women, their adaptability and their want of adaptability (n. 766, *etc.* [*C. L.*, n. 227-229, 246, 271, *seq.*]). (*See* AFFECTION, SIMILITUDE.)

Discourse of the wise concerning the beauty of the female sex (*Memorab.*, n. 1018 [*C. L.*, n. 56]).

Distinction between the love of the sex as it is with men and as it is with beasts (n. 1194-1251 [*C. L.*, n. 48, 94-96, 133]). (*See* BEAST.)

(*Concerning the love of the sex, see* LOVE OF THE SEX.)

Changes of state with man and with woman, especially through marriage (n. 1252-1285 [*C. L.*, n. 184-206]). (*See* STATE.)

Various things concerning the signs that male and female wish to become one (n. 1262, 1278).

State of consorts after death (n. 1719-1736 [*C. L.*, n. 45-54]). (*See* MARRIAGE.)

The love of the sex remains with every man after death such as it was interiorly with him (n. 1721-1723 [*C. L.*, n. 46, 47]). (*See* MARRIAGE.)

Three French orators on the beauty of the female sex (*Memorab.*, n. 1727 (*C. L.*, n. 381-384]).

The perception and wisdom proper to the man and proper to the woman, and concerning the conjunction of man and woman through them (n. 2007-2022 [*C. L.*, n. 156[*] 181]).

Man has a faculty of knowing, of understanding, and of being wise, that woman does not have (n. 2008-2009 [*C. L.*, n. 168, 174, 175]).

Woman has a faculty of knowing, of understanding, and of being wise, that man does not have (n. 2010, 2011 [*C. L.*, n. 168, 174, 175]).

In the woman there is the inclination to love the things which are of knowledge, intelligence, and wisdom with the man, in the man (n. 2011 [*C. L.*, n. 159]).

The man has the inclination to love the things which are of knowledge, intelligence and wisdom with the woman, in the woman (n. 2012).

It is from creation that the faculties and inclinations of the two may be conjoined into one (n. 2013, 2014 [*C. L.*, n. 156[*], 157]).

The conjunction is inspired by the woman according to her love, and it is received by the man according to his wisdom (n. 2015 [*C. L.*, n. 161]).

Inclination to conjoin the man to herself is constant and perpetual with the woman, but its reception is various and alternate with the man (n. 2016 [*C. L.*, n. 160, 169]).

Perceptions of the inclinations and affections of the man, and, together with this, prudence in regulating them, is woman's wisdom (n. 2017 [*C. L.*, n. 166, 168]).

Women hide this wisdom of theirs within themselves, and do not disclose it at all to the man, for the sake of causes that are necessities; so that conjugial love, friendship, and confidence, and thus the union of souls and minds and the consequent bliss of living together, and the happiness of the life of both parties, may be preserved and strengthened (n. 2018 [*C. L.*, n. 167]).

As woman is beautiful, so she is tender; and as she is tender, so she has ability to perceive the delights of conjugial love; and as she is able to perceive these delights, so she is a faithful custodian of the common good, and as she is a custodian of the common good, and the man is wise, so she looks after the prosperity and happiness of the home (n. 2019).

Man's perception and the wisdom therefrom cannot be given in woman; and woman's perception and the wisdom therefrom cannot be given in man (n. 2020 [*C. L.*, n. 168]).

The perception and wisdom of both of them are conjoined through the marriage of one man with one wife; and this conjunction is according to the quality of their conjugial love; and according to this conjunction a man [*homo*] becomes more and more or less and less a man (n. 2021, 2022 [*C. L.*, n. 176–178]).

Duties proper to man and proper to woman, and the conjunction of both by them (n. 2023–2033 [*C. L.*, n. 174–176]).

There are duties proper to man and proper to woman; the duties proper to man may be called public duties, and those proper to woman may be called domestic duties (n. 2024 [*C. L.*, n. 90, 91, 174, 175]).

Man from the wisdom that is proper to himself inclines to his own duties, and woman from the wisdom proper to her inclines to her duties (n. 2024 [*C. L.*, n. 33]).

Man's duties are matters of interior judgment, and woman's duties are of exterior (n. 2026 [*C. L.*, n. 175]).

A woman cannot enter into the duties of man, nor can a man enter into the duties of woman, and perform them aright (n. 2027, 2028 [*C. L.*, n. 174, 175]).

Wise women are not loved (n. 2028 [*C. L.*, n. 17 5; *Arc. Cœlest.*, n. 8994]).

The conjunction of their duties is a mutual help (n. 2029 [*C. L.*, n. 176]).

A man and a woman by this mutual assistance, make a home which is coherent as one (n. 2030 [*C. L.*, n. 176]).

The duties of the two make up as it were a single form of government (n. 2031).

The duties of the man refer to wisdom; the duties of the woman refer to doing the man's delights of wisdom, and thus they refer to the man (n. 2032).

All these are done more perfectly, or more imperfectly, according to the state of conjugial love between them (n. 2033 [*C. L.*, n. 118, 162]).

The inclinations and affections of men and women, through which conjunction is effected (*many articles*, n. 2047 [*C. L.*, n. 163–180]).

Difficulties in knowing the conjunctions of consorts (*articles*, n. 2050).

SIMILITUDE (*Similitudo*).—Conjugial similitude and dissimilitude (n. 765–882).

Various things respecting concordance and discordance of affections (n. 766–840 [*C. L.*, n. 227–229, 246, 271, *seq.*]). (*See* AFFECTION.)

There is compatibility and there is incompatibility between the affections of men and women (n. 841-844).

Hence there is conjugial similitude and dissimilitude (n. 845-852).

There are various similitudes of conjugial love, and there are various dissimilitudes of it (n. 853-859 [*C. L.*, n. 227]).

The various similitudes of conjugial love can be accommodated and conjoined, but not with the various dissimilitudes (n. 860-*809** [*C. L.*, n. 228]).

With those who go to the Lord, and who have a desire for love truly conjugial, a conjugial similitude is provided by Him (*810-817* [*C. L.*, n. 49, 229]).

Similitude and dissimilitude effect nothing with those who are in scortatory love (n. *818-822*).

There are external similitudes, for the sake of which matrimonies are formed in the world; but if they are not at the same time internal, those matrimonies are dissolved after death (n. *822-833* [*C. L.*, n. 48, 49, 274]).

Of external similitudes, eight kinds are enumerated (n. *823-833*).

An exterior cause of coldness between consorts is dissimilitude of external minds (*animorum*) and of manners (n. 929-934 [*C. L.*, n. 246]);

Also inequalities of state and condition of the two parties in external things (n. 935-938 [*C. L.*, n. 250]).

Various things concerning similitude of souls and of minds, also concerning similitude of external minds (*animorum*) and manners, and of state and condition in society (n. 1606, 1607, [*C. L.*, n. 49]).

Union of souls according to similitudes (n. 1607).

[SON and DAUGHTER (*Filius et Filia*).—(*See the other Index.*)]

SOUL (*Anima*).—(*See the other Index also.*)

The soul is the man himself, as to love and wisdom (n. 5 [*C. L.*, n. 28-31]).

Man has soul, spirit, and body: concerning the soul (n. 474-476 [*C. L.*, n. 101]).

---

*EDITOR'S NOTE.—The references underlined are underlined in the original manuscript.

Various things concerning the state of the soul (n. 490–497 [*C. L.*, n. 315]).

The soul is in a state of perpetual fructification and multiplication (n. 498–501 [*C. L.*, n. 220]).

Various things respecting influx, formation of seed, and the opening of the interiors of the mind (n. 539–548 [*C. L.*, n. 220]). (*See* SEED.)

Reasonings respecting the soul, where its seat is, and what its quality (*Memorab.*, n. 1641 [*C. L.*, n. 315]).

SPHERE (*Sphaera.*)—(*See also the other Index.*)

The universal sphere of conjugial love, from the Lord (n. 2 [*C. L.*, n. 92, 222]). (*See also* MARRIAGE.)

Some things about spheres (n. 252–257 [*C. L.*, n. 54, 92, 171, 220, 222, 224, 225, 321, 355, 386, 434, 435, 437, 438, 455]).

Universal spheres (n. 344–352 [*C. L.*, n. 386–400]).

From the Lord proceeds the Divine providence for the preservation of the created universe, and for its continuance to eternity (n. 1644–1647 [*C. L.*, n. 386]).

There are two spheres through which the Lord's Divine providence operates in these things; one is the sphere of procreating and of continuing one's kind, and the other is the sphere of protecting and sustaining, and thus of preserving the species that have been procreated: in relation to the human race, one is called the sphere of conjugial love, and the other is called the sphere of the love of infants (*concerning these spheres, see* n. 1648–1652 [*C. L.*, n. 386]).

These two spheres proceed solely from the Lord, and they inflow universally and particularly into all things of heaven and of the world, from their firsts even to their lasts (n. 1653 [*C. L.*, n. 387–390]).

The sphere of the love of infants which proceeds from the Lord is the sphere of protection and support of those who are unable to protect and support themselves (n. 1658–1662 [*C. L.*, n. 391]).

Various things respecting those spheres (n. 1658–1662).

The sphere of the love of infants inflows into all living and animate things in the universe, and fills them with a love of innocence and peace, which is received by them in their own time[1] (n. 1663–1666 [*C. L.*, n. 392–397]).

(*See more concerning these spheres, under* PARENTAL LOVE.)
(*Concerning the sphere of innocence and peace, see* PARENTAL LOVE.)

SPIRIT (*Spiritus*).—(*See also* MIND.) (*See the other Index.*) Man's spirit is his mind: this is in the whole body (*illustrated*, n. 58–60 [*C. L.*, n. 178, 260]).

SPIRITUAL (*Spirituale*).—Various things concerning the spiritual and the natural, the difference between them, and their conjunction (n. 575 [*C. L.*, n. 31, 52, 326–329]).

What the spiritual is (n. 577 [*C. L.*, n. 326–329]).

Various things concerning the spiritual world and its influx into the natural world (n. 577, 578 [*C. L.*, n. 380]).

The difference between the spiritual and the natural, as to language, mode of writing, and thought (*Memorab.*, n. 1699 [*C. L.*, n. 326–329]).

Spiritual things are substantial (*Memorab.*, n. 1909 [*C. L.*, n. 207]).

SPIRITUAL MARRIAGE, WHICH IS THE MARRIAGE OF GOOD AND TRUTH (*Conjugium spirituale, quod est boni et veri*).—The union of love and wisdom, or of good and truth, is in the Lord alone (n. 36–38 [*C. L.*, n. 84]).

This union is from the Lord, and it is the Lord with man (n. 39, 40 [*C. L.*, n. 85]).

Reciprocal union of wisdom and love can be given only with a male and a female together (n. 42–45 [*C. L.*, n. 100–102]).

This union with them is the image of God (n. 46–50 [*C. L.*, n. 84–86]).

The image of God is the inmost origin of conjugial love (n. 51–56 [*C. L.*, n. 84–86]).

(*That such is the origin of conjugial love, see* CONJUGIAL LOVE.)

Conjugial love is from religion (n. 131–135, 140–145 [*C. L.*, n. 531]). (*See* CONJUGIAL LOVE, *also* RELIGION.)

Masculine conjugial love and feminine, specifically; also the intelligence of each (n. 223–301 [*C. L.*, n. 89–91]). (*See* SEX.)

A paper on which was written, "The marriage of good and truth,"—how it appeared on its way from heaven to earth; also more things concerning that marriage (*Memorab.*, n. 301 [*C.L.*, n. 115]).

The marriage of good and truth (n. 304–407 [*C. L.*, n. 83–102]).

Marriages are from the marriage of good and truth (n. 304 [*C. L.*, 83–102]).

What is properly meant by spiritual marriage is between the good of truth and the truth of good (n. 324, 325 [*C. L.*, n. 93, 100]).

Between these two is the love which is properly called conjugial love (n. 326–329 [*C. L.*, n. 65, 92, 93]).

Concerning its prolification (n. 330–337 [*C. L.*, n. 51, 65]). (*See* OFFSPRING.)

In this marriage there is reciprocal action and reaction, from which the one becomes the other's; it is mutual (n. 338–340 [*C. L.*, n. 61, 293]).

All things of marriage derive their origin from the marriage of good and truth (n. 344, *seq.* [*C. L.*, n. 60–63]).

The marriage of good and truth descends from the Lord through three degrees; in each of these degrees it proceeds from what is greatest to what is least; hence there is infinite variety in that marriage (n. 373–375).

The three degrees of marriages and of adulteries (n. 373–388). (*See* DEGREES.)

Celestial marriages, spiritual marriages, and natural marriages: and distinctions (n. 373–388). (*See* DEGREES.)

Genuine marriages with men altogether make a one with the marriage of good and truth with them (n. 389–392 [*C. L.*, n. 62, 65, 83, 115]).

The marriage of good and truth is in all things and in every single thing of the Word, of the church and of religion (n. 393–397 [*C. L.*, n. 62, 115, 163, 176, 516]).

Therefore marriages with men are altogether in accordance with the states of the church and of religion with them (n. 398–401 [*C. L.*, n. 70–72, 76, 130, 238, 531, 534]).

Therefore each one has heaven according to his conjugial love (n. 402–406 [*C. L.*, n. 531]).

Conjugial love in its first origin is to them the love for the propagation of good and truth (n. 502–512 [*C. L.*, n. 220]).

There is spiritual conjugial love, and there is natural (n. 575–578 [*C. L.*, n. 148]).

There is spiritual conjugial love from which, in which, and into which a man is conceived, and into which he grows, and is formed (n. 579–584).

They who are in love truly conjugial become forms of celestial, natural and spiritual love and wisdom (n. 679–682, *seq.*).

Love and wisdom increase with those who are in conjugial love (n. 723–724 [*C. L.*, n. 98, 188, 211, 212, 355]).

The marriage of the Lord with the church (n. 1301–1344 [*C. L.*, n. 21, 116–131]). (*See* CHURCH.)

The correspondence of the marriage of the Lord and the church with marriages in the heavens and on earth (n. 1347–1358 [*C. L.*, n. 125–127]). (*See* CORRESPONDENCE.)

Conjugial love and potency, natural and spiritual (n. 1459–1652 [*C. L.*, n. 220, 221, 355, 433]).

Various things respecting the spiritual marriage of good and truth (n. 1916).

Various things respecting the delight of good and truth with the male, and also with the female (n. 1916, 1917).

Correspondence of whoredoms and adulteries with the violation of spiritual marriage, or the marriage of good and truth (n. 1950–2000 [*C. L.*, n. 515–520]). (*See* CORRESPONDENCE.)

Many other things respecting spiritual marriage (n. 1952, *seq.* [*C. L.*, n. 516]).

STATE (*Status*), and CHANGES OF STATE (*status mutationes*).—

Change of the state of life with man and with woman, by marriage (n. 1252–1285 [*C. L.*, n. 184–206]).

The states of the life of man are continually and successively changing, from infancy even to old age (n. 1254–1256 [*C. L.*, n. 185]).

The internal form of men is changed according to the states which the mind or spirit undergoes, and from this the external form, which is that of the face, body, and manners (n. 1257, 1258 [*C. L.*, n. 186]).

The changes of the state of life are not alike with men and with women (n. 1258-1260 [*C. L.*, n. 187-189]).

Various things respecting the successive changes of state (n. 1259 [*C. L.*, n. 187]).

But the states of life with men and with women agree in this,—that, in the case of each, they regard a state of reciprocal unition, or one state together (n. 1261-1264).

The first state of the life of men is the state of the thought and understanding of truth (n. 1265, 1266).

The second state of men is the state of the union of the understanding and will, or of the thought of truth and the affection for good (n. 1267-1271).

The third state is the state of the will and the consequent state of the understanding, or the state of the affection for good and the thought of truth therefrom (n. 1272-1274).

This state is the very human state for which man was created; and provision has been made for this in the marriage of a man with one wife (n. 1275-1277).

The male or the young man by marriage with one wife actually changes his state; and in like manner the female or the virgin: and through this change the male from being a young man becomes a husband, and the female from being a virgin becomes a wife (n. 1278, 1279 [*C. L.*, n. 193-199]).

By means of such marriage the husband becomes a form of wisdom, and the wife a form of the love of the wisdom of the man and hence of the husband, and the two forms are reciprocally united and become as one (n. 1280).

Man, both male and female, changes states and is formed according to the quality of the marriage (n. 1281 [*C. L.*, n. 200, 201]).

Each of them, the male and the female, induces opposite states in himself or herself according to the quality of the violation of marriage (n. 1284, 1285).

STORGE.—(*See* PARENTAL LOVE.)

SUBSTANCE (*Substantia*).—Substance is form; substances are of three degrees (n. 154-158 [*C. L.*, n. 66]).

Good and truth are not given apart from substances, and substances are not given apart from forms; thus substance is form, and form is substance (n. 341-343 [*C. L.*, n. 66]). Some things concerning substances (n. 333, *seq.*). Propagations therefore are substantial and material (n. 344). (*See* OFFSPRING.)
Love, wisdom and use are in substance, and substances are forms (n. 695-697, 698).
Substance becomes a subject through form (n. 700-708 [*C. L.*, n. 361]).
Spiritual things are substantial (*Memorab.*, n. 1909 [*C. L.*, n. 207]).

SUN (*Sol*).—The centre and the expanse of nature and of life (*Memorab.*, n. 568 [*C. L.*, n. 380]).

TOUCH (*Tactus*).—The delights of conjugial love are of the sense of touch (n. 116-119 [*C. L.*, n. 210, 396]).

[TREE (*Arbor*).—(*See second Index.*)]

TRUTH (*Verum*).—(*See* GOOD.)
How many kinds of truth there are; as celestial, spiritual, political, etc. (n. 488 [*C. L.*, n. 130]).
They have conjugial love who are in truths through the Word, and wish to propagate them, etc. (n. 516-521 [*C. L.*, n. 128]).

[TURNING (*Conversio*).—(*See the other Index.*)]

ULTIMATE (*Ultimum.*)
LAST (*Ultimum*).   }—(*See* EXTREME.)
OUTMOST (*Ultimum*).

UNCLEAN (*Immundus*).—Various things respecting the unclean things of hell and the clean things of heaven (n. 1922, 1923 [*C. L.*, n. 430, 495, 500]).

UNDERSTANDING (*Intellectus*).—(*See* WISDOM.) (*See also the other Index.*)

INTELLIGENCE (*Intelligentia*).—How man receives influx from the Lord, first with the understanding; and how he receives love, by means of this (*illustrated*, n. 75 [*C. L.*, n. 267]).

- Very many things concerning the human rational, even to fifty various changes (n. 427 [*C. L.*, n. 145, 233, 436]).
- Various things concerning the will and the understanding, and concerning the changes and inversions of the state of the latter (n. 1267–1277). (*See* STATE.)
- Adulterers enjoy the faculty of understanding, or rationality, equally with those who are not adulterers; but[1] they abuse their rationality to confirm adulteries (n. 1904–1908 [*C. L.*, n. 498, 499]).
- The wisdom proper to men and proper to women (n. 2007–2022 [*C. L.*, n. 163–173]).
- Some reasons why wise women are not loved by men (n. 2028 [*C. L.*, n. 175; *Arcana Cœlestia*, n. 8994]).
- They who are in the pride of their own intelligence cannot love the wife nor the neighbor (*many and various things*, n. 2042–2045 [*C. L.*, n. 193]).
- The transcription of the love of proprium with the man into conjugial love with the wife (*articles*, n. 2036 [*C. L.*, n. 32, 88, 156, 193, 253, 293]).
- Things proper to the will, and things proper to the understanding[2] therefrom, from which there is conjunction (*articles*, n. 2048 [*C. L.*, n. 32, 156, 163–173]).
- Concerning man's own intelligence or prudence, that it is nothing (*Memorab.*, n. 2051 [*C. L.*, n. 353]).
- Whether conjugial love and the love of [one's own] beauty, also whether conjugial love and the love of one's own wisdom, are given (*Memorab.*, n. 2052 [*C. L.*, n. 330, 331]).

USE (*Usus.*)—The most excellent use is from conjugial love (n. 128–130 [*C. L.*, n. 68, 143, 183, 305]).
- Various uses (n. 128 [*C. L.*, n. 18]).
- Conjugial love in its first origin is the love of the propagation of good and truth (n. 502).
- Man's soul is in a state of perpetual fructification (n. 498–501 [*C. L.*, n. 220]).
- Man is a form of love, of wisdom, and of use (n. 683–690 [*C. L.*, n. 16, 183, 361]).

Man is a single series of all the uses in the universe (n. 691–693).

These uses cohere in man in most perfect order (n. 694).

The uses of love and wisdom are given in substances, and thus in forms (n. 695–697 [*C. L.*, n. 66, 361]).

There is nothing which is not a form of use (n. 697 [*C. L.*, n. 183]).

Love forms wisdom, and through wisdom it forms use; thus every form is essentially a form of love (n. 700–708).

A conversation concerning love, wisdom and use (*Memorab.*, n. 763 [*C. L.*, n. 183]).

Uses and their affections distinguish men from one another (n. 773–779 [*C. L.*, n. 18]).

A cause of coldness between consorts is, that there is no determination of the mind to any study or business; whence comes either stupidity or wandering desire (n. 951–957 [*C. L.*, n. 249]).

VARIETY (*Varietas*).—Excessive lust for varieties in the love of the sex not only destroys the human conjugial, but also the whole man (n. 1811–1873[1] [*C. L.*, n. 506–510]).

Their lot after death (n. 1813 [*C. L.*, n. 510]).

VIOLATION (*Violatio*).—The lust of violation destroys the human conjugial (n. 1819–1822 [*C. L.*, n. 511]).

Their lot after death (n. 1822 [*C. L.*, n. 512]).

VIRGINITY (*Virginitas*).—The strongest desire for defloration ruins the human conjugial (n. 1814–1818 [*C. L.*, n. 501–505]).

Their lot after death (n. 1816–1818 [*C. L.*, 505]).

Various things respecting virginity (n. 1808, 1814 [*C. L.*, 503]).

WHOREDOM. (*See* ADULTERY.)

WIDOW (*Vidua*).—The state of widowers and of widows, and concerning repeated marriages (n. 1287–1299 [*C. L.*, n. 317–325]).

The state of widowhood is not the same as the state of marriage, and it differs from it in general and in particular according to the state of the marriage in which one has been (n. 1289-1292 [*C. L.*, n. 319, 320]).

The state of the widow is not the same as the state of the widower, but differs from it (n. 1294 [*C. L.*, n. 325]).

It is allowable for any one to enter upon another marriage after the death of a consort (n. 1295 [*C. L.*, n. 54, 318-320]).

But they who have lived in love truly conjugial do not desire to enter upon another marriage after the consort's death, and they therefore cannot do so (n. 1296 [*C. L.*, n. 320, 321]).

The state of the marriage of a young man with a widow is different from the state of marriage with a virgin; so, too, the state of the marriage of a virgin with a widower; also of a widower with a widow (n. 1297-1299 [*C. L.*, n. 322, 323]).

WISDOM (*Sapientia*).—(*See also* UNDERSTANDING.)

Man is a form of love, wisdom, and use (*see* MAN, USE).

The love of his own wisdom sinks man down (n. 734-739 [*C. L.*, n. 88, 193, 353]).

Discourse of the wise on the causes of the beauty of the female sex (*Memorab*, n. 1018 [*C. L.*, n. 56]).

Some reasons why learned women are not loved by men (n. 2028 [*C. L.*, n. 175; *Arc. Cœlest.*, n. 8994]).

They who are in the pride of their own intelligence cannot possibly love the wife (*much concerning this*, n. 2042-2045 [*C. L.*, n. 193]).

The proper perception and wisdom of the man and of the woman, and conjunction by means of them (*articles*, n. 2007, *etc.* [*C. L.*, n. 156[*]—181]). (*See* SEX.)

WORD (*Verbum*).—The Word is the medium of conjunction with the Lord; also with whom: also many other things concerning the Word (n. 1342, 1343 [*C. L.*, n. 24, 128, 516, 532]). (*See* CHURCH.)

The Word consists of correspondences (n. 1345 [*C. L.*, n. 515, 532]).

Various things concerning the violation of the Word (n. 1977, *etc.* [*C. L.*, n. 515-520]).

WORLD, SPIRITUAL AND NATURAL (*Mundus spiritualis et naturalis*.—(*See* SPIRITUAL AND NATURAL.)

ZEAL (*Zelus*). } —Concerning jealousy (n. 1738-1791
JEALOUSY (*Zelotypia*). } [*C. L.*, n. 357-379]).

Jealousy is zeal; and zeal regarded in itself is as the fire of love burning (n. 1741-1743 [*C. L.*, n. 358]).

The burning or flame of that love, which is zeal, is a spiritual burning or flame, arising from an infestation and assault of the love (n. 1744-1747 [*C. L.*, n. 359-361]).

One's zeal is such as the love is; thus of one kind to one who has a love of good, and of another with one who has a love of evil (n. 1748-1750 [*C. L.*, n. 362]).

The zeal of the love of good and the zeal of the love of evil appear alike in externals, and both of them seem like anger and wrath (n. 1751-1754 [*C. L.*, n. 363, 364]);

But in internals the zeal of the love of good and the zeal of the love of evil are altogether unlike (n. 1755-1757 [*C. L.*, n. 363, 364]).

The zeal of the love of good conceals in its internals its own good, charity, and friendship; but the zeal of the love of evil conceals in its internals its own evil, revenge, and hatred (n. 1758-1760 [*C. L.*, n. 365-366]).

The zeal of conjugial love is called jealousy (n. 1761-1764 [*C. L.*, n. 367]).

Jealousy is as a fire against those who infest the love with a consort; and it is as a horrible fear for the loss of that love (n. 1765, 1766 [*C. L.*, n. 368]).

There is spiritual jealousy with monogamists, and natural with polygamists; there is also jealousy with beasts and with birds (n. 1767-1772 [*C. L.*, n. 369, 370, 378]).

They have jealousy who love their consorts, and they also who do not love them (n. 1773 [*C. L.*, n. 371, 372]).

There is jealousy also for mistresses, but not such as there is for wives (n. 1774 [*C. L.*, n. 377]).

Jealousy with those who love their consorts is a just pain from sound reason, lest conjugial love should be divided and thus should perish (n. 1775, 1776 [*C. L.*, n. 371]).

Jealousy with those who do not love their consorts is from various causes (*concerning which*, n. 1777, 1778 [*C. L.*, n. 373, 375]).

With some it is from various sickness of the mind (n. 1779–1785 [*C. L.*, n. 374, 375]).

With some there is no jealousy, and this too from various causes (n. 1786 [*C. L.*, n. 376]).

Jealousy with women and wives is not the same as with men and husbands (n. 1787–1790 [*C. L.*, n. 379]).

SECOND INDEX.

ANGEL (*Angelus*).—No angel was created an angel; but angels were all born men (n. 23 [*C. L.*, n. 30, 31]). (*See* MAN.)

BEAST (*Bestia*).—Some things respecting the difference between men and beasts: also concerning influx through the natural world into beasts, and through the spiritual and higher world with man (n. 75 [*C. L.*, n. 134]).

CAUSE (*Causa*).—The love, which is the end, progresses through causes to effect, and to further effects even to the last; and from this it returns to the first effect, but by another way, and produces an image of love,—a semblance of the first love (n. 80).

Illustrated by the circulation of the blood from the heart through the arteries into the veins, and so back to the heart; also by the circulation of the blood into the lungs, and its return to the heart (n. 81).

There are end, cause and effect in each and all things that have been created; also in things civil and moral, whence the mind[1] becomes rational (n. 83).

CONJUGIAL LOVE (*Amor conjugialis*).—*A Relation.*—There were seen two angels, from the third heaven, who were in love truly conjugial; these are described: they left a parchment on which there was a writing concerning conjugial love (*Memorab.*, n. 1 [*C. L.*, n. 42, 43]).

Love is the image of one in the other; not an image of the person, but of quality; this is friendship's love (n. 18).

Between consorts there is not merely an image, but also a similitude which has its seat in their souls, and manifests itself variously in the body (n. 18, 19).

From this the man recognizes that one is to be his wife; this similitude manifests itself (*illustrated*, n. 20).

There is providence of the Lord in respect to marriages (n. 21 [*C. L.*, n. 229]).

A Relation.—The delights of love truly conjugial were represented with what was flame-like, with colors, with odors, with flower-gardens, with trees,[1] with flying things and with animals (*described*, n. 29, 30 [*C. L.*, n. 76]).
Marriages in heaven (n. 2–30 [*C. L.*, n. 27–41]).
Origin of conjugial love (n. 31–76 [*C. L.*, n. 83–102]).
The delights of conjugial love (n. 77–146 [*C. L.*, n. 68, 69]).
The connection of conjugial love with all the loves of heaven (n. 147–222 [*C. L.*, n. 65–67]).
Conjugial love is not now on the earth, but still it can be raised up with those who will be of the New Jerusalem (n. 31 [*C. L.*, n. 59, 70–72, 81, 534]).
Reciprocal union of wisdom and love can be given only with a male and a female, for that union is conjugial love (n. 42 [*C. L.*, n. 88–93]).
How love and wisdom descend from the Lord into male and female (n. 43 [*C. L.*, n. 90, 91]).
The internal influx of conjugial love from the Lord is not perceived, but it becomes more perceptible and gives the more enjoyment as it descends; and from them in the ultimate effect it becomes the delight of delights (n. 58 [*C. L.*, n. 69, 183]).
It becomes such delight from the highest end,[1] which is in the Lord; namely, the propagation of the human race, and the angelic heaven therefrom, conjunction there with Himself, and eternal happiness (n. 58 [*C. L.*, n. 68]).
This love is spiritual, because it is the conjunction of minds; it therefore remains after death (n. 59 [*C. L.*, n. 46]).
Conjugial love of minds, which is spiritual, makes conjugial love of bodies, which is natural (*illustrated in various ways*, n. 62).
Conjugial love becomes more fully conjugial love by descent into ultimates (n. 63 [*C. L.*, n. 179]).
Conjugial love in the bosom, its quality (*described and illustrated*, n. 64 [*C. L.*, n. 180]).
The quality of love in the loins described, because this enters the province formed by the members of generation (n. 65).

Thus there is descent in a series through causes to effects (n. 66).

What love truly conjugial is, is unknown, from four causes; men have not gone to the Lord, they have separated faith from charity, therefore there is no love toward the neighbor, and thus no love truly conjugial (n. 67).

Angels have said that there is no[1] love truly conjugial except with those who go to the Lord, thus unless consorts are in the spiritual marriage: thence is inmost friendship between consorts; and where there is not[2] this, neither can the love be given that descends to the loins (n. 68).

Where conjugial love is perpetual, there is perpetual potency (n. 68 at end [*C. L.*, n. 113, 115]).

Conjunction with the Lord becomes full through love truly conjugial: not full, however, from the male alone nor from the female alone (n. 74).

How the interiors of man's mind are opened, and will and understanding or love and wisdom conjoined, with those who receive love truly conjugial (n. 75, *at end*).

CONVERSION.—(*See* TURNING.)

DAUGHTER.—(*See* SON.)

DELIGHTS (*Deliciae*).—The delights of conjugial love (n. 77–146 [*C. L.*, n. 68, 69]). (*See* CONJUGIAL LOVE.)

By delights are meant beatitudes, satisfactions, happiness, enjoyments, and pleasures; in general, joys and gladnesses (n. 77).

Whence come delights (n. 77 [*C. L.*, n. 461]). (*See* LOVE.)

Enjoyment is the life of love (n. 78 [*C. L.*, n. 461]).

The enjoyments of love follow in order, as end, cause and effect. What the case is with delights, while the end or love is progressing, is tarrying, and is at a stand (n. 82).

EFFECT (*Effectus*).—(*See* CAUSE.)

END (*Finis*).—Love is the end; its progression through causes to effects (n. 81). (*See* LOVE.)

In the end are all things that follow; and in the effect are all things that precede; the end is the all in all things that follow (n. 82).

There are end, cause, and effect in each and all things that have been created (n. 83). (*See* CAUSE.)

EVIL (*Malum*).—Shunning evils as sins (n. 73). (*See* REPENTANCE.)

EXTERNAL (*Externum*).—Divine operation takes place from firsts by ultimates, and thus in fulness (n. 75).

FEMININE (*Femina*). WOMAN (*Femina*). {—What the masculine is, and what the feminine. With the male, love veils itself with wisdom; and with woman, this wisdom veils itself with love; thus woman is the love of the wisdom which is in man, and thus she was taken out of man (*shown*, n. 6, 7, 52 [*C. L.*, n. 88–91]).

The love of the sex is the most universal of all, and hence in every smallest particular; without it the world would perish (n. 14, 15 [*C. L.*, n. 37, 38]).

Masculine and feminine are implanted from creation in all the subjects of the vegetable kingdom and of the animal kingdom; they are implanted most interiorly, and this from creation (n. 16).

The love of the sex is primarily in the souls of men (n. 17).

The male is born into the capacity of loving to know, to understand, and to be wise; and the female into the love of these in the husband (*illustrated*, n. 53 [*C. L.*, n. 90, 91]).

Consequently they become a one by marriage (n. 54 [*C. L.*, n. 91]).

These reasons why they were so created: *first*, that there may be propagation of offspring and of wisdom; *second*, it is from the love of the Lord towards the human race, that they may be happy; *third*, because they would otherwise love themselves (n 54).

Description of the quality of the will and the understanding with man, and their quality with woman, before and after marriage (n. 55).

GARDEN (*Hortus*).—Description of a certain garden called the nuptial garden, that appeared near houses where there were nuptials (*Memorab.*, n. 76 [*C. L.*, n. 183]).

GENERATION (*Generatio*).
ORGANS OF GENERATION (*Generationis organa*). }—The organs of generation are distinct from all others in man (n. 65).

The procreation of offspring takes place on earth, because fulness is there; and the Divine operation is from firsts by ultimates (n. 75 [*C. L.*, n. 52]).

By man are procreated offspring in whose inmost is the image of God (n. 75).

HEAVEN (*Caelum*).—The entire heaven, and hell also, have been formed according to the varieties of love (n. 13 [*C. L.*, n. 36]). (*See* LOVE.)

IMAGE (*Imago*).—The union of love and wisdom with male and female together is an image of God and a likeness of God (n. 46, 47, 74).

The image is the recipient form or receptacle; and the likeness of God is the perception with man that he acts as from himself, although from the Lord (*illustrated*, n. 46 [*C. L.*, n. 132]).

The image of God has not been lost on the part of God with man; most interiorly with man there still is ability to understand such things as are of God: but His image has been lost on the part of man (n. 48 [*C. L.*, n. 269]).

How lost (n. 49). (*See* TREE.)

This shown and illustrated (n. 50 [*C. L.*, n. 135]). (*See* TREE.)

IMMORTALITY (*Immortalitas*).—A man lives a man after death; and this, so that he loses nothing, but believes that he is in the world as before (n. 3 [*C. L.*, n. 28–31]).

This is unknown in the Christian world; and yet it is known from common perception (*illustrated*, n. 3 [*C. L.*, n. 28]).

The same shown from the Word (n. 4 [*C. L.*, n. 28]).

Every one's love lives after death (n. 9–13 [*C. L.*, n. 34–36]). (*See* LOVE.)

A man lives a man after death (*illustrated*, n. 22-24 [*C. L.*, n. 28-31]). (*See* MAN.)

INFLUX (*Influxus*.) Man feels that to be his own which inflows from the Lord; and by this means conjunction is effected (n. 40 [*C. L.*, n. 122]).

The unition of the Lord and man takes place by means of influx, as a force acting into its organ. There is adjunction, and there is communication (n. 51).

There is influx from the secondary Divine essence that is round about the Lord, in the sun, in the midst of which He is (n. 51).

How the influx of the Lord into man's soul takes place, and thence into the higher parts of the mind, and through these into the lower parts of the mind, and thence into the body, and makes conatus; which, when opportunity offers, becomes act (*illustrated*, n. 57).

The influx of conjugial love into the inmosts, and thence into what follows in order, to ultimates (n. 58). (*See* CONJUGIAL LOVE.)

There is no descent or influx from the brains or from the head into the body; for the mind of man is his spirit, which is a perfect man, and to the body it is everywhere within; so that the terms descent and influx are used from appearance (n. 60, 61 [*C. L.*, n. 315]).

Man's mind or spirit acts instantaneously into the body; it acts simultaneously, and not successively, for the spiritual is not in place; it is received by the material body, not in an instant, but in a moment (n. 60, 61).

There are[1] three degrees in the mind, which are clothed with materials in the body (n. 60, 61).

No one can love the Lord from himself, but from the Lord, and this as from himself: illustrated; also by the laws of influx (*concerning which, see* n. 70).

How this is accomplished (n. 71). (*See* MIND AND TURNING.)

Difference between men and beasts, from influx and its reception (*illustrated*, n. 75 [*C. L.*, n. 134]).

INTELLIGENCE.—(*See* UNDERSTANDING.)

LIFE (*Vita*).—Life in itself is the Lord, and man is an organ of life (n. 43).
The life of the Lord is the union of love and wisdom (n. 43).
Life in its fulness is to be wise from love, and to love from wisdom (n. 43).
It is an enormous crime to believe that man is life in itself (n. 43).

LORD (*Dominus*).—All love and all wisdom, or all good and truth, are[1] from the Lord (n. 33 [*C. L.*, n. 121]).
The name *Lord* is used throughout, because the Lord is Jehovah, or the Lord from eternity, who took upon Himself the Human in time (n. 35).
The union of love and wisdom, or of good and truth, is in the Lord alone, and it is the Lord (n. 36 [*C. L.*, n. 121]).
The union is reciprocal (*shown*, n. 36 [*C. L.*, n. 122]).
How the reciprocal union of love and wisdom, or of good and truth, is effected (n. 37 [*C. L.*, n. 123])
The reciprocal union of the Lord and man (n. 39, 40 [*C. L.*, n. 123, 124]). (*See* LOVE.)
The union of love and wisdom, and the reciprocal union of wisdom and love, is in the Lord alone; and man is an image or organ of it (n. 43[2]).
The influx of the Lord with man; its quality (n. 51). (*See* INFLUX.)
Something concerning the marriage of the Lord and the church (n. 69, 70 [*C. L.*, n. 129, 130]).
No one can love the Lord from himself, but he can love Him as from himself; illustrated by the laws of influx (*concerning which, see* n. 70).
How man loves the Lord as from Himself, and yet from the Lord (n. 71). (*See* MIND, TURNING.)
No one can love the Lord as He is in Himself; but he can love good which is from Him, by doing it (n. 72, 73).
Full conjunction with the Lord is wrought by conjugial love (n. 74). (*See* MARRIAGE.)
Divine operation is from firsts by lasts, and thus in fulness (n. 75).

LOVE (*Amor*).—Every man is his own love, and he remains his own love after death,—illustrated by the consideration that the enjoyments of life are enjoyments of man's love, and man lives from enjoyments (n. 9 [*C. L.*, n. 34-36, 461]).

The love which lives after death is the love of man's spirit; and the exterior draws from this love, so far as they act in unity (n. 10, 11 [*C. L.*, n. 36]).

Of what quality the love becomes after death with the evil, and of what quality with the good; the love of man's spirit makes [all to be] concordant with itself (n. 11 [*C. L.*, n. 36]).

Love makes one with knowledge, intelligence, and wisdom; for by these it exists (*illustrated*, n. 12 [*C. L.*, n. 36]).

Therefore the whole heaven, in general and in particular, is formed according to loves; and hell likewise (n. 13 [*C. L.*, n. 36]).

Hence also man after death becomes the form of his love (n. 13).

The love of the sex is the most universal of all, and consequently is in the most minute particulars (n. 14 [*C. L.*, n. 37]).

All enjoyments are from love (n. 29, 30).

The things which are beautiful and pleasant correspond to the enjoyments of celestial love, and the things which are unbeautiful and unpleasant to the enjoyments of infernal love (n. 30).

All love and all wisdom, or all good and truth, are from the Lord (n. 33).

Love is as multiform as men are. In general there is the love of self, the love of the world, and the love of use. The love of self is corporeal, the love of the world material, and the love of uses spiritual (n. 34 [*C. L.*, n. 35]).

The love of self and the love of the world separate from the love of uses are infernal; but when they are not separated, the love of uses rules, and the other two serve (n. 34).

The reciprocal union of love and wisdom or of good and truth in the Lord (n. 36 [*C. L.*, n. 60, 84]).

There must be the reciprocal, that there may be indissoluble union (*illustrated*, n. 37);

Illustrated by comparison with a chain (n. 38 [*C. L.*, n. 85]).

This union is with man from the Lord, and it is the Lord with him (n. 39 [*C. L.*, n. 90]).

There is a reciprocal union of the Lord and man (*shown*, n. 40).

Reciprocal conjunction with the Lord is effected by man's feeling to be his own that which flows in (n. 40 [*C. L.*, n. 122⚜]).

All delights derive their origins from the will's love; and they are marked with their names in the wisdom of the understanding (n. 77).

Love lives from enjoyments, so that enjoyment is the life of love (n. 78 [*C. L.*, n. 461]).

All love derives its highest origin from the Divine love of the Lord towards the human race; but this origin is veiled and is bent in various ways; still it is there inmostly, and gives the love of understanding (*and more besides*, n. 79).

Love progresses through causes to effects, and to further effects, even to the ultimate; and thence it returns to the first effect, but not by the same way; and so the first love sees itself in an image in another love; the first love produces this (n. 80).

This circulation of love illustrated by the circulation of the blood from the heart into the heart through the body, also through the lungs (n. 81).

Love is the end; and its enjoyments progress as end, cause, and effect: how it is with its enjoyments if the progression be interrupted (*illustrated*, n. 82). (*See* END.)

MALE (*Masculus*).
MASCULINE (*Masculinum*). { —What the masculine is, and what the feminine (n. 6 [*C. L.*, n. 90, 91]). (*See* WOMAN.)

Hence the male is born to become intellectual; and he is different from the woman in face, in sound of voice, in body, in manners (n. 7 [*C. L.*, n. 90]).

MAN (*Homo*).—Love and wisdom in form are man; and a man is a recipient of this; which is called an image (n. 5).

After death a male is a male, and a female is a female; the sex cannot be changed (n. 6 [*C. L.*, n. 32, 33]).

A man lives a man after death, but a spiritual man (n. 22, 23 [*C. L.*, n. 28]).

There would be a more miserable state for man after death than for a beast, if he were to be a breath, floating in the universe, or kept in somewhere (*pu*) even till the Last Judgment; but for him who lives well, a happier state after death has been provided (n. 24 [*C. L.*, n. 29]).

A man lives a man after death; from personal observation (*illustrated*, n. 25 [*C. L.*, n. 28]).

Man feels that to be his own which inflows from the Lord; and by this means there is conjunction (n. 40 [*C. L.*, n. 122]).

Man is an image and an organ of the Lord's love and wisdom (n. 43).

The Lord's influx with man (n. 51). (*See* INFLUX.)

The inmosts of man, which are of his soul, are turned upwards to the Lord; the lower parts are turned to the world; and the lowest to himself: and in consequence of this, man feels that which inflows as if it were in himself (n.

How man becomes rational; and how will and understanding, or love and wisdom, are conjoined in him: also that thus he can receive love truly conjugial (n. 75, *at end*).

Distinction between beasts and men, from influx and the reception of it (n. 75 [*C. L.*, n. 134]).

MARRIAGE (*Conjugium*).—Something respecting the conjunction of female and male from creation (n. 6, 7, 26, 522[1]). (*See* FEMALE AND MALE.)

The conjugial of feminine and masculine is implanted from creation in minds[2], and also in the vegetative and in the animal soul; otherwise there would cease to be a world (n. 15, 16). (*See* WOMAN.)

There is similitude between consorts (*concerning this*, n. 20 [*C. L.*, n. 227, 228]).

It is of the Lord's providence that like should be conjoined with like (n. 21 [*C. L.*, n. 229]).

There are marriages in the heavens (*illustrated*, n. 22, 24 [*C. L.*, n. 27-41]).

There are marriages after death (*from personal observation*, n. 25 [*C. L.*, n. 45-54]).

From marriages in the heavens are born spiritual offspring only, which belong to good and truth (*illustrated*, n. 26 [*C. L.*, n. 51, 52*]*).

Two consorts are not two angels, but are one angel (*illustrated*, n. 26, 28 [*C. L.*, n. 178]).

How the wisdom of the husband grows in his wife's presence (n. 27).

That two consorts are one man is illustrated by the various things in man which are two and still make one (n. 44 [*C. L.*, n. 316]).

This shown from the Word, and illustrated (n. 45).

The reciprocal union of love and wisdom with male and female together, is an image of God and a likeness of God (n. 46). (*See* IMAGE.)

The quality of the masculine and the feminine which become one by marriage (n. 53-55 [*C. L.*, n. 88, 89]). (*See* WOMAN.)

Something respecting the marriage of the Lord and the church (n. 69, 70).

Neither with the male alone nor with the female alone is there full conjunction with the Lord; but with both together, through love truly conjugial (*illustrated*, n. 74).

The Lord's providence is peculiarly in marriages (*illustrated in various ways, Memorab.*, n. 76 [*C. L.*, n. 229]).

The conjugial is with man in the whole and in every part, but of one kind in the male and of another in the female: that there are conjunctions, illustrated by the marriage of will and understanding, and by the many pairs in the body (*Memorab.*, n. 76 [*C. L.*, n. 316]).

The conjugial is also in the most minute things that have their birth from the earth (n. 76, *at end*).

The delights of conjugial love (n. 77-146 [*C. L.*, n. 68, 69]).

MASCULINE.—(*See* MALE.)

MIND (*Mens*).—Man's mind is his [spirit]. How it inflows into the body (*illustrated*, n. 60, 61 [*C. L.*, n. 315]). Man cannot inflow into the Lord, by affections of love and by thoughts of wisdom; for a lower cannot flow into a higher, for it is contrary to order: but the Lord inflows, and man receives it, and acts as from himself (n. 70, 71).

ONE.—(*See* UNIT.)

PERCEPTION (*Perceptio*).—Something about common perception (n. 3).

PROVIDENCE (*Providentia*).—The Lord's providence respecting marriages is most minute in every particular and is most universal (*illustrated by various things, Memorab.*, n. 76 [*C. L.*, n. 316]).

REPENTANCE (*Paenitentia.*).—So far as one shuns evils as sins, so far he does goods (*illustrated*, n. 73).

SON (*Filius*).
DAUGHTER (*Filia*).
{ —Whence it is that "son" signifies the truth of the church, and "daughter" its good[1] (n. 28).

SOUL (*Anima*).—The soul of man is a recipient of love and wisdom; thus it is an image of God (*illustrated*, n. 5 [*C. L.*, n. 132]).

SPHERE (*Sphaera*).—The most universal sphere of propagation, which is accomplished through conjugial love, perpetually inflows from the Lord (n. 2).

SPIRIT (*Spiritus*).—The influx of man's mind or spirit into the body (n. 60, 61 [*C. L.*, n. 315]). (*See* INFLUX.)

TREE (*Arbor*).—"To eat of the tree of the knowledge of good and evil," is to persuade oneself[2] that he wills and thinks and does good from himself and not from God, and thus that he is as God: that the antediluvians were in that persuasion, shown from the Word and illustrated (n. 49 [*C. L.*, n. 135]).

Man was cast out of the garden of Eden, that he might not have wisdom concerning God from his own love, for thus there is eternal damnation: wherefore they who are in sensual love are able to talk about God, but still they do not acknowledge God (*shown*, n. 50).

TURNING (*Conversio*).
CONVERSION (*Conversio*).
{ —The inmost things of man which are of his soul, are turned upward and thus to the Lord; the lower are turned forward, to the world; and the lowest, downwards to himself: hence man is sensible of the things that inflow as being in himself (n. 71, 72).

UNDERSTANDING (*Intellectus*).
INTELLIGENCE (*Intelligentia*).
{ —Love makes for itself wisdom, intelligence and knowledge, that it may exist (*illustrated*, n. 12). (*See* LOVE.)

All love and all wisdom, or all good and truth, are from the Lord (n. 33 [*C. L.*, n 84]).

The reciprocal union of love and wisdom, or of good and truth (n. 36–38 [*C. L.*, n. 89]). (*See* LOVE.)

This union in man is from the Lord (n. 39, 40 [*C. L.*, n. 92]). (*See* LOVE.)

Description of the quality of the will and the understanding with man, and with woman, before and after marriage (n. 54 [*C L.*, n. 90]).

Concerning the highest intellectual, the higher, and the lower, in man; and concerning its influx, successively (n. 57). (*See* INFLUX.)

Every unit in the understanding consists of myriads (n. 68 [*C. L.*, n. 329]).

How the wisdom of the understanding is conjoined with the will's love (*illustrated*, n. 75 *at end* [*C. L.*, n. 92, 93]).

UNIT (*Unum*).—Every unit with men consists of myriads (*illustrated*, n. 68 [*C. L.*, L. 329]).

WOMAN.—(*See* FEMININE.)

EDITOR'S NOTE.

This list of Swedenborg's Works is compiled from Hyde's *Bibliography*, to which some items have been added from the *Chronological List of Swedenborg's Works* by Alfred H. Stroh, A.M. The object in view in preparing this list is to give, in a brief compass, a bird's eye view of the remarkable range of Swedenborg's studies in science, philosophy and theology; also to show the wonderful productive powers of his literary genius, and the wide circulation of his works in reprints and translations.

For the details concerning the various books and editions, we must refer the reader to Hyde's *Bibliography*, and to the researches of Mr. Stroh, whose new and extensive discoveries of "Swedenborgiana" will shortly be published. Many state papers by Swedenborg and concerning him, and other matters of interest connected with Swedenborg, have been brought to light; but these are not yet accessible for use in this list.

We have included the list of Swedenborg's inventions as described in his correspondence; but the original papers, descriptions and drawings are for the most part lost.

An examination of the list of Swedenborg's Works will dispel the notion that Swedenborg was a mere dreamer, an idea fostered by the frequent naming of Swedenborg as a mystic. His works reveal him as a profound and laborious scholar, who based his conclusions on vast researches in the various fields in which he labored.

JOHN WHITEHEAD, *Editor.*

A BRIEF BIBLIOGRAPHY

OF

SWEDENBORG'S WORKS.

Swedenborg was born at Stockholm, Sweden, January 29, 1688, and died in London, England, March 29, 1772.

CONTRACTIONS USED IN THIS LIST.

A., Arabic; Cz., Czechic; D., Danish; Du., Dutch; E., English; F., French; G., German; Gr., Greek; Gu., Gujerati; H., Hindu; I., Italian; Ic., Icelandic; Jap., Japanese; L., Latin; M., Magyar; P., Polish; R., Russian; S., Swedish; Sp., Spanish; W., Welsh; Photo., Photolithograph or Phototype; MS., Manuscript; P. T. W., *Posthumous Theological Works*; A. E., *Apocalypse Explained*.

I. PERIOD OF EDUCATION 1688–1715.

No. of Work	Date when Written	Title and Other Information	Date when First Published
		Opera Poetica S. & L.	1910 S. & L.
		This includes Nos. 1–4, 6–11, 26, 28, 30, 38, 74, 76, 77, 80, 108, 118.	
1	1700	Kolmodin's Marriage S.	1700 S.
2	1700	Verses to Notman S.	1700 S.
3	1707	Verses to Bredberg L.	1707 L.
4	1709	Verses to Eric Benzelius, Sr. L.	1709 L.
5	1709	Selected Sentences L. & Gr.	1709 L. & Gr.
6	1709	Rule of Youth L.	1709 L.
7	1710	Stenbock's Victory L. Editions, L. & E.	1710 L.
8	1710	Verses to Unge L.	1710 L.

568   BIBLIOGRAPHY OF SWEDENBORG'S WORKS

No. of Work	Date when Written	Title and Other Information	Date when First Published
9	1710	Verses to Casaubon L	1875 L. & E.
		(See Tafel *Documents* I. pp. 207-8.)	
10	1710	To Sophia Brenner L	1713 L.
11	1712	Verses on Father's Portrait L	1714 L.
		Swedenborg's Inventions. See Nos. 12–25, 36, 37, 39, 41–44.	
12	1714	Submarine Ship.	
13	1714	New Siphon.	
14	1714	Lifting Weights.	
15	1714	Constructing Sluices.	
16	1714	Machine for Throwing Water.	
17	1714	Draw-Bridge.	
18	1714	Air-Pumps.	
19	1714	Air-Guns.	
20	1714	Universal Musical Instrument.	
21	1714	Art of Shade Drawing.	
22	1714	Water-Clock.	
23	1714	Mechanical Carriage.	
24	1714	Inclinations of the Mind.	
25	1714	Cords and Springs.	
26	1714	Heliconian Sports or Miscellaneous. Poems (*Ludus Heliconius*) L	1714 L.
27	1714	Festal Ode on Charles XII. L	1714 L.
28	1715	Northern Muse (*Camena Borea*) L	1715 L.

II. PERIOD OF SCIENCE AND PHILOSOPHY 1716-1745.

29	1716–1718	Northern Daedalus (Daedalus Hyperboreus)	1716–18 S.
30	1716	Epigram on Northern Daedalus S	1716 S.
31	1716	Youth's Honor S	1716 S.
32	1716	Reflections on Perspective.	
33	1716	Society of Sciences S	1869 Photo. S.
34	1716	Soils and Muds S	1869 Photo. S.
		Translation E. 1908, in *Scientific and Philosophical Treatises*.	
35	1716	Fossils S	1869 S. Photo.
		Translation E. 1906, in *Scientific and Philosophical Treatises*.	
36	1716	Flying Machine MS	1869 Photo. S.
37	1716	Siphon S	1869 Photo. S.
38	1716	Sapphic Ode L	1716 L.
		Translation E. See *Intellectual Repository* 1844.	
39	1716	Sailing up Stream S	1869 Photo. S.
40	1716	Experiments	1869 Photo. S.
41	1716	Screw Jack	1869 Photo. S.

… BIBLIOGRAPHY OF SWEDENBORG'S WORKS

No. of Work	Date when Written	Title and Other Information	Date when First Published
42	1716	Stereometry	1869 Photo. S.
43	1716	Weights.	
44	1716	Crane	1869 Photo. S.
45	1716	Echo	1869 Photo. S.
46	1717	Causes of Things. Translation, E., 1906 in *Scientific and Philosophical Treatises*.	1869 Photo. S.
47	1717	Salt Boileries	1869 Photo. S.
48	1717	Tin-Work	1717 S.
49	1717	Stoppage of the Earth	1869 Photo. S.
50	1717	Improvements at Carlscrona	1869 Photo. S.
51	1717	Instituting an Observatory	1869 Photo. S.
52	1717	Commerce and Manufactures	1869 Photo. S.
53	1717	Fire and Colors. Translation, E. 1906 in *Scientific and Philosophical Treatises*.	1869 Photo. S.
54	1718	Algebra S. (*Regel-Konsten*)	1718 S.
55	1718	To Find the Longitude S	1718 S.
56	1718	New Arithmetic MS. S.	
57	1718	Literary Society S	1869 Photo. S.
58	1718	Welfare of a Country S	1869 Photo. S.
59	1718	Essence of Nature S	1910 Photo. S.
60	1719	Earth's Revolution S. Translation, E. 1900.	1719 S.
61	1719	Height of Water S. Translation, E. 1906 in *Scientific and Philosophical Treatises*. L. 1907.	1719 S.
62	1719	Motive and Vital Essence (Tremulation) S. Translation, E. 1899.	1869 Photo. S.
63	1719	Blast-Furnaces S	1903 S.
64	1719	Money and Measures S.	1719 S. 1795 S.
65	1719	Discovering Mines S. Translation, E. in *Scientific and Philosophical Treatises*.	1869 Photo. S.
66	1719	Docks, Sluice and Salt Works S	1719 S.
67	1719	Geometry and Algebra L	1870 Photo. L.
68	1720	First Principles or Minor Principia (*Principia Rerum Naturalium*) L. Minor Principia, translation E. 1913.	1870 Photo. L.
69	1720	Fall and Rise of Lake Wenner L. Translation, E. 1906 in *Scientific and Philosophical Treatises*.	1720 L.

BIBLIOGRAPHY OF SWEDENBORG'S WORKS

No. of Work	Date when Written	Title and Other Information	Date when First Published
70	1721	Indications of the Deluge (A Letter to Jacob Melle). L	1721 L.
		Translations E. 1742, 1743, 1749. In *Miscellaneous Observations* 1847.	
71	1721	Principles of Natural Things, new attempts to explain the Phenomena of Chemistry and Physics by Geometry (*Prodromus Principiorum Rerum Naturalium*) L	1721 L.
		1911 L. Translation, E. 1847.	
72	1721	Iron and Fire (*Ferrum et Ignem*) L	1721 L.
		1911 L. Translation, E. 1847 in No. 71.	
73	1721	Finding Longitudes, A new method of, L	1721 L.
		1911 L. Translation, E. 1847 in No. 71.	
74	1721	Postscript to Miscellaneous Observations L	1869 Photo. L.
75	1721	Miscellaneous Observations L	1722 L.
		L. 1907; Translation E. 1847.	
76	1722	Love and Metamorphoses of Urania L	1722 L.
		See *Opera Poetica*, 1910.	
77	1722	Verses entitled Augustinus L	1910 L.
78	1722	Conserving Heat L	1722 L.
		Translation, 1847 in *Miscellaneous Observations*.	
79	1722	Working Copper S	1869 Photo. S.
		Translation, E. in Tafel *Documents*.	
80	1722	Festal Ode to Fredrik I. L	1869 Photo. L.
81	1722	Reply to Quesnel L	1722 L.
82	1722	The Magnet MS. L. pp. 338	
83	1722	Calculation Concerning Currency MS. pp. 10.	
84	1722	Swedish Money S	1722 S.
85	1722	Hydrostatics L	1722 L.
		Translation E. in *Miscellaneous Observations*. 1847.	
86	1722	The Genuine Treatment of Metals. L. MS. Prospectus of a large work. See Nos. 91–94.	
87	1723	Swedish Finance MS	1875 E.
		Translation E. 1875 in Tafel *Documents* Vol. I. pp. 471–474.	

BIBLIOGRAPHY OF SWEDENBORG'S WORKS

No. of Work	Date when Written	Title and Other Information	Date when First Published
88	1723	Mining Copper and Iron MS. L.... Translation, E. 1875 in Tafel Documents Vol. I. pp. 475–476.	1875 E.
89	1723	Establishing Iron Works MS. L.... Translation, E. 1875 in Tafel Documents Vol. I. pp. 480–482.	1875 E.
90	1723	Production of Iron MS. L......... Translation, E. 1875 in Tafel Documents Vol. I. pp. 477–480.	1875 L.
91	1724	On Copper MS. L. This and the following MS. pp. 363.	
92	1724	On Silver MS. L.	
93	1724	On Vitriol MS. L. pp. 450˙	
94	1724	On Sulphur and Pyrites MS. L. pp. 335.	
95	1725	On Salt. MS. L. pp. 343.........	1910 L.
96	1729	First Principles (*Principia Rerum Naturalium*). MS. pp. 560 L... L. *Opera Quaedam* 1908 pp. 1–191.	1870 Photo. L.
97	1729	Index to Various Philosophical Subjects. MS. 265 pp. L.......	1869 Photo. L.
98	1733	Various Philosophical and Anatomical Subjects and Itineraries. MS. pp. 716 L..................	Part published 1869 Photo. L. 1870 Photo. L.
99	1733	Motion of the Elements. MS. pp. 5, L. See No. 98............. Translation, E. 1908 in *Scientific and Philosophical Treatises*.	1908 E.
100	1733	Wolff's Ontology and the Principia. MS. L. See No. 98.	
101	1733	Empirical Psychology MS. L.	
102	1734	Philosophical and Mineralogical Works....................... Vol. I. Principia L. 1908. Translation, E. 1845–6, 1912......... Vol. II. Iron. Translation, F. Sec. 4, 1762...................... Vol. III. Copper................	1734 L. 1734 L. 1734 L. 1734 L.
103	1734	The Infinite..., ... Translations E. 1795, 1847, 1848, 1902.	1734 L.

No. of Work	Date when Written	Title and Other Information	Date when First Published
104	1734	Mechanism of Soul and Body. MS. See No. 98. Translation, E. 1905. In *Philosophical and Scientific Treatises*.	1870 Photo. L.
105	1734	Journal........................ See No. 98. Translation, E. in Tafel *Documents* Vol. II.	1840 L.
106	1734	Human Body................... See No. 98. Translation, E. 1905 in *Scientific and Philosophical Treatises*	1870 Photo. L.
107	1734	Declaring War against Russia MS. S. 1875 E. Tafel *Documents* Vol. I. pp. 486–493.	
108	1735	Verses to Julin..................	1735 L.
109	1736	Abstract (or Summary) of the Principia I,........................ L. 1908. Translation, E. *New Philosophy* 1903.	1870 Photo. L.
110	1738	The Infinite and the Finite. MS. 5 pp. L...................... Translation E. 1905. *Scientific and Philosophical Treatises*.	1870 Photo. L.
111	1739	Journeys. MS. and Photo S...... Translation, E. Tafel *Documents* Vol. II. See No. 98............	1844 L.
112	1739	Muscles in General. MS. 20 pp. L. See No. 119.	
113	1739	Knowledge of the Soul. L........ Translation, E. in *Posthumous Tracts* 1847, 1905.	1846 L.
114	1739	Faith and Good Works........... Translation, E. in *Posthumous Tracts*, 1847.	1846 L.
115	1740–1741	Economy of the Animal Kingdom.. Translations, E. 1845, 1846, 1868, 1903.......................	Part I 1740 L. Part II 1741 L.
116	1740	Anatomical and Physiological Subjects........................ Brain MS. pp. 566. Diseases of the Brain MS. pp. 63. Skin, etc. MS. pp. 12.	1869 Photo. L.
117	1740	The Skin and the Tongue......... See No. 116.	1870 Photo. L.
118	1740	In Celebration of Printing........ Translation, E. in *Intellectual Repository*, Lond., 1841, p. 81.	1740 L.

BIBLIOGRAPHY OF SWEDENBORG'S WORKS 573

No. of Work	Date when Written	Title and Other Information	Date when First Published
119	1735–1738	Anatomical, Physiological and Philosophical Subjects. MS. L.	1870 Photo. L.
120	1740	The Brain. MS. 1486 pp.; 62 pp.; 564 pp.	1870 Photo. L.
		See No. 116, 119. L. 1847. Translation E. Vol. I, 1882; Vol. II. 1887.	1869 Photo L.
121	1740	Various Anatomical, Physiological and Philosophical Subjects. MS. 129 pp.	1869 Photo. L.
122	1740–1741	Anatomical, Physiological and Philosophical Subjects. MS. 80 pp.; 433 pp.	Part published 1846 L. 1847 L.
123	1740	Corpuscular Philosophy in Brief E. 1905. See No. 121. L. and E. New Philosophy, 1899	1875 E.
124	1740	Declination of the Needle. MS. S. 11 pp. See Tafel's *Documents* Vol. I. pp. 568–577.	
125	1740	Letter to Nordberg (Memoir of Charles XII)	1740 S.
		See Nordberg's History of Charles XII. Translations E., F., G.	
126	1740	Characteristic and Mathematical Philosophy of Universals. See No. 121.	
127	1741	Divine Prudence. A proposed work, MS. lost.	
128	1740–1744	Various Philosophical, Theological, Mathematical, etc. Subjects. MS. 277 pp.	1869 Photo L. 1870 Photo. L.
129	1741	Mathematics and Physics. See No. 128.	
130	1741	Philosophical and Theological Notes. See No. 128.	
131	1741	Introduction to Rational Psychology	1870 Photo. L.
		(On Correspondences and Representations). See No. 128.	
132	1741	Soul and Body. MS. 80 pp.	1846 L.
		See No. 122. Translation E. in *Posthumous Tracts*, 1847.	

574 BIBLIOGRAPHY OF SWEDENBORG'S WORKS

No. of Work	Date when Written	Title and Other Information	Date when First Published
133	1741	Animal Spirit. MS. 24 pp. Translation, E. in *Posthumous Tracts*, 1847. See No. 122.	1846 L.
134	1741	Red Blood. MS. 24 pp. Translation, E. in *Posthumous Tracts*, 1847. See No. 122.	1846 L.
135	1741	Sensation. MS. 13 pp. Translation, E. in *Posthumous Tracts*, 1847. See No. 122.	1846 L.
136	1741	Action. MS. 32 pp. Translation, E. in *Posthumous Tracts*, 1847.	1846 L.
137	1741	Origin of the Soul. MS. 5 pp. Translation in *Posthumous Tracts*, 1847.	1846 L.
138	1741–1742	Physiological and Metaphysical Subjects. L. 1. *De Anima*. See No. 139. 2. *Ontologia*. See No. 140.	
139	1742	Rational Psychology (*De Anima*) L. Translation E. 1887, 1900.	1849 L.
140	1742	Ontology (*Ontologia*). Translation E. 1880, 1901.	1869 Photo. L.
141	1742	Common Place Book. MS. 264 pp. L. (Various Scientific Subjects).	
142	1742.	Metaphysics. MS. 255 pp.	
143	1742	Hieroglyphic Key (*Clavis Hieroglyphica*). Translations E. 1792, 1826, 1847; S. 1795, 1855.	1784 L.
144	1743	Anatomical and Physiological Subjects. MS. 371 pp. (*Regnum Animale* vi. 1, 2.) Generation, Generative Organs. Translations E. 1852, 1912.	{ 1849 L. 1869 Photo. L.
145	1743	Anatomy of the Body (Generation) L. See No. 144.	
146	1743	Swammerdam's Book of Nature (Notes on). L. MS. 47 pp.	1869 Photo. L.
147	1744	Physiological and Theological Matters. L. MS. 144 pp.	1870 Photo. L.
148	1743	Anatomical, Physiological and Physical Subjects. MS. 241 pp. L.	

BIBLIOGRAPHY OF SWEDENBORG'S WORKS 575

No. of Work	Date when Written	Title and Other Information	Date when First Published
149	1744	Sense in General. MS. 99 pp. L.....1848 L. Photo. Vol. VI. 1869. Translation, E. 1914.	
150	1744	The Brain II. MS. 123 pp. L......1869 Photo. L.	
151	1744	Muscles of the Face and Abdomen. MS. 6 p......................1869 Photo L.	
152	1744	Dreams. MS. 108 pp., S..........1859 S. Translation. Extracts E. in The Dawn 1861–1862; Tafel *Documents* Vol. II.	
153	1744–1745	Animal Kingdom (*Regnum Animale*)....................... { Part I. 1744 L. " II. 1744 L. " III. 1745 L. Translation, E. 1844–1845, 1850, 1858.	
154	1745	Worship and Love of God. (*De Cultu et Amore Dei*)............1745 L. Photo. 1870 L.; L. 1791, 1883. Translations, E. 1801, 1816, 1828, 1832, 1864, 1885, 1914. S. 1816, 1902.	

III. PERIOD OF THEOLOGY 1745–1772.

155	1745–1747	Explanations of the Word. (*Adversaria*)........................1842–1854 L. Vol. I. Genesis. Vol. II. Genesis and Exodus. Vol. III. Exodus to Kings. Vol. IV. Isaiah and Jeremiah.	
156	1745	History of Creation..............1847 L. See No. 155. Translation E.	
157	1745	The Messiah. MS. 64 pp.........1870 Photo. L.	
158	1746	Historical Word. (*Adversaria*).....1842–1854 L. See No. 155. Translations, Extracts, E., *Intellectual Repository* 1841–1842, G. in *Neukirchenblatt* 1896–1903.	
159	1746–1748	Bible Index (*Index Biblicus*).......1859–1868 L.	
160	1746	Bible Index. 4 Vols.............. See No. 159.	
161	1747	Gad and Asher. MS. 1 p...........Photo. L. Privately Printed Translation E. 1914, in *Posthumous Theological Works* Vol. I.	

576 BIBLIOGRAPHY OF SWEDENBORG'S WORKS

No. of Work	Date when Written	Title and Other Information	Date when First Published
162	1747	Isaiah and Jeremiah Explained. See No. 155.	
163	1747	Bible Index. See No. 159.	
164	1746	Marginal Notes .... 1872 Photo. L. On Margin of Swedenborg's Latin Bible.	
165	1748	Bible Index. See No. 159.	
166	1748	Bible Index. See No. 159.	
167	1748	Bible Index. See No. 159.	
168	1747–1763	Spiritual Diary. 9 Vols .... 1843–1860 L. Translations E. in 5 Vols., Lond. 1883–1902; G. Vol. I. 1902.	
169	1747–1753	Arcana Cœlestia .... 1749-1756 L. Latin Reprint Tubingen 1833– 8 Vols. 4° 1942 in 13 Vols. Translations many Editions E., F., G., S. In MS. R.	
170	1749	Spiritual Diary. See No. 168.	
171	1751	Spiritual Diary. See No. 168.	
172	1751	Index to Spiritual Diary. See No. 168.	
173	1755	Liquor Trade in Sweden MS. S. ... 1875 E. See Tafel *Documents* Vol. I. pp. 494–5.	
174	1756	Index to Arcana Cœlestia .... 1815 L. Translations. Many Editions E., F.	
175	1758	Earths in the Universe. (*De Telluribus*) L .... 1758 L. Translations, many editions E., D., F., G., I., S.	
176	1758	Heaven and Hell. (*De Coelo et de Inferno.*) L .... 1758 L. Translations, many editions, E., A., D., Du., F., G., H., I., P., R., S., W.; Extracts, Gu.	
177	1758	Last Judgment. (*De Ultimo Judicio.*) L .... 1758 L. Translations, many editions, E., D., F., G., S.	

BIBLIOGRAPHY OF SWEDENBORG'S WORKS

No. of Work	Date when Written	Title and Other Information	Date when First Published
178	1758	Heavenly Doctrine. L............ (The New Jerusalem and its Heavenly Doctrine.) Translations, many editions, E., D., Du., F., G., I., Ic., R., S., W.; Extracts, Sp.	1758 L.
179	1758	White Horse. L................. Translations, many editions, E., Du., F., G., R., S.	1758 L.
180	1757–1759	Apocalypse Explained. MS. and Photo. L. Translations, many editions, E., F., G.; Extracts, S... 4 Vols.	1785–1789 L.
181	1759	Various Theological Works. L. No. 1. Charity. See No. 215...... 1870 Photo. L. No. 2. Concerning the Lord. Translation E in Vol. VI. A. E..... 1840 L. No. 3. Concerning the Athanasian Creed E. in Vol. VI. A. E...................... 1840 L. No. 4. Canons. See No. 224...... 1840 L. No. 5. Five Memorable Relations. See No. 215.	
182	1760	Athanasian Creed. L............ Translations E., See No. 181.	1840 L.
183	1760	The Lord. (*De Domino*).......... Translations, E. See No: 181.	1840 L.
184	1760	Metallic Currency. S............ Translation E. See Tafel *Documents* Vol. I. pp. 497–503.	1875 E.
185	1760	Restoration of the Coinage. S..... Translations, E., F., G. See Tafel *Documents* Vol. I. pp. 504–505.	1875 E.
186	1760	Course of Exchange. S........... Translation, E. Tafel *Documents* Vol. I. pp. 505–506.	1875 E.
187	1760	Exportation of Copper. S......... Translation E. Tafel *Documents* Vol. I. pp. 507–508.	1875 E.
188	1761	Criticism of Nordencrantz's Book. S........................... Translations E., F., G. See Tafel *Documents* Vol. I. pp. 511–515.	1849 S.
189	1761	Preservation of Freedom S........ Translations E., F., G. See Tafel *Documents* Vol. I. pp. 538–542.	1842 S.

BIBLIOGRAPHY OF SWEDENBORG'S WORKS

No. of Work	Date when Written	Title and Other Information	Date when First Published
190	1761	Prophets and Psalms. MS. and Photo. L....................	1784 L.
		Translations, many editions; E., F., G., S.	
191	1761	Omnipotence, Omnipresence, &c. Referred to but no MS. or edition has been found.	
192	1761	Concerning Life. Referred to but no MS. or edition has been found.	
193	1762	Various Theological Subjects. MS. Photo. L.	
		No. 1. The Sacred Scripture or Word of the Lord, from Experience.	
		No. 2. The Last Judgment (*Posthumous*).	
		No. 3. The Spiritual World.	
		No. 4. The Precepts of the Decalogue.	
		Nos. 1–3 in Vol. I, No. 4 in Vol. II. P. T. W.	
194	1762	Sacred Scripture. (Or Word of the Lord, from Experience.) MS. and Photo. L.................	1846 L.
		See No. 193 (No. 1). Translations; many editions, E., S.	
195	1762	Precepts of the Decalogue. MS. and Photo....................	1846 L.
		See No. 193 (No. 4). Translations E., S.	
196	1762	Last Judgment (Posthumous). MS., Photo. L.....................	1846 L.
		Translations, E. See No. 193 (No. 2).	
197	1762–1763	The Divine Love and the Divine Wisdom. MS. and Photo. L...	1870 Photo. L.
		L. in Vol. V. A. E.	
		E. in Vol. VI. A. E.	
198	1762	Divine Love. MS. and Photo. L...	1870 Photo. L.
		See No. 197. Latin editions. Translations; many editions, E., F., G.	
199	1763	Divine Wisdom. MS. and Photo. L..	1870 Photo. L.
		See No. 197. Latin editions. Translations; E., F., G., many editions.	

No. of Work	Date when Written	Title and Other Information	Date when First Published
200	1763	Inlaying Tables. S. Translation, Tafel's *Documents* Vol. I. pp. 586-590.	1763 S.
201	1763	Doctrine of the Lord. L. (Doctrine of the New Jerusalem Concerning the Lord.) Translations; many editions, E., D., F., G., R., S., W.	1763 L.
202	1763	Doctrine of the Sacred Scripture. L. (Doctrine of the New Jerusalem Concerning the Sacred Scripture.) Translations; many editions, E., D., F., G., R., S., W.	1763 L.
203	1763	Doctrine of Life. L. (Doctrine of the New Jerusalem Concerning Life.) Translations; many editions; E., D., F., G., I., M., R., Sp., S.	1763 L.
204	1763	Doctrine of Faith. L. (Doctrine of the New Jerusalem Concerning Faith.) Translations; many editions, E., D., F., G., R.,S.	1763 L.
205	1763	Continuation of the Last Judgment. Translations; many editions, E., D., F., G., S.	1763 L.
206	1763	Divine Love and Wisdom. L. Translations; many editions, E., D., F., G., I., Ic., R., S.	1763 L.
207	1763	Divine Providence. L. Translations; many editions, E., D., F., G., I., P., R., S.	1764 L.
208	1765	Spiritual Diary. MS. and Photo. L. See No. 168. Translations E., S.	1844 L.
209	1765	Genealogy of the Swedenborg Family. MS. S. In *Narratiunculæ de Vitis Hominum in E. S. Diario* by A. Kahl	1859 L.
210	1766	Index to Spiritual Diary. MS. Photo. L. See No. 168.	1845 L.
211	1766	Apocalypse Revealed. Latin editions; Translations, many editions, E., D., F., G., R., S.	1766 L.
212	1766	Index to Apocalypse Revealed. MS. Translations; many editions, E., F., G., S.	1813 L.

No. of Work	Date when Written	Title and Other Information	Date when First Published
213	1766	Conversations with Angels. MS. and Photo. L.	1846 L.
		Translations. E. 1846, 1914. In P. T. W. Vol. I.	
214	1766	Doctrine of Charity. MS. and Photo. L.	1840 L.
		Translations, many editions, E., A., F., G., Ic., S. See No. 181.	
215	1766	Five Memorable Relations. L.	1846 L.
		See No. 181. Translations E. S.	
216	1767	Marriage (De Conjugio).	1860 L.
		Translations E. 1865, 1914. In P. T. W. Vol. II.	
217	1767	Answers to Three Questions.	1787 S.
		Letter to Beyer. Translations E., F., G. In P. T. W. Vol. I.	
218	1767	Indexes to Marriage (The missing treatise).	1870 Photo. L.
		(These were possibly Indexes to the first draught of *Conjugial Love*.) Latin editions; Translations, E. In P. T. W. Vol. II.	
219	1767	Conjugial Love. (*Amor Conjugialis*).	1768 L.
		Translations, many editions, E., D., F., G., R., S. Extracts E., F., G., Gu., S.	
220	1768	Natural and Spiritual Sense of the Word.	1770 L.
		Translations, E., F., G., S. See Tafel *Documents* Vol. II. pp. 269–271. In P. T. W. Vol. I. p. 569.	
221	1768–1771	Various Theological Works. MS. L.	1846 L.
		No. 1. Justification and Good Works with Roman Catholics, from the Council of Trent.	
		No. 2. Conversation with Calvin.	
		No. 3. Remission of Sins; Canons.	
		No. 4. Summary of the Coronis.	
		No. 5. On God the Saviour Jesus Christ.	
		No. 6. That the Faith of the Reformed is from the Roman Catholics.	
		See *Posthumous Theological Works* (1914) Vol. I.	

BIBLIOGRAPHY OF SWEDENBORG'S WORKS

No. of Work	Date when Written	Title and Other Information	Date when First Published
222	1769	Brief Exposition of the Doctrine of the New Church. L. Translations; many editions, E., D., F., G., I., S.	1769 L.
223	1769	Letter to Beyer. Translation Tafel *Documents*, Vol. II. p. 305.	1769 S.
224	1769	Canons of the New Church. L. Translations; many editions, E., G.	1840 L.
225	1769	Intercourse of Soul and Body. Translations; many editions, E., D., F., G., I., S.	1769 L.
226	1769	Answer to a Letter. Translations; many editions, E., A., D., Du., F., G., H., R. See Vol. I. p. 5 *Posthumous Theological Works*, 1914.	1769 L.
227	1769	Appendix to White Horse. Translations; many editions, E., F.	1859 L.
228	1769	Scripture Confirmations. (*Dicta Probantia*). Translations; E. 1906, 1914. In P. T. W. Vol. II.	1845 L.
229	1769	Index to Formula Concordia. MS. L.	1870 Photo. L.
230	1770	Memorabilia in the True Christian Religion. (Additions to the True Christian Religion.) In *Posthumous Theological Works* Vol. I. 1914 E.	1890 E.
231	1770	History of the New Church. L. Translations, E. Tafel *Documents*, 1890. See *Posthumous Theological Works* Vol. I., 1914.	1870 Photo. L.
232	1771	True Christian Religion. L. Translations; many editions, E., D., F., G., I., R., S. Extracts, E., F., I., R., Sp., S.	1771 L.
233	1771	Nine Questions. L. Translations, many editions, E., D., F., S.	1785 L.
234	1771	Reply to Ernesti L. Translations; E., F., G.	1771 L.

No. of Work	Date when Written	Title and Other Information	Date when First Published
235	1771	Crown (Coronis). L..............1780 L. Translations, many editions, E., F., G., S.	
236	1771	Consummation of the Age. (Invitation to the New Church.).......1846 L. Translations; E., F., S.	
237	1772(?)	Miracles. Referred to by Pernety. Otherwise not known. Possibly it refers to the article on Miracles in the Coronis.	